# ROTHMANS
# SNOOKER YEARBOOK
# 1989-90

### Editor: Janice Hale

ROTHMANS

Queen Anne Press

A *Queen Anne Press* BOOK

© **Rothmans Publications Ltd 1989**

First published in Great Britain in 1989 by
Queen Anne Press, a division of
Macdonald & Co (Publishers) Ltd
66–73 Shoe Lane
London EC4P 4AB

A member of Maxwell Pergamon Publishing Corporation plc

*Front cover photograph*: Alex Higgins (Eric Whitehead Picture Agency).

*Back cover photograph*: Steve Davis and Alex Higgins at the Rothmans Grand Prix 1988 (Eric Whitehead Picture Agency).

*Black and white photographs*: p. 304: Middlesbrough Evening Gazette; all other photographs, Eric Whitehead.

British Library Cataloguing in Publication Data

Rothmans snooker yearbook. — 1989–90—
1. Snooker — Serials
794.7′35′05

ISBN 0-356-17922-7

Typeset by SB Datagraphics, Colchester, Essex
(An Ician Communications Group company)

Printed and bound in Great Britain by BPCC Hazell Books Ltd, Aylesbury, Buckinghamshire

# CONTENTS

# ACKNOWLEDGEMENTS

The editor would like to thank the following for their assistance in compiling this book:
Clive Everton, editor of *Snooker Scene* magazine
Julie Kane, whose statistical research has been invaluable

## FOREWORD
## FROM ROTHMANS PUBLICATIONS LTD

It doesn't seem that long ago that we launched the first *Rothmans Snooker Yearbook*. Now we are pleased to present the fifth edition, and to confirm that the *Yearbook* has firmly established itself as *the* snooker reference work.

Rothmans' overall commitment and involvement with snooker continues at all levels, with the pinnacle being the Rothmans Grand Prix, held annually at the Hexagon in Reading. Support at amateur level encompasses a wide variety of events, and in particular two of the leading tournaments on the circuit, namely the Rothmans Scottish Snooker Championship and the Rothmans National Amateur Snooker Championship.

Perhaps it is not idle to speculate that in the near future we may be able to report in this book that a player who started his tournament career in a Rothmans amateur event went on to win the Rothmans Grand Prix.

Our thanks go once again to editor Janice Hale, who we think you will agree has produced yet another superb book containing a wealth of useful facts and figures for you to enjoy.

# PARROTT REACHES SECOND PERCH

Steve Acteson, snooker correspondent of *The Times* and *Today*

When John Parrott, Liverpool's favourite snooker son, first entered the professional ranks as a wide-eyed, Beatle-fringed 19-year-old in 1983 he was immediately hailed, by the let's-get-on-the-bandwagon-quick-brigade, as the new Steve Davis. There was nothing, apparently, that John was not going to achieve in record time, including the World Championship and Davis's crown as the world number one. Some even staked money on it – and lost it.

Six years on, Parrott begins the 1989–90 season as world number two, his highest position, and with a coveted first ranking title, the ICI European Open, in his pocket. Davis remains the world champion and world number one but there is only one Steve Davis and there is only one John Parrott, an individual character and champion in his own right.

Parrott's upwardly-mobile progress has been steady rather than spectacular, but that was only what both Parrott and his close friend and personal manager, Phil Miller, always expected. Others, not all with Merseyside accents, squawked on Parrott's behalf, as they had for Jimmy White before him and Stephen Hendry after him – but the players, the true stars in the snooker firmament, let their cues do the talking. Last season, Parrott's was positively garrulous until the Embassy World Championship final when Davis took his haul of world crowns to six, winning the most one-sided modern world final 18-3.

It was a mark of Parrott's very special personality that he agreed without demur to play an exhibition with Davis in the dead evening session. This smacked of throwing escaping Christians back to the lions, but he employed his marvellous sense of humour to the full, mainly at his own expense. You could have cried for him. All he wanted to do was to get back to Liverpool, to find sanctuary in family, friends and his fiancée – now wife – Karen. But the show had to go on and it did.

It should also be remembered that the Hillsborough disaster that blighted the World Championship had hit Parrott much harder than most. A fanatical supporter of both Everton and Liverpool, although in that order, he grew up on the terraces at both Goodison Park and Anfield. To him the 95 who died are all 'relatives'. They're like that in Liverpool. He had desperately wanted to take the crown back to them, although there were those of us in the press room who considered he had done marvellously just to reach the final in the circumstances. Snooker is an emotional game and Parrott's well must have been very nearly dry even at the start of the final.

Phil Miller discovered the then 16-year-old Parrott nine years ago playing at Liverpool's Dudley Institute where he used to coach his own son, Duncan.

'What first attracted me was that he had such a nice way about him. He was a very naive kid in lots of ways, but I mean nothing detrimental by that,' Miller said.

'There were other talented kids around, although not with John's talent. It wouldn't have been worth the bother of looking after them. John always had so much commonsense, you see, even at that age. He'd give you an argument now and then if he didn't want to do something, but there was always so much reason in what he said that I'd usually have to be the one to change my tack.

'My first priority was to get him away from Merseyside, playing-wise that is. I wanted him to play better and more varied opponents for the experience. It's no good trying to thump things into players. They have to learn by experience.

'The year before he turned professional he played in 22 tournaments – and in those days it was hard to even find that many decent events. He won 17 of them and came runner-up in two others, including the English Amateur Championship.

'He wasn't very mature in those days, though. Snooker is all ups and downs. He wasn't very good at getting up from the downs. He wasn't like Jimmy White, who would just shrug his shoulders and forget it, but he's learned to cope alright now.'

Parrott's father, Alan, has also been a great influence upon his development. The only reason that he is rarely, if ever, seen at tournaments is simply that when he used to accompany John the pair of them became ridiculously nervous. They decided mutually that it was better for Alan to stay at home.

Parrott has never been one for the bright lights that attract some professionals like moths. He once told me: 'I'm so good and boring when I'm away from home that I get monks banging on my hotel bedroom door asking me how I do it.'

Some have questioned Parrott's unashamed admiration of Davis, whom he even calls 'The Guv'nor', but he has enough self-belief to admire and respect a true genius without being frightened of it.

He waited a long time for real success. The 1987 Mercantile Credit Classic final saw him recover from 9-5 down to lead 11-10 before Davis let loose with tournament-winning breaks of 83, 68 and 99. Victory over Martin Clark in the final of the 1988 Kent Cup in Beijing, though not a major success, was a further stepping-stone, but he started last season badly, losing to Les Dodd in the first ranking tournament, the Fidelity International, and to Ray Edmonds at the Rothmans Grand Prix.

Quarter-final defeats in the Canadian Masters and the Tennents UK Open were followed by further disappointments at the last hurdle in the Everest World Matchplay, again to Davis, and the Benson and Hedges Masters, to Hendry, with another quarter-final defeat, by Wayne Jones at the Mercantile, in between.

But after woe at Wembley there came delight in Deauville as Parrott defeated Terry Griffiths 9-8 to lift a ranking title at long last.

'Thank God I've got that under my belt. It's a terrible feeling when people point fingers at you and accuse you of having no bottle. They don't know what they are talking about because very few players even reach a major final,' he said with feeling.

He should not have worried. Just a few weeks earlier his closest friend, Tony Shirley, had visited a fortune teller, purely out of curiosity. She had asked him: 'Who are John and Alan? Tell them something special will happen in February.'

For Parrott nothing was more special than winning that elusive ranking title and nothing, professionally speaking, will be again until he finally proves right the people who willed him to world title success too early in his career.

Parrott has done it all in his own time but Miller insists there is much more to come. 'You haven't seen the best of him yet and I don't think you will for at least a year or 18 months.'

# HOW A TOURNAMENT HAPPENS

Janice Hale

Snooker's travelling circus takes everything with it except a big top. Its chief ports of call include Stoke, Reading, Preston, Blackpool, Derby and Sheffield. Having no permanent stadia, it has to make its temporary home in theatres or multi-purpose auditoria.

The players just turn up to play but the promoters, sponsors and television people have to do a great deal of pre-planning to create an arena in which the playing conditions are right, the spectators adequately catered for, the television facilities as good as they can be and the sponsor happy that his image is being projected.

It is not just the conditions front of house and in the arena that are important. Snooker needs considerable backstage facilities, some of which have to be converted from rehearsal rooms to press rooms, from chair stores to television studios.

Months before the circus hits town, the venue itself has to be briefed, a hotel needs to be chosen. Eating facilities have to be arranged, parking arrangements organised, planning permission for AA signs sought and the pre-tournament publicity campaign in the local media set into motion.

The hotel has to be willing to cope with the nocturnal habits of snooker people. After all, if you finish playing, refereeing, broadcasting or writing at midnight, you cannot just go to bed. You want a drink, something to eat, a pleasant hour or two in which to unwind. And if you go to bed in the early hours, you do not want chambermaids asking if they can clean your room only six hours after you have gone to sleep. This is swings and roundabouts for the hotel. If they keep on a late chef, there can be nights when he is rushing around making steak sandwiches and others when no one wants to eat.

The other eating arrangement that has to be made is for dining between the afternoon and evening sessions. Sometimes this can be a leisurely affair but more often it is a rushed meal likely to aggravate any chronic dyspepsia sufferer. A restaurant may be persuaded to open early; outside caterers may be brought in; sometimes the venue itself can cope.

Priority is always given to the parking of the television scanners, the mobile control rooms. If the venue cannot cope with these, it cannot cope with snooker. At the Embassy World Championship in Sheffield, special permission has to be obtained so that they can park on the pavement. At other venues, loading bays have to be used. Spectators are not forgotten in the parking stakes either. Parking must be handy and not inordinately expensive. It proved so costly at one venue that the parking charges were more than the price of admission to the snooker.

Two days before the World Championship, the stage of the Crucible Theatre has to be lowered, not only to improve the atmosphere but also to provide an extra 34 seats. TV technicians come in to lay down miles of cables, erect the scaffolding for the commentary boxes and instal the special lighting rigs.

. The tables, too, have to be installed on a specially laid wool carpet so that there is no static or fluff. The tables arrive in pieces and require a skilful fitter to make them of championship standard.

Then, from the sponsor's point of view, comes the most important part, the erection of the set, months in the planning and designed to promote their product and image at its most advantageous. They have to work within certain parameters. The IBA and BBC have standard regulations. Tobacco companies obey their own voluntary code in addition. Basically, only two banners naming the product may be used. These cannot be in 'master shot', the basic 'full frontal' camera view of the whole table as opposed to particular close-ups.

The precise colour of the set is of primary importance to the sponsor: television can subtly alter shades of colour. Tests are taken at other tournaments so that the colour on the screen is exactly the one desired. The flowers which augment the basic set receive special attention. If they are real, they are sealed in a greenhouse for a week and 'bombed' with sulphur so that there is no possibility of insects being attracted to the table and disturbing play. One sponsor thought he had avoided this problem when he ordered silk flowers but these, it turned out, were not quite the right shade so an official solved the problem by spraying them with the right shade of car paint.

When a player arrives, he will be allotted a dressing-room. He will not share with his opponent but possibly with another player. Care is taken that it is not someone he does not like. A practice table is provided as similar as possible to the match table. This may be in a chair store (as at Derby for the British Open) or in the television studio (as at Sheffield for the World Championship).

Players' foibles also have to be catered for. Lucozade is specially purchased for Willie Thorne. Officials may well scurry round for a hairspray – they are, after all, also in the entertainment business – or a shirt button. Wet and dry towels will be out in the arena ready for wiping hands and cues, although Steve Davis prefers to bring his own. And, of course, everyone knows that Cliff Thorburn will have to wash his hands just one more time, seconds before the start.

The spectators expect to be able to buy a programme and to settle comfortably in their seats. At most venues, they will have travelled no more than 40 miles and will not have taken out a season ticket. But for the World Championship they will have come from Cornwall and Canada, Holland and Harrow. They will occupy some 500 hotel rooms, instead of the circus's usual 80 or so, and Sheffield estimates that the 17 days of the championship bring in as much as £1½ million in extra revenue to the city. The Crucible only seats 968, so many ticket applications meet with disappointment.

Within minutes of a trophy being presented and victor and vanquished leaving the arena, the set will be struck. De-rigging will begin and it all comes down a lot quicker than it went up.

# EDITOR'S REVIEW OF THE SEASON

Janice Hale

No one player dominated the 1988–89 season, although at its commencement it seemed that Steve Davis would. He won the first event, the Fidelity International at Stoke, by beating Jimmy White 10-6 in the final and added the second, the Rothmans Grand Prix at Reading, with a 10-6 victory over a temporarily revitalised Alex Higgins.

He also reached the final of the third, the BCE Canadian Masters, the first of the World Professional Billiards and Snooker Association's new overseas ranking events, but lost 9-4 to White. It was to take Davis until the end of the season to regain his best form although he did win the Everest World Matchplay Championship, a new event for the twelve players who earned most ranking points the previous season, and another new event, the Norwich Union European Grand Prix.

Meanwhile, a sentimental, courageous and heartwarming fairytale unfolded. Doug Mountjoy, 46 years old and sliding down the world rankings, had spent the summer completely rebuilding his game, working with Frank Callan, a coach who many professionals believe has brought fresh insights into the art of analysing snooker technique. In the depths of winter, it all came together for him. He won the Tennents UK Open, beating Stephen Hendry 16-12 in the final, and, as if victory in one ranking event was not sweet enough, he won another, the Mercantile Classic, in the New Year, beating his former sparring partner, Wayne Jones, 13-11.

Hendry, who won two ranking events the previous season, won the prestigious but non-ranking Benson and Hedges Masters at Wembley; but John Parrott, whom he beat 9-6 in that final, won the next ranking event, the inaugural European Open at Deauville Casino, France, a venue far off snooker's beaten track to which few spectators were attracted. From this springboard, Parrott's consistency earned him second place in the world rankings by the end of the season.

The amount of play this involved, though, was to tell by the time the Embassy World Championship came to its conclusion at the Crucible Theatre, Sheffield. Davis, who had withdrawn from the European Open pleading mental exhaustion, looked supreme throughout, winning two matches with a whole session to spare. He came to the final with his re-charged reservoir of nervous energy little depleted. Parrott, however, was utterly jaded and Davis beat him by a record 18-3 margin to win his sixth world title, equalling Ray Reardon's modern-day record.

In the meantime, the other ranking event had been won by Tony Meo, another player who had seemed to be inexorably slipping down the rankings. He beat Dean Reynolds 13-6 in the Anglian British Open final and ended a season he had begun in 31st place with a top 16 ranking.

The most emotional event of the year was the Benson and Hedges Irish Masters, an invitation tournament won by the hobbling figure of Alex Higgins, who had broken bones in his foot after a fall from a second floor window in mid-season. In front of an Irish crowd seemingly hanging from the rafters at Goffs, Kill in Co. Kildare, the 40-year-old former world champion beat Hendry 9-8 from two down with three to play.

The following day he fell metaphorically to earth at Preston Guild Hall when he failed to qualify for the Sheffield phase of the Embassy World Championship. Having to face qualifying for the first time since he won the title in his debut season in 1972, he lost 10-8 to the 1987 world amateur champion, Darren Morgan. After re-experiencing the sweet smell of success, it must have seemed a long fortnight away from the spotlight of the Crucible.

While snooker had provided tales of the expected (Davis winning), the unexpected (Mountjoy and Meo winning ranking events) and the overdue (Parrott's first ranking title), there were growing concerns over the game's long- and short-term futures. By the end of the season, the WPBSA found itself without three sponsors whose prize-money in that season totalled £975,000. Tennents, despite a 13.2m peak audience for their final, did not renew their contract for the UK Open; Anglian Windows pulled out of the British Open after only one year; and following ITV's decision not to cover their event, Fidelity Unit Trusts also withdrew.

While three domestic events developed problems, all was not right with the new overseas ranking events either. The Canadian Masters cost the WPBSA at least £120,000 and the European Open £100,000. The Canadian television slot, so promisingly held for four years, was lost; the Dubai Classic, which replaced it in the calendar, failed to attract entries from any of Barry Hearn's eight players as the overseas ranking events became one of the chief battle grounds between the WPBSA and snooker's most powerful private entrepreneur. Serious problems arose, too, with the new Australian Open but the Asian Open in Bangkok looked set to get off the ground without untoward incident.

The WPBSA also found itself under heavy criticism by some of its own lower ranked professionals for its conduct of affairs.

All sport has its political wrangles, its power battles. Amidst them, snooker maintained in all the arenas on the circuit a display of high-quality sportsmanship and skill. Even this priceless asset may soon be undermined unless the WPBSA can regain the confidence of the sponsorship world at large.

## EDITOR'S NOTE

Because of the volume of statistics which modern snooker is constantly creating, the *Rothmans Snooker Yearbook* has had to limit to a certain extent which items are included under the various sections.

To qualify for inclusion in the 'Players' section, matches must have been played in a bona fide tournament with at least four competitors and be of the best of nine frames or more.

The 'Circuit' section is more comprehensive in that we have tended to record at least the result of the final in events where either the earlier rounds consisted of an insufficient number of frames or were played on a round robin basis.

# RANKING LIST

As both the number of professionals and the number of tournaments have increased, the game's governing body, the World Professional Billiards and Snooker Association, have had to devise some form of ranking list, not only to quantify the standings of the players but also to enable them to seed tournaments.

The ranking list is drawn up at the end of each season and is based on performances over the past two seasons in events which are designated ranking tournaments.

To qualify for ranking status, a tournament must be open to all 128 tournament members of the WPBSA with any vacancies in the field going, in order of merit, to non-tournament professionals (except for the World Championship which is open to all snooker members of the WPBSA). For the 1988–89 season there were eight ranking events: Fidelity International, Rothmans Grand Prix, BCE Canadian Masters, Tennents UK Open, Mercantile Credit Classic, European Open, Anglian British Open and Embassy World Championship. For the 1989–90 season three more events have been added: the Australian Open, the Asian Open and the Dubai Classic, with the Canadian Masters being deleted.

When seedings are decided for each tournament, the defending titleholder is automatically seeded one with the world champion, if he is not the defending titleholder, two. The remaining seeds are then taken, in order, from the ranking list.

To separate players who tie on ranking points, merit points, 'A' points and 'frames won' in the first round have also been introduced to the system which also favours performances in the immediate preceding season.

Players seeded 1–16 are exempt until the last 32 of the World Championship but in the other five events, players seeded 1–32 are exempt only until the last 64.

The various points are awarded as follows. World Championship: winner – 10 ranking points; runner-up – 8 ranking points; losing semi-finalists – 6 ranking points; losing quarter-finalists – 4 ranking points; losers in last 16 – 2 ranking points; losers in last 32 – 1 ranking point (if qualifier), 2 merit points (if exempt); losers in last qualifying round – 2 merit points; losers in 2nd preliminary round – 1 merit point; losers in 3rd preliminary round – 1 'A' point; losers in 1st preliminary round: number of frames won. Other ranking events: winner – 6 ranking points; runner-up – 5 ranking points; losing semi-finalists – 4 ranking points; losing quarter-finalists – 3 ranking points; fifth round losers – 2 ranking points; fourth round losers – 1 ranking point; third round losers – 1 merit point; second round losers – 1 'A' point; first round losers: number

# WORLD RANKING LIST 1989

Figure in brackets denotes previous year's ranking

| | 1988–89 | | | | | | | | | | | | 1987–88 | | | |
|---|---|---|---|---|---|---|---|---|---|---|---|---|---|---|---|---|
| | Frames | A Points | Merit Points | Ranking Points | World | Anglian British | European | Mercantile | Tennents | BCE Canadian | Rothmans | Fidelity | Frames | A Points | Merit Points | Ranking Points |
| 1(1) Steve Davis | 0 | 0 | 2 | 64 | 10R | 3R | — | 1M | 4R | 5R | 6R | 6R | 0 | 0 | 1 | 30 |
| 2(7) John Parrott | 0 | 0 | 1 | 48 | 8R | 4R | 6R | 3R | 3R | 3R | 1R | 1M | 0 | 0 | 0 | 20 |
| 3(4) Stephen Hendry | 0 | 0 | 1 | 46 | 6R | 2R | 2R | 3R | 5R | 4R | 1R | 2R | 0 | 0 | 1 | 21 |
| 4(2) Jimmy White | 0 | 0 | 1 | 43 | 4R | 1R | 4R | 1M | 1R | 6R | 3R | 5R | 0 | 0 | 0 | 19 |
| 5(5) Terry Griffiths | 0 | 0 | 2 | 39 | 4R | 1M | 5R | 2R | 4R | 3R | 3R | 1M | 0 | 0 | 0 | 18 |
| 6(9) Mike Hallett | 0 | 0 | 4 | 33 | 4R | 4R | 4R | 1M | 1M | 4R | 2R | 1R | 0 | 0 | 2 | 14 |
| 7(6) Cliff Thorburn | 0 | 0 | 2 | 33 | 2M | 2R | 3R | 4R | 3R | 3R | — | — | 0* | 0 | 0 | 20 |
| 8(10) Dennis Taylor | 0 | 0 | 1 | 29 | 2R | 1M | 1R | 1R | 2R | 3R | 4R | 3R | 0 | 0 | 0 | 13 |
| 9(13) Willie Thorne | 0 | 1 | 1 | 28 | 2R | 2R | 2R | 4R | 2R | 1R | 1M | 2R | 0 | 0 | 0 | 13 |
| 10(24) Doug Mountjoy | 0 | 0 | 4 | 25 | 1R | 2R | 2R | 6R | 6R | 2R | 2R | 1R | 0 | 0 | 4 | 3 |
| 11(11) Joe Johnson | 0 | 0 | 3 | 24 | 2M | 3R | 2R | 2R | 2R | 1R | 1R | 3R | 0 | 0 | 1 | 10 |

*–2

| Rank (Prev) | Name |  |  |  |  |  |  |  |  |  |  |  | Pts |  |  |  |
|---|---|---|---|---|---|---|---|---|---|---|---|---|---|---|---|---|
| 12(8) | Tony Knowles | 16 | 0 | 0 | 1R | 2R | 1M | 2R | 2R | 1M | 1R | 2M | 24 | 4 | 0 | 0 |
| 13(15) | John Virgo | 9 | 0 | 0 | 1R | 1M | 2R | 3R | 2R | 2R | 1R | 2R | 22 | 1 | 0 | 0 |
| 14(31) | Tony Meo | 3 | 4 | 0 | 3R | 1R | 1M | 1M | 1R | 1M | 6R | 6R | 20 | 7 | 0 | 0 |
| 15(22) | Dean Reynolds | 1 | 6 | 0 | 4R | 1R | 1R | 2R | 1R | — | 5R | 4R | 19 | 6 | 0 | 0 |
| 16(32) | Steve James | 7 | 2 | 1 | 4R | 1R | 2R | 1R | 1R | 1M | 1M | 1R | 17 | 4 | 1 | 0 |
| 17(41) | Martin Clark | 5 | 2 | 0 | 1M | 1M | 1R | 1R | 3R | 3R | 3R | 2M | 16 | 4 | 0 | 8 |
| 18(16) | Cliff Wilson | 7 | 0 | 0 | 1M | 2R | 2R | 1R | 1R | 1R | 2R | 2M | 16 | 3 | 0 | 0 |
| 19(25) | Steve Newbury | 8 | 4 | 0 | 2R | 1R | 1R | 1M | 2R | 1M | 1M | 1R | 15 | 7 | 0 | 0 |
| 20(3) | Neal Foulds | 8 | 2 | 0 | 1R | 2R | 1R | 1R | 1R | 1M | 2R | 2M | 15 | 6 | 0 | 0 |
| 21(26) | Barry West | 5 | 2 | 0 | 3R | 1R | 1M | 3R | 1M | 1M | 2R | 2M | 14 | 7 | 0 | 0 |
| 22(19) | Eddie Charlton | 7 | 3 | 0 | 1M | 1R | 1R | 1M | 1M | 3R | 1M | 2R | 14 | 7 | 0 | 0 |
| 23(12) | Silvino Francisco | 8 | 2 | 0 | 1R | 1M | 1M | 1R | 2R | 1M | 1M | 2R | 14 | 6 | 0 | 0 |
| 24(17) | Alex Higgins | 4 | 3 | 0 | 1M | 5R | 1M | 1R | 1R | 1R | 1R | 2M | 13 | 7 | 0 | 0 |
| 25(14) | Peter Francisco | 9 | 1 | 0 | 1M | 1M | 1M | 1R | 1M | 1R | 3R | 2M | 13 | 8 | 0 | 0 |
| 26(39) | David Roe | 6 | 0 | 2 | 1M | 1M | 1M | 2R | 1M | 1M | 1R | 2R | 12 | 4 | 2 | 0 |
| 27(21) | Eugene Hughes | 4 | 5 | 0 | 1R | 2R | 1M | 1M | 1M | 1R | 1R | 1R | 11 | 7 | 0 | 0 |
| 28(23) | Dene O'Kane | 5 | 1 | 3 | 1R | 1R | 1M | 1R | 1R | 1R | 1R | 1R | 11 | 3 | 3 | 0 |
| 29(29) | Robert Chaperon | 6 | 2 | 0 | 2R | 1R | 1M | 1M | 1R | 1M | 1M | 1R | 11 | 6 | 0 | 0 |
| 30(20) | Tony Drago | 7 | 3 | 0 | 1R | 1R | 1M | 1M | 1R | 1M | 1R | 2M | 11 | 8 | 0 | 0 |
| 31(34) | Wayne Jones | 2 | 3 | 1 | 1M | 1R | 1A | 1M | 5R | 1M | 1M | 2R | 10 | 7 | 2 | 0 |
| 32(18) | Rex Williams | 3 | 6 | 0 | 2R | 3R | 1M | 1R | 1M | 1R | 1M | 2M | 10 | 11 | 0 | 0 |
| 33(28) | David Taylor | 3 | 4 | 0 | 2R | 1M | 2R | 1M | 2R | 1M | 1M | 2M | 9 | 10 | 0 | 0 |

*Figure in brackets denotes previous year's ranking*

| | Player | 1987–88 | | | | 1988–89 | | | | | | | | 1988–89 | | | |
|---|---|---|---|---|---|---|---|---|---|---|---|---|---|---|---|---|---|
| | | Ranking Points | Merit Points | A Points | Frames | Fidelity | Rothmans | BCE Canadian | Tennents | Mercantile | European | Anglian British | World | Ranking Points | Merit Points | A Points | Frames |
| 34(30) | Steve Longworth | 4 | 2 | 0 | 0 | 1R | 1M | 2R | 1M | 1M | 1R | 1R | 2M | 9 | 7 | 0 | 0 |
| 35(102) | Alain Robidoux | 0 | 1 | 0 | 0 | 1R | 4R | 1M | 1M | 1A | 2R | 1R | 2M | 8 | 5 | 1 | 0 |
| 36(43) | Danny Fowler | 3 | 3 | 1 | 0 | 1M | 1M | 1R | 2R | 1M | 2R | 1M | 1M | 8 | 8 | 1 | 0 |
| 37(38) | Jim Wych | 3 | 2 | 1 | 0 | 2R | 1A | 1M | 1M | 1A | 3R | 1M | 1M | 8 | 6 | 3 | 0 |
| 38(45) | Gary Wilkinson | 4 | 2 | 1 | 9 | 1A | 1R | 1M | 1R | 1M | 1R | 1M | 1R | 8 | 5 | 2 | 9 |
| 39(27) | John Spencer | 4 | 4 | 0 | 0 | 2R | 1R | 1R | 1M | 1M | — | 1M | 2M | 8 | 9 | 0 | 0 |
| 40(35) | Joe O'Boye | 6 | 2 | 2 | 0 | 1M | 1M | 1M | 1R | 1A | 1M | 1A | 1R | 8 | 6 | 4 | 0 |
| 41(51) | Tony Chappel | 3 | 5 | 0 | 0 | 1M | 1M | 1M | 1M | 2R | 1R | 1R | 1A | 7 | 9 | 1 | 0 |
| 42(33) | John Campbell | 4 | 3 | 0 | 0 | 1R | 1M | 1A | 1M | 1A | 2R | 1M | 1A | 7 | 6 | 3 | 0 |
| 43(50) | Steve Duggan | 0 | 3 | 4 | 0 | 1R | 1R | 1R | 1R | 1M | 1M | 1A | 2R | 6 | 5 | 5 | 0 |
| 44(54) | Paddy Browne | 1 | 1 | 4 | 0 | 1A | 1A | 1M | 1A | 3R | 1R | 1M | 1R | 6 | 3 | 7 | 0 |
| 45(45) | Murdo Macleod | 2 | 6 | 0 | 0 | 1R | 1M | 1R | 1A | 1M | 1R | 1R | 1M | 6 | 9 | 1 | 0 |
| 46(56) | Nigel Gilbert | 2 | 2 | 1 | 5 | 1M | 3R | 1M | 1R | 1M | 1A | 1M | 2M | 6 | 8 | 2 | 5 |
| 47(52) | Mark Bennett | 1 | 4 | 2 | 0 | 1M | 1A | 1R | 2R | 1A | 1R | 1M | 1A | 5 | 6 | 5 | 0 |

| | | | | | | | | | | | | | | | | |
|---|---|---|---|---|---|---|---|---|---|---|---|---|---|---|---|---|
| 48(67) | Colin Roscoe | 1 | 2 | 2 | 4 | 1A | 1F | 1R | 1M | 1A | 1R | 9M | 4 | 3 | 4 | 14 |
| 49(55) | Ray Edmonds | 2 | 1 | 3 | 0 | 1M | 2R | 1A | 1M | 1A | 1A | 1M | 4 | 5 | 6 | 0 |
| 50(37) | Kirk Stevens | 3 | 2 | 0 | 0 | 1M | 1M | 1R | 1M | 1M | 1A | 1M | 4 | 8 | 1 | 0 |
| 51(46) | Graham Cripsey | 3 | 5 | 0 | 0 | 1M | 1A | 1A | 1A | 1M | 1M | 1A | 4 | 8 | 4 | 0 |
| 52(—) | Mark Johnston-Allen | — | — | — | — | 1M | 1M | 1A | 1A | 1A | 1M | 1A | 3 | 2 | 4 | 0 |
| 53(—) | Darren Morgan | — | — | — | — | 3F | 1A | 1R | 1A | 1R | 2R | 1R | 3 | 0 | 4 | 3 |
| 54(40) | Ray Reardon | 1 | 4 | 1 | 0 | 1M | 1A | 1R | 1M | 1M | 1R | 1M | 3 | 9 | 2 | 0 |
| 55(44) | Warren King | 1 | 2 | 3 | 0 | 1M | 1A | 2R | 1M | 1M | 1A | 1A | 3 | 6 | 6 | 0 |
| 56(36) | Dave Martin | 3 | 6 | 0 | 0 | 1M | 1M | 1M | 1M | 1M | 1A | 1M | 3 | 12 | 2 | 0 |
| 57(42) | Tommy Murphy | 3 | 3 | 1 | 0 | 1M | 1A | 1M | 1M | 1M | 1A | 1M | 3 | 9 | 3 | 0 |
| 58(64) | Jack McLaughlin | 0 | 2 | 4 | 0 | 1M | 2R | 1A | 1M | 1M | 1A | 1M | 2 | 7 | 6 | 0 |
| 59(—) | Ian Graham | — | — | — | — | 2F | 4F | 4F | 1A | 1A | 1M | 2M | 2 | 3 | 2 | 10 |
| 60(64) | Jim Chambers | 1 | 1 | 2 | 5 | 1M | 1M | 1A | 1A | 1R | 1M | 1A | 2 | 3 | 6 | 7 |
| 61(60) | Roger Bales | 1 | 0 | 5 | 0 | 1A | 1A | 1A | 1A | 1A | 2F | 1A | 2 | 0 | 12 | 0 |
| 62(49) | Tony Jones | 2 | 3 | 2 | 0 | 1M | 1A | 1A | 1M | 1A | 1R | 1A | 2 | 10 | 4 | 0 |
| 63(57) | Dave Gilbert | 2 | 2 | 3 | 0 | 1A | 1M | 1M | 1A | 1M | 1M | 2M | 2 | 7 | 7 | 0 |
| 64(58) | Mick Fisher | 2 | 0 | 3 | 5 | 1M | 1M | 1A | 1M | 1A | 1A | 1A | 2 | 2 | 9 | 5 |

65(62) Les Dodd 1-12-2-0; 66(81) John Rea 1-8-3-12; 67(61) Jon Wright 1-7-7-0; 68(63) Marcel Gauvreau 1-3-10-0; 69(—) Craig Edwards 1-2-3-5; 70(119) Robert Marshall 1-1-5-18; 71(—) Tony Wilson 1-1-3-12; 72(—) Nick Terry 1-1-4-4; 73(90) George Scott 1-1-6-14; 74(116) Anthony Harris 1-0-8-18; 75(53) Ken Owers 1-7-6-0; 76(72) Martin Smith 1-6-4-7; 77(66) Robby Foldvari 1-6-6-8; 78(65) Graham Miles 1-5-6-10; 79(70) Brian Rowswell 1-4-7-6;

80(68) Paul Medati 1-3-7-15; 81(59) Pat Houlihan 1-3-10-0; 82(69) Paul Gibson 1-2-3-4; 83(71) Vic Harris 1-0-6-14; 84(74) Jim Donnelly 1-0-4-30; 85(84) Bill Oliver 0-6-6-11; 86(82) Mario Morra 0-6-3-16; 87(75) Malcolm Bradley 0-5-7-11; 88(86) Jim Bear 0-5-3-27; 89(83) Fred Davis 0-5-5-13; 90(—) Mick Price 0-3-3-4; 91(95) Glen Wilkinson 0-3-5-14; 92(89) Ian Williamson 0-3-7-15; 93(77) Bob Harris 0-3-6-11; 94(85) Eddie Sinclair 0-3-5-34; 95(92) John Dunning 0-3-4-28; 96(93) Eric Lawlor 0-3-5-16; 97(76) Mark Wildman 0-3-6-13; 98(—) Steve Campbell 0-2-3-16; 99(—) Mark Rowing 0-2-2-5; 100(101) Terry Whitthread 0-2-6-14; 101(80) Tony Kearney 0-2-6-18; 102(100) Mike Darrington 0-2-4-27; 103(87) Jimmy Van Rensberg 0-2-4-25; 104(118) Jason Smith 0-1-8-19; 105(113) François Ellis 0-1-6-13; 106(114) Jack Fitzmaurice 0-1-5-14; 107(117) Steve Meakin 0-1-4-21; 108(111) Dennis Hughes 0-1-4-17; 109(115) Dessie Sheehan 0-1-3-39; 110(108) Mike Watterson 0-1-2-25; 111(NT) Paul Thornley 0-1-1-7; 112(88) Matt Gibson 0-1-9-14; 113(79) Robbie Grace 0-1-7-19; 114(98) Paul Watchorn 0-1-6-21; 115(94) Jim Meadowcroft 0-1-6-16; 116(91) Gino Rigitano 0-1-5-25; 117(99) Jack Rea 0-1-2-23; 118(78) Geoff Foulds 0-0-9-17; 119(110) Billy Kelly 0-0-6-14; 120(104) Greg Jenkins 0-0-4-23; 121(96) Ian Black 0-0-4-15; 122(97) Bernie Mikkelsen 0-0-3-18; 123(103) Patsy Fagan 0-0-3-21; 124(105) Pascal Burke 0-0-2-22; 125(112) Dave Chalmers 0-0-2-29; 126(107) Ian Anderson 0-0-2-11; 127(106) Frank Jonik 0-0-2-8; 128(121) Derek Mienie 0-0-1-19; 129(109) Jim Rempe 0-0-1-16; 130(—) Joe Grech 0-0-1-0; 131(123) Derek Heaton 0-0-1-15; 132(120) Clive Everton 0-0-1-10; 133(125) David Greaves 0-0-0-12; 134(129) Bernard Bennett 0-0-0-9; 135(127) Maurice Parkin 0-0-0-6; 136(122) John Hargreaves 0-0-0-4; 137(128) Bert Demarco 0-0-0-2; 138(131) Eddie McLaughlin 0-0-0-1

*Those ranked 119 and below are non-tournament members of the WPBSA as are also Joe Caggianello, Mike Hines, Lou Condo, Mannie Francisco, James Giannaros, Steve Mizerak, Paddy Morgan, Wayne Saunderson, Gerry Watson, Sam Frangie and Vladimir Potasnik.*

# MONEY LIST 1988-89

The *'Ranking'* column takes into account the Fidelity International, Rothmans Grand Prix, Canadian Masters, Tennents UK Open, Mercantile Credit Classic, European Open and Anglian British Open. *'Sanctioned'* consists of national championships, Everest World Matchplay, Benson and Hedges Masters, Fersina World Cup and Benson and Hedges Irish Masters. *'Others'* comprises events set up primarily or even exclusively for the members of particular management camps. They include Barry Hearn's Matchroom tournament, the Matchroom League, LEP Hong Kong Masters, Dubai Duty Free Masters, Fosters Professional, Norwich Union European Open and the WPBSA's non-ranking tournaments.

| | World | Ranking | Sanctioned | Breaks | Total | Others |
|---|---|---|---|---|---|---|
| 1 S. Davis | 105,000.00 | 169,703.12 | 144,716.01 | 9,500.00 | 428,919.03 | 225,571.00 |
| 2 J. Parrott | 63,000.00 | 91,382.80 | 97,316.01 | 11,300.00 | 262,998.81 | 39,721.00 |
| 3 S. Hendry | 31,500.00 | 83,023.43 | 101,464.46 | 21,433.78 | 237,421.67 | 33,500.00 |
| 4 D. Mountjoy | 4,429.68 | 153,304.68 | 15,000.00 | 9,200.00 | 181,934.36 | – |
| 5 J. White | 15,750.00 | 97,218.74 | 53,105.78 | 2,714.00 | 168,788.52 | 88,071.00 |
| 6 T. Griffiths | 15,750.00 | 70,390.62 | 40,205.78 | – | 126,346.40 | 36,321.00 |
| 7 T. Meo | 31,500.00 | 86,062.49 | 575.00 | – | 118,137.49 | 40,321.00 |
| 8 M. Hallett | 15,750.00 | 55,007.80 | 38,955.78 | – | 109,713.58 | 12,500.00 |
| 9 A. Higgins | 3,445.31 | 52,726.55 | 34,942.25 | – | 91,014.11 | 9,550.00 |
| 10 D. Reynolds | 15,750.00 | 69,249.99 | 1,250.00 | 1,125.00 | 87,374.99 | – |
| 11 C. Thorburn | 4,429.68 | 45,750.00 | 28,691.11 | 1,750.00 | 80,620.79 | 38,750.00 |
| 12 Dennis Taylor | 7,850.00 | 44,382.81 | 23,641.11 | 4,000.00 | 79,873.92 | 49,643.00 |
| 13 N. Foulds | 4,429.68 | 20,593.74 | 45,105.78 | – | 70,129.20 | 68,714.20 |
| 14 W. Thorne | 7,850.00 | 37,484.37 | 14,250.00 | – | 59,584.37 | 41,813.00 |
| 15 J. Johnson | 4,429.68 | 35,460.93 | 19,250.00 | – | 59,140.61 | – |
| 16 W. Jones | 7,850.00 | 40,414.05 | 750.00 | 5,500.00 | 54,514.05 | 250.00 |
| 17 T. Knowles | 4,429.68 | 22,320.30 | 23,441.11 | – | 50,191.09 | 250.00 |
| 18 J. Virgo | 7,850.00 | 29,117.17 | 7,325.00 | – | 44,292.17 | – |
| 19 A. Robidoux | 3,445.31 | 30,695.30 | 6,750.00 | – | 40,890.61 | 625.00 |
| 20 C. Wilson | 4,429.68 | 22,585.93 | 12,000.00 | – | 39,015.61 | – |
| 21 M. Clark | 3,445.31 | 32,968.74 | 575.00 | – | 36,989.05 | 750.00 |
| 22 S. Francisco | 7,850.00 | 14,882.80 | 15,750.00 | 5,400.00 | 36,817.80 | – |
| 23 P. Francisco | 4,429.68 | 19,734.36 | 11,750.00 | – | 35,914.04 | 4,100.00 |
| 24 B. West | 3,445.31 | 30,101.55 | 575.00 | – | 34,121.86 | 250.00 |
| 25 S. James | 4,429.68 | 28,593.74 | 575.00 | – | 33,598.42 | – |
| 26 D. O'Kane | 4,429.68 | 17,007.79 | 9,000.00 | – | 30,437.47 | 250.00 |
| 27 E. Charlton | 7,850.00 | 16,554.67 | 3,450.00 | – | 27,854.67 | 250.00 |
| 28 T. Drago | 3,445.31 | 14,882.79 | 9,000.00 | – | 27,328.10 | 250.00 |
| 29 D. Roe | 7,850.00 | 15,812.48 | 1,250.00 | 1,750.00 | 26,662.48 | 3,050.00 |
| 30 R. Williams | 3,445.31 | 22,546.87 | 575.00 | – | 26,567.18 | – |
| 31 E. Hughes | 4,429.68 | 17,671.79 | 3,600.00 | – | 25,701.47 | 5,850.00 |
| 32 R. Chaperon | 4,429.68 | 14,218.74 | 5,125.00 | – | 23,773.42 | – |
| 33 S. Newbury | 4,429.68 | 16,742.18 | 2,500.00 | – | 23,617.86 | – |
| 34 N. Gilbert | 3,445.31 | 18,218.74 | – | 1,375.00 | 23,039.05 | 200.00 |
| 35 Gary Wilkinson | 4,429.68 | 12,570.30 | 5,000.00 | – | 21,999.28 | 5,300.00 |
| 36 S. Duggan | 7,850.00 | 13,218.73 | – | – | 21,068.73 | – |
| 37 S. Longworth | 3,445.31 | 14,882.79 | 2,500.00 | – | 20,828.10 | 600.00 |
| 38 P. Browne | 4,429.68 | 12,593.75 | 3,600.00 | – | 20,623.43 | 5,975.00 |
| 39 D. Fowler | 1,804.68 | 16,078.11 | 1,250.00 | – | 19,132.79 | 350.00 |
| 40 J. Wych | 1,804.68 | 13,531.25 | 3,750.00 | – | 19,085.93 | – |
| 41 J. McLaughlin | 1,804.68 | 9,687.49 | 6,691.11 | – | 18,183.28 | 450.00 |
| 42 M. Macleod | 1,804.68 | 12,070.29 | 3,950.00 | – | 17,824.79 | 225.00 |
| 43 David Taylor | 3,445.31 | 13,078.12 | 575.00 | – | 17,098.43 | 5,000.00 |
| 44 J. Spencer | 3,445.31 | 12,945.30 | 575.00 | – | 16,965.61 | – |
| 45 M. Johnston-Allen | – | 9,593.74 | – | 7,000.00 | 16,593.74 | 350.00 |
| 46 K. Stevens | 1,804.68 | 8,249.99 | 5,625.00 | – | 15,679.67 | – |
| 47 T. Chappel | – | 14,484.36 | 150.00 | – | 14,634.36 | 1,975.00 |
| 48 J. Campbell | – | 9,882.80 | 4,700.00 | – | 14,582.80 | 650.00 |
| 49 T. Jones | 3,445.31 | 10,007.80 | – | – | 13,453.11 | – |
| 50 J. O'Boye | 4,429.68 | 8,031.24 | – | – | 13,335.92 | – |

|  | World | Ranking | Sanctioned | Breaks | Total | Others |
|---|---|---|---|---|---|---|
| 51  L. Dodd | 3,445.31 | 9,835.42 | – | – | 13,281.23 | 800.00 |
| 52  D. Morgan | 4,429.68 | 5,328.12 | 750.00 | 2,625.00 | 13,132.80 | 1,500.00 |
| 53  M. Bennett | – | 10,453.12 | 2,500.00 | – | 12,953.12 | – |
| 54  R. Reardon | 1,804.68 | 9,742.18 | 750.00 | – | 12,296.86 | – |
| 55  W. King | – | 7,812.49 | 3,450.00 | – | 11,262.49 | 600.00 |
| 56  T. Murphy | 1,804.68 | 5,687.49 | 3,150.00 | 300.00 | 10,942.17 | 725.00 |
| 57  John Rea | 3,445.31 | 5,460.93 | 2,000.00 | – | 10,906.24 | 250.00 |
| 58  C. Roscoe | – | 10,406.24 | 150.00 | – | 10,556.24 | 350.00 |
| 59  R. Edmonds | 1,804.68 | 8,484.37 | – | – | 10,289.05 | – |
| 60  I. Graham | 3,445.31 | 4,531.25 | 1,250.00 | – | 9,226.56 | 100.00 |
| 61  D. Martin | 1,804.68 | 6,234.36 | 575.00 | – | 8,614.04 | – |
| 62  D. Gilbert | 3,445.31 | 4,046.87 | 577.00 | – | 8,067.18 | 475.00 |
| 63  B. Rowswell | 3,445.31 | 1,750.00 | 2,500.00 | – | 7,695.31 | 1,875.00 |
| 64  G. Cripsey | – | 6,054.68 | 1,250.00 | – | 7,304.68 | 525.00 |
| 65  K. Owers | 1,804.68 | 5,140.62 | – | – | 6,945.30 | 450.00 |

66 C. Edwards £6,523 (£600); 67 M. Smith £5,851 (£800); 68 J. Wright £5,179 (£1,275); 69 R. Marshall £5,168 (£300); 70 M. Price £4,914 (£425); 71 T. Kearney £4,900 (£575); 72 P. Medati £4,621 (£575); 73 R. Foldvari £4,203 (£675); 74 M. Gauvreau £4,093 (£175); 75 N. Terry £4,085; 76 M. Morra £3,921 (£475); 77 M. Rowing £3,554 (£175); 78 P. Houlihan £3,528; 79 J. Donnelly £3,450 (£775); 80 R. Bales £3,390; 81 J. Chambers £3,359 (£300); 82 A. Harris £3,239 (£975); 83 Glen Wilkinson £3,207 (£625); 84 T. Wilson £2,921 (£300); 85 G. Miles £2,762 (£675); 86 M. Bradley £2,624 (£625); 87 M. Fisher £2,406 (£925); 88 Jim Bear £2,156; 89 S. Campbell £2,078 (£575); 90 B. Mikkelsen £2,000 (£450); 91 I. Williamson £1,996 (£625); 92 G. Scott £1,937; 93 P. Thornley £1,804; 94 B. Harris £1,750; 95 B. Oliver £1,750; (£450); 96 T. Whitthread £1,531 (£125); 97 M. Watterson £1,421 (£375); 98 F. Ellis £1,421 (£125); 99 D. Sheehan £1,353; 100 M. Darrington £1,203 (£300); 101 D. Hughes £1,203; 102 J. Smith £1,203 (£200); 103 E. Sinclair £1,187 (£1,300); 104 F. Jonik £1,125; 105 S. Meakin £984 (£3,000); 106 E. Lawlor £875; 107 J. Dunning £875 (£375); 108 J. Fitzmaurice £875 (£225); 109 M. Gibson £750 (£750); 110 I. Anderson £500; 111 G. Jenkins £500; 112 Jack Rea £450 (£125); 113 P. Watchorn £450 (£800); 114 I. Black £312 (£125); 115 P. Burke £150 (£250); 116 B. Kelly £150 (£325); 117 B. Werbeniuk (£750); 118 V. Harris (£425); 119 G. Rigitano (£375); 120 D. Greaves (£350); 121 R. Grace (£325); 122 D. Heaton (£225); 123 E. McLaughlin (£200); 124 P. Gibson (£175); 125 J. Grech (£175); 126 J. Giannaros (£125); 127 M. Hines (£125); 128 V. Potaznik (£125); 129 B. Bennett (£100); 130 B. Demarco (£100); 131 C. Everton (£100); 132 S. Frangie (£100); 133 D. Chalmers, F. Davis, P. Fagan, G. Foulds, J. Rempe, J. Van Rensberg, G. Watson, M. Wildman (£0)

# THE PLAYERS

(WS) = *World Series. Figure in brackets denotes previous season's ranking.*

## IAN ANDERSON (Australia)
**Born** 2.4.46. **Turned professional** 1974. **World ranking** 126 (107).

| 1974 | v Mans | 1-8 | 1st round | World Championship |
|---|---|---|---|---|
| 1975 | v Condo | 15-8 | 1st round | World Championship |
| | v Williams | 4-15 | 2nd round | World Championship |
| 1976 | v Jack Rea | 5-8 | Qualifying | Embassy World Championship |
| 1979 | v S. Davis | 1-9 | Prelim | Embassy World Championship |
| 1981 | v Martin | 3-9 | Qualifying | Embassy World Championship |
| 1982 | v Houlihan | 5-9 | Qualifying | Embassy World Championship |
| | v Sinclair | 2-5 | Qualifying | Jameson International |
| | v David Taylor | 1-5 | 1st round | Professional Players Tournament |
| 1983 | v King | 6-10 | Qualifying | Embassy World Championship |
| | v Oliver | 9-1 | Qualifying | Coral UK Championship |
| | v Dunning | 2-9 | Qualifying | Coral UK Championship |
| 1984 | v Watson | 10-4 | Qualifying | Embassy World Championship |
| | v Donnelly | 6-10 | Qualifying | Embassy World Championship |
| 1985 | v Kearney | 10-8 | Qualifying | Embassy World Championship |
| | v Browne | 5-10 | Qualifying | Embassy World Championship |
| | v King | 2-8 | Quarter-final | Australian Championship |
| 1986 | v Charlton | 2-6 | Quarter-final | Australian Championship |
| | v John Rea | 1-5 | 2nd round | BCE International |
| | v Oliver | 5-4 | 1st round | Rothmans Grand Prix |
| | v Murphy | 5-4 | 2nd round | Rothmans Grand Prix |
| 1987 | v Charlton | 2-6 | Quarter-final | Australian Championship |
| | v Watterson | 5-3 | 1st round | Fidelity·International |
| | v Cripsey | 4-5 | 2nd round | Fidelity International |
| | v Jenkins | 5-2 | 1st round | Rothmans Grand Prix |
| | v Bales | 1-5 | 2nd round | Rothmans Grand Prix |
| | v Donnelly | 4-9 | 1st round | Tennents UK Open |
| 1988 | v Giannaros | 5-2 | 2nd round | Australian Championship |
| | v J. Campbell | 0-5 | Quarter-final | Australian Championship |
| 1989 | v Chambers | 7-10 | Qualifying | Embassy World Championship |

## ROGER BALES (England)
**Born** 15.8.48. **Turned professional** 1984. **World ranking** 61 (60). **Best professional performances** Last 32 1989 Anglian British Open, 1987 Rothmans Grand Prix, 1986 Dulux British Open, 1986 Fidelity International.

| 1984 | v Sheehan | 5-2 | Qualifying | Jameson International |
|---|---|---|---|---|
| | v Murphy | 5-4 | Qualifying | Jameson International |
| | v Fisher | 5-3 | Qualifying | Jameson International |
| | v Reynolds | 4-5 | Qualifying | Jameson International |
| | v Higgins | 1-5 | 1st round | Rothmans Grand Prix |
| | v Chalmers | 9-2 | Qualifying | Coral UK Open |
| | v E. McLaughlin | 9-4 | Qualifying | Coral UK Open |
| | v Gauvreau | 8-9 | Qualifying | Coral UK Open |
| 1985 | v Bennett | 5-1 | Qualifying | Mercantile Credit Classic |
| | v Kelly | 5-3 | Qualifying | Mercantile Credit Classic |
| | v Virgo | 1-5 | Qualifying | Mercantile Credit Classic |

|  | v Dodd | 3-9 | Qualifying | Tolly Cobbold English Championship |
|---|---|---|---|---|
|  | v Black | 6-4 | Qualifying | Dulux British Open |
|  | v Higgins | 3-6 | 1st round | Dulux British Open |
|  | v Chaperon | 7-10 | Qualifying | Embassy World Championship |
|  | v Drago | 5-2 | 1st round | Goya Matchroom Trophy |
|  | v Edmonds | 5-0 | 2nd round | Goya Matchroom Trophy |
|  | v S. Davis | 2-5 | 3rd round | Goya Matchroom Trophy |
|  | v Smith | 5-1 | 1st round | Rothmans Grand Prix |
|  | v Fisher | 5-3 | 2nd round | Rothmans Grand Prix |
|  | v Wilson | 1-5 | 3rd round | Rothmans Grand Prix |
|  | v Simngam | 2-9 | 1st round | Coral UK Open |
| 1986 | v Parkin | 5-0 | 1st round | Mercantile Credit Classic |
|  | v Fowler | 4-5 | 2nd round | Mercantile Credit Classic |
|  | v V. Harris | 9-7 | 2nd round | Tolly Cobbold English Championship |
|  | v Knowles | 4-9 | 3rd round | Tolly Cobbold English Championship |
|  | v Parkin | 5-1 | 1st round | Dulux British Open |
|  | v Dunning | wo | 2nd round | Dulux British Open |
|  | v Dennis Taylor | 5-4 | 3rd round | Dulux British Open |
|  | v Williams | 4-5 | 4th round | Dulux British Open |
|  | v Gilbert | 7-10 | Qualifying | Embassy World Championship |
|  | v F. Davis | 5-4 | 2nd round | BCE International |
|  | v Stevens | 5-3 | 3rd round | BCE International |
|  | v Wilson | 1-5 | 4th round | BCE International |
|  | v F. Davis | 4-5 | 2nd round | Rothmans Grand Prix |
|  | v Cripsey | 6-9 | 2nd round | Tennents UK Open |
| 1987 | v Murphy | 2-5 | 2nd round | Mercantile Credit Classic |
|  | v Owers | 5-6 | 2nd round | Tolly Ales English Championship |
|  | v Gauvreau | 0-5 | 2nd round | Dulux British Open |
|  | v Spencer | 3-10 | Qualifying | Embassy World Championship |
|  | v John Rea | 2-5 | 2nd round | Fidelity International |
|  | v Anderson | 5-1 | 2nd round | Rothmans Grand Prix |
|  | v J. Campbell | 5-3 | 3rd round | Rothmans Grand Prix |
|  | v Thorne | 2-5 | 4th round | Rothmans Grand Prix |
|  | v Dunning | 8-9 | 2nd round | Tennents UK Open |
| 1988 | v John Rea | 0-5 | 2nd round | Mercantile Credit Classic |
|  | v D. Gilbert | 2-6 | 2nd round | English Championship |
|  | v Gary Wilkinson | 1-5 | 2nd round | MIM Britannia British Open |
|  | v Miles | 7-10 | Qualifying | Embassy World Championship |
|  | v John Rea | 2-5 | 2nd round | Fidelity International |
|  | v Robidoux | 1-5 | 2nd round | Rothmans Grand Prix |
|  | v S. Campbell | 2-5 | 2nd round | Canadian Masters |
|  | v Robidoux | 4-9 | 2nd round | Tennents UK Open |
| 1989 | v J. Smith | 1-5 | 2nd round | Mercantile Credit Classic |
|  | v Chambers | 1-5 | 2nd round | European Open |
|  | v Medati | 3-5 | 2nd round | English Championship |
|  | v Fitzmaurice | 5-1 | 2nd round | Anglian British Open |
|  | v Newbury | 5-3 | 3rd round | Anglian British Open |
|  | v Hallett | 0-5 | 4th round | Anglian British Open |
|  | v Glen Wilkinson | 1-10 | Qualifying | Embassy World Championship |

## JIM BEAR (Canada)

**Born** 21.1.40. **Turned professional** 1983. **World ranking** 88 (86). **Amateur career** Runner-up 1982 World Amateur Championship.

| 1983 | v Morra | 9-8 | 2nd round | Canadian Championship |
|---|---|---|---|---|
|  | v John Bear | 9-5 | Quarter-final | Canadian Championship |
|  | v Stevens | 8-9 | Semi-final | Canadian Championship |
| 1985 | v Caggianello | 4-5 | 1st round | Canadian Championship |
|  | v Houlihan | 5-2 | 1st round | Goya Matchroom Trophy |
|  | v Donnelly | 5-2 | 2nd round | Goya Matchroom Trophy |

| | | | |
|---|---|---|---|
| v Johnson | 1-5 | 3rd round | Goya Matchroom Trophy |
| v Kearney | 3-5 | 1st round | Rothmans Grand Prix |
| v Demarco | 9-1 | 1st round | Coral UK Open |
| v Watterson | 9-0 | 2nd round | Coral UK Open |
| 1986 v Kearney | 0-5 | 1st round | Mercantile Credit Classic |
| v O'Boye | 1-5 | 1st round | Dulux British Open |
| v Burke | 10-8 | Qualifying | Embassy World Championship |
| v Gauvreau | 5-10 | Qualifying | Embassy World Championship |
| v Chaperon | 3-6 | 1st round | Canadian Championship |
| v Watchorn | 5-1 | 1st round | BCE International |
| v Duggan | 4-5 | 2nd round | BCE International |
| v B. Bennett | 5-2 | 1st round | Rothmans Grand Prix |
| v Fowler | 5-2 | 2nd round | Rothmans Grand Prix |
| v Williams | 2-5 | 3rd round | Rothmans Grand Prix |
| v Everton | 9-1 | 1st round | Tennents UK Open |
| v Edmonds | 6-9 | 2nd round | Tennents UK Open |
| 1987 v Jack Rea | 10-5 | Qualifying | Embassy World Championship |
| v Gauvreau | 5-10 | Qualifying | Embassy World Championship |
| v Mikkelsen | 6-0 | 1st round | Canadian Championship |
| v Wych | 6-4 | Quarter-final | Canadian Championship |
| v Stevens | 7-2 | Semi-final | Canadian Championship |
| v Thorburn | 4-8 | Final | Canadian Championship |
| v Clark | 2-5 | 1st round | Fidelity International |
| v Greaves | 5-0 | 1st round | Rothmans Grand Prix |
| v B. Harris | 5-3 | 2nd round | Rothmans Grand Prix |
| v Thorne | 1-5 | 3rd round | Rothmans Grand Prix |
| v Chalmers | 9-5 | 1st round | Tennents UK Open |
| v B. Harris | 9-4 | 2nd round | Tennents UK Open |
| v Johnson | 5-9 | 3rd round | Tennents UK Open |
| 1988 v J. Smith | 5-3 | 1st round | Mercantile Credit Classic |
| v Scott | 3-5 | 2nd round | Mercantile Credit Classic |
| v A. Harris | 5-2 | 1st round | MIM Britannia British Open |
| v Houlihan | 5-0 | 2nd round | MIM Britannia British Open |
| v S. Francisco | 0-5 | 3rd round | MIM Britannia British Open |
| v Mienie | 10-4 | Qualifying | Embassy World Championship |
| v G. Foulds | 10-2 | Qualifying | Embassy World Championship |
| v F. Davis | 4-10 | Qualifying | Embassy World Championship |
| v Caggianello | 3-6 | 1st round | BCE Canadian Championship |
| v Heaton | 5-1 | 1st round | Fidelity International |
| v Edmonds | 1-5 | 2nd round | Fidelity International |
| v Jenkins | 4-5 | 1st round | Rothmans Grand Prix |
| v Ellis | 7-9 | 1st round | Tennents UK Open |
| 1989 v A. Harris | 3-5 | 1st round | Mercantile Credit Classic |
| v Kelly | 0-5 | 1st round | European Open |
| v Jack Rea | 5-4 | 1st round | Anglian British Open |
| v Martin | 5-2 | 2nd round | Anglian British Open |
| v Drago | 2-5 | 3rd round | Anglian British Open |
| v Edwards | 7-10 | Qualifying | Embassy World Championship |

## MARK BENNETT (Wales)

**Born** 23.9.63. **Turned professional** 1986. **World ranking** 47 (52). **Amateur career** 1985 Welsh champion. **Best professional performance** Last 16 1988 Tennents UK Open.

| | | | |
|---|---|---|---|
| 1986 v Smith | 5-4 | 1st round | BCE International |
| v Browne | 5-1 | 2nd round | BCE International |
| v Virgo | 1-5 | 3rd round | BCE International |
| v Watterson | 5-1 | 1st round | Rothmans Grand Prix |
| v O'Kane | 5-2 | 2nd round | Rothmans Grand Prix |
| v Macleod | 5-1 | 3rd round | Rothmans Grand Prix |

|          |                 |       |              |                               |
|----------|-----------------|-------|--------------|-------------------------------|
|          | v Browne        | 0-5   | 4th round    | Rothmans Grand Prix           |
|          | v Sheehan       | 8-9   | 1st round    | Tennents UK Open              |
| 1987     | v Sheehan       | 5-3   | 1st round    | Mercantile Credit Classic     |
|          | v Black         | 5-3   | 2nd round    | Mercantile Credit Classic     |
|          | v Virgo         | 3-5   | 3rd round    | Mercantile Credit Classic     |
|          | v W. Jones      | 3-6   | 1st round    | Matchroom Welsh Championship  |
|          | v Morra         | 4-5   | 1st round    | Dulux British Open            |
|          | v Hargreaves    | 10-6  | Qualifying   | Embassy World Championship    |
|          | v Mikkelsen     | 10-4  | Qualifying   | Embassy World Championship    |
|          | v W. Jones      | 10-3  | Qualifying   | Embassy World Championship    |
|          | v Werbeniuk     | 10-8  | Qualifying   | Embassy World Championship    |
|          | v Dennis Taylor | 4-10  | 1st round    | Embassy World Championship    |
|          | v Chalmers      | 5-0   | 2nd round    | Fidelity International         |
|          | v White         | 3-5   | 3rd round    | Fidelity International         |
|          | v Medati        | 5-4   | 2nd round    | Rothmans Grand Prix           |
|          | v Hendry        | 1-5   | 3rd round    | Rothmans Grand Prix           |
|          | v V. Harris     | 7-9   | 2nd round    | Tennents UK Open              |
| 1988     | v G. Miles      | 5-1   | 2nd round    | Mercantile Credit Classic     |
|          | v Stevens       | 5-2   | 3rd round    | Mercantile Credit Classic     |
|          | v Clark         | 2-5   | 4th round    | Mercantile Credit Classic     |
|          | v Everton       | 6-0   | 1st round    | Welsh Championship            |
|          | v Mountjoy      | 3-6   | Quarter-final| Welsh Championship            |
|          | v Morra         | 2-5   | 2nd round    | MIM Britannia British Open    |
|          | v Rigitano      | 10-4  | Qualifying   | Embassy World Championship    |
|          | v Wych          | 10-5  | Qualifying   | Embassy World Championship    |
|          | v Stevens       | 7-10  | Qualifying   | Embassy World Championship    |
|          | v Marshall      | 5-1   | 2nd round    | Fidelity International         |
|          | v Newbury       | 0-5   | 3rd round    | Fidelity International         |
|          | v Watterson     | 3-5   | 2nd round    | Rothmans Grand Prix           |
|          | v John Rea      | 5-4   | 2nd round    | BCE Canadian Masters          |
|          | v E. Hughes     | 5-2   | 3rd round    | BCE Canadian Masters          |
|          | v White         | 3-5   | 4th round    | BCE Canadian Masters          |
|          | v V. Harris     | 9-7   | 2nd round    | Tennents UK Open              |
|          | v David Taylor  | 9-4   | 3rd round    | Tennents UK Open              |
|          | v White         | 9-6   | 4th round    | Tennents UK Open              |
|          | v West          | 4-9   | 5th round    | Tennents UK Open              |
| 1989     | v Terry         | 3-5   | 2nd round    | Mercantile Credit Classic     |
|          | v F. Davis      | 5-2   | 2nd round    | European Open                 |
|          | v Drago         | 5-1   | 3rd round    | European Open                 |
|          | v J. Campbell   | 3-5   | 4th round    | European Open                 |
|          | v Roscoe        | 6-3   | 1st round    | Senator Welsh Championship    |
|          | v C. Wilson     | 6-1   | Quarter-final| Senator Welsh Championship    |
|          | v Mountjoy      | 5-9   | Semi-final   | Senator Welsh Championship    |
|          | v J. Smith      | 5-4   | 2nd round    | Anglian British Open          |
|          | v Meo           | 1-5   | 3rd round    | Anglian British Open          |
|          | v Price         | 9-10  | Qualifying   | Embassy World Championship    |

## IAN BLACK (Scotland)

**Born** 11.12.54. **Turned professional** 1981. **World ranking** 121 (96). **Best professional performance** 1981 Scottish champion.

|          |                 |       |              |                               |
|----------|-----------------|-------|--------------|-------------------------------|
| 1981     | v Macleod       | 5-4   | Quarter-final| Scottish Championship         |
|          | v E. McLaughlin | 6-3   | Semi-final   | Scottish Championship         |
|          | **v Gibson**    | **11-7** | **Final** | **Scottish Championship**     |
|          | v E. McLaughlin | 5-3   | Qualifying   | Jameson International          |
|          | v Houlihan      | 4-9   | Qualifying   | Coral UK Championship         |
| 1982     | v Parkin        | 9-6   | Qualifying   | Embassy World Championship    |
|          | v Williams      | 2-9   | Qualifying   | Embassy World Championship    |
|          | v Macleod       | 6-0   | Quarter-final| Scottish Championship         |
|          | v Ross          | 6-4   | Semi-final   | Scottish Championship         |

| | | | | |
|---|---|---|---|---|
| | v Sinclair | 7-11 | Final | Scottish Championship |
| | v Fitzmaurice | 3-5 | Qualifying | Jameson International |
| | v Virgo | 2-5 | 1st round | Professional Players Tournament |
| | v Fisher | 3-9 | Qualifying | Coral UK Championship |
| 1983 | v Morra | 10-9 | Qualifying | Embassy World Championship |
| | v Medati | 10-4 | Qualifying | Embassy World Championship |
| | v Mans | 3-10 | 1st round | Embassy World Championship |
| | v E. McLaughlin | 6-4 | 1st round | Scottish Championship |
| | v Macleod | 2-6 | Semi-final | Scottish Championship |
| | v King | 3-5 | Qualifying | Jameson International |
| | v Spencer | 2-5 | 1st round | Professional Players Tournament |
| | v Williamson | 9-6 | Qualifying | Coral UK Championship |
| | v White | 1-9 | 1st round | Coral UK Championship |
| 1984 | v Hines | 5-10 | Qualifying | Embassy World Championship |
| | v Browne | 5-4 | Qualifying | Jameson International |
| | v Watterson | 5-3 | Qualifying | Jameson International |
| | v Macleod | 3-5 | Qualifying | Jameson International |
| | v P. Francisco | 4-5 | Qualifying | Rothmans Grand Prix |
| | v Chappel | 3-9 | Qualifying | Coral UK Open |
| 1985 | v J. McLaughlin | 0-5 | Qualifying | Mercantile Credit Classic |
| | v M. Gibson | 2-6 | 1st round | Scottish Championship |
| | v Bales | 4-6 | Qualifying | Dulux British Open |
| | v Chalmers | 4-10 | Qualifying | Embassy World Championship |
| | v Rigitano | 5-4 | 2nd round | Goya Matchroom Trophy |
| | v Mans | 5-4 | 3rd round | Goya Matchroom Trophy |
| | v Duggan | 1-5 | 4th round | Goya Matchroom Trophy |
| | v G. Foulds | 3-5 | 2nd round | Rothmans Grand Prix |
| | v V. Harris | 3-9 | 2nd round | Coral UK Open |
| 1986 | v G. Foulds | 2-5 | 2nd round | Mercantile Credit Classic |
| | v Gibson | 5-0 | 2nd round | Dulux British Open |
| | v S. Davis | 2-5 | 3rd round | Dulux British Open |
| | v E. McLaughlin | 6-4 | Quarter-final | Canada Dry Scottish Championship |
| | v Hendry | 2-6 | Semi-final | Canada Dry Scottish Championship |
| | v B. Harris | 10-8 | Qualifying | Embassy World Championship |
| | v Newbury | 2-10 | Qualifying | Embassy World Championship |
| | v Wright | 5-1 | 2nd round | BCE International |
| | v Charlton | 0-5 | 3rd round | BCE International |
| | v Morra | 4-5 | 2nd round | Rothmans Grand Prix |
| | v Watterson | 3-9 | 2nd round | Tennents UK Open |
| 1987 | v M. Bennett | 3-5 | 2nd round | Mercantile Credit Classic |
| | v John Rea | 1-6 | 1st round | Scottish Championship |
| | v Roe | 0-5 | 2nd round | Dulux British Open |
| | v Williamson | 10-8 | Qualifying | Embassy World Championship |
| | v O'Kane | 2-10 | Qualifying | Embassy World Championship |
| | v N. Gilbert | 3-5 | 1st round | Fidelity International |
| | v M. Smith | 0-5 | 1st round | Rothmans Grand Prix |
| | v J. Smith | 9-8 | 1st round | Tennents UK Open |
| | v Werbeniuk | 5-9 | 2nd round | Tennents UK Open |
| 1988 | v P. Gibson | 2-5 | 1st round | Mercantile Credit Classic |
| | v M. Gibson | 2-6 | Quarter-final | Scottish Championship |
| | v Gary Wilkinson | 2-5 | 1st round | MIM Britannia British Open |
| | v Fowler | 1-10 | Qualifying | Embassy World Championship |
| | v Robidoux | 1-5 | 1st round | Fidelity International |
| | v S. Campbell | 1-5 | 1st round | Rothmans Grand Prix |
| | v Marshall | 1-5 | 1st round | BCE Canadian Masters |
| | v Robidoux | 2-9 | 1st round | Tennents UK Open |
| 1989 | v Marshall | 0-5 | 1st round | Mercantile Credit Classic |
| | v Fagan | 5-1 | 1st round | European Open |
| | v Macleod | 1-5 | 2nd round | European Open |
| | v John Rea | 3-5 | 1st round | Scottish Championship |
| | v Edwards | 3-5 | 1st round | Anglian British Open |
| | v Sheehan | 10-8 | Qualifying | Embassy World Championship |
| | v Edmonds | 3-10 | Qualifying | Embassy World Championship |

## MALCOLM BRADLEY (England)

**Born** 8.7.48. **Turned professional** 1984. **World ranking** 87 (75). **Best professional performance** Last 16 1985 Dulux British Open.

| | | | | |
|---|---|---|---|---|
| **1984** | v Darrington | 5-3 | Qualifying | Jameson International |
| | v Jack Rea | 5-2 | Qualifying | Jameson International |
| | v Morra | 3-5 | Qualifying | Jameson International |
| | v Jonik | 5-1 | Qualifying | Rothmans Grand Prix |
| | v Virgo | 0-5 | 1st round | Rothmans Grand Prix |
| | v V. Harris | 9-8 | Qualifying | Coral UK Open |
| | v Kelly | 9-6 | Qualifying | Coral UK Open |
| | v Meadowcroft | 9-7 | Qualifying | Coral UK Open |
| | v Hallett | 8-9 | Qualifying | Coral UK Open |
| **1985** | v Browne | 3-5 | Qualifying | Mercantile Credit Classic |
| | v Williamson | 9-8 | Qualifying | Tolly Cobbold English Championship |
| | v Knowles | 8-9 | Qualifying | Tolly Cobbold English Championship |
| | v Morra | 6-2 | Qualifying | Dulux British Open |
| | v David Taylor | 6-3 | 1st round | Dulux British Open |
| | v Fowler | 5-4 | 2nd round | Dulux British Open |
| | v S. Davis | 2-5 | 3rd round | Dulux British Open |
| | v Mienie | 10-4 | Qualifying | Embassy World Championship |
| | v Mikkelsen | 10-9 | Qualifying | Embassy World Championship |
| | v Wych | 7-10 | Qualifying | Embassy World Championship |
| | v John Rea | 5-1 | 2nd round | Goya Matchroom Trophy |
| | v Hallett | 5-4 | 3rd round | Goya Matchroom Trophy |
| | v Johnson | 2-5 | 4th round | Goya Matchroom Trophy |
| | v Gibson | 4-5 | 2nd round | Rothmans Grand Prix |
| | v Jenkins | 9-3 | 2nd round | Coral UK Open |
| | v White | 4-9 | 1st round | Coral UK Open |
| **1986** | v Oliver | 5-3 | 2nd round | Mercantile Credit Classic |
| | v N. Foulds | 3-5 | 3rd round | Mercantile Credit Classic |
| | v Gilbert | 9-5 | 2nd round | Tolly Cobbold English Championship |
| | v S. Davis | 3-9 | 3rd round | Tolly Cobbold English Championship |
| | v Jack Rea | 5-1 | 2nd round | Dulux British Open |
| | v Higgins | 3-5 | 3rd round | Dulux British Open |
| | v Gilbert | 7-10 | Qualifying | Embassy World Championship |
| | v Wilkinson | 5-4 | 2nd round | BCE International |
| | v Wych | 2-5 | 3rd round | BCE International |
| | v Wright | 0-5 | 2nd round | Rothmans Grand Prix |
| | v Meadowcroft | 9-2 | 2nd round | Tennents UK Open |
| | v Parrott | 4-9 | 3rd round | Tennents UK Open |
| **1987** | v Rowswell | 5-4 | 2nd round | Mercantile Credit Classic |
| | v David Taylor | 5-1 | 3rd round | Mercantile Credit Classic |
| | v White | 0-5 | 4th round | Mercantile Credit Classic |
| | v D. Gilbert | 6-3 | 2nd round | Tolly Ales English Championship |
| | v Fowler | 3-6 | 3rd round | Tolly Ales English Championship |
| | v O'Boye | 1-5 | 2nd round | Dulux British Open |
| | v Rowswell | 10-6 | Qualifying | Embassy World Championship |
| | v O'Boye | 10-7 | Qualifying | Embassy World Championship |
| | v Wych | 7-10 | Qualifying | Embassy World Championship |
| | v J. Smith | 5-1 | 2nd round | Fidelity International |
| | v Dennis Taylor | 0-5 | 3rd round | Fidelity International |
| | v John Rea | 1-5 | 2nd round | Rothmans Grand Prix |
| | v Watchorn | 5-9 | 2nd round | Tennents UK Open |
| **1988** | v Everton | 5-2 | 2nd round | Mercantile Credit Classic |
| | v Thorne | 1-5 | 3rd round | Mercantile Credit Classic |
| | v Lawlor | 5-6 | 2nd round | English Championship |
| | v Williamson | 3-5 | 2nd round | MIM Britannia British Open |
| | v Williamson | 10-9 | Qualifying | Embassy World Championship |
| | v Werbeniuk | 8-10 | Qualifying | Embassy World Championship |
| | v Sheehan | 4-5 | 1st round | Fidelity International |

| | | | |
|---|---|---|---|
| v Rowing | 5-3 | 1st round | Rothmans Grand Prix |
| v Murphy | 5-3 | 2nd round | Rothmans Grand Prix |
| v Johnson | 2-5 | 3rd round | Rothmans Grand Prix |
| v Meakin | 5-0 | 1st round | BCE Canadian Masters |
| v Browne | 2-5 | 2nd round | BCE Canadian Masters |
| v T. Wilson | 9-7 | 1st round | Tennents UK Open |
| v J. McLaughlin | 3-9 | 2nd round | Tennents UK Open |
| 1989 v Fagan | 5-3 | 1st round | Mercantile Credit Classic |
| v T. Jones | 5-4 | 2nd round | Mercantile Credit Classic |
| v Newbury | 3-5 | 3rd round | Mercantile Credit Classic |
| v Rempe | 5-4 | 1st round | European Open |
| v O'Boye | 3-5 | 2nd round | European Open |
| v Chambers | 5-2 | 1st round | English Championship |
| v D. Gilbert | 4-5 | 2nd round | English Championship |
| v Everton | 5-0 | 1st round | Anglian British Open |
| v Cripsey | 4-5 | 2nd round | Anglian British Open |
| v Thornley | 7-10 | Qualifying | Embassy World Championship |

## PADDY BROWNE (Republic of Ireland)

**Born** 1.4.65. **Turned professional** 1983. **World ranking** 44 (54). **Amateur career** 1982 Republic of Ireland champion. **Best professional performance** Quarter-finals 1989 Mercantile Credit Classic.

| | | | |
|---|---|---|---|
| 1983 v Murphy | 2-5 | Qualifying | Professional Players Tournament |
| 1984 v Duggan | 10-9 | Qualifying | Embassy World Championship |
| v Roscoe | 10-4 | Qualifying | Embassy World Championship |
| v Sinclair | 1-10 | Qualifying | Embassy World Championship |
| v John Rea | 5-2 | Qualifying | Jameson International |
| v Black | 4-5 | Qualifying | Jameson International |
| v Duggan | 2-5 | Qualifying | Rothmans Grand Prix |
| v G. Foulds | 9-5 | Qualifying | Coral UK Open |
| v King | 5-9 | Qualifying | Coral UK Open |
| 1985 v Bradley | 5-3 | Qualifying | Mercantile Credit Classic |
| v Everton | 5-0 | Qualifying | Mercantile Credit Classic |
| v Miles | 5-3 | Qualifying | Mercantile Credit Classic |
| v White | 2-5 | 1st round | Mercantile Credit Classic |
| v Newbury | 0-6 | Qualifying | Dulux British Open |
| v Murphy | 3-6 | Qualifying | Irish Championship |
| v Anderson | 10-5 | Qualifying | Embassy World Championship |
| v Morra | 6-10 | Qualifying | Embassy World Championship |
| v B. Harris | 3-5 | 2nd round | Goya Matchroom Trophy |
| v B. Harris | 3-5 | 2nd round | Rothmans Grand Prix |
| v Chalmers | 9-4 | 2nd round | Coral UK Open |
| v Thorne | 6-9 | 3rd round | Coral UK Open |
| 1986 v Everton | 5-0 | 2nd round | Mercantile Credit Classic |
| v Wilson | 5-3 | 3rd round | Mercantile Credit Classic |
| v Gauvreau | 3-5 | 4th round | Mercantile Credit Classic |
| v Hendry | 5-0 | 2nd round | Dulux British Open |
| v Spencer | 5-0 | 3rd round | Dulux British Open |
| v Charlton | 1-5 | 4th round | Dulux British Open |
| v Hendry | 9-10 | Qualifying | Embassy World Championship |
| v Burke | 4-5 | 1st round | Strongbow Irish Championship |
| v M. Bennett | 1-5 | 2nd round | BCE International |
| v Sheehan | 5-4 | 2nd round | Rothmans Grand Prix |
| v Johnson | 5-2 | 3rd round | Rothmans Grand Prix |
| v M. Bennett | 5-0 | 4th round | Rothmans Grand Prix |
| v Hendry | 3-5 | 5th round | Rothmans Grand Prix |
| v Williamson | 4-9 | 2nd round | Tennents UK Open |
| 1987 v Dunning | 5-1 | 2nd round | Mercantile Credit Classic |
| v J. Campbell | 2-5 | 3rd round | Mercantile Credit Classic |
| v Rigitano | 4-5 | 2nd round | Dulux British Open |

| | | | |
|---|---|---|---|
| v Wright | 6-10 | Qualifying | Embassy World Championship |
| v Jack Rea | 5-3 | 1st round | Matchroom Irish Championship |
| v Burke | 6-2 | Quarter-final | Matchroom Irish Championship |
| v Dennis Taylor | 1-6 | Semi-final | Matchroom Irish Championship |
| v Roscoe | 2-5 | 2nd round | Fidelity International |
| v Meadowcroft | 3-5 | 2nd round | Rothmans Grand Prix |
| v M. Smith | 4-9 | 2nd round | Tennents UK Open |
| 1988 v M. Smith | 1-5 | 2nd round | Mercantile Credit Classic |
| v Jack Rea | 5-0 | 1st round | Irish Championship |
| v Murphy | 6-5 | Quarter-final | Irish Championship |
| v Dennis Taylor | 5-6 | Semi-final | Irish Championship |
| v Chalmers | 5-2 | 2nd round | MIM Britannia British Open |
| v Martin | 5-4 | 3rd round | MIM Britannia British Open |
| v O'Kane | 2-5 | 4th round | MIM Britannia British Open |
| v Kelly | 10-8 | Qualifying | Embassy World Championship |
| v James | 1-10 | Qualifying | Embassy World Championship |
| v T. Wilson | 3-5 | 2nd round | Fidelity International |
| v Johnston-Allen | 2-5 | 2nd round | Rothmans Grand Prix |
| v Bradley | 5-2 | 2nd round | BCE Canadian Masters |
| v Longworth | 4-5 | 3rd round | BCE Canadian Masters |
| v Kearney | 6-9 | 2nd round | Tennents UK Open |
| 1989 v Williamson | 5-3 | 2nd round | Mercantile Credit Classic |
| v Hallett | 5-2 | 3rd round | Mercantile Credit Classic |
| v James | 5-4 | 4th round | Mercantile Credit Classic |
| v Chappel | 5-1 | 5th round | Mercantile Credit Classic |
| v Mountjoy | 3-5 | Quarter-final | Mercantile Credit Classic |
| v J. Smith | 5-4 | 2nd round | European Open |
| v Reynolds | wo | 3rd round | European Open |
| v Hallett | 4-5 | 4th round | European Open |
| v Sheehan | 5-2 | 1st round | Irish Championship |
| v Murphy | 5-3 | Quarter-final | Irish Championship |
| v J. McLaughlin | 3-6 | Semi-final | Irish Championship |
| v Sinclair | 5-3 | 2nd round | Anglian British Open |
| v Thorburn | 0-5 | 3rd round | Anglian British Open |
| v Meakin | 10-9 | Qualifying | Embassy World Championship |
| v Macleod | 10-6 | Qualifying | Embassy World Championship |
| v Longworth | 10-0 | Qualifying | Embassy World Championship |
| v Thorne | 5-10 | 1st round | Embassy World Championship |

## PASCAL BURKE (Republic of Ireland)

**Born** 19.6.32. **Turned professional** 1982. **World ranking** 124 (105). **Amateur career** 1974 and 1976 Republic of Ireland champion.

| | | | |
|---|---|---|---|
| 1983 v E. Hughes | 2-6 | Quarter-final | Irish Championship |
| v Meo | 0-5 | 1st round | Benson & Hedges Irish Masters |
| v Morgan | 9-10 | Qualifying | Embassy World Championship |
| v G. Foulds | 2-5 | Qualifying | Jameson International |
| v G. Foulds | 5-4 | Qualifying | Professional Players Tournament |
| v Johnson | 3-5 | 1st round | Professional Players Tournament |
| 1984 v Kelly | 10-7 | Qualifying | Embassy World Championship |
| v B. Harris | 10-4 | Qualifying. | Embassy World Championship |
| v Hallett | 5-10 | Qualifying | Embassy World Championship |
| v Kearney | 5-4 | Qualifying | Jameson International |
| v Newbury | 0-5 | Qualifying | Jameson International |
| v Darrington | 5-3 | Qualifying | Rothmans Grand Prix |
| v Meo | 1-5 | 1st round | Rothmans Grand Prix |
| v Longworth | 4-9 | Qualifying | Coral UK Open |
| 1985 v Newbury | 1-5 | Qualifying | Mercantile Credit Classic |
| v Chalmers | 5-6 | Qualifying | Dulux British Open |
| v Kearney | 6-4 | Qualifying | Irish Championship |
| v Higgins | 0-6 | Quarter-final | Irish Championship |

| | | | |
|---|---|---|---|
| | v Newbury | 3-10 | Qualifying | Embassy World Championship |
| | v Rempe | 3-5 | 1st round | Goya Matchroom Trophy |
| | v Newbury | 3-5 | 2nd round | Rothmans Grand Prix |
| | v Jenkins | 5-9 | 1st round | Coral UK Open |
| 1986 | v D. Hughes | 5-3 | 1st round | Mercantile Credit Classic |
| | v Chaperon | 2-5 | 2nd round | Mercantile Credit Classic |
| | v Gilbert | 1-5 | 1st round | Dulux British Open |
| | v Jim Bear | 8-10 | Qualifying | Embassy World Championship |
| | v Browne | 5-4 | 1st round | Strongbow Irish Championship |
| | v E. Hughes | 3-6 | Quarter-final | Strongbow Irish Championship |
| | v Fitzmaurice | 5-4 | 1st round | BCE International |
| | v T. Jones | 5-4 | 2nd round | BCE International |
| | v Thorburn | 0-5 | 3rd round | BCE International |
| | v Roscoe | 5-3 | 1st round | Rothmans Grand Prix |
| | v Spencer | 3-5 | 2nd round | Rothmans Grand Prix |
| | v Watterson | 0-9 | 1st round | Tennents UK Open |
| 1987 | v King | 0-5 | 2nd round | Mercantile Credit Classic |
| | v Scott | 2-5 | 2nd round | Dulux British Open |
| | v Oliver | 5-10 | Qualifying | Embassy World Championship |
| | v Fagan | 5-3 | 1st round | Matchroom Irish Championship |
| | v Browne | 2-6 | Quarter-final | Matchroom Irish Championship |
| | v Jack Rea | 1-5 | 1st round | Fidelity International |
| | v Everton | 5-1 | 1st round | Rothmans Grand Prix |
| | v Reardon | 2-5 | 2nd round | Rothmans Grand Prix |
| | v Oliver | 1-9 | 1st round | Tennents UK Open |
| 1988 | v Oliver | 2-5 | 1st round | Mercantile Credit Classic |
| | v J. McLaughlin | 3-5 | 1st round | Irish Championship |
| | v Darrington | 4-5 | 1st round | MIM Britannia British Open |
| | v Sinclair | 2-10 | Qualifying | Embassy World Championship |
| | v V. Harris | 2-5 | 1st round | Fidelity International |
| | v M. Gibson | 4-5 | 1st round | Rothmans Grand Prix |
| | v Foldvari | 2-5 | 1st round | BCE Canadian Masters |
| | v Foldvari | 0-9 | 1st round | Tennents UK Open |
| 1989 | v Rowswell | 2-5 | 1st round | Mercantile Credit Classic |
| | v Rigitano | 2-5 | 1st round | European Open |
| | v Watchorn | 4-5 | 1st round | Irish Championship |
| | v P. Gibson | wo | 1st round | Anglian British Open |
| | v Owers | 2-5 | 2nd round | Anglian British Open |
| | v Rowswell | 0-10 | Qualifying | Embassy World Championship |

## JOHN CAMPBELL (Australia)

**Born** 10.4.53. **Turned professional** 1982. **World ranking** 42 (33). **Amateur career** 1979 Australian champion. **Best professional performances** 1985 and 1988 Australian champion; last 16 1989 European Open, 1987 Tennents UK Open, 1987 Mercantile Credit Classic, 1986 Dulux British Open, 1985 Rothmans Grand Prix, 1985 Goya Matchroom Trophy.

| | | | |
|---|---|---|---|
| 1983 | v Watterson | 10-6 | Qualifying | Embassy World Championship |
| | v Donnelly | 10-2 | Qualifying | Embassy World Championship |
| | v Thorburn | 5-10 | 1st round | Embassy World Championship |
| | v E. McLaughlin | 2-5 | Qualifying | Jameson International |
| | v Mountjoy | 5-3 | 1st round | Professional Players Tournament |
| | v Miles | 5-2 | 2nd round | Professional Players Tournament |
| | v Martin | 5-0 | 3rd round | Professional Players Tournament |
| | v Knowles | 3-5 | Quarter-final | Professional Players Tournament |
| 1984 | v White | 1-5 | Qualifying | Lada Classic |
| | v Gauvreau | 7-10 | Qualifying | Embassy World Championship |
| | v G. Foulds | 5-3 | Qualifying | Jameson International |
| | v S. Davis | 1-5 | 1st round | Jameson International |
| | v W. Jones | 5-4 | 1st round | Rothmans Grand Prix |

|        |   |                |  |          |                         |
|--------|---|----------------|-------|---------------|------------------------------|
|        | v | Thorburn       | 1-5   | 2nd round     | Rothmans Grand Prix          |
|        | v | Donnelly       | 9-6   | Qualifying    | Coral UK Open                |
|        | v | White          | 7-9   | 1st round     | Coral UK Open                |
| 1985   | v | Scott          | 4-5   | Qualifying    | Mercantile Credit Classic    |
|        | v | O'Kane         | 4-6   | 1st round     | Dulux British Open           |
|        | v | Morra          | 10-9  | Qualifying    | Embassy World Championship   |
|        | v | Charlton       | 3-10  | 1st round     | Embassy World Championship   |
|        | v | Charlton       | 5-4   | Quarter-final | Winfield Australian Masters  |
|        | v | Parrott        | 6-4   | Semi-final    | Winfield Australian Masters  |
|        | v | Meo            | 2-7   | Final         | Winfield Australian Masters  |
|        | v | Foldvari       | 8-5   | Quarter-final | Australian Championship      |
|        | v | King           | 9-6   | Semi-final    | Australian Championship      |
|        | **v** | **Charlton** | **10-7** | **Final**  | **Australian Championship**  |
|        | v | Morra          | 5-2   | 3rd round     | Goya Matchroom Trophy        |
|        | v | Mountjoy       | 5-1   | 4th round     | Goya Matchroom Trophy        |
|        | v | Thorburn       | 0-5   | 5th round     | Goya Matchroom Trophy        |
|        | v | Van Rensberg   | 5-4   | 3rd round     | Rothmans Grand Prix          |
|        | v | Mountjoy       | 5-2   | 4th round     | Rothmans Grand Prix          |
|        | v | Knowles        | 2-5   | 5th round     | Rothmans Grand Prix          |
|        | v | Medati         | 9-7   | 3rd round     | Coral UK Open                |
|        | v | David Taylor   | 4-9   | 4th round     | Coral UK Open                |
| 1986   | v | Donnelly       | 5-2   | 3rd round     | Mercantile Credit Classic    |
|        | v | Mikkelsen      | 5-2   | 4th round     | Mercantile Credit Classic    |
|        | v | N. Foulds      | 1-5   | 5th round     | Mercantile Credit Classic    |
|        | v | West           | 5-4   | 3rd round     | Dulux British Open           |
|        | v | Medati         | 5-4   | 4th round     | Dulux British Open           |
|        | v | S. Davis       | 0-5   | 5th round     | Dulux British Open           |
|        | v | Van Rensberg   | 10-6  | Qualifying    | Embassy World Championship   |
|        | v | Reardon        | 10-8  | 1st round     | Embassy World Championship   |
|        | v | Thorne         | 9-13  | 2nd round     | Embassy World Championship   |
|        | v | Wilkinson      | 6-1   | Quarter-final | Australian Championship      |
|        | v | Foldvari       | 8-3   | Semi-final    | Australian Championship      |
|        | v | King           | 3-10  | Final         | Australian Championship      |
|        | v | Duggan         | 3-5   | 3rd round     | BCE International            |
|        | v | G. Foulds      | 5-0   | 3rd round     | Rothmans Grand Prix          |
|        | v | Griffiths      | 1-5   | 4th round     | Rothmans Grand Prix          |
|        | v | W. Jones       | 3-9   | 3rd round     | Tennents UK Open             |
| 1987   | v | Browne         | 5-2   | 3rd round     | Mercantile Credit Classic    |
|        | v | Spencer        | 5-3   | 4th round     | Mercantile Credit Classic    |
|        | v | Griffiths      | 3-5   | 5th round     | Mercantile Credit Classic    |
|        | v | James          | 1-5   | 3rd round     | Dulux British Open           |
|        | v | Chappel        | 10-6  | Qualifying    | Embassy World Championship   |
|        | v | S. Francisco   | 3-10  | 1st round     | Embassy World Championship   |
|        | v | Wilkinson      | 6-4   | Quarter-final | Australian Championship      |
|        | v | Charlton       | 6-8   | Semi-final    | Australian Championship      |
|        | v | James          | 4-5   | 3rd round     | Fidelity International       |
|        | v | Bales          | 3-5   | 3rd round     | Rothmans Grand Prix          |
|        | v | Chambers       | 9-7   | 3rd round     | Tennents UK Open             |
|        | v | M. Smith       | 9-8   | 4th round     | Tennents UK Open             |
|        | v | Thorburn       | 4-9   | 5th round     | Tennents UK Open             |
| 1988   | v | Murphy         | 3-5   | 3rd round     | Mercantile Credit Classic    |
|        | v | W. Jones       | 5-3   | 3rd round     | MIM Britannia British Open   |
|        | v | O'Boye         | 1-5   | 4th round     | MIM Britannia British Open   |
|        | v | F. Davis       | 10-3  | Qualifying    | Embassy World Championship   |
|        | v | White          | 3-10  | 1st round     | Embassy World Championship   |
|        | v | Anderson       | 5-0   | Quarter-final | Australian Championship      |
|        | v | Charlton       | 8-6   | Semi-final    | Australian Championship      |
|        | **v** | **Foldvari** | **9-7** | **Final** | **Australian Championship**  |
|        | v | Dennis Taylor  | 4-5   | 4th round     | Fidelity International       |
|        | v | W. Jones       | 2-5   | 3rd round     | Rothmans Grand Prix          |
|        | v | Oliver         | 3-5   | 2nd round     | BCE Canadian Masters         |
|        | v | Foldvari       | 9-7   | 2nd round     | Tennents UK Open             |
|        | v | White          | 5-9   | 3rd round     | Tennents UK Open             |

| **1989** | v S. Campbell | 2-5 | 2nd round | Mercantile Credit Classic |
| | v Watchorn | 5-1 | 2nd round | European Open |
| | v P. Francisco | 5-0 | 3rd round | European Open |
| | v M. Bennett | 5-3 | 4th round | European Open |
| | v Parrott | 0-5 | 5th round | European Open |
| | v M. Gibson | 5-2 | 2nd round | Anglian British Open |
| | v P. Francisco | 2-5 | 3rd round | Anglian British Open |
| | v D. Morgan | 4-10 | Qualifying | Embassy World Championship |

## STEVE CAMPBELL (England)

**Born** 7.3.66. **Turned professional** 1988. **World ranking** 98.

| **1988** | v F. Davis | 4-5 | 1st round | Fidelity International |
| | v Black | 5-1 | 1st round | Rothmans Grand Prix |
| | v Stevens | 3-5 | 2nd round | Rothmans Grand Prix |
| | v Kearney | 5-2 | 1st round | BCE Canadian Masters |
| | v Bales | 5-2 | 2nd round | BCE Canadian Masters |
| | v Hendry | 2-5 | 3rd round | BCE Canadian Masters |
| | v Dunning | 9-5 | 1st round | Tennents UK Open |
| | v Clark | 3-9 | 2nd round | Tennents UK Open |
| **1989** | v Oliver | 5-4 | 1st round | Mercantile Credit Classic |
| | v J. Campbell | 5-2 | 2nd round | Mercantile Credit Classic |
| | v C. Wilson | 3-5 | 3rd round | Mercantile Credit Classic |
| | v Morra | 3-5 | 1st round | European Open |
| | v Dunning | 5-3 | 1st round | English Championship |
| | v Fowler | 1-5 | 2nd round | English Championship |
| | v Medati | 5-3 | 1st round | Anglian British Open |
| | v Reardon | 4-5 | 2nd round | Anglian British Open |
| | v M. Smith | 9-10 | Qualifying | Embassy World Championship |

## DAVE CHALMERS (England)

**Born** 14.7.48. **Turned professional** 1984. **World ranking** 125 (112). **Amateur career** 1982 English champion.

| **1984** | v Oliver | 5-4 | Qualifying | Jameson International |
| | v Meadowcroft | 1-5 | Qualifying | Jameson International |
| | v Andrewartha | 5-2 | Qualifying | Rothmans Grand Prix |
| | v Williams | 0-5 | 1st round | Rothmans Grand Prix |
| | v Bales | 2-9 | Qualifying | Coral UK Open |
| **1985** | v Mikkelsen | 1-5 | Prelim | Mercantile Credit Classic |
| | v Meadowcroft | 9-3 | Qualifying | Tolly Cobbold English Championship |
| | v White | 5-9 | Qualifying | Tolly Cobbold English Championship |
| | v Burke | 6-5 | Qualifying | Dulux British Open |
| | v Griffiths | 0-6 | 1st round | Dulux British Open |
| | v Greaves | 10-3 | Qualifying | Embassy World Championship |
| | v E. McLaughlin | 10-9 | Qualifying | Embassy World Championship |
| | v Black | 10-4 | Qualifying | Embassy World Championship |
| | v Hallett | 1-10 | Qualifying | Embassy World Championship |
| | v Chaperon | 2-5 | 2nd round | Goya Matchroom Trophy |
| | v Scott | 2-5 | 2nd round | Rothmans Grand Prix |
| | v Browne | 4-9 | 2nd round | Coral UK Open |
| **1986** | v Donnelly | 0-5 | 2nd round | Mercantile Credit Classic |
| | v Fisher | 9-2 | 2nd round | Tolly Cobbold English Championship |
| | v Hallett | 1-9 | 3rd round | Tolly Cobbold English Championship |
| | v Scott | 1-5 | 2nd round | Dulux British Open |
| | v F. Davis | 6-10 | Qualifying | Embassy World Championship |
| | v Houlihan | 1-5 | 1st round | BCE International |
| | v Agrawal | 5-1 | 1st round | Rothmans Grand Prix |
| | v Chaperon | 2-5 | 2nd round | Rothmans Grand Prix |

|      | v Oliver          | 6-9  | 1st round  | Tennents UK Open              |
|------|-------------------|------|------------|-------------------------------|
| 1987 | v G. Foulds       | 4-5  | 1st round  | Mercantile Credit Classic     |
|      | v Wright          | 5-6  | 1st round  | Tolly Ales English Championship |
|      | v Wildman         | 0-5  | 2nd round  | Dulux British Open            |
|      | v T. Jones        | 1-10 | Qualifying | Embassy World Championship    |
|      | v Fitzmaurice     | 5-4  | 1st round  | Fidelity International        |
|      | v M. Bennett      | 0-5  | 2nd round  | Fidelity International        |
|      | v Darrington      | 2-5  | 1st round  | Rothmans Grand Prix           |
|      | v Bear            | 5-9  | 1st round  | Tennents UK Open              |
| 1988 | v Glen Wilkinson  | 3-5  | 1st round  | Mercantile Credit Classic     |
|      | v Browne          | 2-5  | 2nd round  | MIM Britannia British Open    |
|      | v Oliver          | 9-10 | Qualifying | Embassy World Championship    |
|      | v Williamson      | 2-5  | 1st round  | BCE Canadian Masters          |
| 1989 | v Oliver          | 4-5  | 1st round  | European Open                 |
|      | v Miles           | 4-5  | 1st round  | Anglian British Open          |

## JIM CHAMBERS (England)

**Born** 7.2.57. **Turned professional** 1987. **World ranking** 60 (73). **Best professional performances** Last 32 1989 European Open, 1987 Rothmans Grand Prix.

|      | v Grace           | 4-5  | 2nd round  | Fidelity International        |
|------|-------------------|------|------------|-------------------------------|
| 1987 | v Fitzmaurice     | 5-2  | 1st round  | Rothmans Grand Prix           |
|      | v O'Boye          | 5-3  | 2nd round  | Rothmans Grand Prix           |
|      | v Mountjoy        | 5-2  | 3rd round  | Rothmans Grand Prix           |
|      | v Hendry          | 1-5  | 4th round  | Rothmans Grand Prix           |
|      | v Roscoe          | 9-4  | 1st round  | Tennents UK Open              |
|      | v Wildman         | 9-5  | 2nd round  | Tennents UK Open              |
|      | v J. Campbell     | 7-9  | 3rd round  | Tennents UK Open              |
| 1988 | v Rowswell        | 2-5  | 1st round  | Mercantile Credit Classic     |
|      | v P. Gibson       | 6-0  | 1st round  | English Championship          |
|      | v Scott           | 6-2  | 2nd round  | English Championship          |
|      | v Longworth       | 4-6  | 3rd round  | English Championship          |
|      | v Roe             | 3-5  | 1st round  | MIM Britannia British Open    |
|      | v Watterson       | 10-3 | Qualifying | Embassy World Championship    |
|      | v Wright          | 2-10 | Qualifying | Embassy World Championship    |
|      | v Graham          | 5-2  | 1st round  | Fidelity International        |
|      | v Gary Wilkinson  | 5-4  | 2nd round  | Fidelity International        |
|      | v Thorne          | 2-5  | 3rd round  | Fidelity International        |
|      | v Meakin          | 5-0  | 1st round  | Rothmans Grand Prix           |
|      | v Owers           | 5-3  | 2nd round  | Rothmans Grand Prix           |
|      | v West            | 3-5  | 3rd round  | Rothmans Grand Prix           |
|      | v Fagan           | 5-2  | 1st round  | BCE Canadian Masters          |
|      | v Murphy          | 3-5  | 2nd round  | BCE Canadian Masters          |
|      | v Owers           | 4-9  | 2nd round  | Tennents UK Open              |
| 1989 | v Mienie          | 5-2  | 1st round  | Mercantile Credit Classic     |
|      | v Reardon         | 4-5  | 2nd round  | Mercantile Credit Classic     |
|      | v Mikkelsen       | 5-3  | 1st round  | European Open                 |
|      | v Bales           | 5-1  | 2nd round  | European Open                 |
|      | v S. Davis        | wo   | 3rd round  | European Open                 |
|      | v Charlton        | 2-5  | 4th round  | European Open                 |
|      | v Bradley         | 2-5  | 1st round  | English Championship          |
|      | v Marshall        | 2-5  | 1st round  | Anglian British Open          |
|      | v Anderson        | 10-7 | Qualifying | Embassy World Championship    |
|      | v Stevens         | 8-10 | Qualifying | Embassy World Championship    |

## ROBERT CHAPERON (Canada)

**Born** 18.5.58. **Turned professional** 1983. **World ranking** 29 (29). **Amateur career** 1981 Canadian champion. **Best professional performance** Quarter-finals 1987 Rothmans Grand Prix.

| **1983** | v Watson | 9-5 | 1st round | Canadian Championship |
|---|---|---|---|---|
| | v Jonik | 4-9 | 2nd round | Canadian Championship |
| **1984** | v Fowler | 0-5 | Qualifying | Jameson International |
| | v Kearney | 5-1 | Qualifying | Rothmans Grand Prix |
| | v Gibson | 5-4 | Qualifying | Rothmans Grand Prix |
| | v Martin | 4-5 | Qualifying | Rothmans Grand Prix |
| | v T. Jones | 1-9 | Qualifying | Coral UK Open |
| **1985** | v G. Foulds | 3-5 | Qualifying | Mercantile Credit Clasic |
| | v Fagan | 6-5 | Qualifying | Dulux British Open |
| | v Werbeniuk | 6-1 | 1st round | Dulux British Open |
| | v W. Jones | 5-2 | 2nd round | Dulux British Open |
| | v S. Francisco | 2-5 | 3rd round | Dulux British Open |
| | v Bales | 10-7 | Qualifying | Embassy World Championship |
| | v Heywood | 10-1 | Qualifying | Embassy World Championship |
| | v Morgan | 10-3 | Qualifying | Embassy World Championship |
| | v F. Davis | 9-10 | Qualifying | Embassy World Championship |
| | v Thornley | 5-1 | 1st round | Canadian Championship |
| | v Stevens | 6-4 | Quarter-final | Canadian Championship |
| | v Jonik | 6-3 | Semi-final | Canadian Championship |
| | v Thorburn | 4-6 | Final | Canadian Championship |
| | v Chalmers | 5-2 | 2nd round | Goya Matchroom Trophy |
| | v S. Francisco | 5-3 | 3rd round | Goya Matchroom Trophy |
| | v Macleod | 4-5 | 4th round | Goya Matchroom Trophy |
| | v O'Boye | 3-5 | 2nd round | Rothmans Grand Prix |
| | v J. McLaughlin | 5-9 | 2nd round | Coral UK Open |
| **1986** | v Burke | 5-2 | 2nd round | Mercantile Credit Classic |
| | S. Davis | 1-5 | 3rd round | Mercantile Credit Classic |
| | v V. Harris | 5-0 | 2nd round | Dulux British Open |
| | v Wilson | 3-5 | 3rd round | Dulux British Open |
| | v Jonik | 10-8 | Qualifying | Embassy World Championship |
| | v Gauvreau | 8-10 | Qualifying | Embassy World Championship |
| | v Bear | 6-3 | 1st round | Canadian Championship |
| | v Jonik | 3-6 | 2nd round | Canadian Championship |
| | v N. Gilbert | 5-3 | 2nd round | BCE International |
| | v Martin | 5-4 | 3rd round | BCE International |
| | v Drago | 5-1 | 4th round | BCE International |
| | v E. Hughes | 0-5 | 5th round | BCE International |
| | v Chalmers | 5-2 | 2nd round | Rothmans Grand Prix |
| | v Reardon | 5-3 | 3rd round | Rothmans Grand Prix |
| | v Hendry | 2-5 | 4th round | Rothmans Grand Prix |
| | v Dodd | 9-4 | 2nd round | Tennents UK Open |
| | v David Taylor | 8-9 | 3rd round | Tennents UK Open |
| **1987** | v Roe | 5-4 | 2nd round | Mercantile Credit Classic |
| | v Stevens | 3-5 | 3rd round | Mercantile Credit Classic |
| | v Fisher | 5-2 | 2nd round | Dulux British Open |
| | v Stevens | 4-5 | 3rd round | Dulux British Open |
| | v Fitzmaurice | 10-2 | Qualifying | Embassy World Championship |
| | v Spencer | 4-10 | Qualifying | Embassy World Championship |
| | v Morra | 5-6 | 1st round | Canadian Championship |
| | v V. Harris | 5-4 | 2nd round | Fidelity International |
| | v West | 5-4 | 3rd round | Fidelity International |
| | v Parrott | 1-5 | 4th round | Fidelity International |
| | v Rowswell | 5-4 | 2nd round | Rothmans Grand Prix |
| | v Reynolds | 5-4 | 3rd round | Rothmans Grand Prix |
| | v Houlihan | 5-0 | 4th round | Rothmans Grand Prix |
| | v Fisher | 5-2 | 5th round | Rothmans Grand Prix |
| | v Parrott | 2-5 | Quarter-final | Rothmans Grand Prix |
| | v Jack Rea | 9-6 | 2nd round | Tennents UK Open |
| | v David Taylor | 6-9 | 3rd round | Tennents UK Open |
| **1988** | v Medati | 5-3 | 2nd round | Mercantile Credit Classic |
| | v N. Foulds | 1-5 | 3rd round | Mercantile Credit Classic |
| | v Rigitano | 5-2 | 2nd round | MIM Britannia British Open |

|  | v Stevens | *wo* | 3rd round | MIM Britannia British Open |
|---|---|---|---|---|
|  | v T. Jones | 4-5 | 4th round | MIM Britannia British Open |
|  | v Marshall | 10-3 | Qualifying | Embassy World Championship |
|  | v Murphy | 10-5 | Qualifying | Embassy World Championship |
|  | v David Taylor | 10-6 | Qualifying | Embassy World Championship |
|  | v Hallett | 2-10 | 1st round | Embassy World Championship |
|  | v Robidoux | 3-6 | 1st round | BCE Canadian Championship |
|  | v Fisher | 5-3 | 3rd round | Fidelity International |
|  | v S. Francisco | 5-2 | 4th round | Fidelity International |
|  | v Meo | 4-5 | 5th round | Fidelity International |
|  | v Martin | 5-0 | 3rd round | Rothmans Grand Prix |
|  | v Dennis Taylor | 4-5 | 4th round | Rothmans Grand Prix |
|  | v Reardon | 4-5 | 3rd round | BCE Canadian Masters |
|  | v Gary Wilkinson | 0-9 | 3rd round | Tennents UK Open |
| 1989 | v J. McLaughlin | 5-3 | 3rd round | Mercantile Credit Classic |
|  | v Virgo | 1-5 | 4th round | Mercantile Credit Classic |
|  | v Edwards | 3-5 | 3rd round | European Open |
|  | v Clark | 10-4 | Qualifying | Embassy World Championship |
|  | v Griffiths | 6-10 | 1st round | Embassy World Championship |

## TONY CHAPPEL (Wales)

**Born** 28.5.60. **Turned professional** 1984. **World ranking** 41 (51). **Best professional performances** Last 16 1989 Mercantile Credit Classic, 1987 Tennents UK Open.

| 1984 | v Mikkelsen | 4-5 | Qualifying | Jameson International |
|---|---|---|---|---|
|  | v Scott | 5-1 | Qualifying | Rothmans Grand Prix |
|  | v Stevens | 3-5 | 1st round | Rothmans Grand Prix |
|  | v Houlihan | 9-3 | Qualifying | Coral UK Open |
|  | v Black | 9-3 | Qualifying | Coral UK Open |
|  | v Reynolds | 9-6 | Qualifying | Coral UK Open |
|  | v Stevens | 7-9 | 1st round | Coral UK Open |
|  | v Giannaros | 2-5 | Qualifying | Mercantile Credit Classic |
|  | v Williamson | 6-5 | Qualifying | Dulux British Open |
|  | v S. Davis | 5-6 | 1st round | Dulux British Open |
|  | v Hines | 8-10 | Qualifying | Embassy World Championship |
|  | v M. Owen | 6-0 | 1st round | BCE Welsh Championship |
|  | v Griffiths | 0-6 | Quarter-final | BCE Welsh Championship |
| 1985 | v Meadowcroft | 5-2 | 2nd round | Goya Matchroom Trophy |
|  | v Stevens | 5-3 | 3rd round | Goya Matchroom Trophy |
|  | v Wilson | 0-5 | 4th round | Goya Matchroom Trophy |
|  | v Dodd | 5-2 | 2nd round | Rothmans Grand Prix |
|  | v Mountjoy | 1-5 | 3rd round | Rothmans Grand Prix |
|  | v O'Kane | 9-5 | 1st round | Coral UK Open |
|  | v White | 5-9 | 2nd round | Coral UK Open |
| 1986 | v Murphy | 4-5 | 2nd round | Mercantile Credit Classic |
|  | v Griffiths | 4-6 | Quarter-final | Zetters Welsh Championship |
|  | v Fowler | 4-5 | 2nd round | Dulux British Open |
|  | v Wych | 6-10 | Qualifying | Embassy World Championship |
|  | v Roscoe | 5-3 | 2nd round | BCE International |
|  | v E. Hughes | 4-5 | 3rd round | BCE International |
|  | v Kearney | 5-1 | 2nd round | Rothmans Grand Prix |
|  | v Meo | 1-5 | 3rd round | Rothmans Grand Prix |
|  | v Wilkinson | 9-2 | 2nd round | Tennents UK Open |
|  | v S. Davis | 7-9 | 3rd round | Tennents UK Open |
| 1987 | v Wright | 4-5 | 2nd round | Mercantile Credit Classic |
|  | v Reardon | 6-4 | Quarter-final | Matchroom Welsh Championship |
|  | v Mountjoy | 2-9 | Semi-final | Matchroom Welsh Championship |
|  | v Kearney | 5-3 | 2nd round | Dulux British Open |
|  | v White | 1-5 | 3rd round | Dulux British Open |
|  | v Morra | 10-8 | Qualifying | Embassy World Championship |
|  | v Duggan | 10-3 | Qualifying | Embassy World Championship |

| | | | |
|---|---|---|---|
| v J. Campbell | 6-10 | Qualifying | Embassy World Championship |
| v M. Gibson | 5-2 | 2nd round | Fidelity International |
| v Parrott | 1-5 | 3rd round | Fidelity International |
| v Jonik | 5-4 | 2nd round | Rothmans Grand Prix |
| v Spencer | 5-1 | 3rd round | Rothmans Grand Prix |
| v Griffiths | 3-5 | 4th round | Rothmans Grand Prix |
| v D. Gilbert | 9-2 | 2nd round | Tennents UK Open |
| v Reynolds | 9-5 | 3rd round | Tennents UK Open |
| v Longworth | 9-6 | 4th round | Tennents UK Open |
| v Johnson | 4-9 | 5th round | Tennents UK Open |
| **1988** v D. Hughes | 5-3 | 2nd round | Mercantile Credit Classic |
| v Johnson | 2-5 | 3rd round | Mercantile Credit Classic |
| v Roscoe | 6-4 | 1st round | Welsh Championship |
| v Griffiths | 4-6 | Quarter-final | Welsh Championship |
| v Ellis | 5-0 | 2nd round | MIM Britannia British Open |
| v Hendry | 1-5 | 3rd round | MIM Britannia British Open |
| v N. Gilbert | 10-8 | Qualifying | Embassy World Championship |
| v Miles | 10-7 | Qualifying | Embassy World Championship |
| v Drago | 7-10 | Qualifying | Embassy World Championship |
| v Watchorn | 5-4 | 2nd round | Fidelity International |
| v Dennis Taylor | 1-5 | 3rd round | Fidelity International |
| v T. Wilson | 5-4 | 2nd round | Rothmans Grand Prix |
| v C. Wilson | 2-5 | 3rd round | Rothmans Grand Prix |
| v Darrington | 5-1 | 2nd round | BCE Canadian Masters |
| v Thorburn | 1-5 | 3rd round | BCE Canadian Masters |
| v J. Smith | 9-6 | 2nd round | Tennents UK Open |
| v Reynolds | 4-9 | 3rd round | Tennents UK Open |
| **1989** v Johnston-Allen | 5-2 | 2nd round | Mercantile Credit Classic |
| v S. Davis | 5-3 | 3rd round | Mercantile Credit Classic |
| v A. Harris | 5-1 | 4th round | Mercantile Credit Classic |
| v Browne | 1-5 | 5th round | Mercantile Credit Classic |
| v Darrington | 5-0 | 2nd round | European Open |
| v O'Kane | 5-0 | 3rd round | European Open |
| v Griffiths | 2-5 | 4th round | European Open |
| v D. Morgan | 5-6 | 1st round | Senator Welsh Championship |
| v Lawlor | 5-2 | 2nd round | Anglian British Open |
| v James | 5-3 | 3rd round | Anglian British Open |
| v Wilson | 3-5 | 4th round | Anglian British Open |
| v Edwards | 7-10 | Qualifying | Embassy World Championship |

## EDDIE CHARLTON A.M. (Australia)

**Born** 31.10.29. **Turned professional** 1960. **World ranking** 22 (19). **Best professional performances** Runner-up 1973 World Championship, 1975 World Championship; 1964–67, 1969–84 Australian champion.

| | | | |
|---|---|---|---|
| **1970** v Simpson | 22-27 | Semi-final | World Championship |
| **1972** v David Taylor | 31-25 | Quarter-final | World Championship |
| v Spencer | 32-37 | Semi-final | World Championship |
| **1973** v Mans | 16-8 | 2nd round | World Championship |
| v Miles | 16-6 | Quarter-final | World Championship |
| v Higgins | 23-9 | Semi-final | World Championship |
| v Reardon | 32-38 | Final | World Championship |
| **1974** v Dunning | 13-15 | 2nd round | World Championship |
| **1975** v F. Davis | 5-3 | Quarter-final | Benson & Hedges Masters |
| v Spencer | 2-5 | Semi-final | Benson & Hedges Masters |
| v Werbeniuk | 15-11 | 2nd round | World Championship |
| v Thorburn | 19-12 | Quarter-final | World Championship |
| v Dennis Taylor | 19-12 | Semi-final | World Championship |
| v Reardon | 30-31 | Final | World Championship |
| **1976** v Williams | 4-1 | 2nd round | Benson & Hedges Masters |
| v Reardon | 4-5 | Semi-final | Benson & Hedges Masters |

|      | v Pulman        | 15-9  | 1st round     | Embassy World Championship      |
|------|-----------------|-------|---------------|---------------------------------|
|      | v F. Davis      | 15-13 | Quarter-final | Embassy World Championship      |
|      | v Higgins       | 18-20 | Semi-final    | Embassy World Championship      |
| 1977 | v David Taylor  | 13-5  | 1st round     | Embassy World Championship      |
|      | v Thorburn      | 12-13 | Quarter-final | Embassy World Championship      |
| 1978 | v Thorne        | 13-12 | 1st round     | Embassy World Championship      |
|      | v Thorburn      | 13-12 | Quarter-final | Embassy World Championship      |
|      | v Reardon       | 14-18 | Semi-final    | Embassy World Championship      |
| 1979 | v Higgins       | 2-5   | Quarter-final | Benson & Hedges Masters         |
|      | v Mountjoy      | 13-6  | 1st round     | Embassy World Championship      |
|      | v F. Davis      | 13-4  | Quarter-final | Embassy World Championship      |
|      | v Griffiths     | 17-19 | Semi-final    | Embassy World Championship      |
| 1980 | v Spencer       | 2-5   | Quarter-final | Benson & Hedges Masters         |
|      | v Virgo         | 13-12 | 2nd round     | Embassy World Championship      |
|      | v Stevens       | 7-13  | Quarter-final | Embassy World Championship      |
| 1981 | v Mountjoy      | 0-5   | 1st round     | Benson & Hedges Masters         |
|      | v Mountjoy      | 7-13  | 2nd round     | Embassy World Championship      |
|      | v Martin        | 2-5   | 3rd round     | Jameson International            |
| 1982 | v White         | 5-4   | 1st round     | Benson & Hedges Masters         |
|      | v Higgins       | 1-5   | Quarter-final | Benson & Hedges Masters         |
|      | v Wilson        | 10-5  | 1st round     | Embassy World Championship      |
|      | v Werbeniuk     | 13-5  | 2nd round     | Embassy World Championship      |
|      | v Knowles       | 13-11 | Quarter-final | Embassy World Championship      |
|      | v Reardon       | 11-16 | Semi-final    | Embassy World Championship      |
|      | v Virgo         | 4-5   | 1st round     | Jameson International            |
|      | v D. Hughes     | 5-2   | 1st round     | Professional Players Tournament |
|      | v Williams      | 5-2   | 2nd round     | Professional Players Tournament |
|      | v Meo           | 5-3   | 3rd round     | Professional Players Tournament |
|      | v Reynolds      | 5-2   | Quarter-final | Professional Players Tournament |
|      | v Reardon       | 7-10  | Semi-final    | Professional Players Tournament |
| 1983 | v Virgo         | 5-2   | 1st round     | Lada Classic                    |
|      | v S. Davis      | 4-5   | Quarter-final | Lada Classic                    |
|      | v Meo           | 5-3   | 1st round     | Benson & Hedges Masters         |
|      | v Werbeniuk     | 5-3   | Quarter-final | Benson & Hedges Masters         |
|      | v Thorburn      | 5-6   | Semi-final    | Benson & Hedges Masters         |
|      | v David Taylor  | 5-4   | 1st round     | Benson & Hedges Irish Masters   |
|      | v S. Davis      | 1-5   | Quarter-final | Benson & Hedges Irish Masters   |
|      | v Dodd          | 10-7  | 1st round     | Embassy World Championship      |
|      | v Spencer       | 13-11 | 2nd round     | Embassy World Championship      |
|      | v S. Davis      | 5-13  | Quarter-final | Embassy World Championship      |
|      | v Johnson       | 5-2   | 1st round     | Jameson International            |
|      | v Morra         | 5-3   | 2nd round     | Jameson International            |
|      | v Thorne        | 5-0   | Quarter-final | Jameson International            |
|      | v S. Davis      | 2-9   | Semi-final    | Jameson International            |
|      | v E. McLaughlin | 5-0   | 1st round     | Professional Players Tournament |
|      | v Fisher        | 5-4   | 2nd round     | Professional Players Tournament |
|      | v Johnson       | 0-5   | 3rd round     | Professional Players Tournament |
| 1984 | v Wilson        | 5-0   | Qualifying    | Lada Classic                    |
|      | v White         | 5-3   | 1st round     | Lada Classic                    |
|      | v Wildman       | 4-5   | Quarter-final | Lada Classic                    |
|      | v White         | 2-5   | 1st round     | Benson & Hedges Masters         |
|      | v Higgins       | 2-5   | 1st round     | Benson & Hedges Irish Masters   |
|      | v Stevens       | 3-5   | 1st round     | Tolly Cobbold Classic           |
|      | v Andrewartha   | 10-4  | 1st round     | Embassy World Championship      |
|      | v White         | 7-13  | 2nd round     | Embassy World Championship      |
|      | v David Taylor  | 5-4   | Quarter-final | Winfield Australian Masters     |
|      | v Knowles       | 0-6   | Semi-final    | Winfield Australian Masters     |
|      | v Johnson       | 1-5   | 1st round     | Jameson International            |
|      | v Everton       | 5-1   | 1st round     | Rothmans Grand Prix             |
|      | v Parrott       | 5-1   | 2nd round     | Rothmans Grand Prix             |
|      | v Mountjoy      | 4-5   | 3rd round     | Rothmans Grand Prix             |
|      | v S. Francisco  | 9-4   | 1st round     | Coral UK Open                   |
|      | v Thorne        | 7-9   | 2nd round     | Coral UK Open                   |

| | | | | |
|---|---|---|---|---|
| **1985** | v Macleod | 1-5 | 1st round | Mercantile Credit Classic |
| | v Spencer | 3-5 | 1st round | Benson & Hedges Masters |
| | v B. Harris | 3-6 | 1st round | Dulux British Open |
| | v Dennis Taylor | 5-4 | 1st round | Benson & Hedges Irish Masters |
| | v Knowles | 3-5 | Quarter-final | Benson & Hedges Irish Masters |
| | v J. Campbell | 10-3 | 1st round | Embassy World Championship |
| | v Dennis Taylor | 6-13 | 2nd round | Embassy World Championship |
| | v J. Campbell | 4-5 | Quarter-final | Winfield Australian Masters |
| | v Wilkinson | 8-2 | Quarter-final | Australian Championship |
| | v Morgan | 9-3 | Semi-final | Australian Championship |
| | v J. Campbell | 7-10 | Final | Australian Championship |
| | v Gibson | 4-5 | 3rd round | Goya Matchroom Trophy |
| | v G. Foulds | 5-1 | 3rd round | Rothmans Grand Prix |
| | v Drago | 3-5 | 4th round | Rothmans Grand Prix |
| | v P. Francisco | 5-9 | 3rd round | Coral UK Open |
| **1986** | v P. Francisco | 1-5 | 3rd round | Mercantile Credit Classic |
| | v Stevens | 5-4 | 1st round | Benson & Hedges Masters |
| | v Knowles | 4-5 | Quarter-final | Benson & Hedges Masters |
| | v Gilbert | 5-2 | 3rd round | Dulux British Open |
| | v Browne | 5-1 | 4th round | Dulux British Open |
| | v Virgo | 4-5 | 5th round | Dulux British Open |
| | v Wilson | 10-6 | 1st round | Embassy World Championship |
| | v Stevens | 12-13 | 2nd round | Embassy World Championship |
| | v Anderson | 6-2 | Quarter-final | Australian Championship |
| | v King | 6-8 | Semi-final | Australian Championship |
| | v Black | 5-0 | 3rd round | BCE International |
| | v Knowles | 1-5 | 4th round | BCE International |
| | v Drago | 4-5 | 3rd round | Rothmans Grand Prix |
| | v V. Harris | 9-2 | 3rd round | Tennents UK Open |
| | v S. Davis | 6-9 | 4th round | Tennents UK Open |
| **1987** | v Fisher | 5-0 | 3rd round | Mercantile Credit Classic |
| | v Williams | 5-4 | 4th round | Mercantile Credit Classic |
| | v Parrott | 4-5 | 5th round | Mercantile Credit Classic |
| | v Medati | 5-4 | 3rd round | Dulux British Open |
| | v Dennis Taylor | 1-5 | 4th round | Dulux British Open |
| | v King | 4-10 | Qualifying | Embassy World Championship |
| | v Anderson | 6-2 | Quarter-final | Australian Championship |
| | v J. Campbell | 8-6 | Semi-final | Australian Championship |
| | v King | 7-10 | Final | Australian Championship |
| | v Reardon | 5-4 | 3rd round | Fidelity International |
| | v Griffiths | 5-2 | 4th round | Fidelity International |
| | v N. Gilbert | 5-0 | 5th round | Fidelity International |
| | v Hallett | 4-5 | Quarter-final | Fidelity International |
| | v Van Rensberg | 5-3 | 3rd round | Rothmans Grand Prix |
| | v Edmonds | 5-3 | 4th round | Rothmans Grand Prix |
| | v Knowles | 0-5 | 5th round | Rothmans Grand Prix |
| | v O'Kane | 8-9 | 3rd round | Tennents UK Open |
| **1988** | v Roscoe | 3-5 | 3rd round | Mercantile Credit Classic |
| | v James | 2-5 | 3rd round | MIM Britannia British Open |
| | v B. Harris | 10-4 | Qualifying | Embassy World Championship |
| | v S. Francisco | 10-7 | 1st round | Embassy World Championship |
| | v Knowles | 7-13 | 2nd round | Embassy World Championship |
| | v Jenkins | 5-0 | Quarter-final | Australian Championship |
| | v J. Campbell | 6-8 | Semi-final | Australian Championship |
| | v Robidoux | 2-5 | 3rd round | Fidelity International |
| | v Houlihan | 5-3 | 3rd round | Rothmans Grand Prix |
| | v N. Gilbert | 0-5 | 4th round | Rothmans Grand Prix |
| | v Wych | 5-4 | 3rd round | BCE Canadian Masters |
| | v Graham | 2-5 | 4th round | BCE Canadian Masters |
| | v Stevens | 7-9 | 3rd round | Tennents UK Open |
| **1989** | v Reardon | 1-5 | 3rd round | Mercantile Credit Classic |
| | v Duggan | 5-2 | 3rd round | European Open |
| | v Chambers | 5-2 | 4th round | European Open |

| v Virgo | 5-4 | 5th round | European Open |
|---------|-----|-----------|---------------|
| v Parrott | 1-5 | Quarter-final | European Open |
| v D. Morgan | 3-5 | 3rd round | Anglian British Open |
| v Dodd | 10-6 | Qualifying | Embassy World Championship |
| v Thorburn | 10-9 | 1st round | Embassy World Championship |
| v Meo | 8-13 | 2nd round | Embassy World Championship |

## MARTIN CLARK (England)

**Born** 27.10.68. **Turned professional** 1987. **World ranking** 17 (41). **Best professional performances** Quarter-finals 1989 Anglian British Open, 1989 European Open, 1989 Mercantile Credit Classic.

| | | | | |
|------|-------------|------|-----------|---------------------------|
| 1987 | v Bear | 5-2 | 1st round | Fidelity International |
| | v Duggan | 5-2 | 2nd round | Fidelity International |
| | v Drago | 5-2 | 3rd round | Fidelity International |
| | v Dennis Taylor | 5-0 | 4th round | Fidelity International |
| | v O'Boye | 2-5 | 5th round | Fidelity International |
| | v Williamson | 5-1 | 1st round | Rothmans Grand Prix |
| | v Grace | 5-1 | 2nd round | Rothmans Grand Prix |
| | v N. Foulds | 5-4 | 3rd round | Rothmans Grand Prix |
| | v Fisher | 4-5 | 4th round | Rothmans Grand Prix |
| | v Foldvari | 8-9 | 1st round | Tennents UK Open |
| 1988 | v Wych | 5-2 | 2nd round | Mercantile Credit Classic |
| | v Hallett | 5-4 | 3rd round | Mercantile Credit Classic |
| | v Bennett | 5-2 | 4th round | Mercantile Credit Classic |
| | v Newbury | 2-5 | 5th round | Mercantile Credit Classic |
| | v G. Foulds | 6-0 | 2nd round | English Championship |
| | v White | 5-6 | 3rd round | English Championship |
| | v Fisher | 5-1 | 1st round | MIM Britannia British Open |
| | v Grace | 5-0 | 2nd round | MIM Britannia British Open |
| | v White | 2-5 | 3rd round | MIM Britannia British Open |
| | v Parrott | 1-5 | Final | Kent Cup |
| | v Darrington | 10-5 | Qualifying | Embassy World Championship |
| | v Scott | 10-4 | Qualifying | Embassy World Championship |
| | v King | 9-10 | Qualifying | Embassy World Championship |
| | v Kearney | 5-3 | 2nd round | Fidelity International |
| | v White | 2-5 | 3rd round | Fidelity International |
| | v Whitthread | 5-1 | 2nd round | Rothmans Grand Prix |
| | v E. Hughes | 3-5 | 3rd round | Rothmans Grand Prix |
| | v T. Wilson | 5-3 | 2nd round | BCE Canadian Masters |
| | v Higgins | 3-5 | 3rd round | BCE Canadian Masters |
| | v S. Campbell | 9-3 | 2nd round | Tennents UK Open |
| | v Hallett | 9-6 | 3rd round | Tennents UK Open |
| | v Fowler | 6-9 | 4th round | Tennents UK Open |
| 1989 | v Morgan | 5-1 | 2nd round | Mercantile Credit Classic |
| | v Spencer | 5-2 | 3rd round | Mercantile Credit Classic |
| | v N. Foulds | 5-4 | 4th round | Mercantile Credit Classic |
| | v Johnson | 5-3 | 5th round | Mercantile Credit Classic |
| | v Thorne | 4-5 | Quarter-final | Mercantile Credit Classic |
| | v Rowing | 5-0 | 2nd round | European Open |
| | v N. Foulds | 5-3 | 3rd round | European Open |
| | v E. Hughes | 5-1 | 4th round | European Open |
| | v Johnson | 5-4 | 5th round | European Open |
| | v Griffiths | 1-5 | Quarter-final | European Open |
| | v Oliver | 5-2 | 2nd round | English Championship |
| | v Thorne | 1-5 | 3rd round | English Championship |
| | v Darrington | 5-2 | 2nd round | Anglian British Open |
| | v David Taylor | 5-2 | 3rd round | Anglian British Open |
| | v Virgo | 5-1 | 4th round | Anglian British Open |
| | v N. Foulds | 5-4 | 5th round | Anglian British Open |
| | v Hallett | 3-5 | Quarter-final | Anglian British Open |

*Martin Clark*

| | | | |
|---|---|---|---|
| v Morra | 10-6 | Qualifying | Embassy World Championship |
| v Martin | 10-2 | Qualifying | Embassy World Championship |
| v Chaperon | 4-10 | Qualifying | Embassy World Championship |

## GRAHAM CRIPSEY (England)

**Born** 8.12.54. **Turned professional** 1982. **World ranking** 51 (46). **Best professional performance** Last 16 1987 Rothmans Grand Prix.

| | | | | |
|---|---|---|---|---|
| 1982 | v French | 1-5 | Qualifying | Jameson International |
| | v B. Harris | 6-9 | Qualifying | Coral UK Championship |
| 1983 | v D. Hughes | 10-2 | Qualifying | Embassy World Championship |
| | v Meadowcroft | 6-10 | Qualifying | Embassy World Championship |
| | v Ganim | 4-5 | Qualifying | Professional Players Tournament |
| | v Darrington | 3-9 | Qualifying | Coral UK Championship |
| 1984 | v Parkin | 10-4 | Qualifying | Embassy World Championship |
| | v Gauvreau | 1-10 | Qualifying | Embassy World Championship |
| | v Thornley | 5-3 | Qualifying | Jameson Internaitonal |
| | v Dunning | 3-5 | Qualifying | Jameson International |
| | v Morra | 3-5 | Qualifying | Rothmans Grand Prix |
| | v Foldvari | 9-7 | Qualifying | Coral UK Open |
| | v Fitzmaurice | 8-9 | Qualifying | Coral UK Open |
| 1985 | v Medati | 4-5 | Qualifying | Mercantile Credit Classic |
| | v Bennett ˙ | 9-0 | Qualifying | Tolly Cobbold English Championship |
| | v David Taylor | 5-9 | 1st round | Tolly Cobbold English Championship |
| | v O'Kane | 4-6 | Qualifying | Dulux British Open |
| | v Longworth | 8-10 | Qualifying | Embassy World Championship |
| | v Bennett | 5-3 | 1st round | Goya Matchroom Trophy |
| | v Medati | 5-2 | 2nd round | Goya Matchroom Trophy |
| | v Dennis Taylor | 1-5 | 3rd round | Goya Matchroom Trophy |
| | v Hargreaves | 1-5 | 1st round | Rothmans Grand Prix |
| | v Greaves | 9-4 | 1st round | Coral UK Open |
| | v Dunning | wo | 2nd round | Coral UK Open |
| | v Wilson | 9-7 | 3rd round | Coral UK Open |
| | v Dennis Taylor | 2-9 | 4th round | Coral UK Open |
| 1986 | v Drago | 5-4 | 1st round | Mercantile Credit Classic |
| | v Newbury | 5-4 | 2nd round | Mercantile Credit Classic |
| | v Spencer | 5-1 | 3rd round | Mercantile Credit Classic |
| | v Higgins | 2-5 | 4th round | Mercantile Credit Classic |
| | v Meadowcroft | 9-1 | 2nd round | Tolly Cobbold English Championship |
| | v Wildman | 5-9 | 3rd round | Tolly Cobbold English Championship |
| | v Darrington | 5-4 | 1st round | Dulux British Open |
| | v Williamson | 4-5 | 2nd round | Dulux British Open |
| | v Drago | 4-10 | Qualifying | Embassy World Championship |
| | v Houlihan | 1-5 | 2nd round | BCE International |
| | v P. Gibson | 5-3 | 2nd round | Rothmans Grand Prix |
| | v Parrott | 4-5 | 3rd round | Rothmans Grand Prix |
| | v Bales | 9-6 | 2nd round | Tennents UK Open |
| | v N. Foulds | 7-9 | 3rd round | Tennents UK Open |
| 1987 | v Mienie | 5-0 | 2nd round | Mercantile Credit Classic |
| | v Thorburn | 0-5 | 3rd round | Mercantile Credit Classic |
| | v Dunning | 6-1 | 2nd round | Tolly Ales English Championship |
| | v White | 4-6 | 3rd round | Tolly Ales English Championship |
| | v Watchorn | 5-4 | 2nd round | Dulux British Open |
| | v Werbeniuk | 5-2 | 3rd round | Dulux British Open |
| | v Thorburn | 2-5 | 4th round | Dulux British Open |
| | v Meadowcroft | 10-9 | Qualifying | Embassy World Championship |
| | v M. Gibson | 10-4 | Qualifying | Embassy World Championship |
| | v David Taylor | 7-10 | Qualifying | Embassy World Championship |
| | v Anderson | 5-4 | 2nd round | Fidelity International |
| | v Werbeniuk | 1-5 | 3rd round | Fidelity International |
| | v M. Gibson | 5-2 | 2nd round | Rothmans Grand Prix |

|      | v West         | 5-3   | 3rd round  | Rothmans Grand Prix              |
|------|----------------|-------|------------|----------------------------------|
|      | v P. Gibson    | 5-4   | 4th round  | Rothmans Grand Prix              |
|      | v P. Francisco | 1-5   | 5th round  | Rothmans Grand Prix              |
|      | v P. Gibson    | 9-6   | 2nd round  | Tennents UK Open                 |
|      | v Thorburn     | 6-9   | 3rd round  | Tennents UK Open                 |
| 1988 | v M. Gibson    | 5-4   | 2nd round  | Mercantile Credit Classic        |
|      | v P. Francisco | 2-5   | 3rd round  | Mercantile Credit Classic        |
|      | v Greaves      | 4-6   | 2nd round  | English Championship             |
|      | v Donnelly     | 5-4   | 2nd round  | MIM Britannia British Open       |
|      | v E. Hughes    | 5-3   | 3rd round  | MIM Britannia British Open       |
|      | v Hallett      | 2-5   | 4th round  | MIM Britannia British Open       |
|      | v Meadowcroft  | 10-3  | Qualifying | Embassy World Championship       |
|      | v Houlihan     | 10-4  | Qualifying | Embassy World Championship       |
|      | v Longworth    | 2-10  | Qualifying | Embassy World Championship       |
|      | v Johnson      | 3-5   | 3rd round  | Fidelity International           |
|      | v M. Smith     | 0-5   | 2nd round  | Rothmans Grand Prix              |
|      | v Medati       | 0-5   | 2nd round  | BCE Canadian Masters             |
|      | v John Rea     | 2-9   | 2nd round  | Tennents UK Open                 |
| 1989 | v Kearney      | 5-2   | 2nd round  | Mercantile Credit Classic        |
|      | v Longworth    | 5-3   | 3rd round  | Mercantile Credit Classic        |
|      | v Thorburn     | 1-5   | 4th round  | Mercantile Credit Classic        |
|      | v Roscoe       | 5-4   | 2nd round  | European Open                    |
|      | v Johnson      | 2-5   | 3rd round  | European Open                    |
|      | v Whitthread   | 5-2   | 2nd round  | English Championship             |
|      | v James        | 5-3   | 3rd round  | English Championship             |
|      | v N. Foulds    | 1-5   | 4th round  | English Championship             |
|      | v Bradley      | 5-4   | 2nd round  | Anglian British Open             |
|      | v S. Davis     | 1-5   | 3rd round  | Anglian British Open             |
|      | v Graham       | 2-10  | Qualifying | Embassy World Championship       |

## MIKE DARRINGTON (England)

**Born** 13.9.31. **Turned professional** 1982. **World ranking** 102 (100).

|      | v Williams      | 0-10  | Qualifying | Embassy World Championship            |
|------|-----------------|-------|------------|---------------------------------------|
| 1983 | v Williamson    | 5-3   | Qualifying | Jameson International                  |
|      | v S. Francisco  | 2-5   | Qualifying | Jameson International                  |
|      | v Duggan        | 4-5   | Qualifying | Professional Players Tournament        |
|      | v Cripsey       | 9-3   | Qualifying | Coral UK Championship                  |
|      | v Hallett       | 1-9   | Qualifying | Coral UK Championship                  |
| 1984 | v Caggianello   | 7-10  | Qualifying | Embassy World Championship             |
|      | v Bradley       | 3-5   | Qualifying | Jameson International                  |
|      | v Burke         | 3-5   | Qualifying | Rothmans Grand Prix                    |
|      | v Longworth     | 5-9   | Qualifying | Coral UK Open                          |
| 1985 | v Hargreaves    | 2-5   | Qualifying | Mercantile Credit Classic              |
|      | v Virgo         | 0-9   | 1st round  | Tolly Cobbold English Championship     |
|      | v Scott         | 3-6   | Qualifying | Dulux British Open                     |
|      | v T. Jones      | 2-10  | Qualifying | Embassy World Championship             |
|      | v Gilbert       | 5-2   | 1st round  | Goya Matchroom Trophy                  |
|      | v Sinclair      | 0-5   | 2nd round  | Goya Matchroom Trophy                  |
|      | v Greaves       | 5-2   | 1st round  | Rothmans Grand Prix                    |
|      | v Foldvari      | 5-3   | 2nd round  | Rothmans Grand Prix                    |
|      | v N. Foulds     | 0-5   | 3rd round  | Rothmans Grand Prix                    |
|      | v Foldvari      | 9-6   | 2nd round  | Coral UK Open                          |
|      | v Martin        | 3-9   | 3rd round  | Coral UK Open                          |
| 1986 | v O'Boye        | 0-5   | 1st round  | Mercantile Credit Classic              |
|      | v Fowler        | 3-9   | 2nd round  | Tolly Cobbold English Championship     |
|      | v Cripsey       | 4-5   | 1st round  | Dulux British Open                     |
|      | v Meadowcroft   | 10-6  | Qualifying | Embassy World Championship             |
|      | v Edmonds       | 5-10  | Qualifying | Embassy World Championship             |
|      | v Jack Rea      | 4-5   | 1st round  | BCE International                      |
|      | v Watchorn      | 2-5   | 1st round  | Rothmans Grand Prix                    |
|      | v Whitthread    | 9-8   | 1st round  | Tennents UK Open                       |

|      | | | | |
|------|-----------|-------|-----------|--------------------------------|
|      | v Fowler | 6-9 | 2nd round | Tennents UK Open |
| 1987 | v Roe | 0-5 | 1st round | Mercantile Credit Classic |
|      | v V. Harris | 3-6 | 2nd round | Tolly Ales English Championship |
|      | v James | 3-5 | 1st round | Dulux British Open |
|      | v Demarco | 10-6 | Qualifying | Embassy World Championship |
|      | v Hendry | 7-10 | 2nd round | Embassy World Championship |
|      | v Kelly | 4-5 | 1st round | Fidelity International |
|      | v Chalmers | 5-2 | 1st round | Rothmans Grand Prix |
|      | v Kearney | 0-5 | 2nd round | Rothmans Grand Prix |
|      | v Watchorn | 2-9 | 1st round | Tennents UK Open |
| 1988 | v Meakin | 4-5 | 1st round | Mercantile Credit Classic |
|      | v Meakin | 3-6 | 1st round | English Championship |
|      | v Burke | 5-4 | 1st round | MIM Britannia British Open |
|      | v Dodd | 5-4 | 2nd round | MIM Britannia British Open |
|      | v P. Francisco | 1-5 | 3rd round | MIM Britannia British Open |
|      | v Clark | 5-10 | Qualifying | Embassy World Championship |
|      | v Williamson | 1-5 | 1st round | Fidelity International |
|      | v John Rea | 4-5 | 1st round | Rothmans Grand Prix |
|      | v V. Harris | 5-0 | 1st round | BCE Canadian Masters |
|      | v Chappel | 1-5 | 2nd round | BCE Canadian Masters |
|      | v Roscoe | 7-9 | 1st round | Tennents UK Open |
| 1989 | v Morra | 5-2 | 1st round | Mercantile Credit Classic |
|      | v Houlihan | 5-4 | 2nd round | Mercantile Credit Classic |
|      | v David Taylor | 2-5 | 3rd round | Mercantile Credit Classic |
|      | v Dunning | 5-4 | 1st round | European Open |
|      | v Chappel | 0-5 | 2nd round | European Open |
|      | v Graham | 3-5 | 1st round | English Championship |
|      | v Scott | 5-4 | 1st round | Anglian British Open |
|      | v Clark | 2-5 | 2nd round | Anglian British Open |
|      | v M. Gibson | 0-10 | Qualifying | Embassy World Championship |

## FRED DAVIS O.B.E. (England)

**Born** 14.8.13. **Turned professional** 1930. **World ranking** 89 (83). **Best professional performances** World champion 1948–49, 1951–56.

|      | | | | |
|------|------------------|-------|---------------|--------------------------------|
| 1969 | v Reardon | 25-24 | Quarter-final | World Championship |
|      | v G. Owen | 28-45 | Semi-final | World Championship |
| 1970 | v Reardon | 26-31 | Quarter-final | World Championship |
| 1972 | v Spencer | 21-31 | Quarter-final | World Championship |
| 1973 | v Greaves | 16-1 | 2nd round | World Championship |
|      | v Higgins | 14-16 | Quarter-final | World Championship |
| 1974 | v Werbeniuk | 15-5 | 2nd round | World Championship |
|      | v Higgins | 15-14 | Quarter-final | World Championship |
|      | v Reardon | 3-15 | Semi-final | World Championship |
| 1975 | v Charlton | 3-5 | Quarter-final | Benson & Hedges Masters |
|      | v Dennis Taylor | 14-15 | 2nd round | World Championship |
| 1976 | v Thorburn | 4-2 | 1st round | Benson & Hedges Masters |
|      | v Spencer | 0-4 | 2nd round | Benson & Hedges Masters |
|      | v Werbeniuk | 15-12 | 1st round | Embassy World Championship |
|      | v Charlton | 13-15 | Quarter-final | Embassy World Championship |
| 1977 | v Mountjoy | 2-4 | Quarter-final | Benson & Hedges Masters |
|      | v Pulman | 12-13 | 1st round | Embassy World Championship |
|      | v Fagan | 0-5 | 2nd round | Super Crystalate UK Championship |
| 1978 | v Miles | 3-4 | 1st round | Benson & Hedges Masters |
|      | v Virgo | 9-8 | Qualifying | Embassy World Championship |
|      | v Dennis Taylor | 13-9 | 1st round | Embassy World Championship |
|      | v Fagan | 13-10 | Quarter-final | Embassy World Championship |
|      | v Mans | 16-18 | Semi-final | Embassy World Championship |
|      | v Dunning | 9-2 | 1st round | Coral UK Championship |
|      | v Higgins | 4-9 | Quarter-final | Coral UK Championship |
| 1979 | v Mountjoy | 2-5 | 1st round | Benson & Hedges Masters |

| | | | | |
|---|---|---|---|---|
| | v Stevens | 13-8 | 1st round | Embassy World Championship |
| | v Charlton | 4-13 | Quarter-final | Embassy World Championship |
| | v Edmonds | 6-9 | 3rd round | Coral UK Championship |
| 1980 | v David Taylor | 5-13 | 2nd round | Embassy World Championship |
| | v Wildman | 9-6 | 2nd round | Coral UK Championship |
| | v Higgins | 6-9 | Quarter-final | Coral UK Championship |
| 1981 | v Stevens | 5-4 | 1st round | Benson & Hedges Masters |
| | v Griffiths | 2-5 | Quarter-final | Benson & Hedges Masters |
| | v Edmonds | 6-9 | 1st round | John Courage English |
| | v David Taylor | 3-13 | 2nd round | Embassy World Championship |
| | v Williams | 0-5 | 2nd round | Jameson International |
| | v Knowles | 6-9 | 2nd round | Coral UK Championship |
| 1982 | v Reynolds | 7-10 | 1st round | Embassy World Championship |
| | v Fisher | 3-5 | Qualifying | Jameson International |
| | v Sinclair | 2-5 | 1st round | Professional Players Tournament |
| | v Hallett | 7-9 | 1st round | Coral UK Open |
| 1983 | v Williams | 1-10 | Qualifying | Embassy World Championship |
| | v Kelly | 5-1 | Qualifying | Jameson International |
| | v Morgan | 3-5 | Qualifying | Jameson International |
| | v Fisher | 4-5 | 1st round | Professional Players Tournament |
| | v Watterson | 6-9 | Qualifying | Coral UK Championship |
| | v Donnelly | 10-5 | Qualifying | Embassy World Championship |
| | v Werbeniuk | 4-10 | 1st round | Embassy World Championship |
| 1984 | v Dunning | 5-4 | Qualifying | Jameson International |
| | v Virgo | 3-5 | Qualifying | Jameson International |
| | v V. Harris | 1-5 | Qualifying | Rothmans Grand Prix |
| | v Fowler | 4-9 | Qualifying | Coral UK Open |
| 1985 | v E. McLaughlin | 1-5 | Qualifying | Mercantile Credit Classic |
| | v G. Foulds | 2-9 | Qualifying | Tolly Cobbold English Championship |
| | v Longworth | 1-6 | Qualifying | Dulux British Open |
| | v Chaperon | 10-9 | Qualifying | Embassy World Championship |
| | v Williams | 6-10 | Qualifying | Embassy World Championship |
| | v Duggan | 1-5 | 2nd round | Goya Matchroom Trophy |
| | v Simngam | 2-5 | 2nd round | Rothmans Grand Prix |
| | v John Rea | 9-8 | 2nd round | Coral UK Open |
| | v Werbeniuk | 9-7 | 3rd round | Coral UK Open |
| | v Higgins | 2-9 | 4th round | Coral UK Open |
| 1986 | v Kelly | 5-3 | 2nd round | Mercantile Credit Classic |
| | v Stevens | 5-2 | 3rd round | Mercantile Credit Classic |
| | v E. Hughes | 3-5 | 4th round | Mercantile Credit Classic |
| | v D. Hughes | 9-6 | 2nd round | Tolly Cobbold English Championship |
| | v Martin | 8-9 | 3rd round | Tolly Cobbold English Championship |
| | v Kelly | 5-4 | 2nd round | Dulux British Open |
| | v Macleod | 4-5 | 3rd round | Dulux British Open |
| | v Chalmers | 10-6 | Qualifying | Embassy World Championship |
| | v P. Francisco | 1-10 | Qualifying | Embassy World Championship |
| | v Bales | 4-5 | 2nd round | BCE International |
| | v Bales | 5-4 | 2nd round | Rothmans Grand Prix |
| | v Higgins | 0-5 | 3rd round | Rothmans Grand Prix |
| | v Rowswell | 4-9 | 2nd round | Tennents UK Open |
| 1987 | v Fisher | 2-5 | 2nd round | Mercantile Credit Classic |
| | v James | 2-6 | 2nd round | Tolly Ales English Championship |
| | v Owers | 3-5 | 2nd round | Dulux British Open |
| | v Owers | 5-10 | Qualifying | Embassy World Championship |
| | v Roe | 3-5 | 2nd round | Fidelity International |
| | v Fisher | 0-5 | 2nd round | Rothmans Grand Prix |
| | v Ellis | 9-6 | 2nd round | Tennents UK Open |
| | v Virgo | 4-9 | 3rd round | Tennents UK Open |
| 1988 | v Meakin | 5-4 | 2nd round | Mercantile Credit Classic |
| | v Mountjoy | 0-5 | 3rd round | Mercantile Credit Classic |
| | v N. Gilbert | 6-5 | 2nd round | English Championship |
| | v Meo | 3-6 | 3rd round | English Championship |
| | v D. Hughes | 5-2 | 2nd round | MIM Britannia British Open |

|  | v Spencer | 0-5 | 3rd round | MIM Britannia British Open |
|---|---|---|---|---|
|  | v Fitzmaurice | 10-8 | Qualifying | Embassy World Championship |
|  | v Bear | 10-4 | Qualifying | Embassy World Championship |
|  | v J. Campbell | 3-10 | Qualifying | Embassy World Championship |
|  | v S. Campbell | 5-4 | 1st round | Fidelity International |
|  | v Murphy | 1-5 | 2nd round | Fidelity International |
|  | v Kelly | 3-5 | 1st round | Rothmans Grand Prix |
|  | v Morgan | 2-5 | 1st round | BCE Canadian Masters |
|  | v Sheehan | 7-9 | 1st round | Tennents UK Open |
| 1989 | v Everton | 5-0 | 1st round | European Open |
|  | v M. Bennett | 2-5 | 2nd round | European Open |
|  | v Lawlor | 2-5 | 1st round | English Championship |
|  | v T. Wilson | 1-5 | 1st round | Anglian British Open |
|  | v B. Bennett | 10-4 | Qualifying | Embassy World Championship |
|  | v Duggan | 3-10 | Qualifying | Embassy World Championship |

## STEVE DAVIS M.B.E. (England)

**Born** 22.8.57. **Turned professional** 1978. **World ranking** 1 (1). **Best professional performances** Winner Embassy World Championship 1981, 1983, 1984, 1987, 1988, 1989, Coral UK Championship 1980, 1981, 1984, 1985, Tennents UK Open 1986, 1987; winner of 10 other ranking tournaments, 20 non-ranking tournaments, 2 English Championships.

| 1979 | v Anderson | 9-1 | Prelim | Embassy World Championship |
|---|---|---|---|---|
|  | v Fagan | 9-2 | Qualifying | Embassy World Championship |
|  | v Dennis Taylor | 11-13 | 1st round | Embassy World Championship |
|  | v Dunning | 9-3 | 2nd round | Coral UK Championship |
|  | v Mountjoy | 9-5 | 3rd round | Coral UK Championship |
|  | v Virgo | 7-9 | Quarter-final | Coral UK Championship |
| 1980 | v Morgan | 9-0 | Qualifying | Embassy World Championship |
|  | v Fagan | 10-6 | 1st round | Embassy World Championship |
|  | v Griffiths | 13-10 | 2nd round | Embassy World Championship |
|  | v Higgins | 9-13 | Quarter-final | Embassy World Championship |
|  | v Hallett | 9-1 | 1st round | Coral UK Championship |
|  | v Werbeniuk | 9-3 | 2nd round | Coral UK Championship |
|  | v Meo | 9-5 | Quarter-final | Coral UK Championship |
|  | v Griffiths | 9-0 | Semi-final | Coral UK Championship |
|  | **v Higgins** | **16-6** | **Final** | **Coral UK Championship** |
| 1981 | v Mans | 3-5 | 1st round | Benson & Hedges Masters |
|  | v Dennis Taylor | 5-2 | Semi-final | Yamaha International Masters |
|  | **v David Taylor** | **9-6** | **Final** | **Yamaha International Masters** |
|  | v Meadowcroft | 9-2 | 1st round | John Courage English |
|  | v Spencer | 9-7 | 2nd round | John Courage English |
|  | v Edmonds | 9-0 | Semi-final | John Courage English |
|  | **v Meo** | **9-3** | **Final** | **John Courage English** |
|  | v White | 10-8 | 1st round | Embassy World Championship |
|  | v Higgins | 13-8 | 2nd round | Embassy World Championship |
|  | v Griffiths | 13-9 | Quarter-final | Embassy World Championship |
|  | v Thorburn | 16-10 | Semi-final | Embassy World Championship |
|  | **v Mountjoy** | **18-12** | **Final** | **Embassy World Championship** |
|  | v Mountjoy | 5-0 | Quarter-final | Langs Scottish Masters |
|  | v White | 5-6 | Semi-final | Langs Scottish Masters |
|  | v Mans | 5-3 | 3rd round | Jameson International |
|  | v David Taylor | 5-1 | Quarter-final | Jameson International |
|  | v Higgins | 9-8 | Semi-final | Jameson International |
|  | **v Dennis Taylor** | **9-0** | **Final** | **Jameson International** |
|  | v Higgins | 5-2 | 1st round | Northern Ireland Classic |
|  | v Griffiths | 9-6 | Semi-final | Northern Ireland Classic |
|  | v White | 9-11 | Final | Northern Ireland Classic |
|  | v Thorne | 9-2 | 3rd round | Coral UK Championship |

*Steve Davis*

|        |                |       |              |                                |
|--------|----------------|-------|--------------|--------------------------------|
|        | v Werbeniuk    | 9-5   | Quarter-final | Coral UK Championship         |
|        | v White        | 9-0   | Semi-final    | Coral UK Championship         |
|        | **v Griffiths**| **16-3** | **Final**  | **Coral UK Championship**     |
| 1982   | v Spencer      | 5-2   | 1st round     | Lada Classic                  |
|        | v Reardon      | 5-4   | Semi-final    | Lada Classic                  |
|        | v Griffiths    | 8-9   | Final         | Lada Classic                  |
|        | v Mountjoy     | 5-2   | Quarter-final | Benson & Hedges Masters       |
|        | v Meo          | 6-4   | Semi-final    | Benson & Hedges Masters       |
|        | **v Griffiths**| **9-5** | **Final**   | **Benson & Hedges Masters**   |
|        | **v Griffiths**| **9-7** | **Final**   | **Yamaha International Masters** |
|        | v Miles        | 5-2   | Semi-final    | Tolly Cobbold Classic         |
|        | **v Dennis Taylor** | **8-3** | **Final** | **Tolly Cobbold Classic**  |
|        | v Mountjoy     | 5-2   | Quarter-final | Benson & Hedges Irish Masters |
|        | v Higgins      | 6-2   | Semi-final    | Benson & Hedges Irish Masters |
|        | v Griffiths    | 5-9   | Final         | Benson & Hedges Irish Masters |
|        | v Knowles      | 1-10  | 1st round     | Embassy World Championship    |
|        | v Knowles      | 5-4   | 1st round     | Langs Scottish Masters        |
|        | v Dennis Taylor| 6-1   | Semi-final    | Langs Scottish Masters        |
|        | **v Higgins**  | **9-4** | **Final**   | **Langs Scottish Masters**    |
|        | v Roscoe       | 5-0   | 1st round     | Jameson International          |
|        | v Reynolds     | 5-0   | 2nd round     | Jameson International          |
|        | v David Taylor | 3-5   | Quarter-final | Jameson International          |
|        | v Williams     | 9-6   | 1st round     | Coral UK Open                 |
|        | v Fagan        | 9-3   | 2nd round     | Coral UK Open                 |
|        | v Griffiths    | 6-9   | Quarter-final | Coral UK Open                 |
| 1983   | v Dennis Taylor| 5-2   | 1st round     | Lada Classic                  |
|        | v Charlton     | 5-4   | Quarter-final | Lada Classic                  |
|        | v Spencer      | 5-4   | Semi-final    | Lada Classic                  |
|        | **v Werbeniuk**| **9-5** | **Final**   | **Lada Classic**              |
|        | v Wildman      | 5-2   | 1st round     | Benson & Hedges Masters       |
|        | v Mountjoy     | 4-5   | Quarter-final | Benson & Hedges Masters       |
|        | v Dennis Taylor| 5-1   | Semi-final    | Tolly Cobbold Classic         |
|        | **v Griffiths**| **7-5** | **Final**   | **Tolly Cobbold Classic**     |
|        | v Charlton     | 5-1   | Quarter-final | Benson & Hedges Irish Masters |
|        | v Griffiths    | 6-2   | Semi-final    | Benson & Hedges Irish Masters |
|        | **v Reardon**  | **9-2** | **Final**   | **Benson & Hedges Irish Masters** |
|        | v Williams     | 10-4  | 1st round     | Embassy World Championship    |
|        | v Dennis Taylor| 13-11 | 2nd round     | Embassy World Championship    |
|        | v Charlton     | 13-5  | Quarter-final | Embassy World Championship    |
|        | v Higgins      | 16-5  | Semi-final    | Embassy World Championship    |
|        | **v Thorburn** | **18-6** | **Final**  | **Embassy World Championship** |
|        | v Macleod      | 5-1   | 1st round     | Langs Scottish Masters        |
|        | v Higgins      | 6-2   | Semi-final    | Langs Scottish Masters        |
|        | **v Knowles**  | **9-6** | **Final**   | **Langs Scottish Masters**    |
|        | v E. Hughes    | 5-1   | 1st round     | Jameson International          |
|        | v Watterson    | 5-0   | 2nd round     | Jameson International          |
|        | v S. Francisco | 5-1   | Quarter-final | Jameson International          |
|        | v Charlton     | 9-2   | Semi-final    | Jameson International          |
|        | **v Thorburn** | **9-4** | **Final**   | **Jameson International**      |
|        | v Donnelly     | 5-1   | 1st round     | Professional Players Tournament |
|        | v Hallett      | 2-5   | 2nd round     | Professional Players Tournament |
|        | v G. Foulds    | 9-1   | 1st round     | Coral UK Championship         |
|        | v Thorne       | 9-3   | 2nd round     | Coral UK Championship         |
|        | v Meo          | 9-4   | Quarter-final | Coral UK Championship         |
|        | v White        | 9-4   | Semi-final    | Coral UK Championship         |
|        | v Higgins      | 15-16 | Final         | Coral UK Championship         |
| 1984   | v Spencer      | 5-2   | 1st round     | Lada Classic                  |
|        | v Griffiths    | 5-4   | Quarter-final | Lada Classic                  |
|        | v Parrott      | 5-4   | Semi-final    | Lada Classic                  |
|        | **v Meo**      | **9-8** | **Final**   | **Lada Classic**              |
|        | v Meo          | 5-0   | 1st round     | Benson & Hedges Masters       |
|        | v Stevens      | 3-5   | Quarter-final | Benson & Hedges Masters       |

|      |  |  |  |  |
|------|----------|-------|-------|------------|
|      | v Meo | 5-4 | Quarter-final | Benson & Hedges Irish Masters |
|      | v Higgins | 6-4 | Semi-final | Benson & Hedges Irish Masters |
|      | **v Griffiths** | **9-1** | **Final** | **Benson & Hedges Irish Masters** |
|      | v Thorne | 5-2 | 1st round | Tolly Cobbold Classic |
|      | v Stevens | 5-4 | Semi-final | Tolly Cobbold Classic |
|      | **v Knowles** | **8-2** | **Final** | **Tolly Cobbold Classic** |
|      | v King | 10-3 | 1st round | Embassy World Championship |
|      | v Spencer | 13-5 | 2nd round | Embassy World Championship |
|      | v Griffiths | 13-10 | Quarter-final | Embassy World Championship |
|      | v Dennis Taylor | 16-9 | Semi-final | Embassy World Championship |
|      | **v White** | **18-16** | **Final** | **Embassy World Championship** |
|      | v Thorburn | 5-2 | 1st round | Langs Supreme Scottish Masters |
|      | v Higgins | 6-4 | Semi-final | Langs Supreme Scottish Masters |
|      | **v White** | **9-4** | **Final** | **Langs Supreme Scottish Masters** |
|      | v J. Campbell | 5-1 | 1st round | Jameson International |
|      | v David Taylor | 5-1 | 2nd round | Jameson International |
|      | v Higgins | 5-1 | Quarter-final | Jameson International |
|      | v E. Hughes | 9-3 | Semi-final | Jameson International |
|      | **v Knowles** | **9-2** | **Final** | **Jameson International** |
|      | v Morra | 5-2 | 1st round | Rothmans Grand Prix |
|      | v Miles | 5-0 | 2nd round | Rothmans Grand Prix |
|      | v David Taylor | 5-1 | 3rd round | Rothmans Grand Prix |
|      | v Reynolds | 5-0 | Quarter-final | Rothmans Grand Prix |
|      | v Thorburn | 7-9 | Semi-final | Rothmans Grand Prix |
|      | v Murphy | 9-1 | 1st round | Coral UK Open |
|      | v Meo | 9-7 | 2nd round | Coral UK Open |
|      | v White | 9-4 | Quarter-final | Coral UK Open |
|      | v Stevens | 9-2 | Semi-final | Coral UK Open |
|      | **v Higgins** | **16-8** | **Final** | **Coral UK Open** |
| 1985 | v S. Francisco | 5-0 | 1st round | Mercantile Credit Classic |
|      | v Higgins | 5-2 | 2nd round | Mercantile Credit Classic |
|      | v Reardon | 5-1 | Quarter-final | Mercantile Credit Classic |
|      | v Thorne | 8-9 | Semi-final | Mercantile Credit Classic |
|      | v Higgins | 4-5 | 1st round | Benson & Hedges Masters |
|      | v Fowler | 9-3 | 1st round | Tolly Cobbold English Championship |
|      | v Williams | 9-2 | 2nd round | Tolly Cobbold English Championship |
|      | v Virgo | 9-2 | Quarter-final | Tolly Cobbold English Championship |
|      | v Meo | 9-8 | Semi-final | Tolly Cobbold English Championship |
|      | **v Knowles** | **9-2** | **Final** | **Tolly Cobbold English Championship** |
|      | v Chappel | 6-5 | 1st round | Dulux British Open |
|      | v Virgo | 5-2 | 2nd round | Dulux British Open |
|      | v Bradley | 5-2 | 3rd round | Dulux British Open |
|      | v O'Kane | 5-1 | Quarter-final | Dulux British Open |
|      | v Stevens | 7-9 | Semi-final | Dulux British Open |
|      | v E. Hughes | 5-4 | Quarter-final | Benson & Hedges Irish Masters |
|      | v Higgins | 2-6 | Semi-final | Benson & Hedges Irish Masters |
|      | v N. Foulds | 10-8 | 1st round | Embassy World Championship |
|      | v David Taylor | 13-4 | 2nd round | Embassy World Championship |
|      | v Griffiths | 13-6 | Quarter-final | Embassy World Championship |
|      | v Reardon | 16-5 | Semi-final | Embassy World Championship |
|      | v Dennis Taylor | 17-18 | Final | Embassy World Championship |
|      | v Bales | 5-2 | 3rd round | Goya Matchroom Trophy |
|      | v Virgo | 5-1 | 4th round | Goya Matchroom Trophy |
|      | v Macleod | 5-1 | 5th round | Goya Matchroom Trophy |
|      | v White | 3-5 | Quarter-final | Goya Matchroom Trophy |
|      | v Agrawal | 5-0 | 3rd round | Rothmans Grand Prix |
|      | v Fowler | 5-1 | 4th round | Rothmans Grand Prix |
|      | v Higgins | 5-0 | 5th round | Rothmans Grand Prix |
|      | v S. Francisco | 5-2 | Quarter-final | Rothmans Grand Prix |
|      | v Thorburn | 9-5 | Semi-final | Rothmans Grand Prix |
|      | **v Dennis Taylor** | **10-9** | **Final** | **Rothmans Grand Prix** |
|      | v Griffiths | 5-4 | 1st round | BCE Canadian Masters |

|         |                |        |              |                                   |
|---------|----------------|--------|--------------|-----------------------------------|
|         | v Thorburn     | 8-1    | Semi-final   | BCE Canadian Masters              |
|         | v Dennis Taylor| 5-9    | Final        | BCE Canadian Masters              |
|         | v Sheehan      | 9-1    | 3rd round    | Coral UK Open                     |
|         | v Drago        | 9-2    | 4th round    | Coral UK Open                     |
|         | v Meo          | 9-5    | 5th round    | Coral UK Open                     |
|         | v West         | 9-1    | Quarter-final| Coral UK Open                     |
|         | v White        | 9-5    | Semi-final   | Coral UK Open                     |
|         | **v Thorne**   | **16-14** | **Final** | **Coral UK Open**                 |
|         | v Reardon      | 5-2    | 1st round    | Kit Kat                           |
|         | v Higgins      | 6-1    | Semi-final   | Kit Kat                           |
|         | v Dennis Taylor| 5-9    | Final        | Kit Kat                           |
| **1986**| v Chaperon     | 5-1    | 3rd round    | Mercantile Credit Classic         |
|         | v Van Rensberg | 5-1    | 4th round    | Mercantile Credit Classic         |
|         | v P. Francisco | 5-0    | 5th round    | Mercantile Credit Classic         |
|         | v White        | 2-5    | Quarter-final| Mercantile Credit Classic         |
|         | v Griffiths    | 2-5    | 1st round    | BCE Belgian Classic               |
|         | v David Taylor | 5-4    | 1st round    | Benson & Hedges Masters           |
|         | v Thorne       | 5-4    | Quarter-final| Benson & Hedges Masters           |
|         | v White        | 3-6    | Semi-final   | Benson & Hedges Masters           |
|         | v Bradley      | 9-3    | 3rd round    | Tolly Cobbold English Championship|
|         | v Martin       | 9-4    | 4th round    | Tolly Cobbold English Championship|
|         | v Virgo        | 9-2    | Quarter-final| Tolly Cobbold English Championship|
|         | v Meo          | 7-9    | Semi-final   | Tolly Cobbold English Championship|
|         | v Black        | 5-2    | 3rd round    | Dulux British Open                |
|         | v Martin       | 5-1    | 4th round    | Dulux British Open                |
|         | v J. Campbell  | 5-0    | 5th round    | Dulux British Open                |
|         | v Wych         | 5-2    | Quarter-final| Dulux British Open                |
|         | v Higgins      | 9-3    | Semi-final   | Dulux British Open                |
|         | **v Thorne**   | **12-7** | **Final** | **Dulux British Open**            |
|         | v Edmonds      | 10-4   | 1st round    | Embassy World Championship        |
|         | v Mountjoy     | 13-5   | 2nd round    | Embassy World Championship        |
|         | v White        | 13-5   | Quarter-final| Embassy World Championship        |
|         | v Thorburn     | 16-12  | Semi-final   | Embassy World Championship        |
|         | v Johnson      | 12-18  | Final        | Embassy World Championship        |
|         | v Thorne       | 2-5    | Semi-final   | Camus Hong Kong Masters           |
|         | v Griffiths    | 6-2    | Semi-final   | Matchroom Trophy                  |
|         | v Thorne       | 9-10   | Final        | Matchroom Trophy                  |
|         | v John Rea     | 5-1    | 3rd round    | BCE International                 |
|         | v King         | 5-4    | 4th round    | BCE International                 |
|         | v Williams     | 5-4    | 5th round    | BCE International                 |
|         | v E. Hughes    | 4-5    | Quarter-final| BCE International                 |
|         | v M. Gibson    | 5-1    | 3rd round    | Rothmans Grand Prix               |
|         | v Drago        | 5-1    | 4th round    | Rothmans Grand Prix               |
|         | v Griffiths    | 5-2    | 5th round    | Rothmans Grand Prix               |
|         | v Williams     | 1-5    | Quarter-final| Rothmans Grand Prix               |
|         | v White        | 5-2    | 1st round    | BCE Canadian Masters              |
|         | v Higgins      | 8-2    | Semi-final   | BCE Canadian Masters              |
|         | **v Thorne**   | **9-3** | **Final**   | **BCE Canadian Masters**          |
|         | v Chappel      | 9-7    | 3rd round    | Tennents UK Open                  |
|         | v Charlton     | 9-6    | 4th round    | Tennents UK Open                  |
|         | v Reynolds     | 9-5    | 5th round    | Tennents UK Open                  |
|         | v Drago        | 9-8    | Quarter-final| Tennents UK Open                  |
|         | v Higgins      | 9-3    | Semi-final   | Tennents UK Open                  |
|         | **v N. Foulds**| **16-7** | **Final** | **Tennents UK Open**              |
| **1987**| v Jenkins      | 5-0    | 3rd round    | Mercantile Credit Classic         |
|         | v Virgo        | 5-2    | 4th round    | Mercantile Credit Classic         |
|         | v Meo          | 5-2    | 5th round    | Mercantile Credit Classic         |
|         | v Parrott      | 5-4    | Quarter-final| Mercantile Credit Classic         |
|         | v Hendry       | 9-3    | Semi-final   | Mercantile Credit Classic         |
|         | **v White**    | **13-12** | **Final**| **Mercantile Credit Classic**     |
|         | v Mountjoy     | 2-5    | 1st round    | Benson & Hedges Masters           |
|         | v Gauvreau     | 5-0    | 3rd round    | Dulux British Open                |

|      |               |       |              |                                |
|------|---------------|-------|--------------|--------------------------------|
|      | v Virgo       | 4-5   | 4th round    | Dulux British Open             |
|      | v Meo         | 5-2   | Quarter-final| Benson & Hedges Irish Masters  |
|      | v Griffiths   | 6-2   | Semi-final   | Benson & Hedges Irish Masters  |
|      | **v Thorne**  | **9-1** | **Final**  | **Benson & Hedges Irish Masters** |
|      | v King        | 10-7  | 1st round    | Embassy World Championship     |
|      | v Reardon     | 13-4  | 2nd round    | Embassy World Championship     |
|      | v Griffiths   | 13-5  | Quarter-final| Embassy World Championship     |
|      | v White       | 16-11 | Semi-final   | Embassy World Championship     |
|      | **v Johnson** | **18-14** | **Final** | **Embassy World Championship** |
|      | v Dennis Taylor | 5-4 | Semi-final   | Riley Hong Kong Masters (WS)   |
|      | **v Hendry**  | **9-3** | **Final**  | **Riley Hong Kong Masters (WS)** |
|      | v O'Kane      | 5-2   | 3rd round    | Fidelity International          |
|      | v Meo         | 5-3   | 4th round    | Fidelity International          |
|      | v Parrott     | 5-2   | 5th round    | Fidelity International          |
|      | v Virgo       | 5-2   | Quarter-final| Fidelity International          |
|      | v Hallett     | 9-3   | Semi-final   | Fidelity International          |
|      | **v Thorburn**| **12-5** | **Final** | **Fidelity International**      |
|      | v Miles       | 5-1   | 3rd round    | Rothmans Grand Prix            |
|      | v Wych        | 5-1   | 4th round    | Rothmans Grand Prix            |
|      | v Hendry      | 2-5   | 5th round    | Rothmans Grand Prix            |
|      | v Dennis Taylor | 1-5 | 1st round    | Labatts Canadian Masters (WS)  |
|      | v Meo         | 6-5   | 1st round    | Matchroom Trophy               |
|      | v Dennis Taylor | 3-6 | Semi-final   | Matchroom Trophy               |
|      | v King        | 9-2   | 3rd round    | Tennents UK Open               |
|      | v P. Francisco| 9-6   | 4th round    | Tennents UK Open               |
|      | v Higgins     | 9-2   | 5th round    | Tennents UK Open               |
|      | v Parrott     | 9-5   | Quarter-final| Tennents UK Open               |
|      | v Thorne      | 9-2   | Semi-final   | Tennents UK Open               |
|      | **v White**   | **16-14** | **Final** | **Tennents UK Open**           |
| 1988 | v Dodd        | 5-0   | 3rd round    | Mercantile Credit Classic      |
|      | v Donnelly    | 5-0   | 4th round    | Mercantile Credit Classic      |
|      | v Higgins     | 5-0   | 5th round    | Mercantile Credit Classic      |
|      | v Hendry      | 5-3   | Quarter-final| Mercantile Credit Classic      |
|      | v Newbury     | 9-2   | Semi-final   | Mercantile Credit Classic      |
|      | **v Parrott** | **13-11** | **Final** | **Mercantile Credit Classic**  |
|      | v Reynolds    | 5-2   | 1st round    | Benson and Hedges Masters      |
|      | v Griffiths   | 5-0   | Quarter-final| Benson and Hedges Masters      |
|      | v Johnson     | 6-3   | Semi-final   | Benson and Hedges Masters      |
|      | **v Hallett** | **9-0** | **Final**  | **Benson and Hedges Masters**  |
|      | v Reardon     | 0-5   | 3rd round    | MIM Britannia British Open     |
|      | v Johnson     | 5-0   | Quarter-final| Benson and Hedges Irish Masters |
|      | v Higgins     | 6-2   | Semi-final   | Benson and Hedges Irish Masters |
|      | **v N. Foulds** | **9-4** | **Final** | **Benson and Hedges Irish Masters** |
|      | v Virgo       | 10-8  | 1st round    | Embassy World Championship     |
|      | v Hallett     | 13-1  | 2nd round    | Embassy World Championship     |
|      | v Drago       | 13-4  | Quarter-final| Embassy World Championship     |
|      | v Thorburn    | 16-8  | Semi-final   | Embassy World Championship     |
|      | **v Griffiths** | **18-11** | **Final** | **Embassy World Championship** |
|      | v W. Jones    | 5-1   | 3rd round    | Fidelity International          |
|      | v Robidoux    | 5-4   | 4th round    | Fidelity International          |
|      | v David Taylor| 5-1   | 5th round    | Fidelity International          |
|      | v Dennis Taylor | 5-2 | Quarter-final| Fidelity International          |
|      | v James       | 9-1   | Semi-final   | Fidelity International          |
|      | **v White**   | **12-6** | **Final** | **Fidelity International**      |
|      | v Newbury     | 5-1   | 4th round    | Rothmans Grand Prix            |
|      | v C. Wilson   | 5-1   | 5th round    | Rothmans Grand Prix            |
|      | v Griffiths   | 5-3   | Quarter-final| Rothmans Grand Prix            |
|      | v Dennis Taylor | 9-1 | Semi-final   | Rothmans Grand Prix            |
|      | **v Higgins** | **10-6** | **Final** | **Rothmans Grand Prix**        |
|      | v M. Smith    | 5-0   | 3rd round    | BCE Canadian Masters           |
|      | v Scott       | 5-1   | 4th round    | BCE Canadian Masters           |
|      | v James       | 5-0   | 5th round    | BCE Canadian Masters           |

| | | | |
|---|---|---|---|
| v Griffiths | 5-3 | Quarter-final | BCE Canadian Masters |
| v Hendry | 9-5 | Semi-final | BCE Canadian Masters |
| v White | 4-9 | Final | BCE Canadian Masters |
| v Thorne | 6-2 | 1st round | LEP Matchroom Championship |
| v White | 6-4 | Semi-final | LEP Matchroom Championship |
| **v Dennis Taylor** | **10-7** | **Final** | **LEP Matchroom Championship** |
| v Thorne | 5-2 | Semi-final | Dubai Duty Free Masters |
| v N. Foulds | 4-5 | Final | Dubai Duty Free Masters |
| v King | 9-7 | 3rd round | Tennents UK Open |
| v Gary Wilkinson | 9-3 | 4th round | Tennents UK Open |
| v Fowler | 9-6 | 5th round | Tennents UK Open |
| v Parrott | 9-4 | Quarter-final | Tennents UK Open |
| v Hendry | 3-9 | Semi-final | Tennents UK Open |
| v Hallett | 9-2 | Quarter-final | Everest World Matchplay |
| v White | 9-5 | Semi-final | Everest World Matchplay |
| **v Parrott** | **9-5** | **Final** | **Everest World Matchplay** |
| **v White** | **5-4** | **Final** | **Norwich Union European Grand Prix** |
| 1989 v Chappel | 3-5 | 3rd round | Mercantile Credit Classic |
| v C. Wilson | 5-2 | 1st round | Benson and Hedges Masters |
| v Knowles | 5-0 | Quarter-final | Benson and Hedges Masters |
| v Hendry | 3-6 | Semi-final | Benson and Hedges Masters |
| v Cripsey | 5-1 | 3rd round | Anglian British Open |
| v Higgins | 5-0 | 4th round | Anglian British Open |
| v Thorne | 5-0 | 5th round | Anglian British Open |
| v Parrott | 1-5 | Quarter-final | Anglian British Open |
| v Hallett | 5-4 | Quarter-final | Benson and Hedges Irish Masters |
| v Hendry | 4-6 | Semi-final | Benson and Hedges Irish Masters |
| v Newbury | 10-5 | 1st round | Embassy World Championship |
| v Duggan | 13-3 | 2nd round | Embassy World Championship |
| v Hallett | 13-3 | Quarter-final | Embassy World Championship |
| v Hendry | 16-9 | Semi-final | Embassy World Championship |
| **v Parrott** | **18-3** | **Final** | **Embassy World Championship** |

## LES DODD (England)

**Born** 11.2.54. **Turned professional** 1982. **World ranking** 65 (62). **Best professional performances** Runner-up 1987 Tolly Ales English Championship; last 32 1983 Embassy World Championship, 1987 Mercantile Credit Classic, 1986 Rothmans Grand Prix.

| | | | |
|---|---|---|---|
| 1982 v Macleod | 5-1 | Qualifying | Jameson International |
| v Fitzmaurice | 5-3 | Qualifying | Jameson International |
| v Mans | 3-5 | 1st round | Jameson International |
| v Williamson | 9-1 | Qualifying | Coral UK Championship |
| v French | 9-7 | Qualifying | Coral UK Championship |
| v David Taylor | 7-9 | 1st round | Coral UK Championship |
| 1983 v Williamson | 10-9 | Qualifying | Embassy World Championship |
| v Charlton | 7-10 | 1st round | Embassy World Championship |
| v Gibson | 1-5 | Qualifying | Jameson International |
| v Griffiths | 3-5 | 1st round | Professional Players Tournament |
| v G. Foulds | 7-9 | Qualifying | Coral UK Championship |
| 1984 v Giannaros | 10-1 | Qualifying | Embassy World Championship |
| v N. Foulds | 4-10 | Qualifying | Embassy World Championship |
| v Foldvari | 5-3 | Qualifying | Jameson International |
| v Wilson | 5-1 | Qualifying | Jameson International |
| v Reardon | 4-5 | 1st round | Jameson International |
| v Medati | 4-5 | Qualifying | Rothmans Grand Prix |
| v Newbury | 9-6 | Qualifying | Coral UK Open |
| v Wilson | 8-9 | Qualifying | Coral UK Open |
| 1985 v T. Jones | 1-5 | Qualifying | Mercantile Credit Classic |
| v Bales | 9-5 | Qualifying | Tolly Cobbold English Championship |

|  | v Thorne | 1-9 | 1st round | Tolly Cobbold English Championship |
|---|---|---|---|---|
|  | v V. Harris | 1-6 | Qualifying | Dulux British Open |
|  | v O'Kane | 7-10 | Qualifying | Embassy World Championship |
|  | v Simngam | 5-4 | 2nd round | Goya Matchroom Trophy |
|  | v N. Foulds | 3-5 | 3rd round | Goya Matchroom Trophy |
|  | v Chappel | 2-5 | 2nd round | Rothmans Grand Prix |
|  | v Thorburn | 4-9 | 3rd round | Coral UK Open |
| 1986 | v Rigitano | 3-5 | 2nd round | Mercantile Credit Classic |
|  | v Oliver | 5-9 | 2nd round | Tolly Cobbold English Championship |
|  | v Jonik | 5-4 | 2nd round | Dulux British Open |
|  | v Thorne | 2-5 | 3rd round | Dulux British Open |
|  | v Fitzmaurice | 10-6 | Qualifying | Embassy World Championship |
|  | v Watterson | 10-1 | Qualifying | Embassy World Championship |
|  | v Mans | 7-10 | Qualifying | Embassy World Championship |
|  | v Reynolds | 2-5 | 3rd round | BCE International |
|  | v Scott | 5-2 | 2nd round | Rothmans Grand Prix |
|  | v Stevens | 5-4 | 3rd round | Rothmans Grand Prix |
|  | v Hallett | 2-5 | 4th round | Rothmans Grand Prix |
|  | v Chaperon | 4-9 | 2nd round | Tennents UK Open |
| 1987 | v Medati | 5-4 | 2nd round | Mercantile Credit Classic |
|  | v Mountjoy | 5-4 | 3rd round | Mercantile Credit Classic |
|  | v Wilson | 4-5 | 4th round | Mercantile Credit Classic |
|  | v Smith | 6-3 | 2nd round | Tolly Ales English Championship |
|  | v Knowles | 6-2 | 3rd round | Tolly Ales English Championship |
|  | v West | 6-3 | 4th round | Tolly Ales English Championship |
|  | v Hallett | 6-5 | Quarter-final | Tolly Ales English Championship |
|  | v Johnson | 9-5 | Semi-final | Tolly Ales English Championship |
|  | v Meo | 5-9 | Final | Tolly Ales English Championship |
|  | v Fowler | 1-5 | 2nd round | Dulux British Open |
|  | v Newbury | 7-10 | Qualifying | Embassy World Championship |
|  | v Morra | 3-5 | 2nd round | Fidelity International |
|  | v Kelly | 5-2 | 2nd round | Rothmans Grand Prix |
|  | v Parrott | 1-5 | 3rd round | Rothmans Grand Prix |
|  | v Medati | 9-6 | 2nd round | Tennents UK Open |
|  | v Dennis Taylor | 8-9 | 3rd round | Tennents UK Open |
| 1988 | v Roe | 2-5 | 2nd round | Mercantile Credit Classic |
|  | v S. Davis | 0-5 | 3rd round | Mercantile Credit Classic |
|  | v Heaton | 6-0 | 2nd round | English Championship |
|  | v Virgo | 3-6 | 3rd round | English Championship |
|  | v Darrington | 4-5 | 2nd round | MIM Britannia British Open |
|  | v Medati | 10-6 | Qualifying | Embassy World Championship |
|  | v Fowler | 8-10 | Qualifying | Embassy World Championship |
|  | v Roscoe | 5-1 | 2nd round | Fidelity International |
|  | v Parrott | 5-4 | 3rd round | Fidelity International |
|  | v West | 3-5 | 4th round | Fidelity International |
|  | v M. Gibson | 5-1 | 2nd round | Rothmans Grand Prix |
|  | v Reynolds | 3-5 | 3rd round | Rothmans Grand Prix |
|  | v Marshall | 5-3 | 2nd round | BCE Canadian Masters |
|  | v David Taylor | 3-5 | 3rd round | BCE Canadian Masters |
|  | v Glen Wilkinson | 9-6 | 2nd round | Tennents UK Open |
|  | v Higgins | 7-9 | 3rd round | Tennents UK Open |
| 1989 | v Sinclair | 5-3 | 2nd round | Mercantile Credit Classic |
|  | v Virgo | 2-5 | 3rd round | Mercantile Credit Classic |
|  | v Higgins | 2-5 | 3rd round | European Open |
|  | v Edwards | 1-5 | 2nd round | English Championship |
|  | v Rempe | 5-0 | 2nd round | Anglian British Open |
|  | v Reynolds | 2-5 | 3rd round | Anglian British Open |
|  | v Grech | 10-9 | Qualifying | Embassy World Championship |
|  | v Glen Wilkinson | 10-4 | Qualifying | Embassy World Championship |
|  | v Charlton | 6-10 | Qualifying | Embassy World Championship |

## JIM DONNELLY (Scotland)

**Born** 13.6.46. **Turned professional** 1981. **World ranking** 84 (74). **Amateur career** 1978 Scottish champion. **Best professional performances** Last 32 1982 Embassy World Championship, 1988 Mercantile Credit Classic; runner-up 1987 Scottish Championship.

| | | | |
|---|---|---|---|
| **1981** | v Johnson | 4-5 | Qualifying | Jameson International |
| | v Sinclair | 5-0 | Quarter-final | Scottish Championship |
| | v Gibson | 4-6 | Semi-final | Scottish Championship |
| | v Medati | 7-9 | Qualifying | Coral UK Championship |
| **1982** | v Gibson | 9-8 | Qualifying | Embassy World Championship |
| | v Sinclair | 9-8 | Qualifying | Embassy World Championship |
| | v Reardon | 5-10 | 1st round | Embassy World Championship |
| | v Macleod | 5-6 | 1st round | Scottish Championship |
| | v Williamson | 3-5 | Qualifying | Jameson International |
| | v Watterson | 4-5 | 1st round | Professional Players Tournament |
| | v Ross | 9-5 | Qualifying | Coral UK Championship |
| | v Knowles | 6-9 | 1st round | Coral UK Championship |
| **1983** | v Sheehan | 10-6 | Qualifying | Embassy World Championship |
| | v Campbell | 2-10 | Qualifying | Embassy World Championship |
| | v Demarco | 6-4 | 1st round | Scottish Championship |
| | v Sinclair | 5-6 | Semi-final | Scottish Championship |
| | v Bennett | 5-1 | Qualifying | Jameson International |
| | v Wilson | 5-1 | Qualifying | Jameson International |
| | v David Taylor | 5-3 | 1st round | Jameson International |
| | v S. Francisco | 1-5 | 2nd round | Jameson International |
| | v S. Davis | 1-5 | 1st round | Professional Players Tournament |
| | v Murphy | 4-9 | Qualifying | Coral UK Championship |
| **1984** | v Watchorn | 10-7 | Qualifying | Embassy World Championship |
| | v Anderson | 10-6 | Qualifying | Embassy World Championship |
| | v F. Davis | 5-10 | Qualifying | Embassy World Championship |
| | v G. Foulds | 3-5 | Qualifying | Jameson International |
| | v Hargreaves | 5-4 | Qualifying | Rothmans Grand Prix |
| | v Wilson | 2-5 | 1st round | Rothmans Grand Prix |
| | v Gibson | 9-6 | Qualifying | Coral UK Open |
| | v Campbell | 6-9 | Qualifying | Coral UK Open |
| **1985** | v Watchorn | 5-1 | Qualifying | Mercantile Credit Classic |
| | v Williams | 3-5 | Qualifying | Mercantile Credit Classic |
| | v John Rea | 2-6 | 1st round | Scottish Championship |
| | v W. Jones | 1-6 | Qualifying | Dulux British Open |
| | v Fowler | 0-10 | Qualifying | Embassy World Championship |
| | v Jim Bear | 2-5 | 2nd round | Goya Matchroom Trophy |
| | v Kelly | 4-5 | 2nd round | Rothmans Grand Prix |
| | v Drago | 8-9 | 1st round | Coral UK Open |
| **1986** | v Chalmers | 5-0 | 2nd round | Mercantile Credit Classic |
| | v Campbell | 2-5 | 3rd round | Mercantile Credit Classic |
| | v Wilkinson | 5-4 | 2nd round | Dulux British Open |
| | v Meo | 3-5 | 3rd round | Dulux British Open |
| | v John Rea | 1-6 | Quarter-final | Canada Dry Scottish Championship |
| | v Smith | 10-6 | Qualifying | Embassy World Championship |
| | v West | 5-10 | Qualifying | Embassy World Championship |
| | v Murphy | 2-5 | 2nd round | BCE International |
| | v N. Gilbert | 5-1 | 1st round | Rothmans Grand Prix |
| | v King | 2-5 | 2nd round | Rothmans Grand Prix |
| | v N. Gilbert | 8-9 | 1st round | Tennents UK Open |
| **1987** | v Watchorn | 0-5 | 1st round | Mercantile Credit Classic |
| | v Macleod | 6-2 | 1st round | Scottish Championship |
| | v Sinclair | 6-4 | Semi-final | Scottish Championship |
| | v Hendry | 7-10 | Final | Scottish Championship |
| | v T. Jones | 2-5 | 2nd round | Dulux British Open |
| | v W. Jones | 3-10 | Qualifying | Embassy World Championship |

|      | v M. Smith | 3-5 | 1st round | Fidelity International |
|------|------------|-----|-----------|----------------------|
|      | v D. Hughes | 5-1 | 1st round | Rothmans Grand Prix |
|      | v W. Jones | 3-5 | 2nd round | Rothmans Grand Prix |
|      | v Anderson | 9-4 | 1st round | Tennents UK Open |
|      | v O'Boye | 2-9 | 2nd round | Tennents UK Open |
| 1988 | v N. Gilbert | 5-2 | 1st round | Mercantile Credit Classic |
|      | v Duggan | 5-4 | 2nd round | Mercantile Credit Classic |
|      | v Macleod | 5-4 | 3rd round | Mercantile Credit Classic |
|      | v S. Davis | 0-5 | 4th round | Mercantile Credit Classic |
|      | v Macleod | 5-6 | Quarter-final | Scottish Championship |
|      | v Greaves | 5-4 | 1st round | MIM Britannia British Open |
|      | v Cripsey | 4-5 | 2nd round | MIM Britannia British Open |
|      | v J. Smith | 4-10 | Qualifying | Embassy World Championship |
|      | v J. Smith | 5-2 | 1st round | Fidelity International |
|      | v Reardon | 1-5 | 2nd round | Fidelity International |
|      | v Watterson | 0-5 | 1st round | Rothmans Grand Prix |
|      | v Terry | 1-5 | 1st round | BCE Canadian Masters |
|      | v Whitthread | 8-9 | 1st round | Tennents UK Open |
| 1989 | v Ellis | 0-5 | 1st round | Mercantile Credit Classic |
|      | v Johnston-Allen | 3-5 | 1st round | European Open |
|      | v Demarco | 5-1 | 1st round | Scottish Championship |
|      | v John Rea | 1-5 | Semi-final | Scottish Championship |
|      | v Whitthread | 4-5 | 1st round | Anglian British Open |
|      | v Whitthread | 7-10 | Qualifying | Embassy World Championship |

## TONY DRAGO (Malta)

**Born** 22.9.65. **Turned professional** 1985. **World ranking** 32 (20). **Amateur career** 1984 Malta champion. **Best professional performances** Quarter-finals 1988 Embassy World Championship, 1986 Tennents UK Open.

|      |  |  |  |  |
|------|---------|-----|-----------|----------------------|
| 1985 | v Bales | 2-5 | 1st round | Goya Matchroom Trophy |
|      | v Watchorn | 5-2 | 1st round | Rothmans Grand Prix |
|      | v King | 5-4 | 2nd round | Rothmans Grand Prix |
|      | v Macleod | 5-3 | 3rd round | Rothmans Grand Prix |
|      | v Charlton | 5-3 | 4th round | Rothmans Grand Prix |
|      | v Wilson | 2-5 | 5th round | Rothmans Grand Prix |
|      | v Gilbert | 9-5 | 1st round | Coral UK Open |
|      | v Donnelly | 9-8 | 2nd round | Coral UK Open |
|      | v Wildman | 9-5 | 3rd round | Coral UK Open |
|      | v S. Davis | 2-9 | 4th round | Coral UK Open |
| 1986 | v Cripsey | 4-5 | 1st round | Mercantile Credit Classic |
|      | v Gauvreau | 5-3 | 2nd round | Dulux British Open |
|      | v Williams | 1-5 | 3rd round | Dulux British Open |
|      | v Cripsey | 10-4 | Qualifying | Embassy World Championship |
|      | v P. Francisco | 4-10 | Qualifying | Embassy World Championship |
|      | v Morra | 5-3 | 2nd round | BCE International |
|      | v Thorne | 5-2 | 3rd round | BCE International |
|      | v Chaperon | 1-5 | 4th round | BCE International |
|      | v Watchorn | 5-3 | 2nd round | Rothmans Grand Prix |
|      | v Charlton | 5-4 | 3rd round | Rothmans Grand Prix |
|      | v S. Davis | 1-5 | 4th round | Rothmans Grand Prix |
|      | v Morra | 9-6 | 2nd round | Tennents UK Open |
|      | v Williams | 9-7 | 3rd round | Tennents UK Open |
|      | v Virgo | 9-6 | 4th round | Tennents UK Open |
|      | v Thorne | 9-5 | 5th round | Tennents UK Open |
|      | v S. Davis | 8-9 | Quarter-final | Tennents UK Open |
| 1987 | v Jonik | 2-5 | 2nd round | Mercantile Credit Classic |
|      | v Oliver | 5-1 | 2nd round | Dulux British Open |
|      | v Johnson | 0-5 | 3rd round | Dulux British Open |
|      | v Sinclair | 9-10 | Qualifying | Embassy World Championship |
|      | v Clark | 2-5 | 3rd round | Fidelity International |

|      | v Meadowcroft | 5-1 | 3rd round | Rothmans Grand Prix |
|------|---------------|-----|-----------|---------------------|
|      | v Thorne | 2-5 | 4th round | Rothmans Grand Prix |
|      | v Murphy | 7-9 | 3rd round | Tennents UK Open |
| 1988 | v Scott | 5-3 | 3rd round | Mercantile Credit Classic |
|      | v Dennis Taylor | 0-5 | 4th round | Mercantile Credit Classic |
|      | v Roe | 3-5 | 3rd round | MIM Britannia British Open |
|      | v Chappel | 10-7 | Qualifying | Embassy World Championship |
|      | v Higgins | 10-2 | 1st round | Embassy World Championship |
|      | v Dennis Taylor | 13-5 | 2nd round | Embassy World Championship |
|      | v S. Davis | 4-13 | Quarter-final | Embassy World Championship |
|      | v Fowler | 5-3 | 3rd round | Fidelity International |
|      | v Thorne | 2-5 | 4th round | Fidelity International |
|      | v Foldvari | 5-3 | 3rd round | Rothmans Grand Prix |
|      | v C. Wilson | 4-5 | 4th round | Rothmans Grand Prix |
|      | v Fowler | 1-5 | 3rd round | BCE Canadian Masters |
|      | v Duggan | 7-9 | 3rd round | Tennents UK Open |
| 1989 | v Marshall | 5-1 | 3rd round | Mercantile Credit Classic |
|      | v Griffiths | 0-5 | 4th round | Mercantile Credit Classic |
|      | v M. Bennett | 1-5 | 3rd round | European Open |
|      | v Bear | 5-2 | 3rd round | Anglian British Open |
|      | v Johnson | 3-5 | 4th round | Anglian British Open |
|      | v Gary Wilkinson | 9-10 | Qualifying | Embassy World Championship |

## STEVE DUGGAN (England)

**Born** 10.4.58. **Turned professional** 1983. **World ranking** 43 (50). **Best professional performances** Last 16 1989 Embassy World Championship; quarter-finals 1985 Goya Matchroom Trophy.

|      | v Darrington | 5-4 | Qualifying | Professional Players Tournament |
|------|--------------|-----|------------|---------------------------------|
| 1983 | v Darrington | 5-4 | Qualifying | Professional Players Tournament |
|      | v Dunning | 5-2 | 1st round | Professional Players Tournament |
|      | v Reardon | 2-5 | 2nd round | Professional Players Tournament |
|      | v G. Foulds | 8-9 | Qualifying | Coral UK Championship |
| 1984 | v Browne | 9-10 | Qualifying | Embassy World Championship |
|      | v T. Jones | 5-2 | Qualifying | Jameson International |
|      | v Sinclair | 0-5 | Qualifying | Jameson International |
|      | v Browne | 5-2 | Qualifying | Rothmans Grand Prix |
|      | v S. Francisco | 3-5 | 1st round | Rothmans Grand Prix |
|      | v O'Kane | 6-9 | Qualifying | Coral UK Open |
| 1985 | v W. Jones | 5-0 | Qualifying | Mercantile Credit Classic |
|      | v King | 4-5 | Qualifying | Mercantile Credit Classic |
|      | v B. Harris | 9-8 | Qualifying | Tolly Cobbold English Championship |
|      | v Hallett | 4-9 | 1st round | Tolly Cobbold English Championship |
|      | v Foldvari | 4-6 | Qualifying | Dulux British Open |
|      | v T. Jones | 8-10 | Qualifying | Embassy World Championship |
|      | v F. Davis | 5-1 | 2nd round | Goya Matchroom Trophy |
|      | v Reardon | 5-3 | 3rd round | Goya Matchroom Trophy |
|      | v Black | 5-1 | 4th round | Goya Matchroom Trophy |
|      | v Thorne | 5-4 | 5th round | Goya Matchroom Trophy |
|      | v Thorburn | 2-5 | Quarter-final | Goya Matchroom Trophy |
|      | v Gauvreau | 5-4 | 2nd round | Rothmans Grand Prix |
|      | v Wildman | 4-5 | 3rd round | Rothmans Grand Prix |
|      | v Wych | 5-9 | 2nd round | Coral UK Open |
| 1986 | v King | 2-5 | 2nd round | Mercantile Credit Classic |
|      | v Longworth | 4-9 | 2nd round | Tolly Cobbold English Championship |
|      | v Murphy | 5-1 | 2nd round | Dulux British Open |
|      | v Hallett | 3-5 | 3rd round | Dulux British Open |
|      | v Fisher | 10-3 | Qualifying | Embassy World Championship |
|      | v Wych | 5-10 | Qualifying | Embassy World Championship |
|      | v Bear | 5-4 | 2nd round | BCE International |
|      | v Campbell | 5-3 | 3rd round | BCE International |
|      | v Williams | 4-5 | 4th round | BCE International |

|        |                |  |          |                       |
|--------|----------------|-------|---------------|---------------------------------|
|        | v Whitthread   | 5-1   | 2nd round     | Rothmans Grand Prix             |
|        | v Thorne       | 0-5   | 3rd round     | Rothmans Grand Prix             |
|        | v O'Boye       | 4-9   | 2nd round     | Tennents UK Open                |
| 1987   | v Watchorn     | 5-1   | 2nd round     | Mercantile Credit Classic       |
|        | v N. Foulds    | 5-3   | 3rd round     | Mercantile Credit Classic       |
|        | v Werbeniuk    | 5-0   | 4th round     | Mercantile Credit Classic       |
|        | v White        | 2-5   | 5th round     | Mercantile Credit Classic       |
|        | v Fisher       | 6-0   | 2nd round     | Tolly Ales English Championship |
|        | v Meo          | 3-6   | 3rd round     | Tolly Ales English Championship |
|        | v P. Gibson    | 5-3   | 2nd round     | Dulux British Open              |
|        | v Longworth    | 5-2   | 3rd round     | Dulux British Open              |
|        | v Thorne       | 2-5   | 4th round     | Dulux British Open              |
|        | v Roscoe       | 10-7  | Qualifying    | Embassy World Championship      |
|        | v Chappel      | 3-10  | Qualifying    | Embassy World Championship      |
|        | v Clark        | 2-5   | 2nd round     | Fidelity International          |
|        | v P. Gibson    | 4-5   | 2nd round     | Rothmans Grand Prix             |
|        | v Williamson   | 9-7   | 2nd round     | Tennents UK Open                |
|        | v Higgins      | 4-9   | 3rd round     | Tennents UK Open                |
| 1988   | v Donnelly     | 4-5   | 2nd round     | Mercantile Credit Classic       |
|        | v Williamson   | 6-2   | 2nd round     | English Championship            |
|        | v Hallett      | 3-6   | 3rd round     | English Championship            |
|        | v M. Gibson    | 2-5   | 2nd round     | MIM Britannia British Open      |
|        | v A. Harris    | 10-4  | Qualifying    | Embassy World Championship      |
|        | v P. Gibson    | 10-9  | Qualifying    | Embassy World Championship      |
|        | v Virgo        | 5-10  | Qualifying    | Embassy World Championship      |
|        | v Oliver       | 5-3   | 2nd round     | Fidelity International          |
|        | v C. Wilson    | 5-2   | 3rd round     | Fidelity International          |
|        | v Williams     | 4-5   | 4th round     | Fidelity International          |
|        | v Edwards      | 5-4   | 2nd round     | Rothmans Grand Prix             |
|        | v David Taylor | 5-1   | 3rd round     | Rothmans Grand Prix             |
|        | v N. Foulds    | 4-5   | 4th round     | Rothmans Grand Prix             |
|        | v Wildman      | 5-1   | 2nd round     | BCE Canadian Masters            |
|        | v West         | 5-3   | 3rd round     | BCE Canadian Masters            |
|        | v King         | 4-5   | 4th round     | BCE Canadian Masters            |
|        | v Morra        | 9-8   | 2nd round     | Tennents UK Open                |
|        | v Drago        | 9-7   | 3rd round     | Tennents UK Open                |
|        | v Griffiths    | 2-9   | 4th round     | Tennents UK Open                |
| 1989   | v Dunning      | 5-2   | 2nd round     | Mercantile Credit Classic       |
|        | v Reynolds     | 1-5   | 3rd round     | Mercantile Credit Classic       |
|        | v D. Morgan    | 5-4   | 2nd round     | European Open                   |
|        | v Charlton     | 2-5   | 3rd round     | European Open                   |
|        | v Graham       | 2-5   | 2nd round     | English Championship            |
|        | v Graham       | 2-5   | 2nd round     | Anglian British Open            |
|        | v F. Davis     | 10-3  | Qualifying    | Embassy World Championship      |
|        | v Rowing       | 10-6  | Qualifying    | Embassy World Championship      |
|        | v C. Wilson    | 10-1  | 1st round     | Embassy World Championship      |
|        | v S. Davis     | 3-13  | 2nd round     | Embassy World Championship      |

## JOHN DUNNING (England)

**Born** 18.4.27. **Turned professional** 1970. **World ranking** 95 (92). **Best professional performance** Quarter-finals 1974 World Championship.

|        |                |  |          |                  |
|--------|----------------|-------|---------------|----------------------------|
| 1972   | v Houlihan     | 11-10 | Qualifying    | World Championship         |
|        | v Miles        | 11-5  | Qualifying    | World Championship         |
|        | v Pulman       | 7-19  | 1st round     | World Championship         |
| 1973   | v David Taylor | 4-9   | 1st round     | World Championship         |
| 1974   | v David Taylor | 8-6   | 1st round     | World Championship         |
|        | v Charlton     | 15-13 | 2nd round     | World Championship         |
|        | v Miles        | 13-15 | Quarter-final | World Championship         |
| 1975   | v G. Owen      | 8-15  | 2nd round     | World Championship         |
| 1976   | v Reardon      | 7-15  | 1st round     | Embassy World Championship |

| | | | | |
|---|---|---|---|---|
| **1977** | v Virgo | 6-11 | Qualifying | Embassy World Championship |
| | v Parkin | 5-4 | 1st round | Super Crystalate UK Championship |
| | v Higgins | 0-5 | Quarter-final | Super Crystalate UK Championship |
| **1978** | v Fagan | 5-9 | Qualifying | Embassy World Championship |
| | v Greaves | 9-3 | Qualifying | Coral UK Championship |
| | v F. Davis | 2-9 | 1st round | Coral UK Championship |
| **1979** | v Jack Rea | 9-5 | Prelim | Embassy World Championship |
| | v David Taylor | 8-9 | Qualifying | Embassy World Championship |
| | v Greaves | 9-8 | 1st round | Coral UK Championship |
| | v S. Davis | 3-9 | 2nd round | Coral UK Championship |
| **1980** | v Johnson | 6-9 | Qualifying | Coral UK Championship |
| **1981** | v Greaves | 9-4 | Qualifying | John Courage English |
| | v David Taylor | 9-8 | 1st round | John Courage English |
| | v Thorne | 0-9 | 2nd round | John Courage English |
| | v Bennett | 9-6 | Qualifying | Embassy World Championship |
| | v Fagan | 9-7 | Qualifying | Embassy World Championship |
| | v Stevens | 4-10 | 1st round | Embassy World Championship |
| | v Gibson | 5-3 | Qualifying | Jameson International |
| | v Martin | 2-5 | 1st round | Jameson International |
| **1982** | v Macleod | 9-4 | Qualifying | Embassy World Championship |
| | v Spencer | 4-10 | 1st round | Embassy World Championship |
| | v Roscoe | 2-5 | Qualifying | Jameson International |
| | v Wildman | 4-5 | 1st round | Professional Players Tournament |
| **1983** | v B. Harris | 3-5 | Qualifying | Jameson International |
| | v Duggan | 2-5 | 1st round | Professional Players Tournament |
| | v Andrewartha | 9-2 | Qualifying | Coral UK Championship |
| | v Spencer | 7-9 | 1st round | Coral UK Championship |
| **1984** | v Oliver | 3-10 | Qualifying | Embassy World Championship |
| | v Cripsey | 5-3 | Qualifying | Jameson International |
| | v F. Davis | 4-5 | Qualifying | Jameson International |
| | v D. Hughes | 5-0 | Qualifying | Rothmans Grand Prix |
| | v Mans | 5-4 | 1st round | Rothmans Grand Prix |
| | v Knowles | 1-5 | 2nd round | Rothmans Grand Prix |
| | v John Rea | 3-9 | Qualifying | Coral UK Open |
| **1985** | v W. Jones | 6-10 | Qualifying | Embassy World Championship |
| | v Everton | 5-2 | 2nd round | Goya Matchroom Trophy |
| | v Meo | 0-5 | 3rd round | Goya Matchroom Trophy |
| | v Agrawal | 0-5 | 2nd round | Rothmans Grand Prix |
| **1986** | v West | 3-10 | Qualifying | Embassy World Championship |
| | v Demarco | 5-4 | 1st round | BCE International |
| | v Newbury | 4-5 | 2nd round | BCE International |
| | v P. Gibson | 1-5 | 1st round | Rothmans Grand Prix |
| | v Kearney | 9-6 | 1st round | Tennents UK Open |
| | v M. Gibson | 2-9 | 2nd round | Tennents UK Open |
| **1987** | v B. Bennett | 5-2 | 1st round | Mercantile Credit Classic |
| | v Browne | 1-5 | 2nd round | Mercantile Credit Classic |
| | v Cripsey | 1-6 | 2nd round | Tolly Ales English Championship |
| | v Watchorn | 2-5 | 1st round | Dulux British Open |
| | v Caggianello | 10-7 | Qualifying | Embassy World Championship |
| | v Scott | 7-10 | Qualifying | Embassy World Championship |
| | v Sheehan | 5-1 | 1st round | Fidelity International |
| | v W. Jones | 1-5 | 2nd round | Fidelity International |
| | v Foldvari | 0-5 | 1st round | Rothmans Grand Prix |
| | v Fagan | 9-4 | 1st round | Tennents UK Open |
| | v Bales | 9-8 | 2nd round | Tennents UK Open |
| | v White | 0-9 | 3rd round | Tennents UK Open |
| **1988** | v Jonik | 2-5 | 1st round | Mercantile Credit Classic |
| | v Williamson | 5-6 | 1st round | English Championship |
| | v Jonik | 5-3 | 1st round | MIM Britannia British Open |
| | v Scott | 5-3 | 2nd round | MIM Britannia British Open |
| | v West | 0-5 | 3rd round | MIM Britannia British Open |
| | v Rigitano | 7-10 | Qualifying | Embassy World Championship |
| | v Kelly | 5-0 | 1st round | Fidelity International |

|        |               |       |              |                              |
|--------|---------------|-------|--------------|------------------------------|
|        | v N. Gilbert  | 0-5   | 2nd round    | Fidelity International        |
|        | v Heaton      | 5-1   | 1st round    | Rothmans Grand Prix          |
|        | v Edmonds     | 3-5   | 2nd round    | Rothmans Grand Prix          |
|        | v Sheehan     | 5-3   | 1st round    | BCE Canadian Masters         |
|        | v Werbeniuk   | 3-5   | 2nd round    | BCE Canadian Masters         |
|        | v Parrott     | 2-5*  | 3rd round    | BCE Canadian Masters         |
| 1989   | v Price       | 5-3   | 1st round    | Mercantile Credit Classic    |
|        | v Duggan      | 2-5   | 2nd round    | Mercantile Credit Classic    |
|        | v Darrington  | 4-5   | 1st round    | European Open                |
|        | v S. Campbell | 3-5   | 1st round    | English Championship         |
|        | v Fitzmaurice | 1-5   | 1st round    | Anglian British Open         |
|        | v Rowing      | 9-10  | Qualifying   | Embassy World Championship   |

\* Dunning deemed lucky loser after Werbeniuk suspended for contravening drug regulations.

## RAY EDMONDS (England)

**Born** 28.5.36. **Turned professional** 1978. **World ranking** 49 (55). **Amateur career** 1972, 1974 World Champion; 1969, 1974 English champion. **Best professional performance** Quarter-finals 1979 Coral UK Championship.

|        |                 |        |               |                                    |
|--------|-----------------|--------|---------------|------------------------------------|
| 1978   | v Virgo         | 4-9    | Qualifying    | Coral UK Championship              |
| 1979   | v Meadowcroft   | 9-3    | 2nd round     | Coral UK Championship              |
|        | v F. Davis      | 9-6    | 3rd round     | Coral UK Championship              |
|        | v Werbeniuk     | 8-9    | Quarter-final | Coral UK Championship              |
| 1980   | v Hood          | 9-6    | Qualifying    | Embassy World Championship         |
|        | v David Taylor  | 3-10   | 1st round     | Embassy World Championship         |
|        | v Hallett       | 8-9    | Qualifying    | Coral UK Championship              |
| 1981   | v Hallett       | 9-3    | Qualifying    | John Courage English               |
|        | v F. Davis      | 9-6    | 1st round     | John Courage English               |
|        | v Johnson       | 9-5    | 2nd round     | John Courage English               |
|        | v S. Davis      | 0-9    | Semi-final    | John Courage English               |
|        | v Wildman       | 9-3    | Qualifying    | Embassy World Championship         |
|        | v Williams      | 9-7    | Qualifying    | Embassy World Championship         |
|        | v Spencer       | 9-10   | 1st round     | Embassy World Championship         |
|        | v E. Hughes     | 5-4    | 1st round     | Jameson International               |
|        | v Spencer       | 3-5    | 2nd round     | Jameson International               |
|        | v Thorne        | 4-9    | 2nd round     | Coral UK Championship              |
| 1982   | v Reynolds      | 6-9    | Qualifying    | Embassy World Championship         |
|        | v D. Hughes     | 5-0    | Qualifying    | Jameson International               |
|        | v Miles         | 5-1    | Qualifying    | Jameson International               |
|        | v Spencer       | 2-5    | 1st round     | Jameson International               |
|        | v Dennis Taylor | 4-5    | 1st round     | Professional Players Tournament    |
|        | v Fisher        | 8-9    | Qualifying    | Coral UK Championship              |
| 1983   | v Jonik         | 10-4   | Qualifying    | Embassy World Championship         |
|        | v Reynolds      | 6-10   | Qualifying    | Embassy World Championship         |
|        | v Jack Rea      | 5-1    | Qualifying    | Jameson International               |
|        | v E. McLaughlin | 5-1    | Qualifying    | Jameson International               |
|        | v Knowles       | 1-5    | 1st round     | Jameson International               |
|        | v Stevens       | 1-5    | 1st round     | Professional Players Tournament    |
|        | v Medati        | 7-9    | Qualifying    | Coral UK Championship              |
| 1984   | v Greaves       | 10-0   | Qualifying    | Embassy World Championship         |
|        | v Van Rensberg  | 9-10   | Qualifying    | Embassy World Championship         |
|        | v Foldvari      | 1-5    | Qualifying    | Jameson International               |
|        | v Rigitano      | 3-5    | Qualifying    | Rothmans Grand Prix                |
|        | v John Rea      | 6-9    | Qualifying    | Coral UK Open                      |
| 1985   | v Hargreaves    | 5-2    | Qualifying    | Mercantile Credit Classic          |
|        | v Watterson     | 5-2    | Qualifying    | Mercantile Credit Classic          |
|        | v Johnson       | 4-5    | Qualifying    | Mercantile Credit Classic          |
|        | v Longworth     | 4-9    | Qualifying    | Tolly Cobbold English Championship |
|        | v Mienie        | 6-1    | Qualifying    | Dulux British Open                 |
|        | v Miles         | 1-6    | 1st round     | Dulux British Open                 |
|        | v Foldvari      | 10-3   | Qualifying    | Embassy World Championship         |
|        | v Wildman       | 10-7   | Qualifying    | Embassy World Championship         |

| | | | |
|---|---|---|---|
| v Stevens | 8-10 | 1st round | Embassy World Championship |
| v Bales | 0-5 | 2nd round | Goya Matchroom Trophy |
| v Kearney | 5-2 | 2nd round | Rothmans Grand Prix |
| v O'Kane | 5-2 | 3rd round | Rothmans Grand Prix |
| v Knowles | 3-5 | 4th round | Rothmans Grand Prix |
| v Van Rensberg | 9-5 | 2nd round | Coral UK Open |
| v Higgins | 8-9 | 3rd round | Coral UK Open |
| 1986 v Smith | 2-5 | 2nd round | Mecantile Credit Classic |
| v Smith | 9-8 | 2nd round | Tolly Cobbold English Championship |
| v David Taylor | 9-6 | 3rd round | Tolly Cobbold English Championship |
| v N. Foulds | 4-9 | 4th round | Tolly Cobbold English Championship |
| v Hargreaves | 3-5 | 2nd round | Dulux British Open |
| v Kelly | 10-0 | Qualifying | Embassy World Championship |
| v Darrington | 10-5 | Qualifying | Embassy World Championship |
| v Wildman | 10-9 | Qualifying | Embassy World Championship |
| v S. Davis | 4-10 | 1st round | Embassy World Championship |
| v James | 5-2 | 2nd round | BCE International |
| v David Taylor | 4-5 | 3rd round | BCE International |
| v O'Boye | 2-5 | 2nd round | Rothmans Grand Prix |
| v Bear | 9-6 | 2nd round | Tennents UK Open |
| v White | 4-9 | 3rd round | Tennents UK Open |
| 1987 v Williamson | 2-5 | 2nd round | Mercantile Credit Classic |
| v Bennett | 6-1 | 2nd round | Tolly Ales English Championship |
| v Reynolds | 3-6 | 3rd round | Tolly Ales English Championship |
| v G. Foulds | 3-5 | 2nd round | Dulux British Open |
| v James | 10-1 | Qualifying | Embassy World Championship |
| v Sinclair | 10-6 | Qualifying | Embassy World Championship |
| v Macleod | 7-10 | Qualifying | Embassy World Championship |
| v Sinclair | 4-5 | 2nd round | Fidelity International |
| v Sinclair | 5-2 | 2nd round | Rothmans Grand Prix |
| v Williams | 5-3 | 3rd round | Rothmans Grand Prix |
| v Charlton | 3-5 | 4th round | Rothmans Grand Prix |
| v D. Hughes | 9-4 | 2nd round | Tennents UK Open |
| v Macleod | 9-4 | 3rd round | Tennents UK Open |
| v Griffiths | 5-9 | 4th round | Tennents UK Open |
| 1988 v Foldvari | 5-4 | 2nd round | Mercantile Credit Classic |
| v Longworth | 3-5 | 3rd round | Mercantile Credit Classic |
| v Gary Wilkinson | 3-6 | 2nd round | English Championship |
| v Roe | 1-5 | 2nd round | MIM Britannia British Open |
| v Morra | 8-10 | Qualifying | Embassy World Championship |
| v Bear | 5-1 | 2nd round | Fidelity International |
| v Hendry | 1-5 | 3rd round | Fidelity International |
| v Dunning | 5-2 | 2nd round | Rothmans Grand Prix |
| v Longworth | 5-3 | 3rd round | Rothmans Grand Prix |
| v Parrott | 5-3 | 4th round | Rothmans Grand Prix |
| v Williams | 3-5 | 5th round | Rothmans Grand Prix |
| v Scott | 2-5 | 2nd round | BCE Canadian Masters |
| v Wildman | 9-4 | 2nd round | Tennents UK Open |
| v C. Wilson | 1-9 | 3rd round | Tennents UK Open |
| 1989 v Marshall | 2-5 | 2nd round | Mercantile Credit Classic |
| v Grace | 5-1 | 2nd round | European Open |
| v Thorburn | 2-5 | 3rd round | European Open |
| v Price | 4-5 | 2nd round | English Championship |
| v Johnston-Allen | 4-5 | 2nd round | Anglian British Open |
| v Black | 10-3 | Qualifying | Embassy World Championship |
| v John Rea | 7-10 | Qualifying | Embassy World Championship |

## CRAIG EDWARDS (England)

**Born** 23.12.68. **Turned professional** 1988. **World ranking** 69. **Best professional performance** Last 32 1989 European Open.

| 1988 | v John Rea | 2-5 | 1st round | Fidelity International |
|---|---|---|---|---|
| | v Duggan | 4-5 | 2nd round | Rothmans Grand Prix |
| | v Medati | 3-5 | 1st round | BCE Canadian Masters |
| | v Sinclair | 9-8 | 1st round | Tennents UK Open |
| | v Stevens | 4-9 | 2nd round | Tennents UK Open |
| 1989 | v Lawlor | 5-1 | 1st round | Mercantile Credit Classic |
| | v Stevens | 4-5 | 2nd round | Mercantile Credit Classic |
| | v M. Smith | 4-5 | 1st round | European Open |
| | v Werbeniuk | wo | 2nd round | European Open |
| | v Chaperon | 5-3 | 3rd round | European Open |
| | v Virgo | 3-5 | 4th round | European Open |
| | v Watterson | 5-0 | 1st round | English Championship |
| | v Dodd | 5-1 | 2nd round | English Championship |
| | v Spencer | 5-1 | 3rd round | English Championship |
| | v Johnson | 0-5 | 4th round | English Championship |
| | v Black | 5-3 | 1st round | Anglian British Open |
| | v O'Boye | 5-4 | 2nd round | Anglian British Open |
| | v Hendry | 0-5 | 3rd round | Anglian British Open |
| | v Giannaros | 10-4 | Qualifying | Embassy World Championship |
| | v Bear | 10-7 | Qualifying | Embassy World Championship |
| | v Chappel | 10-7 | Qualifying | Embassy World Championship |
| | v N. Gilbert | 8-10 | Qualifying | Embassy World Championship |

## FRANÇOIS ELLIS (South Africa)

**Born** 11.9.59. **Turned professional** 1983. **World ranking** 105 (113). **Amateur career** 1979, 1980 South African champion.

| 1986 | v Mans | 7-6 | 2nd round | South African Championship |
|---|---|---|---|---|
| | v Van Rensberg | 8-2 | Semi-final | South African Championship |
| | v S. Francisco | 1-9 | Final | South African Championship |
| | v Morra | 3-5 | 1st round | BCE International |
| | v Wildman | 1-5 | 2nd round | Rothmans Grand Prix |
| | v D. Hughes | 6-9 | 1st round | Tennents UK Open |
| 1987 | v Morra | 1-5 | 1st round | Mercantile Credit Classic |
| | v Smith | 5-2 | 1st round | Dulux British Open |
| | v Medati | 0-5 | 2nd round | Dulux British Open |
| | v Roe | 4-5 | 1st round | Fidelity International |
| | v Sinclair | 4-5 | 1st round | Rothmans Grand Prix |
| | v Sheehan | 9-8 | 1st round | Tennents UK Open |
| | v F. Davis | 6-9 | 2nd round | Tennents UK Open |
| 1988 | v V. Harris | 1-5 | 1st round | Mercantile Credit Classic |
| | v Chappel | 0-5 | 2nd round | MIM Britannia British Open |
| | v G. Foulds | 2-5 | 1st round | Fidelity International |
| | v Lawlor | 5-4 | 1st round | Rothmans Grand Prix |
| | v Gauvreau | 5-2 | 2nd round | Rothmans Grand Prix |
| | v Dennis Taylor | 1-5 | 3rd round | Rothmans Grand Prix |
| | v Rowswell | 1-5 | 1st round | BCE Canadian Masters |
| | v Bear | 9-7 | 1st round | Tennents UK Open |
| | v Fowler | 3-9 | 2nd round | Tennents UK Open |
| 1989 | v Donnelly | 5-0 | 1st round | Mercantile Credit Classic |
| | v Roe | 0-5 | 2nd round | Mercantile Credit Classic |
| | v Kearney | 5-4 | 1st round | European Open |
| | v D. Gilbert | 2-5 | 2nd round | European Open |
| | v Rowswell | 1-5 | 1st round | Anglian British Open |
| | v Wildman | 10-7 | Qualifying | Embassy World Championship |
| | v J. McLaughlin | 9-10 | Qualifying | Embassy World Championship |

## PATSY FAGAN (Republic of Ireland)

**Born** 15.1.51. **Turned professional** 1976. **World ranking** 123 (103). **Best professional performance** Winner 1977 Super Crystalate UK Championship.

| 1977 | v Meadowcroft | 11-9 | Qualifying | Embassy World Championship |
|------|---------------|------|------------|----------------------------|
| | v Reardon | 7-13 | 1st round | Embassy World Championship |
| | v Jack Rea | 5-1 | 1st round | Super Crystalate UK Championship |
| | v F. Davis | 5-0 | 2nd round | Super Crystalate UK Championship |
| | v Meadowcroft | 5-4 | Quarter-final | Super Crystalate UK Championship |
| | v Virgo | 9-8 | Semi-final | Super Crystalate UK Championship |
| | **v Mountjoy** | **12-9** | **Final** | **Super Crystalate UK Championship** |
| 1978 | v Pulman | 2-4 | 1st round | Benson & Hedges Masters |
| | v Dunning | 9-5 | Qualifying | Embassy World Championship |
| | v Higgins | 13-12 | 1st round | Embassy World Championship |
| | v F. Davis | 10-13 | Quarter-final | Embassy World Championship |
| | v David Taylor | 7-9 | 1st round | Coral UK Championship |
| 1979 | v S. Davis | 2-9 | Qualifying | Embassy World Championship |
| | v Hallett | 9-4 | 2nd round | Coral UK Championship |
| | v Miles | 9-5 | 3rd round | Coral UK Championship |
| | v Dennis Taylor | 6-9 | Quarter-final | Coral UK Championship |
| 1980 | v S. Davis | 6-10 | 1st round | Embassy World Championship |
| | v Johnson | 9-4 | 1st round | Coral UK Championship |
| | v Griffiths | 8-9 | 2nd round | Coral UK Championship |
| 1981 | v Dunning | 7-9 | Qualifying | Embassy World Championship |
| | v Watterson | 5-2 | Qualifying | Jameson International |
| | v Higgins | 3-5 | 2nd round | Jameson International |
| | v Hallett | 5-9 | Qualifying | Coral UK Championship |
| 1982 | v Murphy | 2-6 | Quarter-final | Irish Championship |
| | v French | 9-6 | Qualifying | Embassy World Championship |
| | v David Taylor | 10-9 | 1st round | Embassy World Championship |
| | v Stevens | 7-13 | 2nd round | Embassy World Championship |
| | v Watterson | 1-5 | Qualifying | Jameson International |
| | v Everton | 2-5 | 1st round | Professional Players Tournament |
| | v B. Harris | 9-6 | 1st round | Coral UK Championship |
| | v S. Davis | 3-9 | 2nd round | Coral UK Championship |
| 1983 | v Murphy | 6-4 | Quarter-final | Irish Championship |
| | v Dennis Taylor | 1-6 | Semi-final | Irish Championship |
| | v Fisher | 8-10 | Qualifying | Embassy World Championship |
| | v Martin | 0-5 | Qualifying | Jameson International |
| | v Parrott | 2-5 | 1st round | Professional Players Tournament |
| 1984 | v Higgins | 3-5 | Qualifying | Lada Classic |
| | v Wych | 3-10 | Qualifying | Embassy World Championship |
| | v Newbury | 0-5 | Qualifying | Jameson International |
| | v T. Jones | 2-9 | Qualifying | Coral UK Open |
| 1985 | v Williamson | 5-1 | Qualifying | Mercantile Credit Classic |
| | v Wildman | 5-3 | Qualifying | Mercantile Credit Classic |
| | v Griffiths | 0-5 | 1st round | Mercantile Credit Classic |
| | v Murphy | 6-2 | Quarter-final | Irish Championship |
| | v Higgins | 3-6 | Semi-final | Irish Championship |
| | v Gibson | 10-8 | Qualifying | Embassy World Championship |
| | v Wilson | 10-9 | Qualifying | Embassy World Championship |
| | v Thorne | 10-6 | 1st round | Embassy World Championship |
| | v Reardon | 9-13 | 2nd round | Embassy World Championship |
| | v Mienie | 5-4 | 2nd round | Goya Matchroom Trophy |
| | v White | 2-5 | 3rd round | Goya Matchroom Trophy |
| | v Oliver | 4-5 | 2nd round | Rothmans Grand Prix |
| | v B. Harris | 9-2 | 2nd round | Coral UK Open |
| | v N. Foulds | 5-9 | 3rd round | Coral UK Open |
| 1986 | v Fitzmaurice | 3-5 | 2nd round | Mercantile Credit Classic |
| | v Fitzmaurice | 5-4 | 2nd round | Dulux British Open |
| | v Mountjoy | 5-1 | 3rd round | Dulux British Open |
| | v Parrott | 0-5 | 4th round | Dulux British Open |
| | v Knowles | 5-4 | Quarter-final | Benson & Hedges Irish Masters |
| | v White | 0-6 | Semi-final | Benson & Hedges Irish Masters |
| | v Thornley | 7-10 | Qualifying | Embassy World Championship |
| | v Kearney | 0-5 | 1st round | Strongbow Irish Championship |

|      |                |  |       |                    |
|------|----------------|-------|------------|------------------------------|
|      | v Sinclair     | 0-5   | 2nd round  | BCE International            |
|      | v Grace        | 5-3   | 2nd round  | Rothmans Grand Prix          |
|      | v Virgo        | 2-5   | 3rd round  | Rothmans Grand Prix          |
|      | v Wright       | 0-9   | 2nd round  | Tennents UK Open             |
| 1987 | v Grace        | 3-5   | 2nd round  | Dulux British Open           |
|      | v Oliver       | 2-10  | Qualifying | Embassy World Championship   |
|      | v Burke        | 3-5   | 1st round  | Matchroom Irish Championship |
|      | v O'Boye       | 1-5   | 2nd round  | Fidelity International        |
|      | v P. Gibson    | 0-5   | 1st round  | Rothmans Grand Prix          |
|      | v Dunning      | 4-9   | 1st round  | Tennents UK Open             |
| 1988 | v Whitthread   | 2-5   | 1st round  | Mercantile Credit Classic    |
|      | v Kearney      | 3-5   | 1st round  | Irish Championship           |
|      | v D. Hughes    | 4-5   | 1st round  | MIM Britannia British Open   |
|      | v Greaves      | 10-3  | Qualifying | Embassy World Championship   |
|      | v B. Harris    | 1-10  | Qualifying | Embassy World Championship   |
|      | v Oliver       | 0-5   | 1st round  | Fidelity International        |
|      | v Wildman      | 1-5   | 1st round  | Rothmans Grand Prix          |
|      | v Chambers     | 2-5   | 1st round  | BCE Canadian Masters         |
|      | v Scott        | 2-9   | 1st round  | Tennents UK Open             |
| 1989 | v Bradley      | 3-5   | 1st round  | Mercantile Credit Classic    |
|      | v Black        | 1-5   | 1st round  | European Open                |
|      | v Grace        | 2-5   | 1st round  | Anglian British Open         |
|      | v G. Foulds    | 10-6  | Qualifying | Embassy World Championship   |
|      | v D. Gilbert   | 4-10  | Qualifying | Embassy World Championship   |

## MICK FISHER (England)

**Born** 12.7.44. **Turned professional** 1982. **World ranking** 64 (58). **Best professional performance** Last 16 1987 Rothmans Grand Prix.

|      |                 |  |       |                           |
|------|-----------------|-------|------------|-------------------------------------|
| 1982 | v Murphy        | 5-1   | Qualifying | Jameson International               |
|      | v F. Davis      | 5-3   | Qualifying | Jameson International               |
|      | v David Taylor  | 1-5   | 1st round  | Jameson International               |
|      | v Black         | 9-3   | Qualifying | Coral UK Championship               |
|      | v Edmonds       | 9-8   | Qualifying | Coral UK Championship               |
|      | v Reynolds      | 6-9   | 1st round  | Coral UK Championship               |
| 1983 | v Fagan         | 10-8  | Qualifying | Embassy World Championship          |
|      | v E. McLaughlin | 10-9  | Qualifying | Embassy World Championship          |
|      | v Stevens       | 2-10  | 1st round  | Embassy World Championship          |
|      | v E. Hughes     | 4-5   | Qualifying | Jameson International               |
|      | v F. Davis      | 5-4   | 1st round  | Professional Players Tournament     |
|      | v Charlton      | 4-5   | 2nd round  | Professional Players Tournament     |
|      | v Parrott       | 0-9   | Qualifying | Coral UK Championship               |
| 1984 | v Thornley      | 10-8  | Qualifying | Embassy World Championship          |
|      | v Gibson        | 7-10  | Qualifying | Embassy World Championship          |
|      | v Bales         | 3-5   | Qualifying | Jameson International               |
|      | v Newbury       | 0-5   | Qualifying | Rothmans Grand Prix                 |
|      | v Watchorn      | 9-5   | Qualifying | Coral UK Open                       |
|      | v Williams      | 8-9   | Qualifying | Coral UK Open                       |
| 1985 | v Longworth     | 1-5   | Qualifying | Mercantile Credit Classic           |
|      | v French        | 9-8   | Qualifying | Tolly Cobbold English Championship  |
|      | v Meo           | 3-9   | 1st round  | Tolly Cobbold English Championship  |
|      | v John Rea      | 0-6   | Qualifying | Dulux British Open                  |
|      | v Rigitano      | 2-10  | Qualifying | Embassy World Championship          |
|      | v Mikkelsen     | 3-5   | 1st round  | Goya Matchroom Trophy               |
|      | v Bales         | 3-5   | 2nd round  | Rothmans Grand Prix                 |
|      | v Simngam       | 4-9   | 2nd round  | Coral UK Open                       |
| 1986 | v Jack Rea      | 5-3   | 2nd round  | Mercantile Credit Classic           |
|      | v Higgins       | 0-5   | 3rd round  | Mercantile Credit Classic           |
|      | v Chalmers      | 2-9   | 2nd round  | Tolly Cobbold English Championship  |

|      |                 |      |           |                               |
|------|-----------------|------|-----------|-------------------------------|
|      | v J. McLaughlin | 3-5  | 2nd round | Dulux British Open            |
|      | v Duggan        | 3-10 | Qualifying| Embassy World Championship    |
|      | v Hines         | 2-5  | 1st round | BCE International             |
|      | v Wright        | 1-5  | 1st round | Rothmans Grand Prix           |
|      | v Greaves       | 9-4  | 1st round | Tennents UK Open              |
|      | v V. Harris     | 4-9  | 2nd round | Tennents UK Open              |
| 1987 | v Demarco       | 5-0  | 1st round | Mercantile Credit Classic     |
|      | v F. Davis      | 5-2  | 2nd round | Mercantile Credit Classic     |
|      | v Charlton      | 0-5  | 3rd round | Mercantile Credit Classic     |
|      | v Whitthread    | 6-3  | 1st round | Tolly Ales English Championship|
|      | v Duggan        | 0-6  | 2nd round | Tolly Ales English Championship|
|      | v Chaperon      | 2-5  | 2nd round | Dulux British Open            |
|      | v Owers         | 5-10 | Qualifying| Embassy World Championship    |
|      | v Newbury       | 0-5  | 2nd round | Fidelity International         |
|      | v Watchorn      | 5-4  | 1st round | Rothmans Grand Prix           |
|      | v F. Davis      | 5-0  | 2nd round | Rothmans Grand Prix           |
|      | v E. Hughes     | 5-4  | 3rd round | Rothmans Grand Prix           |
|      | v Clark         | 5-4  | 4th round | Rothmans Grand Prix           |
|      | v Chaperon      | 2-5  | 5th round | Rothmans Grand Prix           |
|      | v Wych          | 6-9  | 2nd round | Tennents UK Open              |
| 1988 | v Owers         | 0-5  | 2nd round | Mercantile Credit Classic     |
|      | v Wright        | 2-6  | 2nd round | English Championship          |
|      | v Clark         | 1-5  | 1st round | MIM Britannia British Open    |
|      | v A. Harris     | 4-10 | Qualifying| Embassy World Championship    |
|      | v Glen Wilkinson| 5-4  | 2nd round | Fidelity International         |
|      | v Chaperon      | 3-5  | 3rd round | Fidelity International         |
|      | v J. Smith      | 5-3  | 2nd round | Rothmans Grand Prix           |
|      | v Mountjoy      | 1-5  | 3rd round | Rothmans Grand Prix           |
|      | v Robidoux      | 0-5  | 2nd round | BCE Canadian Masters          |
|      | v Medati        | 3-9  | 2nd round | Tennents UK Open              |
| 1989 | v Sheehan       | 3-5  | 2nd round | Mercantile Credit Classic     |
|      | v Robidoux      | 1-5  | 2nd round | European Open                 |
|      | v Miles         | 4-5  | 2nd round | English Championship          |
|      | v Foldvari      | 0-5  | 2nd round | Anglian British Open          |
|      | v Robidoux      | 2-10 | Qualifying| Embassy World Championship    |

## JACK FITZMAURICE (England)

**Born** 25.4.28. **Turned professional** 1981. **World ranking** 106 (114). **Best professional performance** Last 32 1982 Embassy World Championship.

|      |             |       |           |                                  |
|------|-------------|-------|-----------|----------------------------------|
| 1981 | v Bennett   | 5-1   | Qualifying| Jameson International             |
|      | v E. Hughes | 3-5   | Qualifying| Jameson International             |
|      | v Gibson    | 6-9   | Qualifying| Coral UK Championship            |
| 1982 | v Morra     | 9-7   | Qualifying| Embassy World Championship       |
|      | v Stevens   | 4-10  | 1st round | Embassy World Championship       |
|      | v Black     | 5-3   | Qualifying| Jameson International             |
|      | v Dodd      | 3-5   | Qualifying| Jameson International             |
|      | v Sheehan   | 5-1   | 1st round | Professional Players Tournament  |
|      | v Reynolds  | 0-5   | 2nd round | Professional Players Tournament  |
|      | v Kelly     | 0-8   | Qualifying| Coral UK Championship            |
|      |             | *retd*|           |                                  |
| 1983 | v E. Hughes | 7-10  | Qualifying| Embassy World Championship       |
|      | v Morgan    | 4-5   | Qualifying| Jameson International             |
|      | v Martin    | 0-5   | 1st round | Professional Players Tournament  |
|      | v B. Harris | 3-9   | Qualifying| Coral UK Championship            |
| 1984 | v Murphy    | 8-10  | Qualifying| Embassy World Championship       |
|      | v O'Kane    | 4-5   | Qualifying| Jameson International             |
|      | v John Rea  | 2-5   | Qualifying| Rothmans Grand Prix              |
|      | v Cripsey   | 9-8   | Qualifying| Coral UK Open                    |
|      | v Parrott   | 6-9   | Qualifying| Coral UK Open                    |

| 1985 | v G. Foulds | 1-5 | Qualifying | Mercantile Credit Classic |
|------|-------------|-----|------------|---------------------------|
|      | v Greaves | 9-3 | Qualifying | Tolly Cobbold English Championship |
|      | v Reynolds | 2-9 | 1st round | Tolly Cobbold English Championship |
|      | v Watterson | 1-6 | Qualifying | Dulux British Open |
|      | v T. Jones | 4-10 | Qualifying | Embassy World Championship |
|      | v Watterson | 5-2 | 2nd round | Goya Matchroom Trophy |
|      | v Macleod | 1-5 | 3rd round | Goya Matchroom Trophy |
|      | v Sinclair | 5-3 | 2nd round | Rothmans Grand Prix |
|      | v White | 0-5 | 3rd round | Rothmans Grand Prix |
|      | v W. Jones | 3-9 | 2nd round | Coral UK Open |
| 1986 | v Fagan | 5-3 | 2nd round | Mercantile Credit Classic |
|      | v Dennis Taylor | 1-5 | 3rd round | Mercantile Credit Classic |
|      | v Miles | 5-9 | 2nd round | Tolly Cobbold English Championship |
|      | v Fagan | 4-5 | 2nd round | Dulux British Open |
|      | v Dodd | 6-10 | Qualifying | Embassy World Championship |
|      | v Burke | 4-5 | 1st round | BCE International |
|      | v Mienie | 2-5 | 1st round | Rothmans Grand Prix |
|      | v Hines | 9-4 | 1st round | Tennents UK Open |
|      | v T. Jones | 0-9 | 2nd round | Tennents UK Open |
| 1987 | v Wilkinson | 2-5 | 1st round | Mercantile Credit Classic |
|      | v Scott | 6-2 | 2nd round | Tolly Ales English Championship |
|      | v David Taylor | 1-6 | 3rd round | Tolly Ales English Championship |
|      | v Wilkinson | 0-5 | 1st round | Dulux British Open |
|      | v Everton | 10-2 | Qualifying | Embassy World Championship |
|      | v Chaperon | 2-10 | Qualifying | Embassy World Championship |
|      | v Chalmers | 4-5 | 1st round | Fidelity International |
|      | v Chambers | 2-5 | 1st round | Rothmans Grand Prix |
|      | v Lawlor | 0-9 | 1st round | Tennents UK Open |
| 1988 | v M. Smith | 2-5 | 1st round | Mercantile Credit Classic |
|      | v Marshall | 1-6 | 1st round | English Championship |
|      | v T. Jones | 3-5 | 2nd round | MIM Britannia British Open |
|      | v Parkin | 10-6 | Qualifying | Embassy World Championship |
|      | v F. Davis | 8-10 | Qualifying | Embassy World Championship |
|      | v Mikkelsen | 2-5 | 1st round | Fidelity International |
|      | v Oliver | 3-5 | 1st round | Rothmans Grand Prix |
|      | v Van Rensberg | 5-3 | 1st round | BCE Canadian Masters |
|      | v J. McLaughlin | 5-2 | 2nd round | BCE Canadian Masters |
|      | v Thorne | 0-5 | 3rd round | BCE Canadian Masters |
|      | v Lawlor | 1-9 | 1st round | Tennents UK Open |
| 1989 | v Meadowcroft | 5-2 | 1st round | Mercantile Credit Classic |
|      | v N. Gilbert | 3-5 | 2nd round | Mercantile Credit Classic |
|      | v Lawlor | 0-5 | 1st round | European Open |
|      | v B. Harris | 5-4 | 1st round | English Championship |
|      | v Houlihan | 4-5 | 2nd round | English Championship |
|      | v Dunning | 5-1 | 1st round | Anglian British Open |
|      | v Bales | 1-5 | 2nd round | Anglian British Open |
|      | v Roscoe | 10-9 | Qualifying | Embassy World Championship |
|      | v Reardon | 5-10 | Qualifying | Embassy World Championship |

## ROBBY FOLDVARI (Australia)

**Born** 2.6.60. **Turned professional** 1984. **World ranking** 77 (66). **Best professional performances** Last 32 1987 Fidelity International, 1987 Rothmans Grand Prix.

| 1984 | v Rigitano | 5-2 | Qualifying | Jameson International |
|------|-----------|-----|------------|----------------------|
|      | v Edmonds | 5-1 | Qualifying | Jameson International |
|      | v Dodd | 3-5 | Qualifying | Jameson International |
|      | v Gauvreau | 2-5 | Qualifying | Rothmans Grand Prix |
|      | v Greaves | 9-5 | Qualifying | Coral UK Open |
|      | v Cripsey | 7-9 | Qualifying | Coral UK Open |
| 1985 | v Houlihan | 5-1 | Qualifying | Mercantile Credit Classic |
|      | v Jack Rea | 5-4 | Qualifying | Mercantile Credit Classic |

| | | | | |
|---|---|---|---|---|
| | v Martin | 5-2 | Qualifying | Mercantile Credit Classic |
| | v Thorne | 2-5 | 1st round | Mercantile Credit Classic |
| | v Duggan | 6-4 | Qualifying | Dulux British Open |
| | v Meo | 0-6 | 1st round | Dulux British Open |
| | v Oliver | 10-3 | Qualifying | Embassy World Championship |
| | v Edmonds | 3-10 | Qualifying | Embassy World Championship |
| | v Robinson | 7-2 | 2nd round | Australian Championship |
| | v Campbell | 5-8 | Quarter-final | Australian Championship |
| | v V. Harris | 5-4 | 2nd round | Goya Matchroom Trophy |
| | v Spencer | 4-5 | 3rd round | Goya Matchroom Trophy |
| | v Darrington | 3-5 | 2nd round | Rothmans Grand Prix |
| | v Darrington | 6-9 | 2nd round | Coral UK Open |
| 1986 | v Houlihan | 4-5 | 2nd round | Mercantile Credit Classic |
| | v Kearney | 5-2 | 2nd round | Dulux British Open |
| | v Werbeniuk | 4-5 | 3rd round | Dulux British Open |
| | v Rigitano | 10-6 | Qualifying | Embassy World Championship |
| | v Miles | 10-7 | Qualifying | Embassy World Championship |
| | v Parrott | 6-10 | Qualifying | Embassy World Championship |
| | v Jenkins | 6-3 | 2nd round | Australian Championship |
| | v Morgan | 6-2 | Quarter-final | Australian Championship |
| | v Campbell | 3-8 | Semi-final | Australian Championship |
| | v B. Harris | 5-0 | 2nd round | BCE International |
| | v Dennis Taylor | 1-5 | 3rd round | BCE International |
| | v W. Jones | 3-5 | 2nd round | Rothmans Grand Prix |
| | v Spencer | 6-9 | 2nd round | Tennents UK Open |
| 1987 | v Mikkelsen | 1-5 | 2nd round | Mercantile Credit Classic |
| | v Mikkelsen | 5-3 | 2nd round | Dulux British Open |
| | v Williams | 4-5 | 3rd round | Dulux British Open |
| | v Wildman | 5-10 | Qualifying | Embassy World Championship |
| | v King | 1-8 | Semi-final | Australian Championship |
| | v Meakin | 3-5 | 1st round | Fidelity International |
| | v Kearney | 5-1 | 2nd round | Fidelity International |
| | v Williams | 5-0 | 3rd round | Fidelity International |
| | v D. Gilbert | 4-5 | 4th round | Fidelity International |
| | v Dunning | 5-0 | 1st round | Rothmans Grand Prix |
| | v King | 5-4 | 2nd round | Rothmans Grand Prix |
| | v Werbeniuk | 1-5 | 3rd round | Rothmans Grand Prix |
| | v Clark | 9-8 | 1st round | Tennents UK Open |
| | v Newbury | 5-9 | 2nd round | Tennents UK Open |
| 1988 | v Greaves | 5-3 | 1st round | Mercantile Credit Classic |
| | v Edmonds | 4-5 | 2nd round | Mercantile Credit Classic |
| | v Heaton | 5-1 | 1st round | MIM Britannia British Open |
| | v G. Foulds | 5-3 | 2nd round | MIM Britannia British Open |
| | v Parrott | 1-5 | 3rd round | MIM Britannia British Open |
| | v Rempe | 10-4 | Qualifying | Embassy World Championship |
| | v T. Jones | 10-9 | Qualifying | Embassy World Championship |
| | v Wildman | 10-1 | Qualifying | Embassy World Championship |
| | v P. Francisco | 5-10 | Qualifying | Embassy World Championship |
| | v Potaszyk | 5-3 | Quarter-final | Australian Championship |
| | v King | 8-4 | Semi-final | Australian Championship |
| | v J. Campbell | 7-9 | Final | Australian Championship |
| | v A. Harris | 5-1 | 1st round | Fidelity International |
| | v T. Jones | 4-5 | 2nd round | Fidelity International |
| | v Price | 5-1 | 1st round | Rothmans Grand Prix |
| | v Wright | 5-4 | 2nd round | Rothmans Grand Prix |
| | v Drago | 3-5 | 3rd round | Rothmans Grand Prix |
| | v Burke | 5-2 | 1st round | BCE Canadian Masters |
| | v Wych | 2-5 | 2nd round | BCE Canadian Masters |
| | v Burke | 9-0 | 1st round | Tennents UK Open |
| | v J. Campbell | 7-9 | 2nd round | Tennents UK Open |
| 1989 | v T. Wilson | 5-4 | 1st round | Mercantile Credit Classic |
| | v Martin | 2-5 | 2nd round | Mercantile Credit Classic |
| | v Rowing | 4-5 | 1st round | European Open |

| v Sheehan | 5-1 | 1st round | Anglian British Open |
| v Fisher | 5-0 | 2nd round | Anglian British Open |
| v Higgins | 1-5 | 3rd round | Anglian British Open |
| v J. Smith | 4-10 | Qualifying | Embassy World Championship |

## GEOFF FOULDS (England)

**Born** 20.11.39. **Turned professional** 1981. **World ranking** 118 (78). **Best professional performance** Last 32 1986 BCE International.

| | | | | |
|---|---|---|---|---|
| **1981** | v French | 2-5 | Qualifying | Jameson International |
| | v Kelly | 9-7 | Qualifying | Coral UK Championship |
| | v Knowles | 1-9 | Qualifying | Coral UK Championship |
| **1982** | v Wildman | 8-9 | Qualifying | Embassy World Championship |
| | v Kelly | 4-5 | Qualifying | Jameson International |
| | v Spencer | 1-5 | 1st round | Professional Players Tournament |
| | v Gibson | 9-3 | Qualifying | Coral UK Championship |
| | v Williams | 7-9 | Qualifying | Coral UK Championship |
| **1983** | v Gibson | 10-6 | Qualifying | Embassy World Championship |
| | v Meo | 4-10 | Qualifying | Embassy World Championship |
| | v Burke | 5-2 | Qualifying | Jameson International |
| | v E. Hughes | 1-5 | Qualifying | Jameson International |
| | v Burke | 4-5 | Qualifying | Professional Players Tournament |
| | v Duggan | 9-8 | Qualifying | Coral UK Championship |
| | v Dodd | 9-7 | Qualifying | Coral UK Championship |
| | v S. Davis | 1-9 | 1st round | Coral UK Championship |
| **1984** | v Morra | 2-10 | Qualifying | Embassy World Championship |
| | v P. Francisco | 5-4 | Qualifying | Jameson International |
| | v Williamson | 5-4 | Qualifying | Jameson International |
| | v Donnelly | 5-3 | Qualifying | Jameson International |
| | v Campbell | 3-5 | Qualifying | Jameson International |
| | v Murphy | 1-5 | Qualifying | Rothmans Grand Prix |
| | v D. Hughes | 9-7 | Qualifying | Coral UK Open |
| | v Browne | 5-9 | Qualifying | Coral UK Open |
| **1985** | v Chaperon | 5-3 | Qualifying | Mercantile Credit Classic |
| | v Jonik | 5-2 | Qualifying | Mercantile Credit Classic |
| | v Fitzmaurice | 5-1 | Qualifying | Mercantile Credit Classic |
| | v Hallett | 4-5 | Qualifying | Mercantile Credit Classic |
| | v F. Davis | 9-2 | Qualifying | Tolly Cobbold English Championship |
| | v Parrott | 4-9 | 1st round | Tolly Cobbold English Championship |
| | v T. Jones | 0-6 | Qualifying | Dulux British Open |
| | v Parkin | 10-6 | Qualifying | Embassy World Championship |
| | v Everton | 10-2 | Qualifying | Embassy World Championship |
| | v Roscoe | 10-7 | Qualifying | Embassy World Championship |
| | v Johnson | 6-10 | Qualifying | Embassy World Championship |
| | v Roscoe | 3-5 | 2nd round | Goya Matchroom Trophy |
| | v Black | 5-3 | 2nd round | Rothmans Grand Prix |
| | v Charlton | 1-5 | 3rd round | Rothmans Grand Prix |
| | v Sinclair | 4-9 | 2nd round | Coral UK Open |
| **1986** | v Black | 5-2 | 2nd round | Mercantile Credit Classic |
| | v Werbeniuk | 3-5 | 3rd round | Mercantile Credit Classic |
| | v Watterson | 9-1 | 2nd round | Tolly Cobbold English Championship |
| | v N. Foulds | 4-9 | 3rd round | Tolly Cobbold English Championship |
| | v P. Francisco | 2-5 | 2nd round | Dulux British Open |
| | v Roscoe | 3-10 | Qualifying | Embassy World Championship |
| | v V. Harris | 5-4 | 2nd round | BCE International |
| | v Werbeniuk | 5-2 | 3rd round | BCE International |
| | v N. Foulds | 0-5 | 4th round | BCE International |
| | v Wilkinson | 5-3 | 1st round | Rothmans Grand Prix |
| | v Mikkelsen | 5-1 | 2nd round | Rothmans Grand Prix |
| | v Campbell | 0-5 | 3rd round | Rothmans Grand Prix |
| | v Roe | 1-7 *retd* | 1st round | Tennents UK Open |

| 1987 | v Chalmers | 5-4 | 1st round | Mercantile Credit Classic |
|---|---|---|---|---|
| | v O'Kane | 5-4 | 2nd round | Mercantile Credit Classic |
| | v Martin | 4-5 | 3rd round | Mercantile Credit Classic |
| | v B. Harris | 1-6 | 2nd round | Tolly Ales English Championship |
| | v Edmonds | 5-3 | 2nd round | Dulux British Open |
| | v Wilson | 3-5 | 3rd round | Dulux British Open |
| | v Watchorn | 10-6 | Qualifying | Embassy World Championship |
| | v Fowler | 6-10 | Qualifying | Embassy World Championship |
| | v Jack Rea | 1-5 | 2nd round | Fidelity International |
| | v James | 0-5 | 2nd round | Rothmans Grand Prix |
| | v N. Gilbert | 4-9 | 2nd round | Tennents UK Open |
| 1988 | v Whitthread | 3-5 | 2nd round | Mercantile Credit Classic |
| | v Clark | 0-6 | 2nd round | English Championship |
| | v Foldvari | 3-5 | 2nd round | MIM Britannia British Open |
| | v Bear | 2-10 | Qualifying | Embassy World Championship |
| | v Ellis | 5-2 | 1st round | Fidelity International |
| | v Miles | 3-5 | 2nd round | Fidelity International |
| | v J. Smith | 3-5 | 1st round | Rothmans Grand Prix |
| | v J. Smith | 1-5 | 1st round | BCE Canadian Masters |
| | v Rowing | 4-9 | 1st round | Tennents UK Open |
| 1989 | v Everton | 5-0 | 1st round | Mercantile Credit Classic |
| | v Wright | 4-5 | 2nd round | Mercantile Credit Classic |
| | v Jack Rea | 5-4 | 1st round | European Open |
| | v Wych | 0-5 | 2nd round | European Open |
| | v Oliver | 1-5 | 1st round | English Championship |
| | v J. Smith | 3-5 | 1st round | Anglian British Open |
| | v Fagan | 6-10 | Qualifying | Embassy World Championship |

## NEAL FOULDS (England)

**Born** 13.7.63. **Turned professional** 1983. **World ranking** 20 (3). **Best professional performances** Winner 1986 BCE International; runner-up 1986 Tennents UK Open, 1987 Dulux British Open.

| 1983 | v French | 2-5 | Qualifying | Professional Players Tournament |
|---|---|---|---|---|
| | v Roscoe | 9-2 | Qualifying | Coral UK Championship |
| | v Meadowcroft | 9-2 | Qualifying | Coral UK Championship |
| | v David Taylor | 4-9 | 1st round | Coral UK Championship |
| 1984 | v French | 10-5 | Qualifying | Embassy World Championship |
| | v Dodd | 10-4 | Qualifying | Embassy World Championship |
| | v Meadowcroft | 10-2 | Qualifying | Embassy World Championship |
| | v Higgins | 10-9 | 1st round | Embassy World Championship |
| | v Mountjoy | 6-13 | 2nd round | Embassy World Championship |
| | v Bennett | 5-0 | Qualifying | Jameson International |
| | v Griffiths | 3-5 | 1st round | Jameson International |
| | v Demarco | 5-2 | 1st round | Rothmans Grand Prix |
| | v T. Jones | 5-0 | 2nd round | Rothmans Grand Prix |
| | v Thorne | 5-1 | 3rd round | Rothmans Grand Prix |
| | v Knowles | 5-2 | Quarter-final | Rothmans Grand Prix |
| | v Dennis Taylor | 3-9 | Semi-final | Rothmans Grand Prix |
| | v Fowler | 6-9 | Qualifying | Coral UK Open |
| 1985 | v Longworth | 3-5 | Qualifying | Mercantile Credit Classic |
| | v D. Hughes | 9-3 | 1st round | Tolly Cobbold English Championship |
| | v White | 7-9 | 2nd round | Tolly Cobbold English Championship |
| | v Hargreaves | 6-1 | 1st round | Dulux British Open |
| | v Higgins | 1-5 | 2nd round | Dulux British Open |
| | v Rigitano | 10-8 | Qualifying | Embassy World Championship |
| | v S. Davis | 8-10 | 1st round | Embassy World Championship |
| | v Dodd | 5-3 | 3rd round | Goya Matchroom Trophy |
| | v Knowles | 5-3 | 4th round | Goya Matchroom Trophy |
| | v David Taylor | 5-4 | 5th round | Goya Matchroom Trophy |

|      |               |       |              |                                 |
|------|---------------|-------|--------------|---------------------------------|
|      | v Johnson     | 5-2   | Quarter-final | Goya Matchroom Trophy          |
|      | v White       | 5-9   | Semi-final   | Goya Matchroom Trophy           |
|      | v Darrington  | 5-0   | 3rd round    | Rothmans Grand Prix             |
|      | v Higgins     | 3-5   | 4th round    | Rothmans Grand Prix             |
|      | v Fagan       | 9-5   | 3rd round    | Coral UK Open                   |
|      | v Johnson     | 9-8   | 4th round    | Coral UK Open                   |
|      | v Dennis Taylor | 5-9 | 5th round    | Coral UK Open                   |
| 1986 | v Bradley     | 5-3   | 3rd round    | Mercantile Credit Classic       |
|      | v Hendry      | 5-4   | 4th round    | Mercantile Credit Classic       |
|      | v Campbell    | 5-1   | 5th round    | Mercantile Credit Classic       |
|      | v Mountjoy    | 3-5   | Quarter-final | Mercantile Credit Classic      |
|      | v G. Foulds   | 9-4   | 3rd round    | Tolly Cobbold English Championship |
|      | v Edmonds     | 9-4   | 4th round    | Tolly Cobbold English Championship |
|      | v White       | 9-4   | Quarter-final | Tolly Cobbold English Championship |
|      | v Hallett     | 9-8   | Semi-final   | Tolly Cobbold English Championship |
|      | v Meo         | 7-9   | Final        | Tolly Cobbold English Championship |
|      | v Hargreaves  | 5-4   | 3rd round    | Dulux British Open              |
|      | v Griffiths   | 3-5   | 4th round    | Dulux British Open              |
|      | v P. Francisco | 10-9 | Qualifying   | Embassy World Championship      |
|      | v Knowles     | 9-10  | 1st round    | Embassy World Championship      |
|      | v Thorne      | 3-6   | 1st round    | Matchroom Trophy                |
|      | v Miles       | 5-2   | 3rd round    | BCE International                |
|      | v G. Foulds   | 5-0   | 4th round    | BCE International                |
|      | v Owers       | 5-1   | 5th round    | BCE International                |
|      | v Reynolds    | 5-2   | Quarter-final | BCE International               |
|      | v E. Hughes   | 9-8   | Semi-final   | BCE International                |
|      | **v Thorburn** | **12-9** | **Final** | **BCE International**          |
|      | v Miles       | 5-1   | 3rd round    | Rothmans Grand Prix             |
|      | v Wilson      | 5-0   | 4th round    | Rothmans Grand Prix             |
|      | v Thorne      | 5-3   | 5th round    | Rothmans Grand Prix             |
|      | v Meo         | 5-3   | Quarter-final | Rothmans Grand Prix            |
|      | v Williams    | 8-9   | Semi-final   | Rothmans Grand Prix             |
|      | v Cripsey     | 9-7   | 3rd round    | Tennents UK Open                |
|      | v Wych        | 9-3   | 4th round    | Tennents UK Open                |
|      | v White       | 9-7   | 5th round    | Tennents UK Open                |
|      | v Thorburn    | 9-2   | Quarter-final | Tennents UK Open               |
|      | v Parrott     | 9-2   | Semi-final   | Tennents UK Open                |
|      | v S. Davis    | 7-16  | Final        | Tennents UK Open                |
| 1987 | v Duggan      | 3-5   | 3rd round    | Mercantile Credit Classic       |
|      | v Dennis Taylor | 2-5 | 1st round    | Benson & Hedges Masters         |
|      | v Owers       | 3-6   | 3rd round    | Tolly Ales English Championship |
|      | v Roe         | 5-1   | 3rd round    | Dulux British Open              |
|      | v King        | 5-4   | 4th round    | Dulux British Open              |
|      | v Thorne      | 5-2   | 5th round    | Dulux British Open              |
|      | v Virgo       | 5-3   | Quarter-final | Dulux British Open             |
|      | v Knowles     | 9-2   | Semi-final   | Dulux British Open              |
|      | v White       | 9-13  | Final        | Dulux British Open              |
|      | v Virgo       | 10-4  | 1st round    | Embassy World Championship      |
|      | v Dennis Taylor | 13-10 | 2nd round  | Embassy World Championship      |
|      | v Hallett     | 13-9  | Quarter-final | Embassy World Championship     |
|      | v Johnson     | 9-16  | Semi-final   | Embassy World Championship      |
|      | v Johnson     | 4-5   | 1st round    | Carling Champions               |
|      | v Griffiths   | 4-5   | 1st round    | Langs Scottish Masters          |
|      | v P. Gibson   | 5-2   | 3rd round    | Fidelity International           |
|      | v Hendry      | 2-5   | 4th round    | Fidelity International           |
|      | v Clark       | 4-5   | 3rd round    | Rothmans Grand Prix             |
|      | v Griffiths   | 5-4   | 1st round    | Labatts Canadian Masters (WS)   |
|      | v White       | 7-8   | Semi-final   | Labatts Canadian Masters (WS)   |
|      | v Griffiths   | 6-2   | 1st round    | Matchroom Trophy                |
|      | v Thorne      | 5-6   | Semi-final   | Matchroom Trophy                |
|      | v Fowler      | 5-9   | 3rd round    | Tennents UK Open                |
| 1988 | v Chaperon    | 5-1   | 3rd round    | Mercantile Credit Classic       |
|      | v Virgo       | 3-5   | 4th round    | Mercantile Credit Classic       |

| | | | |
|---|---|---|---|
| v Parrott | 4-5 | 1st round | Benson & Hedges Masters |
| v Gary Wilkinson | 6-3 | 3rd round | English Championship |
| v Fowler | 6-1 | 4th round | English Championship |
| v Thorne | 6-2 | Quarter-final | English Championship |
| v West | 9-6 | Semi-final | English Championship |
| v Reynolds | 5-9 | Final | English Championship |
| v Fowler | 5-3 | 3rd round | MIM Britannia British Open |
| v P. Francisco | 5-3 | 4th round | MIM Britannia British Open |
| v Parrott | 0-5 | 5th round | MIM Britannia British Open |
| v Knowles | 5-3 | Quarter-final | Benson & Hedges Irish Masters |
| v Griffiths | 6-4 | Semi-final | Benson & Hedges Irish Masters |
| v S. Davis | 4-9 | Final | Benson & Hedges Irish Masters |
| v W. Jones | 10-7 | 1st round | Embassy World Championship |
| v Mountjoy | 13-1 | 2nd round | Embassy World Championship |
| v Griffiths | 9-13 | Quarter-final | Embassy World Championship |
| v Thorne | 5-4 | Semi-final | LEP Hong Kong Masters |
| v White | 3-6 | Final | LEP Hong Kong Masters |
| v Murphy | 5-3 | 3rd round | Fidelity International |
| v Reynolds | 3-5 | 4th round | Fidelity International |
| v Meo | 5-4 | Semi-final | Dubai Duty Free Masters |
| **v S. Davis** | **5-4** | **Final** | **Dubai Duty Free Masters** |
| v Griffiths | 6-4 | 1st round | LEP Matchroom Championship |
| v Dennis Taylor | 3-6 | Semi-final | LEP Matchroom Championship |
| v Terry | 5-4 | 3rd round | Rothmans Grand Prix |
| v Duggan | 5-4 | 4th round | Rothmans Grand Prix |
| v Higgins | 3-5 | 5th round | Rothmans Grand Prix |
| v King | 3-5 | 3rd round | BCE Canadian Masters |
| v Rowing | 9-4 | 3rd round | Tennents UK Open |
| v Mountjoy | 4-9 | 4th round | Tennents UK Open |
| **1989** v Martin | 5-1 | 3rd round | Mercantile Credit Classic |
| v Clark | 4-5 | 4th round | Mercantile Credit Classic |
| v P. Francisco | 5-2 | 1st round | Benson and Hedges Masters |
| v Thorburn | 5-2 | Quarter-final | Benson and Hedges Masters |
| v Parrott | 5-6 | Semi-final | Benson and Hedges Masters |
| v Clark | 3-5 | 3rd round | European Open |
| v Medati | 5-3 | 3rd round | English Championship |
| v Cripsey | 5-1 | 4th round | English Championship |
| v Thorne | 3-5 | Quarter-final | English Championship |
| v Reardon | 5-1 | 3rd round | Anglian British Open |
| v Robidoux | 5-1 | 4th round | Anglian British Open |
| v Clark | 4-5 | 5th round | Anglian British Open |
| v Higgins | 2-5 | Quarter-finals | Benson and Hedges Irish Masters |
| v W. Jones | 9-10 | 1st round | Embassy World Championship |

## DANNY FOWLER (England)

**Born** 30.7.56. **Turned professional** 1984. **World ranking** 36 (43). **Best professional performances** Last 16 1989 European Open, 1987, 1988 Tennents UK Open.

| | | | |
|---|---|---|---|
| **1984** v Chaperon | 5-0 | Qualifying | Jameson International |
| v Andrewartha | 5-0 | Qualifying | Jameson International |
| v Martin | 5-0 | Qualifying | Jameson International |
| v Dennis Taylor | 0-5 | 1st round | Jameson International |
| v Reynolds | 2-5 | 1st round | Rothmans Grand Prix |
| v Demarco | 9-3 | Qualifying | Coral UK Open |
| v Oliver | 9-3 | Qualifying | Coral UK Open |
| v F. Davis | 9-4 | Qualifying | Coral UK Open |
| v N. Foulds | 9-6 | Qualifying | Coral UK Open |
| v Reardon | 2-9 | 1st round | Coral UK Open |
| **1985** v Rigitano | 5-0 | Qualifying | Mercantile Credit Classic |
| v Murphy | 5-0 | Qualifying | Mercantile Credit Classic |
| v Meadowcroft | 5-2 | Qualifying | Mercantile Credit Classic |

| | | | | |
|---|---|---|---|---|
| | v Wilson | 4-5 | Qualifying | Mercantile Credit Classic |
| | v Oliver | 9-7 | Qualifying | Tolly Cobbold English Championship |
| | v S. Davis | 3-9 | 1st round | Tolly Cobbold English Championship |
| | v Everton | 6-1 | Qualifying | Dulux British Open |
| | v Williams | 6-4 | 1st round | Dulux British Open |
| | v Bradley | 4-5 | 2nd round | Dulux British Open |
| | v Hargreaves | 10-0 | Qualifying | Embassy World Championship |
| | v Donnelly | 10-0 | Qualifying | Embassy World Championship |
| | v Parrott | 2-10 | Qualifying | Embassy World Championship |
| | v Agrawal | 5-2 | 2nd round | Goya Matchroom Trophy |
| | v Thorne | 1-5 | 3rd round | Goya Matchroom Trophy |
| | v Jonik | 5-4 | 2nd round | Rothmans Grand Prix |
| | v Werbeniuk | 5-1 | 3rd round | Rothmans Grand Prix |
| | v S. Davis | 1-5 | 4th round | Rothmans Grand Prix |
| | v Wilkinson | 9-6 | 2nd round | Coral UK Open |
| | v Mans | 9-2 | 3rd round | Coral UK Open |
| | v Meo | 2-9 | 4th round | Coral UK Open |
| **1986** | v Bales | 5-4 | 2nd round | Mercantile Credit Classic |
| | v White | 1-5 | 3rd round | Mercantile Credit Classic |
| | v Darrington | 9-3 | 2nd round | Tolly Cobbold English Championship |
| | v Johnson | 7-9 | 3rd round | Tolly Cobbold English Championship |
| | v Chappel | 5-4 | 2nd round | Dulux British Open |
| | v Virgo | 1-5 | 3rd round | Dulux British Open |
| | v Oliver | 10-8 | Qualifying | Embassy World Championship |
| | v Scott | 10-7 | Qualifying | Embassy World Championship |
| | v Macleod | 10-6 | Qualifying | Embassy World Championship |
| | v Griffiths | 2-10 | 1st round | Embassy World Championship |
| | v J. McLaughlin | 2-5 | 2nd round | BCE International |
| | v Bear | 2-5 | 2nd round | Rothmans Grand Prix |
| | v Darrington | 9-6 | 2nd round | Tennents UK Open |
| | v Thorburn | 7-9 | 3rd round | Tennents UK Open |
| **1987** | v Wilkinson | 5-1 | 2nd round | Mercantile Credit Classic |
| | v Knowles | 5-4 | 3rd round | Mercantile Credit Classic |
| | v Hallett | 5-4 | 4th round | Mercantile Credit Classic |
| | v Hendry | 4-5 | 5th round | Mercantile Credit Classic |
| | v Bradley | 6-3 | 3rd round | Tolly Ales English Championship |
| | v Meo | 0-6 | 4th round | Tolly Ales English Championship |
| | v Dodd | 5-1 | 2nd round | Dulux British Open |
| | v Knowles | 4-5 | 3rd round | Dulux British Open |
| | v G. Foulds | 10-6 | Qualifying | Embassy World Championship |
| | v B. Harris | 10-6 | Qualifying | Embassy World Championship |
| | v Parrott | 3-10 | Qualifying | Embassy World Championship |
| | v Watchorn | 5-1 | 2nd round | Fidelity International |
| | v Knowles | 4-5 | 3rd round | Fidelity International |
| | v D. Gilbert | 5-1 | 2nd round | Rothmans Grand Prix |
| | v S. Francisco | 1-5 | 3rd round | Rothmans Grand Prix |
| | v Kearney | 9-7 | 2nd round | Tennents UK Open |
| | v N. Foulds | 9-5 | 3rd round | Tennents UK Open |
| | v Miles | 9-4 | 4th round | Tennents UK Open |
| | v Hallett | 4-9 | 5th round | Tennents UK Open |
| **1988** | v Rigitano | 2-5 | 2nd round | Mercantile Credit Classic |
| | v Medati | 6-1 | 2nd round | English Championship |
| | v Spencer | 6-3 | 3rd round | English Championship |
| | v Foulds | 1-6 | 4th round | English Championship |
| | v Kearney | 5-1 | 2nd round | MIM Britannia British Open |
| | v N. Foulds | 3-5 | 3rd round | MIM Britannia British Open |
| | v Black | 10-1 | Qualifying | Embassy World Championship |
| | v Dodd | 10-8 | Qualifying | Embassy World Championship |
| | v Macleod | 10-3 | Qualifying | Embassy World Championship |
| | v Knowles | 8-10 | 1st round | Embassy World Championship |
| | v Grace | 5-3 | 2nd round | Fidelity International |
| | v Drago | 3-5 | 3rd round | Fidelity International |
| | v Kelly | 5-4 | 2nd round | Rothmans Grand Prix |

|        |                 |      |           |                             |
|--------|-----------------|------|-----------|-----------------------------|
|        | v White         | 0-5  | 3rd round | Rothmans Grand Prix         |
|        | v Rowswell      | 5-4  | 2nd round | BCE Canadian Masters        |
|        | v Drago         | 5-1  | 3rd round | BCE Canadian Masters        |
|        | v Hendry        | 2-5  | 4th round | BCE Canadian Masters        |
|        | v Ellis         | 9-3  | 2nd round | Tennents UK Open            |
|        | v Longworth     | 9-8  | 3rd round | Tennents UK Open            |
|        | v Clark         | 9-6  | 4th round | Tennents UK Open            |
|        | v S. Davis      | 6-9  | 5th round | Tennents UK Open            |
| 1989   | v Dennis Taylor | 3-5  | 3rd round | Mercantile Credit Classic   |
|        | v A. Harris     | 5-1  | 2nd round | European Open               |
|        | v Knowles       | 5-2  | 3rd round | European Open               |
|        | v T. Wilson     | 5-2  | 4th round | European Open               |
|        | v Wych          | 4-5  | 5th round | European Open               |
|        | v S. Campbell   | 5-1  | 2nd round | English Championship        |
|        | v Meo           | 5-3  | 3rd round | English Championship        |
|        | v Parrott       | 4-5  | 4th round | English Championship        |
|        | v Van Rensberg  | 5-1  | 2nd round | Anglian British Open        |
|        | v Virgo         | 2-5  | 3rd round | Anglian British Open        |
|        | v Whitthread    | 10-6 | Qualifying| Embassy World Championship  |
|        | v O'Boye        | 6-10 | Qualifying| Embassy World Championship  |

## PETER FRANCISCO (South Africa)

**Born** 14.2.62. **Turned professional** 1984. **World ranking** 25 (14). **Amateur career** 1981-83 South African champion. **Best professional performances** Semi-finals 1987 Rothmans Grand Prix, 1986 BCE International.

|        |                 |      |           |                             |
|--------|-----------------|------|-----------|-----------------------------|
| 1984   | v G. Foulds     | 4-5  | Qualifying| Jameson International        |
|        | v Black         | 5-4  | Qualifying| Rothmans Grand Prix         |
|        | v Spencer       | 5-2  | 1st round | Rothmans Grand Prix         |
|        | v Reynolds      | 4-5  | 2nd round | Rothmans Grand Prix         |
|        | v Sheehan       | 9-5  | Qualifying| Coral UK Open               |
|        | v Williamson    | 9-2  | Qualifying| Coral UK Open               |
|        | v Sinclair      | 8-9  | Qualifying| Coral UK Open               |
| 1985   | v Longworth     | 4-5  | Qualifying| Mercantile Credit Classic   |
|        | v Kelly         | 6-3  | Qualifying| Dulux British Open          |
|        | v Virgo         | 2-6  | 1st round | Dulux British Open          |
|        | v Demarco       | 10-4 | Qualifying| Embassy World Championship  |
|        | v Murphy        | 10-4 | Qualifying| Embassy World Championship  |
|        | v Meadowcroft   | 10-5 | Qualifying| Embassy World Championship  |
|        | v Macleod       | 7-10 | Qualifying| Embassy World Championship  |
|        | v Gibson        | 4-5  | 2nd round | Goya Matchroom Trophy       |
|        | v Everton       | 5-0  | 2nd round | Rothmans Grand Prix         |
|        | v Virgo         | 5-4  | 3rd round | Rothmans Grand Prix         |
|        | v W. Jones      | 5-3  | 4th round | Rothmans Grand Prix         |
|        | v Griffiths     | 2-5  | 5th round | Rothmans Grand Prix         |
|        | v Charlton      | 9-5  | 3rd round | Coral UK Open               |
|        | v Williams      | 7-9  | 4th round | Coral UK Open               |
| 1986   | v Jonik         | 5-2  | 2nd round | Mercantile Credit Classic   |
|        | v Charlton      | 5-1  | 3rd round | Mercantile Credit Classic   |
|        | v Martin        | 5-2  | 4th round | Mercantile Credit Classic   |
|        | v S. Davis      | 0-5  | 5th round | Mercantile Credit Classic   |
|        | v G. Foulds     | 5-2  | 2nd round | Dulux British Open          |
|        | v White         | 5-4  | 3rd round | Dulux British Open          |
|        | v Longworth     | 5-2  | 4th round | Dulux British Open          |
|        | v Higgins       | 2-5  | 5th round | Dulux British Open          |
|        | v Drago         | 10-4 | Qualifying| Embassy World Championship  |
|        | v F. Davis      | 10-1 | Qualifying| Embassy World Championship  |
|        | v N. Foulds     | 9-10 | Qualifying| Embassy World Championship  |
|        | v Grace         | 7-1  | 2nd round | South African Championship  |
|        | v S. Francisco  | 3-8  | Semi-final| South African Championship  |
|        | v Wildman       | 5-2  | 3rd round | BCE International            |

| | | | |
|---|---|---|---|
| v Higgins | 5-4 | 4th round | BCE International |
| v Gauvreau | 5-2 | 5th round | BCE International |
| v S. Francisco | 5-3 | Quarter-final | BCE International |
| v Thorburn | 7-9 | Semi-final | BCE International |
| v Medati | 5-1 | 3rd round | Rothmans Grand Prix |
| v Knowles | 3-5 | 4th round | Rothmans Grand Prix |
| v Watterson | 9-4 | 3rd round | Tennents UK Open |
| v White | 5-9 | 4th round | Tennents UK Open |
| **1987** v Gauvreau | 5-3 | 3rd round | Mercantile Credit Classic |
| v Johnson | 5-3 | 4th round | Mercantile Credit Classic |
| v S. Francisco | 1-5 | 5th round | Mercantile Credit Classic |
| v Sinclair | 5-3 | 3rd round | Dulux British Open |
| v Mountjoy | 3-5 | 4th round | Dulux British Open |
| v O'Kane | 5-10 | Qualifying | Embassy World Championship |
| v Newbury | 2-5 | 3rd round | Fidelity International |
| v John Rea | 5-3 | 3rd round | Rothmans Grand Prix |
| v Johnson | 5-2 | 4th round | Rothmans Grand Prix |
| v Cripsey | 5-1 | 5th round | Rothmans Grand Prix |
| v Thorne | 5-3 | Quarter-final | Rothmans Grand Prix |
| v Dennis Taylor | 4-9 | Semi-final | Rothmans Grand Prix |
| v Lawlor | 9-4 | 3rd round | Tennents UK Open |
| v S. Davis | 6-9 | 4th round | Tennents UK Open |
| **1988** v Cripsey | 5-2 | 3rd round | Mercantile Credit Classic |
| v Owers | 5-0 | 4th round | Mercantile Credit Classic |
| v Dennis Taylor | 3-5 | 5th round | Mercantile Credit Classic |
| v Darrington | 5-1 | 3rd round | MIM Britannia British Open |
| v N. Foulds | 3-5 | 4th round | MIM Britannia British Open |
| v Foldvari | 10-5 | Qualifying | Embassy World Championship |
| v Thorne | 6-10 | 1st round | Embassy World Championship |
| v John Rea | 0-5 | 3rd round | Fidelity International |
| v J. McLaughlin | 2-5 | 3rd round | Rothmans Grand Prix |
| v Graham | 3-5 | 3rd round | BCE Canadian Masters |
| v John Rea | 9-2 | 3rd round | Tennents UK Open |
| v Roe | 7-9 | 4th round | Tennents UK Open |
| v Griffiths | 7-9 | 1st round | Everest World Matchplay |
| **1989** v Terry | 4-5 | 3rd round | Mercantile Credit Classic |
| v N. Foulds | 2-5 | 1st round | Benson and Hedges Masters |
| v J. Campbell | 0-5 | 3rd round | European Open |
| v J. Campbell | 5-2 | 3rd round | Anglian British Open |
| v Roe | 5-3 | 4th round | Anglian British Open |
| v West | 5-1 | 5th round | Anglian British Open |
| v Meo | 3-5 | Quarter-final | Anglian British Open |
| v Reynolds | 7-10 | 1st round | Embassy World Championship |

## SILVINO FRANCISCO (South Africa)

**Born** 3.5.46. **Turned professional** 1978. **World ranking** 23 (12). **Amateur career** 1968, 1969, 1974, 1977 South African champion. **Best professional performances** Winner 1985 Dulux British Open, 1986 South African Championship.

| | | | |
|---|---|---|---|
| **1982** v Ross | 9-0 | Qualifying | Embassy World Championship |
| v Morgan | 9-1 | Qualifying | Embassy World Championship |
| v Dennis Taylor | 10-7 | 1st round | Embassy World Championship |
| v Reynolds | 13-8 | 2nd round | Embassy World Championship |
| v Reardon | 8-13 | Quarter-final | Embassy World Championship |
| **1983** v Kelly | 10-5 | Qualifying | Embassy World Championship |
| v Dennis Taylor | 9-10 | 1st round | Embassy World Championship |
| v Darrington | 5-2 | Qualifying | Jameson International |
| v Donnelly | 5-1 | 2nd round | Jameson International |
| v S. Davis | 1-5 | Quarter-final | Jameson International |
| v Morra | 5-3 | 1st round | Professional Players Tournament |
| v Scott | 5-1 | 2nd round | Professional Players Tournament |

|  |  |  |  |
|---|---|---|---|
| v Knowles | 0-5 | 3rd round | Professional Players Tournament |
| **1984** v Thorburn | 5-1 | Qualifying | Lada Classic |
| v Wildman | 1-5 | 1st round | Lada Classic |
| v Van Rensberg | 10-3 | Qualifying | Embassy World Championship |
| v Meo | 10-5 | 1st round | Embassy World Championship |
| v Reardon | 8-13 | 2nd round | Embassy World Championship |
| v Kelly | 5-3 | Qualifying | Jameson International |
| v Spencer | 5-2 | 1st round | Jameson International |
| v Virgo | 5-2 | 2nd round | Jameson International |
| v Knowles | 6-9 | Semi-final | Jameson International |
| v Duggan | 5-3 | 1st round | Rothmans Grand Prix |
| v White | 5-1 | 2nd round | Rothmans Grand Prix |
| v Reynolds | 1-5 | 3rd round | Rothmans Grand Prix |
| v Sinclair | 9-4 | Qualifying | Coral UK Open |
| v Charlton | 4-9 | 1st round | Coral UK Open |
| **1985** v T. Jones | 5-1 | Qualifying | Mercantile Credit Classic |
| v S. Davis | 0-5 | 1st round | Mercantile Credit Classic |
| v Kearney | 6-4 | 1st round | Dulux British Open |
| v White | 5-4 | 2nd round | Dulux British Open |
| v Chaperon | 5-2 | 3rd round | Dulux British Open |
| v Meo | 5-4 | Quarter-final | Dulux British Open |
| v Higgins | 9-6 | Semi-final | Dulux British Open |
| **v Stevens** | **12-9** | **Final** | **Dulux British Open** |
| v Medati | 10-7 | Qualifying | Embassy World Championship |
| v Dennis Taylor | 2-10 | 1st round | Embassy World Championship |
| v Parrott | 3-4 | 1st round | Winfield Australian Masters |
| v Knowles | 5-4 | 1st round | Langs Scottish Masters |
| v Thorburn | 0-6 | Semi-final | Langs Scottish Masters |
| v Chaperon | 3-5 | 3rd round | Goya Matchroom Trophy |
| v Kelly | 5-2 | 3rd round | Rothmans Grand Prix |
| v Martin | 5-3 | 4th round | Rothmans Grand Prix |
| v White | 5-4 | 5th round | Rothmans Grand Prix |
| v S. Davis | 2-5 | Quarter-final | Rothmans Grand Prix |
| v Wych | 9-8 | 3rd round | Coral UK Open |
| v Martin | 9-6 | 4th round | Coral UK Open |
| v Griffiths | 5-9 | 5th round | Coral UK Open |
| **1986** v Hendry | 4-5 | 3rd round | Mercantile Credit Classic |
| v Knowles | 1-5 | 1st round | Benson & Hedges Masters |
| v T. Jones | 5-2 | 3rd round | Dulux British Open |
| v Macleod | 1-5 | 4th round | Dulux British Open |
| v Williams | 10-4 | 1st round | Embassy World Championship |
| v Knowles | 10-13 | 2nd round | Embassy World Championship |
| v P. Francisco | 8-3 | Semi-final | South African Championship |
| **v Ellis** | **9-1** | **Final** | **South African Championship** |
| v Newbury | 5-4 | 3rd round | BCE International |
| v Virgo | 5-0 | 4th round | BCE International |
| v Dennis Taylor | 5-0 | 5th round | BCE International |
| v P. Francisco | 3-5 | Quarter-final | BCE International |
| v Spencer | 5-4 | 3rd round | Rothmans Grand Prix |
| v W. Jones | 5-4 | 4th round | Rothmans Grand Prix |
| v Newbury | 5-2 | 5th round | Rothmans Grand Prix |
| v Knowles | 5-2 | Quarter-final | Rothmans Grand Prix |
| v White | 6-9 | Semi-final | Rothmans Grand Prix |
| **1987** v Van Rensberg | 5-4 | 3rd round | Mercantile Credit Classic |
| v B. Harris | 5-3 | 4th round | Mercantile Credit Classic |
| v P. Francisco | 5-1 | 5th round | Mercantile Credit Classic |
| v Hendry | 0-5 | Quarter-final | Mercantile Credit Classic |
| v Knowles | 5-2 | 1st round | Benson & Hedges Masters |
| v Dennis Taylor | 3-5 | Quarter-final | Benson & Hedges Masters |
| v Rowswell | 5-0 | 3rd round | Dulux British Open |
| v Wilson | 4-5 | 4th round | Dulux British Open |
| v J. Campbell | 10-3 | 1st round | Embassy World Championship |
| v Hallett | 9-13 | 2nd round | Embassy World Championship |

| | | | |
|---|---|---|---|
| v King | 5-2 | 3rd round | Fidelity International |
| v Werbeniuk | 5-3 | 4th round | Fidelity International |
| v E. Hughes | 4-5 | 5th round | Fidelity International |
| v Fowler | 5-1 | 3rd round | Rothmans Grand Prix |
| v Gary Wilkinson | 3-5 | 4th round | Rothmans Grand Prix |
| v Reardon | 9-3 | 3rd round | Tennents UK Open |
| v Wilson | 9-1 | 4th round | Tennents UK Open |
| v Griffiths | 3-9 | 5th round | Tennents UK Open |
| 1988 v Rowswell | 5-3 | 3rd round | Mercantile Credit Classic |
| v Longworth | 5-2 | 4th round | Mercantile Credit Classic |
| v Hendry | 3-5 | 5th round | Mercantile Credit Classic |
| v Griffiths | 3-5 | 1st round | Benson & Hedges Masters |
| v Bear | 5-0 | 3rd round | MIM Britannia British Open |
| v Gary Wilkinson | 3-5 | 4th round | MIM Britannia British Open |
| v Charlton | 7-10 | 1st round | Embassy World Championship |
| v Owers | 5-1 | 3rd round | Fidelity International |
| v Chaperon | 2-5 | 4th round | Fidelity International |
| v N. Gilbert | 4-5 | 3rd round | Rothmans Grand Prix |
| v Macleod | 4-5 | 3rd round | BCE Canadian Masters |
| v Medati | 9-8 | 3rd round | Tennents UK Open |
| v West | 4-9 | 4th round | Tennents UK Open |
| 1989 v Werbeniuk | wo | 3rd round | Mercantile Credit Classic |
| v Meo | 5-1 | 4th round | Mercantile Credit Classic |
| v Parrott | 1-5 | 5th round | Mercantile Credit Classic |
| v Griffiths | 1-5 | 1st round | Benson and Hedges Masters |
| v Wych | 1-5 | 3rd round | European Open |
| v Macleod | 4-5 | 3rd round | Anglian British Open |
| v O'Boye | 10-6 | 1st round | Embassy World Championship |
| v Griffiths | 9-13 | 2nd round | Embassy World Championship |

## MARCEL GAUVREAU (Canada)

**Born** 9.1.55. **Turned professional** 1983. **World ranking** 68 (63). **Best professional performances** Last 16 1986 Mercantile Credit Classic, 1986 BCE International.

| | | | |
|---|---|---|---|
| 1983 v Rigitano | 6-9 | 1st round | Canadian Championship |
| v Miles | 3-5 | 1st round | Professional Players Tournament |
| 1984 v J. Campbell | 10-7 | Qualifying | Embassy World Championship |
| v Cripsey | 10-1 | Qualifying | Embassy World Championship |
| v Macleod | 10-6 | Qualifying | Embassy World Championship |
| v David Taylor | 5-10 | 1st round | Embassy World Championship |
| v Jonik | 5-1 | Qualifying | Jameson International |
| v Parrott | 5-4 | Qualifying | Jameson International |
| v Stevens | 5-1 | 1st round | Jameson International |
| v Thorne | 3-5 | 2nd round | Jameson International |
| v Foldvari | 5-2 | Qualifying | Rothmans Grand Prix |
| v Parrott | 3-5 | 1st round | Rothmans Grand Prix |
| v Bales | 9-8 | Qualifying | Coral UK Open |
| v Mans | 9-6 | Qualifying | Coral UK Open |
| v Knowles | 5-9 | 1st round | Coral UK Open |
| 1985 v Giannaros | 5-3 | Qualifying | Mercantile Credit Classic |
| v Sinclair | 5-1 | Qualifying | Mercantile Credit Classic |
| v Higgins | 3-5 | 1st round | Mercantile Credit Classic |
| v Greaves | 6-3 | Qualifying | Dulux British Open |
| v Stevens | 3-6 | 1st round | Dulux British Open |
| v Van Rensberg | 10-9 | Qualifying | Embassy World Championship |
| v Reynolds | 1-10 | Qualifying | Embassy World Championship |
| v D. Hughes | 4-5 | 2nd round | Goya Matchroom Trophy |
| v Duggan | 4-5 | 2nd round | Rothmans Grand Prix |
| v O'Boye | 5-9 | 2nd round | Coral UK Open |
| 1986 v Simngam | 5-1 | 2nd round | Mercantile Credit Classic |
| v David Taylor | 5-3 | 3rd round | Mercantile Credit Classic |

|      | v Browne       | 5-3   | 4th round     | Mercantile Credit Classic   |
|------|----------------|-------|---------------|-----------------------------|
|      | v White        | 2-5   | 5th round     | Mercantile Credit Classic   |
|      | v Drago        | 3-5   | 2nd round     | Dulux British Open          |
|      | v Jim Bear     | 10-5  | Qualifying    | Embassy World Championship  |
|      | v Chaperon     | 10-8  | Qualifying    | Embassy World Championship  |
|      | v Williams     | 3-10  | Qualifying    | Embassy World Championship  |
|      | v Jenkins      | 5-1   | 2nd round     | BCE International           |
|      | v Macleod      | 5-4   | 3rd round     | BCE International           |
|      | v Reardon      | 5-2   | 4th round     | BCE International           |
|      | v P. Francisco | 2-5   | 5th round     | BCE International           |
|      | v J. McLaughlin | 3-5  | 2nd round     | Rothmans Grand Prix         |
|      | v J. McLaughlin | 8-9  | 2nd round     | Tennents UK Open            |
| 1987 | v Rigitano     | 5-0   | 2nd round     | Mercantile Credit Classic   |
|      | v P. Francisco | 3-5   | 3rd round     | Mercantile Credit Classic   |
|      | v Bales        | 5-0   | 2nd round     | Dulux British Open          |
|      | v S. Davis     | 0-5   | 3rd round     | Dulux British Open          |
|      | v Bear         | 10-3  | Qualifying    | Embassy World Championship  |
|      | v Medati       | 3-10  | Qualifying    | Embassy World Championship  |
|      | v Caggianello  | 3-6   | 1st round     | Canadian Championship       |
|      | v Williamson   | 1-5   | 2nd round     | Fidelity International      |
|      | v M. Smith     | 5-3   | 2nd round     | Rothmans Grand Prix         |
|      | v Virgo        | 1-5   | 3rd round     | Rothmans Grand Prix         |
|      | v A. Harris    | 9-3   | 2nd round     | Tennents UK Open            |
|      | v West         | 6-9   | 3rd round     | Tennents UK Open            |
| 1988 | v Morra        | 4-5   | 2nd round     | Mercantile Credit Classic   |
|      | v Medati       | 1-5   | 2nd round     | MIM Britannia British Open  |
|      | v P. Gibson    | 9-10  | Qualifying    | Embassy World Championship  |
|      | v Meakin       | 3-5   | 2nd round     | Fidelity International      |
|      | v Ellis        | 2-5   | 2nd round     | Rothmans Grand Prix         |
|      | v Williamson   | 5-1   | 2nd round     | BCE Canadian Masters        |
|      | v Meo          | 5-0   | 3rd round     | BCE Canadian Masters        |
|      | v Hallett      | 3-5   | 4th round     | BCE Canadian Masters        |
|      | v Rowswell     | 7-9   | 2nd round     | Tennents UK Open            |
| 1989 | v Miles        | 3-5   | 2nd round     | Mercantile Credit Classic   |
|      | v T. Wilson    | 3-5   | 2nd round     | European Open               |
|      | v Kelly        | 5-0   | 2nd round     | Anglian British Open        |
|      | v Mountjoy     | 0-5   | 3rd round     | Anglian British Open        |
|      | v Rowswell     | 7-10  | Qualifying    | Embassy World Championship  |

## MATT GIBSON (Scotland)

**Born** 7.5.53. **Turned professional** 1981. **World ranking** 112 (88). **Amateur career** 1980 Scottish champion. **Best professional performance** Last 32 1985 Goya Matchroom Trophy.

|      | v Hood          | 5-3   | Qualifying     | Jameson International                |
|------|-----------------|-------|----------------|--------------------------------------|
| 1981 | v Hood          | 5-3   | Qualifying     | Jameson International                |
|      | v Parkin        | 5-3   | Qualifying     | Jameson International                |
|      | v Dunning       | 3-5   | Qualifying     | Jameson International                |
|      | v Demarco       | 5-3   | Quarter-final  | Scottish Championship                |
|      | v Donnelly      | 6-4   | Semi-final     | Scottish Championship                |
|      | v Black         | 7-11  | Final          | Scottish Championship                |
|      | v Fitzmaurice   | 9-6   | Qualifying     | Coral UK Championship                |
|      | v Everton       | 7-9   | Qualifying     | Coral UK Championship                |
| 1982 | v Donnelly      | 8-9   | Qualifying     | Embassy World Championship           |
|      | v E. McLaughlin | 6-3   | Quarter-final  | Scottish Championship                |
|      | v Sinclair      | 2-6   | Semi-final     | Scottish Championship                |
|      | v Wildman       | 1-5   | Qualifying     | Jameson International                |
|      | v Martin        | 2-5   | 1st round      | Professional Players Tournament      |
|      | v G. Foulds     | 3-9   | Qualifying     | Coral UK Championship                |
| 1983 | v G. Foulds     | 6-10  | Qualifying     | Embassy World Championship           |
|      | v Macleod       | 5-6   | 1st round      | Scottish Championship                |
|      | v Dodd          | 5-1   | Qualifying     | Jameson International                |

| | | | | |
|---|---|---|---|---|
| | v Scott | 3-5 | Qualifying | Jameson International |
| | v Morgan | 4-5 | Qualifying | Professional Players Tournament |
| | v Johnson | 6-9 | Qualifying | Coral UK Championship |
| 1984 | v Rigitano | 10-7 | Qualifying | Embassy World Championship |
| | v Fisher | 10-7 | Qualifying | Embassy World Championship |
| | v Johnson | 3-10 | Qualifying | Embassy World Championship |
| | v Medati | 5-3 | Qualifying | Jameson International |
| | v W. Jones | 2-5 | Qualifying | Jameson International |
| | v Chaperon | 4-5 | Qualifying | Rothmans Grand Prix |
| | v Hargreaves | 9-8 | Qualifying | Coral UK Open |
| | v Donnelly | 6-9 | Qualifying | Coral UK Open |
| 1985 | v T. Jones | 0-5 | Qualifying | Mercantile Credit Classic |
| | v Black | 6-2 | 1st round | Scottish Championship |
| | v Macleod | 4-6 | Semi-final | Scottish Championship |
| | v Demarco | 6-1 | Qualifying | Dulux British Open |
| | v Wildman | 1-6 | 1st round | Dulux British Open |
| | v Hines | 10-7 | Qualifying | Embassy World Championship |
| | v Fagan | 8-10 | Qualifying | Embassy World Championship |
| | v P. Francisco | 5-4 | 2nd round | Goya Matchroom Trophy |
| | v Charlton | 5-4 | 3rd round | Goya Matchroom Trophy |
| | v Reynolds | 0-5 | 4th round | Goya Matchroom Trophy |
| | v Bradley | 5-4 | 2nd round | Rothmans Grand Prix |
| | v Knowles | 1-5 | 3rd round | Rothmans Grand Prix |
| | v Longworth | 2-9 | 2nd round | Coral UK Open |
| 1986 | v Virgo | 3-5 | 3rd round | Mercantile Credit Classic |
| | v Black | 0-5 | 2nd round | Dulux British Open |
| | v Sinclair | 6-4 | Quarter-final | Canada Dry Scottish Championship |
| | v John Rea | 6-0 | Semi-final | Canada Dry Scottish Championship |
| | v Hendry | 5-10 | Final | Canada Dry Scottish Championship |
| | v Jenkins | 10-4 | Qualifying | Embassy World Championship |
| | v Morra | 10-9 | Qualifying | Embassy World Championship |
| | v Medati | 6-10 | Qualifying | Embassy World Championship |
| | v Hines | 5-1 | 2nd round | BCE International |
| | v Mountjoy | 3-5 | 3rd round | BCE International |
| | v Mienie | 5-4 | 2nd round | Rothmans Grand Prix |
| | v S. Davis | 1-5 | 3rd round | Rothmans Grand Prix |
| | v Dunning | 9-2 | 2nd round | Tennents UK Open |
| | v Reardon | 6-9 | 3rd round | Tennents UK Open |
| 1987 | v J. McLaughlin | 3-5 | 2nd round | Mercantile Credit Classic |
| | v Sinclair | 2-6 | 1st round | Scottish Championship |
| | v J. McLaughlin | 1-5 | 2nd round | Dulux British Open |
| | v Kelly | 10-9 | Qualifying | Embassy World Championship |
| | v Cripsey | 4-10 | Qualifying | Embassy World Championship |
| | v Chappel | 2-5 | 2nd round | Fidelity International |
| | v Cripsey | 2-5 | 2nd round | Rothmans Grand Prix |
| | v Murphy | 0-9 | 2nd round | Tennents UK Open |
| 1988 | v Cripsey | 4-5 | 2nd round | Mercantile Credit Classic |
| | v Black | 6-2 | Quarter-final | Scottish Championship |
| | v Hendry | 1-6 | Semi-final | Scottish Championship |
| | v Duggan | 5-2 | 2nd round | MIM Britannia British Open |
| | v Knowles | 4-5 | 3rd round | MIM Britannia British Open |
| | v Watchorn | 7-10 | Qualifying | Embassy World Championship |
| | v T. Wilson | 1-5 | 1st round | Fidelity International |
| | v Burke | 5-4 | 1st round | Rothmans Grand Prix |
| | v Dodd | 1-5 | 2nd round | Rothmans Grand Prix |
| | v D. Hughes | 5-1 | 1st round | BCE Canadian Masters |
| | v King | 3-5 | 2nd round | BCE Canadian Masters |
| | v A. Harris | 9-8 | 1st round | Tennents UK Open |
| | v Roe | 3-9 | 2nd round | Tennents UK Open |
| 1989 | v Jack Rea | 3-5 | 1st round | Mercantile Credit Classic |
| | v T. Wilson | 3-5 | 1st round | European Open |
| | v Sinclair | 5-4 | 1st round | Scottish Championship |
| | v Macleod | 1-5 | Semi-final | Scottish Championship |

| v Rowing | 5-0 | 1st round | Anglian British Open |
|---|---|---|---|
| v J. Campbell | 2-5 | 2nd round | Anglian British Open |
| v Darrington | 10-0 | Qualifying | Embassy World Championship |
| v Martin | 7-10 | Qualifying | Embassy World Championship |

## PAUL GIBSON (England)

**Born** 9.6.63. **Turned professional** 1986. **World ranking** 82 (69). **Best professional performance** Last 32 1987 Rothmans Grand Prix.

| 1986 | v Meadowcroft | 5-2 | 1st round | BCE International |
|---|---|---|---|---|
| | v Hendry | 2-5 | 2nd round | BCE International |
| | v Dunning | 5-1 | 1st round | Rothmans Grand Prix |
| | v Cripsey | 3-5 | 2nd round | Rothmans Grand Prix |
| | v Agrawal | 9-6 | 1st round | Tennents UK Open |
| | v Mans | wo | 2nd round | Tennents UK Open |
| | v Griffiths | 3-9 | 3rd round | Tennents UK Open |
| 1987 | v B. Harris | 3-5 | 2nd round | Mercantile Credit Classic |
| | v D. Hughes | 6-3 | 1st round | Tolly Ales English Championship |
| | v Medati | 2-6 | 2nd round | Tolly Ales English Championship |
| | v Agrawal | 5-0 | 1st round | Dulux British Open |
| | v Duggan | 3-5 | 2nd round | Dulux British Open |
| | v Morra | 6-10 | Qualifying | Embassy World Championship |
| | v Glen Wilkinson | 5-3 | 1st round | Fidelity International |
| | v T. Jones | 5-4 | 2nd round | Fidelity International |
| | v N. Foulds | 2-5 | 3rd round | Fidelity International |
| | v Fagan | 5-0 | 1st round | Rothmans Grand Prix |
| | v Duggan | 5-4 | 2nd round | Rothmans Grand Prix |
| | v Hallett | 5-4 | 3rd round | Rothmans Grand Prix |
| | v Cripsey | 4-5 | 4th round | Rothmans Grand Prix |
| | v Rigitano | 9-5 | 1st round | Tennents UK Open |
| | v Cripsey | 6-9 | 2nd round | Tennents UK Open |
| 1988 | v Black | 5-2 | 1st round | Mercantile Credit Classic |
| | v J. McLaughlin | 4-5 | 2nd round | Mercantile Credit Classic |
| | v Chambers | 0-6 | 1st round | English Championship |
| | v Roscoe | 4-5 | 1st round | MIM Britannia British Open |
| | v Sheehan | 10-9 | Qualifying | Embassy World Championship |
| | v Gauvreau | 10-9 | Qualifying | Embassy World Championship |
| | v Duggan | 9-10 | Qualifying | Embassy World Championship |
| 1989 | v Marshall | 10-3 | Qualifying | Embassy World Championship |
| | v Owers | 8-10 | Qualifying | Embassy World Championship |

## DAVE GILBERT (England)

**Born** 15.8.61. **Turned professional** 1985. **World ranking** 63 (57). **Best professional performance** Last 16 1987 Fidelity International.

| 1985 | v Darrington | 2-5 | 1st round | Goya Matchroom Trophy |
|---|---|---|---|---|
| | v Wilkinson | 5-4 | 1st round | Rothmans Grand Prix |
| | v Williamson | 5-4 | 2nd round | Rothmans Grand Prix |
| | v Johnson | 2-5 | 3rd round | Rothmans Grand Prix |
| | v Drago | 5-9 | 1st round | Coral UK Open |
| 1986 | v Watson | 5-4 | 1st round | Mercantile Credit Classic |
| | v T. Jones | 3-5 | 2nd round | Mercantile Credit Classic |
| | v West | 9-8 | 1st round | Tolly Cobbold English Championship |
| | v Bradley | 5-9 | 2nd round | Tolly Cobbold English Championship |
| | v Burke | 5-1 | 1st round | Dulux British Open |
| | v Morra | 5-4 | 2nd round | Dulux British Open |
| | v Charlton | 2-5 | 3rd round | Dulux British Open |
| | v Bales | 10-7 | Qualifying | Embassy World Championship |
| | v Bradley | 10-7 | Qualifying | Embassy World Championship |

|      |                  |       |              |                                |
|------|------------------|-------|--------------|--------------------------------|
|      | v T. Jones       | 10-7  | Qualifying   | Embassy World Championship     |
|      | v Martin         | 5-10  | Qualifying   | Embassy World Championship     |
|      | v James          | 2-5   | 1st round    | BCE International              |
|      | v Rowswell       | 5-1   | 1st round    | Rothmans Grand Prix           |
|      | v Newbury        | 1-5   | 2nd round    | Rothmans Grand Prix           |
|      | v Owers          | 8-9   | 1st round    | Tennents UK Open              |
| 1987 | v Spencer        | 4-5   | 2nd round    | Mercantile Credit Classic     |
|      | v Bradley        | 3-6   | 2nd round    | Tolly Ales English Championship |
|      | v Murphy         | 4-5   | 2nd round    | Dulux British Open            |
|      | v O'Kane         | 2-10  | Qualifying   | Embassy World Championship     |
|      | v A. Harris      | 5-4   | 1st round    | Fidelity International         |
|      | v Houlihan       | 5-3   | 2nd round    | Fidelity International         |
|      | v Martin         | 5-2   | 3rd round    | Fidelity International         |
|      | v Wilson         | 5-1   | 4th round    | Fidelity International         |
|      | v Hendry         | 0-5   | 5th round    | Fidelity International         |
|      | v Lawlor         | 5-2   | 1st round    | Rothmans Grand Prix           |
|      | v Fowler         | 1-5   | 2nd round    | Rothmans Grand Prix           |
|      | v Heaton         | 9-5   | 1st round    | Tennents UK Open              |
|      | v Chappel        | 2-9   | 2nd round    | Tennents UK Open              |
| 1988 | v Jack Rea       | 5-2   | 1st round    | Mercantile Credit Classic     |
|      | v B. Harris      | 5-4   | 2nd round    | Mercantile Credit Classic     |
|      | v C. Wilson      | 3-5   | 3rd round    | Mercantile Credit Classic     |
|      | v Whitthread     | 6-1   | 1st round    | English Championship          |
|      | v Bales          | 6-2   | 2nd round    | English Championship          |
|      | v Reynolds       | 3-6   | 3rd round    | English Championship          |
|      | v Wright         | 5-2   | 2nd round    | MIM Britannia British Open    |
|      | v Macleod        | 4-5   | 3rd round    | MIM Britannia British Open    |
|      | v Heaton         | 10-2  | Qualifying   | Embassy World Championship     |
|      |                  |       |              | (withdrew from 2nd qualifying round) |
|      | v Johnston-Allen | 3-5   | 2nd round    | Fidelity International         |
|      | v Mienie         | 5-0   | 2nd round    | Rothmans Grand Prix           |
|      | v O'Kane         | 4-5   | 3rd round    | Rothmans Grand Prix           |
|      | v Price          | 4-5   | 2nd round    | BCE Canadian Masters          |
|      | v Lawlor         | 9-2   | 2nd round    | Tennents UK Open              |
|      | v Thorne         | 3-9   | 3rd round    | Tennents UK Open              |
| 1989 | v A. Harris      | 4-5   | 2nd round    | Mercantile Credit Classic     |
|      | v Ellis          | 5-2   | 2nd round    | European Open                 |
|      | v Hallett        | 3-5   | 3rd round    | European Open                 |
|      | v Bradley        | 5-4   | 2nd round    | English Championship          |
|      | v Johnson        | 2-5   | 3rd round    | English Championship          |
|      | v John Rea       | 3-5   | 2nd round    | Anglian British Open          |
|      | v Fagan          | 10-4  | Qualifying   | Embassy World Championship     |
|      | v Thornley       | 10-4  | Qualifying   | Embassy World Championship     |
|      | v Mountjoy       | 7-10  | Qualifying   | Embassy World Championship     |

## NIGEL GILBERT (England)

**Born** 20.3.59. **Turned professional** 1986. **World ranking** 46 (56). **Best professional performance** Quarter-finals 1988 Rothmans Grand Prix.

|      |                  |       |              |                                |
|------|------------------|-------|--------------|--------------------------------|
| 1986 | v Agrawal        | 5-0   | 1st round    | BCE International              |
|      | v Chaperon       | 3-5   | 2nd round    | BCE International              |
|      | v Donnelly       | 1-5   | 1st round    | Rothmans Grand Prix           |
|      | v Donnelly       | 8-9   | 1st round    | Tennents UK Open              |
| 1987 | v Smith          | 5-0   | 1st round    | Mercantile Credit Classic     |
|      | v Van Rensberg   | 3-5   | 2nd round    | Mercantile Credit Classic     |
|      | v B. Bennett     | 5-6   | 1st round    | Tolly Ales English Championship |
|      | v Houlihan       | 5-4   | 1st round    | Dulux British Open            |
|      | v W. Jones       | 5-3   | 2nd round    | Dulux British Open            |
|      | v Reynolds       | 2-5   | 3rd round    | Dulux British Open            |
|      | v Sheehan        | 10-6  | Qualifying   | Embassy World Championship     |
|      | v O'Boye         | 5-10  | Qualifying   | Embassy World Championship     |

|        |                 |      |              |                           |
|--------|-----------------|------|--------------|---------------------------|
|        | v Black         | 5-3  | 1st round    | Fidelity International     |
|        | v J. McLaughlin | 5-4  | 2nd round    | Fidelity International     |
|        | v Macleod       | 5-1  | 3rd round    | Fidelity International     |
|        | v W. Jones      | 5-4  | 4th round    | Fidelity International     |
|        | v Charlton      | 0-5  | 5th round    | Fidelity International     |
|        | v Jonik         | 3-5  | 1st round    | Rothmans Grand Prix        |
|        | v Sinclair      | 9-8  | 1st round    | Tennents UK Open           |
|        | v G. Foulds     | 9-4  | 2nd round    | Tennents UK Open           |
|        | v E. Hughes     | 7-9  | 3rd round    | Tennents UK Open           |
| 1988   | v Donnelly      | 2-5  | 1st round    | Mercantile Credit Classic  |
|        | v A. Harris     | 6-3  | 1st round    | English Championship       |
|        | v F. Davis      | 5-6  | 2nd round    | English Championship       |
|        | v Sheehan       | 5-3  | 1st round    | MIM Britannia British Open |
|        | v Werbeniuk     | 5-1  | 2nd round    | MIM Britannia British Open |
|        | v Williams      | 2-5  | 3rd round    | MIM Britannia British Open |
|        | v John Rea      | 10-5 | Qualifying   | Embassy World Championship |
|        | v Chappel       | 8-10 | Qualifying   | Embassy World Championship |
|        | v Dunning       | 5-0  | 2nd round    | Fidelity International     |
|        | v Meo           | 1-5  | 3rd round    | Fidelity International     |
|        | v Oliver        | 5-4  | 2nd round    | Rothmans Grand Prix        |
|        | v S. Francisco  | 5-4  | 3rd round    | Rothmans Grand Prix        |
|        | v Charlton      | 5-0  | 4th round    | Rothmans Grand Prix        |
|        | v Knowles       | 5-4  | 5th round    | Rothmans Grand Prix        |
|        | v Robidoux      | 4-5  | Quarter-final| Rothmans Grand Prix        |
|        | v Johnston-Allen| 5-4  | 2nd round    | BCE Canadian Masters       |
|        | v Newbury       | 3-5  | 3rd round    | BCE Canadian Masters       |
|        | v Whitthread    | 9-5  | 2nd round    | Tennents UK Open           |
|        | v Spencer       | 9-7  | 3rd round    | Tennents UK Open           |
|        | v Parrott       | 8-9  | 4th round    | Tennents UK Open           |
| 1989   | v Fitzmaurice   | 5-3  | 2nd round    | Mercantile Credit Classic  |
|        | v O'Kane        | 2-5  | 3rd round    | Mercantile Credit Classic  |
|        | v Morra         | 1-5  | 2nd round    | European Open              |
|        | v Marshall      | 4-5  | 2nd round    | English Championship       |
|        | v T. Wilson     | 5-2  | 2nd round    | Anglian British Open       |
|        | v Hallett       | 3-5  | 3rd round    | Anglian British Open       |
|        | v Terry         | 10-5 | Qualifying   | Embassy World Championship |
|        | v Edwards       | 10-8 | Qualifying   | Embassy World Championship |
|        | v Newbury       | 7-10 | Qualifying   | Embassy World Championship |

## ROBBIE GRACE (South Africa)

**Born** 14.6.54. **Turned professional** 1985. **World ranking** 113 (79). **Best professional performance** Last 32 1986 Tennents UK Open.

|        |                 |       |            |                            |
|--------|-----------------|-------|------------|----------------------------|
| 1986   | v Parkin        | 10-8  | Qualifying | Embassy World Championship |
|        | v W. Jones      | 3-10  | Qualifying | Embassy World Championship |
|        | v P. Francisco  | 1-7   | 2nd round  | South African Championship |
|        | v Houlihan      | 5-1   | 1st round  | Rothmans Grand Prix        |
|        | v Fagan         | 3-5   | 2nd round  | Rothmans Grand Prix        |
|        | v Houlihan      | 9-6   | 1st round  | Tennents UK Open           |
|        | v Medati        | 9-5   | 2nd round  | Tennents UK Open           |
|        | v Macleod       | 9-6   | 3rd round  | Tennents UK Open           |
|        | v Thorne        | 1-9   | 4th round  | Tennents UK Open           |
| 1987   | v Rigitano      | 4-5   | 1st round  | Mercantile Credit Classic  |
|        | v Meadowcroft   | 5-4   | 1st round  | Dulux British Open         |
|        | v Fagan         | 5-3   | 2nd round  | Dulux British Open         |
|        | v West          | 2-5   | 3rd round  | Dulux British Open         |
|        | v Jenkins       | 9-10  | Qualifying | Embassy World Championship |
|        | v Chambers      | 5-4   | 2nd round  | Fidelity International      |
|        | v Thorburn      | 1-5   | 3rd round  | Fidelity International      |
|        | v Clark         | 1-5   | 2nd round  | Rothmans Grand Prix        |
|        | v Gary Wilkinson| 5-9   | 2nd round  | Tennents UK Open           |

| 1988 | v Van Rensberg | 3-5 | 2nd round | Mercantile Credit Classic |
|------|----------------|-----|-----------|---------------------------|
|      | v Clark        | 0-5 | 2nd round | MIM Britannia British Open |
|      | v Fowler       | 3-5 | 2nd round | Fidelity International |
|      | v Whitthread   | 4-5 | 1st round | Rothmans Grand Prix |
|      | v T. Wilson    | 2-5 | 1st round | BCE Canadian Masters |
|      | v Price        | 3-9 | 1st round | Tennents UK Open |
| 1989 | v Graham       | 4-5 | 1st round | Mercantile Credit Classic |
|      | v Meakin       | 5-4 | 1st round | European Open |
|      | v Edmonds      | 1-5 | 2nd round | European Open |
|      | v Fagan        | 5-2 | 1st round | Anglian British Open |
|      | v Wright       | 1-5 | 2nd round | Anglian British Open |
|      | v Watchorn     | 6-10 | Qualifying | Embassy World Championship |

## IAN GRAHAM (England)

**Born** 17.2.67. **Turned professional** 1988. **World ranking** 59. **Best professional performance** Last 16 BCE Canadian Masters.

| 1988 | v Chambers       | 2-5 | 1st round | Fidelity International |
|------|------------------|-----|-----------|------------------------|
|      | v Glen Wilkinson | 4-5 | 1st round | Rothmans Grand Prix |
|      | v Sinclair       | 5-3 | 1st round | BCE Canadian Masters |
|      | v Wright         | 5-2 | 2nd round | BCE Canadian Masters |
|      | v P. Francisco   | 5-3 | 3rd round | BCE Canadian Masters |
|      | v Charlton       | 5-2 | 4th round | BCE Canadian Masters |
|      | v Thorburn       | 4-5 | 5th round | BCE Canadian Masters |
|      | v B. Harris      | 4-9 | 1st round | Tennents UK Open |
| 1989 | v Grace          | 5-4 | 1st round | Mercantile Credit Classic |
|      | v Macleod        | 4-5 | 2nd round | Mercantile Credit Classic |
|      | v Scott          | 5-1 | 1st round | European Open |
|      | v Gary Wilkinson | 3-5 | 2nd round | European Open |
|      | v Heaton         | 5-1 | Prelim | English Championship |
|      | v Darrington     | 5-3 | 1st round | English Championship |
|      | v Duggan         | 5-2 | 2nd round | English Championship |
|      | v Williams       | 5-3 | 3rd round | English Championship |
|      | v Gary Wilkinson | 1-5 | 4th round | English Championship |
|      | v Williamson     | 5-4 | 1st round | Anglian British Open |
|      | v Duggan         | 5-2 | 2nd round | Anglian British Open |
|      | v West           | 1-5 | 3rd round | Anglian British Open |
|      | v Greaves        | 10-0 | Qualifying | Embassy World Championship |
|      | v B. Harris      | wo  | Qualifying | Embassy World Championship |
|      | v Cripsey        | 10-2 | Qualifying | Embassy World Championship |
|      | v M. Smith       | 10-6 | Qualifying | Embassy World Championship |
|      | v Reynolds       | 5-10 | Qualifying | Embassy World Championship |

## TERRY GRIFFITHS (Wales)

**Born** 16.10.47. **Turned professional** 1978. **World ranking** 5 (5). **Amateur career** 1975 Welsh champion, 1977 & 1978 English champion. **Best professional performances** Winner 1979 Embassy World Championship, 1982 Coral UK Championship, 1985 & 1986 Welsh Championship, 1982 Lada Classic, 1980 Benson & Hedges Masters, 1980, 1981, 1982 Benson & Hedges Irish Masters, 1986 BCE Belgian Classic.

| 1978 | v Williams      | 8-9   | Qualifying | Coral UK Championship |
|------|-----------------|-------|------------|------------------------|
| 1979 | v Bennett       | 9-2   | Prelim | Embassy World Championship |
|      | v Meadowcroft   | 9-6   | Qualifying | Embassy World Championship |
|      | v Mans          | 13-8  | 1st round | Embassy World Championship |
|      | v Higgins       | 13-12 | Quarter-final | Embassy World Championship |

*Terry Griffiths*

| | | | | |
|---|---|---|---|---|
| | v Charlton | 19-17 | Semi-final | Embassy World Championship |
| | **v Dennis Taylor** | **24-16** | **Final** | **Embassy World Championship** |
| | v Wilson | 9-4 | 3rd round | Coral UK Championship |
| | v Higgins | 9-7 | Quarter-final | Coral UK Championship |
| | v Werbeniuk | 9-3 | Semi-final | Coral UK Championship |
| | v Virgo | 13-14 | Final | Coral UK Championship |
| **1980** | v Thorburn | 5-3 | Quarter-final | Benson & Hedges Masters |
| | v Spencer | 5-0 | Semi-final | Benson & Hedges Masters |
| | **v Higgins** | **9-5** | **Final** | **Benson & Hedges Masters** |
| | v Mountjoy | 6-9 | 1st round | Woodpecker Welsh Championship |
| | **v Mountjoy** | **9-8** | **Final** | **Benson & Hedges Irish Masters** |
| | v S. Davis | 10-13 | 2nd round | Embassy World Championship |
| | v Fagan | 9-8 | 2nd round | Coral UK Championship |
| | v Dennis Taylor | 9-7 | Quarter-final | Coral UK Championship |
| | v S. Davis | 0-9 | Semi-final | Coral UK Championship |
| **1981** | v F. Davis | 5-2 | Quarter-final | Benson & Hedges Masters |
| | v Spencer | 6-5 | Semi-final | Benson & Hedges Masters |
| | v Higgins | 6-9 | Final | Benson & Hedges Masters |
| | v Reardon | 6-9 | Semi-final | Woodpecker Welsh Championship |
| | v Thorburn | 6-5 | Semi-final | Benson & Hedges Irish Masters |
| | **v Reardon** | **9-7** | **Final** | **Benson & Hedges Irish Masters** |
| | v Meo | 13-6 | 2nd round | Embassy World Championship |
| | v S. Davis | 9-13 | Quarter-final | Embassy World Championship |
| | v Spencer | 5-2 | 3rd round | Jameson International |
| | v Higgins | 2-5 | Quarter-final | Jameson International |
| | v Stevens | 5-0 | 1st round | Northern Ireland Classic |
| | v S. Davis | 6-9 | Semi-final | Northern Ireland Classic |
| | v Miles | 9-4 | 3rd round | Coral UK Championship |
| | v Knowles | 9-5 | Quarter-final | Coral UK Championship |
| | v Meo | 9-3 | Semi-final | Coral UK Championship |
| | v S. Davis | 3-16 | Final | Coral UK Championship |
| **1982** | v Thorburn | 5-1 | 1st round | Lada Classic |
| | v Higgins | 5-1 | Semi-final | Lada Classic |
| | **v S. Davis** | **9-8** | **Final** | **Lada Classic** |
| | v Reardon | 5-3 | Quarter-final | Benson & Hedges Masters |
| | v Higgins | 6-4 | Semi-final | Benson & Hedges Masters |
| | v S. Davis | 5-9 | Final | Benson & Hedges Masters |
| | v S. Davis | 7-9 | Final | Yamaha International Masters |
| | v Roscoe | 6-2 | 1st round | Woodpecker Welsh Championship |
| | v Wilson | 9-6 | Semi-final | Woodpecker Welsh Championship |
| | v Mountjoy | 8-9 | Final | Woodpecker Welsh Championship |
| | v Meo | 5-3 | Quarter-final | Benson & Hedges Irish Masters |
| | v Reardon | 6-3 | Semi-final | Benson & Hedges Irish Masters |
| | **v S. Davis** | **9-5** | **Final** | **Benson & Hedges Irish Masters** |
| | v Thorne | 6-10 | 1st round | Embassy World Championship |
| | v Reardon | 5-3 | 1st round | Langs Scottish Masters |
| | v Higgins | 5-6 | Semi-final | Langs Scottish Masters |
| | v Williams | 5-2 | 1st round | Jameson International |
| | v Higgins | 5-2 | 2nd round | Jameson International |
| | v Stevens | 3-5 | Quarter-final | Jameson International |
| | v Roscoe | 5-1 | 1st round | Professional Players Tournament |
| | v Watterson | 5-2 | 2nd round | Professional Players Tournament |
| | v Sinclair | 5-3 | 3rd round | Professional Players Tournament |
| | v White | 2-5 | Quarter-final | Professional Players Tournament |
| | v Johnson | 9-1 | 1st round | Coral UK Championship |
| | v Dennis Taylor | 9-7 | 2nd round | Coral UK Championship |
| | v S. Davis | 9-6 | Quarter-final | Coral UK Championship |
| | v Meo | 9-7 | Semi-final | Coral UK Championship |
| | **v Higgins** | **16-15** | **Final** | **Coral UK Championship** |
| **1983** | v Mountjoy | 1-5 | 1st round | Lada Classic |
| | v Stevens | 5-3 | 1st round | Benson & Hedges Masters |
| | v Thorburn | 3-5 | Quarter-final | Benson & Hedges Masters |

| | | | |
|---|---|---|---|
| v Everton | 6-1 | Quarter-final | Woodpecker Welsh Championship |
| v Reardon | 4-9 | Semi-final | Woodpecker Welsh Championship |
| v Werbeniuk | 5-3 | Semi-final | Tolly Cobbold Classic |
| v S. Davis | 5-7 | Final | Tolly Cobbold Classic |
| v Mountjoy | 5-4 | Quarter-final | Benson & Hedges Irish Masters |
| v S. Davis | 2-6 | Semi-final | Benson & Hedges Irish Masters |
| v Wildman | 10-8 | 1st round | Embassy World Championship |
| v Thorburn | 12-13 | 2nd round | Embassy World Championship |
| v Thorburn | 1-5 | 1st round | Langs Scottish Masters |
| v Miles | 5-2 | 1st round | Jameson International |
| v Scott | 5-0 | 2nd round | Jameson International |
| v Spencer | 5-4 | Quarter-final | Jameson International |
| v Thorburn | 8-9 | Semi-final | Jameson International |
| v Dodd | 5-3 | 1st round | Professional Players Tournament |
| v Parrott | 5-1 | 2nd round | Professional Players Tournament |
| v E. Hughes | 2-5 | 3rd round | Professional Players Tournament |
| v Martin | 9-4 | 1st round | Coral UK Championship |
| v Hallett | 9-5 | 2nd round | Coral UK Championship |
| v Johnson | 9-2 | Quarter-final | Coral UK Championship |
| v Higgins | 4-9 | Semi-final | Coral UK Championship |
| **1984** v Reynolds | 5-2 | Qualifying | Lada Classic |
| v Roscoe | 5-2 | 1st round | Lada Classic |
| v S. Davis | 4-5 | Quarter-final | Lada Classic |
| v Werbeniuk | 5-1 | 1st round | Benson & Hedges Masters |
| v Spencer | 5-4 | Quarter-final | Benson & Hedges Masters |
| v Knowles | 6-4 | Semi-final | Benson & Hedges Masters |
| v White | 5-9 | Final | Benson & Hedges Masters |
| v Andrewartha | 6-1 | 1st round | Strongbow Welsh Championship |
| v Mountjoy | 5-9 | Semi-final | Strongbow Welsh Championship |
| v Werbeniuk | 5-2 | 1st round | Benson & Hedges Irish Masters |
| v Knowles | 5-0 | Quarter-final | Benson & Hedges Irish Masters |
| v Dennis Taylor | 5-4 | Semi-final | Benson & Hedges Irish Masters |
| v S. Davis | 1-9 | Final | Benson & Hedges Irish Masters |
| v Mifsud | 10-2 | 1st round | Embassy World Championship |
| v Werbeniuk | 10-5 | 2nd round | Embassy World Championship |
| v S. Davis | 10-13 | Quarter-final | Embassy World Championship |
| v Knowles | 3-5 | 1st round | Langs Scottish Masters |
| v N. Foulds | 5-3 | 1st round | Jameson International |
| v Higgins | 4-5 | 2nd round | Jameson International |
| v T. Jones | 3-5 | 1st round | Rothmans Grand Prix |
| v Wilson | 6-9 | 1st round | Coral UK Open |
| **1985** v Fagan | 5-0 | 1st round | Mercantile Credit Classic |
| v Williams | 5-3 | 2nd round | Mercantile Credit Classic |
| v Thorburn | 4-5 | Quarter-final | Mercantile Credit Classic |
| v Werbeniuk | 5-2 | 1st round | Benson & Hedges Masters |
| v Higgins | 5-1 | Quarter-final | Benson & Hedges Masters |
| v Mountjoy | 2-6 | Semi-final | Benson & Hedges Masters |
| v Chalmers | 6-0 | 1st round | Dulux British Open |
| v Newbury | 3-5 | 2nd round | Dulux British Open |
| v Higgins | 2-5 | 1st round | Benson & Hedges Irish Masters |
| v Williams | 10-3 | 1st round | Embassy World Championship |
| v Higgins | 13-7 | 2nd round | Embassy World Championship |
| v S. Davis | 6-13 | Quarter-final | Embassy World Championship |
| v Chappel | 6-0 | Quarter-final | BCE Welsh Championship |
| v Reardon | 9-3 | Semi-final | BCE Welsh Championship |
| **v Mountjoy** | **9-4** | **Final** | **BCE Welsh Championship** |
| v Newbury | 5-2 | 3rd round | Goya Matchroom Trophy |
| v Spencer | 5-1 | 4th round | Goya Matchroom Trophy |
| v Parrott | 1-5 | 5th round | Goya Matchroom Trophy |
| v J. McLaughlin | 5-4 | 3rd round | Rothmans Grand Prix |
| v B. Harris | 5-3 | 4th round | Rothmans Grand Prix |
| v P. Francisco | 5-2 | 5th round | Rothmans Grand Prix |

| | | | | |
|---|---|---|---|---|
| | v Thorburn | 1-5 | Quarter-final | Rothmans Grand Prix |
| | v S. Davis | 4-5 | 1st round | BCE Canadian Masters |
| | v T. Jones | 9-5 | 3rd round | Coral UK Open |
| | v Reynolds | 9-7 | 4th round | Coral UK Open |
| | v S. Francisco | 9-5 | 5th round | Coral UK Open |
| | v Thorne | 7-9 | Quarter-final | Coral UK Open |
| | v Reardon | 5-2 | 1st round | Kit Kat |
| | v Dennis Taylor | 4-6 | Semi-final | Kit Kat |
| 1986 | v V. Harris | 3-5 | 3rd round | Mercantile Credit Classic |
| | v S. Davis | 5-2 | 1st round | BCE Belgian Classic |
| | v Knowles | 5-2 | Semi-final | BCE Belgian Classic |
| | **v Stevens** | **9-7** | **Final** | **BCE Belgian Classic** |
| | v Higgins | 5-4 | 1st round | Benson & Hedges Masters |
| | v Thorburn | 2-5 | Quarter-final | Benson & Hedges Masters |
| | v Chappel | 6-4 | Quarter-final | Zetters Welsh Championship |
| | v Wilson | 9-1 | Semi-final | Zetters Welsh Championship |
| | **v Mountjoy** | **9-3** | **Final** | **Zetters Welsh Championship** |
| | v Scott | 5-3 | 3rd round | Dulux British Open |
| | v N. Foulds | 5-3 | 4th round | Dulux British Open |
| | v Macleod | 5-2 | 5th round | Dulux British Open |
| | v Thorne | 4-5 | Quarter-final | Dulux British Open |
| | v Thorne | 2-5 | 1st round | Benson & Hedges Irish Masters |
| | v Fowler | 10-2 | 1st round | Embassy World Championship |
| | v Higgins | 13-12 | 2nd round | Embassy World Championship |
| | v Johnson | 12-13 | Quarter-final | Embassy World Championship |
| | v Dennis Taylor | 4-5 | Semi-final | Camus Hong Kong Masters |
| | v Meo | 6-3 | 1st round | Matchroom Trophy |
| | v S. Davis | 2-6 | Semi-final | Matchroom Trophy |
| | v Medati | 5-3 | 3rd round | BCE International |
| | v West | 5-1 | 4th round | BCE International |
| | v Thorburn | 4-5 | 5th round | BCE International |
| | v Morra | 5-3 | 3rd round | Rothmans Grand Prix |
| | v J. Campbell | 5-1 | 4th round | Rothmans Grand Prix |
| | v S. Davis | 2-5 | 5th round | Rothmans Grand Prix |
| | v P. Gibson | 9-3 | 3rd round | Tennents UK Open |
| | v O'Kane | 9-0 | 4th round | Tennents UK Open |
| | v Knowles | 6-9 | 5th round | Tennents UK Open |
| 1987 | v O'Boye | 5-1 | 3rd round | Mercantile Credit Classic |
| | v Martin | 5-4 | 4th round | Mercantile Credit Classic |
| | v J. Campbell | 5-3 | 5th round | Mercantile Credit Classic |
| | v White | 3-5 | Quarter-final | Mercantile Credit Classic |
| | v Higgins | 4-5 | 1st round | Benson & Hedges Masters |
| | v W. Jones | 6-2 | Quarter-final | Matchroom Welsh Championship |
| | v Newbury | 6-9 | Semi-final | Matchroom Welsh Championship |
| | v John Rea | 5-2 | 3rd round | Dulux British Open |
| | v T. Jones | 5-3 | 4th round | Dulux British Open |
| | v Dennis Taylor | 4-5 | 5th round | Dulux British Open |
| | v Higgins | 5-1 | 1st round | Benson & Hedges Irish Masters |
| | v Johnson | 5-0 | Quarter-final | Benson & Hedges Irish Masters |
| | v S. Davis | 2-6 | Semi-final | Benson & Hedges Irish Masters |
| | v Wych | 10-4 | 1st round | Embassy World Championship |
| | v Higgins | 13-10 | 2nd round | Embassy World Championship |
| | v S. Davis | 5-13 | Quarter-final | Embassy World Championship |
| | v Dennis Taylor | 3-6 | Final | British Caledonian Tokyo Masters (WS) |
| | v N. Foulds | 5-4 | 1st round | Langs Scottish Masters |
| | v White | 6-2 | Semi-final | Langs Scottish Masters |
| | v Johnson | 7-9 | Final | Langs Scottish Masters |
| | v Wildman | 5-1 | 3rd round | Fidelity International |
| | v Charlton | 2-5 | 4th round | Fidelity International |
| | v Kearney | 5-0 | 3rd round | Rothmans Grand Prix |
| | v Chappel | 5-3 | 4th round | Rothmans Grand Prix |
| | v Parrott | 4-5 | 5th round | Rothmans Grand Prix |

| | | | |
|---|---|---|---|
| v N. Foulds | 4-5 | 1st round | Labatts Canadian Masters (WS) |
| v N. Foulds | 2-6 | 1st round | Matchroom Trophy |
| v Gary Wilkinson | 9-5 | 3rd round | Tennents UK Open |
| v Edmonds | 9-5 | 4th round | Tennents UK Open |
| v S. Francisco | 9-3 | 5th round | Tennents UK Open |
| v White | 7-9 | Quarter-final | Tennents UK Open |
| 1988 v Van Rensberg | 5-2 | 3rd round | Mercantile Credit Classic |
| v C. Wilson | 5-2 | 4th round | Mercantile Credit Classic |
| v West | 5-2 | 5th round | Mercantile Credit Classic |
| v Newbury | 4-5 | Quarter-final | Mercantile Credit Classic |
| v S. Francisco | 5-3 | 1st round | Benson and Hedges Masters |
| v S. Davis | 0-5 | Quarter-final | Benson and Hedges Masters |
| v Chappel | 6-4 | Quarter-final | Welsh Championship |
| v C. Wilson | 9-7 | Semi-final | Welsh Championship |
| **v W. Jones** | **9-3** | **Final** | **Welsh Championship** |
| v Morra | 5-1 | 3rd round | MIM Britannia British Open |
| v Hendry | 1-5 | 4th round | MIM Britannia British Open |
| v Williams | 5-1 | 1st round | Benson & Hedges Irish Masters |
| v White | 5-2 | Quarter-final | Benson & Hedges Irish Masters |
| v N. Foulds | 4-6 | Semi-final | Benson & Hedges Irish Masters |
| v Longworth | 10-1 | 1st round | Embassy World Championship |
| v Thorne | 13-9 | 2nd round | Embassy World Championship |
| v N. Foulds | 13-9 | Quarter-final | Embassy World Championship |
| v White | 16-11 | Semi-final | Embassy World Championship |
| v S. Davis | 11-18 | Final | Embassy World Championship |
| v Wych | 0-5 | 3rd round | Fidelity International |
| v N. Foulds | 4-6 | 1st round | LEP Matchroom Championship |
| v Watterson | 5-3 | 3rd round | Rothmans Grand Prix |
| v West | 5-1 | 4th round | Rothmans Grand Prix |
| v E. Hughes | 5-2 | 5th round | Rothmans Grand Prix |
| v S. Davis | 3-5 | Quarter-final | Rothmans Grand Prix |
| v Oliver | 5-4 | 3rd round | BCE Canadian Masters |
| v Reardon | 5-2 | 4th round | BCE Canadian Masters |
| v Mountjoy | 5-4 | 5th round | BCE Canadian Masters |
| v S. Davis | 3-5 | Quarter-final | BCE Canadian Masters |
| v Owers | 9-2 | 3rd round | Tennents UK Open |
| v Duggan | 9-2 | 4th round | Tennents UK Open |
| v Reynolds | 9-6 | 5th round | Tennents UK Open |
| v West | 9-5 | Quarter-final | Tennents UK Open |
| v Mountjoy | 4-9 | Semi-final | Tennents UK Open |
| v P. Francisco | 9-7 | 1st round | Everest World Matchplay |
| v White | 5-9 | Quarter-final | Everest World Matchplay |
| 1989 v King | 5-2 | 3rd round | Mercantile Credit Classic |
| v Drago | 5-0 | 4th round | Mercantile Credit Classic |
| v Thorne | 1-5 | 5th round | Mercantile Credit Classic |
| v S. Francisco | 5-1 | 1st round | Benson and Hedges Masters |
| v Hendry | 3-5 | Quarter-final | Benson and Hedges Masters |
| v J. McLaughlin | 5-3 | 3rd round | European Open |
| v Chappel | 5-2 | 4th round | European Open |
| v Robidoux | 5-3 | 5th round | European Open |
| v Clark | 5-1 | Quarter-final | European Open |
| v White | 5-4 | Semi-final | European Open |
| v Parrott | 8-9 | Final | European Open |
| v D. Morgan | 6-5 | Quarter-final | Senator Welsh Championship |
| v Newbury | 9-7 | Semi-final | Senator Welsh Championship |
| v Mountjoy | 6-9 | Final | Senator Welsh Championship |
| v Johnston-Allen | 1-5 | 3rd round | Anglian British Open |
| v J. McLaughlin | 5-4 | 1st round | Benson and Hedges Irish Masters |
| v Hendry | 2-5 | Quarter-final | Benson and Hedges Irish Masters |
| v Chaperon | 10-6 | 1st round | Embassy World Championship |
| v S. Francisco | 13-9 | 2nd round | Embassy World Championship |
| v Hendry | 5-13 | Quarter-final | Embassy World Championship |

## MIKE HALLETT (England)

**Born** 6.7.59. **Turned professional** 1979. **World ranking** 6 (9). **Best professional performances** Runner-up 1988 MIM Britannia British Open; winner 1988 Fosters Professional, 1989 English Championship.

| | | | | |
|---|---|---|---|---|
| **1979** | v Parkin | 9-1 | 1st round | Coral UK Championship |
| | v Fagan | 4-9 | 2nd round | Coral UK Championship |
| **1980** | v Stevens | 3-9 | Qualifying | Embassy World Championship |
| | v Bennett | 9-4 | Qualifying | Coral UK Championship |
| | v Edmonds | 9-8 | Qualifying | Coral UK Championship |
| | v S. Davis | 1-9 | 1st round | Coral UK Championship |
| **1981** | v Edmonds | 3-9 | Qualifying | John Courage English |
| | v Jonik | 9-1 | Qualifying | Embassy World Championship |
| | v Meo | 4-9 | Qualifying | Embassy World Championship |
| | v Demarco | 5-4 | Qualifying | Jameson International |
| | v Knowles | 2-5 | 1st round | Jameson International |
| | v V. Harris | 9-4 | Qualifying | Coral UK Championship |
| | v D. Hughes | 9-6 | Qualifying | Coral UK Championship |
| | v Fagan | 9-5 | Qualifying | Coral UK Championship |
| | v Stevens | 4-9 | 2nd round | Coral UK Championship |
| **1982** | v Johnson | 9-8 | Qualifying | Embassy World Championship |
| | v Virgo | 4-10 | 1st round | Embassy World Championship |
| | v Jonik | 5-2 | Qualifying | Jameson International |
| | v Wildman | 2-5 | Qualifying | Jameson International |
| | v V. Harris | 5-3 | 1st round | Professional Players Tournament |
| | v Virgo | 2-5 | 2nd round | Professional Players Tournament |
| | v Demarco | 9-1 | Qualifying | Coral UK Championship |
| | v F. Davis | 9-7 | 1st round | Coral UK Championship |
| | v Reardon | 8-9 | 2nd round | Coral UK Championship |
| **1983** | v Andrewartha | 10-7 | Qualifying | Embassy World Championship |
| | v King | 10-6 | Qualifying | Embassy World Championship |
| | v Spencer | 7-10 | 1st round | Embassy World Championship |
| | v Roscoe | 5-2 | Qualifying | Jameson International |
| | v Morra | 3-5 | Qualifying | Jameson International |
| | v Kelly | 5-0 | 1st round | Professional Players Tournament |
| | v S. Davis | 5-2 | 2nd round | Professional Players Tournament |
| | v Meo | 3-5 | 3rd round | Professional Players Tournament |
| | v Darrington | 9-1 | Qualifying | Coral UK Championship |
| | v Miles | 9-4 | 1st round | Coral UK Championship |
| | v Griffiths | 5-9 | 2nd round | Coral UK Championship |
| **1984** | v Dennis Taylor | 5-4 | Qualifying | Lada Classic |
| | v Knowles | 3-5 | 1st round | Lada Classic |
| | v Burke | 10-5 | Qualifying | Embassy World Championship |
| | v Mountjoy | 4-10 | 1st round | Embassy World Championship |
| | v O'Kane | 4-5 | Qualifying | Jameson International |
| | v Sheehan | 5-1 | 1st round | Rothmans Grand Prix |
| | v Higgins | 5-3 | 2nd round | Rothmans Grand Prix |
| | v Stevens | 3-5 | 3rd round | Rothmans Grand Prix |
| | v Bradley | 9-8 | Qualifying | Coral UK Open |
| | v Mountjoy | 2-9 | 1st round | Coral UK Open |
| **1985** | v G. Foulds | 5-4 | Qualifying | Mercantile Credit Classic |
| | v Reardon | 3-5 | 1st round | Mercantile Credit Classic |
| | v Duggan | 9-4 | 1st round | Tolly Cobbold English Championship |
| | v Meo | 4-9 | 2nd round | Tolly Cobbold English Championship |
| | v Meo | 4-5 | 2nd round | Dulux British Open |
| | v Chalmers | 10-1 | Qualifying | Embassy World Championship |
| | v Thorburn | 8-10 | 1st round | Embassy World Championship |
| | v Bradley | 4-5 | 3rd round | Goya Matchroom Trophy |
| | v Mikkelsen | 5-3 | 3rd round | Rothmans Grand Prix |
| | v Johnson | 4-5 | 4th round | Rothmans Grand Prix |
| | v Meadowcroft | 9-1 | 3rd round | Coral UK Open |

*Mike Hallett*

|  | v Stevens | 5-9 | 4th round | Coral UK Open |
| 1986 | v John Rea | 5-2 | 3rd round | Mercantile Credit Classic |
|  | v Thorburn | 3-5 | 4th round | Mercantile Credit Classic |
|  | v Chalmers | 9-1 | 3rd round | Tolly Cobbold English Championship |
|  | v Knowles | 9-5 | 4th round | Tolly Cobbold English Championship |
|  | v Johnson | 9-6 | Quarter-final | Tolly Cobbold English Championship |
|  | v N. Foulds | 8-9 | Semi-final | Tolly Cobbold English Championship |
|  | v Duggan | 5-3 | 3rd round | Dulux British Open |
|  | v Higgins | 1-5 | 4th round | Dulux British Open |
|  | v Wych | 10-7 | Qualifying | Embassy World Championship |
|  | v Dennis Taylor | 10-6 | 1st round | Embassy World Championship |
|  | v Johnson | 6-13 | 2nd round | Embassy World Championship |
|  | v O'Kane | 1-5 | 3rd round | BCE International |
|  | v V. Harris | 5-2 | 3rd round | Rothmans Grand Prix |
|  | v Dodd | 5-2 | 4th round | Rothmans Grand Prix |
|  | v White | 3-5 | 5th round | Rothmans Grand Prix |
|  | v King | 9-5 | 3rd round | Tennents UK Open |
|  | v Meo | 9-4 | 4th round | Tennents UK Open |
|  | v Higgins | 7-9 | 5th round | Tennents UK Open |
| 1987 | v Mikkelsen | 5-3 | 3rd round | Mercantile Credit Classic |
|  | v Fowler | 4-5 | 4th round | Mercantile Credit Classic |
|  | v Williamson | 2-6 | 3rd round | Tolly Ales English Championship |
|  | v Owers | 6-2 | 4th round | Tolly Ales English Championship |
|  | v Dodd | 5-6 | Quarter-final | Tolly Ales English Championship |
|  | v Rigitano | 5-0 | 3rd round | Dulux British Open |
|  | v White | 2-5 | 4th round | Dulux British Open |
|  | v Newbury | 10-4 | Qualifying | Embassy World Championship |
|  | v Knowles | 10-6 | 1st round | Embassy World Championship |
|  | v S. Francisco | 13-9 | 2nd round | Embassy World Championship |
|  | v N. Foulds | 9-13 | Quarter-final | Embassy World Championship |
|  | v Roscoe | 5-3 | 3rd round | Fidelity International |
|  | v Longworth | 5-1 | 4th round | Fidelity International |
|  | v White | 5-4 | 5th round | Fidelity International |
|  | v Charlton | 5-4 | Quarter-final | Fidelity International |
|  | v S. Davis | 3-9 | Semi-final | Fidelity International |
|  | v P. Gibson | 4-5 | 3rd round | Rothmans Grand Prix |
|  | v T. Jones | 9-2 | 3rd round | Tennents UK Open |
|  | v Meo | 9-5 | 4th round | Tennents UK Open |
|  | v Fowler | 9-4 | 5th round | Tennents UK Open |
|  | v Johnson | 7-9 | Quarter-final | Tennents UK Open |
| 1988 | v Clark | 4-5 | 3rd round | Mercantile Credit Classic |
|  | v Dennis Taylor | 5-3 | 1st round | Benson & Hedges Masters |
|  | v Higgins | 5-2 | Quarter-final | Benson & Hedges Masters |
|  | v Parrott | 6-5 | Semi-final | Benson & Hedges Masters |
|  | v S. Davis | 0-9 | Final | Benson & Hedges Masters |
|  | v Duggan | 6-3 | 3rd round | English Championship |
|  | v Williams | 6-3 | 4th round | English Championship |
|  | v West | 5-6 | Quarter-final | English Championship |
|  | v Williamson | 5-0 | 3rd round | MIM Britannia British Open |
|  | v Cripsey | 5-2 | 4th round | MIM Britannia British Open |
|  | v Macleod | 5-2 | 5th round | MIM Britannia British Open |
|  | v O'Boye | 5-4 | Quarter-final | MIM Britannia British Open |
|  | v Parrott | 9-8 | Semi-final | MIM Britannia British Open |
|  | v Hendry | 2-13 | Final | MIM Britannia British Open |
|  | v Chaperon | 10-2 | 1st round | Embassy World Championship |
|  | v S. Davis | 1-13 | 2nd round | Embassy World Championship |
|  | v O'Kane | 5-1 | 1st round | New Zealand Masters |
|  | v Knowles | 5-3 | Semi-final | New Zealand Masters |
|  | v Hendry | 1-6 | Final | New Zealand Masters |
|  | v O'Boye | 5-3 | 3rd round | Fidelity International |
|  | v Meo | 3-5 | 4th round | Fidelity International |
|  | v Parrott | 5-3 | 1st round | Fosters Professional |
|  | **v Hendry** | **8-5** | **Final** | **Fosters Professional** |

|      |                   |       |              |                                  |
|------|-------------------|-------|--------------|----------------------------------|
|      | v T. Jones        | 5-2   | 3rd round    | Rothmans Grand Prix              |
|      | v James           | 5-2   | 4th round    | Rothmans Grand Prix              |
|      | v Dennis Taylor   | 2-5   | 5th round    | Rothmans Grand Prix              |
|      | v O'Boye          | 5-0   | 3rd round    | BCE Canadian Masters             |
|      | v Gauvreau        | 5-3   | 4th round    | BCE Canadian Masters             |
|      | v King            | 5-2   | 5th round    | BCE Canadian Masters             |
|      | v Parrott         | 5-3   | Quarter-final| BCE Canadian Masters             |
|      | v White           | 2-9   | Semi-final   | BCE Canadian Masters             |
|      | v Clark           | 6-9   | 3rd round    | Tennents UK Open                 |
|      | v Thorne          | 9-8   | 1st round    | Everest World Matchplay          |
|      | v S. Davis        | 2-9   | Quarter-final| Everest World Matchplay          |
| 1989 | v Browne          | 2-5   | 3rd round    | Mercantile Credit Classic        |
|      | v Knowles         | 3-5   | 1st round    | Benson and Hedges Masters        |
|      | v D. Gilbert      | 5-3   | 3rd round    | European Open                    |
|      | v Browne          | 5-4   | 4th round    | European Open                    |
|      | v Hendry          | 5-3   | 5th round    | European Open                    |
|      | v Wych            | 5-3   | Quarter-final| European Open                    |
|      | v Parrott         | 4-5   | Semi-final   | European Open                    |
|      | v Houlihan        | 5-2   | 3rd round    | English Championship             |
|      | v Price           | 5-4   | 4th round    | English Championship             |
|      | v Longworth       | 5-1   | Quarter-final| English Championship             |
|      | v Gary Wilkinson  | 5-3   | Semi-final   | English Championship             |
|      | **v Parrott**     | **9-7** | **Final**  | **English Championship**         |
|      | v N. Gilbert      | 5-3   | 3rd round    | Anglian British Open             |
|      | v Bales           | 5-0   | 4th round    | Anglian British Open             |
|      | v Thorburn        | 5-4   | 5th round    | Anglian British Open             |
|      | v Clark           | 5-3   | Quarter-final| Anglian British Open             |
|      | v Meo             | 8-9   | Semi-final   | Anglian British Open             |
|      | v Knowles         | 5-0   | 1st round    | Benson and Hedges Irish Masters  |
|      | v S. Davis        | 4-5   | Quarter-final| Benson and Hedges Irish Masters  |
|      | v Mountjoy        | 10-7  | 1st round    | Embassy World Championship       |
|      | v Roe             | 13-12 | 2nd round    | Embassy World Championship       |
|      | v S. Davis        | 3-13  | Quarter-final| Embassy World Championship       |

## ANTHONY HARRIS (England)

**Born** 19.4.68. **Turned professional** 1987. **World ranking** 74 (116). **Amateur career** 1986 English champion. **Best professional performance** Last 32 1989 Mercantile Credit Classic.

|      |                   |       |            |                                  |
|------|-------------------|-------|------------|----------------------------------|
| 1987 | v D. Gilbert      | 4-5   | 1st round  | Fidelity International            |
|      | v Meadowcroft     | 3-5   | 1st round  | Rothmans Grand Prix               |
|      | v Morra           | 9-8   | 1st round  | Tennents UK Open                  |
|      | v Gauvreau        | 3-9   | 2nd round  | Tennents UK Open                  |
| 1988 | v Jenkins         | 5-4   | 1st round  | Mercantile Credit Classic         |
|      | v T. Jones        | 2-5   | 2nd round  | Mercantile Credit Classic         |
|      | v N. Gilbert      | 3-5   | 1st round  | English Championship              |
|      | v Bear            | 2-5   | 1st round  | MIM Britannia British Open        |
|      | v Mizerak         | 10-3  | Preliminary| Embassy World Championship        |
|      | v Fisher          | 10-4  | Qualifying | Embassy World Championship        |
|      | v Duggan          | 4-10  | Qualifying | Embassy World Championship        |
|      | v Foldvari        | 1-5   | 1st round  | Fidelity International             |
|      | v Kearney         | 5-2   | 1st round  | Rothmans Grand Prix               |
|      | v Werbeniuk       | 1-5   | 2nd round  | Rothmans Grand Prix               |
|      | v Morra           | 5-3   | 1st round  | BCE Canadian Masters              |
|      | v O'Boye          | 3-5   | 2nd round  | BCE Canadian Masters              |
|      | v M. Gibson       | 8-9   | 1st round  | Tennents UK Open                  |
| 1989 | v Bear            | 5-3   | 1st round  | Mercantile Credit Classic         |
|      | v D. Gilbert      | 5-4   | 2nd round  | Mercantile Credit Classic         |
|      | v West            | 5-4   | 3rd round  | Mercantile Credit Classic         |
|      | v Chappel         | 1-5   | 4th round  | Mercantile Credit Classic         |
|      | v Glen Wilkinson  | 5-4   | 1st round  | European Open                     |

| v Fowler | 1-5 | 2nd round | European Open |
|---|---|---|---|
| v T. Jones | 5-3 | 2nd round | English Championship |
| v Reynolds | 1-5 | 3rd round | English Championship |
| v Wildman | 5-4 | 1st round | Anglian British Open |
| v Wych | 4-5 | 2nd round | Anglian British Open |
| v Van Rensberg | 10-7 | Qualifying | Embassy World Championship |
| v W. Jones | 4-10 | Qualifying | Embassy World Championship |

## BOB HARRIS (England)

**Born** 12.3.56. **Turned professional** 1982. **World ranking** 93 (77). **Best professional performances** Last 32 1985 Goya Matchroom Trophy, 1985 Rothmans Grand Prix, 1987 Mercantile Credit Classic.

| | | | |
|---|---|---|---|
| **1982** v Scott | 4-5 | Qualifying | Jameson International |
| v Cripsey | 9-6 | Qualifying | Coral UK Championship |
| v Watterson | 9-3 | Qualifying | Coral UK Championship |
| v Fagan | 6-9 | 1st round | Coral UK Championship |
| **1983** v Wildman | 7-10 | Qualifying | Embassy World Championship |
| v Dunning | 5-3 | Qualifying | Jameson International |
| v Wildman | 2-5 | Qualifying | Jameson International |
| v King | 3-5 | Qualifying | Professional Players Tournament |
| v E. McLaughlin | 9-8 | Qualifying | Coral UK Championship |
| v Fitzmaurice | 9-3 | Qualifying | Coral UK Championship |
| v Reardon | 7-9 | 1st round | Coral UK Championship |
| **1984** v Sheehan | 10-3 | Qualifying | Embassy World Championship |
| v Burke | 4-10 | Qualifying | Embassy World Championship |
| v Watchorn | 7-9 | Qualifying | Coral UK Open |
| **1985** v Duggan | 8-9 | Qualifying | Tolly Cobbold English Championship |
| v Meadowcroft | 6-1 | Qualifying | Dulux British Open |
| v Charlton | 6-3 | 1st round | Dulux British Open |
| v E. Hughes | 4-5 | 2nd round | Dulux British Open |
| v Rigitano | 4-10 | Qualifying | Embassy World Championship |
| v Browne | 5-3 | 2nd round | Goya Matchroom Trophy |
| v O'Kane | 5-3 | 3rd round | Goya Matchroom Trophy |
| v Dennis Taylor | 3-5 | 4th round | Goya Matchroom Trophy |
| v Browne | 5-3 | 2nd round | Rothmans Grand Prix |
| v Spencer | 5-2 | 3rd round | Rothmans Grand Prix |
| v Griffiths | 3-5 | 4th round | Rothmans Grand Prix |
| v Fagan | 2-9 | 2nd round | Coral UK Open |
| **1986** v Morra | 5-3 | 2nd round | Mercantile Credit Classic |
| v Johnson | 4-5 | 3rd round | Mercantile Credit Classic |
| v T. Jones | 5-9 | 2nd round | Tolly Cobbold English Championship |
| v Sinclair | 5-3 | 2nd round | Dulux British Open |
| v Martin | 1-5 | 3rd round | Dulux British Open |
| v Black | 8-10 | Qualifying | Embassy World Championship |
| v Foldvari | 0-5 | 2nd round | BCE International |
| v Jack Rea | 5-0 | 2nd round | Rothmans Grand Prix |
| v Mountjoy | 2-5 | 3rd round | Rothmans Grand Prix |
| v Jack Rea | 9-5 | 2nd round | Tennents UK Open |
| v Wych | 6-9 | 3rd round | Tennents UK Open |
| **1987** v P. Gibson | 5-3 | 2nd round | Mercantile Credit Classic |
| v Wych | 5-3 | 3rd round | Mercantile Credit Classic |
| v S. Francisco | 3-5 | 4th round | Mercantile Credit Classic |
| v G. Foulds | 6-1 | 2nd round | Tolly Ales English Championship |
| v Thorne | 2-6 | 3rd round | Tolly Ales English Championship |
| v Kelly | 5-2 | 2nd round | Dulux British Open |
| v Thorne | 1-5 | 3rd round | Dulux British Open |
| v D. Hughes | 10-2 | Qualifying | Embassy World Championship |
| v Fowler | 6-10 | Qualifying | Embassy World Championship |
| v James | 0-5 | 2nd round | Fidelity International |
| v Bear | 3-5 | 2nd round | Rothmans Grand Prix |
| v Bear | 4-9 | 2nd round | Tennents UK Open |

| 1988 | v D. Gilbert | 4-5 | 2nd round | Mercantile Credit Classic |
| | v M. Smith | 4-6 | 2nd round | English Championship |
| | v Lawlor | 2-5 | 2nd round | MIM Britannia British Open |
| | v Fagan | 10-1 | Qualifying | Embassy World Championship |
| | v Sinclair | 10-0 | Qualifying | Embassy World Championship |
| | v Charlton | 4-10 | Qualifying | Embassy World Championship |
| | v Watchorn | 2-5 | 1st round | Fidelity International |
| | v Jack Rea | 5-2 | 1st round | Rothmans Grand Prix |
| | v Roe | 2-5 | 2nd round | Rothmans Grand Prix |
| | v Johnston-Allen | 4-5 | 1st round | BCE Canadian Masters |
| | v Graham | 9-4 | 1st round | Tennents UK Open |
| | v Macleod | 9-8 | 2nd round | Tennents UK Open |
| | v Williams | 4-9 | 3rd round | Tennents UK Open |
| 1989 | v Robidoux | 1-5 | 1st round | Mercantile Credit Classic |
| | v Watchorn | 4-5 | 1st round | European Open |
| | v Fitzmaurice | 4-5 | 1st round | English Championship |
| | v Robidoux | 0-5 | 1st round | Anglian British Open |

## VIC HARRIS (England)

**Born** 16.8.45. **Turned professional** 1981. **World ranking** 83 (71). **Amateur career** 1981 English champion. **Best professional performances** Last 32 1987 Tennents UK Open, 1986 Mercantile Credit Classic.

| 1981 | v Sheehan | 1-5 | Qualifying | Jameson International |
| | v Higgins | 3-5 | Quarter-final | Langs Scottish Masters |
| | v Hallett | 4-9 | Qualifying | Coral UK Championship |
| | v Johnson | 4-9 | Qualifying | Embassy World Championship |
| 1982 | v Hallett | 3-5 | 1st round | Professional Players Tournament |
| | v M. Owen | 9-4 | Qualifying | Coral UK Championship |
| | v Johnson | 8-9 | Qualifying | Coral UK Championship |
| | v Sheehan | 5-3 | Qualifying | Jameson International |
| | v Virgo | 2-5 | Qualifying | Jameson International |
| 1983 | v Meo | 0-10 | Qualifying | Embassy World Championship |
| | v Medati | 0-5 | Qualifying | Jameson International |
| | v Thorburn | 1-5 | 1st round | Professional Players Tournament |
| | v Houlihan | 9-6 | Qualifying | Coral UK Championship |
| | v Williams | 6-9 | Qualifying | Coral UK Championship |
| 1984 | v Van Rensberg | 7-10 | Qualifying | Embassy World Championship |
| | v Williamson | 0-5 | Qualifying | Jameson International |
| | v F. Davis | 5-1 | Qualifying | Rothmans Grand Prix |
| | v Knowles | 1-5 | 1st round | Rothmans Grand Prix |
| | v Bradley | 8-9 | Qualifying | Coral UK Open |
| 1985 | v Newbury | 3-5 | Qualifying | Mercantile Credit Classic |
| | v Scott | 7-9 | Qualifying | Tolly Cobbold English Championship |
| | v Dodd | 6-1 | Qualifying | Dulux British Open |
| | v Mountjoy | 6-5 | 1st round | Dulux British Open |
| | v O'Kane | 3-5 | 2nd round | Dulux British Open |
| | v O'Kane | 5-10 | Qualifying | Embassy World Championship |
| | v Foldvari | 4-5 | 2nd round | Goya Matchroom Trophy |
| | v Wych | 5-3 | 2nd round | Rothmans Grand Prix |
| | v Higgins | 1-5 | 3rd round | Rothmans Grand Prix |
| | v Black | 9-3 | 2nd round | Coral UK Open |
| | v Spencer | 5-9 | 3rd round | Coral UK Open |
| 1986 | v Roscoe | 5-1 | 2nd round | Mercantile Credit Classic |
| | v Griffiths | 5-3 | 3rd round | Mercantile Credit Classic |
| | v Williams | 1-5 | 4th round | Mercantile Credit Classic |
| | v Bales | 7-9 | 2nd round | Tolly Cobbold English Championship |
| | v Chaperon | 0-5 | 2nd round | Dulux British Open |
| | v T. Jones | 7-10 | Qualifying | Embassy World Championship |
| | v G. Foulds | 4-5 | 2nd round | BCE International |
| | v Kelly | 5-3 | 2nd round | Rothmans Grand Prix |

| | | | |
|---|---|---|---|
| v Hallett | 2-5 | 3rd round | Rothmans Grand Prix |
| v Fisher | 9-4 | 2nd round | Tennents UK Open |
| v Charlton | 2-9 | 3rd round | Tennents UK Open |
| 1987 v O'Boye | 1-5 | 2nd round | Mercantile Credit Classic |
| v Darrington | 6-3 | 2nd round | Tolly Ales English Championship |
| v West | 3-6 | 3rd round | Tolly Ales English Championship |
| v Sheehan | 5-4 | 2nd round | Dulux British Open |
| v E. Hughes | 1-5 | 3rd round | Dulux British Open |
| v Rigitano | 6-10 | Qualifying | Embassy World Championship |
| v Marshall | 5-1 | 1st round | Fidelity International |
| v Chaperon | 4-5 | 2nd round | Fidelity International |
| v Gary Wilkinson | 0-5 | 1st round | Rothmans Grand Prix |
| v Greaves | 9-1 | 1st round | Tennents UK Open |
| v M. Bennett | 9-7 | 2nd round | Tennents UK Open |
| v Martin | 9-7 | 3rd round | Tennents UK Open |
| v Roe | 5-9 | 4th round | Tennents UK Open |
| 1988 v Ellis | 5-1 | 1st round | Mercantile Credit Classic |
| v Murphy | 2-5 | 2nd round | Mercantile Credit Classic |
| v J. Smith | 3-6 | 1st round | English Championship |
| v Thornley | 4-5 | 1st round | MIM Britannia British Open |
| v M. Smith | 6-10 | Qualifying | Embassy World Championship |
| v Burke | 5-2 | 1st round | Fidelity International |
| v Wych | 3-5 | 2nd round | Fidelity International |
| v Marshall | 5-3 | 1st round | Rothmans Grand Prix |
| v J. McLaughlin | 4-5 | 2nd round | Rothmans Grand Prix |
| v Darrington | 0-5 | 1st round | BCE Canadian Masters |
| v Mikkelsen | 9-3 | 1st round | Tennents UK Open |
| v M. Bennett | 7-9 | 2nd round | Tennents UK Open |
| 1989 v D. Morgan | 3-5 | 1st round | Mercantile Credit Classic |
| v Terry | 5-2 | 1st round | European Open |
| v Roe | 1-5 | 2nd round | European Open |
| v Rowswell | 3-5 | 1st round | English Championship |
| v Johnston-Allen | 1-5 | 1st round | Anglian British Open |
| v Watterson | 10-5 | Qualifying | Embassy World Championship |
| v Gary Wilkinson | 6-10 | Qualifying | Embassy World Championship |

## STEPHEN HENDRY (Scotland)

**Born** 13.1.69. **Turned professional** 1985. **World ranking** 3 (4). **Amateur career** 1984 and 1985 Scottish champion. **Best professional performances** Winner 1987 Rothmans Grand Prix, 1988 MIM Britannia British Open, 1989 Benson and Hedges Masters; Scottish champion 1986–88.

| | | | |
|---|---|---|---|
| 1985 v West | 5-4 | 1st round | Goya Matchroom Trophy |
| v E. McLaughlin | 3-5 | 2nd round | Goya Matchroom Trophy |
| v O'Boye | 4-5 | 1st round | Rothmans Grand Prix |
| v Agrawal | 2-9 | Qualifying | Coral UK Open |
| 1986 v Sheehan | 5-2 | 1st round | Mercantile Credit Classic |
| v Miles | 5-1 | 2nd round | Mercantile Credit Classic |
| v S. Francisco | 5-4 | 3rd round | Mercantile Credit Classic |
| v N. Foulds | 4-5 | 4th round | Mercantile Credit Classic |
| v D. Hughes | 5-1 | 1st round | Dulux British Open |
| v Browne | 0-5 | 2nd round | Dulux British Open |
| v Demarco | 6-1 | 1st round | Canada Dry Scottish Championship |
| v Macleod | 6-5 | Quarter-final | Canada Dry Scottish Championship |
| v Black | 6-2 | Semi-final | Canada Dry Scottish Championship |
| **v Gibson** | **10-5** | **Final** | **Canada Dry Scottish Championship** |
| v Demarco | 10-7 | Qualifying | Embassy World Championship |
| v Browne | 10-9 | Qualifying | Embassy World Championship |
| v W. Jones | 10-8 | Qualifying | Embassy World Championship |
| v O'Kane | 10-9 | Qualifying | Embassy World Championship |
| v Thorne | 8-10 | 1st round | Embassy World Championship |

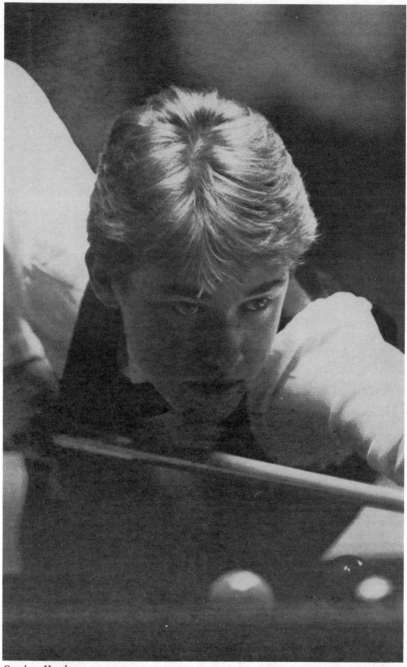

*Stephen Hendry*

|  | v White | 1-5 | 1st round | Langs Scottish Masters |
|---|---|---|---|---|
|  | v P. Gibson | 5-2 | 2nd round | BCE International |
|  | v Parrott | 5-3 | 3rd round | BCE International |
|  | v Dennis Taylor | 3-5 | 4th round | BCE International |
|  | v Williamson | 5-1 | 2nd round | Rothmans Grand Prix |
|  | v E. Hughes | 5-1 | 3rd round | Rothmans Grand Prix |
|  | v Chaperon | 5-2 | 4th round | Rothmans Grand Prix |
|  | v M. Bennett | 5-3 | 5th round | Rothmans Grand Prix |
|  | v White | 4-5 | Quarter-final | Rothmans Grand Prix |
|  | v Oliver | 9-1 | 2nd round | Tennents UK Open |
|  | v Higgins | 8-9 | 3rd round | Tennents UK Open |
| 1987 | v Jack Rea | 5-1 | 2nd round | Mercantile Credit Classic |
|  | v Reardon | 5-3 | 3rd round | Mercantile Credit Classic |
|  | v Wright | 5-1 | 4th round | Mercantile Credit Classic |
|  | v Fowler | 5-4 | 5th round | Mercantile Credit Classic |
|  | v S. Francisco | 5-0 | Quarter-final | Mercantile Credit Classic |
|  | v S. Davis | 3-9 | Semi-final | Mercantile Credit Classic |
|  | v Demarco | 6-2 | 1st round | Scottish Championship |
|  | v John Rea | 6-0 | Semi-final | Scottish Championship |
|  | **v Donnelly** | **10-7** | **Final** | **Scottish Championship** |
|  | v Sinclair | 2-5 | 2nd round | Dulux British Open |
|  | v Darrington | 10-7 | Qualifying | Embassy World Championship |
|  | v Rempe | 10-4 | Qualifying | Embassy World Championship |
|  | v Martin | 10-7 | Qualifying | Embassy World Championship |
|  | v Thorne | 10-7 | 1st round | Embassy World Championship |
|  | v Longworth | 13-7 | 2nd round | Embassy World Championship |
|  | v Johnson | 12-13 | Quarter-final | Embassy World Championship |
|  | v White | 5-2 | Semi-final | Riley Hong Kong Masters (WS) |
|  | v S. Davis | 3-9 | Final | Riley Hong Kong Masters (WS) |
|  | v Dennis Taylor | 3-5 | 1st round | Carling Champions |
|  | v Johnson | 2-5 | 1st round | Langs Scottish Masters |
|  | v Gary Wilkinson | 5-4 | 3rd round | Fidelity International |
|  | v N. Foulds | 5-2 | 4th round | Fidelity International |
|  | v D. Gilbert | 5-0 | 5th round | Fidelity International |
|  | v O'Boye | 5-2 | Quarter-final | Fidelity International |
|  | v Thorburn | 1-9 | Semi-final | Fidelity International |
|  | v M. Bennett | 5-1 | 3rd round | Rothmans Grand Prix |
|  | v Chambers | 5-1 | 4th round | Rothmans Grand Prix |
|  | v S. Davis | 5-2 | 5th round | Rothmans Grand Prix |
|  | v Knowles | 5-2 | Quarter-final | Rothmans Grand Prix |
|  | v Parrott | 9-7 | Semi-final | Rothmans Grand Prix |
|  | **v Dennis Taylor** | **10-7** | **Final** | **Rothmans Grand Prix** |
|  | v Wych | 7-9 | 3rd round | Tennents UK Open |
| 1988 | v Werbeniuk | 5-2 | 3rd round | Mercantile Credit Classic |
|  | v Johnson | 5-3 | 4th round | Mercantile Credit Classic |
|  | v S. Francisco | 5-3 | 5th round | Mercantile Credit Classic |
|  | v S. Davis | 3-5 | Quarter-final | Mercantile Credit Classic |
|  | v Demarco | 6-0 | Quarter-final | Scottish Championship |
|  | v M. Gibson | 6-1 | Semi-final | Scottish Championship |
|  | **v Macleod** | **10-4** | **Final** | **Scottish Championship** |
|  | v Chappel | 5-1 | 3rd round | MIM Britannia British Open |
|  | v Griffiths | 5-1 | 4th round | MIM Britannia British Open |
|  | v T. Jones | 5-3 | 5th round | MIM Britannia British Open |
|  | v White | 5-4 | Quarter-final | MIM Britannia British Open |
|  | v Thorburn | 9-5 | Semi-final | MIM Britannia British Open |
|  | **v Hallett** | **13-2** | **Final** | **MIM Britannia British Open** |
|  | v Wright | 10-4 | Qualifying | Embassy World Championship |
|  | v Reynolds | 10-6 | 1st round | Embassy World Championship |
|  | v White | 12-13 | 2nd round | Embassy World Championship |
|  | v D. Morgan | 5-2 | 1st round | New Zealand Masters |
|  | v Johnson | 5-2 | Semi-final | New Zealand Masters |
|  | **v Hallett** | **6-1** | **Final** | **New Zealand Masters** |
|  | v Edmonds | 5-1 | 3rd round | Fidelity International |

|      |                  |       |              |                               |
|------|------------------|-------|--------------|-------------------------------|
|      | v Longworth      | 5-3   | 4th round    | Fidelity International        |
|      | v James          | 2-5   | 5th round    | Fidelity International        |
|      | v E. Hughes      | 5-1   | 1st round    | Fosters Professional          |
|      | v Hallett        | 5-8   | Final        | Fosters Professional          |
|      | v Williamson     | 5-2   | 3rd round    | Rothmans Grand Prix           |
|      | v Mountjoy       | 1-5   | 4th round    | Rothmans Grand Prix           |
|      | v S. Campbell    | 5-2   | 3rd round    | BCE Canadian Masters          |
|      | v Fowler         | 5-2   | 4th round    | BCE Canadian Masters          |
|      | v C. Wilson      | 5-1   | 5th round    | BCE Canadian Masters          |
|      | v Thorburn       | 5-4   | Quarter-final| BCE Canadian Masters          |
|      | v S. Davis       | 5-9   | Semi-final   | BCE Canadian Masters          |
|      | v Murphy         | 9-4   | 3rd round    | Tennents UK Open              |
|      | v Roscoe         | 9-3   | 4th round    | Tennents UK Open              |
|      | v Thorne         | 9-4   | 5th round    | Tennents UK Open              |
|      | v Thorburn       | 9-2   | Quarter-final| Tennents UK Open              |
|      | v Davis          | 9-3   | Semi-final   | Tennents UK Open              |
|      | v Mountjoy       | 12-16 | Final        | Tennents UK Open              |
|      | v Dennis Taylor  | 9-7   | Quarter-final| Everest World Matchplay       |
|      | v Parrott        | 6-9   | Semi-final   | Everest World Matchplay       |
| 1989 | v Murphy         | 5-2   | 3rd round    | Mercantile Credit Classic     |
|      | v Reardon        | 5-4   | 4th round    | Mercantile Credit Classic     |
|      | v Newbury        | 5-1   | 5th round    | Mercantile Credit Classic     |
|      | v Thorburn       | 4-5   | Quarter-final| Mercantile Credit Classic     |
|      | v Thorne         | 5-2   | 1st round    | Benson and Hedges Masters     |
|      | v Griffiths      | 5-3   | Quarter-final| Benson and Hedges Masters     |
|      | v S. Davis       | 6-3   | Semi-final   | Benson and Hedges Masters     |
|      | **v Parrott**    | **9-6** | **Final**  | **Benson and Hedges Masters** |
|      | v O'Boye         | 5-2   | 3rd round    | European Open                 |
|      | v Longworth      | 5-0   | 4th round    | European Open                 |
|      | v Hallett        | 3-5   | 5th round    | European Open                 |
|      | v Edwards        | 5-0   | 3rd round    | Anglian British Open          |
|      | v O'Kane         | 5-2   | 4th round    | Anglian British Open          |
|      | v Meo            | 3-5   | 5th round    | Anglian British Open          |
|      | v Griffiths      | 5-2   | Quarter-final| Benson and Hedges Irish Masters |
|      | v S. Davis       | 6-4   | Semi-final   | Benson and Hedges Irish Masters |
|      | v Higgins        | 8-9   | Final        | Benson and Hedges Irish Masters |
|      | v Gary Wilkinson | 10-9  | 1st round    | Embassy World Championship    |
|      | v Thorne         | 10-4  | 2nd round    | Embassy World Championship    |
|      | v Griffiths      | 13-5  | Quarter-final| Embassy World Championship    |
|      | v S. Davis       | 9-16  | Semi-final   | Embassy World Championship    |

## ALEX HIGGINS (Northern Ireland)

**Born** 18.3.49. **Turned professional** 1971. **World ranking** 24 (17). **Amateur career** 1968 Northern Ireland champion. **Best professional performances** Winner 1972 World Championship, 1982 Embassy World Championship, 1983 Coral UK Championship, 1978 and 1981 Benson & Hedges Masters, 1980 British Gold Cup, 1989 Benson and Hedges Irish Masters, 1983 and 1989 Irish Championship.

|      |                 |       |              |                      |
|------|-----------------|-------|--------------|----------------------|
| 1972 | v Gross         | 15-6  | Qualifying   | World Championship   |
|      | v Parkin        | 11-3  | Qualifying   | World Championship   |
|      | v Jack Rea      | 19-11 | 1st round    | World Championship   |
|      | v Pulman        | 31-23 | Quarter-final| World Championship   |
|      | v Williams      | 31-30 | Semi-final   | World Championship   |
|      | **v Spencer**   | **37-32** | **Final**| **World Championship** |
| 1973 | v Houlihan      | 16-3  | 2nd round    | World Championship   |
|      | v Davis         | 16-14 | Quarter-final| World Championship   |
|      | v Charlton      | 9-23  | Semi-final   | World Championship   |
|      | v Spencer       | 2-8   | Semi-final   | Norwich Union Open   |
| 1974 | v Bennett       | 15-4  | 2nd round    | World Championship   |
|      | v F. Davis      | 14-15 | Quarter-final| World Championship   |
|      | v Dennis Taylor | 5-1   | 1st round    | Norwich Union Open   |

| | | | | |
|---|---|---|---|---|
| | v Werbeniuk | 5-4 | Quarter-final | Norwich Union Open |
| | v Reardon | 8-9 | Semi-final | Norwich Union Open |
| 1975 | v Werbeniuk | 5-0 | 1st round | Benson & Hedges Masters |
| | v Williams | 3-5 | Quarter-final | Benson & Hedges Masters |
| | v David Taylor | 15-2 | 2nd round | World Championship |
| | v Williams | 19-12 | Quarter-final | World Championship |
| | v Reardon | 14-19 | Semi-final | World Championship |
| 1976 | v Miles | 1-4 | 2nd round | Benson & Hedges Masters |
| | v Thorburn | 15-14 | 1st round | Embassy World Championship |
| | v Spencer | 15-14 | Quarter-final | Embassy World Championship |
| | v Charlton | 20-18 | Semi-final | Embassy World Championship |
| | v Reardon | 16-27 | Final | Embassy World Championship |
| 1977 | v Mans | 4-2 | Quarter-final | Benson & Hedges Masters |
| | v Mountjoy | 3-5 | Semi-final | Benson & Hedges Masters |
| | v Mountjoy | 12-13 | 1st round | Embassy World Championship |
| | v David Taylor | 5-4 | 2nd round | Super Crystalate UK Championship |
| | v Dunning | 5-0 | Quarter-final | Super Crystalate UK Championship |
| | v Mountjoy | 2-9 | Semi-final | Super Crystalate UK Championship |
| 1978 | v Dennis Taylor | 4-3 | Quarter-final | Benson & Hedges Masters |
| | v Reardon | 5-1 | Semi-final | Benson & Hedges Masters |
| | **v Thorburn** | **7-5** | **Final** | **Benson & Hedges Masters** |
| | v Fagan | 12-13 | 1st round | Embassy World Championship |
| | v Meadowcroft | 9-6 | 1st round | Coral UK Championship |
| | v F. Davis | 9-4 | Quarter-final | Coral UK Championship |
| | v David Taylor | 5-9 | Semi-final | Coral UK Championship |
| 1979 | v Miles | 3-6 | Semi-final | Holsten Lager International |
| | v Charlton | 5-2 | Quarter-final | Benson & Hedges Masters |
| | v Mountjoy | 5-1 | Semi-final | Benson & Hedges Masters |
| | v Mans | 4-8 | Final | Benson & Hedges Masters |
| | v David Taylor | 13-5 | 1st round | Embassy World Championship |
| | v Griffiths | 12-13 | Quarter-final | Embassy World Championship |
| | v Houlihan | 9-3 | 3rd round | Coral UK Championship |
| | v Griffiths | 7-9 | Quarter-final | Coral UK Championship |
| 1980 | v F. Davis | 5-1 | 1st round | Benson & Hedges Masters |
| | v Mans | 5-1 | Quarter-final | Benson & Hedges Masters |
| | v Reardon | 5-2 | Semi-final | Benson & Hedges Masters |
| | v Griffiths | 5-9 | Final | Benson & Hedges Masters |
| | **v Reardon** | **5-1** | **Final** | **British Gold Cup** |
| | v Meo | 10-9 | 1st round | Embassy World Championship |
| | v Mans | 13-6 | 2nd round | Embassy World Championship |
| | v S. Davis | 13-9 | Quarter-final | Embassy World Championship |
| | v Stevens | 16-13 | Semi-final | Embassy World Championship |
| | v Thorburn | 16-18 | Final | Embassy World Championship |
| | v Thorne | 9-7 | 2nd round | Coral UK Championship |
| | v F. Davis | 9-6 | Quarter-final | Coral UK Championship |
| | v Reardon | 9-7 | Semi-final | Coral UK Championship |
| | v S. Davis | 6-16 | Final | Coral UK Championship |
| 1981 | v Mountjoy | 5-1 | Quarter-final | Benson & Hedges Masters |
| | v Thorburn | 6-5 | Semi-final | Benson & Hedges Masters |
| | **v Griffiths** | **9-6** | **Final** | **Benson & Hedges Masters** |
| | v Reardon | 5-6 | Semi-final | Benson & Hedges Irish Masters |
| | v S. Davis | 8-13 | 2nd round | Embassy World Championship |
| | v V. Harris | 5-3 | Quarter-final | Langs Scottish Masters |
| | v Thorburn | 2-6 | Semi-final | Langs Scottish Masters |
| | v Fagan | 5-3 | 2nd round | Jameson International |
| | v Mountjoy | 5-1 | 3rd round | Jameson International |
| | v Griffiths | 5-2 | Quarter-final | Jameson International |
| | v S. Davis | 8-9 | Semi-final | Jameson International |
| | v S. Davis | 2-5 | 1st round | Northern Ireland Classic |
| | v Martin | 9-7 | 2nd round | Coral UK Championship |
| | v David Taylor | 9-5 | 3rd round | Coral UK Championship |
| | v Meo | 4-9 | Quarter-final | Coral UK Championship |
| 1982 | v Dennis Taylor | 5-1 | 1st round | Lada Classic |

|  | v Griffiths | 1-5 | Semi-final | Lada Classic |
|---|---|---|---|---|
|  | v Charlton | 5-1 | Quarter-final | Benson & Hedges Masters |
|  | v Griffiths | 4-6 | Semi-final | Benson & Hedges Masters |
|  | v D. Hughes | 6-2 | Semi-final | Irish Championship |
|  | v Dennis Taylor | 13-16 | Final | Irish Championship |
|  | v Wych | 5-3 | 1st round | Benson & Hedges Irish Masters |
|  | v Thorburn | 5-4 | Quarter-final | Benson & Hedges Irish Masters |
|  | v S. Davis | 2-6 | Semi-final | Benson & Hedges Irish Masters |
|  | v Meadowcroft | 10-5 | 1st round | Embassy World Championship |
|  | v Mountjoy | 13-12 | 2nd round | Embassy World Championship |
|  | v Thorne | 13-10 | Quarter-final | Embassy World Championship |
|  | v White | 16-15 | Semi-final | Embassy World Championship |
|  | **v Reardon** | **18-15** | **Final** | **Embassy World Championship** |
|  | v Sinclair | 5-1 | 1st round | Langs Scottish Masters |
|  | v Griffiths | 6-5 | Semi-final | Langs Scottish Masters |
|  | v S. Davis | 4-9 | Final | Langs Scottish Masters |
|  | v Kelly | 5-3 | 1st round | Jameson International |
|  | v Griffiths | 2-5 | 2nd round | Jameson International |
|  | v French | 5-3 | 1st round | Professional Players Tournament |
|  | v Reardon | 2-5 | 2nd round | Professional Players Tournament |
|  | v Martin | 9-7 | 1st round | Coral UK Championship |
|  | v Reynolds | 9-8 | 2nd round | Coral UK Championship |
|  | v Spencer | 9-5 | Quarter-final | Coral UK Championship |
|  | v Reardon | 9-6 | Semi-final | Coral UK Championship |
|  | v Griffiths | 15-16 | Final | Coral UK Championship |
| 1983 | v Werbeniuk | 4-5 | 1st round | Lada Classic |
|  | v Werbeniuk | 4-5 | 1st round | Benson & Hedges Masters |
|  | v Jack Rea | 6-3 | Quarter-final | Irish Championship |
|  | v E. Hughes | 6-2 | Semi-final | Irish Championship |
|  | **v Dennis Taylor** | **16-11** | **Final** | **Irish Championship** |
|  | v White | 5-2 | Quarter-final | Benson & Hedges Irish Masters |
|  | v Reardon | 3-6 | Semi-final | Benson & Hedges Irish Masters |
|  | v Reynolds | 10-4 | 1st round | Embassy World Championship |
|  | v Thorne | 13-8 | 2nd round | Embassy World Championship |
|  | v Werbeniuk | 13-11 | Quarter-final | Embassy World Championship |
|  | v S. Davis | 5-16 | Semi-final | Embassy World Championship |
|  | v White | 5-3 | 1st round | Langs Supreme Scottish Masters |
|  | v S. Davis | 2-6 | Semi-final | Langs Supreme Scottish Masters |
|  | v Martin | 2-5 | 1st round | Jameson International |
|  | v Watterson | 2-5 | 1st round | Professional Players Tournament |
|  | v Macleod | 9-6 | 1st round | Coral UK Championship |
|  | v Medati | 9-1 | 2nd round | Coral UK Championship |
|  | v Knowles | 9-5 | Quarter-final | Coral UK Championship |
|  | v Griffiths | 9-4 | Semi-final | Coral UK Championship |
|  | **v S. Davis** | **16-15** | **Final** | **Coral UK Championship** |
| 1984 | v Fagan | 5-3 | Qualifying | Lada Classic |
|  | v Parrott | 2-5 | 1st round | Lada Classic |
|  | v Mountjoy | 5-2 | 1st round | Benson & Hedges Masters |
|  | v Knowles | 1-5 | Quarter-final | Benson & Hedges Masters |
|  | v Charlton | 5-2 | 1st round | Benson & Hedges Irish Masters |
|  | v Reardon | 5-2 | Quarter-final | Benson & Hedges Irish Masters |
|  | v S. Davis | 4-6 | Semi-final | Benson & Hedges Irish Masters |
|  | v N. Foulds | 9-10 | 1st round | Embassy World Championship |
|  | v Stevens | 5-2 | 1st round | Langs Supreme Scottish Masters |
|  | v S. Davis | 4-6 | Semi-final | Langs Supreme Scottish Masters |
|  | v Knowles | 3-5 | 1st round | Carlsberg Challenge |
|  | v Sinclair | 5-1 | 1st round | Jameson International |
|  | v Griffiths | 5-4 | 2nd round | Jameson International |
|  | v S. Davis | 1-5 | Quarter-final | Jameson International |
|  | v Bales | 5-1 | 1st round | Rothmans Grand Prix |
|  | v Hallett | 3-5 | 2nd round | Rothmans Grand Prix |
|  | v T. Jones | 9-7 | 1st round | Coral UK Open |
|  | v Williams | 9-7 | 2nd round | Coral UK Open |

|  | v Thorne | 9-5 | Quarter-final | Coral UK Open |
|---|---|---|---|---|
|  | v Thorburn | 9-7 | Semi-final | Coral UK Open |
|  | v S. Davis | 8-16 | Final | Coral UK Open |
| 1985 | v Gauvreau | 5-3 | 1st round | Mercantile Credit Classic |
|  | v S. Davis | 2-5 | 2nd round | Mercantile Credit Classic |
|  | v S. Davis | 5-4 | 1st round | Benson & Hedges Masters |
|  | v Griffiths | 1-5 | Quarter-final | Benson & Hedges Masters |
|  | v Bales | 6-3 | 1st round | Dulux British Open |
|  | v N. Foulds | 5-1 | 2nd round | Dulux British Open |
|  | v Thorburn | 5-2 | 3rd round | Dulux British Open |
|  | v E. Hughes | 5-2 | Quarter-final | Dulux British Open |
|  | v S. Francisco | 6-9 | Semi-final | Dulux British Open |
|  | v Griffiths | 5-2 | 1st round | Benson & Hedges Irish Masters |
|  | v Stevens | 5-3 | Quarter-final | Benson & Hedges Irish Masters |
|  | v S. Davis | 6-2 | Semi-final | Benson & Hedges Irish Masters |
|  | v White | 5-9 | Final | Benson & Hedges Irish Masters |
|  | v Burke | 6-0 | Quarter-final | Irish Championship |
|  | v Fagan | 6-3 | Semi-final | Irish Championship |
|  | v Dennis Taylor | 5-10 | Final | Irish Championship |
|  | v Reynolds | 10-4 | 1st round | Embassy World Championship |
|  | v Griffiths | 7-13 | 2nd round | Embassy World Championship |
|  | v Thorburn | 5-4 | Semi-final | Carlsberg Challenge |
|  | v White | 3-8 | Final | Carlsberg Challenge |
|  | v White | 0-5 | 1st round | Langs Scottish Masters |
|  | v D. Hughes | 5-1 | 3rd round | Goya Matchroom Trophy |
|  | v Murphy | 5-2 | 4th round | Goya Matchroom Trophy |
|  | v Dennis Taylor | 1-5 | 5th round | Goya Matchroom Trophy |
|  | v V. Harris | 5-1 | 3rd round | Rothmans Grand Prix |
|  | v N. Foulds | 5-3 | 4th round | Rothmans Grand Prix |
|  | v S. Davis | 0-5 | 5th round | Rothmans Grand Prix |
|  | v Edmonds | 9-8 | 3rd round | Coral UK Open |
|  | v F. Davis | 9-2 | 4th round | Coral UK Open |
|  | v White | 6-9 | 5th round | Coral UK Open |
|  | v Thorburn | 5-4 | 1st round | Kit Kat |
|  | v S. Davis | 1-6 | Semi-final | Kit Kat |
| 1986 | v Fisher | 5-0 | 3rd round | Mercantile Credit Classic |
|  | v Cripsey | 5-2 | 4th round | Mercantile Credit Classic |
|  | v Dennis Taylor | 5-4 | 5th round | Mercantile Credit Classic |
|  | v Williams | 2-5 | Quarter-final | Mercantile Credit Classic |
|  | v Dennis Taylor | 5-1 | 1st round | BCE Belgian Classic |
|  | v Stevens | 4-5 | Semi-final | BCE Belgian Classic |
|  | v Griffiths | 4-5 | 1st round | Benson & Hedges Masters |
|  | v Bradley | 5-3 | 3rd round | Dulux British Open |
|  | v Hallett | 5-1 | 4th round | Dulux British Open |
|  | v P. Francisco | 5-2 | 5th round | Dulux British Open |
|  | v Werbeniuk | 5-1 | Quarter-final | Dulux British Open |
|  | v S. Davis | 3-9 | Semi-final | Dulux British Open |
|  | v Meo | 4-5 | 1st round | Benson & Hedges Irish Masters |
|  | v Spencer | 10-7 | 1st round | Embassy World Championship |
|  | v Griffiths | 12-13 | 2nd round | Embassy World Championship |
|  | v J. McLaughlin | 6-2 | Quarter-final | Strongbow Irish Championship |
|  | v E. Hughes | 6-2 | Semi-final | Strongbow Irish Championship |
|  | v Dennis Taylor | 7-10 | Final | Strongbow Irish Championship |
|  | v White | 1-5 | 1st round | Carlsberg Challenge |
|  | v Johnson | 5-2 | 1st round | Langs Scottish Masters |
|  | v Stevens | 6-2 | Semi-final | Langs Scottish Masters |
|  | v Thorburn | 8-9 | Final | Langs Scottish Masters |
|  | v Sinclair | 5-3 | 3rd round | BCE International |
|  | v P. Francisco | 4-5 | 4th round | BCE International |
|  | v F. Davis | 5-0 | 3rd round | Rothmans Grand Prix |
|  | v Martin | 5-2 | 4th round | Rothmans Grand Prix |
|  | v Williams | 1-5 | 5th round | Rothmans Grand Prix |
|  | v Johnson | 5-3 | 1st round | BCE Canadian Masters |

|      |                  |       |              |                              |
|------|------------------|-------|--------------|------------------------------|
|      | v S. Davis       | 2-8   | Semi-final   | BCE Canadian Masters         |
|      | v Hendry         | 9-8   | 3rd round    | Tennents UK Open             |
|      | v Martin         | 9-6   | 4th round    | Tennents UK Open             |
|      | v Hallett        | 9-7   | 5th round    | Tennents UK Open             |
|      | v W. Jones       | 9-5   | Quarter-final | Tennents UK Open            |
|      | v S. Davis       | 3-9   | Semi-final   | Tennents UK Open             |
| 1987 | v Roscoe         | 5-2   | 3rd round    | Mercantile Credit Classic    |
|      | v Parrott        | 2-5   | 4th round    | Mercantile Credit Classic    |
|      | v Griffiths      | 5-4   | 1st round    | Benson & Hedges Masters      |
|      | v Johnson        | 5-1   | Quarter-final | Benson & Hedges Masters     |
|      | v Meo            | 6-2   | Semi-final   | Benson & Hedges Masters      |
|      | v Dennis Taylor  | 8-9   | Final        | Benson & Hedges Masters      |
|      | v J. McLaughlin  | 4-5   | 3rd round    | Dulux British Open           |
|      | v Griffiths      | 1-5   | 1st round    | Benson & Hedges Irish Masters |
|      | v Wright         | 10-6  | 1st round    | Embassy World Championship   |
|      | v Griffiths      | 10-13 | 2nd round    | Embassy World Championship   |
|      | v White          | 3-5   | 1st round    | Langs Scottish Masters       |
|      | v Duggan         | 9-4   | 3rd round    | Tennents UK Open             |
|      | v David Taylor   | 9-6   | 4th round    | Tennents UK Open             |
|      | v S. Davis       | 2-9   | 5th round    | Tennents UK Open             |
| 1988 | v T. Jones       | 5-0   | 3rd round    | Mercantile Credit Classic    |
|      | v S. Davis       | 0-5   | 4th round    | Mercantile Credit Classic    |
|      | v Knowles        | 5-4   | 1st round    | Benson & Hedges Masters      |
|      | v Hallett        | 2-5   | 2nd round    | Benson & Hedges Masters      |
|      | v O'Boye         | 4-6   | Quarter-final | Irish Championship          |
|      | v T. Jones       | 3-5   | 3rd round    | MIM Britannia British Open   |
|      | v Dennis Taylor  | 5-3   | 1st round    | Benson & Hedges Irish Masters |
|      | v Thorburn       | 5-3   | Quarter-final | Benson & Hedges Irish Masters |
|      | v Davis          | 2-6   | Semi-final   | Benson & Hedges Irish Masters |
|      | v Drago          | 2-10  | 1st round    | Embassy World Championship   |
|      | v Macleod        | 2-5   | 3rd round    | Fidelity International        |
|      | v Roe            | 5-4   | 3rd round    | Rothmans Grand Prix          |
|      | v O'Kane         | 5-0   | 4th round    | Rothmans Grand Prix          |
|      | v N. Foulds      | 5-3   | 5th round    | Rothmans Grand Prix          |
|      | v Williams       | 5-4   | Quarter-final | Rothmans Grand Prix         |
|      | v Robidoux       | 9-7   | Semi-final   | Rothmans Grand Prix          |
|      | v S. Davis       | 6-10  | Final        | Rothmans Grand Prix          |
|      | v Clark          | 3-5   | 3rd round    | BCE Canadian Masters         |
|      | v Dodd           | 9-7   | 3rd round    | Tennents UK Open             |
|      | v Knowles        | 6-9   | 4th round    | Tennents UK Open             |
| 1989 | v Macleod        | 5-2   | 3rd round    | Mercantile Credit Classic    |
|      | v Johnson        | 0-5   | 4th round    | Mercantile Credit Classic    |
|      | v Dodd           | 5-2   | 3rd round    | European Open                |
|      | v Thorne         | 1-5   | 4th round    | European Open                |
|      | v Watchorn       | 5-2   | Quarter-final | Irish Championship          |
|      | v E. Hughes      | 6-2   | Semi-final   | Irish Championship           |
|      | **v J. McLaughlin** | **9-7** | **Final** | **Irish Championship**    |
|      | v Foldvari       | 5-1   | 3rd round    | Anglian British Open         |
|      | v S. Davis       | 0-5   | 4th round    | Anglian British Open         |
|      | v Thorburn       | 5-4   | 1st round    | Benson and Hedges Irish Masters |
|      | v N. Foulds      | 5-2   | Quarter-final | Benson and Hedges Irish Masters |
|      | v Parrott        | 6-4   | Semi-final   | Benson and Hedges Irish Masters |
|      | **v Hendry**     | **9-8** | **Final**  | **Benson and Hedges Irish Masters** |
|      | v D. Morgan      | 8-10  | Qualifying   | Embassy World Championship   |

## PAT HOULIHAN (England)

**Born** 7.11.29. **Turned professional** 1969. **World ranking** 81 (59). **Amateur career** 1965 English champion. **Best professional performance** Last 32 1987 Rothmans Grand Prix.

| 1972 | v Dunning | 10-11 | Qualifying | World Championship |
|------|-----------|-------|------------|--------------------|

| 1973 | v Jack Rea | 9-2 | 1st round | World Championship |
|---|---|---|---|---|
| | v Higgins | 3-16 | 2nd round | World Championship |
| 1977 | v Meadowcroft | 1-5 | 1st round | Super Crystalate UK |
| 1978 | v Ross | 9-1 | Prelim | Embassy World Championship |
| | v Meadowcroft | 9-6 | Qualifying | Embassy World Championship |
| | v Thorburn | 8-13 | 1st round | Embassy World Championship |
| | v Andrewartha | 3-9 | Qualifying | Coral UK Championship |
| 1979 | v Barrie | 9-5 | Prelim | Embassy World Championship |
| | v Mountjoy | 6-9 | Qualifying | Embassy World Championship |
| | v Jack Rea | 9-3 | 2nd round | Coral UK Championship |
| | v Higgins | 3-9 | 3rd round | Coral UK Championship |
| 1980 | v Meo | 1-9 | Qualifying | Embassy World Championship |
| | v Meo | 1-9 | 1st round | Coral UK Championship |
| 1981 | v Spencer | 1-9 | 1st round | John Courage English |
| | v French | 3-5 | Qualifying | Jameson International |
| | v Kennerley | 9-1 | Qualifying | Coral UK Championship |
| | v Black | 9-4 | Qualifying | Coral UK Championship |
| | v Meadowcroft | 9-4 | Qualifying | Coral UK Championship |
| | v Miles | 3-9 | 2nd round | Coral UK Championship |
| 1982 | v Anderson | 9-5 | Qualifying | Embassy World Championship |
| | v Martin | 3-9 | Qualifying | Embassy World Championship |
| | v E. McLaughlin | 2-5 | Qualifying | Jameson International |
| | v Knowles | 4-5 | 1st round | Professional Players Tournament |
| | v Mountjoy | 3-9 | 1st round | Coral UK Championship |
| 1983 | v Murphy | 9-10 | Qualifying | Embassy World Championship |
| | v Scott | 0-5 | Qualifying | Jameson International |
| | v Sheehan | 2-5 | Qualifying | Professional Players Tournament |
| | v V. Harris | 6-9 | Qualifying | Coral UK Championship |
| 1984 | v Williamson | 5-10 | Qualifying | Embassy World Championship |
| | v Hargreaves | 2-5 | Qualifying | Jameson International |
| | v Everton | 3-5 | Qualifying | Rothmans Grand Prix |
| | v Chappel | 3-9 | Qualifying | Coral UK Open |
| 1985 | v Foldvari | 1-5 | Qualifying | Mercantile Credit Classic |
| | v T. Jones | 1-9 | Qualifying | Tolly Cobbold English Championship |
| | v Bear | 2-5 | 1st round | Goya Matchroom Trophy |
| | v Robinson | 5-0 | 1st round | Rothmans Grand Prix |
| | v T. Jones | 4-5 | 2nd round | Rothmans Grand Prix |
| | v Watson | 9-4 | 1st round | Coral UK Open |
| | v Newbury | 3-9 | 2nd round | Coral UK Open |
| 1986 | v Bennett | 5-0 | 1st round | Mercantile Credit Classic |
| | v Foldvari | 5-4 | 2nd round | Mercantile Credit Classic |
| | v Reynolds | 1-5 | 3rd round | Mercantile Credit Classic |
| | v Hargreaves | 9-5 | 1st round | Tolly Cobbold English Championship |
| | v Dunning | wo | 2nd round | Tolly Cobbold English Championship |
| | v Spencer | 5-9 | 3rd round | Tolly Cobbold English Championship |
| | v Longworth | 3-5 | 2nd round | Dulux British Open |
| | v Sheehan | 7-10 | Qualifying | Embassy World Championship |
| | v Chalmers | 5-1 | 1st round | BCE International |
| | v Cripsey | 5-1 | 2nd round | BCE International |
| | v Meo | 5-4 | 3rd round | BCE International |
| | v E. Hughes | 1-5 | 4th round | BCE International |
| | v Grace | 1-5 | 1st round | Rothmans Grand Prix |
| 1987 | v Owers | 1-5 | 1st round | Mercantile Credit Classic |
| | v N. Gilbert | 4-5 | 1st round | Dulux British Open |
| | v Wright | 4-10 | Qualifying | Embassy World Championship |
| | v D. Gilbert | 3-5 | 2nd round | Fidelity International |
| | v Heaton | 5-0 | 2nd round | Rothmans Grand Prix |
| | v Reynolds | 5-4 | 3rd round | Rothmans Grand Prix |
| | v Chaperon | 0-5 | 4th round | Rothmans Grand Prix |
| | v Miles | 3-9 | 2nd round | Tennents UK Open |
| 1988 | v James | 2-5 | 2nd round | Mercantile Credit Classic |
| | v Marshall | 4-6 | 2nd round | English Championship |
| | v Bear | 0-5 | 2nd round | MIM Britannia British Open |

|      |                |       |             |                             |
|------|----------------|-------|-------------|-----------------------------|
|      | v Cripsey      | 4-10  | Qualifying  | Embassy World Championship  |
|      | v Robidoux     | 2-5   | 2nd round   | Fidelity International       |
|      | v John Rea     | 5-1   | 2nd round   | Rothmans Grand Prix         |
|      | v Charlton     | 3-5   | 3rd round   | Rothmans Grand Prix         |
|      | v M. Smith     | 2-5   | 2nd round   | BCE Canadian Masters        |
|      | v Roscoe       | 8-9   | 2nd round   | Tennents UK Open            |
| 1989 | v Darrington   | 4-5   | 2nd round   | Mercantile Credit Classic   |
|      | v Sinclair     | 1-5   | 2nd round   | European Open               |
|      | v Fitzmaurice  | 5-4   | 2nd round   | English Championship        |
|      | v Hallett      | 2-5   | 3rd round   | English Championship        |
|      | v Terry        | 5-2   | 2nd round   | Anglian British Open        |
|      | v John Rea     | 5-10  | Qualifying  | Embassy World Championship  |

## DENNIS HUGHES (England)
**Born** 30.1.37. **Turned professional** 1981. **World ranking** 108 (111).

|      |                |       |             |                                    |
|------|----------------|-------|-------------|------------------------------------|
| 1981 | v Jack Rea     | 5-4   | Qualifying  | Jameson International              |
|      | v Demarco      | 1-5   | Qualifying  | Jameson International              |
|      | v Hallett      | 6-9   | Qualifying  | Coral UK Championship              |
| 1982 | v Higgins      | 2-6   | Semi-final  | Irish Championship                 |
|      | v Everton      | 9-4   | Qualifying  | Embassy World Championship         |
|      | v Meo          | 4-9   | Qualifying  | Embassy World Championship         |
|      | v Edmonds      | 0-5   | Qualifying  | Jameson International              |
|      | v Charlton     | 2-5   | 1st round   | Professional Players Tournament    |
|      | v Meadowcroft  | 8-9   | Qualifying  | Coral UK Championship              |
| 1983 | v Parkin       | 5-0   | Qualifying  | Jameson International              |
|      | v Johnson      | 1-5   | Qualifying  | Jameson International              |
|      | v Medati       | 1-5   | Qualifying  | Professional Players Tournament    |
|      | v Medati       | 2-9   | Qualifying  | Coral UK Championship              |
| 1984 | v Parrott      | 3-10  | Qualifying  | Embassy World Championship         |
|      | v Oliver       | 4-5   | Qualifying  | Jameson International              |
|      | v Dunning      | 0-5   | Qualifying  | Rothmans Grand Prix                |
|      | v G. Foulds    | 7-9   | Qualifying  | Coral UK Open                      |
| 1985 | v Watchorn     | 0-5   | Prelim      | Mercantile Credit Classic          |
|      | v Watterson    | 9-5   | Qualifying  | Tolly Cobbold English Championship |
|      | v N. Foulds    | 3-9   | 1st round   | Tolly Cobbold English Championship |
|      | v Mikkelsen    | 0-6   | Qualifying  | Dulux British Open                 |
|      | v French       | 10-5  | Qualifying  | Embassy World Championship         |
|      | v Newbury      | 9-10  | Qualifying  | Embassy World Championship         |
|      | v Kearney      | 5-1   | 1st round   | Goya Matchroom Trophy              |
|      | v Gauvreau     | 5-4   | 2nd round   | Goya Matchroom Trophy              |
|      | v Higgins      | 1-5   | 3rd round   | Goya Matchroom Trophy              |
|      | v Bennett      | 5-4   | 1st round   | Rothmans Grand Prix                |
|      | v Morra        | 2-5   | 2nd round   | Rothmans Grand Prix                |
|      | v Kearney      | 9-8   | 1st round   | Coral UK Open                      |
|      | v King         | 0-9   | 2nd round   | Coral UK Open                      |
| 1986 | v Burke        | 3-5   | 1st round   | Mercantile Credit Classic          |
|      | v F. Davis     | 6-9   | 2nd round   | Tolly Cobbold English Championship |
|      | v Hendry       | 1-5   | 1st round   | Dulux British Open                 |
|      | v Agrawal      | 6-10  | Qualifying  | Embassy World Championship         |
|      | v Roe          | 2-5   | 1st round   | BCE International                  |
|      | v Jack Rea     | 2-5   | 1st round   | Rothmans Grand Prix                |
|      | v Ellis        | 9-6   | 1st round   | Tennents UK Open                   |
|      | v Murphy       | 0-9   | 2nd round   | Tennents UK Open                   |
| 1987 | v Wright       | 2-5   | 1st round   | Mercantile Credit Classic          |
|      | v P. Gibson    | 3-6   | 1st round   | Tolly Ales English Championship    |
|      | v Whitthread   | 1-5   | 1st round   | Dulux British Open                 |
|      | v Parkin       | 10-5  | Qualifying  | Embassy World Championship         |
|      | v B. Harris    | 2-10  | Qualifying  | Embassy World Championship         |
|      | v Rowswell     | 1-5   | 1st round   | Fidelity International             |
|      | v Donnelly     | 1-5   | 1st round   | Rothmans Grand Prix                |
|      | v Edmonds      | 4-9   | 2nd round   | Tennents UK Open                   |

| | | | | |
|---|---|---|---|---|
| **1988** | v Williamson | 5-3 | 1st round | Mercantile Credit Classic |
| | v Chappel | 3-5 | 2nd round | Mercantile Credit Classic |
| | v Fitzmaurice | 6-1 | 1st round | English Championship |
| | v Wildman | 6-0 | 2nd round | English Championship |
| | v Williams | 1-6 | 3rd round | English Championship |
| | v Fagan | 5-4 | 1st round | MIM Britannia British Open |
| | v F. Davis | 2-5 | 2nd round | MIM Britannia British Open |
| | v Miles | 3-10 | Qualifying | Embassy World Championship |
| | v Rigitano | 5-4 | 1st round | Fidelity International |
| | v Stevens | 2-5 | 2nd round | Fidelity International |
| | v Mikkelsen | 4-5 | 1st round | Rothmans Grand Prix |
| | v M. Gibson | 1-5 | 1st round | BCE Canadian Masters |
| | v Morra | 2-9 | 1st round | Tennents UK Open |
| **1989** | v O'Boye | 5-1 | 2nd round | Mercantile Credit Classic |
| | v Mountjoy | 0-5 | 3rd round | Mercantile Credit Classic |
| | v Williamson | 1-5 | 1st round | European Open |
| | v Whitthread | 1-5 | 1st round | English Championship |
| | v M. Smith | 1-5 | 1st round | Anglian British Open |
| | v John Rea | 3-10 | Qualifying | Embassy World Championship |

## EUGENE HUGHES (Republic of Ireland)

**Born** 4.11.55. **Turned professional** 1981. **World ranking** 27 (21). **Amateur career** 1978, 1979 Republic of Ireland champion. **Best professional performances** Semi-finals 1984 Jameson International, 1986 BCE International.

| | | | | |
|---|---|---|---|---|
| **1981** | v M. Owen | 5-1 | Qualifying | Jameson International |
| | v Fitzmaurice | 5-3 | Qualifying | Jameson International |
| | v Sinclair | 5-2 | Qualifying | Jameson International |
| | v Edmonds | 4-5 | 1st round | Jameson International |
| **1982** | v Mountjoy | 4-5 | 1st round | Benson & Hedges Irish Masters |
| | v Jack Rea | 6-1 | Quarter-final | Irish Championship |
| | v Higgins | 2-6 | Semi-final | Irish Championship |
| | v Knowles | 7-9 | Qualifying | Embassy World Championship |
| | v Parkin | 5-2 | Qualifying | Jameson International |
| | v Martin | 5-4 | Qualifying | Jameson International |
| | v Reardon | 3-5 | 1st round | Jameson International |
| | v Stevens | 2-5 | 1st round | Professional Players Tournament |
| **1983** | v Burke | 6-2 | Quarter-final | Irish Championship |
| | v Higgins | 2-6 | Semi-final | Irish Championship |
| | v Fitzmaurice | 10-7 | Qualifying | Embassy World Championship |
| | v Sinclair | 10-8 | Qualifying | Embassy World Championship |
| | v Reardon | 7-10 | 1st round | Embassy World Championship |
| | v Fisher | 5-4 | Qualifying | Jameson International |
| | v G. Foulds | 5-1 | Qualifying | Jameson International |
| | v S. Davis | 1-5 | 1st round | Jameson International |
| | v Sinclair | 5-4 | 1st round | Professional Players Tournament |
| | v Werbeniuk | 5-0 | 2nd round | Professional Players Tournament |
| | v Griffiths | 5-2 | 3rd round | Professional Players Tournament |
| | v Thorne | 1-5 | Quarter-final | Professional Players Tournament |
| **1984** | v Knowles | 1-5 | Qualifying | Lada Classic |
| | v Dennis Taylor | 1-5 | 1st round | Benson & Hedges Irish Masters |
| | v Mifsud | 5-10 | Qualifying | Embassy World Championship |
| | v Roscoe | 5-1 | Qualifying | Jameson International |
| | v Mountjoy | 5-1 | 1st round | Jameson International |
| | v Reardon | 5-1 | 2nd round | Jameson International |
| | v Thorne | 5-2 | Quarter-final | Jameson International |
| | v S. Davis | 3-9 | Semi-final | Jameson International |
| | v John Rea | 4-5 | 1st round | Rothmans Grand Prix |
| | v Morra | 9-8 | Qualifying | Coral UK Open |
| | v Meo | 4-9 | 1st round | Coral UK Open |
| **1985** | v Newbury | 5-3 | Qualifying | Mercantile Credit Classic |

|  | v Meo | 5-4 | 1st round | Mercantile Credit Classic |
|---|---|---|---|---|
|  | v Reardon | 1-5 | 2nd round | Mercantile Credit Classic |
|  | v Watchorn | 6-4 | 1st round | Dulux British Open |
|  | v B. Harris | 5-4 | 2nd round | Dulux British Open |
|  | v Macleod | 5-2 | 3rd round | Dulux British Open |
|  | v Higgins | 2-5 | Quarter-final | Dulux British Open |
|  | v Reardon | 5-0 | 1st round | Benson & Hedges Irish Masters |
|  | v S. Davis | 4-5 | Quarter-final | Benson & Hedges Irish Masters |
|  | v Kelly | 6-2 | Quarter-final | Irish Championship |
|  | v Dennis Taylor | 5-6 | Semi-final | Irish Championship |
|  | v Newbury | 10-6 | Qualifying | Embassy World Championship |
|  | v Reardon | 9-10 | 1st round | Embassy World Championship |
|  | v Murphy | 3-5 | 3rd round | Goya Matchroom Trophy |
|  | v Simngam | 5-1 | 3rd round | Rothmans Grand Prix |
|  | v Meo | 3-5 | 4th round | Rothmans Grand Prix |
|  | v West | 3-9 | 3rd round | Coral UK Open |
| 1986 | v Wych | 5-2 | 3rd round | Mercantile Credit Classic |
|  | v F. Davis | 5-3 | 4th round | Mercantile Credit Classic |
|  | v Johnson | 1-5 | 5th round | Mercantile Credit Classic |
|  | v Longworth | 4-5 | 3rd round | Dulux British Open |
|  | v Reardon | 5-2 | 1st round | Benson & Hedges Irish Masters |
|  | v Thorburn | 1-5 | Quarter-final | Benson & Hedges Irish Masters |
|  | v Murphy | 10-7 | Qualifying | Embassy World Championship |
|  | v David Taylor | 10-7 | 1st round | Embassy World Championship |
|  | v Thorburn | 6-13 | 2nd round | Embassy World Championship |
|  | v Sheehan | 5-0 | 1st round | Strongbow Irish Championship |
|  | v Burke | 6-3 | Quarter-final | Strongbow Irish Championship |
|  | v Higgins | 2-6 | Semi-final | Strongbow Irish Championship |
|  | v Chappel | 5-4 | 3rd round | BCE International |
|  | v Houlihan | 5-1 | 4th round | BCE International |
|  | v Chaperon | 5-0 | 5th round | BCE International |
|  | v S. Davis | 5-4 | Quarter-final | BCE International |
|  | v N. Foulds | 8-9 | Semi-final | BCE International |
|  | v Hendry | 1-5 | 3rd round | Rothmans Grand Prix |
|  | v Roscoe | 9-8 | 3rd round | Tennents UK Open |
|  | v Reardon | 9-5 | 4th round | Tennents UK Open |
|  | v W. Jones | 5-9 | 5th round | Tennents UK Open |
| 1987 | v Wright | 4-5 | 3rd round | Mercantile Credit Classic |
|  | v V. Harris | 5-0 | 3rd round | Dulux British Open |
|  | v Johnson | 3-5 | 4th round | Dulux British Open |
|  | v Dennis Taylor | 4-5 | 1st round | Benson & Hedges Irish Masters |
|  | v Medati | 10-2 | Qualifying | Embassy World Championship |
|  | v Johnson | 9-10 | 1st round | Embassy World Championship |
|  | v Watchorn | 5-2 | 1st round | Matchroom Irish Championship |
|  | v Kearney | 6-1 | Quarter-final | Matchroom Irish Championship |
|  | v O'Boye | 3-6 | Semi-final | Matchroom Irish Championship |
|  | v Owers | 5-4 | 3rd round | Fidelity International |
|  | v Wych | 5-4 | 4th round | Fidelity International |
|  | v S. Francisco | 5-4 | 5th round | Fidelity International |
|  | v Thorburn | 1-5 | Quarter-final | Fidelity International |
|  | v Fisher | 4-5 | 3rd round | Rothmans Grand Prix |
|  | v N. Gilbert | 9-7 | 3rd round | Tennents UK Open |
|  | v White | 4-9 | 4th round | Tennents UK Open |
| 1988 | v Newbury | 1-5 | 3rd round | Mercantile Credit Classic |
|  | v Watchorn | 2-5 | 1st round | Irish Championship |
|  | v Cripsey | 3-5 | 3rd round | MIM Britannia British Open |
|  | v Johnson | 4-5 | 1st round | Benson & Hedges Irish Masters |
|  | v James | 6-10 | Qualifying | Embassy World Championship |
|  | v Meakin | 5-0 | 3rd round | Fidelity International |
|  | v White | 1-5 | 4th round | Fidelity International |
|  | v Hendry | 1-5 | 1st round | Fosters Professional |
|  | v Clark | 5-3 | 3rd round | Rothmans Grand Prix |
|  | v Johnson | 5-2 | 4th round | Rothmans Grand Prix |

| | v Griffiths | 2-5 | 5th round | Rothmans Grand Prix |
|---|---|---|---|---|
| | v M. Bennett | 2-5 | 3rd round | BCE Canadian Masters |
| | v O'Boye | 8-9 | 3rd round | Tennents UK Open |
| 1989 | v Miles | 5-2 | 3rd round | Mercantile Credit Classic |
| | v W. Jones | 1-5 | 4th round | Mercantile Credit Classic |
| | v Morra | 5-1 | 3rd round | European Open |
| | v Clark | 1-5 | 4th round | European Open |
| | v Kearney | 5-1 | Quarter-final | Irish Championship |
| | v Higgins | 2-6 | Semi-final | Irish Championship |
| | v W. Jones | 5-2 | 3rd round | Anglian British Open |
| | v Johnston-Allen | 2-5 | 4th round | Anglian British Open |
| | v Rowswell | 10-9 | Qualifying | Embassy World Championship |
| | v Dennis Taylor | 3-10 | 1st round | Embassy World Championship |

## STEVE JAMES (England)

**Born** 2.5.61. **Turned professional** 1986. **World ranking** 16 (32). **Best professional performances** Semi-finals 1988 Fidelity International; quarter-finals 1988 Embassy World Championship.

| | | | | |
|---|---|---|---|---|
| 1986 | v N. Gilbert | 5-2 | 1st round | BCE International |
| | v Edmonds | 2-5 | 2nd round | BCE International |
| | v Morra | 3-5 | 1st round | Rothmans Grand Prix |
| | v Rigitano | 9-5 | 1st round | Tennents UK Open |
| | v King | 8-9 | 2nd round | Tennents UK Open |
| 1987 | v Jonik | 4-5 | 1st round | Mercantile Credit Classic |
| | v Hargreaves | 6-5 | 1st round | Tolly Ales English Championship |
| | v F. Davis | 6-2 | 2nd round | Tolly Ales English Championship |
| | v Longworth | 6-2 | 3rd round | Tolly Ales English Championship |
| | v Johnson | 3-6 | 4th round | Tolly Ales English Championship |
| | v Darrington | 5-3 | 1st round | Dulux British Open |
| | v Miles | 5-2 | 2nd round | Dulux British Open |
| | v J. Campbell | 5-1 | 3rd round | Dulux British Open |
| | v Williams | 2-5 | 4th round | Dulux British Open |
| | v Watterson | 10-2 | Qualifying | Embassy World Championship |
| | v Edmonds | 1-10 | Qualifying | Embassy World Championship |
| | v B. Harris | 5-0 | 2nd round | Fidelity International |
| | v J. Campbell | 5-4 | 3rd round | Fidelity International |
| | v Row | 3-5 | 4th round | Fidelity International |
| | v G. Foulds | 5-0 | 2nd round | Rothmans Grand Prix |
| | v Johnson | 4-5 | 3rd round | Rothmans Grand Prix |
| | v T. Jones | 6-9 | 2nd round | Tennents UK Open |
| 1988 | v Houlihan | 5-2 | 2nd round | Mercantile Credit Classic |
| | v White | 1-5 | 3rd round | Mercantile Credit Classic |
| | v Greaves | 5-6 | 1st round | English Championship |
| | v King | 5-2 | 2nd round | MIM Britannia British Open |
| | v Charlton | 5-2 | 3rd round | MIM Britannia British Open |
| | v White | 1-5 | 4th round | MIM Britannia British Open |
| | v O'Boye | 10-7 | Qualifying | Embassy World Championship |
| | v Browne | 10-1 | Qualifying | Embassy World Championship |
| | v E. Hughes | 10-6 | Qualifying | Embassy World Championship |
| | v Williams | 10-6 | 1st round | Embassy World Championship |
| | v Johnson | 13-9 | 2nd round | Embassy World Championship |
| | v Thorburn | 11-13 | Quarter-final | Embassy World Championship |
| | v Wright | 5-3 | 3rd round | Fidelity International |
| | v Macleod | 5-2 | 4th round | Fidelity International |
| | v Hendry | 5-2 | 5th round | Fidelity International |
| | v Meo | 5-1 | Quarter-final | Fidelity International |
| | v S. Davis | 1-9 | Semi-final | Fidelity International |
| | v M. Smith | 5-3 | 3rd round | Rothmans Grand Prix |
| | v Hallett | 2-5 | 4th round | Rothmans Grand Prix |
| | v Murphy | 5-3 | 3rd round | BCE Canadian Masters |

*Steve James*

|  | v Johnson | 5-4 | 4th round | BCE Canadian Masters |
|  | v S. Davis | 0-5 | 5th round | BCE Canadian Masters |
|  | v Kearney | 9-1 | 3rd round | Tennents UK Open |
|  | v Thorburn | 6-9 | 4th round | Tennents UK Open |
| 1989 | v Gary Wilkinson | 5-1 | 3rd round | Mercantile Credit Classic |
|  | v Browne | 4-5 | 4th round | Mercantile Credit Classic |
|  | v Johnston-Allen | 1-5 | 3rd round | European Open |
|  | v Cripsey | 3-5 | 3rd round | English Championship |
|  | v Chappel | 3-5 | 3rd round | Anglian British Open |
|  | v John Rea | 10-7 | Qualifying | Embassy World Championship |
|  | v Parrott | 9-10 | 1st round | Embassy World Championship |

## GREG JENKINS (Australia)

**Turned professional** 1985. **World ranking** 120 (104).

| 1985 | v Wilkinson | 2-6 | 1st round | Australian Championship |
|  | v Burke | 9-5 | 1st round | Coral UK Open |
|  | v Bradley | 3-9 | 2nd round | Coral UK Open |
| 1986 | v Watterson | 2-5 | 2nd round | Mercantile Credit Classic |
|  | v Demarco | 5-1 | 1st round | Dulux British Open |
|  | v Meadowcroft | 5-2 | 2nd round | Dulux British Open |
|  | v Wildman | 4-5 | 3rd round | Dulux British Open |
|  | v Gibson | 4-10 | Qualifying | Embassy World Championship |
|  | v Foldvari | 3-6 | 2nd round | Australian Championship |
|  | v Everton | 5-3 | 1st round | BCE International |
|  | v Gauvreau | 1-5 | 2nd round | BCE International |
|  | v Kearney | 3-5 | 1st round | Rothmans Grand Prix |
|  | v Mienie | 9-6 | 1st round | Tennents UK Open |
|  | v O'Kane | 5-9 | 2nd round | Tennents UK Open |
| 1987 | v Parkin | 5-2 | 1st round | Mercantile Credit Classic |
|  | v Scott | 5-4 | 2nd round | Mercantile Credit Classic |
|  | v S. Davis | 0-5 | 3rd round | Mercantile Credit Classic |
|  | v Rowswell | 1-5 | 1st round | Dulux British Open |
|  | v Grace | 10-9 | Qualifying | Embassy World Championship |
|  | v Murphy | 4-10 | Qualifying | Embassy World Championship |
|  | v King | 4-6 | Quarter-final | Australian Championship |
|  | v Whitthread | 5-1 | 1st round | Fidelity International |
|  | v Wych | 4-5 | 2nd round | Fidelity International |
|  | v Anderson | 2-5 | 1st round | Rothmans Grand Prix |
|  | v Gary Wilkinson | 3-9 | 1st round | Tennents UK Open |
| 1988 | v A. Harris | 4-5 | 1st round | Mercantile Credit Classic |
|  | v J. Smith | 5-3 | 1st round | MIM Britannia British Open |
|  | v O'Boye | 1-5 | 2nd round | MIM Britannia British Open |
|  | v P. Morgan | 5-3 | 2nd round | Australian Championship |
|  | v Charlton | 0-5 | Quarter-final | Australian Championship |
|  | v Wildman | 5-1 | 1st round | Fidelity International |
|  | v Owers | 1-5 | 2nd round | Fidelity International |
|  | v Bear | 5-4 | 1st round | Rothmans Grand Prix |
|  | v O'Boye | 1-5 | 2nd round | Rothmans Grand Prix |
|  | v Wildman | 1-5 | 1st round | BCE Canadian Masters |
|  | v Rowswell | 4-9 | 1st round | Tennents UK Open |
| 1989 | v Williamson | 2-5 | 1st round | Mercantile Credit Classic |
|  | v Miles | 3-5 | 1st round | European Open |
|  | v Meadowcroft | 4-5 | 1st round | Anglian British Open |

## JOE JOHNSON (England)

**Born** 29.7.52. **Turned professional** 1979. **World ranking** 11 (11). **Amateur career** Runner-up 1978 World Championship. **Best professional performances** Winner 1986 Embassy World Championship; runner-up 1987 Embassy World Championship.

| | | | | |
|---|---|---|---|---|
| **1979** | v Werbeniuk | 3-9 | 2nd round | Coral UK Championship |
| **1980** | v Dunning | 9-6 | Qualifying | Coral UK Championship |
| | v Fagan | 4-9 | 1st round | Coral UK Championship |
| **1981** | v Knowles | 9-2 | Qualifying | John Courage English |
| | Johnson | *wo* | 1st round | John Courage English |
| | v Edmonds | 5-9 | 2nd round | John Courage English |
| | v Meo | 8-9 | Qualifying | Embassy World Championship |
| | v Donnelly | 5-4 | Qualifying | Jameson International |
| | v Macleod | 5-1 | Qualifying | Jameson International |
| | v Wych | 5-2 | 1st round | Jameson International |
| | v Miles | 3-5 | 2nd round | Jameson International |
| | v Murphy | 9-1 | Qualifying | Coral UK Championship |
| | v Watterson | 9-3 | Qualifying | Coral UK Championship |
| | v Wilson | 9-5 | Qualifying | Coral UK Championship |
| | v Spencer | 9-5 | 2nd round | Coral UK Championship |
| | v Reardon | 7-9 | 3rd round | Coral UK Championship |
| **1982** | v Harris | 9-4 | Qualifying | Embassy World Championship |
| | v Hallett | 8-9 | Qualifying | Embassy World Championship |
| | v Wilson | 4-5 | Qualifying | Jameson International |
| | v Miles | 5-1 | 1st round | Professional Players Tournament |
| | v Stevens | 5-1 | 2nd round | Professional Players Tournament |
| | v Wildman | 5-4 | 3rd round | Professional Players Tournament |
| | v Virgo | 1-5 | Quarter-final | Professional Players Tournament |
| | v V. Harris | 9-8 | Qualifying | Coral UK Championship |
| | v Griffiths | 1-9 | 1st round | Coral UK Championship |
| **1983** | v Thorburn | 2-5 | 1st round | Benson & Hedges Masters |
| | v Watchorn | 10-0 | Qualifying | Embassy World Championship |
| | v Wilson | 8-10 | Qualifying | Embassy World Championship |
| | v D. Hughes | 5-1 | Qualifying | Jameson International |
| | v Charlton | 2-5 | 1st round | Jameson International |
| | v Burke | 5-3 | 1st round | Professional Players Tournament |
| | v White | 5-3 | 2nd round | Professional Players Tournament |
| | v Charlton | 5-0 | 3rd round | Professional Players Tournament |
| | v Thorburn | 5-1 | Quarter-final | Professional Players Tournament |
| | v Meo | 9-6 | Semi-final | Professional Players Tournament |
| | v Knowles | 8-9 | Final | Professional Players Tournament |
| | v Gibson | 9-6 | Qualifying | Coral UK Championship |
| | v Virgo | 9-6 | 1st round | Coral UK Championship |
| | v David Taylor | 9-3 | 2nd round | Coral UK Championship |
| | v Griffiths | 2-9 | Quarter-final | Coral UK Championship |
| **1984** | v Spencer | 4-5 | Qualifying | Lada Classic |
| | v Gibson | 10-3 | Qualifying | Embassy World Championship |
| | v Dennis Taylor | 1-10 | 1st round | Embassy World Championship |
| | v Morra | 5-0 | Qualifying | Jameson International |
| | v Charlton | 5-1 | 1st round | Jameson International |
| | v Dennis Taylor | 2-5 | 2nd round | Jameson International |
| | v Medati | 5-1 | 1st round | Rothmans Grand Prix |
| | v Williamson | 4-5 | 2nd round | Rothmans Grand Prix |
| | v John Rea | 9-6 | Qualifying | Coral UK Open |
| | v Spencer | 9-6 | 1st round | Coral UK Open |
| | v Stevens | 2-9 | 2nd round | Coral UK Open |
| **1985** | v Edmonds | 5-4 | Qualifying | Mercantile Credit Classic |
| | v Knowles | 5-1 | 1st round | Mercantile Credit Classic |
| | v Wilson | 5-0 | 2nd round | Mercantile Credit Classic |
| | v King | 5-3 | Quarter-final | Mercantile Credit Classic |
| | v Thorburn | 2-9 | Semi-final | Mercantile Credit Classic |
| | v Scott | 9-1 | 1st round | Tolly Cobbold English Championship |
| | v Virgo | 4-9 | 2nd round | Tolly Cobbold English Championship |
| | v W. Jones | 5-6 | 1st round | Dulux British Open |
| | v G. Foulds | 10-6 | Qualifying | Embassy World Championship |
| | v Werbeniuk | 8-10 | 1st round | Embassy World Championship |
| | v White | 4-5 | Quarter-final | Winfield Australian Masters |
| | v Bear | 5-1 | 3rd round | Goya Matchroom Trophy |

|        |  |  |  |  |
|--------|----------|-------|-------|------------|
|        | v Bradley | 5-2 | 4th round | Goya Matchroom Trophy |
|        | v Wilson | 5-1 | 5th round | Goya Matchroom Trophy |
|        | v N. Foulds | 2-5 | Quarter-final | Goya Matchroom Trophy |
|        | v Gilbert | 5-2 | 3rd round | Rothmans Grand Prix |
|        | v Hallett | 5-4 | 4th round | Rothmans Grand Prix |
|        | v Thorburn | 1-5 | 5th round | Rothmans Grand Prix |
|        | v Simngam | 9-4 | 3rd round | Coral UK Open |
|        | v N. Foulds | 8-9 | 4th round | Coral UK Open |
| 1986   | v B. Harris | 5-4 | 3rd round | Mercantile Credit Classic |
|        | v Mans | 5-2 | 4th round | Mercantile Credit Classic |
|        | v E. Hughes | 5-1 | 5th round | Mercantile Credit Classic |
|        | v Thorburn | 4-5 | Quarter-final | Mercantile Credit Classic |
|        | v Thorburn | 3-5 | 1st round | Benson & Hedges Masters |
|        | v Fowler | 9-7 | 3rd round | Tolly Cobbold English Championship |
|        | v Spencer | 9-7 | 4th round | Tolly Cobbold English Championship |
|        | v Hallett | 6-9 | Quarter-final | Tolly Cobbold English Championship |
|        | v J. McLaughlin | 5-2 | 3rd round | Dulux British Open |
|        | v Werbeniuk | 5-2 | 4th round | Dulux British Open |
|        | v Martin | 10-3 | 1st round | Embassy World Championship |
|        | v Hallett | 13-6 | 2nd round | Embassy World Championship |
|        | v Griffiths | 13-12 | Quarter-final | Embassy World Championship |
|        | v Knowles | 16-8 | Semi-final | Embassy World Championship |
|        | **v S. Davis** | **18-12** | **Final** | **Embassy World Championship** |
|        | v Dennis Taylor | 3-5 | 1st round | Carlsberg Challenge |
|        | v Higgins | 2-5 | 1st round | Langs Scottish Masters |
|        | v Murphy | 5-4 | 3rd round | BCE International |
|        | v David Taylor | 3-5 | 4th round | BCE International |
|        | v Browne | 2-5 | 3rd round | Rothmans Grand Prix |
|        | v Higgins | 3-5 | 1st round | BCE Canadian Masters |
|        | v Parrott | 1-9 | 3rd round | Tennents UK Open |
| 1987   | v Sinclair | 5-0 | 3rd round | Mercantile Credit Classic |
|        | v P. Francisco | 3-5 | 4th round | Mercantile Credit Classic |
|        | v Reardon | 5-2 | 1st round | Benson & Hedges Masters |
|        | v Higgins | 1-5 | Quarter-final | Benson & Hedges Masters |
|        | v Miles | 6-3 | 3rd round | Tolly Ales English Championship |
|        | v James | 6-2 | 4th round | Tolly Ales English Championship |
|        | v Williams | 6-5 | Quarter-final | Tolly Ales English Championship |
|        | v Dodd | 5-9 | Semi-final | Tolly Ales English Championship |
|        | v Drago | 5-0 | 3rd round | Dulux British Open |
|        | v E. Hughes | 5-3 | 4th round | Dulux British Open |
|        | v Spencer | 3-5 | 5th round | Dulux British Open |
|        | v Griffiths | 0-5 | Quarter-final | Benson & Hedges Irish Masters |
|        | v E. Hughes | 10-9 | 1st round | Embassy World Championship |
|        | v Macleod | 13-7 | 2nd round | Embassy World Championship |
|        | v Hendry | 13-12 | Quarter-final | Embassy World Championship |
|        | v N. Foulds | 16-9 | Semi-final | Embassy World Championship |
|        | v S. Davis | 14-18 | Final | Embassy World Championship |
|        | v N. Foulds | 5-4 | 1st round | Carling Champions |
|        | v Dennis Taylor | 5-8 | Final | Carling Champions |
|        | v Hendry | 5-2 | 1st round | Langs Scottish Masters |
|        | v Thorburn | 6-3 | Semi-final | Langs Scottish Masters |
|        | **v Griffiths** | **9-7** | **Final** | **Langs Scottish Masters** |
|        | v Wych | 4-5 | 3rd round | Fidelity International |
|        | v James | 5-4 | 3rd round | Rothmans Grand Prix |
|        | v P. Francisco | 2-5 | 4th round | Rothmans Grand Prix |
|        | v Thorburn | 3-5 | 1st round | Labatts Canadian Masters (WS) |
|        | v Bear | 9-5 | 3rd round | Tennents UK Open |
|        | v West | 9-6 | 4th round | Tennents UK Open |
|        | v Chappel | 9-4 | 5th round | Tennents UK Open |
|        | v Hallett | 9-7 | Quarter-final | Tennents UK Open |
|        | v White | 4-9 | Semi-final | Tennents UK Open |
| 1988   | v Chappel | 5-2 | 3rd round | Mercantile Credit Classic |
|        | v Hendry | 3-5 | 4th round | Mercantile Credit Classic |

*Joe Johnson*

| | | | |
|---|---|---|---|
| v Thorne | 5-4 | 1st round | Benson & Hedges Masters |
| v White | 5-3 | Quarter-final | Benson & Hedges Masters |
| v S. Davis | 3-6 | Semi-final | Benson & Hedges Masters |
| v J. Smith | 6-5 | 3rd round | English Championship |
| v Martin | 6-4 | 4th round | English Championship |
| v Knowles | 6-4 | Quarter-final | English Championship |
| v Reynolds | 8-9 | Semi-final | English Championship |
| v Lawlor | 5-1 | 3rd round | MIM Britannia British Open |
| v Rowswell | 5-2 | 4th round | MIM Britannia British Open |
| v O'Kane | 2-5 | 5th round | MIM Britannia British Open |
| v E. Hughes | 5-4 | 1st round | Benson & Hedges Irish Masters |
| v S. Davis | 0-5 | Quarter-final | Benson & Hedges Irish Masters |
| v C. Wilson | 10-7 | 1st round | Embassy World Championship |
| v James | 9-13 | 2nd round | Embassy World Championship |
| v Reynolds | 5-4 | 1st round | New Zealand Masters |
| v Hendry | 2-5 | 2nd round | New Zealand Masters |
| v Knowles | 5-4 | Play-off for 3rd | New Zealand Masters |
| v Cripsey | 5-3 | 3rd round | Fidelity International |
| v Mountjoy | 5-4 | 4th round | Fidelity International |
| v Newbury | 5-2 | 5th round | Fidelity International |
| v Reynolds | 1-5 | Quarter-final | Fidelity International |
| v Bradley | 5-2 | 3rd round | Rothmans Grand Prix |
| v E. Hughes | 2-5 | 4th round | Rothmans Grand Prix |
| v Robidoux | 5-1 | 3rd round | BCE Canadian Masters |
| v James | 4-5 | 4th round | BCE Canadian Masters |
| v M. Smith | 9-2 | 3rd round | Tennents UK Open |
| v Williams | 9-7 | 4th round | Tennents UK Open |
| v Mountjoy | 5-9 | 5th round | Tennents UK Open |
| v Thorburn | 9-4 | 1st round | Everest World Matchplay |
| v Parrott | 7-9 | Quarter-final | Everest World Matchplay |
| 1989 v Sheehan | 5-2 | 3rd round | Mercantile Credit Classic |
| v Higgins | 5-0 | 4th round | Mercantile Credit Classic |
| v Clark | 3-5 | 5th round | Mercantile Credit Classic |
| v Thorburn | 2-5 | 1st round | Benson and Hedges Masters |
| v Cripsey | 5-2 | 3rd round | European Open |
| v Roe | 5-2 | 4th round | European Open |
| v Clark | 4-5 | 5th round | European Open |
| v D. Gilbert | 5-2 | 3rd round | English Championship |
| v Edwards | 5-0 | 4th round | English Championship |
| v Parrott | 4-5 | Quarter-final | English Championship |
| v Whitthread | 5-2 | 3rd round | Anglian British Open |
| v Drago | 5-3 | 4th round | Anglian British Open |
| v Johnston-Allen | 5-2 | 5th round | Anglian British Open |
| v Reynolds | 4-5 | Quarter-final | Anglian British Open |
| v Meo | 5-10 | 1st round | Embassy World Championship |

## MARK JOHNSTON-ALLEN (England)

**Born** 28.12.68. **Turned professional** 1988. **World ranking** 52. **Best professional performance** Last 16 Anglian British Open.

| | | | |
|---|---|---|---|
| 1988 v Scott | 5-2 | 1st round | Fidelity International |
| v D. Gilbert | 5-3 | 2nd round | Fidelity International |
| v O'Kane | 3-5 | 3rd round | Fidelity International |
| v Roscoe | 5-1 | 1st round | Rothmans Grand Prix |
| v Browne | 5-2 | 2nd round | Rothmans Grand Prix |
| v Spencer | 3-5 | 3rd round | Rothmans Grand Prix |
| v B. Harris | 5-4 | 1st round | BCE Canadian Masters |
| v N. Gilbert | 4-5 | 2nd round | BCE Canadian Masters |
| v Van Rensberg | 9-4 | 1st round | Tennents UK Open |
| v W. Jones | 8-9 | 2nd round | Tennents UK Open |
| 1989 v Scott | 5-0 | 1st round | Mercantile Credit Classic |

| v Chappel | 2-5 | 2nd round | Mercantile Credit Classic |
|---|---|---|---|
| v Donnelly | 5-3 | 1st round | European Open |
| v Wright | 5-4 | 2nd round | European Open |
| v James | 5-1 | 3rd round | European Open |
| v Wych | 4-5 | 4th round | European Open |
| v B. Bennett | 5-2 | Prelim | English Championship |
| v Price | 4-5 | 1st round | English Championship |
| v V. Harris | 5-1 | 1st round | Anglian British Open |
| v Edmonds | 5-4 | 2nd round | Anglian British Open |
| v Griffiths | 5-1 | 3rd round | Anglian British Open |
| v E. Hughes | 5-2 | 4th round | Anglian British Open |
| v Johnson | 2-5 | 5th round | Anglian British Open |
| v E. McLaughlin | 10-3 | Qualifying | Embassy World Championship |
| v Rigitano | 10-3 | Qualifying | Embassy World Championship |
| v Wych | 3-10 | Qualifying | Embassy World Championship |

## TONY JONES (England)

**Born** 15.4.60. **Turned professional** 1983. **World ranking** 62 (49). **Amateur career** 1983 English champion. **Best professional performance** Last 16 1988 MIM Britannia British Open.

| 1983 | v Oliver | 5-2 | Qualifying | Professional Players Tournament |
|---|---|---|---|---|
| | v Werbeniuk | 4-5 | 1st round | Professional Players Tournament |
| | v Sinclair | 9-3 | Qualifying | Coral UK Championship |
| | v Knowles | 5-9 | 1st round | Coral UK Championship |
| 1984 | v King | 9-10 | Qualifying | Embassy World Championship |
| | v French | 5-1 | Qualifying | Jameson International |
| | v Duggan | 2-5 | Qualifying | Jameson International |
| | v Sinclair | 5-4 | Qualifying | Rothmans Grand Prix |
| | v Griffiths | 5-3 | 1st round | Rothmans Grand Prix |
| | v N. Foulds | 0-5 | 2nd round | Rothmans Grand Prix |
| | v Chaperon | 9-1 | Qualifying | Coral UK Open |
| | v Fagan | 9-2 | Qualifying | Coral UK Open |
| | v Wildman | 9-2 | Qualifying | Coral UK Open |
| | v Higgins | 7-9 | 1st round | Coral UK Open |
| 1985 | v Greaves | 5-2 | Qualifying | Mercantile Credit Classic |
| | v Gibson | 5-0 | Qualifying | Mercantile Credit Classic |
| | v Dodd | 5-1 | Qualifying | Mercantile Credit Classic |
| | v S. Francisco | 1-5 | Qualifying | Mercantile Credit Classic |
| | v Houlihan | 9-1 | Qualifying | Tolly Cobbold English Championship |
| | v Williams | 6-9 | 1st round | Tolly Cobbold English Championship |
| | v G. Foulds | 6-0 | Qualifying | Dulux British Open |
| | v White | 5-6 | 1st round | Dulux British Open |
| | v Darrington | 10-2 | Qualifying | Embassy World Championship |
| | v Duggan | 10-8 | Qualifying | Embassy World Championship |
| | v Fitzmaurice | 10-4 | Qualifying | Embassy World Championship |
| | v Sinclair | 10-2 | Qualifying | Embassy World Championship |
| | v Knowles | 8-10 | 1st round | Embassy World Championship |
| | v Kelly | 5-3 | 2nd round | Goya Matchroom Trophy |
| | v David Taylor | 4-5 | 3rd round | Goya Matchroom Trophy |
| | v Houlihan | 5-4 | 2nd round | Rothmans Grand Prix |
| | v Meo | 2-5 | 3rd round | Rothmans Grand Prix |
| | v Jonik | 9-4 | 2nd round | Coral UK Open |
| | v Griffiths | 5-9 | 3rd round | Coral UK Open |
| 1986 | v Gilbert | 5-3 | 2nd round | Mercantile Credit Classic |
| | v Thorne | 5-3 | 3rd round | Mercantile Credit Classic |
| | v Werbeniuk | 3-5 | 4th round | Mercantile Credit Classic |
| | v B. Harris | 9-5 | 2nd round | Tolly Cobbold English Championship |
| | v Virgo | 7-9 | 3rd round | Tolly Cobbold English Championship |
| | v O'Boye | 5-2 | 2nd round | Dulux British Open |
| | v S. Francisco | 2-5 | 3rd round | Dulux British Open |

|  | v V. Harris | 10-7 | Qualifying | Embassy World Championship |
|---|---|---|---|---|
|  | v Gilbert | 7-10 | Qualifying | Embassy World Championship |
|  | v Burke | 4-5 | 2nd round | BCE International |
|  | v Smith | 5-0 | 2nd round | Rothmans Grand Prix |
|  | v White | 0-5 | 3rd round | Rothmans Grand Prix |
|  | v Fitzmaurice | 9-0 | 2nd round | Tennents UK Open |
|  | v West | 9-4 | 3rd round | Tennents UK Open |
|  | v Knowles | 2-9 | 4th round | Tennents UK Open |
| 1987 | v Oliver | 5-0 | 2nd round | Mercantile Credit Classic |
|  | v Parrott | 2-5 | 3rd round | Mercantile Credit Classic |
|  | v Oliver | 6-1 | 2nd round | Tolly Ales English Championship |
|  | v Williams | 4-6 | 3rd round | Tolly Ales English Championship |
|  | v Donnelly | 5-2 | 2nd round | Dulux British Open |
|  | v Macleod | 5-4 | 3rd round | Dulux British Open |
|  | v Griffiths | 3-5 | 4th round | Dulux British Open |
|  | v Chalmers | 10-1 | Qualifying | Embassy World Championship |
|  | v Van Rensberg | 10-0 | Qualifying | Embassy World Championship |
|  | v Virgo | 9-10 | Qualifying | Embassy World Championship |
|  | v P. Gibson | 4-5 | 2nd round | Fidelity International |
|  | v Roscoe | 5-1 | 2nd round | Rothmans Grand Prix |
|  | v Thorburn | 2-5 | 3rd round | Rothmans Grand Prix |
|  | v James | 9-6 | 2nd round | Tennents UK Open |
|  | v Hallett | 2-9 | 3rd round | Tennents UK Open |
| 1988 | v A. Harris | 5-2 | 2nd round | Mercantile Credit Classic |
|  | v Higgins | 0-5 | 3rd round | Mercantile Credit Classic |
|  | v J. Smith | 0-5 | 2nd round | English Championship |
|  | v Fitzmaurice | 5-3 | 2nd round | MIM Britannia British Open |
|  | v Higgins | 5-3 | 3rd round | MIM Britannia British Open |
|  | v Chaperon | 5-4 | 4th round | MIM Britannia British Open |
|  | v Hendry | 3-5 | 5th round | MIM Britannia British Open |
|  | v Foldvari | 9-10 | Qualifying | Embassy World Championship |
|  | v Foldvari | 5-4 | 2nd round | Fidelity International |
|  | v Reynolds | 4-5 | 3rd round | Fidelity International |
|  | v Mikkelsen | 5-3 | 2nd round | Rothmans Grand Prix |
|  | v Hallett | 2-5 | 3rd round | Rothmans Grand Prix |
|  | v D. Morgan | 0-5 | 2nd round | BCE Canadian Masters |
|  | v Scott | 9-5 | 2nd round | Tennents UK Open |
|  | v West | 5-9 | 3rd round | Tennents UK Open |
| 1989 | v Bradley | 4-5 | 2nd round | Mercantile Credit Classic |
|  | v Medati | 5-2 | 2nd round | European Open |
|  | v C. Wilson | 3-5 | 3rd round | European Open |
|  | v A. Harris | 3-5 | 2nd round | English Championship |
|  | v Meadowcroft | 5-1 | 2nd round | Anglian British Open |
|  | v O'Kane | 4-5 | 3rd round | Anglian British Open |
|  | v J. Smith | 10-7 | Qualifying | Embassy World Championship |
|  | v Stevens | 10-2 | Qualifying | Embassy World Championship |
|  | v Meo | 7-10 | Qualifying | Embassy World Championship |

## WAYNE JONES (Wales)

**Born** 24.12.59. **Turned professional** 1984. **World ranking** 31 (34). **Amateur career** 1983 Welsh champion. **Best professional performance** Runner-up 1989 Mercantile Credit Classic.

| 1984 | v Watchorn | 5-0 | Qualifying | Jameson International |
|---|---|---|---|---|
|  | v Gibson | 5-2 | Qualifying | Jameson International |
|  | v Scott | 5-0 | Qualifying | Jameson International |
|  | v Wildman | 5-0 | Qualifying | Jameson International |
|  | v David Taylor | 4-5 | 1st round | Jameson International |
|  | v Watterson | 5-3 | Qualifying | Rothmans Grand Prix |
|  | v J. Campbell | 4-5 | 1st round | Rothmans Grand Prix |
|  | v O'Kane | 7-9 | Qualifying | Coral UK Open |

| | | | |
|---|---|---|---|
| **1985** v O'Kane | 5-0 | Qualifying | Mercantile Credit Classic |
| v Duggan | 0-5 | Qualifying | Mercantile Credit Classic |
| v Donnelly | 6-1 | Qualifying | Dulux British Open |
| v Johnson | 6-5 | 1st round | Dulux British Open |
| v Chaperon | 2-5 | 2nd round | Dulux British Open |
| v Jack Rea | 10-3 | Qualifying | Embassy World Championship |
| v Dunning | 10-6 | Qualifying | Embassy World Championship |
| v Watterson | 10-5 | Qualifying | Embassy World Championship |
| v Miles | 10-8 | Qualifying | Embassy World Championship |
| v White | 4-10 | 1st round | Embassy World Championship |
| v Newbury | 2-6 | 1st round | BCE Welsh Championship |
| v Smith | 5-3 | 2nd round | Goya Matchroom Trophy |
| v Parrott | 3-5 | 3rd round | Goya Matchroom Trophy |
| v John Rea | 5-0 | 2nd round | Rothmans Grand Prix |
| v Thorne | 5-0 | 3rd round | Rothmans Grand Prix |
| v P. Francisco | 3-5 | 4th round | Rothmans Grand Prix |
| v Fitzmaurice | 9-3 | 2nd round | Coral UK Open |
| v Virgo | 7-9 | 3rd round | Coral UK Open |
| **1986** v Van Rensberg | 4-5 | 2nd round | Mercantile Credit Classic |
| v Everton | 6-2 | 1st round | Zetters Welsh Championship |
| v Reardon | 6-4 | Quarter-final | Zetters Welsh Championship |
| v Mountjoy | 7-9 | Semi-final | Zetters Welsh Championship |
| v Rigitano | 5-1 | 2nd round | Dulux British Open |
| v Mans | 2-5 | 3rd round | Dulux British Open |
| v Grace | 10-3 | Qualifying | Embassy World Championship |
| v Hendry | 8-10 | Qualifying | Embassy World Championship |
| v Jack Rea | 5-1 | 2nd round | BCE International |
| v Reardon | 4-5 | 3rd round | BCE International |
| v Foldvari | 5-3 | 2nd round | Rothmans Grand Prix |
| v David Taylor | 5-1 | 3rd round | Rothmans Grand Prix |
| v S. Francisco | 4-5 | 4th round | Rothmans Grand Prix |
| v Hargreaves | 9-0 | 2nd round | Tennents UK Open |
| v J. Campbell | 9-3 | 3rd round | Tennents UK Open |
| v Dennis Taylor | 9-2 | 4th round | Tennents UK Open |
| v E. Hughes | 9-5 | 5th round | Tennents UK Open |
| v Higgins | 5-9 | Quarter-final | Tennents UK Open |
| **1987** v Everton | 5-0 | 2nd round | Mercantile Credit Classic |
| v Dennis Taylor | 5-2 | 3rd round | Mercantile Credit Classic |
| v Kearney | 5-1 | 4th round | Mercantile Credit Classic |
| v Wilson | 3-5 | 5th round | Mercantile Credit Classic |
| v M. Bennett | 6-3 | 1st round | Matchroom Welsh Championship |
| v Griffiths | 2-6 | Quarter-final | Matchroom Welsh Championship |
| v Gilbert | 3-5 | 2nd round | Dulux British Open |
| v Donnelly | 10-3 | Qualifying | Embassy World Championship |
| v M. Bennett | 3-10 | Qualifying | Embassy World Championship |
| v Dunning | 5-1 | 2nd round | Fidelity International |
| v Reynolds | 5-4 | 3rd round | Fidelity International |
| v N. Gilbert | 4-5 | 4th round | Fidelity International |
| v Donnelly | 5-3 | 2nd round | Rothmans Grand Prix |
| v Stevens | 1-5 | 3rd round | Rothmans Grand Prix |
| v Meakin | 9-1 | 2nd round | Tennents UK Open |
| v Wilson | 6-9 | 3rd round | Tennents UK Open |
| **1988** v Roscoe | 4-5 | 2nd round | Mercantile Credit Classic |
| v Reardon | 6-5 | Quarter-final | Welsh Championship |
| v Mountjoy | 9-5 | Semi-final | Welsh Championship |
| v Griffiths | 3-9 | Final | Welsh Championship |
| v John Rea | 5-3 | 2nd round | MIM Britannia British Open |
| v J. Campbell | 3-5 | 3rd round | MIM Britannia British Open |
| v Glen Wilkinson | 10-4 | Qualifying | Embassy World Championship |
| v Morra | 10-8 | Qualifying | Embassy World Championship |
| v Martin | 10-5 | Qualifying | Embassy World Championship |
| v N. Foulds | 7-10 | 1st round | Embassy World Championship |
| v M. Smith | 5-2 | 2nd round | Fidelity International |

|      | v S. Davis | 1-5 | 3rd round | Fidelity International |
|------|------------|-----|-----------|----------------------|
|      | v Rigitano | 5-3 | 2nd round | Rothmans Grand Prix |
|      | v J. Campbell | 5-2 | 3rd round | Rothmans Grand Prix |
|      | v White | 1-5 | 4th round | Rothmans Grand Prix |
|      | v Roscoe | 4-5 | 3rd round | BCE Canadian Masters |
|      | v Johnston-Allen | 9-8 | 2nd round | Tennents UK Open |
|      | v Mountjoy | 7-9 | 3rd round | Tennents UK Open |
| 1989 | v Rowswell | 5-3 | 2nd round | Mercantile Credit Classic |
|      | v White | 5-3 | 3rd round | Mercantile Credit Classic |
|      | v E. Hughes | 5-1 | 4th round | Mercantile Credit Classic |
|      | v David Taylor | 5-3 | 5th round | Mercantile Credit Classic |
|      | v Parrott | 5-4 | Quarter-final | Mercantile Credit Classic |
|      | v Thorne | 9-4 | Semi-final | Mercantile Credit Classic |
|      | v Mountjoy | 11-13 | Final | Mercantile Credit Classic |
|      | v Newbury | 5-6 | Quarter-final | Senator Welsh Championship |
|      | v Rowswell | 5-0 | 2nd round | Anglian British Open |
|      | v E. Hughes | 2-5 | 3rd round | Anglian British Open |
|      | v A. Harris | 10-4 | Qualifying | Embassy World Championship |
|      | v Wych | 10-9 | Qualifying | Embassy World Championship |
|      | v David Taylor | 10-7 | Qualifying | Embassy World Championship |
|      | v N. Foulds | 10-9 | 1st round | Embassy World Championship |
|      | v Reynolds | 3-13 | 2nd round | Embassy World Championship |

## FRANK JONIK (Canada)

**Born** 2.12.57. **Turned professional** 1979. **World ranking** 127 (106).

|      | v Wildman | 9-7 | Qualifying | Embassy World Championship |
|------|-----------|-----|------------|----------------------------|
| 1980 | v Wildman | 9-7 | Qualifying | Embassy World Championship |
|      | v Wilson | 6-9 | Qualifying | Embassy World Championship |
| 1981 | v Hallett | 1-9 | Qualifying | Embassy World Championship |
| 1982 | v John Bear | 4-9 | Qualifying | Embassy World Championship |
|      | v Hallett | 2-5 | Qualifying | Jameson International |
|      | v Mountjoy | 5-3 | 1st round | Professional Players Tournament |
|      | v Meo | 0-5 | 2nd round | Professional Players Tournament |
| 1983 | v Edmonds | 4-10 | Qualifying | Embassy World Championship |
|      | v Chaperon | 9-4 | 2nd round | Canadian Championship |
|      | v Wych | 9-5 | Quarter-final | Canadian Championship |
|      | v Thorburn | 9-6 | Semi-final | Canadian Championship |
|      | **v Stevens** | **8-9** | **Final** | **Canadian Championship** |
|      | v Wildman | 4-5 | 1st round | Professional Players Tournament |
| 1984 | v Mikkelsen | 9-10 | Qualifying | Embassy World Championship |
|      | v J. McLaughlin | 5-2 | Qualifying | Jameson International |
|      | v Gauvreau | 1-5 | Qualifying | Jameson International |
|      | v Bradley | 1-5 | Qualifying | Rothmans Grand Prix |
|      | v Newbury | 3-9 | Qualifying | Coral UK Open |
| 1985 | v G. Foulds | 2-5 | Qualifying | Mercantile Credit Classic |
|      | v J. McLaughlin | 6-2 | Qualifying | Dulux British Open |
|      | v Spencer | 0-6 | 1st round | Dulux British Open |
|      | v O'Kane | 5-10 | Qualifying | Embassy World Championship |
|      | v Mikkelsen | 6-4 | Quarter-final | Canadian Championship |
|      | v Chaperon | 3-6 | Semi-final | Canadian Championship |
|      | v Newbury | 4-5 | 2nd round | Goya Matchroom Trophy |
|      | v Fowler | 4-5 | 2nd round | Rothmans Grand Prix |
|      | v T. Jones | 4-9 | 2nd round | Coral UK Open |
| 1986 | v P. Francisco | 2-5 | 2nd round | Mercantile Credit Classic |
|      | v Dodd | 4-5 | 2nd round | Dulux British Open |
|      | v Chaperon | 8-10 | Qualifying | Embassy World Championship |
|      | v Rigitano | 6-1 | 1st round | Canadian Championship |
|      | v Chaperon | 6-3 | 2nd round | Canadian Championship |
|      | v Thorburn | 3-6 | Semi-final | Canadian Championship |
|      | v Miles | 1-5 | 2nd round | Rothmans Grand Prix |
|      | v Wilkinson | 8-9 | 1st round | Tennents UK Open |
| 1987 | v James | 5-4 | 1st round | Mercantile Credit Classic |

|        | v Drago     | 5-2 | 2nd round     | Mercantile Credit Classic       |
|--------|-------------|-----|---------------|---------------------------------|
|        | v West      | 4-5 | 3rd round     | Mercantile Credit Classic       |
|        | v Owers     | 4-5 | 1st round     | Dulux British Open              |
|        | v Morra     | 2-6 | Quarter-final | Canadian Championship           |
|        | v N. Gilbert| 5-3 | 1st round     | Rothmans Grand Prix             |
|        | v Chappel   | 4-5 | 2nd round     | Rothmans Grand Prix             |
|        | v M. Smith  | 5-9 | 1st round     | Tennents UK Open                |
| 1988   | v Dunning   | 2-5 | 1st round     | Mercantile Credit Classic       |
|        | v Wildman   | 4-5 | 2nd round     | Mercantile Credit Classic       |
|        | v Dunning   | 3-5 | 1st round     | MIM Britannia British Open      |
|        | v Thorburn  | 4-6 | Quarter-final | BCE Canadian Championship       |

## TONY KEARNEY (Republic of Ireland)

**Born** 24.6.54. **Turned professional** 1984. **World ranking** 101 (80). **Amateur career** 1981 Republic of Ireland champion. **Best professional performance** Last 32 1987 Mercantile Credit Classic.

|        | v Burke        | 4-5   | Qualifying     | Jameson International            |
|--------|----------------|-------|----------------|----------------------------------|
| 1984   | v Chaperon     | 1-5   | Qualifying     | Rothmans Grand Prix              |
|        | v Murphy       | 2-9   | Qualifying     | Coral UK Open                    |
| 1985   | v French       | 5-1   | Qualifying     | Mercantile Credit Classic        |
|        | v Williamson   | 3-5   | Qualifying     | Mercantile Credit Classic        |
|        | v Watterson    | 6-4   | Qualifying     | Dulux British Open               |
|        | v S. Francisco | 4-6   | 1st round      | Dulux British Open               |
|        | v Burke        | 4-6   | Qualifying     | Irish Championship               |
|        | v Anderson     | 8-10  | Qualifying     | Embassy World Championship       |
|        | v D. Hughes    | 1-5   | 1st round      | Goya Matchroom Trophy            |
|        | v Bear         | 5-3   | 1st round      | Rothmans Grand Prix              |
|        | v Edmonds      | 2-5   | 2nd round      | Rothmans Grand Prix              |
|        | v D. Hughes    | 8-9   | 1st round      | Coral UK Open                    |
| 1986   | v Jim Bear     | 5-0   | 1st round      | Mercantile Credit Classic        |
|        | v Medati       | 2-5   | 2nd round      | Mercantile Credit Classic        |
|        | v Smith        | 5-2   | 1st round      | Dulux British Open               |
|        | v Foldvari     | 5-2   | 2nd round      | Dulux British Open               |
|        | v Wilkinson    | 10-5  | Qualifying     | Embassy World Championship       |
|        | v Scott        | 8-10  | Qualifying     | Embassy World Championship       |
|        | v Fagan        | 5-0   | 1st round      | Strongbow Irish Championship     |
|        | v Murphy       | 2-6   | Quarter-final  | Strongbow Irish Championship     |
|        | v Medati       | 3-5   | 2nd round      | BCE International                |
|        | v Jenkins      | 5-3   | 1st round      | Rothmans Grand Prix              |
|        | v Chappel      | 1-5   | 2nd round      | Rothmans Grand Prix              |
|        | v Dunning      | 6-9   | 1st round      | Tennents UK Open                 |
| 1987   | v Agrawal      | 5-0   | 1st round      | Mercantile Credit Classic        |
|        | v Wildman      | 5-3   | 2nd round      | Mercantile Credit Classic        |
|        | v Macleod      | 5-0   | 3rd round      | Mercantile Credit Classic        |
|        | v W. Jones     | 1-5   | 4th round      | Mercantile Credit Classic        |
|        | v Chappel      | 3-5   | 2nd round      | Dulux British Open               |
|        | v Medati       | 8-10  | Qualifying     | Embassy World Championship       |
|        | v Murphy       | 5-1   | 1st round      | Matchroom Irish Championship     |
|        | v E. Hughes    | 1-6   | Quarter-final  | Matchroom Irish Championship     |
|        | v Foldvari     | 1-5   | 2nd round      | Fidelity International           |
|        | v Darrington   | 5-0   | 2nd round      | Rothmans Grand Prix              |
|        | v Griffiths    | 0-5   | 3rd round      | Rothmans Grand Prix              |
|        | v Fowler       | 7-9   | 2nd round      | Tennents UK Open                 |
| 1988   | v Newbury      | 1-5   | 2nd round      | Mercantile Credit Classic        |
|        | v Fagan        | 5-3   | 1st round      | Irish Championship               |
|        | v Dennis Taylor| 3-6   | Quarter-final  | Irish Championship               |
|        | v Fowler       | 1-5   | 2nd round      | MIM Britannia British Open       |
|        | v Kelly        | 4-10  | Qualifying     | Embassy World Championship       |
|        | v Watterson    | 5-1   | 1st round      | Fidelity International           |

| | | | | |
|---|---|---|---|---|
| | v Clark | 3-5 | 2nd round | Fidelity International |
| | v A. Harris | 2-5 | 1st round | Rothmans Grand Prix |
| | v S. Campbell | 2-5 | 1st round | BCE Canadian Masters |
| | v Watterson | 9-3 | 1st round | Tennents UK Open |
| | v Browne | 9-6 | 2nd round | Tennents UK Open |
| | v James | 1-9 | 3rd round | Tennents UK Open |
| 1989 | v Kelly | 5-3 | 1st round | Mercantile Credit Classic |
| | v Cripsey | 2-5 | 2nd round | Mercantile Credit Classic |
| | v Ellis | 4-5 | 1st round | European Open |
| | v Kelly | 5-2 | 1st round | Irish Championship |
| | v E. Hughes | 1-5 | Quarter-final | Irish Championship |
| | v Terry | 3-5 | 1st round | Anglian British Open |
| | v Meakin | 3-10 | Qualifying | Embassy World Championship |

## BILLY KELLY (Republic of Ireland)
**Born** 1.5.45. **Turned professional** 1981. **World ranking** 119 (110).

| | | | | |
|---|---|---|---|---|
| 1981 | v Macleod | 1-5 | Qualifying | Jameson International |
| | v G. Foulds | 7-9 | Qualifying | Coral UK Championship |
| 1982 | v Sinclair | 8-9 | Qualifying | Embassy World Championship |
| | v G. Foulds | 5-4 | Qualifying | Jameson International |
| | v Williamson | 5-1 | Qualifying | Jameson International |
| | v Higgins | 3-5 | 1st round | Jameson International |
| | v Wych | 0-5 | 1st round | Professional Players Tournament |
| | v Fitzmaurice | 8-0 retd | Qualifying | Coral UK Championship |
| | v Virgo | 2-9 | 1st round | Coral UK Championship |
| 1983 | v Dennis Taylor | 0-6 | Quarter-final | Irish Championship |
| | v Demarco | 10-4 | Qualifying | Embassy World Championship |
| | v S. Francisco | 5-10 | Qualifying | Embassy World Championship |
| | v F. Davis | 1-5 | Qualifying | Jameson International |
| | v Hallett | 0-5 | 1st round | Professional Players Tournament |
| 1984 | v Burke | 7-10 | Qualifying | Embassy World Championship |
| | v Hargreaves | 5-2 | Qualifying | Jameson International |
| | v King | 5-4 | Qualifying | Jameson International |
| | v S. Francisco | 3-5 | Qualifying | Jameson International |
| | v O'Kane | 4-5 | Qualifying | Rothmans Grand Prix |
| | v Bradley | 6-9 | Qualifying | Coral UK Open |
| | v Bales | 3-5 | Qualifying | Mercantile Credit Classic |
| | v P. Francisco | 3-6 | Qualifying | Dulux British Open |
| | v Watchorn | 6-2 | Qualifying | Irish Championship |
| | v E. Hughes | 2-6 | Quarter-final | Irish Championship |
| | v Rigitano | 6-10 | Qualifying | Embassy World Championship |
| 1985 | v P. Francisco | 3-6 | Qualifying | Dulux British Open |
| | v Watchorn | 6-2 | Qualifying | Irish Championship |
| | v E. Hughes | 2-6 | Quarter-final | Irish Championship |
| | v Rigitano | 6-10 | Qualifying | Embassy World Championship |
| | v T. Jones | 3-5 | 2nd round | Goya Matchroom Trophy |
| | v Donnelly | 5-4 | 2nd round | Rothmans Grand Prix |
| | v S. Francisco | 2-5 | 3rd round | Rothmans Grand Prix |
| | v Medati | 1-9 | 2nd round | Coral UK Open |
| 1986 | v F. Davis | 3-5 | 2nd round | Mercantile Credit Classic |
| | v F. Davis | 4-5 | 2nd round | Dulux British Open |
| | v Edmonds | 0-10 | Qualifying | Embassy World Championship |
| | v Jack Rea | 5-0 | 1st round | Strongbow Irish Championship |
| | v Dennis Taylor | 1-6 | Quarter-final | Strongbow Irish Championship |
| | v Whitthread | 5-1 | 1st round | BCE International |
| | v Van Rensberg | 1-5 | 2nd round | BCE International |
| | v Parkin | 5-2 | 1st round | Rothmans Grand Prix |
| | v V. Harris | 3-5 | 2nd round | Rothmans Grand Prix |

|      | v Watchorn       | 8-9   | 1st round     | Tennents UK Open               |
|------|------------------|-------|---------------|--------------------------------|
| 1987 | v Jack Rea       | 3-5   | 1st round     | Mercantile Credit Classic      |
|      | v B. Bennett     | 5-2   | 1st round     | Dulux British Open             |
|      | v B. Harris      | 2-5   | 2nd round     | Dulux British Open             |
|      | v B. Bennett     | 10-0  | Qualifying    | Embassy World Championship     |
|      | v Gibson         | 9-10  | Qualifying    | Embassy World Championship     |
|      | v O'Boye         | 0-5   | 1st round     | Matchroom Irish Championship   |
|      | v Darrington     | 5-4   | 1st round     | Fidelity International         |
|      | v Wright         | 2-5   | 2nd round     | Fidelity International         |
|      | v Dodd           | 2-5   | 2nd round     | Rothmans Grand Prix            |
|      | v Williamson     | 5-9   | 1st round     | Tennents UK Open               |
| 1988 | v Roe            | 1-5   | 1st round     | Mercantile Credit Classic      |
|      | v Murphy         | 1-5   | 1st round     | Irish Championship             |
|      | v Meadowcroft    | 1-5   | 1st round     | MIM Britannia British Open     |
|      | v Kearney        | 10-4  | Qualifying    | Embassy World Championship     |
|      | v Browne         | 8-10  | Qualifying    | Embassy World Championship     |
|      | v Dunning        | 0-5   | 1st round     | Fidelity International         |
|      | v F. Davis       | 5-3   | 1st round     | Rothmans Grand Prix            |
|      | v Fowler         | 4-5   | 2nd round     | Rothmans Grand Prix            |
|      | v Stevens        | 1-5   | 2nd round     | BCE Canadian Masters           |
|      | v Oliver         | 2-9   | 1st round     | Tennents UK Open               |
| 1989 | v Kearney        | 3-5   | 1st round     | Mercantile Credit Classic      |
|      | v Bear           | 0-5   | 1st round     | European Open                  |
|      | v Kearney        | 2-5   | 1st round     | Irish Championship             |
|      | v Oliver         | 5-4   | 1st round     | Anglian British Open           |
|      | v Gauvreau       | 0-5   | 2nd round     | Anglian British Open           |
|      | v Glen Wilkinson | 2-10  | Qualifying    | Embassy World Championship     |

## WARREN KING (Australia)

**Born** 1.4.55. **Turned professional** 1982. **World ranking** 55 (44). **Amateur career** 1980, 1981 Australian champion. **Best professional performances** Australian champion 1986–87; last 16 1988 BCE Canadian Masters.

|      | v Anderson       | 10-6  | Qualifying    | Embassy World Championship      |
|------|------------------|-------|---------------|---------------------------------|
| 1983 | v Anderson       | 10-6  | Qualifying    | Embassy World Championship      |
|      | v Hallett        | 6-10  | Qualifying    | Embassy World Championship      |
|      | v Black          | 5-3   | Qualifying    | Jameson International            |
|      | v Miles          | 3-5   | Qualifying    | Jameson International            |
|      | v B. Harris      | 5-3   | Qualifying    | Professional Players Tournament |
|      | v Meo            | 2-5   | 1st round     | Professional Players Tournament |
| 1984 | v Jones          | 10-9  | Qualifying    | Embassy World Championship      |
|      | v Watterson      | 10-8  | Qualifying    | Embassy World Championship      |
|      | v Martin         | 10-8  | Qualifying    | Embassy World Championship      |
|      | v S. Davis       | 3-10  | 1st round     | Embassy World Championship      |
|      | v Kelly          | 4-5   | Qualifying    | Jameson International            |
|      | v Greaves        | 5-0   | Qualifying    | Rothmans Grand Prix             |
|      | v Macleod        | 4-5   | 1st round     | Rothmans Grand Prix             |
|      | v Browne         | 9-5   | Qualifying    | Coral UK Open                   |
|      | v Virgo          | 9-4   | Qualifying    | Coral UK Open                   |
|      | v Dennis Taylor  | 5-9   | 1st round     | Coral UK Open                   |
| 1985 | v Duggan         | 5-4   | Qualifying    | Mercantile Credit Classic       |
|      | v Reynolds       | 5-2   | Qualifying    | Mercantile Credit Classic       |
|      | v Spencer        | 5-2   | 1st round     | Mercantile Credit Classic       |
|      | v White          | 5-2   | 2nd round     | Mercantile Credit Classic       |
|      | v Johnson        | 3-5   | Quarter-final | Mercantile Credit Classic       |
|      | v Medati         | 6-4   | Qualifying    | Dulux British Open              |
|      | v Reardon        | 5-6   | 1st round     | Dulux British Open              |
|      | v Medati         | 9-10  | Qualifying    | Embassy World Championship      |
|      | v Anderson       | 8-2   | Quarter-final | Australian Championship         |
|      | v J. Campbell    | 6-9   | Semi-final    | Australian Championship         |

|  | | | | |
|---|---|---|---|---|
| | v Caggianello | 5-0 | 2nd round | Goya Matchroom Trophy |
| | v Williams | 5-3 | 3rd round | Goya Matchroom Trophy |
| | v White | 2-5 | 4th round | Goya Matchroom Trophy |
| | v Drago | 4-5 | 2nd round | Rothmans Grand Prix |
| | v D. Hughes | 9-0 | 2nd round | Coral UK Open |
| | v Williams | 5-9 | 3rd round | Coral UK Open |
| 1986 | v Duggan | 5-2 | 2nd round | Mercantile Credit Classic |
| | v Mountjoy | 4-5 | 3rd round | Mercantile Credit Classic |
| | v John Rea | 1-5 | 2nd round | Dulux British Open |
| | v Sheehan | 10-4 | Qualifying | Embassy World Championship |
| | v Roscoe | 10-5 | Qualifying | Embassy World Championship |
| | v Reynolds | 7-10 | Qualifying | Embassy World Championship |
| | v Charlton | 8-6 | Semi-final | Australian Championship |
| | **v J. Campbell** | **10-3** | **Final** | **Australian Championship** |
| | v Rigitano | 5-0 | 2nd round | BCE International |
| | v Longworth | 5-0 | 3rd round | BCE International |
| | v S. Davis | 4-5 | 4th round | BCE International |
| | v Donnelly | 5-2 | 2nd round | Rothmans Grand Prix |
| | v Werbeniuk | 5-2 | 3rd round | Rothmans Grand Prix |
| | v Thorne | 2-5 | 4th round | Rothmans Grand Prix |
| | v James | 9-8 | 2nd round | Tennents UK Open |
| | v Hallett | 5-9 | 3rd round | Tennents UK Open |
| 1987 | v Burke | 5-0 | 2nd round | Mercantile Credit Classic |
| | v Reynolds | 4-5 | 3rd round | Mercantile Credit Classic |
| | v Williamson | 5-3 | 2nd round | Dulux British Open |
| | v Parrott | 5-1 | 3rd round | Dulux British Open |
| | v N. Foulds | 4-5 | 4th round | Dulux British Open |
| | v Roe | 10-4 | Qualifying | Embassy World Championship |
| | v Owers | 10-4 | Qualifying | Embassy World Championship |
| | v Charlton | 10-4 | Qualifying | Embassy World Championship |
| | v S. Davis | 7-10 | 1st round | Embassy World Championship |
| | v Jenkins | 6-4 | Quarter-final | Australian Championship |
| | v Foldvari | 8-1 | Semi-final | Australian Championship |
| | **v Charlton** | **10-7** | **Final** | **Australian Championship** |
| | v M. Smith | 5-3 | 2nd round | Fidelity International |
| | v S. Francisco | 2-5 | 3rd round | Fidelity International |
| | v Foldvari | 4-5 | 2nd round | Rothmans Grand Prix |
| | v Meadowcroft | 9-4 | 2nd round | Tennents UK Open |
| | v S. Davis | 2-9 | 3rd round | Tennents UK Open |
| 1988 | v Oliver | 3-5 | 2nd round | Mercantile Credit Classic |
| | v James | 2-5 | 2nd round | MIM Britannia British Open |
| | v Watchorn | 10-4 | Qualifying | Embassy World Championship |
| | v Clark | 10-9 | Qualifying | Embassy World Championship |
| | v Spencer | 10-7 | Qualifying | Embassy World Championship |
| | v Parrott | 4-10 | 1st round | Embassy World Championship |
| | v Frangie | 5-4 | Quarter-final | Australian Championship |
| | v Foldvari | 4-8 | Semi-final | Australian Championship |
| | v Knowles | 4-5 | 1st round | New Zealand Masters |
| | v Morra | 5-4 | 2nd round | Fidelity International |
| | v West | 4-5 | 3rd round | Fidelity International |
| | v Medati | 1-5 | 2nd round | Rothmans Grand Prix |
| | v M. Gibson | 5-3 | 2nd round | BCE Canadian Masters |
| | v N. Foulds | 5-3 | 3rd round | BCE Canadian Masters |
| | v Duggan | 5-4 | 4th round | BCE Canadian Masters |
| | v Hallett | 2-5 | 5th round | BCE Canadian Masters |
| | v Terry | 9-7 | 2nd round | Tennents UK Open |
| | v S. Davis | 7-9 | 3rd round | Tennents UK Open |
| 1989 | v Rowing | 5-4 | 2nd round | Mercantile Credit Classic |
| | v Griffiths | 2-5 | 3rd round | Mercantile Credit Classic |
| | v Miles | 5-2 | 2nd round | European Open |
| | v Williams | 2-5 | 3rd round | European Open |
| | v Robidoux | 2-5 | 2nd round | Anglian British Open |
| | v Rowing | 7-10 | Qualifying | Embassy World Championship |

## TONY KNOWLES (England)

**Born** 13.6.55. **Turned professional** 1980. **World ranking** 12 (8). **Best professional performances** Winner 1982 Jameson International, 1983 Professional Players Tournament.

| | | | | |
|---|---|---|---|---|
| **1980** | v Andrewartha | 8-9 | Qualifying | Coral UK Championship |
| **1981** | v Johnson | 2-9 | Qualifying | John Courage English Professional |
| | v Ross | 7-0 | Qualifying | Embassy World Championship |
| | v Wych | 9-3 | Qualifying | Embassy World Championship |
| | v Miles | 8-10 | 1st round | Embassy World Championship |
| | v Hallet | 5-2 | 1st round | Jameson International |
| | v Virgo | 2-5 | 2nd round | Jameson International |
| | v G. Foulds | 9-1 | Qualifying | Coral UK Championship |
| | v F. Davis | 9-6 | 2nd round | Coral UK Championship |
| | v Mountjoy | 9-6 | 3rd round | Coral UK Championship |
| | v Griffiths | 5-9 | Quarter-final | Coral UK Championship |
| **1982** | v Dennis Taylor | 2-5 | Semi-final | Tolly Cobbold Classic |
| | v E. Hughes | 9-7 | Qualifying | Embassy World Championship |
| | v S. Davis | 10-1 | 1st round | Embassy World Championship |
| | v Miles | 13-7 | 2nd round | Embassy World Championship |
| | v Charlton | 11-13 | Quarter-final | Embassy World Championship |
| | v S. Davis | 4-5 | 1st round | Langs Scottish Masters |
| | v Sinclair | 5-2 | 1st round | Jameson International |
| | v Reardon | 5-2 | 2nd round | Jameson International |
| | v Wilson | 5-4 | Quarter-final | Jameson International |
| | v Stevens | 9-8 | Semi-final | Jameson International |
| | **v David Taylor** | **9-6** | **Final** | **Jameson International** |
| | v Houlihan | 5-4 | 1st round | Professional Players Tournament |
| | v Wilson | 4-5 | 2nd round | Professional Players Tournament |
| | v Donnelly | 9-6 | 1st round | Coral UK Championship |
| | v Spencer | 6-9 | 2nd round | Coral UK Championship |
| **1983** | v Stevens | 0-5 | 1st round | Lada Classic |
| | v Mountjoy | 1-5 | 1st round | Benson & Hedges Irish Masters |
| | v Miles | 10-3 | 1st round | Embassy World Championship |
| | v Reardon | 13-12 | 2nd round | Embassy World Championship |
| | v Meo | 13-9 | Quarter-final | Embassy World Championship |
| | v Thorburn | 15-16 | Semi-final | Embassy World Championship |
| | v Werbeniuk | 0-5 | Semi-final | Winfield Masters |
| | v Meo | 5-4 | 1st round | Langs Scottish Masters |
| | v Thorburn | 6-2 | Semi-final | Langs Scottish Masters |
| | v S. Davis | 6-9 | Final | Langs Scottish Masters |
| | v Edmonds | 5-1 | 1st round | Jameson International |
| | v Spencer | 4-5 | 2nd round | Jameson International |
| | v Medati | 5-1 | 1st round | Professional Players Tournament |
| | v Williams | 5-4 | 2nd round | Professional Players Tournament |
| | v S. Francisco | 5-0 | 3rd round | Professional Players Tournament |
| | v J. Campbell | 5-3 | Quarter-final | Professional Players Tournament |
| | v Thorne | 9-7 | Semi-final | Professional Players Tournament |
| | **v Johnson** | **9-8** | **Final** | **Professional Players Tournament** |
| | v T. Jones | 9-5 | 1st round | Coral UK Championship |
| | v Mountjoy | 9-5 | 2nd round | Coral UK Championship |
| | v Higgins | 5-9 | Quarter-final | Coral UK Championship |
| **1984** | v E. Hughes | 5-1 | Qualifying | Lada Classic |
| | v Hallett | 5-3 | 1st round | Lada Classic |
| | v Parrott | 1-5 | Quarter-final | Lada Classic |
| | v Dennis Taylor | 5-2 | 1st round | Benson & Hedges Masters |
| | v Higgins | 5-1 | Quarter-final | Benson & Hedges Masters |
| | v Griffiths | 4-6 | Semi-final | Benson & Hedges Masters |
| | v Griffiths | 0-5 | Quarter-final | Benson & Hedges Irish Masters |
| | v White | 5-1 | 1st round | Tolly Cobbold Classic |
| | v Thorburn | 5-3 | Semi-final | Tolly Cobbold Classic |

*Tony Knowles*

| | | | |
|---|---|---|---|
| v S. Davis | 2-8 | Final | Tolly Cobbold Classic |
| v Parrott | 7-10 | 1st round | Embassy World Championship |
| v White | 5-3 | Quarter-final | Winfield Australian Masters |
| v Charlton | 6-0 | Semi-final | Winfield Australian Masters |
| **v Virgo** | **7-3** | **Final** | **Winfield Australian Masters** |
| v Griffiths | 5-3 | 1st round | Langs Scottish Masters |
| v White | 5-6 | Semi-final | Langs Scottish Masters |
| v Higgins | 5-3 | 1st round | Carlsberg Challenge |
| v White | 7-9 | Final | Carlsberg Challenge |
| v Reynolds | 5-1 | 1st round | Jameson International |
| v Newbury | 5-4 | 2nd round | Jameson International |
| v White | 5-4 | Quarter-final | Jameson International |
| v S. Francisco | 9-6 | Semi-final | Jameson International |
| v S. Davis | 2-9 | Final | Jameson International |
| v V. Harris | 5-1 | 1st round | Rothmans Grand Prix |
| v Dunning | 5-1 | 2nd round | Rothmans Grand Prix |
| v Williamson | 5-2 | 3rd round | Rothmans Grand Prix |
| v N. Foulds | 2-5 | Quarter-final | Rothmans Grand Prix |
| v Gauvreau | 9-5 | 1st round | Coral UK Open |
| v Dennis Taylor | 9-2 | 2nd round | Coral UK Open |
| v Stevens | 7-9 | Quarter-final | Coral UK Open |
| **1985** v Johnson | 1-5 | 1st round | Mercantile Credit Classic |
| v Mountjoy | 3-5 | 1st round | Benson & Hedges Masters |
| v Bradley | 9-8 | 1st round | Tolly Cobbold English Championship |
| v Martin | 9-3 | 2nd round | Tolly Cobbold English Championship |
| v David Taylor | 9-2 | Quarter-final | Tolly Cobbold English Championship |
| v Longworth | 9-6 | Semi-final | Tolly Cobbold English Championship |
| v S. Davis | 2-9 | Final | Tolly Cobbold English Championship |
| v French | 6-2 | 1st round | Dulux British Open |
| v Longworth | 5-2 | 2nd round | Dulux British Open |
| v Meo | 2-5 | 3rd round | Dulux British Open |
| v Charlton | 5-3 | Quarter-final | Benson & Hedges Irish Masters |
| v White | 4-6 | Semi-final | Benson & Hedges Irish Masters |
| v T. Jones | 10-8 | 1st round | Embassy World Championship |
| v Mountjoy | 13-6 | 2nd round | Embassy World Championship |
| v White | 13-10 | Quarter-final | Embassy World Championship |
| v Dennis Taylor | 5-16 | Semi-final | Embassy World Championship |
| v S. Francisco | 4-5 | 1st round | Langs Scottish Masters |
| v E. McLaughlin | 5-1 | 3rd round | Goya Matchroom Trophy |
| v N. Foulds | 4-5 | 4th round | Goya Matchroom Trophy |
| v Gibson | 5-1 | 3rd round | Rothmans Grand Prix |
| v Edmonds | 5-3 | 4th round | Rothmans Grand Prix |
| v J. Campbell | 5-2 | 5th round | Rothmans Grand Prix |
| v Stevens | 5-4 | Quarter-final | Rothmans Grand Prix |
| v Dennis Taylor | 6-9 | Semi-final | Rothmans Grand Prix |
| v Reardon | 5-2 | 1st round | BCE Canadian Masters |
| v O'Boye | 9-5 | 3rd round | Coral UK Open |
| v Spencer | 9-7 | 4th round | Coral UK Open |
| v David Taylor | 9-7 | 5th round | Coral UK Open |
| v White | 4-9 | Quarter-final | Coral UK Open |
| **1986** v Rigitano | 5-4 | 3rd round | Mercantile Credit Classic |
| v Macleod | 5-4 | 4th round | Mercantile Credit Classic |
| v Williams | 2-5 | 5th round | Mercantile Credit Classic |
| v White | 5-3 | 1st round | BCE Belgian Classic |
| v Griffiths | 2-5 | Semi-final | BCE Belgian Classic |
| v S. Francisco | 5-1 | 1st round | Benson & Hedges Masters |
| v Charlton | 5-4 | Quarter-final | Benson & Hedges Masters |
| v Thorburn | 4-6 | Semi-final | Benson & Hedges Masters |
| v Bales | 9-4 | 3rd round | Tolly Cobbold English Championship |
| v Hallett | 5-9 | 4th round | Tolly Cobbold English Championship |
| v Williamson | 5-1 | 3rd round | Dulux British Open |
| v Wych | 4-5 | 4th round | Dulux British Open |
| v Fagan | 4-5 | Quarter-final | Benson & Hedges Irish Masters |

|  |  |  |  |  |
|---|---|---|---|---|
| | v N. Foulds | 10-9 | 1st round | Embassy World Championship |
| | v S. Francisco | 13-10 | 2nd round | Embassy World Championship |
| | v Stevens | 13-9 | Quarter-final | Embassy World Championship |
| | v Johnson | 8-16 | Semi-final | Embassy World Championship |
| | v Stevens | 3-5 | 1st round | Langs Scottish Masters |
| | v Spencer | 5-0 | 3rd round | BCE International |
| | v Charlton | 5-1 | 4th round | BCE International |
| | v Wilson | 4-5 | 5th round | BCE International |
| | v Roe | 5-3 | 3rd round | Rothmans Grand Prix |
| | v P. Francisco | 5-3 | 4th round | Rothmans Grand Prix |
| | v Mountjoy | 5-1 | 5th round | Rothmans Grand Prix |
| | v S. Francisco | 2-5 | Quarter-final | Rothmans Grand Prix |
| | v Thorburn | 5-1 | 1st round | BCE Canadian Masters |
| | v Thorne | 7-8 | Semi-final | BCE Canadian Masters |
| | v John Rea | 9-4 | 3rd round | Tennents UK Open |
| | v T. Jones | 9-2 | 4th round | Tennents UK Open |
| | v Griffiths | 9-6 | 5th round | Tennents UK Open |
| | v Parrott | 4-9 | Quarter-final | Tennents UK Open |
| 1987 | v Fowler | 4-5 | 3rd round | Mercantile Credit Classic |
| | v S. Francisco | 2-5 | 1st round | Benson & Hedges Masters |
| | v Dodd | 2-6 | 3rd round | Tolly Ales English Championship |
| | v Fowler | 5-4 | 3rd round | Dulux British Open |
| | v Reynolds | 5-0 | 4th round | Dulux British Open |
| | v Murphy | 5-3 | 5th round | Dulux British Open |
| | v Dennis Taylor | 5-4 | Quarter-final | Dulux British Open |
| | v N. Foulds | 2-9 | Semi-final | Dulux British Open |
| | v Meo | 2-5 | 1st round | Benson & Hedges Irish Masters |
| | v Hallett | 6-10 | 1st round | Embassy World Championship |
| | v Fowler | 5-4 | 3rd round | Fidelity International |
| | v David Taylor | 5-2 | 4th round | Fidelity International |
| | v Virgo | 2-5 | 5th round | Fidelity International |
| | v J. McLaughlin | 5-0 | 3rd round | Rothmans Grand Prix |
| | v Roe | 5-2 | 4th round | Rothmans Grand Prix |
| | v Charlton | 5-0 | 5th round | Rothmans Grand Prix |
| | v Hendry | 2-5 | Quarter-final | Rothmans Grand Prix |
| | v White | 1-5 | 1st round | Labatts Canadian Masters (WS) |
| | v John Rea | 9-6 | 3rd round | Tennents UK Open |
| | v Stevens | 9-8 | 4th round | Tennents UK Open |
| | v Parrott | 4-9 | 5th round | Tennents UK Open |
| 1988 | v Wright | 5-1 | 3rd round | Mercantile Credit Classic |
| | v Roscoe | 5-0 | 4th round | Mercantile Credit Classic |
| | v Murphy | 5-3 | 5th round | Mercantile Credit Classic |
| | v Dennis Taylor | 5-1 | Quarter-final | Mercantile Credit Classic |
| | v Parrott | 4-9 | Semi-final | Mercantile Credit Classic |
| | v Higgins | 4-5 | 1st round | Benson & Hedges Masters |
| | v Wright | 6-2 | 3rd round | English Championship |
| | v Owers | 6-4 | 4th round | English Championship |
| | v Johnson | 4-6 | Quarter-final | English Championship |
| | v M. Gibson | 5-4 | 3rd round | MIM Britannia British Open |
| | v Macleod | 4-5 | 4th round | MIM Britannia British Open |
| | v Thorne | 5-3 | 1st round | Benson & Hedges Irish Masters |
| | v N. Foulds | 3-5 | Quarter-final | Benson & Hedges Irish Masters |
| | v Fowler | 10-8 | 1st round | Embassy World Championship |
| | v Charlton | 13-7 | 2nd round | Embassy World Championship |
| | v White | 6-13 | Quarter-final | Embassy World Championship |
| | v King | 5-4 | 1st round | New Zealand Masters |
| | v Hallett | 3-5 | Semi-final | New Zealand Masters |
| | v Miles | 5-4 | 3rd round | Fidelity International |
| | v Newbury | 4-5 | 4th round | Fidelity International |
| | v O'Boye | 5-4 | 3rd round | Rothmans Grand Prix |
| | v Reynolds | 5-3 | 4th round | Rothmans Grand Prix |
| | v N. Gilbert | 4-5 | 5th round | Rothmans Grand Prix |
| | v Roscoe | 2-5 | 3rd round | BCE Canadian Masters |

| v Wych | 9-4 | 3rd round | Tennents UK Open |
|---|---|---|---|
| v Higgins | 9-6 | 4th round | Tennents UK Open |
| v Virgo | 3-9 | 5th round | Tennents UK Open |
| v Dennis Taylor | 7-9 | 1st round | Everest World Matchplay |
| 1989 v Roscoe | 5-4 | 3rd round | Mercantile Credit Classic |
| v Reynolds | 5-4 | 4th round | Mercantile Credit Classic |
| v Mountjoy | 4-5 | 5th round | Mercantile Credit Classic |
| v Hallett | 5-3 | 1st round | Benson and Hedges Masters |
| v S. Davis | 0-5 | Quarter-final | Benson and Hedges Masters |
| v Fowler | 2-5 | 3rd round | European Open |
| v Williamson | 5-2 | 3rd round | English Championship |
| v Longworth | 4-5 | 4th round | English Championship |
| v Wych | 5-2 | 3rd round | Anglian British Open |
| v West | 0-5 | 4th round | Anglian British Open |
| v Hallett | 0-5 | 1st round | Benson and Hedges Irish Masters |
| v Roe | 6-10 | 1st round | Embassy World Championship |

## ERIC LAWLOR (England)

**Born** 1.7.37. **Turned professional** 1987. **World ranking** 96 (93).

| 1987 v Roscoe | 4-5 | 1st round | Fidelity International |
|---|---|---|---|
| v D. Gilbert | 2-5 | 1st round | Rothmans Grand Prix |
| v Fitzmaurice | 9-0 | 1st round | Tennents UK Open |
| v Wright | 9-7 | 2nd round | Tennents UK Open |
| v P. Francisco | 4-9 | 3rd round | Tennents UK Open |
| 1988 v Sinclair | 3-5 | 1st round | Mercantile Credit Classic |
| v Roe | 6-5 | 1st round | English Championship |
| v Bradley | 6-5 | 2nd round | English Championship |
| v Parrott | 3-6 | 3rd round | English Championship |
| v Sinclair | 5-3 | 1st round | MIM Britannia British Open |
| v B. Harris | 5-2 | 2nd round | MIM Britannia British Open |
| v Johnson | 1-5 | 3rd round | MIM Britannia British Open |
| v Newbury | 3-10 | Qualifying | Embassy World Championship |
| v Jack Rea | 5-2 | 1st round | Fidelity International |
| v J. McLaughlin | 3-5 | 2nd round | Fidelity International |
| v Ellis | 4-5 | 1st round | Rothmans Grand Prix |
| v Mikkelsen | 5-2 | 1st round | BCE Canadian Masters |
| v Owers | 2-5 | 2nd round | BCE Canadian Masters |
| v Fitzmaurice | 9-1 | 1st round | Tennents UK Open |
| v D. Gilbert | 2-9 | 2nd round | Tennents UK Open |
| 1989 v Edwards | 1-5 | 1st round | Mercantile Credit Classic |
| v Fitzmaurice | 5-0 | 1st round | European Open |
| v Owers | 5-4 | 2nd round | European Open |
| v Parrott | scr | 3rd round | European Open |
| v F. Davis | 5-2 | 1st round | English Championship |
| v Roe | 1-5 | 2nd round | English Championship |
| v Watterson | 5-9 | 1st round | Anglian British Open |
| v Chappel | 2-5 | 2nd round | Anglian British Open |
| v D. Morgan | 2-10 | Qualifying | Embassy World Championship |

## STEVE LONGWORTH (England)

**Born** 27.7.48. **Turned professional** 1984. **World ranking** 34 (30). **Amateur career** 1984 English champion. **Best professional performances** Last 16 1988 BCE Canadian Masters, 1987 Embassy World Championship, 1986 Tennents UK Open, 1985 Rothmans Grand Prix.

| 1984 v Newbury | 4-5 | Qualifying | Jameson International |
|---|---|---|---|
| v E. McLaughlin | 2-5 | Qualifying | Rothmans Grand Prix |
| v Darrington | 9-5 | Qualifying | Coral UK Open |

|  |  |  |  |  |
|---|---|---|---|---|
|  | v Burke | 9-4 | Qualifying | Coral UK Open |
|  | v Morra | 1-9 | Qualifying | Coral UK Open |
| 1985 | v P. Francisco | 5-4 | Qualifying | Mercantile Credit Classic |
|  | v Oliver | 5-1 | Qualifying | Mercantile Credit Classic |
|  | v Fisher | 5-1 | Qualifying | Mercantile Credit Classic |
|  | v N. Foulds | 5-3 | Qualifying | Mercantile Credit Classic |
|  | v David Taylor | 5-4 | 1st round | Mercantile Credit Classic |
|  | v Thorburn | 3-5 | 2nd round | Mercantile Credit Classic |
|  | v Edmonds | 9-4 | Qualifying | Tolly Cobbold English Championship |
|  | v Wildman | 9-3 | 1st round | Tolly Cobbold English Championship |
|  | v Medati | 9-7 | 2nd round | Tolly Cobbold English Championship |
|  | v White | 9-5 | Quarter-final | Tolly Cobbold English Championship |
|  | v Knowles | 6-9 | Semi-final | Tolly Cobbold English Championship |
|  | v F. Davis | 6-1 | Qualifying | Dulux British Open |
|  | v Wilson | 6-3 | 1st round | Dulux British Open |
|  | v Knowles | 2-5 | 2nd round | Dulux British Open |
|  | v Giannaros | 10-1 | Qualifying | Embassy World Championship |
|  | v Cripsey | 10-8 | Qualifying | Embassy World Championship |
|  | v Van Rensberg | 7-10 | Qualifying | Embassy World Championship |
|  | v Wilkinson | 5-0 | 2nd round | Goya Matchroom Trophy |
|  | v Thorburn | 3-5 | 3rd round | Goya Matchroom Trophy |
|  | v Hargreaves | 5-2 | 2nd round | Rothmans Grand Prix |
|  | v Parrott | 5-2 | 3rd round | Rothmans Grand Prix |
|  | v David Taylor | 5-1 | 4th round | Rothmans Grand Prix |
|  | v Stevens | 3-5 | 5th round | Rothmans Grand Prix |
|  | v Gibson | 9-2 | 2nd round | Coral UK Open |
|  | v Meo | 5-9 | 3rd round | Coral UK Open |
| 1986 | v O'Boye | 1-5 | 2nd round | Mercantile Credit Classic |
|  | v Duggan | 9-4 | 2nd round | Tolly Cobbold English Championship |
|  | v Reynolds | 5-9 | 3rd round | Tolly Cobbold English Championship |
|  | v Houlihan | 5-3 | 2nd round | Dulux British Open |
|  | v E. Hughes | 5-4 | 3rd round | Dulux British Open |
|  | v P. Francisco | 2-5 | 4th round | Dulux British Open |
|  | v Watchorn | 10-7 | Qualifying | Embassy World Championship |
|  | v John Rea | 10-4 | Qualifying | Embassy World Championship |
|  | v Virgo | 8-10 | Qualifying | Embassy World Championship |
|  | v King | 0-5 | 3rd round | BCE International |
|  | v Wildman | 2-5 | 3rd round | Rothmans Grand Prix |
|  | v Rowswell | 9-3 | 3rd round | Tennents UK Open |
|  | v Mountjoy | 9-1 | 4th round | Tennents UK Open |
|  | v Parrott | 6-9 | 5th round | Tennents UK Open |
| 1987 | v Murphy | 5-3 | 3rd round | Mercantile Credit Classic |
|  | v Meo | 0-5 | 4th round | Mercantile Credit Classic |
|  | v James | 2-6 | 3rd round | Tolly Ales English Championship |
|  | v Duggan | 2-5 | 3rd round | Dulux British Open |
|  | v Murphy | 10-2 | Qualifying | Embassy World Championship |
|  | v Stevens | 10-4 | 1st round | Embassy World Championship |
|  | v Hendry | 7-13 | 2nd round | Embassy World Championship |
|  | v Williamson | 5-4 | 3rd round | Fidelity International |
|  | v White | 1-5 | 4th round | Fidelity International |
|  | v Gary Wilkinson | 4-5 | 3rd round | Rothmans Grand Prix |
|  | v Werbeniuk | 9-5 | 3rd round | Tennents UK Open |
|  | v Chappel | 6-9 | 4th round | Tennents UK Open |
| 1988 | v Edmonds | 5-3 | 3rd round | Mercantile Credit Classic |
|  | v S. Francisco | 2-5 | 4th round | Mercantile Credit Classic |
|  | v Chambers | 6-4 | 3rd round | English Championship |
|  | v Meo | 4-6 | 4th round | English Championship |
|  | v Rowswell | 4-5 | 3rd round | MIM Britannia British Open |
|  | v Cripsey | 10-2 | Qualifying | Embassy World Championship |
|  | v Griffiths | 1-10 | 1st round | Embassy World Championship |
|  | v Price | 5-4 | 3rd round | Fidelity International |
|  | v Hendry | 3-5 | 4th round | Fidelity International |
|  | v Edmonds | 3-5 | 3rd round | Rothmans Grand Prix |

|      | v Browne   | 5-4  | 3rd round    | BCE Canadian Masters         |
|------|------------|------|--------------|------------------------------|
|      | v Macleod  | 5-3  | 4th round    | BCE Canadian Masters         |
|      | v White    | 3-5  | 5th round    | BCE Canadian Masters         |
|      | v Fowler   | 8-9  | 3rd round    | Tennents UK Open             |
| 1989 | v Cripsey  | 3-5  | 3rd round    | Mercantile Credit Classic    |
|      | v Hendry   | 0-5  | 4th round    | European Open                |
|      | v Marshall | 5-3  | 3rd round    | English Championship         |
|      | v Knowles  | 5-4  | 4th round    | English Championship         |
|      | v Hallett  | 1-5  | Quarter-final| English Championship         |
|      | v Owers    | 5-1  | 3rd round    | Anglian British Open         |
|      | v Parrott  | 1-5  | 4th round    | Anglian British Open         |
|      | v Browne   | 0-10 | Qualifying   | Embassy World Championship   |

## JACK McLAUGHLIN (Northern Ireland)

**Born** 29.1.59. **Turned professional** 1984. **World ranking** 58 (64). **Amateur career** 1983, 1984 Northern Ireland champion. **Best professional performances** Winner 1988 Irish Championship; last 16 1988 Rothmans Grand Prix.

|      |               |      |              |                               |
|------|---------------|------|--------------|-------------------------------|
| 1984 | v Greaves     | 5-3  | Qualifying   | Jameson International          |
|      | v Jonik       | 2-5  | Qualifying   | Jameson International          |
|      | v Meadowcroft | 5-1  | Qualifying   | Rothmans Grand Prix           |
|      | v Wildman     | 3-5  | 1st round    | Rothmans Grand Prix           |
|      | v French      | 9-3  | Qualifying   | Coral UK Open                 |
|      | v Roscoe      | 9-8  | Qualifying   | Coral UK Open                 |
|      | v Miles       | 9-8  | Qualifying   | Coral UK Open                 |
|      | v Thorburn    | 4-9  | 1st round    | Coral UK Open                 |
| 1985 | v Demarco     | 5-1  | Qualifying   | Mercantile Credit Classic     |
|      | v Black       | 5-0  | Qualifying   | Mercantile Credit Classic     |
|      | v Scott       | 4-5  | Qualifying   | Mercantile Credit Classic     |
|      | v Jonik       | 2-6  | Qualifying   | Dulux British Open            |
|      | v Sheehan     | 6-3  | Qualifying   | Irish Championship            |
|      | v Williamson  | 3-5  | 2nd round    | Goya Matchroom Trophy         |
|      | v Medati      | 5-2  | 2nd round    | Rothmans Grand Prix           |
|      | v Griffiths   | 4-5  | 3rd round    | Rothmans Grand Prix           |
|      | v Chaperon    | 9-5  | Qualifying   | Coral UK Open                 |
|      | v Reynolds    | 7-9  | 1st round    | Coral UK Open                 |
| 1986 | v E. McLaughlin | 5-2 | 2nd round   | Mercantile Credit Classic     |
|      | v Thorburn    | 1-5  | 3rd round    | Mercantile Credit Classic     |
|      | v Fisher      | 5-3  | 2nd round    | Dulux British Open            |
|      | v Johnson     | 2-5  | 3rd round    | Dulux British Open            |
|      | v Murphy      | 7-10 | Qualifying   | Embassy World Championship    |
|      | v Watchorn    | 5-0  | 1st round    | Strongbow Irish Championship  |
|      | v Higgins     | 2-6  | Quarter-final| Strongbow Irish Championship  |
|      | v B. Bennett  | 5-0  | 1st round    | BCE International             |
|      | v Fowler      | 5-2  | 2nd round    | BCE International             |
|      | v Wilson      | 2-5  | 3rd round    | BCE International             |
|      | v Owers       | 5-2  | 1st round    | Rothmans Grand Prix           |
|      | v Gauvreau    | 5-3  | 2nd round    | Rothmans Grand Prix           |
|      | v West        | 5-1  | 3rd round    | Rothmans Grand Prix           |
|      | v White       | 2-5  | 4th round    | Rothmans Grand Prix           |
|      | v Gauvreau    | 9-8  | 2nd round    | Tennents UK Open              |
|      | v Mountjoy    | 6-9  | 3rd round    | Tennents UK Open              |
| 1987 | v M. Gibson   | 5-3  | 2nd round    | Mercantile Credit Classic     |
|      | v Werbeniuk   | 1-5  | 3rd round    | Mercantile Credit Classic     |
|      | v Gibson      | 5-1  | 2nd round    | Dulux British Open            |
|      | v Higgins     | 5-4  | 3rd round    | Dulux British Open            |
|      | v David Taylor| 2-5  | 4th round    | Dulux British Open            |
|      | v Van Rensberg| 6-10 | Qualifying   | Embassy World Championship    |
|      | v Sheehan     | 4-5  | 1st round    | Matchroom Irish Championship  |
|      | v N. Gilbert  | 4-5  | 2nd round    | Fidelity International         |
|      | v Oliver      | 5-2  | 2nd round    | Rothmans Grand Prix           |

|      |                | | | |
|------|----------------|------|------------|--------------------------------|
|      | v Knowles      | 0-5  | 3rd round  | Rothmans Grand Prix            |
|      | v John Rea     | 5-9  | 2nd round  | Tennents UK Open               |
| 1988 | v P. Gibson    | 5-4  | 2nd round  | Mercantile Credit Classic      |
|      | v Martin       | 2-5  | 3rd round  | Mercantile Credit Classic      |
|      | v Burke        | 5-3  | 1st round  | Irish Championship             |
|      | v Watchorn     | 6-5  | Quarter-final | Irish Championship          |
|      | v O'Boye       | 6-4  | Semi-final | Irish Championship             |
|      | **v Dennis Taylor** | **9-4** | **Final** | **Irish Championship**    |
|      | v Rowswell     | 2-5  | 2nd round  | MIM Britannia British Open     |
|      | v M. Smith     | 3-10 | Qualifying | Embassy World Championship     |
|      | v Lawlor       | 5-3  | 2nd round  | Fidelity International         |
|      | v Virgo        | 0-5  | 3rd round  | Fidelity International         |
|      | v V. Harris    | 5-4  | 2nd round  | Rothmans Grand Prix            |
|      | v P. Francisco | 5-2  | 3rd round  | Rothmans Grand Prix            |
|      | v Spencer      | 5-3  | 4th round  | Rothmans Grand Prix            |
|      | v White        | 2-5  | 5th round  | Rothmans Grand Prix            |
|      | v Fitzmaurice  | 2-5  | 2nd round  | BCE Canadian Masters           |
|      | v Bradley      | 9-3  | 2nd round  | Tennents UK Open               |
|      | v Dennis Taylor | 5-9 | 3rd round  | Tennents UK Open               |
| 1989 | v Watterson    | 5-3  | 2nd round  | Mercantile Credit Classic      |
|      | v Chaperon     | 3-5  | 3rd round  | Mercantile Credit Classic      |
|      | v Price        | 5-3  | 2nd round  | European Open                  |
|      | v Griffiths    | 3-5  | 3rd round  | European Open                  |
|      | v Jack Rea     | 5-0  | Quarter-final | Irish Championship          |
|      | v Browne       | 6-3  | Semi-final | Irish Championship             |
|      | v Higgins      | 7-9  | Final      | Irish Championship             |
|      | v Griffiths    | 4-5  | 1st round  | Benson and Hedges Irish Masters |
|      | v Ellis        | 10-0 | Qualifying | Embassy World Championship     |
|      | v Robidoux     | 2-10 | Qualifying | Embassy World Championship     |

## MURDO MACLEOD (Scotland)

**Born** 14.1.47. **Turned professional** 1981. **World ranking** 45 (48). **Best professional performances** Winner 1983 and 1985 Scottish Championship; last 16 1988 MIM Britannia British Open, 1987 Embassy World Championship, 1985 Coral UK Open, 1985 Goya Matchroom Trophy.

|      |                 | | | |
|------|-----------------|------|------------|--------------------------------|
| 1981 | v Kelly         | 5-1  | Qualifying | Jameson International          |
|      | v Johnson       | 1-5  | Qualifying | Jameson International          |
|      | v Black         | 4-5  | Quarter-final | Scottish Championship       |
|      | v Roscoe        | 7-9  | Qualifying | Coral UK Championship          |
| 1982 | v E. McLaughlin | 9-8  | Qualifying | Embassy World Championship     |
|      | v Dunning       | 4-9  | Qualifying | Embassy World Championship     |
|      | v Donnelly      | 6-5  | 1st round  | Scottish Championship          |
|      | v Black         | 0-6  | Quarter-final | Scottish Championship       |
|      | v Dodd          | 1-5  | Qualifying | Jameson International          |
|      | v Thorne        | 5-2  | 2nd round  | Professional Players Tournament |
|      | v Reardon       | 2-5  | 3rd round  | Professional Players Tournament |
|      | v Martin        | 6-9  | Qualifying | Coral UK Championship          |
| 1983 | v M. Owen       | 10-5 | Qualifying | Embassy World Championship     |
|      | v Martin        | 7-10 | Qualifying | Embassy World Championship     |
|      | v Gibson        | 6-5  | 1st round  | Scottish Championship          |
|      | v Black         | 6-2  | Semi-final | Scottish Championship          |
|      | **v Sinclair**  | **11-9** | **Final** | **Scottish Championship**  |
|      | v S. Davis      | 1-5  | 1st round  | Langs Supreme Scottish Masters |
|      | v Medati        | 5-3  | Qualifying | Jameson International          |
|      | v Reardon       | 2-5  | 1st round  | Jameson International          |
|      | v Murphy        | 0-5  | 1st round  | Professional Players Tournament |
|      | v Bennett       | 9-0  | Qualifying | Coral UK Championship          |
|      | v Higgins       | 6-9  | 1st round  | Coral UK Championship          |
| 1984 | v David Taylor  | 5-4  | Qualifying | Lada Classic                   |
|      | v Stevens       | 1-5  | 1st round  | Lada Classic                   |

|      |                   |       |              |                                   |
|------|-------------------|-------|--------------|-----------------------------------|
|      | v Gauvreau        | 6-10  | Qualifying   | Embassy World Championship        |
|      | v White           | 0-5   | 1st round    | Langs Supreme Scottish Masters    |
|      | v Black           | 5-3   | Qualifying   | Jameson International              |
|      | v Meo             | 1-5   | 1st round    | Jameson International              |
|      | v King            | 5-4   | 1st round    | Rothmans Grand Prix               |
|      | v Thorne          | 3-5   | 2nd round    | Rothmans Grand Prix               |
|      | v Scott           | 9-5   | Qualifying   | Coral UK Open                     |
|      | v David Taylor    | 6-9   | 1st round    | Coral UK Open                     |
| 1985 | v E. McLaughlin   | 5-4   | Qualifying   | Mercantile Credit Classic         |
|      | v Charlton        | 5-1   | 1st round    | Mercantile Credit Classic         |
|      | v Virgo           | 0-5   | 2nd round    | Mercantile Credit Classic         |
|      | v E. McLaughlin   | 6-4   | 1st round    | Scottish Championship             |
|      | v M. Gibson       | 6-4   | Semi-final   | Scottish Championship             |
|      | **v Sinclair**    | **10-2** | **Final** | **Scottish Championship**         |
|      | v Murphy          | 6-5   | 1st round    | Dulux British Open                |
|      | v Thorne          | 5-0   | 2nd round    | Dulux British Open                |
|      | v E. Hughes       | 2-5   | 3rd round    | Dulux British Open                |
|      | v P. Francisco    | 10-7  | Qualifying   | Embassy World Championship        |
|      | v Mountjoy        | 5-10  | 1st round    | Embassy World Championship        |
|      | v Thorburn        | 1-5   | 1st round    | Langs Scottish Masters            |
|      | v Fitzmaurice     | 5-1   | 3rd round    | Goya Matchroom Trophy             |
|      | v Chaperon        | 5-4   | 4th round    | Goya Matchroom Trophy             |
|      | v S. Davis        | 1-5   | 5th round    | Goya Matchroom Trophy             |
|      | v Drago           | 3-5   | 3rd round    | Rothmans Grand Prix               |
|      | v Murphy          | 9-7   | 3rd round    | Coral UK Open                     |
|      | v Reardon         | 9-5   | 4th round    | Coral UK Open                     |
|      | v West            | 4-9   | 5th round    | Coral UK Open                     |
| 1986 | v Sinclair        | 5-3   | 3rd round    | Mercantile Credit Classic         |
|      | v Knowles         | 4-5   | 4th round    | Mercantile Credit Classic         |
|      | v F. Davis        | 5-4   | 3rd round    | Dulux British Open                |
|      | v S. Francisco    | 5-1   | 4th round    | Dulux British Open                |
|      | v Griffiths       | 2-5   | 5th round    | Dulux British Open                |
|      | v Hendry          | 5-6   | Quarter-final | Canada Dry Scottish Championship |
|      | v Fowler          | 6-10  | Qualifying   | Embassy World Championship        |
|      | v Gauvreau        | 4-5   | 3rd round    | BCE International                 |
|      | v M. Bennett      | 1-5   | 3rd round    | Rothmans Grand Prix               |
|      | v Grace           | 6-9   | 3rd round    | Tennents UK Open                  |
| 1987 | v Kearney         | 0-5   | 3rd round    | Mercantile Credit Classic         |
|      | v Donnelly        | 2-6   | 1st round    | Scottish Championship             |
|      | v T. Jones        | 4-5   | 3rd round    | Dulux British Open                |
|      | v Edmonds         | 10-7  | Qualifying   | Embassy World Championship        |
|      | v Williams        | 10-5  | 1st round    | Embassy World Championship        |
|      | v Johnson         | 7-13  | 2nd round    | Embassy World Championship        |
|      | v N. Gilbert      | 1-5   | 3rd round    | Fidelity International            |
|      | v Wych            | 4-5   | 3rd round    | Rothmans Grand Prix               |
|      | v Edmonds         | 4-9   | 3rd round    | Tennents UK Open                  |
| 1988 | v Donnelly        | 4-5   | 3rd round    | Mercantile Credit Classic         |
|      | v Donnelly        | 6-5   | Quarter-final | Scottish Championship            |
|      | v John Rea        | 6-5   | Semi-final   | Scottish Championship             |
|      | v Hendry          | 4-10  | Final        | Scottish Championship             |
|      | v D. Gilbert      | 5-4   | 3rd round    | MIM Britannia British Open        |
|      | v Knowles         | 5-4   | 4th round    | MIM Britannia British Open        |
|      | v Hallett         | 2-5   | 5th round    | MIM Britannia British Open        |
|      | v Fowler          | 3-10  | Qualifying   | Embassy World Championship        |
|      | v Sheehan         | 5-0   | 2nd round    | Fidelity International            |
|      | v Higgins         | 5-2   | 3rd round    | Fidelity International            |
|      | v James           | 2-5   | 4th round    | Fidelity International            |
|      | v Glen Wilkinson  | 5-2   | 2nd round    | Rothmans Grand Prix               |
|      | v Newbury         | 3-5   | 3rd round    | Rothmans Grand Prix               |
|      | v Watchorn        | 5-1   | 2nd round    | BCE Canadian Masters              |
|      | v S. Francisco    | 5-4   | 3rd round    | BCE Canadian Masters              |
|      | v Longworth       | 3-5   | 4th round    | BCE Canadian Masters              |
|      | v B. Harris       | 8-9   | 2nd round    | Tennents UK Open                  |

| 1989 | v Graham | 5-4 | 2nd round | Mercantile Credit Classic |
|---|---|---|---|---|
| | v Higgins | 2-5 | 3rd round | Mercantile Credit Classic |
| | v Black | 5-1 | 2nd round | European Open |
| | v West | 5-4 | 3rd round | European Open |
| | v Thorburn | 1-5 | 4th round | European Open |
| | v E. McLaughlin | 5-0 | 1st round | Scottish Championship |
| | v M. Gibson | 5-1 | Semi-final | Scottish Championship |
| | v John Rea | 7-9 | Final | Scottish Championship |
| | v M. Smith | 5-4 | 2nd round | Anglian British Open |
| | v S. Francisco | 5-4 | 3rd round | Anglian British Open |
| | v Mountjoy | 0-5 | 4th round | Anglian British Open |
| | v Meadowcroft | 10-9 | Qualifying | Embassy World Championship |
| | v Browne | 6-10 | Qualifying | Embassy World Championship |

## ROBERT MARSHALL (England)
Born 25.8.64. Turned professional 1987. World ranking 70 (119).

| 1987 | v V. Harris | 1-5 | 1st round | Fidelity International |
|---|---|---|---|---|
| | v Sheehan | 5-1 | 1st round | Rothmans Grand Prix |
| | v Wych | 2-5 | 2nd round | Rothmans Grand Prix |
| | v Roe | 3-9 | 1st round | Tennents UK Open |
| 1988 | v Morra | 0-5 | 1st round | Mercantile Credit Classic |
| | v Oliver | 6-3 | 1st round | English Championship |
| | v Houlihan | 6-4 | 2nd round | English Championship |
| | v Thorne | 3-6 | 3rd round | English Championship |
| | v Rigitano | 2-5 | 1st round | MIM Britannia British Open |
| | v Chaperon | 3-10 | Qualifying | Embassy World Championship |
| | v Rowswell | 5-4 | 1st round | Fidelity International |
| | v M. Bennett | 1-5 | 2nd round | Fidelity International |
| | v V. Harris | 3-5 | 1st round | Rothmans Grand Prix |
| | v Black | 5-1 | 1st round | BCE Canadian Masters |
| | v Dodd | 3-5 | 2nd round | BCE Canadian Masters |
| | v M. Smith | 6-9 | 1st round | Tennents UK Open |
| 1989 | v Black | 5-0 | 1st round | Mercantile Credit Classic |
| | v Edmonds | 5-2 | 2nd round | Mercantile Credit Classic |
| | v Drago | 1-5 | 3rd round | Mercantile Credit Classic |
| | v Van Rensberg | 5-1 | 1st round | European Open |
| | v Murphy | 4-5 | 2nd round | European Open |
| | v Terry | 5-3 | 1st round | English Championship |
| | v N. Gilbert | 5-4 | 2nd round | English Championship |
| | v Longworth | 3-5 | 3rd round | English Championship |
| | v Chambers | 5-2 | 1st round | Anglian British Open |
| | v Stevens | 5-4 | 2nd round | Anglian British Open |
| | v Chaperon | 2-5 | 3rd round | Anglian British Open |
| | v Hines | 10-1 | Qualifying | Embassy World Championship |
| | v P. Gibson | 3-10 | Qualifying | Embassy World Championship |

## DAVE MARTIN (England)
Born 9.5.48. Turned professional 1981. World ranking 56 (36). Best professional performances Semi-finals 1981 Jameson International; quarter-finals 1988 Mercantile Credit Classic.

| 1981 | v Anderson | 9-3 | Qualifying | Embassy World Championship |
|---|---|---|---|---|
| | v Pulman | 9-2 | Qualifying | Embassy World Championship |
| | v Werbeniuk | 4-10 | 1st round | Embassy World Championship |
| | v Dunning | 5-2 | 1st round | Jameson International |
| | v Werbeniuk | 5-2 | 2nd round | Jameson International |
| | v Charlton | 5-2 | 3rd round | Jameson International |
| | v Miles | 5-1 | Quarter-final | Jameson International |

|      |                 |       |            |                                      |
|------|-----------------|-------|------------|--------------------------------------|
|      | v Dennis Taylor | 1-9   | Semi-final | Jameson International                 |
|      | v Sinclair      | 9-7   | Qualifying | Coral UK Championship                 |
|      | v Higgins       | 7-9   | 2nd round  | Coral UK Championship                 |
| 1982 | v Houlihan      | 9-3   | Qualifying | Embassy World Championship            |
|      | v Miles         | 5-10  | Qualifying | Embassy World Championship            |
|      | v E. Hughes     | 4-5   | Qualifying | Jameson International                  |
|      | v Gibson        | 5-2   | 1st round  | Professional Players Tournament       |
|      | v Spencer       | 3-5   | 2nd round  | Professional Players Tournament       |
|      | v Macleod       | 9-6   | Qualifying | Coral UK Championship                 |
|      | v Higgins       | 7-9   | 1st round  | Coral UK Championship                 |
| 1983 | v Parkin        | 10-1  | Qualifying | Embassy World Championship            |
|      | v Macleod       | 10-7  | Qualifying | Embassy World Championship            |
|      | v Werbeniuk     | 4-10  | Qualifying | Embassy World Championship            |
|      | v Greaves       | 5-1   | Qualifying | Jameson International                  |
|      | v Fagan         | 5-0   | Qualifying | Jameson International                  |
|      | v Higgins       | 5-2   | 1st round  | Jameson International                  |
|      | v Mountjoy      | 0-5   | 2nd round  | Jameson International                  |
|      | v Fitzmaurice   | 5-0   | 1st round  | Professional Players Tournament       |
|      | v Watterson     | 5-4   | 2nd round  | Professional Players Tournament       |
|      | v J. Campbell   | 0-5   | 3rd round  | Professional Players Tournament       |
|      | v French        | 9-3   | Qualifying | Coral UK Championship                 |
|      | v Griffiths     | 4-9   | Qualifying | Coral UK Championship                 |
| 1984 | v King          | 8-10  | Qualifying | Embassy World Championship            |
|      | v Fowler        | 0-5   | Qualifying | Jameson International                  |
|      | v Chaperon      | 5-4   | 1st round  | Rothmans Grand Prix                   |
|      | v Meo           | 4-5   | 2nd round  | Rothmans Grand Prix                   |
|      | v Murphy        | 8-9   | Qualifying | Coral UK Open                         |
| 1985 | v Foldvari      | 2-5   | Qualifying | Mercantile Credit Classic             |
|      | v Miles         | 9-7   | 1st round  | Tolly Cobbold English Championship    |
|      | v Knowles       | 3-9   | 2nd round  | Tolly Cobbold English Championship    |
|      | v Bennett       | 6-0   | 1st round  | Dulux British Open                    |
|      | v Reardon       | 5-4   | 2nd round  | Dulux British Open                    |
|      | v O'Kane        | 4-5   | 3rd round  | Dulux British Open                    |
|      | v O'Kane        | 8-10  | Qualifying | Embassy World Championship            |
|      | v Sinclair      | 5-1   | 3rd round  | Goya Matchroom Trophy                 |
|      | v Thorburn      | 3-5   | 4th round  | Goya Matchroom Trophy                 |
|      | v Morra         | 5-2   | 3rd round  | Rothmans Grand Prix                   |
|      | v S. Francisco  | 3-5   | 4th round  | Rothmans Grand Prix                   |
|      | v Darrington    | 9-3   | 3rd round  | Coral UK Open                         |
|      | v S. Francisco  | 6-9   | 4th round  | Coral UK Open                         |
| 1986 | v Murphy        | 5-3   | 3rd round  | Mercantile Credit Classic             |
|      | v P. Francisco  | 2-5   | 4th round  | Mercantile Credit Classic             |
|      | v F. Davis      | 9-8   | 3rd round  | Tolly Cobbold English Championship    |
|      | v S. Davis      | 4-9   | 4th round  | Tolly Cobbold English Championship    |
|      | v B. Harris     | 5-1   | 3rd round  | Dulux British Open                    |
|      | v S. Davis      | 1-5   | 4th round  | Dulux British Open                    |
|      | v Gilbert       | 10-5  | Qualifying | Embassy World Championship            |
|      | v Johnson       | 3-10  | 1st round  | Embassy World Championship            |
|      | v Chaperon      | 4-5   | 3rd round  | BCE International                     |
|      | v Higgins       | 2-5   | 4th round  | Rothmans Grand Prix                   |
|      | v Williamson    | 9-5   | 3rd round  | Tennents UK Open                      |
|      | v Higgins       | 6-9   | 4th round  | Tennents UK Open                      |
| 1987 | v G. Foulds     | 5-4   | 3rd round  | Mercantile Credit Classic             |
|      | v Griffiths     | 4-5   | 4th round  | Mercantile Credit Classic             |
|      | v Spencer       | 6-5   | 3rd round  | Tolly Ales English Championship       |
|      | v Thorne        | 3-6   | 4th round  | Tolly Ales English Championship       |
|      | v Scott         | 5-3   | 3rd round  | Dulux British Open                    |
|      | v Spencer       | 2-5   | 4th round  | Dulux British Open                    |
|      | v Hendry        | 7-10  | Qualifying | Embassy World Championship            |
|      | v D. Gilbert    | 2-5   | 3rd round  | Fidelity International                 |
|      | v Roe           | 4-5   | 3rd round  | Rothmans Grand Prix                   |
|      | v V. Harris     | 7-9   | 3rd round  | Tennents UK Open                      |
| 1988 | v J. McLaughlin | 5-2   | 3rd round  | Mercantile Credit Classic             |

| | | | |
|---|---|---|---|
| v Mountjoy | 5-4 | 4th round | Mercantile Credit Classic |
| v White | 5-2 | 5th round | Mercantile Credit Classic |
| v Knowles | 1-5 | Quarter-final | Mercantile Credit Classic |
| v M. Smith | 6-5 | 3rd round | English Championship |
| v Johnson | 4-6 | 4th round | English Championship |
| v Browne | 4-5 | 3rd round | MIM Britannia British Open |
| v W. Jones | 5-10 | Qualifying | Embassy World Championship |
| v Mikkelsen | 5-4 | 2nd round | Fidelity International |
| v Mountjoy | 1-5 | 3rd round | Fidelity International |
| v Wildman | 5-1 | 2nd round | Rothmans Grand Prix |
| v Chaperon | 0-5 | 3rd round | Rothmans Grand Prix |
| v Watterson | 5-1 | 2nd round | BCE Canadian Masters |
| v Reynolds | 0-5 | 3rd round | BCE Canadian Masters |
| v Miles | 9-7 | 2nd round | Tennents UK Open |
| v Parrott | 6-9 | 3rd round | Tennents UK Open |
| 1989 v Foldvari | 5-2 | 2nd round | Mercantile Credit Classic |
| v N. Foulds | 1-5 | 3rd round | Mercantile Credit Classic |
| v Oliver | 4-5 | 2nd round | European Open |
| v Rowswell | 2-5 | 3rd round | English Championship |
| v Bear | 2-5 | 2nd round | Anglian British Open |
| v M. Gibson | 10-7 | Qualifying | Embassy World Championship |
| v Clark | 2-10 | Qualifying | Embassy World Championship |

## JIM MEADOWCROFT (England)

**Born** 15.12.46. **Turned professional** 1971. **World ranking** 115 (94). **Best professional performances** Quarter-finals 1976 Embassy World Championship, 1977 Super Crystalate UK Championship.

| | | | |
|---|---|---|---|
| **1973** v Reardon | 10-16 | 2nd round | World Championship |
| **1974** v Kennerley | 8-5 | 1st round | World Championship |
| v Reardon | 3-15 | 2nd round | World Championship |
| **1975** v Werbeniuk | 9-15 | Qualifying | World Championship |
| **1976** v Wheelwright | 8-1 | Qualifying | Embassy World Championship |
| v Gross | 8-4 | Qualifying | Embassy World Championship |
| v Thorne | 8-5 | Qualifying | Embassy World Championship |
| v Williams | 15-7 | 1st round | Embassy World Championship |
| v Mans | 8-15 | Quarter-final | Embassy World Championship |
| **1977** v Fagan | 9-11 | Qualifying | Embassy World Championship |
| v Houlihan | 5-1 | 1st round | Super Crystalate UK Championship |
| v Reardon | 5-4 | 2nd round | Super Crystalate UK Championship |
| v Fagan | 4-5 | Quarter-final | Super Crystalate UK Championship |
| **1978** v Houlihan | 6-9 | Qualifying | Embassy World Championship |
| v Jack Rea | 9-5 | Qualifying | Coral UK Championship |
| v Higgins | 6-9 | 1st round | Coral UK Championship |
| **1979** v Van Rensberg | 9-7 | Prelim | Embassy World Championship |
| v Griffiths | 6-9 | Qualifying | Embassy World Championship |
| v Edmonds | 3-9 | 2nd round | Coral UK Championship |
| **1980** v Sinclair | 9-1 | Qualifying | Embassy World Championship |
| v Virgo | 2-10 | 1st round | Embassy World Championship |
| v Greaves | 9-1 | Qualifying | Coral UK Championship |
| v Thorne | 1-9 | 1st round | Coral UK Championship |
| **1981** v Barrie | 9-3 | Qualifying | John Courage English |
| v S. Davis | 2-9 | 1st round | John Courage English |
| v White | 8-9 | Qualifying | Embassy World Championship |
| v Roscoe | 5-4 | Qualifying | Jameson International |
| v Wilson | 5-4 | 1st round | Jameson International |
| v Stevens | 1-5 | 2nd round | Jameson International |
| v Houlihan | 4-9 | Qualifying | Coral UK Championship |
| **1982** v Watterson | 9-7 | Qualifying | Embassy World Championship |
| v Higgins | 5-10 | 1st round | Embassy World Championship |
| v Ross | 5-0 | Qualifying | Jameson International |

|      |                  |       |           |                                        |
|------|------------------|-------|-----------|----------------------------------------|
|      | v White          | 1-5   | 1st round | Jameson International                   |
|      | v Bennett        | 5-4   | 1st round | Professional Players Tournament        |
|      | v Sinclair       | 3-5   | 2nd round | Professional Players Tournament        |
|      | v D. Hughes      | 9-8   | Qualifying | Coral UK Championship                 |
|      | v Dennis Taylor  | 7-9   | 1st round | Coral UK Championship                   |
| 1983 | v Bennett        | 10-3  | Qualifying | Embassy World Championship            |
|      | v Cripsey        | 10-6  | Qualifying | Embassy World Championship            |
|      | v David Taylor   | 2-10  | 1st round | Embassy World Championship              |
|      | v Roscoe         | 5-4   | 1st round | Professional Players Tournament        |
|      | v Thorburn       | 1-5   | 2nd round | Professional Players Tournament        |
|      | v N. Foulds      | 2-9   | Qualifying | Coral UK Championship                 |
| 1984 | v Meo            | 1-5   | Qualifying | Lada Classic                          |
|      | v N. Foulds      | 2-10  | Qualifying | Embassy World Championship            |
|      | v Chalmers       | 5-1   | Qualifying | Jameson International                 |
|      | v Williams       | 4-5   | Qualifying | Jameson International                 |
|      | v J. McLaughlin  | 1-5   | Qualifying | Rothmans Grand Prix                   |
|      | v Bradley        | 7-9   | Qualifying | Coral UK Open                         |
| 1985 | v Fowler         | 2-5   | Qualifying | Mercantile Credit Classic             |
|      | v Chalmers       | 3-9   | Qualifying | Tolly Cobbold English Championship    |
|      | v B. Harris      | 1-6   | Qualifying | Dulux British Open                    |
|      | v P. Francisco   | 5-10  | Qualifying | Embassy World Championship            |
|      | v Chappel        | 2-5   | 2nd round | Goya Matchroom Trophy                   |
|      | v West           | 2-5   | 2nd round | Rothmans Grand Prix                     |
|      | v Hargreaves     | 9-8   | 2nd round | Coral UK Open                           |
|      | v Hallett        | 1-9   | 3rd round | Coral UK Open                           |
| 1986 | v West           | 0-5   | 2nd round | Mercantile Credit Classic               |
|      | v Cripsey        | 1-9   | 2nd round | Tolly Cobbold English Championship      |
|      | v Jenkins        | 2-5   | 2nd round | Dulux British Open                      |
|      | v Darrington     | 6-10  | Qualifying | Embassy World Championship            |
|      | v P. Gibson      | 2-5   | 1st round | BCE International                       |
|      | v Greaves        | 5-2   | 1st round | Rothmans Grand Prix                     |
|      | v Mans           | wo    | 2nd round | Rothmans Grand Prix                     |
|      | v Martin         | scr   | 3rd round | Rothmans Grand Prix                     |
|      | v Demarco        | 9-2   | 1st round | Tennents UK Open                        |
|      | v Bradley        | 2-9   | 2nd round | Tennents UK Open                        |
| 1987 | v Newbury        | 1-5   | 2nd round | Mercantile Credit Classic               |
|      | v Grace          | 4-5   | 1st round | Dulux British Open                      |
|      | v Mienie         | 10-3  | Qualifying | Embassy World Championship            |
|      | v Cripsey        | 9-10  | Qualifying | Embassy World Championship            |
|      | v Greaves        | 5-1   | 1st round | Fidelity International                  |
|      | v Owers          | 3-5   | 2nd round | Fidelity International                  |
|      | v A. Harris      | 5-3   | 1st round | Rothmans Grand Prix                     |
|      | v Browne         | 3-5   | 2nd round | Rothmans Grand Prix                     |
|      | v King           | 4-9   | 2nd round | Tennents UK Open                        |
| 1988 | v Everton        | 3-5   | 1st round | Mercantile Credit Classic               |
|      | v Heaton         | 0-6   | 1st round | English Championship                    |
|      | v Kelly          | 5-1   | 1st round | MIM Britannia British Open              |
|      | v Murphy         | 4-5   | 2nd round | MIM Britannia British Open              |
|      | v B. Bennett     | 10-5  | Qualifying | Embassy World Championship            |
|      | v Cripsey        | 3-10  | Qualifying | Embassy World Championship            |
|      | v Whitthread     | 4-5   | 1st round | Fidelity International                  |
|      | v Price          | 0-5   | 1st round | BCE Canadian Masters                    |
|      | v J. Smith       | 7-9   | 1st round | Tennents UK Open                        |
| 1989 | v Fitzmaurice    | 2-5   | 1st round | Mercantile Credit Classic               |
|      | v Robidoux       | 0-5   | 1st round | European Open                           |
|      | v Jenkins        | 5-4   | 1st round | Anglian British Open                    |
|      | v T. Jones       | 1-5   | 2nd round | Anglian British Open                    |
|      | v Mienie         | 10-7  | Qualifying | Embassy World Championship            |
|      | v Macleod        | 9-10  | Qualifying | Embassy World Championship            |

## STEVE MEAKIN (England)

**Born** 19.7.61. **Turned professional** 1987. **World ranking** 107 (117).

| 1987 | v Foldvari | 3-5 | 1st round | Fidelity International |
|------|------------|-----|-----------|----------------------|
| | v Morra | 5-2 | 1st round | Rothmans Grand Prix |
| | v Newbury | 1-5 | 2nd round | Rothmans Grand Prix |
| | v Glen Wilkinson | 9-0 | 1st round | Tennents UK Open |
| | v W. Jones | 1-9 | 2nd round | Tennents UK Open |
| 1988 | v Darrington | 5-4 | 1st round | Mercantile Credit Classic |
| | v F. Davis | 4-5 | 2nd round | Mercantile Credit Classic |
| | v Darrington | 6-3 | 1st round | English Championship |
| | v Owers | 2-6 | 2nd round | English Championship |
| | v Williamson | 1-5 | 1st round | MIM Britannia British Open |
| | v Morra | 5-10 | Qualifying | Embassy World Championship |
| | v Van Rensberg | 5-4 | 1st round | Fidelity International |
| | v Gauvreau | 5-3 | 2nd round | Fidelity International |
| | v E. Hughes | 0-5 | 3rd round | Fidelity International |
| | v Chambers | 0-5 | 1st round | Rothmans Grand Prix |
| | v John Rea | 6-9 | 1st round | Tennents UK Open |
| 1989 | v Sinclair | 1-5 | 1st round | Mercantile Credit Classic |
| | v Grace | 4-5 | 1st round | European Open |
| | v Roscoe | 1-5 | 1st round | Anglian British Open |
| | v Kearney | 10-3 | Qualifying | Embassy World Championship |
| | v Browne | 9-10 | Qualifying | Embassy World Championship |

## PAUL MEDATI (England)

**Born** 14.11.44. **Turned professional** 1981. **World ranking** 80 (68). **Best professional performances** Last 32 1988 MIM Britannia British Open, 1986 Dulux British Open.

| 1981 | v Watterson | 3-5 | Qualifying | Jameson International |
|------|-------------|-----|-----------|----------------------|
| | v E. McLaughlin | 9-5 | Qualifying | Coral UK Championship |
| | v Donnelly | 9-7 | Qualifying | Coral UK Championship |
| | v Thorne | 6-9 | Qualifying | Coral UK Championship |
| 1982 | v Phillips | 9-3 | Qualifying | Embassy World Championship |
| | v Wilson | 5-9 | Qualifying | Embassy World Championship |
| | v Williams | 3-5 | Qualifying | Jameson International |
| | v Thorburn | 1-5 | 1st round | Professional Players Tournament |
| | v Bennett | 9-1 | Qualifying | Coral UK Championship |
| | v White | 7-9 | 1st round | Coral UK Championship |
| 1983 | v John Bear | 10-7 | Qualifying | Embassy World Championship |
| | v Black | 4-10 | Qualifying | Embassy World Championship |
| | v V. Harris | 5-0 | Qualifying | Jameson International |
| | v Macleod | 3-5 | Qualifying | Jameson International |
| | v D. Hughes | 5-1 | Qualifying | Professional Players Tournament |
| | v Knowles | 1-5 | 1st round | Professional Players Tournament |
| | v D. Hughes | 9-2 | Qualifying | Coral UK Championship |
| | v Edmonds | 9-7 | Qualifying | Coral UK Championship |
| | v Reynolds | 9-3 | 1st round | Coral UK Championship |
| | v Higgins | 1-9 | 2nd round | Coral UK Championship |
| 1984 | v Mikkelsen | 8-10 | Qualifying | Embassy World Championship |
| | v Gibson | 3-5 | Qualifying | Jameson International |
| | v Dodd | 5-4 | Qualifying | Rothmans Grand Prix |
| | v Johnson | 1-5 | 1st round | Rothmans Grand Prix |
| | v Hargreaves | 6-9 | Qualifying | Coral UK Open |
| 1985 | v Cripsey | 5-4 | Qualifying | Mercantile Credit Classic |
| | v Roscoe | 5-4 | Qualifying | Mercantile Credit Classic |
| | v Parrott | 5-3 | Qualifying | Mercantile Credit Classic |
| | v Stevens | 4-5 | 1st round | Mercantile Credit Classic |
| | v Hargreaves | 9-8 | Qualifying | Tolly Cobbold English Championship |
| | v Spencer | 9-4 | 1st round | Tolly Cobbold English Championship |
| | v Longworth | 7-9 | 2nd round | Tolly Cobbold English Championship |
| | v King | 4-6 | Qualifying | Dulux British Open |

|  |  |  |  |
|---|---|---|---|
| v Bennett | 10-4 | Qualifying | Embassy World Championship |
| v Williamson | 10-8 | Qualifying | Embassy World Championship |
| v King | 10-9 | Qualifying | Embassy World Championship |
| v S. Francisco | 7-10 | Qualifying | Embassy World Championship |
| v Cripsey | 2-5 | 2nd round | Goya Matchroom Trophy |
| v J. McLaughlin | 2-5 | 2nd round | Rothmans Grand Prix |
| v Kelly | 9-1 | 2nd round | Coral UK Open |
| ❦ v J. Campbell | 7-9 | 3rd round | Coral UK Open |
| 1986 v Kearney | 5-2 | 2nd round | Mercantile Credit Classic |
| v O'Kane | 0-5 | 3rd round | Mercantile Credit Classic |
| v Greaves | 9-4 | 2nd round | Tolly Cobbold English Championship |
| v Thorne | 2-9 | 3rd round | Tolly Cobbold English Championship |
| v Everton | 5-1 | 2nd round | Dulux British Open |
| v David Taylor | 5-1 | 3rd round | Dulux British Open |
| v J. Campbell | 4-5 | 4th round | Dulux British Open |
| v Simngam | 10-9 | Qualifying | Embassy World Championship |
| v Gibson | 10-6 | Qualifying | Embassy World Championship |
| v Wilson | 6-10 | Qualifying | Embassy World Championship |
| v Kearney | 5-3 | 2nd round | BCE International |
| v Griffiths | 3-5 | 3rd round | BCE International |
| v Rigitano | 5-1 | 2nd round | Rothmans Grand Prix |
| v P. Francisco | 1-5 | 3rd round | Rothmans Grand Prix |
| v Grace | 5-9 | 2nd round | Tennents UK Open |
| 1987 v Dodd | 4-5 | 2nd round | Mercantile Credit Classic |
| v N. Gibson | 6-2 | 2nd round | Tolly Ales English Championship |
| v Virgo | 1-6 | 3rd round | Tolly Ales English Championship |
| v Ellis | 5-0 | 2nd round | Dulux British Open |
| v Charlton | 4-5 | 3rd round | Dulux British Open |
| v Kearney | 10-8 | Qualifying | Embassy World Championship |
| v Gauvreau | 10-3 | Qualifying | Embassy World Championship |
| v E. Hughes | 2-10 | Qualifying | Embassy World Championship |
| v Murphy | 3-5 | 2nd round | Fidelity International |
| v M. Bennett | 4-5 | 2nd round | Rothmans Grand Prix |
| v Dodd | 6-9 | 2nd round | Tennents UK Open |
| 1988 v Chaperon | 3-5 | 2nd round | Mercantile Credit Classic |
| v B. Bennett | 6-0 | 1st round | English Championship |
| v Fowler | 1-6 | 2nd round | English Championship |
| v Gauvreau | 5-1 | 2nd round | MIM Britannia British Open |
| v David Taylor | 5-4 | 3rd round | MIM Britannia British Open |
| v Thorburn | 2-5 | 4th round | MIM Britannia British Open |
| v Gary Wilkinson | 10-9 | Qualifying | Embassy World Championship |
| v Dodd | 6-10 | Qualifying | Embassy World Championship |
| v Price | 4-5 | 1st round | Fidelity International |
| v Watchorn | 5-2 | 1st round | Rothmans Grand Prix |
| v King | 5-1 | 2nd round | Rothmans Grand Prix |
| v Williams | 2-5 | 3rd round | Rothmans Grand Prix |
| v Edwards | 5-3 | 1st round | BCE Canadian Masters |
| v Cripsey | 5-0 | 2nd round | BCE Canadian Masters |
| v Virgo | 1-5 | 3rd round | BCE Canadian Masters |
| v Fisher | 9-3 | 2nd round | Tennents UK Open |
| v S. Francisco | 8-9 | 3rd round | Tennents UK Open |
| 1989 v Gary Wilkinson | 1-5 | 2nd round | Mercantile Credit Classic |
| v Sheehan | 5-1 | 1st round | European Open |
| v T. Jones | 2-5 | 2nd round | European Open |
| v Wildman | 5-4 | 1st round | English Championship |
| v Bales | 5-3 | 2nd round | English Championship |
| v N. Foulds | 3-5 | 3rd round | English Championship |
| v S. Campbell | 3-5 | 1st round | Anglian British Open |
| v Terry | 8-10 | Qualifying | Embassy World Championship |

## TONY MEO (England)

**Born** 4.10.59. **Turned professional** 1979. **World ranking** 14 (31). **Best professional performances** Winner 1989 Anglian British Open; runner-up 1984 Lada Classic; winner 1986 and 1987 English Championship.

| Year | Opponent | Score | Round | Tournament |
|---|---|---|---|---|
| 1979 | v David Taylor | 9-7 | 2nd round | Coral UK Championship |
| | v Virgo | 6-9 | 3rd round | Coral UK Championship |
| 1980 | v Van Rensberg | 9-1 | Qualifying | Embassy World Championship |
| | v Houlihan | 9-1 | Qualifying | Embassy World Championship |
| | v Higgins | 9-10 | 1st round | Embassy World Championship |
| | v Hood | 9-5 | Qualifying | Coral UK Championship |
| | v Houlihan | 9-1 | 1st round | Coral UK Championship |
| | v Virgo | 9-1 | 2nd round | Coral UK Championship |
| | v S. Davis | 5-9 | Quarter-final | Coral UK Championship |
| 1981 | v Virgo | 9-6 | Qualifying | John Courage English |
| | v Miles | 9-7 | 2nd round | John Courage English |
| | v Thorne | 9-8 | Semi-final | John Courage English |
| | v S. Davis | 3-9 | Final | John Courage English |
| | v Johnson | 9-8 | Qualifying | Embassy World Championship |
| | v Hallett | 9-4 | Qualifying | Embassy World Championship |
| | v Virgo | 10-6 | 1st round | Embassy World Championship |
| | v Griffiths | 6-13 | 2nd round | Embassy World Championship |
| | v E. McLaughlin | 5-2 | 1st round | Jameson International |
| | v Mans | 3-5 | 2nd round | Jameson International |
| | v Williams | 9-8 | 2nd round | Coral UK Championship |
| | v Thorburn | 9-6 | 3rd round | Coral UK Championship |
| | v Higgins | 9-4 | Quarter-final | Coral UK Championship |
| | v Griffiths | 3-9 | Semi-final | Coral UK Championship |
| 1982 | v David Taylor | 5-2 | 1st round | Benson & Hedges Masters |
| | v Thorburn | 5-0 | Quarter-final | Benson & Hedges Masters |
| | v S. Davis | 4-6 | Semi-final | Benson & Hedges Masters |
| | v Spencer | 5-3 | 1st round | Benson & Hedges Irish Masters |
| | v Griffiths | 3-5 | Quarter-final | Benson & Hedges Irish Masters |
| | v D. Hughes | 9-4 | Qualifying | Embassy World Championship |
| | v Mans | 8-10 | 1st round | Embassy World Championship |
| | v Sinclair | 3-5 | Qualifying | Jameson International |
| | v M. Owen | 5-4 | 1st round | Professional Players Tournament |
| | v Jonik | 5-0 | 2nd round | Professional Players Tournament |
| | v Charlton | 3-5 | 3rd round | Professional Players Tournament |
| | v Scott | 9-5 | Qualifying | Coral UK Championship |
| | v Miles | 9-4 | 1st round | Coral UK Championship |
| | v David Taylor | 9-6 | 2nd round | Coral UK Championship |
| | v Virgo | 9-6 | Quarter-final | Coral UK Championship |
| | v Griffiths | 7-9 | Semi-final | Coral UK Championship |
| 1983 | v Charlton | 3-5 | 1st round | Benson & Hedges Masters |
| | v Burke | 5-0 | 1st round | Benson & Hedges Irish Masters |
| | v Reardon | 4-5 | Quarter-final | Benson & Hedges Irish Masters |
| | v V. Harris | 10-0 | Qualifying | Embassy World Championship |
| | v G. Foulds | 10-4 | Qualifying | Embassy World Championship |
| | v White | 10-8 | 1st round | Embassy World Championship |
| | v Mountjoy | 13-11 | 2nd round | Embassy World Championship |
| | v Knowles | 9-13 | Quarter-final | Embassy World Championship |
| | v Knowles | 4-5 | 1st round | Langs Supreme Scottish Masters |
| | v Watterson | 3-5 | 1st round | Jameson International |
| | v King | 5-2 | 1st round | Professional Players Tournament |
| | v Reynolds | 5-0 | 2nd round | Professional Players Tournament |
| | v Hallett | 5-3 | 3rd round | Professional Players Tournament |
| | v Stevens | 5-3 | Quarter-final | Professional Players Tournament |
| | v Johnson | 6-9 | Semi-final | Professional Players Tournament |
| | v Parrott | 9-7 | 1st round | Coral UK Championship |
| | v Spencer | 9-5 | 2nd round | Coral UK Championship |

*Tony Meo*

| | | | | |
|---|---|---|---|---|
| | v Davis | 4-9 | Quarter-final | Coral UK Championship |
| **1984** | v Meadowcroft | 5-1 | Qualifying | Lada Classic |
| | v Williams | 5-3 | 1st round | Lada Classic |
| | v Stevens | 5-2 | Quarter-final | Lada Classic |
| | v Wildman | 5-3 | Semi-final | Lada Classic |
| | v S. Davis | 8-9 | Final | Lada Classic |
| | v S. Davis | 0-5 | 1st round | Benson & Hedges Masters |
| | v White | 5-4 | 1st round | Benson & Hedges Irish Masters |
| | v S. Davis | 4-5 | Quarter-final | Benson & Hedges Irish Masters |
| | v Thorburn | 4-5 | 1st round | Tolly Cobbold Classic |
| | v S. Francisco | 5-10 | 1st round | Embassy World Championship |
| | v Stevens | 5-1 | Quarter-final | Winfield Australian Masters |
| | v Virgo | 2-6 | Semi-final | Winfield Australian Masters |
| | v Macleod | 5-1 | 1st round | Jameson International |
| | v White | 1-5 | 2nd round | Jameson International |
| | v Burke | 5-1 | 1st round | Rothmans Grand Prix |
| | v Martin | 5-4 | 2nd round | Rothmans Grand Prix |
| | v Thorburn | 4-5 | 3rd round | Rothmans Grand Prix |
| | v E. Hughes | 9-4 | 1st round | Coral UK Open |
| | v S. Davis | 7-9 | 2nd round | Coral UK Open |
| **1985** | v E. Hughes | 4-5 | 1st round | Mercantile Credit Classic |
| | v Fisher | 9-3 | 1st round | Tolly Cobbold English Championship |
| | v Hallett | 9-4 | 2nd round | Tolly Cobbold English Championship |
| | v Reynolds | 9-4 | Quarter-final | Tolly Cobbold English Championship |
| | v S. Davis | 8-9 | Semi-final | Tolly Cobbold English Championship |
| | v Foldvari | 6-0 | 1st round | Dulux British Open |
| | v Hallett | 5-4 | 2nd round | Dulux British Open |
| | v Knowles | 5-2 | 3rd round | Dulux British Open |
| | v S. Francisco | 4-5 | Quarter-final | Dulux British Open |
| | v White | 1-5 | 1st round | Benson & Hedges Irish Masters |
| | v Virgo | 10-6 | 1st round | Embassy World Championship |
| | v White | 11-13 | 2nd round | Embassy World Championship |
| | v Virgo | 5-3 | Quarter-final | Winfield Australian Masters |
| | v White | 6-3 | Semi-final | Winfield Australian Masters |
| | **v J. Campbell** | **7-2** | **Final** | **Winfield Australian Masters** |
| | v Dunning | 5-0 | 3rd round | Goya Matchroom Trophy |
| | v Parrott | 4-5 | 4th round | Goya Matchroom Trophy |
| | v T. Jones | 5-2 | 3rd round | Rothmans Grand Prix |
| | v E. Hughes | 5-3 | 4th round | Rothmans Grand Prix |
| | v Dennis Taylor | 3-5 | 5th round | Rothmans Grand Prix |
| | v Longworth | 9-5 | 3rd round | Coral UK Open |
| | v Fowler | 9-2 | 4th round | Coral UK Open |
| | v S. Davis | 5-9 | 5th round | Coral UK Open |
| **1986** | v O'Boye | 5-3 | 3rd round | Mercantile Credit Classic |
| | v West | 5-1 | 4th round | Mercantile Credit Classic |
| | v Thorburn | 1-5 | 5th round | Mercantile Credit Classic |
| | v White | 4-5 | 1st round | Benson & Hedges Masters |
| | v Scott | 9-1 | 3rd round | Tolly Cobbold English Championship |
| | v Wildman | 9-3 | 4th round | Tolly Cobbold English Championship |
| | v Reynolds | 9-4 | Quarter-final | Tolly Cobbold English Championship |
| | v S. Davis | 9-7 | Semi-final | Tolly Cobbold English Championship |
| | **v N. Foulds** | **9-7** | **Final** | **Tolly Cobbold English Championship** |
| | v Donnelly | 5-3 | 3rd round | Dulux British Open |
| | v Newbury | 5-0 | 4th round | Dulux British Open |
| | v Thorburn | 5-3 | 5th round | Dulux British Open |
| | v Virgo | 3-5 | Quarter-final | Dulux British Open |
| | v Higgins | 5-4 | 1st round | Benson & Hedges Irish Masters |
| | v White | 2-5 | Quarter-final | Benson & Hedges Irish Masters |
| | v Parrott | 6-10 | 1st round | Embassy World Championship |
| | v Griffiths | 3-6 | 1st round | Matchroom Trophy |
| | v Houlihan | 5-1 | 3rd round | BCE International |
| | v Chappel | 5-1 | 3rd round | Rothmans Grand Prix |
| | v Parrott | 5-3 | 4th round | Rothmans Grand Prix |

|      |                  |       |              |                                  |
|------|------------------|-------|--------------|----------------------------------|
|      | v Dennis Taylor  | 5-2   | 5th round    | Rothmans Grand Prix              |
|      | v N. Foulds      | 3-5   | Quarter-final | Rothmans Grand Prix             |
|      | v O'Boye         | 9-3   | 3rd round    | Tennents UK Open                 |
|      | v Hallett        | 4-9   | 4th round    | Tennents UK Open                 |
| 1987 | v John Rea       | 5-4   | 3rd round    | Mercantile Credit Classic        |
|      | v Longworth      | 5-0   | 4th round    | Mercantile Credit Classic        |
|      | v S. Davis       | 2-5   | 5th round    | Mercantile Credit Classic        |
|      | v White          | 5-4   | 1st round    | Benson & Hedges Masters          |
|      | v Mountjoy       | 5-4   | Quarter-final | Benson & Hedges Masters         |
|      | v Higgins        | 2-6   | Semi-final   | Benson & Hedges Masters          |
|      | v Duggan         | 6-3   | 3rd round    | Tolly Ales English Championship  |
|      | v Fowler         | 6-0   | 4th round    | Tolly Ales English Championship  |
|      | v Parrott        | 6-3   | Quarter-final | Tolly Ales English Championship |
|      | v Thorne         | 9-3   | Semi-final   | Tolly Ales English Championship  |
|      | **v Dodd**       | **9-5** | **Final**  | **Tolly Ales English Championship** |
|      | v Spencer        | 1-5   | 3rd round    | Dulux British Open               |
|      | v Knowles        | 5-2   | 1st round    | Benson & Hedges Irish Masters    |
|      | v S. Davis       | 2-5   | Quarter-final | Benson & Hedges Irish Masters   |
|      | v Parrott        | 8-10  | 1st round    | Embassy World Championship       |
|      | v Wright         | 5-2   | 3rd round    | Fidelity International           |
|      | v S. Davis       | 3-5   | 4th round    | Fidelity International           |
|      | v Newbury        | 0-5   | 3rd round    | Rothmans Grand Prix              |
|      | v S. Davis       | 5-6   | 1st round    | Matchroom Trophy                 |
|      | v Watchorn       | 9-1   | 3rd round    | Tennents UK Open                 |
|      | v Hallett        | 5-9   | 4th round    | Tennents UK Open                 |
| 1988 | v Morra          | 5-1   | 3rd round    | Mercantile Credit Classic        |
|      | v Higgins        | 3-5   | 4th round    | Mercantile Credit Classic        |
|      | v F. Davis       | 6-3   | 3rd round    | English Championship             |
|      | v Longworth      | 6-4   | 4th round    | English Championship             |
|      | v Reynolds       | 4-6   | Quarter-final | English Championship            |
|      | v Gary Wilkinson | 2-5   | 3rd round    | MIM Britannia British Open       |
|      | v Werbeniuk      | 4-10  | Qualifying   | Embassy World Championship       |
|      | v N. Gilbert     | 5-1   | 3rd round    | Fidelity International           |
|      | v Hallett        | 5-3   | 4th round    | Fidelity International           |
|      | v Chaperon       | 5-4   | 5th round    | Fidelity International           |
|      | v James          | 1-5   | Quarter-final | Fidelity International           |
|      | v N. Foulds      | 4-5   | Semi-final   | Dubai Duty Free Masters          |
|      | v Stevens        | 5-3   | 3rd round    | Rothmans Grand Prix              |
|      | v Robidoux       | 0-5   | 4th round    | Rothmans Grand Prix              |
|      | v Gauvreau       | 0-5   | 3rd round    | BCE Canadian Masters             |
|      | v Roe            | 6-9   | 3rd round    | Tennents UK Open                 |
| 1989 | v Stevens        | 5-3   | 3rd round    | Mercantile Credit Classic        |
|      | v S. Francisco   | 1-5   | 4th round    | Mercantile Credit Classic        |
|      | v Roe            | 1-5   | 3rd round    | European Open                    |
|      | v Fowler         | 3-5   | 3rd round    | English Championship             |
|      | v M. Bennett     | 5-1   | 3rd round    | Anglian British Open             |
|      | v Roscoe         | 5-3   | 4th round    | Anglian British Open             |
|      | v Hendry         | 5-3   | 5th round    | Anglian British Open             |
|      | v P. Francisco   | 5-3   | Quarter-final | Anglian British Open            |
|      | v Hallett        | 9-8   | Semi-final   | Anglian British Open             |
|      | **v Reynolds**   | **13-6** | **Final** | **Anglian British Open**         |
|      | v T. Jones       | 10-5  | Qualifying   | Embassy World Championship       |
|      | v Johnson        | 10-5  | 1st round    | Embassy World Championship       |
|      | v Charlton       | 13-8  | 2nd round    | Embassy World Championship       |
|      | v Reynolds       | 13-9  | Quarter-final | Embassy World Championship      |
|      | v Parrott        | 7-16  | Semi-final   | Embassy World Championship       |

## BERNIE MIKKELSEN (Canada)

**Born** 11.4.50. **Turned professional** 1979. **World ranking** 122 (97). **Best professional performance** Last 32 1986 Mercantile Credit Classic.

| 1981 | v White | 4-9 | Qualifying | Embassy World Championship |
|---|---|---|---|---|
| 1982 | v Roscoe | 6-9 | Qualifying | Embassy World Championship |
| 1983 | v Rigitano | 9-4 | 2nd round | Canadian Championship |
|  | v Thorburn | 2-9 | Quarter-final | Canadian Championship |
| 1984 | v Medati | 10-8 | Qualifying | Embassy World Championship |
|  | v Jonik | 10-9 | Qualifying | Embassy World Championship |
|  | v Thorne | 3-10 | Qualifying | Embassy World Championship |
|  | v Chappel | 5-4 | Qualifying | Jameson International |
|  | v Everton | 5-0 | Qualifying | Jameson International |
|  | v Roscoe | 1-5 | Qualifying | Jameson International |
|  | v Sheehan | 3-5 | Qualifying | Rothmans Grand Prix |
| 1985 | v Chalmers | 5-1 | Prelim | Mercantile Credit Classic |
|  | v Watchorn | 1-5 | Qualifying | Mercantile Credit Classic |
|  | v D. Hughes | 6-0 | Qualifying | Dulux British Open |
|  | v Bradley | 9-10 | Qualifying | Embassy World Championship |
|  | v Watson | 5-3 | 1st round | Canadian Championship |
|  | v Jonik | 4-6 | Quarter-final | Canadian Championship |
|  | v Fisher | 5-3 | 2nd round | Goya Matchroom Trophy |
|  | v Reynolds | 0-5 | 3rd round | Goya Matchroom Trophy |
|  | v Murphy | 5-4 | 2nd round | Rothmans Grand Prix |
|  | v Hallett | 3-5 | 3rd round | Rothmans Grand Prix |
|  | v Williamson | 9-3 | 2nd round | Coral UK Open |
|  | v David Taylor | 6-9 | 3rd round | Coral UK Open |
| 1986 | v Scott | 5-1 | 2nd round | Mercantile Credit Classic |
|  | v Reardon | 5-3 | 3rd round | Mercantile Credit Classic |
|  | v J. Campbell | 2-5 | 4th round | Mercantile Credit Classic |
|  | v Roscoe | 4-5 | 2nd round | Dulux British Open |
|  | v Hargreaves | 10-7 | Qualifying | Embassy World Championship |
|  | v Watterson | 2-10 | Qualifying | Embassy World Championship |
|  | v Sanderson | 6-1 | 1st round | Canadian Championship |
|  | v Wych | 3-6 | 2nd round | Canadian Championship |
|  | v O'Boye | 4-5 | 2nd round | BCE International |
|  | v G. Foulds | 1-5 | 2nd round | Rothmans Grand Prix |
|  | v Sinclair | 9-8 | 2nd round | Tennents UK Open |
|  | v Reynolds | 6-9 | 3rd round | Tennents UK Open |
| 1987 | v Foldvari | 5-1 | 2nd round | Mercantile Credit Classic |
|  | v Hallett | 3-5 | 3rd round | Mercantile Credit Classic |
|  | v Foldvari | 3-5 | 2nd round | Dulux British Open |
|  | v M. Bennett | 4-10 | Qualifying | Embassy World Championship |
|  | v Bear | 0-6 | 1st round | Canadian Championship |
| 1988 | v Jack Rea | 10-3 | Qualifying | Embassy World Championship |
|  | v Wildman | 5-10 | Qualifying | Embassy World Championship |
|  | v Stevens | 6-5 | Quarter-final | BCE Canadian Championship |
|  | v Robidoux | 3-7 | Semi-final | BCE Canadian Championship |
|  | v Fitzmaurice | 5-2 | 1st round | Fidelity International |
|  | v Martin | 4-5 | 2nd round | Fidelity International |
|  | v D. Hughes | 5-4 | 1st round | Rothmans Grand Prix |
|  | v T. Jones | 3-5 | 2nd round | Rothmans Grand Prix |
|  | v Lawlor | 2-5 | 1st round | BCE Canadian Masters |
|  | v V. Harris | 3-9 | 1st round | Tennents UK Open |
| 1989 | v Miles | 3-5 | 1st round | Mercantile Credit Classic |
|  | v Chambers | 3-5 | 1st round | European Open |
|  | v Sinclair | 3-5 | 1st round | Anglian British Open |
|  | v Morra | 4-10 | Qualifying | Embassy World Championship |

## GRAHAM MILES (England)

**Born** 11.5.41. **Turned professional** 1969. **World ranking** 78 (65). **Best professional performance** Runner-up 1974 World Championship.

| 1972 | v Bennett | 15-6 | Qualifying | World Championship |
|---|---|---|---|---|
|  | v Dunning | 5-11 | Qualifying | World Championship |

| 1973 | v Thompson | 9-5 | 1st round | World Championship |
|------|------------|-----|-----------|--------------------|
|      | v Pulman | 16-10 | 2nd round | World Championship |
|      | v Charlton | 6-16 | Quarter-final | World Championship |
| 1974 | v Morgan | 15-7 | 2nd round | World Championship |
|      | v Dunning | 15-13 | Quarter-final | World Championship |
|      | v Williams | 15-7 | Semi-final | World Championship |
|      | v Reardon | 12-22 | Final | World Championship |
| 1975 | v Reardon | 3-5 | Quarter-final | Benson & Hedges Masters |
|      | v Thorburn | 2-15 | 2nd round | World Championship |
| 1976 | v Spencer | 5-4 | Semi-final | Benson & Hedges Masters |
|      | v Reardon | 3-7 | Final | Benson & Hedges Masters |
|      | v Mans | 10-15 | 1st round | Embassy World Championship |
| 1977 | v Reardon | 2-5 | Semi-final | Benson & Hedges Masters |
|      | v Thorne | 13-4 | 1st round | Embassy World Championship |
|      | v Pulman | 10-13 | Quarter-final | Embassy World Championship |
|      | v Ross | 5-1 | 2nd round | Super Crystalate UK Championship |
|      | v Virgo | 2-5 | Quarter-final | Super Crystalate UK Championship |
| 1978 | v David Taylor | 13-10 | 1st round | Embassy World Championship |
|      | v Mans | 7-13 | Quarter-final | Embassy World Championship |
|      | v Williams | 9-8 | 1st round | Coral UK Championship |
|      | v Thorne | 9-1 | Quarter-final | Coral UK Championship |
|      | v Mountjoy | 1-9 | Semi-final | Coral UK Championship |
| 1979 | v Higgins | 6-3 | Semi-final | Holsten Lager International |
|      | v Spencer | 7-11 | Final | Holsten Lager International |
|      | v Williams | 9-5 | Qualifying | Embassy World Championship |
|      | v Reardon | 8-13 | 1st round | Embassy World Championship |
|      | v Fagan | 5-9 | 3rd round | Coral UK Championship |
| 1980 | v Stevens | 3-10 | 1st round | Embassy World Championship |
|      | v Sinclair | 5-9 | 1st round | Coral UK Championship |
| 1981 | v Hood | 9-1 | 1st round | John Courage English |
|      | v Meo | 7-9 | 2nd round | John Courage English |
|      | v Knowles | 10-8 | 1st round | Embassy World Championship |
|      | v Thorburn | 2-13 | 2nd round | Embassy World Championship |
|      | v Johnson | 5-3 | 2nd round | Jameson International |
|      | v Thorburn | 5-0 | 3rd round | Jameson International |
|      | v Martin | 1-5 | Quarter-final | Jameson International |
|      | v Houlihan | 9-5 | 2nd round | Coral UK Championship |
|      | v Griffiths | 4-9 | 3rd round | Coral UK Championship |
| 1982 | v S. Davis | 2-5 | Semi-final | Tolly Cobbold Classic |
|      | v Martin | 10-5 | 1st round | Embassy World Championship |
|      | v Knowles | 7-13 | 2nd round | Embassy World Championship |
|      | v Edmonds | 1-5 | Qualifying | Jameson International |
|      | v Johnson | 1-5 | 1st round | Professional Players Tournament |
|      | v Meo | 4-9 | 1st round | Coral UK Championship |
| 1983 | v Morgan | 10-6 | Qualifying | Embassy World Championship |
|      | v Knowles | 3-10 | 1st round | Embassy World Championship |
|      | v King | 5-3 | Qualifying | Jameson International |
|      | v Griffiths | 2-5 | 1st round | Jameson International |
|      | v Gauvreau | 5-3 | 1st round | Professional Players Tournament |
|      | v J. Campbell | 2-5 | 2nd round | Professional Players Tournament |
|      | v Hallett | 4-9 | 1st round | Coral UK Championship |
| 1984 | v Williamson | 10-6 | Qualifying | Embassy World Championship |
|      | v Spencer | 3-10 | 1st round | Embassy World Championship |
|      | v Newbury | 1-5 | Qualifying | Jameson International |
|      | v Murphy | 5-3 | 1st round | Rothmans Grand Prix |
|      | v S. Davis | 0-5 | 2nd round | Rothmans Grand Prix |
|      | v J. McLaughlin | 8-9 | Qualifying | Coral UK Open |
| 1985 | v Browne | 3-5 | Qualifying | Mercantile Credit Classic |
|      | v Martin | 7-9 | 1st round | Tolly Cobbold English Championship |
|      | v Edmonds | 6-1 | 1st round | Dulux British Open |
|      | v Spencer | 2-5 | 2nd round | Dulux British Open |
|      | v Stevens | 2-5 | 3rd round | Dulux British Open |
|      | v W. Jones | 8-10 | Qualifying | Embassy World Championship |

| | | | |
|---|---|---|---|
| v O'Boye | 5-2 | 2nd round | Goya Matchroom Trophy |
| v Virgo | 2-5 | 3rd round | Goya Matchroom Trophy |
| v Rigitano | 5-4 | 2nd round | Rothmans Grand Prix |
| v Reynolds | 5-3 | 3rd round | Rothmans Grand Prix |
| v Stevens | 2-5 | 4th round | Rothmans Grand Prix |
| v Oliver | 9-4 | 2nd round | Coral UK Open |
| v Reardon | 4-9 | 3rd round | Coral UK Open |
| **1986** v Hendry | 1-5 | 2nd round | Mercantile Credit Classic |
| v Fitzmaurice | 9-5 | 2nd round | Tolly Cobbold English Championship |
| v Williams | 6-9 | 3rd round | Tolly Cobbold English Championship |
| v Agrawal | 5-4 | 2nd round | Dulux British Open |
| v Stevens | 3-5 | 3rd round | Dulux British Open |
| v Everton | 10-3 | Qualifying | Embassy World Championship |
| v Foldvari | 7-10 | Qualifying | Embassy World Championship |
| v Roe | 5-1 | 2nd round | BCE International |
| v N. Foulds | 2-5 | 3rd round | BCE International |
| v Jonik | 5-1 | 2nd round | Rothmans Grand Prix |
| v N. Foulds | 1-5 | 3rd round | Rothmans Grand Prix |
| v Sheehan | 9-8 | 2nd round | Tennents UK Open |
| v Virgo | 7-9 | 3rd round | Tennents UK Open |
| **1987** v Sinclair | 1-5 | 2nd round | Mercantile Credit Classic |
| v Johnson | 3-6 | 3rd round | Tolly Ales English Championship |
| v Greaves | 10-7 | Qualifying | Embassy World Championship |
| v Murphy | 7-10 | Qualifying | Embassy World Championship |
| v Wildman | 3-5 | 2nd round | Fidelity International |
| v Scott | 5-2 | 2nd round | Rothmans Grand Prix |
| v Davis | 1-5 | 3rd round | Rothmans Grand Prix |
| v Houlihan | 9-3 | 2nd round | Tennents UK Open |
| v Spencer | 9-5 | 3rd round | Tennents UK Open |
| v Fowler | 4-9 | 4th round | Tennents UK Open |
| **1988** v M. Bennett | 1-5 | 2nd round | Mercantile Credit Classic |
| v M. Smith | 1-6 | 1st round | English Championship |
| v Owers | 5-3 | 2nd round | MIM Britannia British Open |
| v Dennis Taylor | 1-5 | 3rd round | MIM Britannia British Open |
| v D. Hughes | 10-3 | Qualifying | Embassy World Championship |
| v Bales | 10-7 | Qualifying | Embassy World Championship |
| v Chappel | 7-10 | Qualifying | Embassy World Championship |
| v G. Foulds | 5-3 | 2nd round | Fidelity International |
| v Knowles | 4-5 | 3rd round | Fidelity International |
| v Terry | 1-5 | 2nd round | Rothmans Grand Prix |
| v Watchorn | 2-5 | 1st round | BCE Canadian Masters |
| v Watchorn | 9-6 | 1st round | Tennents UK Open |
| v Martin | 7-9 | 2nd round | Tennents UK Open |
| **1989** v Mikkelsen | 5-3 | 1st round | Mercantile Credit Classic |
| v Gauvreau | 5-3 | 2nd round | Mercantile Credit Classic |
| v E. Hughes | 2-5 | 3rd round | Mercantile Credit Classic |
| v Jenkins | 5-3 | 1st round | European Open |
| v King | 2-5 | 2nd round | European Open |
| v M. Smith | 5-4 | 1st round | English Championship |
| v M. Fisher | 5-4 | 2nd round | English Championship |
| v Parrott | 3-5 | 3rd round | English Championship |
| v Chalmers | 5-4 | 1st round | Anglian British Open |
| v Gary Wilkinson | 2-5 | 2nd round | Anglian British Open |
| v Robidoux | 8-10 | Qualifying | Embassy World Championship |

## DARREN MORGAN (Wales)

**Born** 3.5.66. **Turned professional** 1988. **World ranking** 53. **Amateur career** 1987 World champion, 1987 Welsh champion. **Best professional performances** Last 32 1988 BCE Canadian Masters, 1989 Anglian British Open, 1989 Embassy World Championship.

| 1988 | v Hendry | 2-5 | 1st round | New Zealand Masters |
|------|----------|-----|-----------|---------------------|
| | v M. Smith | 3-5 | 1st round | Fidelity International |
| | v Rowswell | 5-0 | 1st round | Rothmans Grand Prix |
| | v Gary Wilkinson | 1-5 | 2nd round | Rothmans Grand Prix |
| | v F. Davis | 5-2 | 1st round | BCE Canadian Masters |
| | v T. Jones | 5-0 | 2nd round | BCE Canadian Masters |
| | v O'Kane | 5-3 | 3rd round | BCE Canadian Masters |
| | v Parrott | 3-5 | 4th round | BCE Canadian Masters |
| | v Reardon | 5-9 | 2nd round | Tennents UK Open |
| 1989 | v V. Harris | 5-3 | 1st round | Mercantile Credit Classic |
| | v Clark | 1-5 | 2nd round | Mercantile Credit Classic |
| | v Wildman | 5-1 | 1st round | European Open |
| | v Duggan | 4-5 | 2nd round | European Open |
| | v Chappel | 6-5 | 1st round | Senator Welsh Championship |
| | v Griffiths | 5-6 | Quarter-final | Senator Welsh Championship |
| | v Glen Wilkinson | 5-0 | 1st round | Anglian British Open |
| | v J. McLaughlin | 5-0 | 2nd round | Anglian British Open |
| | v Charlton | 5-3 | 3rd round | Anglian British Open |
| | v Thorburn | 4-5 | 4th round | Anglian British Open |
| | v Frangie | 10-5 | Qualifying | Embassy World Championship |
| | v Lawlor | 10-2 | Qualifying | Embassy World Championship |
| | v J. Campbell | 10-4 | Qualifying | Embassy World Championship |
| | v Owers | 10-8 | Qualifying | Embassy World Championship |
| | v Higgins | 10-8 | Qualifying | Embassy World Championship |
| | v Virgo | 4-10 | 1st round | Embassy World Championship |

## MARIO MORRA (Canada)

**Born** 8.9.53. **Turned professional** 1979. **World ranking** 86 (82). **Best professional performance** Last 16 1983 Jameson International.

| 1981 | v Thorne | 5-9 | Qualifying | Embassy World Championship |
|------|----------|-----|-----------|---------------------|
| | v Wildman | 3-5 | Qualifying | Jameson International |
| 1982 | v Murphy | 9-5 | Qualifying | Embassy World Championship |
| | v Fitzmaurice | 7-9 | Qualifying | Embassy World Championship |
| | v Demarco | 5-2 | Qualifying | Jameson International |
| | v Reynolds | 1-5 | Qualifying | Jameson International |
| | v Wilson | 2-5 | 1st round | Professional Players Tournament |
| 1983 | v Black | 9-10 | Qualifying | Embassy World Championship |
| | v Jim Bear | 8-9 | 2nd round | Canadian Championship |
| | v Watchorn | 5-3 | Qualifying | Jameson International |
| | v Hallett | 5-3 | Qualifying | Jameson International |
| | v White | 5-3 | 1st round | Jameson International |
| | v Charlton | 3-5 | 2nd round | Jameson International |
| | v Hargreaves | 5-0 | Qualifying | Professional Players Tournament |
| | v S. Francisco | 3-5 | 1st round | Professional Players Tournament |
| | v Burke | 5-2 | Qualifying | Lada Classic |
| | v Everton | 5-0 | Qualifying | Lada Classic |
| | v S. Francisco | 1-5 | Qualifying | Lada Classic |
| 1984 | v G. Foulds | 10-2 | Qualifying | Embassy World Championship |
| | v Murphy | 10-5 | Qualifying | Embassy World Championship |
| | v Reynolds | 10-7 | Qualifying | Embassy World Championship |
| | v Thorburn | 3-10 | 1st round | Embassy World Championship |
| | v Bradley | 5-3 | Qualifying | Jameson International |
| | v Johnson | 0-5 | Qualifying | Jameson International |
| | v Cripsey | 5-3 | Qualifying | Rothmans Grand Prix |
| | v S. Davis | 2-5 | 1st round | Rothmans Grand Prix |
| | v Longworth | 9-1 | Qualifying | Coral UK Open |
| | v E. Hughes | 8-9 | Qualifying | Coral UK Open |
| 1985 | v Newbury | 2-5 | Qualifying | Mercantile Credit Classic |

|      |  |  |  |  |
|------|----------|-------|-------|------------|
|      | v Bradley | 2-6 | Qualifying | Dulux British Open |
|      | v Browne | 10-6 | Qualifying | Embassy World Championship |
|      | v J. Campbell | 9-10 | Qualifying | Embassy World Championship |
|      | v John Bear | 4-5 | 1st round | Canadian Championship |
|      | v Oliver | 5-1 | 2nd round | Goya Matchroom Trophy |
|      | v J. Campbell | 2-5 | 3rd round | Goya Matchroom Trophy |
|      | v D. Hughes | 5-2 | 2nd round | Rothmans Grand Prix |
|      | v Martin | 2-5 | 3rd round | Rothmans Grand Prix |
|      | v Agrawal | 9-8 | 2nd round | Coral UK Open |
|      | v Mountjoy | 2-9 | 3rd round | Coral UK Open |
| 1986 | v B. Harris | 3-5 | 2nd round | Mercantile Credit Classic |
|      | v Gilbert | 4-5 | 2nd round | Dulux British Open |
|      | v Gibson | 9-10 | Qualifying | Embassy World Championship |
|      | v Thornley | 4-6 | 1st round | Canadian Championship |
|      | v Ellis | 5-3 | 1st round | BCE International |
|      | v Drago | 3-5 | 2nd round | BCE International |
|      | v James | 5-3 | 1st round | Rothmans Grand Prix |
|      | v Black | 5-4 | 2nd round | Rothmans Grand Prix |
|      | v Griffiths | 3-5 | 3rd round | Rothmans Grand Prix |
|      | v B. Bennett | 9-3 | 1st round | Tennents UK Open |
|      | v Drago | 6-9 | 2nd round | Tennents UK Open |
| 1987 | v Ellis | 5-1 | 1st round | Mercantile Credit Classic |
|      | v Mans | 5-0 | 2nd round | Mercantile Credit Classic |
|      | v Williams | 2-5 | 3rd round | Mercantile Credit Classic |
|      | v M. Bennett | 5-4 | 1st round | Dulux British Open |
|      | v Van Rensberg | 5-1 | 2nd round | Dulux British Open |
|      | v Virgo | 3-5 | 3rd round | Dulux British Open |
|      | v P. Gibson | 10-6 | Qualifying | Embassy World Championship |
|      | v Chappel | 8-10 | Qualifying | Embassy World Championship |
|      | v Chaperon | 6-5 | 1st round | Canadian Championship |
|      | v Jonik | 6-2 | Quarter-final | Canadian Championship |
|      | v Thorburn | 4-7 | Semi-final | Canadian Championship |
|      | v Hargreaves | 5-4 | 1st round | Fidelity International |
|      | v Dodd | 5-3 | 2nd round | Fidelity International |
|      | v David Taylor | 3-5 | 3rd round | Fidelity International |
|      | v Meakin | 2-5 | 1st round | Rothmans Grand Prix |
|      | v A. Harris | 8-9 | 1st round | Tennents UK Open |
| 1988 | v Marshall | 5-0 | 1st round | Mercantile Credit Classic |
|      | v Gauvreau | 5-4 | 2nd round | Mercantile Credit Classic |
|      | v Meo | 1-5 | 3rd round | Mercantile Credit Classic |
|      | v Watchorn | 5-1 | 1st round | MIM Britannia British Open |
|      | v M. Bennett | 5-2 | 2nd round | MIM Britannia British Open |
|      | v Griffiths | 1-5 | 3rd round | MIM Britannia British Open |
|      | v Meakin | 10-5 | Qualifying | Embassy World Championship |
|      | v Edmonds | 10-8 | Qualifying | Embassy World Championship |
|      | v W. Jones | 8-10 | Qualifying | Embassy World Championship |
|      | v Watson | 6-2 | 1st round | BCE Canadian Championship |
|      | v Wych | 4-6 | Quarter-final | BCE Canadian Championship |
|      | v Everton | 5-2 | 1st round | Fidelity International |
|      | v King | 4-5 | 2nd round | Fidelity International |
|      | v Reardon | 5-4 | 2nd round | Rothmans Grand Prix |
|      | v Parrott | 3-5 | 3rd round | Rothmans Grand Prix |
|      | v A. Harris | 3-5 | 1st round | BCE Canadian Masters |
|      | v D. Hughes | 9-2 | 1st round | Tennents UK Open |
|      | v Duggan | 8-9 | 2nd round | Tennents UK Open |
| 1989 | v Darrington | 2-5 | 1st round | Mercantile Credit Classic |
|      | v S. Campbell | 5-3 | 1st round | European Open |
|      | v N. Gilbert | 5-1 | 2nd round | European Open |
|      | v E. Hughes | 1-5 | 3rd round | European Open |
|      | v Rempe | 1-5 | 1st round | Anglian British Open |
|      | v Mikkelsen | 10-4 | Qualifying | Embassy World Championship |
|      | v Clark | 6-10 | Qualifying | Embassy World Championship |

## DOUG MOUNTJOY (Wales)

**Born** 8.6.42. **Turned professional** 1976. **World ranking** 10 (24). **Amateur career** 1976 World champion; 1968 and 1976 Welsh champion. **Best professional performances** Winner 1988 Tennents UK Open, 1989 Mercantile Credit Classic, 1978 Coral UK Championship, 1977 Benson & Hedges Masters, 1979 Benson & Hedges Irish Masters; 1979, 1982, 1984, 1987, 1989 Welsh Championship.

| | | | | |
|---|---|---|---|---|
| 1977 | v Higgins | 5-3 | Semi-final | Benson & Hedges Masters |
| | **v Reardon** | **7-6** | **Final** | **Benson & Hedges Masters** |
| | v Jack Rea | 11-9 | Qualifying | Embassy World Championship |
| | v Higgins | 13-12 | 1st round | Embassy World Championship |
| | v Dennis Taylor | 11-13 | Quarter-final | Embassy World Championship |
| | v Andrewartha | 5-2 | 1st round | Super Crystalate UK Championship |
| | v Spencer | 5-3 | 2nd round | Super Crystalate UK Championship |
| | v Thorne | 5-4 | Quarter-final | Super Crystalate UK Championship |
| | v Higgins | 9-2 | Semi-final | Super Crystalate UK Championship |
| | v Fagan | 9-12 | Final | Super Crystalate UK Championship |
| 1978 | v Spencer | 3-5 | Final | Benson & Hedges Irish Masters |
| | v Andrewartha | 9-3 | Qualifying | Embassy World Championship |
| | v Reardon | 9-13 | 1st round | Embassy World Championship |
| | v Barrie | 9-5 | Qualifying | Coral UK Championship |
| | v Dennis Taylor | 9-4 | 1st round | Coral UK Championship |
| | v Andrewartha | 9-4 | Quarter-final | Coral UK Championship |
| | v Miles | 9-1 | Semi-final | Coral UK Championship |
| | **v David Taylor** | **15-9** | **Final** | **Coral UK Championship** |
| 1979 | v F. Davis | 5-2 | 1st round | Benson & Hedges Masters |
| | v Spencer | 5-0 | Quarter-final | Benson & Hedges Masters |
| | v Higgins | 1-5 | Semi-final | Benson & Hedges Masters |
| | **v Reardon** | **6-5** | **Final** | **Benson & Hedges Irish Masters** |
| | v Mienie | 9-1 | Prelim | Embassy World Championship |
| | v Houlihan | 9-6 | Qualifying | Embassy World Championship |
| | v Charlton | 6-13 | 1st round | Embassy World Championship |
| | v S. Davis | 5-9 | 3rd round | Coral UK Championship |
| | v Griffiths | 9-6 | 1st round | Woodpecker Welsh Championship |
| | **v Reardon** | **9-6** | **Final** | **Woodpecker Welsh Championship** |
| 1980 | v Griffiths | 8-9 | Final | Benson & Hedges Irish Masters |
| | v Wilson | 10-6 | 1st round | Embassy World Championship |
| | v Thorburn | 10-13 | 2nd round | Embassy World Championship |
| | v Williams | 8-9 | 1st round | Coral UK Championship |
| 1981 | v Charlton | 5-0 | 1st round | Benson & Hedges Masters |
| | v Higgins | 1-5 | Quarter-final | Benson & Hedges Masters |
| | v Wilson | 6-9 | Semi-final | Woodpecker Welsh Championship |
| | v Thorne | 10-6 | 1st round | Embassy World Championship |
| | v Charlton | 13-7 | 2nd round | Embassy World Championship |
| | v Dennis Taylor | 13-8 | Quarter-final | Embassy World Championship |
| | v Reardon | 16-10 | Semi-final | Embassy World Championship |
| | v S. Davis | 12-18 | Final | Embassy World Championship |
| | v S. Davis | 0-5 | Quarter-final | Langs Supreme Scottish Masters |
| | v Higgins | 1-5 | 3rd round | Jameson International |
| | v Dennis Taylor | 5-4 | 1st round | Northern Ireland Classic |
| | v White | 8-9 | Semi-final | Northern Ireland Classic |
| | v Knowles | 6-9 | 3rd round | Coral UK Championship |
| 1982 | v Spencer | 5-4 | 1st round | Benson & Hedges Masters |
| | v S. Davis | 2-5 | Quarter-final | Benson & Hedges Masters |
| | v Andrewartha | 6-3 | 1st round | Welsh Championship |
| | v Reardon | 9-7 | Semi-final | Welsh Championship |
| | **v Griffiths** | **9-8** | **Final** | **Welsh Championship** |
| | v E. Hughes | 5-4 | 1st round | Benson & Hedges Irish Masters |
| | v S. Davis | 2-5 | Quarter-final | Benson & Hedges Irish Masters |
| | v Williams | 10-3 | 1st round | Embassy World Championship |

|      |  |  |  |  |
|------|----------|-------|-------|------------|
|      | v Higgins | 12-13 | 2nd round | Embassy World Championship |
|      | v Wilson | 4-5 | 1st round | Jameson International |
|      | v Jonik | 3-5 | 1st round | Professional Players Tournament |
|      | v Houlihan | 9-3 | 1st round | Coral UK Championship |
|      | v Virgo | 5-9 | 2nd round | Coral UK Championship |
| 1983 | v Griffiths | 5-1 | 1st round | Lada Classic |
|      | v Werbeniuk | 2-5 | Quarter-final | Lada Classic |
|      | v Virgo | 5-1 | 1st round | Benson & Hedges Masters |
|      | v S. Davis | 5-4 | Quarter-final | Benson & Hedges Masters |
|      | v Reardon | 3-6 | Semi-final | Benson & Hedges Masters |
|      | v M. Owen | 6-0 | Quarter-final | Woodpecker Welsh Championship |
|      | v Wilson | 9-3 | Semi-final | Woodpecker Welsh Championship |
|      | v Reardon | 1-9 | Final | Woodpecker Welsh Championship |
|      | v Knowles | 5-1 | 1st round | Benson & Hedges Irish Masters |
|      | v Griffiths | 4-5 | Quarter-final | Benson & Hedges Irish Masters |
|      | v Wilson | 10-2 | 1st round | Embassy World Championship |
|      | v Meo | 11-13 | 2nd round | Embassy World Championship |
|      | v Wildman | 5-4 | 1st round | Jameson International |
|      | v Martin | 5-0 | 2nd round | Jameson International |
|      | v Thorburn | 2-5 | Quarter-final | Jameson International |
|      | v J. Campbell | 3-5 | 1st round | Professional Players Tournament |
|      | v Watterson | 9-2 | 1st round | Coral UK Championship |
|      | v Knowles | 5-9 | 2nd round | Coral UK Championship |
| 1984 | v Parrott | 4-5 | Qualifying | Lada Classic |
|      | v Higgins | 2-5 | 1st round | Benson & Hedges Masters |
|      | v Everton | 6-1 | 1st round | Strongbow Welsh Championship |
|      | v Griffiths | 9-5 | Semi-final | Strongbow Welsh Championship |
|      | **v Wilson** | **9-3** | **Final** | **Strongbow Welsh Championship** |
|      | v Hallett | 10-4 | 1st round | Embassy World Championship |
|      | v N. Foulds | 13-6 | 2nd round | Embassy World Championship |
|      | v Dennis Taylor | 8-13 | Quarter-final | Embassy World Championship |
|      | v E. Hughes | 1-5 | 1st round | Jameson International |
|      | v E. McLaughlin | 5-4 | 1st round | Rothmans Grand Prix |
|      | v Wildman | 5-0 | 2nd round | Rothmans Grand Prix |
|      | v Charlton | 5-4 | 3rd round | Rothmans Grand Prix |
|      | v Thorburn | 3-5 | Quarter-final | Rothmans Grand Prix |
|      | v Hallett | 9-2 | 1st round | Coral UK Open |
|      | v White | 2-9 | 2nd round | Coral UK Open |
| 1985 | v Wilson | 4-5 | 1st round | Mercantile Credit Classic |
|      | v Knowles | 5-3 | 1st round | Benson & Hedges Masters |
|      | v Meo | 5-4 | Quarter-final | Benson & Hedges Masters |
|      | v Griffiths | 6-2 | Semi-final | Benson & Hedges Masters |
|      | v Thorburn | 6-9 | Final | Benson & Hedges Masters |
|      | v V. Harris | 5-6 | 1st round | Dulux British Open |
|      | v Macleod | 10-5 | 1st round | Embassy World Championship |
|      | v Knowles | 6-13 | 2nd round | Embassy World Championship |
|      | v Newbury | 6-5 | Quarter-final | BCE Welsh Championship |
|      | v Wilson | 9-2 | Semi-final | BCE Welsh Championship |
|      | v Griffiths | 4-9 | Final | BCE Welsh Championship |
|      | v Wych | 5-1 | 3rd round | Goya Matchroom Trophy |
|      | v J. Campbell | 1-5 | 4th round | Goya Matchroom Trophy |
|      | v Chappel | 5-1 | 3rd round | Rothmans Grand Prix |
|      | v J. Campbell | 2-5 | 4th round | Rothmans Grand Prix |
|      | v Morra | 9-2 | 3rd round | Coral UK Open |
|      | v West | 4-9 | 4th round | Coral UK Open |
| 1986 | v King | 5-4 | 3rd round | Mercantile Credit Classic |
|      | v O'Kane | 5-3 | 4th round | Mercantile Credit Classic |
|      | v Werbeniuk | 5-3 | 5th round | Mercantile Credit Classic |
|      | v N. Foulds | 5-3 | Quarter-final | Mercantile Credit Classic |
|      | v Thorburn | 6-9 | Semi-final | Mercantile Credit Classic |
|      | v Dennis Taylor | 2-5 | 1st round | Benson & Hedges Masters |
|      | v Roscoe | 6-4 | Quarter-final | Zetters Welsh Championship |
|      | v W. Jones | 9-7 | Semi-final | Zetters Welsh Championship |

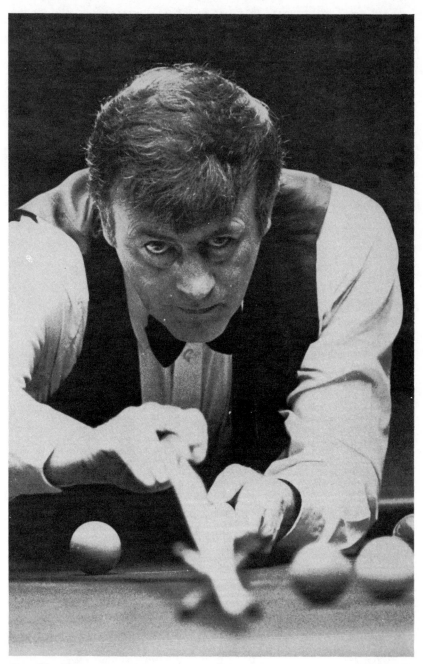

*Doug Mountjoy*

|  | v Griffiths | 3-9 | Final | Zetters Welsh Championship |
|---|---|---|---|---|
|  | v Fagan | 1-5 | 3rd round | Dulux British Open |
|  | v Mans | 10-3 | 1st round | Embassy World Championship |
|  | v S. Davis | 5-13 | 2nd round | Embassy World Championship |
|  | v M. Gibson | 5-3 | 3rd round | BCE International |
|  | v Reynolds | 2-5 | 4th round | BCE International |
|  | v B. Harris | 5-2 | 3rd round | Rothmans Grand Prix |
|  | v Wych | 5-1 | 4th round | Rothmans Grand Prix |
|  | v Knowles | 1-5 | 5th round | Rothmans Grand Prix |
|  | v J. McLaughlin | 9-6 | 3rd round | Tennents UK Open |
|  | v Longworth | 1-9 | 4th round | Tennents UK Open |
| 1987 | v Dodd | 4-5 | 3rd round | Mercantile Credit Classic |
|  | v S. Davis | 2-5 | 1st round | Benson & Hedges Masters |
|  | v Meo | 4-5 | Quarter-final | Benson & Hedges Masters |
|  | v Roscoe | 6-2 | Quarter-final | Matchroom Welsh Championship |
|  | v Chappel | 9-2 | Semi-final | Matchroom Welsh Championship |
|  | **v Newbury** | **9-7** | **Final** | **Matchroom Welsh Championship** |
|  | v Owers | 5-3 | 3rd round | Dulux British Open |
|  | v P. Francisco | 5-3 | 4th round | Dulux British Open |
|  | v Thorburn | 4-5 | 5th round | Dulux British Open |
|  | v David Taylor | 10-5 | 1st round | Embassy World Championship |
|  | v O'Kane | 5-13 | 2nd round | Embassy World Championship |
|  | v Roe | 4-5 | 3rd round | Fidelity International |
|  | v Chambers | 2-5 | 3rd round | Rothmans Grand Prix |
|  | v M. Smith | 7-9 | 3rd round | Tennents UK Open |
| 1988 | v F. Davis | 5-0 | 3rd round | Mercantile Credit Classic |
|  | v Martin | 4-5 | 4th round | Mercantile Credit Classic |
|  | v White | 0-5 | 1st round | Benson & Hedges Masters |
|  | v M. Bennett | 6-3 | Quarter-final | Welsh Championship |
|  | v W. Jones | 5-9 | Semi-final | Welsh Championship |
|  | v O'Kane | 3-5 | 3rd round | MIM Britannia British Open |
|  | v West | 10-6 | 1st round | Embassy World Championship |
|  | v N. Foulds | 1-13 | 2nd round | Embassy World Championship |
|  | v Martin | 5-1 | 3rd round | Fidelity International |
|  | v Johnson | 4-5 | 4th round | Fidelity International |
|  | v Fisher | 5-1 | 3rd round | Rothmans Grand Prix |
|  | v Hendry | 5-1 | 4th round | Rothmans Grand Prix |
|  | v Robidoux | 4-5 | 5th round | Rothmans Grand Prix |
|  | v Price | 5-2 | 3rd round | BCE Canadian Masters |
|  | v Thorne | 5-4 | 4th round | BCE Canadian Masters |
|  | v Griffiths | 4-5 | 5th round | BCE Canadian Masters |
|  | v W. Jones | 9-7 | 3rd round | Tennents UK Open |
|  | v N. Foulds | 9-4 | 4th round | Tennents UK Open |
|  | v Johnson | 9-5 | 5th round | Tennents UK Open |
|  | v Virgo | 9-8 | Quarter-final | Tennents UK Open |
|  | v Griffiths | 9-4 | Semi-final | Tennents UK Open |
|  | **v Hendry** | **16-12** | **Final** | **Tennents UK Open** |
| 1989 | v D. Hughes | 5-0 | 3rd round | Mercantile Credit Classic |
|  | v Terry | 5-4 | 4th round | Mercantile Credit Classic |
|  | v Knowles | 5-4 | 5th round | Mercantile Credit Classic |
|  | v Browne | 5-3 | Quarter-final | Mercantile Credit Classic |
|  | v Thorburn | 9-5 | Semi-final | Mercantile Credit Classic |
|  | **v W. Jones** | **13-11** | **Final** | **Mercantile Credit Classic** |
|  | v Murphy | 5-1 | 3rd round | European Open |
|  | v Dennis Taylor | 5-3 | 4th round | European Open |
|  | v Thorburn | 0-5 | 5th round | European Open |
|  | v Reardon | 6-3 | Quarter-final | Senator Welsh Championship |
|  | v M. Bennett | 9-5 | Semi-final | Senator Welsh Championship |
|  | **v Griffiths** | **9-6** | **Final** | **Senator Welsh Championship** |
|  | **v Gauvreau** | **5-0** | **3rd round** | **Anglian British Open** |
|  | **v Macleod** | **5-0** | **4th round** | **Anglian British Open** |
|  | **v Parrott** | **2-5** | **5th round** | **Anglian British Open** |

| v D. Gilbert | 10-7 | Qualifying | Embassy World Championship |
| v Hallett | 7-10 | 1st round | Embassy World Championship |

## TOMMY MURPHY (Northern Ireland)

**Born** 8.1.62. **Turned professional** 1981. **World ranking** 57 (42). **Amateur career** 1981 Northern Ireland champion. **Best professional performances** Last 16 1988 Mercantile Credit Classic, 1987 Dulux British Open.

| | | | | |
|---|---|---|---|---|
| **1981** | v Johnson | 1-9 | Qualifying | Coral UK Championship |
| **1982** | v Fagan | 6-2 | Quarter-final | Irish Championship |
| | v Dennis Taylor | 0-6 | Semi-final | Irish Championship |
| | v Morra | 5-9 | Qualifying | Embassy World Championship |
| | v Fisher | 1-5 | Qualifying | Jameson International |
| | v Reardon | 0-5 | 1st round | Professional Players Tournament |
| | v Everton | 9-4 | Qualifying | Coral UK Championship |
| | v Sinclair | 5-9 | Qualifying | Coral UK Championship |
| **1983** | v Fagan | 4-6 | Quarter-final | Irish Championship |
| | v Houlihan | 10-9 | Qualifying | Embassy World Championship |
| | v Virgo | 8-10 | Qualifying | Embassy World Championship |
| | v Sheehan | 5-2 | Qualifying | Jameson International |
| | v Thorne | 2-5 | Qualifying | Jameson International |
| | v Macleod | 5-0 | 1st round | Professional Players Tournament |
| | v Stevens | 1-5 | 2nd round | Professional Players Tournament |
| | v Demarco | 9-4 | Qualifying | Coral UK Championship |
| | v Donnelly | 9-4 | Qualifying | Coral UK Championship |
| | v Dennis Taylor | 6-9 | 1st round | Coral UK Championship |
| **1984** | v Fitzmaurice | 10-8 | Qualifying | Embassy World Championship |
| | v Morra | 5-10 | Qualifying | Embassy World Championship |
| | v Bales | 4-5 | Qualifying | Jameson International |
| | v G. Foulds | 5-1 | Qualifying | Rothmans Grand Prix |
| | v Miles | 3-5 | 1st round | Rothmans Grand Prix |
| | v Kearney | 9-2 | Qualifying | Coral UK Open |
| | v Watterson | 9-4 | Qualifying | Coral UK Open |
| | v Martin | 9-8 | Qualifying | Coral UK Open |
| | v S. Davis | 1-9 | 1st round | Coral UK Open |
| **1985** | v Fowler | 0-5 | Qualifying | Mercantile Credit Classic |
| | v Sheehan | 6-3 | Qualifying | Dulux British Open |
| | v Macleod | 5-6 | 1st round | Dulux British Open |
| | v Browne | 6-3 | Qualifying | Irish Championship |
| | v Fagan | 2-6 | Quarter-final | Irish Championship |
| | v P. Francisco | 4-10 | Qualifying | Embassy World Championship |
| | v Jack Rea | 5-1 | 2nd round | Goya Matchroom Trophy |
| | v E. Hughes | 5-3 | 3rd round | Goya Matchroom Trophy |
| | v Higgins | 2-5 | 4th round | Goya Matchroom Trophy |
| | v Mikkelsen | 4-5 | 2nd round | Rothmans Grand Prix |
| | v Everton | 9-4 | 2nd round | Coral UK Open |
| | v Macleod | 7-9 | 3rd round | Coral UK Open |
| **1986** | v Chappel | 5-4 | 2nd round | Mercantile Credit Classic |
| | v Martin | 3-5 | 3rd round | Mercantile Credit Classic |
| | v Duggan | 1-5 | 2nd round | Dulux British Open |
| | v J. McLaughlin | 10-7 | Qualifying | Embassy World Championship |
| | v Thornley | 10-3 | Qualifying | Embassy World Championship |
| | v E. Hughes | 7-10 | Qualifying | Embassy World Championship |
| | v O'Boye | 5-0 | 1st round | Strongbow Irish Championship |
| | v Kearney | 6-2 | Quarter-final | Strongbow Irish Championship |
| | v Dennis Taylor | 3-6 | Semi-final | Strongbow Irish Championship |
| | v Donnelly | 5-2 | 2nd round | BCE International |
| | v Johnson | 4-5 | 3rd round | BCE International |
| | v Anderson | 4-5 | 2nd round | Rothmans Grand Prix |
| | v D. Hughes | 9-0 | 2nd round | Tennents UK Open |

|      |                 |      |              |                              |
|------|-----------------|------|--------------|------------------------------|
|      | v Thorne        | 4-9  | 3rd round    | Tennents UK Open             |
| 1987 | v Bales         | 5-2  | 2nd round    | Mercantile Credit Classic    |
|      | v Longworth     | 3-5  | 3rd round    | Mercantile Credit Classic    |
|      | v D. Gilbert    | 5-4  | 2nd round    | Dulux British Open           |
|      | v Wych          | 5-1  | 3rd round    | Dulux British Open           |
|      | v Reardon       | 5-4  | 4th round    | Dulux British Open           |
|      | v Knowles       | 3-5  | 5th round    | Dulux British Open           |
|      | v Jenkins       | 10-4 | Qualifying   | Embassy World Championship   |
|      | v Miles         | 10-7 | Qualifying   | Embassy World Championship   |
|      | v Longworth     | 2-10 | Qualifying   | Embassy World Championship   |
|      | v Kearney       | 1-5  | 1st round    | Matchroom Irish Championship |
|      | v Medati        | 5-3  | 2nd round    | Fidelity International        |
|      | v Virgo         | 1-5  | 3rd round    | Fidelity International        |
|      | v Van Rensberg  | 4-5  | 2nd round    | Rothmans Grand Prix          |
|      | v M. Gibson     | 9-0  | 2nd round    | Tennents UK Open             |
|      | v Drago         | 9-7  | 3rd round    | Tennents UK Open             |
|      | v Thorne        | 4-9  | 4th round    | Tennents UK Open             |
| 1988 | v V. Harris     | 5-2  | 2nd round    | Mercantile Credit Classic    |
|      | v J. Campbell   | 5-3  | 3rd round    | Mercantile Credit Classic    |
|      | v Reynolds      | 5-4  | 4th round    | Mercantile Credit Classic    |
|      | v Knowles       | 3-5  | 5th round    | Mercantile Credit Classic    |
|      | v Kelly         | 5-1  | 1st round    | Irish Championship           |
|      | v Browne        | 5-6  | Quarter-final| Irish Championship           |
|      | v Meadowcroft   | 5-4  | 2nd round    | MIM Britannia British Open   |
|      | v Virgo         | 1-5  | 3rd round    | MIM Britannia British Open   |
|      | v Roscoe        | 10-8 | Qualifying   | Embassy World Championship   |
|      | v Chaperon      | 5-10 | Qualifying   | Embassy World Championship   |
|      | v F. Davis      | 5-1  | 2nd round    | Fidelity International        |
|      | v N. Foulds     | 3-5  | 3rd round    | Fidelity International        |
|      | v Bradley       | 3-5  | 2nd round    | Rothmans Grand Prix          |
|      | v Chambers      | 5-3  | 2nd round    | BCE Canadian Masters         |
|      | v James         | 3-5  | 3rd round    | BCE Canadian Masters         |
|      | v Price         | 9-6  | 2nd round    | Tennents UK Open             |
|      | v Hendry        | 4-9  | 3rd round    | Tennents UK Open             |
| 1989 | v Jack Rea      | 5-0  | 2nd round    | Mercantile Credit Classic    |
|      | v Hendry        | 2-5  | 3rd round    | Mercantile Credit Classic    |
|      | v Marshall      | 5-4  | 2nd round    | European Open                |
|      | v Mountjoy      | 1-5  | 3rd round    | European Open                |
|      | v Browne        | 3-5  | Quarter-final| Irish Championship           |
|      | v Whitthread    | 2-5  | 2nd round    | Anglian British Open         |
|      | v Oliver        | 10-8 | Qualifying   | Embassy World Championship   |
|      | v Roe           | 7-10 | Qualifying   | Embassy World Championship   |

## STEVE NEWBURY (Wales)

**Born** 21.4.56. **Turned professional** 1984. **World ranking** 19 (25). **Amateur career** 1980 Welsh champion. **Best professional performance** Semi-finals 1988 Mercantile Credit Classic.

|      |              |     |            |                           |
|------|--------------|-----|------------|---------------------------|
| 1984 | v Longworth  | 5-4 | Qualifying | Jameson International      |
|      | v Burke      | 5-0 | Qualifying | Jameson International      |
|      | v Fagan      | 5-0 | Qualifying | Jameson International      |
|      | v Miles      | 5-1 | Qualifying | Jameson International      |
|      | v Werbeniuk  | 5-2 | 1st round  | Jameson International      |
|      | v Knowles    | 4-5 | 2nd round  | Jameson International      |
|      | v Fisher     | 5-0 | Qualifying | Rothmans Grand Prix       |
|      | v Thorne     | 2-5 | 1st round  | Rothmans Grand Prix       |
|      | v Rigitano   | 9-6 | Qualifying | Coral UK Open             |
|      | v Jonik      | 9-3 | Qualifying | Coral UK Open             |
|      | v Dodd       | 6-9 | Qualifying | Coral UK Open             |
| 1985 | v V. Harris  | 5-3 | Qualifying | Mercantile Credit Classic |

*Steve Newbury*

| | | | |
|---|---|---|---|
| v Burke | 5-1 | Qualifying | Mercantile Credit Classic |
| v Morra | 5-2 | Qualifying | Mercantile Credit Classic |
| v E. Hughes | 3-5 | Qualifying | Mercantile Credit Classic |
| v Browne | 6-0 | Qualifying | Dulux British Open |
| v Sinclair | 6-3 | 1st round | Dulux British Open |
| v Griffiths | 5-3 | 2nd round | Dulux British Open |
| v Dennis Taylor | 3-5 | 3rd round | Dulux British Open |
| v D. Hughes | 10-9 | Qualifying | Embassy World Championship |
| v Burke | 10-3 | Qualifying | Embassy World Championship |
| v Scott | 10-2 | Qualifying | Embassy World Championship |
| v E. Hughes | 6-10 | Qualifying | Embassy World Championship |
| v W. Jones | 6-2 | 1st round | BCE Welsh Championship |
| v Mountjoy | 5-6 | Quarter-final | BCE Welsh Championship |
| v Jonik | 5-4 | 2nd round | Goya Matchroom Trophy |
| v Griffiths | 2-5 | 3rd round | Goya Matchroom Trophy |
| v Burke | 5-3 | 2nd round | Rothmans Grand Prix |
| v David Taylor | 2-5 | 3rd round | Rothmans Grand Prix |
| v Houlihan | 9-3 | 2nd round | Coral UK Open |
| v Stevens | 7-9 | 3rd round | Coral UK Open |
| 1986 v Cripsey | 4-5 | 2nd round | Mercantile Credit Classic |
| v Wilson | 4-6 | Quarter-final | Zetters Welsh Championship |
| v Oliver | 5-2 | 2nd round | Dulux British Open |
| v O'Kane | 5-3 | 3rd round | Dulux British Open |
| v Meo | 0-5 | 4th round | Dulux British Open |
| v Agrawal | 10-5 | Qualifying | Embassy World Championship |
| v Black | 10-2 | Qualifying | Embassy World Championship |
| v Spencer | 7-10 | Qualifying | Embassy World Championship |
| v Dunning | 5-4 | 2nd round | BCE International |
| v S. Francisco | 4-5 | 3rd round | BCE International |
| v D. Gilbert | 5-1 | 2nd round | Rothmans Grand Prix |
| v Reynolds | 5-0 | 3rd round | Rothmans Grand Prix |
| v O'Boye | 5-2 | 4th round | Rothmans Grand Prix |
| v S. Francisco | 2-5 | 5th round | Rothmans Grand Prix |
| v Owers | 8-9 | 2nd round | Tennents UK Open |
| 1987 v Meadowcroft | 5-1 | 2nd round | Mercantile Credit Classic |
| v White | 4-5 | 3rd round | Mercantile Credit Classic |
| v Wilson | 6-2 | Quarter-final | Matchroom Welsh Championship |
| v Griffiths | 9-6 | Semi-final | Matchroom Welsh Championship |
| v Mountjoy | 7-9 | Final | Matchroom Welsh Championship |
| v Roscoe | 3-5 | 2nd round | Dulux British Open |
| v Dodd | 10-7 | Qualifying | Embassy World Championship |
| v Rigitano | 10-4 | Qualifying | Embassy World Championship |
| v Hallett | 4-10 | Qualifying | Embassy World Championship |
| v Fisher | 5-0 | 2nd round | Fidelity International |
| v P. Francisco | 5-2 | 3rd round | Fidelity International |
| v Thorburn | 3-5 | 4th round | Fidelity International |
| v Meakin | 5-1 | 2nd round | Rothmans Grand Prix |
| v Meo | 5-0 | 3rd round | Rothmans Grand Prix |
| v Thorburn | 5-0 | 4th round | Rothmans Grand Prix |
| v Gary Wilkinson | 5-3 | 5th round | Rothmans Grand Prix |
| v Dennis Taylor | 2-5 | Quarter-final | Rothmans Grand Prix |
| v Foldvari | 9-5 | 2nd round | Tennents UK Open |
| v Parrott | 5-9 | 3rd round | Tennents UK Open |
| 1988 v Kearney | 5-1 | 2nd round | Mercantile Credit Classic |
| v E. Hughes | 5-1 | 3rd round | Mercantile Credit Classic |
| v Thorburn | 5-3 | 4th round | Mercantile Credit Classic |
| v Clark | 5-2 | 5th round | Mercantile Credit Classic |
| v Griffiths | 5-4 | Quarter-final | Mercantile Credit Classic |
| v S. Davis | 2-9 | Semi-final | Mercantile Credit Classic |
| v C. Wilson | 3-6 | Quarter-final | Welsh Championship |
| v Oliver | 5-3 | 2nd round | MIM Britannia British Open |
| v Thorburn | 2-5 | 3rd round | MIM Britannia British Open |
| v Lawlor | 10-3 | Qualifying | Embassy World Championship |

|      | v M. Smith      | 10-9  | Qualifying    | Embassy World Championship      |
|------|-----------------|-------|---------------|---------------------------------|
|      | v West          | 8-10  | Qualifying    | Embassy World Championship      |
|      | v M. Bennett    | 5-0   | 3rd round     | Fidelity International           |
|      | v Knowles       | 5-4   | 4th round     | Fidelity International           |
|      | v Johnson       | 2-5   | 5th round     | Fidelity International           |
|      | v Macleod       | 5-3   | 3rd round     | Rothmans Grand Prix             |
|      | v S. Davis      | 1-5   | 4th round     | Rothmans Grand Prix             |
|      | v N. Gilbert    | 5-3   | 3rd round     | BCE Canadian Masters            |
|      | v Virgo         | 2-5   | 4th round     | BCE Canadian Masters            |
|      | v Roscoe        | 7-9   | 3rd round     | Tennents UK Open                |
| 1989 | v Bradley       | 5-3   | 3rd round     | Mercantile Credit Classic       |
|      | v Dennis Taylor | 5-4   | 4th round     | Mercantile Credit Classic       |
|      | v Hendry        | 1-5   | 5th round     | Mercantile Credit Classic       |
|      | v Robidoux      | 0-5   | 3rd round     | European Open                   |
|      | v W. Jones      | 6-5   | Quarter-final | Senator Welsh Championship      |
|      | v Griffiths     | 7-9   | Semi-final    | Senator Welsh Championship      |
|      | v Bales         | 3-5   | 3rd round     | Anglian British Open            |
|      | v N. Gilbert    | 10-7  | Qualifying    | Embassy World Championship      |
|      | v S. Davis      | 5-10  | 1st round     | Embassy World Championship      |

## JOE O'BOYE (Republic of Ireland)

**Born** 6.3.60. **Turned professional** 1985. **World ranking** 40 (35). **Amateur career** 1980 English champion. **Best professional performances** Quarter-finals 1987 Fidelity International, 1988 MIM Britannia British Open.

|      |         |    |      |            |
|------|-----------------|-------|---------------|---------------------------------|
| 1985 | v Parkin        | 5-3   | 1st round     | Goya Matchroom Trophy           |
|      | v Miles         | 2-5   | 2nd round     | Goya Matchroom Trophy           |
|      | v Hendry        | 5-4   | 1st round     | Rothmans Grand Prix             |
|      | v Chaperon      | 5-3   | 2nd round     | Rothmans Grand Prix             |
|      | v Mans          | 5-3   | 3rd round     | Rothmans Grand Prix             |
|      | v White         | 4-5   | 4th round     | Rothmans Grand Prix             |
|      | v Bennett       | 9-3   | 1st round     | Coral UK Open                   |
|      | v Gauvreau      | 9-5   | 2nd round     | Coral UK Open                   |
|      | v Knowles       | 5-9   | 3rd round     | Coral UK Open                   |
| 1986 | v Wilkinson     | 5-1   | 1st round     | Mercantile Credit Classic       |
|      | v Longworth     | 5-1   | 2nd round     | Mercantile Credit Classic       |
|      | v Meo           | 3-5   | 3rd round     | Mercantile Credit Classic       |
|      | v Jim Bear      | 5-1   | 1st round     | Dulux British Open              |
|      | v T. Jones      | 2-5   | 2nd round     | Dulux British Open              |
|      | v Oliver        | 8-10  | Qualifying    | Embassy World Championship      |
|      | v Murphy        | 0-5   | 1st round     | Strongbow Irish Championship    |
|      | v Mikkelsen     | 5-4   | 2nd round     | BCE International               |
|      | v Williams      | 0-5   | 3rd round     | BCE International               |
|      | v Edmonds       | 5-2   | 2nd round     | Rothmans Grand Prix             |
|      | v Thorburn      | 5-4   | 3rd round     | Rothmans Grand Prix             |
|      | v Newbury       | 2-5   | 4th round     | Rothmans Grand Prix             |
|      | v Duggan        | 9-4   | 2nd round     | Tennents UK Open                |
|      | v Meo           | 3-9   | 3rd round     | Tennents UK Open                |
| 1987 | v V. Harris     | 5-1   | 2nd round     | Mercantile Credit Classic       |
|      | v Griffiths     | 1-5   | 3rd round     | Mercantile Credit Classic       |
|      | v Bradley       | 5-1   | 2nd round     | Dulux British Open              |
|      | v Reardon       | 5-4   | 3rd round     | Dulux British Open              |
|      | v N. Gilbert    | 10-5  | Qualifying    | Embassy World Championship      |
|      | v Bradley       | 7-10  | Qualifying    | Embassy World Championship      |
|      | v Kelly         | 5-0   | 1st round     | Matchroom Irish Championship    |
|      | v Higgins       | wo    | Quarter-final | Matchroom Irish Championship    |
|      | v E. Hughes     | 6-3   | Semi-final    | Matchroom Irish Championship    |
|      | v Dennis Taylor | 2-9   | Final         | Matchroom Irish Championship    |
|      | v Fagan         | 5-1   | 2nd round     | Fidelity International           |
|      | v Stevens       | 5-1   | 3rd round     | Fidelity International           |

|      |       |  |          |                  |
|------|---------------|-------|---------------|----------------------------|
|      | v Foldvari    | 5-4   | 4th round     | Fidelity International      |
|      | v Clark       | 5-2   | 5th round     | Fidelity International      |
|      | v Hendry      | 2-5   | Quarter-final | Fidelity International      |
|      | v Chambers    | 3-5   | 2nd round     | Rothmans Grand Prix        |
|      | v Donnelly    | 9-2   | 2nd round     | Tennents UK Open           |
|      | v Stevens     | 8-9   | 3rd round     | Tennents UK Open           |
| 1988 | v Sheehan     | 5-3   | 2nd round     | Mercantile Credit Classic  |
|      | v Reynolds    | 3-5   | 3rd round     | Mercantile Credit Classic  |
|      | v Sheehan     | 5-0   | 1st round     | Irish Championship         |
|      | v Higgins     | 6-4   | Quarter-final | Irish Championship         |
|      | v J. McLaughlin | 4-6 | Semi-final    | Irish Championship         |
|      | v Jenkins     | 5-1   | 2nd round     | MIM Britannia British Open |
|      | v Reynolds    | 5-2   | 3rd round     | MIM Britannia British Open |
|      | v J. Campbell | 5-1   | 4th round     | MIM Britannia British Open |
|      | v Roe         | 5-1   | 5th round     | MIM Britannia British Open |
|      | v Hallett     | 4-5   | Quarter-final | MIM Britannia British Open |
|      | v James       | 7-10  | Qualifying    | Embassy World Championship |
|      | v Whitthread  | 5-1   | 2nd round     | Fidelity International      |
|      | v Hallett     | 3-5   | 3rd round     | Fidelity International      |
|      | v Jenkins     | 5-1   | 2nd round     | Rothmans Grand Prix        |
|      | v Knowles     | 4-5   | 3rd round     | Rothmans Grand Prix        |
|      | v A. Harris   | 5-3   | 2nd round     | BCE Canadian Masters       |
|      | v Hallett     | 0-5   | 3rd round     | BCE Canadian Masters       |
|      | v Williamson  | 9-4   | 2nd round     | Tennents UK Open           |
|      | v E. Hughes   | 9-8   | 3rd round     | Tennents UK Open           |
|      | v Dennis Taylor | 4-9 | 4th round    | Tennents UK Open           |
| 1989 | v D. Hughes   | 1-5   | 2nd round     | Mercantile Credit Classic  |
|      | v Bradley     | 5-3   | 2nd round     | European Open              |
|      | v Hendry      | 2-5   | 3rd round     | European Open              |
|      | v Edwards     | 4-5   | 2nd round     | Anglian British Open       |
|      | v T. Wilson   | 10-8  | Qualifying    | Embassy World Championship |
|      | v Fowler      | 10-6  | Qualifying    | Embassy World Championship |
|      | v West        | 10-7  | Qualifying    | Embassy World Championship |
|      | v S. Francisco | 6-10 | 1st round     | Embassy World Championship |

## DENE O'KANE (New Zealand)

**Born** 24.2.63. **Turned professional** 1984. **World ranking** 28 (23). **Amateur career** 1980 New Zealand champion. **Best professional performances** Quarter-finals 1987 Embassy World Championship, 1988 MIM Britannia British Open.

|      |         |  |          |                  |
|------|-----------------|-------|---------------|----------------------------|
| 1984 | v Parkin        | 5-2   | Qualifying    | Jameson International       |
|      | v E. McLaughlin | 5-1   | Qualifying    | Jameson International       |
|      | v Fitzmaurice   | 5-4   | Qualifying    | Jameson International       |
|      | v Hallett       | 5-4   | Qualifying    | Jameson International       |
|      | v Thorne        | 3-5   | 1st round     | Jameson International       |
|      | v Kelly         | 5-4   | Qualifying    | Rothmans Grand Prix        |
|      | v David Taylor  | 1-5   | 1st round     | Rothmans Grand Prix        |
|      | v W. Jones      | 9-7   | Qualifying    | Coral UK Open              |
|      | v Duggan        | 9-6   | Qualifying    | Coral UK Open              |
|      | v Scott         | 7-9   | Qualifying    | Coral UK Open              |
| 1985 | v W. Jones      | 0-5   | Qualifying    | Mercantile Credit Classic  |
|      | v Cripsey       | 6-4   | Qualifying    | Dulux British Open         |
|      | v J. Campbell   | 6-4   | 1st round     | Dulux British Open         |
|      | v V. Harris     | 5-3   | 2nd round     | Dulux British Open         |
|      | v Martin        | 5-4   | 3rd round     | Dulux British Open         |
|      | v S. Davis      | 1-5   | Quarter-final | Dulux British Open         |
|      | v J. McLaughlin | wo    | Qualifying    | Embassy World Championship |
|      | v V. Harris     | 10-5  | Qualifying    | Embassy World Championship |
|      | v Jonik         | 10-5  | Qualifying    | Embassy World Championship |

|        | v Dodd          | 10-7  | Qualifying     | Embassy World Championship     |
|--------|-----------------|-------|----------------|--------------------------------|
|        | v Martin        | 10-8  | Qualifying     | Embassy World Championship     |
|        | v David Taylor  | 4-10  | 1st round      | Embassy World Championship     |
|        | v B. Harris     | 3-5   | 3rd round      | Goya Matchroom Trophy          |
|        | v Edmonds       | 2-5   | 3rd round      | Rothmans Grand Prix            |
|        | v Chappel       | 5-9   | 3rd round      | Coral UK Open                  |
| 1986   | v Medati        | 5-0   | 3rd round      | Mercantile Credit Classic      |
|        | v Mountjoy      | 3-5   | 4th round      | Mercantile Credit Classic      |
|        | v Newbury       | 3-5   | 3rd round      | Dulux British Open             |
|        | v Hendry        | 9-10  | Qualifying     | Embassy World Championship     |
|        | v Oliver        | 5-2   | 2nd round      | BCE International              |
|        | v Hallett       | 5-1   | 3rd round      | BCE International              |
|        | v Owers         | 0-5   | 4th round      | BCE International              |
|        | v M. Bennett    | 2-5   | 2nd round      | Rothmans Grand Prix            |
|        | v Jenkins       | 9-5   | 2nd round      | Tennents UK Open               |
|        | v Werbeniuk     | 9-5   | 3rd round      | Tennents UK Open               |
|        | v Griffiths     | 0-9   | 4th round      | Tennents UK Open               |
| 1987   | v G. Foulds     | 4-5   | 2nd round      | Mercantile Credit Classic      |
|        | v Rowswell      | 4-5   | 2nd round      | Dulux British Open             |
|        | v D. Gilbert    | 10-2  | Qualifying     | Embassy World Championship     |
|        | v Black         | 10-2  | Qualifying     | Embassy World Championship     |
|        | v P. Francisco  | 10-5  | Qualifying     | Embassy World Championship     |
|        | v Thorburn      | 10-5  | 1st round      | Embassy World Championship     |
|        | v Mountjoy      | 13-5  | 2nd round      | Embassy World Championship     |
|        | v White         | 6-13  | Quarter-final  | Embassy World Championship     |
|        | v Van Rensberg  | 5-3   | 2nd round      | Fidelity International         |
|        | v S. Davis      | 2-5   | 3rd round      | Fidelity International         |
|        | v Gary Wilkinson| 2-5   | 2nd round      | Rothmans Grand Prix            |
|        | v Rowswell      | 9-2   | 2nd round      | Tennents UK Open               |
|        | v Charlton      | 9-8   | 3rd round      | Tennents UK Open               |
|        | v Dennis Taylor | 9-7   | 4th round      | Tennents UK Open               |
|        | v Thorne        | 7-9   | 5th round      | Tennents UK Open               |
| 1988   | v Rowswell      | 4-5   | 2nd round      | Mercantile Credit Classic      |
|        | v Whitthread    | 5-2   | 2nd round      | MIM Britannia British Open     |
|        | v Mountjoy      | 5-3   | 3rd round      | MIM Britannia British Open     |
|        | v Browne        | 5-2   | 4th round      | MIM Britannia British Open     |
|        | v Johnson       | 5-2   | 5th round      | MIM Britannia British Open     |
|        | v Parrott       | 2-5   | Quarter-final  | MIM Britannia British Open     |
|        | v Sinclair      | 9-10  | Qualifying     | Embassy World Championship     |
|        | v Hallett       | 1-5   | 1st round      | New Zealand Masters            |
|        | v Johnston-Allen| 5-3   | 3rd round      | Fidelity International         |
|        | v Wych          | 4-5   | 4th round      | Fidelity International         |
|        | v D. Gilbert    | 5-4   | 3rd round      | Rothmans Grand Prix            |
|        | v Higgins       | 0-5   | 4th round      | Rothmans Grand Prix            |
|        | v D. Morgan     | 3-5   | 3rd round      | BCE Canadian Masters           |
|        | v Reardon       | 9-8   | 3rd round      | Tennents UK Open               |
|        | v Virgo         | 8-9   | 4th round      | Tennents UK Open               |
| 1989   | v N. Gilbert    | 5-2   | 3rd round      | Mercantile Credit Classic      |
|        | v Thorne        | 3-5   | 4th round      | Mercantile Credit Classic      |
|        | v Chappel       | 0-5   | 3rd round      | European Open                  |
|        | v T. Jones      | 5-4   | 3rd round      | Anglian British Open           |
|        | v Hendry        | 2-5   | 4th round      | Anglian British Open           |
|        | v Robidoux      | 10-5  | Qualifying     | Embassy World Championship     |
|        | v White         | 7-10  | 1st round      | Embassy World Championship     |

## BILL OLIVER (England)

**Born** 3.12.48. **Turned professional** 1983. **World ranking** 85 (84).

| 1983   | v T. Jones      | 2-5   | Qualifying     | Professional Players Tournament |
|--------|-----------------|-------|----------------|---------------------------------|
|        | v Andrewartha   | 1-9   | Qualifying     | Coral UK Championship           |
| 1984   | v Dunning       | 10-3  | Qualifying     | Embassy World Championship      |

|      |                |       |           |                                   |
|------|----------------|-------|-----------|-----------------------------------|
|      | v Caggianello  | 10-7  | Qualifying | Embassy World Championship       |
|      | v Williams     | 8-10  | Qualifying | Embassy World Championship       |
|      | v D. Hughes    | 5-4   | Qualifying | Jameson International             |
|      | v Chalmers     | 4-5   | Qualifying | Jameson International             |
|      | v Bennett      | 5-3   | Qualifying | Rothmans Grand Prix              |
|      | v White        | 1-5   | 1st round | Rothmans Grand Prix              |
|      | v Fowler       | 3-9   | Qualifying | Coral UK Open                    |
| 1985 | v Longworth    | 1-5   | Qualifying | Mercantile Credit Classic        |
|      | v Fowler       | 7-9   | Qualifying | Tolly Cobbold English Championship |
|      | v Thorne       | 3-6   | 1st round | Dulux British Open               |
|      | v Foldvari     | 3-10  | Qualifying | Embassy World Championship       |
|      | v Morra        | 1-5   | 2nd round | Goya Matchroom Trophy            |
|      | v Fagan        | 5-4   | Rothmans Grand Prix |                        |
|      | v Thorburn     | 0-5   | 3rd round | Rothmans Grand Prix              |
|      | v Miles        | 4-9   | 2nd round | Coral UK Open                    |
| 1986 | v Bradley      | 3-5   | 2nd round | Mercantile Credit Classic        |
|      | v Dodd         | 9-5   | 2nd round | Tolly Cobbold English Championship |
|      | v Parrott      | 0-9   | 3rd round | Tolly Cobbold English Championship |
|      | v Newbury      | 2-5   | 2nd round | Dulux British Open               |
|      | v O'Boye       | 10-8  | Qualifying | Embassy World Championship       |
|      | v Fowler       | 8-10  | Qualifying | Embassy World Championship       |
|      | v Mienie       | 5-4   | 1st round | BCE International                |
|      | v O'Kane       | 2-5   | 2nd round | BCE International                |
|      | v Anderson     | 4-5   | 1st round | Rothmans Grand Prix              |
|      | v Chalmers     | 9-6   | 1st round | Tennents UK Open                 |
|      | v Hendry       | 1-9   | 2nd round | Tennents UK Open                 |
| 1987 | v Greaves      | 5-4   | 1st round | Mercantile Credit Classic        |
|      | v T. Jones     | 0-5   | 2nd round | Mercantile Credit Classic        |
|      | v T. Jones     | 1-6   | 2nd round | Tolly Ales English Championship  |
|      | v Jack Rea     | 5-1   | 1st round | Dulux British Open               |
|      | v Drago        | 1-5   | 2nd round | Dulux British Open               |
|      | v Watchorn     | 3-5   | 1st round | Fidelity International            |
|      | v J. McLaughlin| 2-5   | 2nd round | Rothmans Grand Prix              |
|      | v Burke        | 9-1   | 1st round | Tennents UK Open                 |
|      | v Scott        | 9-4   | 1st round | Tennents UK Open                 |
|      | v Thorne       | 3-9   | 3rd round | Tennents UK Open                 |
| 1988 | v Burke        | 5-2   | 1st round | Mercantile Credit Classic        |
|      | v King         | 5-3   | 2nd round | Mercantile Credit Classic        |
|      | v West         | 3-5   | 3rd round | Mercantile Credit Classic        |
|      | v Marshall     | 3-6   | 1st round | English Championship             |
|      | v M. Smith     | 5-0   | 1st round | MIM Britannia British Open       |
|      | v Newbury      | 3-5   | 2nd round | MIM Britannia British Open       |
|      | v Chalmers     | 10-9  | Qualifying | Embassy World Championship       |
|      | v Reardon      | 10-6  | Qualifying | Embassy World Championship       |
|      | v Robidoux     | 10-2  | Qualifying | Embassy World Championship       |
|      | v C. Wilson    | 6-10  | Qualifying | Embassy World Championship       |
|      | v Fagan        | 5-0   | 1st round | Fidelity International            |
|      | v Duggan       | 3-5   | 2nd round | Fidelity International            |
|      | v Fitzmaurice  | 5-3   | 1st round | Rothmans Grand Prix              |
|      | v N. Gilbert   | 4-5   | 2nd round | Rothmans Grand Prix              |
|      | v Rempe        | 5-3   | 1st round | BCE Canadian Masters             |
|      | v J. Campbell  | 5-3   | 2nd round | BCE Canadian Masters             |
|      | v Griffiths    | 4-5   | 3rd round | BCE Canadian Masters             |
|      | v Kelly        | 9-2   | 1st round | Tennents UK Open                 |
|      | v Wych         | 6-9   | 2nd round | Tennents UK Open                 |
| 1989 | v S. Campbell  | 4-5   | 1st round | Mercantile Credit Classic        |
|      | v Chalmers     | 5-4   | 1st round | European Open                    |
|      | v Martin       | 5-4   | 2nd round | European Open                    |
|      | v Thorne       | 0-5   | 3rd round | European Open                    |
|      | v G. Foulds    | 5-1   | 1st round | English Championship             |
|      | v Clark        | 2-5   | 2nd round | English Championship             |
|      | v Kelly        | 4-5   | 1st round | Anglian British Open             |

| v Rempe | 10-5 | Qualifying | Embassy World Championship |
| v Murphy | 8-10 | Qualifying | Embassy World Championship |

## KEN OWERS (England)

**Born** 30.3.53. **Turned professional** 1986. **World ranking** 75 (53). **Best professional performance** Last 16 1986 BCE International.

| 1986 | v Scott | 5-1 | 2nd round | BCE International |
| | v White | 5-2 | 3rd round | BCE International |
| | v O'Kane | 5-0 | 4th round | BCE International |
| | v N. Foulds | 1-5 | 5th round | BCE International |
| | v J. McLaughlin | 2-5 | 1st round | Rothmans Grand Prix |
| | v D. Gilbert | 9-8 | 1st round | Tennents UK Open |
| | v Newbury | 9-8 | 2nd round | Tennents UK Open |
| | v S. Francisco | 3-9 | 3rd round | Tennents UK Open |
| 1987 | v Houlihan | 5-1 | 1st round | Mercantile Credit Classic |
| | v John Rea | 2-5 | 2nd round | Mercantile Credit Classic |
| | v Bales | 6-5 | 2nd round | Tolly Ales English Championship |
| | v N. Foulds | 6-3 | 3rd round | Tolly Ales English Championship |
| | v Hallett | 2-6 | 4th round | Tolly Ales English Championship |
| | v Jonik | 5-4 | 1st round | Dulux British Open |
| | v F. Davis | 5-3 | 2nd round | Dulux British Open |
| | v Mountjoy | 1-5 | 3rd round | Dulux British Open |
| | v Fisher | 10-5 | Qualifying | Embassy World Championship |
| | v F. Davis | 10-5 | Qualifying | Embassy World Championship |
| | v King | 4-10 | Qualifying | Embassy World Championship |
| | v Meadowcroft | 5-3 | 2nd round | Fidelity International |
| | v E. Hughes | 4-5 | 3rd round | Fidelity International |
| | v Glen Wilkinson | 4-5 | 2nd round | Rothmans Grand Prix |
| | v Roe | 7-9 | 2nd round | Tennents UK Open |
| 1988 | v Fisher | 5-0 | 2nd round | Mercantile Credit Classic |
| | v Williams | 5-3 | 3rd round | Mercantile Credit Classic |
| | v P. Francisco | 0-5 | 4th round | Mercantile Credit Classic |
| | v Meakin | 6-2 | 2nd round | English Championship |
| | v David Taylor | 6-3 | 3rd round | English Championship |
| | v Knowles | 4-6 | 4th round | English Championship |
| | v Miles | 3-5 | 2nd round | MIM Britannia British Open |
| | v Roe | 10-7 | Qualifying | Embassy World Championship |
| | v Wright | 8-10 | Qualifying | Embassy World Championship |
| | v Jenkins | 5-1 | 2nd round | Fidelity International |
| | v S. Francisco | 1-5 | 3rd round | Fidelity International |
| | v Chambers | 3-5 | 2nd round | Rothmans Grand Prix |
| | v Lawlor | 5-2 | 2nd round | BCE Canadian Masters |
| | v Dennis Taylor | 1-5 | 3rd round | BCE Canadian Masters |
| | v Chambers | 9-4 | 2nd round | Tennents UK Open |
| | v Griffiths | 2-9 | 3rd round | Tennents UK Open |
| 1989 | v Roscoe | 3-5 | 2nd round | Mercantile Credit Classic |
| | v Lawlor | 4-5 | 2nd round | European Open |
| | v Williamson | 4-5 | 2nd round | English Championship |
| | v Burke | 5-2 | 2nd round | Anglian British Open |
| | v Longworth | 1-5 | 3rd round | Anglian British Open |
| | v P. Gibson | 10-8 | Qualifying | Embassy World Championship |
| | v D. Morgan | 8-10 | Qualifying | Embassy World Championship |

## JOHN PARROTT (England)

**Born** 11.5.64. **Turned professional** 1983. **World ranking** 2 (7). **Best professional performances** Winner 1989 European Open; runner-up 1989 Embassy World Championship, 1988 Mercantile Credit Classic, 1989 Benson and Hedges Masters, English Championship.

| 1983 | v Watchorn | 5-0 | Qualifying | Professional Players Tournament |
|---|---|---|---|---|
| | v Fagan | 5-2 | 1st round | Professional Players Tournament |
| | v Griffiths | 1-5 | 2nd round | Professional Players Tournament |
| | v Scott | 9-7 | Qualifying | Coral UK Championship |
| | v Fisher | 9-0 | Qualifying | Coral UK Championship |
| | v Meo | 7-9 | 1st round | Coral UK Championship |
| 1984 | v Mountjoy | 5-4 | Qualifying | Lada Classic |
| | v Higgins | 5-2 | 1st round | Lada Classic |
| | v Knowles | 5-1 | Quarter-final | Lada Classic |
| | v S. Davis | 4-5 | Semi-final | Lada Classic |
| | v D. Hughes | 10-3 | Qualifying | Embassy World Championship |
| | v Everton | 10-2 | Qualifying | Embassy World Championship |
| | v Mans | 10-0 | Qualifying | Embassy World Championship |
| | v Knowles | 10-7 | 1st round | Embassy World Championship |
| | v Dennis Taylor | 11-13 | 2nd round | Embassy World Championship |
| | v Gauvreau | 4-5 | Qualifying | Jameson International |
| | v Gauvreau | 5-3 | 1st round | Rothmans Grand Prix |
| | v Charlton | 1-5 | 2nd round | Rothmans Grand Prix |
| | v Fitzmaurice | 9-6 | Qualifying | Coral UK Open |
| | v Thorne | 7-9 | 1st round | Coral UK Open |
| 1985 | v Medati | 3-5 | Qualifying | Mercantile Credit Classic |
| | v G. Foulds | 9-4 | 1st round | Tolly Cobbold English Championship |
| | v David Taylor | 6-9 | 2nd round | Tolly Cobbold English Championship |
| | v John Rea | 6-4 | 1st round | Dulux British Open |
| | v Dennis Taylor | 2-5 | 2nd round | Dulux British Open |
| | v Fowler | 10-2 | Qualifying | Embassy World Championship |
| | v Spencer | 10-3 | 1st round | Embassy World Championship |
| | v Stevens | 13-6 | 2nd round | Embassy World Championship |
| | v Reardon | 12-13 | Quarter-final | Embassy World Championship |
| | v Thorne | 5-0 | Quarter-final | Winfield Australian Masters |
| | v J. Campbell | 4-6 | Semi-final | Winfield Australian Masters |
| | v White | 3-5 | Semi-final | Carlsberg Trophy |
| | v W. Jones | 5-3 | 3rd round | Goya Matchroom Trophy |
| | v Meo | 5-4 | 4th round | Goya Matchroom Trophy |
| | v Griffiths | 5-1 | 5th round | Goya Matchroom Trophy |
| | v Dennis Taylor | 1-5 | Quarter-final | Goya Matchroom Trophy |
| | v Longworth | 2-5 | 3rd round | Rothmans Grand Prix |
| | v Dennis Taylor | 1-5 | 1st round | BCE Canadian Masters |
| | v Sinclair | 9-2 | 3rd round | Coral UK Open |
| | v Thorburn | 6-9 | 4th round | Coral UK Open |
| 1986 | v Van Rensberg | 3-5 | 3rd round | Mercantile Credit Classic |
| | v Oliver | 9-0 | 3rd round | Tolly Cobbold English Championship |
| | v Virgo | 6-9 | 4th round | Tolly Cobbold English Championship |
| | v Roscoe | 5-2 | 3rd round | Dulux British Open |
| | v Fagan | 5-0 | 4th round | Dulux British Open |
| | v Wych | 4-5 | 5th round | Dulux British Open |
| | v Foldvari | 10-6 | Qualifying | Embassy World Championship |
| | v Meo | 10-4 | 1st round | Embassy World Championship |
| | v White | 8-13 | 2nd round | Embassy World Championship |
| | v Thorburn | 1-5 | 1st round | Langs Scottish Masters |
| | v Hendry | 3-5 | 3rd round | BCE International |
| | v Cripsey | 5-4 | 3rd round | Rothmans Grand Prix |
| | v Meo | 3-5 | 4th round | Rothmans Grand Prix |
| | v Bradley | 9-4 | 3rd round | Tennents UK Open |
| | v Johnson | 9-1 | 4th round | Tennents UK Open |
| | v Longworth | 9-6 | 5th round | Tennents UK Open |
| | v Knowles | 9-4 | Quarter-final | Tennents UK Open |
| | v N. Foulds | 3-9 | Semi-final | Tennents UK Open |
| 1987 | v T. Jones | 5-2 | 3rd round | Mercantile Credit Classic |
| | v Higgins | 5-2 | 4th round | Mercantile Credit Classic |
| | v Charlton | 5-4 | 5th round | Mercantile Credit Classic |
| | v S. Davis | 4-5 | Quarter-final | Mercantile Credit Classic |
| | v Wildman | 6-1 | 3rd round | Tolly Ales English Championship |

*John Parrott*

| | | | |
|---|---|---|---|
| v Virgo | 6-2 | 4th round | Tolly Ales English Championship |
| v Meo | 3-6 | Quarter-final | Tolly Ales English Championship |
| v King | 1-5 | 3rd round | Dulux British Open |
| v Fowler | 10-3 | Qualifying | Embassy World Championship |
| v Meo | 10-8 | 1st round | Embassy World Championship |
| v White | 11-13 | 2nd round | Embassy World Championship |
| v Chappel | 5-1 | 3rd round | Fidelity International |
| v Chaperon | 5-1 | 4th round | Fidelity International |
| v S. Davis | 2-5 | 5th round | Fidelity International |
| v Dodd | 5-1 | 3rd round | Rothmans Grand Prix |
| v Stevens | 5-0 | 4th round | Rothmans Grand Prix |
| v Griffiths | 5-4 | 5th round | Rothmans Grand Prix |
| v Chaperon | 5-2 | Quarter-final | Rothmans Grand Prix |
| v Hendry | 7-9 | Semi-final | Rothmans Grand Prix |
| v Newbury | 9-5 | 3rd round | Tennents UK Open |
| v Wych | 9-6 | 4th round | Tennents UK Open |
| v Knowles | 9-4 | 5th round | Tennents UK Open |
| v S. Davis | 5-9 | Quarter-final | Tennents UK Open |
| **1988** v Wildman | 5-2 | 3rd round | Mercantile Credit Classic |
| v David Taylor | 5-0 | 4th round | Mercantile Credit Classic |
| v Virgo | 5-0 | 5th round | Mercantile Credit Classic |
| v Dennis Taylor | 5-1 | Quarter-final | Mercantile Credit Classic |
| v Knowles | 9-4 | Semi-final | Mercantile Credit Classic |
| v S. Davis | 11-13 | Final | Mercantile Credit Classic |
| v Foulds | 5-4 | 1st round | Benson & Hedges Masters |
| v Thorburn | 5-4 | Quarter-final | Benson & Hedges Masters |
| v Hallett | 5-6 | Semi-final | Benson & Hedges Masters |
| v Lawlor | 6-3 | 3rd round | English Championship |
| v Reynolds | 2-6 | 4th round | English Championship |
| v Foldvari | 5-1 | 3rd round | MIM Britannia British Open |
| v Virgo | 5-1 | 4th round | MIM Britannia British Open |
| v N. Foulds | 5-0 | 5th round | MIM Britannia British Open |
| v O'Kane | 5-2 | Quarter-final | MIM Britannia British Open |
| v Hallett | 8-9 | Semi-final | MIM Britannia British Open |
| v Clark | 5-1 | Semi-final | Kent Cup |
| v King | 10-4 | 1st round | Embassy World Championship |
| v Thorburn | 10-13 | 2nd round | Embassy World Championship |
| v Dodd | 4-5 | 3rd round | Fidelity International |
| v Hallett | 3-5 | 1st round | Fosters Professional |
| v Morra | 5-3 | 3rd round | Rothmans Grand Prix |
| v Edmonds | 3-5 | 4th round | Rothmans Grand Prix |
| v Dunning | 5-2 | 3rd round | BCE Canadian Masters |
| v D. Morgan | 5-3 | 4th round | BCE Canadian Masters |
| v Virgo | 5-4 | 5th round | BCE Canadian Masters |
| v Hallett | 3-5 | Quarter-final | BCE Canadian Masters |
| v Martin | 9-6 | 3rd round | Tennents UK Open |
| v N. Gilbert | 9-8 | 4th round | Tennents UK Open |
| v Dennis Taylor | 9-4 | 5th round | Tennents UK Open |
| v S. Davis | 4-9 | Quarter-final | Tennents UK Open |
| v Johnson | 9-7 | Quarter-final | Everest World Matchplay |
| v Hendry | 9-6 | Semi-final | Everest World Matchplay |
| v S. Davis | 5-9 | Final | Everest World Matchplay |
| **1989** v Roe | 5-2 | 3rd round | Mercantile Credit Classic |
| v Wright | 5-2 | 4th round | Mercantile Credit Classic |
| v S. Francisco | 5-1 | 5th round | Mercantile Credit Classic |
| v W. Jones | 4-5 | Quarter-final | Mercantile Credit Classic |
| v Dennis Taylor | 5-1 | 1st round | Benson and Hedges Masters |
| v White | 5-4 | Quarter-final | Benson and Hedges Masters |
| v N. Foulds | 6-5 | Semi-final | Benson and Hedges Masters |
| v Hendry | 6-9 | Final | Benson and Hedges Masters |
| v Gary Wilkinson | 5-2 | 4th round | European Open |
| v J. Campbell | 5-0 | 5th round | European Open |
| v Charlton | 5-1 | Quarter-final | European Open |

| v Hallett | 5-4 | Semi-final | European Open |
| v **Griffiths** | **9-8** | **Final** | **European Open** |
| v Miles | 5-3 | 3rd round | English Championship |
| v Fowler | 5-4 | 4th round | English Championship |
| v Johnson | 5-4 | Quarter-final | English Championship |
| v N. Foulds | 5-4 | Semi-final | English Championship |
| v Hallett | 7-9 | Final | English Championship |
| v Wright | 5-1 | 3rd round | Anglian British Open |
| v Longworth | 5-1 | 4th round | Anglian British Open |
| v Mountjoy | 5-2 | 5th round | Anglian British Open |
| v S. Davis | 5-1 | Quarter-final | Anglian British Open |
| v Reynolds | 8-9 | Semi-final | Anglian British Open |
| v Dennis Taylor | 5-1 | 1st round | Benson and Hedges Irish Masters |
| v White | 5-1 | Quarter-final | Benson and Hedges Irish Masters |
| v Higgins | 4-6 | Semi-final | Benson and Hedges Irish Masters |
| v James | 10-9 | 1st round | Embassy World Championship |
| v Dennis Taylor | 13-10 | 2nd round | Embassy World Championship |
| v White | 13-7 | Quarter-final | Embassy World Championship |
| v Meo | 16-7 | Semi-final | Embassy World Championship |
| v S. Davis | 3-18 | Final | Embassy World Championship |

## MICK PRICE (England)

**Born** 2.6.66. **Turned professional** 1988. **World ranking** 90.

| **1988** | v Medati | 5-4 | 1st round | Fidelity International |
| | v Werbeniuk | 5-2 | 2nd round | Fidelity International |
| | v Longworth | 4-5 | 3rd round | Fidelity International |
| | v Foldvari | 1-5 | 1st round | Rothmans Grand Prix |
| | v Meadowcroft | 5-0 | 1st round | BCE Canadian Masters |
| | v D. Gilbert | 5-4 | 2nd round | BCE Canadian Masters |
| | v Mountjoy | 2-5 | 3rd round | BCE Canadian Masters |
| | v Grace | 9-3 | 1st round | Tennents UK Open |
| | v Murphy | 6-9 | 2nd round | Tennents UK Open |
| **1989** | v Dunning | 3-5 | 1st round | Mercantile Credit Classic |
| | v John Rea | 5-4 | 1st round | European Open |
| | v J. McLaughlin | 3-5 | 2nd round | European Open |
| | v Johnston-Allen | 5-4 | 1st round | English Championship |
| | v Edmonds | 5-4 | 2nd round | English Championship |
| | v David Taylor | 5-1 | 3rd round | English Championship |
| | v Hallett | 4-5 | 4th round | English Championship |
| | v Rigitano | 5-0 | 1st round | Anglian British Open |
| | v Roe | 2-5 | 2nd round | Anglian British Open |
| | v Sinclair | 10-9 | Qualifying | Embassy World Championship |
| | v M. Bennett | 10-9 | Qualifying | Embassy World Championship |
| | v Rowswell | 6-10 | Qualifying | Embassy World Championship |

## JACK REA (Northern Ireland)

**Born** 6.4.21. **Turned professional** 1948. **World ranking** 117 (99). **Amateur career** 1947 Northern Ireland champion. **Best professional performance** Runner-up 1957 World Championship.

| **1969** | v G. Owen | 17-25 | Quarter-final | World Championship |
| **1970** | v Spencer | 15-31 | Quarter-final | World Championship |
| **1972** | v Higgins | 11-19 | 1st round | World Championship |
| **1973** | v Houlihan | 2-9 | 1st round | World Championship |
| **1976** | v Anderson | 8-5 | Qualifying | Embassy World Championship |
| **1977** | v John Rea | 9-11 | Qualifying | Embassy World Championship |
| | v Fagan | 1-5 | 1st round | Super Crystalate UK Championship |
| **1978** | v Meadowcroft | 5-9 | Qualifying | Coral UK Championship |

| 1979 | v Dunning | 5-9 | Prelim | Embassy World Championship |
|---|---|---|---|---|
| | v Bennett | 9-8 | 1st round | Coral UK Championship |
| | v Houlihan | 3-9 | 2nd round | Coral UK Championship |
| 1980 | v Thorne | 1-9 | Qualifying | Embassy World Championship |
| 1981 | v D. Hughes | 4-5 | Qualifying | Jameson International |
| 1982 | v E. Hughes | 1-6 | Quarter-final | Irish Championship |
| | v Bennett | 8-5 | Qualifying | Embassy World Championship |
| | v Werbeniuk | 2-5 | 2nd round | Professional Players Tournament |
| | v Roscoe | 6-9 | Qualifying | Coral UK Championship |
| 1983 | v Higgins | 3-6 | Quarter-final | Irish Championship |
| | v David Taylor | 7-8 | Qualifying | Embassy World Championship |
| | v Edmonds | 1-5 | Qualifying | Jameson International |
| | v French | 5-9 | Qualifying | Coral UK Championship |
| 1984 | v Bradley | 2-5 | Qualifying | Jameson International |
| 1985 | v Foldvari | 4-5 | Qualifying | Mercantile Credit Classic |
| | v Dennis Taylor | 0-6 | Quarter-final | Irish Championship |
| | v Murphy | 1-5 | 2nd round | Goya Matchroom Trophy |
| 1986 | v Fisher | 3-5 | 2nd round | Mercantile Credit Classic |
| | v Bradley | 1-5 | 2nd round | Dulux British Open |
| | v Kelly | 0-5 | 1st round | Strongbow Irish Championship |
| | v Darrington | 5-4 | 1st round | BCE International |
| | v W. Jones | 1-5 | 2nd round | BCE International |
| | v D. Hughes | 5-2 | 1st round | Rothmans Grand Prix |
| | v B. Harris | 0-5 | 2nd round | Rothmans Grand Prix |
| | v B. Harris | 5-9 | 2nd round | Tennents UK Open |
| 1987 | v Kelly | 5-3 | 1st round | Mercantile Credit Classic |
| | v Hendry | 1-5 | 2nd round | Mercantile Credit Classic |
| | v Oliver | 1-5 | 1st round | Dulux British Open |
| | v Bear | 5-10 | Qualifying | Embassy World Championship |
| | v Browne | 3-5 | 1st round | Matchroom Irish Championship |
| | v Burke | 5-1 | 1st round | Fidelity International |
| | v G. Foulds | 5-4 | 2nd round | Fidelity International |
| | v Spencer | 0-5 | 3rd round | Fidelity International |
| | v Rigitano | 4-5 | 1st round | Rothmans Grand Prix |
| | v Watterson | 9-6 | 1st round | Tennents UK Open |
| | v Chaperon | 6-9 | 2nd round | Tennents UK Open |
| 1988 | v D. Gilbert | 2-5 | 1st round | Mercantile Credit Classic |
| | v Browne | 0-5 | 1st round | Irish Championship |
| | v Rowswell | 1-5 | 1st round | MIM Britannia British Open |
| | v Mikkelsen | 3-10 | Qualifying | Embassy World Championship |
| | v Lawlor | 2-5 | 1st round | Fidelity International |
| | v B. Harris | 2-5 | 1st round | Rothmans Grand Prix |
| | v M. Smith | 1-5 | 1st round | BCE Canadian Masters |
| | v Glen Wilkinson | 0-9 | 1st round | Tennents UK Open |
| 1989 | v M. Gibson | 5-3 | 1st round | Mercantile Credit Classic |
| | v Murphy | 0-5 | 2nd round | Mercantile Credit Classic |
| | v G. Foulds | 4-5 | 1st round | European Open |
| | v J. McLaughlin | 0-5 | Quarter-final | Irish Championship |
| | v Bear | 4-5 | 1st round | Anglian British Open |

## JOHN REA (Scotland)

**Born** 5.12.51. **Turned professional** 1984. **World ranking** 66 (81). **Best professional performances** Winner 1989 Scottish Championship; last 32 1988 Fidelity International, 1986 Dulux British Open.

| 1984 | v Browne | 2-5 | Qualifying | Jameson International |
|---|---|---|---|---|
| | v Fitzmaurice | 5-2 | Qualifying | Rothmans Grand Prix |
| | v E. Hughes | 5-4 | 1st round | Rothmans Grand Prix |
| | v David Taylor | 1-5 | 2nd round | Rothmans Grand Prix |
| | v Bennett | 9-5 | Qualifying | Coral UK Open |
| | v Dunning | 9-3 | Qualifying | Coral UK Open |
| | v Edmonds | 9-6 | Qualifying | Coral UK Open |

| | | | | |
|---|---|---|---|---|
| | v Johnson | 6-9 | Qualifying | Coral UK Open |
| 1985 | v Sheehan | 2-5 | Qualifying | Mercantile Credit Classic |
| | v Donnelly | 6-2 | 1st round | Scottish Championship |
| | v Sinclair | 2-6 | Semi-final | Scottish Championship |
| | v Fisher | 6-0 | Qualifying | Dulux British Open |
| | v Parrott | 4-6 | 1st round | Dulux British Open |
| | v W. Jones | 3-10 | Qualifying | Embassy World Championship |
| | v Bradley | 1-5 | 2nd round | Goya Matchroom Trophy |
| | v W. Jones | 0-5 | 2nd round | Rothmans Grand Prix |
| | v F. Davis | 8-9 | 2nd round | Coral UK Open |
| 1986 | v Williamson | 5-4 | 2nd round | Mercantile Credit Classic |
| | v Hallett | 2-5 | 3rd round | Mercantile Credit Classic |
| | v King | 5-1 | 2nd round | Dulux British Open |
| | v Reardon | 5-3 | 3rd round | Dulux British Open |
| | v Virgo | 0-5 | 4th round | Dulux British Open |
| | v Donnelly | 6-1 | Quarter-final | Canada Dry Scottish Championship |
| | v Gibson | 0-6 | Semi-final | Canada Dry Scottish Championship |
| | v E. McLaughlin | 10-6 | Qualifying | Embassy World Championship |
| | v Longworth | 4-10 | Qualifying | Embassy World Championship |
| | v Anderson | 5-1 | 2nd round | BCE International |
| | v S. Davis | 1-5 | 3rd round | BCE International |
| | v Sinclair | 5-4 | 2nd round | Rothmans Grand Prix |
| | v Wych | 2-5 | 3rd round | Rothmans Grand Prix |
| | v N. Gilbert | 9-8 | 2nd round | Tennents UK Open |
| | v Knowles | 4-9 | 3rd round | Tennents UK Open |
| 1987 | v Owers | 5-2 | 2nd round | Mercantile Credit Classic |
| | v Meo | 4-5 | 3rd round | Mercantile Credit Classic |
| | v Black | 6-1 | 1st round | Scottish Championship |
| | v Hendry | 0-6 | Semi-final | Scottish Championship |
| | v Hargreaves | 5-3 | 2nd round | Dulux British Open |
| | v Griffiths | 2-5 | 3rd round | Dulux British Open |
| | v Rempe | 9-10 | Qualifying | Embassy World Championship |
| | v Bales | 5-2 | 2nd round | Fidelity International |
| | v Thorne | 3-5 | 3rd round | Fidelity International |
| | v Bradley | 5-1 | 2nd round | Rothmans Grand Prix |
| | v P. Francisco | 3-5 | 3rd round | Rothmans Grand Prix |
| | v J. McLaughlin | 9-5 | 2nd round | Rothmans Grand Prix |
| | v Knowles | 6-9 | 3rd round | Tennents UK Open |
| 1988 | v Bales | 5-0 | 2nd round | Mercantile Credit Classic |
| | v Spencer | 3-5 | 3rd round | Mercantile Credit Classic |
| | v Sinclair | 6-5 | Quarter-final | Scottish Championship |
| | v W. Jones | 3-5 | 2nd round | MIM Britannia British Open |
| | v N. Gilbert | 5-10 | Qualifying | Embassy World Championship |
| | v Edwards | 5-2 | 1st round | Fidelity International |
| | v Bales | 5-2 | 2nd round | Fidelity International |
| | v P. Francisco | 5-0 | 3rd round | Fidelity International |
| | v David Taylor | 4-5 | 4th round | Fidelity International |
| | v Darrington | 5-4 | 1st round | Rothmans Grand Prix |
| | v Houlihan | 1-5 | 2nd round | Rothmans Grand Prix |
| | v Rowing | 5-2 | 1st round | BCE Canadian Masters |
| | v M. Bennett | 4-5 | 2nd round | BCE Canadian Masters |
| | v Meakin | 9-6 | 1st round | Tennents UK Open |
| | v Cripsey | 9-2 | 2nd round | Tennents UK Open |
| | v P. Fransisco | 2-9 | 3rd round | Tennents UK Open |
| 1989 | v Terry | 3-5 | 1st round | Mercantile Credit Classic |
| | v Price | 4-5 | 1st round | European Open |
| | v Black | 5-3 | 1st round | Scottish Championship |
| | v Donnelly | 5-1 | Semi-final | Scottish Championship |
| | **v Macleod** | **9-7** | **Final** | **Scottish Championship** |
| | v Watchorn | 5-3 | 1st round | Anglian British Open |
| | v D. Gilbert | 3-5 | 2nd round | Anglian British Open |
| | v D. Hughes | 10-3 | Qualifying | Embassy World Championship |
| | v Houlihan | 10-5 | Qualifying | Embassy World Championship |

| v Edmonds | 10-7 | Qualifying | Embassy World Championship |
| v James | 7-10 | Qualifying | Embassy World Championship |

## RAY REARDON M.B.E. (Wales)

**Born** 8.10.32. **Turned professional** 1967. **World ranking** 54 (40). **Amateur career** 1950–55 Welsh champion, 1964 English champion. **Best professional performances** Winner 1970, 1973–76, 1978 World Championship, 1982 Professional Players Tournament, 1976 Benson & Hedges Masters, 1981 and 1983 Welsh Championship.

| | | | | |
|---|---|---|---|---|
| **1969** | v F. Davis | 24-25 | Quarter-final | World Championship |
| **1970** | v F. Davis | 31-26 | Quarter-final | World Championship (Apr) |
| | v Spencer | 37-33 | Semi-final | World Championship (Apr) |
| | **v Pulman** | **39-34** | **Final** | **World Championship (Apr)** |
| | v Spencer | 15-34 | Semi-final | World Championship (Nov) |
| **1972** | v Williams | 23-25 | Quarter-final | World Championship |
| **1973** | v Meadowcroft | 16-10 | 2nd round | World Championship |
| | v G. Owen | 16-6 | Quarter-final | World Championship |
| | v Spencer | 23-22 | Semi-final | World Championship |
| | **v Charlton** | **38-32** | **Final** | **World Championship** |
| **1974** | v Meadowcroft | 15-3 | 2nd round | World Championship |
| | v M. Owen | 15-11 | Quarter-final | World Championship |
| | v F. Davis | 15-3 | Semi-final | World Championship |
| | **v Miles** | **22-12** | **Final** | **World Championship** |
| **1975** | v Miles | 5-3 | Quarter-final | Benson & Hedges Masters |
| | v Williams | 5-4 | Semi-final | Benson & Hedges Masters |
| | v Spencer | 8-9 | Final | Benson & Hedges Masters |
| | v Simpson | 15-11 | 2nd round | World Championship |
| | v Spencer | 19-17 | Quarter-final | World Championship |
| | v Higgins | 19-14 | Semi-final | World Championship |
| | **v Charlton** | **31-30** | **Final** | **World Championship** |
| **1976** | v Charlton | 5-4 | Semi-final | Benson & Hedges Masters |
| | **v Miles** | **7-3** | **Final** | **Benson & Hedges Masters** |
| | v Dunning | 15-7 | 1st round | Embassy World Championship |
| | v Dennis Taylor | 15-2 | Quarter-final | Embassy World Championship |
| | v Mans | 20-10 | Semi-final | Embassy World Championship |
| | **v Higgins** | **27-16** | **Final** | **Embassy World Championship** |
| **1977** | v Miles | 5-2 | Semi-final | Benson & Hedges Masters |
| | v Mountjoy | 6-7 | Final | Benson & Hedges Masters |
| | v Fagan | 13-7 | 1st round | Embassy World Championship |
| | v Spencer | 6-13 | Quarter-final | Embassy World Championship |
| | v Meadowcroft | 4-5 | 2nd round | Super Crystalate UK Championship |
| **1978** | v Higgins | 1-5 | Semi-final | Benson & Hedges Masters |
| | v Mountjoy | 13-9 | 1st round | Embassy World Championship |
| | v Werbeniuk | 13-6 | Quarter-final | Embassy World Championship |
| | v Charlton | 18-14 | Semi-final | Embassy World Championship |
| | **v Mans** | **25-18** | **Final** | **Embassy World Championship** |
| | v Thorne | 6-9 | 1st round | Coral UK Championship |
| **1979** | v David Taylor | 5-2 | Quarter-final | Benson & Hedges Masters |
| | v Mans | 3-5 | Semi-final | Benson & Hedges Masters |
| | v Mountjoy | 5-6 | Final | Benson & Hedges Masters |
| | v Miles | 13-8 | 1st round | Embassy World Championship |
| | v Dennis Taylor | 8-13 | Quarter-final | Embassy World Championship |
| **1980** | v Dennis Taylor | 5-3 | Quarter-final | Benson & Hedges Masters |
| | v Higgins | 2-5 | Semi-final | Benson & Hedges Masters |
| | v Higgins | 1-5 | Final | British Gold Cup |
| | v Wilson | 9-3 | 1st round | Woodpecker Welsh Championship |
| | v Mountjoy | 6-9 | Final | Woodpecker Welsh Championship |
| | v Werbeniuk | 13-6 | 2nd round | Embassy World Championship |
| | v David Taylor | 11-13 | Quarter-final | Embassy World Championship |
| | v Andrewartha | 9-3 | 2nd round | Coral UK Championship |

| | | | | |
|---|---|---|---|---|
| | v Williams | 9-4 | Quarter-final | Coral UK Championship |
| | v Higgins | 7-9 | Semi-final | Coral UK Championship |
| **1981** | v Spencer | 1-5 | Quarter-final | Benson & Hedges Masters |
| | v Griffiths | 9-6 | Semi-final | Woodpecker Welsh Championship |
| | **v Wilson** | **9-6** | **Final** | **Woodpecker Welsh Championship** |
| | v Higgins | 6-5 | Semi-final | Benson & Hedges Irish Masters |
| | v Griffiths | 7-9 | Final | Benson & Hedges Irish Masters |
| | v Spencer | 13-11 | 2nd round | Embassy World Championship |
| | v Werbeniuk | 13-10 | Quarter-final | Embassy World Championship |
| | v Mountjoy | 10-16 | Semi-final | Embassy World Championship |
| | v White | 4-5 | Quarter-final | Langs Supreme Scottish Masters |
| | v Virgo | 3-5 | 3rd round | Jameson International |
| | v Johnson | 9-7 | 3rd round | Coral UK Championship |
| | v White | 8-9 | Quarter-final | Coral UK Championship |
| **1982** | v David Taylor | 5-1 | 1st round | Lada Classic |
| | v S. Davis | 4-5 | Semi-final | Lada Classic |
| | v Dennis Taylor | 5-3 | 1st round | Benson & Hedges Masters |
| | v Griffiths | 3-5 | Quarter-final | Benson & Hedges Masters |
| | v Everton | 6-1 | 1st round | Welsh Championship |
| | v Mountjoy | 7-9 | Semi-final | Welsh Championship |
| | v Dennis Taylor | 5-4 | Quarter-final | Benson & Hedges Irish Masters |
| | v Griffiths | 3-6 | Semi-final | Benson & Hedges Irish Masters |
| | v Donnelly | 10-5 | 1st round | Embassy World Championship |
| | v Virgo | 13-8 | 2nd round | Embassy World Championship |
| | v S. Francisco | 13-8 | Quarter-final | Embassy World Championship |
| | v Charlton | 16-11 | Semi-final | Embassy World Championship |
| | v Higgins | 15-18 | Final | Embassy World Championship |
| | v Griffiths | 3-5 | 1st round | Langs Supreme Scottish Masters |
| | v E. Hughes | 5-3 | 1st round | Jameson International |
| | v Knowles | 2-5 | 2nd round | Jameson International |
| | v Murphy | 5-0 | 1st round | Professional Players Tournament |
| | v Higgins | 5-2 | 2nd round | Professional Players Tournament |
| | v Macleod | 5-2 | 3rd round | Professional Players Tournament |
| | v Werbeniuk | 5-3 | Quarter-final | Professional Players Tournament |
| | v Charlton | 10-7 | Semi-final | Professional Players Tournament |
| | **v White** | **10-5** | **Final** | **Professional Players Tournament** |
| | v Wildman | 9-5 | 1st round | Coral UK Championship |
| | v Hallett | 9-8 | 2nd round | Coral UK Championship |
| | v White | 9-8 | Quarter-final | Coral UK Championship |
| | v Higgins | 6-9 | Semi-final | Coral UK Championship |
| **1983** | v Spencer | 3-5 | 1st round | Lada Classic |
| | v Reynolds | 5-1 | 1st round | Benson & Hedges Masters |
| | v White | 5-2 | Quarter-final | Benson & Hedges Masters |
| | v Mountjoy | 6-3 | Semi-final | Benson & Hedges Masters |
| | v Thorburn | 7-9 | Final | Benson & Hedges Masters |
| | **v White** | **9-6** | **Final** | **Yamaha International Masters** |
| | v Andrewartha | 6-2 | Quarter-final | Woodpecker Welsh Championship |
| | v Griffiths | 9-4 | Semi-final | Woodpecker Welsh Championship |
| | **v Mountjoy** | **9-1** | **Final** | **Woodpecker Welsh Championship** |
| | v Meo | 5-4 | Quarter-final | Benson & Hedges Irish Masters |
| | v Higgins | 6-3 | Semi-final | Benson & Hedges Irish Masters |
| | v S. Davis | 2-9 | Final | Benson & Hedges Irish Masters |
| | v E. Hughes | 10-7 | 1st round | Embassy World Championship |
| | v Knowles | 12-13 | 2nd round | Embassy World Championship |
| | v Macleod | 5-2 | 1st round | Jameson International |
| | v Thorne | 0-5 | 2nd round | Jameson International |
| | v Ganim | 5-4 | 1st round | Professional Players Tournament |
| | v Duggan | 5-2 | 2nd round | Professional Players Tournament |
| | v Thorne | 3-5 | 3rd round | Professional Players Tournament |
| | v B. Harris | 9-7 | 1st round | Coral UK Championship |
| | v Wilson | 9-4 | 2nd round | Coral UK Championship |
| | v White | 4-9 | Quarter-final | Coral UK Championship |
| **1984** | v Williams | 4-5 | Qualifying | Lada Classic |

| | | | |
|---|---|---|---|
| v Virgo | 5-3 | 1st round | Benson & Hedges Masters |
| v White | 3-5 | Quarter-final | Benson & Hedges Masters |
| v M. Owen | 6-1 | 1st round | Strongbow Welsh Championship |
| v Wilson | 4-9 | Semi-final | Strongbow Welsh Championship |
| v Higgins | 2-5 | Quarter-final | Benson & Hedges Irish Masters |
| v Wych | 10-7 | 1st round | Embassy World Championship |
| v S. Francisco | 13-8 | 2nd round | Embassy World Championship |
| v Stevens | 2-13 | Quarter-final | Embassy World Championship |
| v Dodd | 5-4 | 1st round | Jameson International |
| v E. Hughes | 1-5 | 2nd round | Jameson International |
| v Roscoe | 5-1 | 1st round | Rothmans Grand Prix |
| v Wilson | 5-4 | 2nd round | Rothmans Grand Prix |
| v Dennis Taylor | 3-5 | 3rd round | Rothmans Grand Prix |
| v Fowler | 9-2 | 1st round | Coral UK Open |
| v David Taylor | 9-4 | 2nd round | Coral UK Open |
| v Thorburn | 8-9 | Quarter-final | Coral UK Open |
| 1985 v Hallett | 5-3 | 1st round | Mercantile Credit Classic |
| v E. Hughes | 5-1 | 2nd round | Mercantile Credit Classic |
| v S. Davis | 1-5 | Quarter-final | Mercantile Credit Classic |
| v David Taylor | 5-1 | 1st round | Benson & Hedges Masters |
| v Thorburn | 0-5 | Quarter-final | Benson & Hedges Masters |
| v King | 6-5 | 1st round | Dulux British Open |
| v Martin | 4-5 | 2nd round | Dulux British Open |
| v E. Hughes | 0-5 | 1st round | Benson & Hedges Irish Masters |
| v E. Hughes | 10-9 | 1st round | Embassy World Championship |
| v Fagan | 13-9 | 2nd round | Embassy World Championship |
| v Parrott | 13-12 | Quarter-final | Embassy World Championship |
| v S. Davis | 5-16 | Semi-final | Embassy World Championship |
| v Everton | 6-2 | Quarter-final | BCE Welsh Championship |
| v Griffiths | 3-9 | Semi-final | BCE Welsh Championship |
| v Duggan | 3-5 | 3rd round | Goya Matchroom Trophy |
| v Scott | 4-5 | 3rd round | Rothmans Grand Prix |
| v Knowles | 5-2 | 1st round | BCE Canadian Masters |
| v Dennis Taylor | 3-8 | Semi-final | BCE Canadian Masters |
| v Miles | 9-4 | 3rd round | Coral UK Open |
| v Macleod | 5-9 | 4th round | Coral UK Open |
| v Griffiths | 2-5 | 1st round | Kit Kat |
| 1986 v Mikkelsen | 3-5 | 3rd round | Mercantile Credit Classic |
| v Stevens | 1-5 | 1st round | BCE Belgian Classic |
| v Thorne | 4-5 | 1st round | Benson & Hedges Masters |
| v W. Jones | 4-6 | Quarter-final | Zetters Welsh Championship |
| v John Rea | 3-5 | 3rd round | Dulux British Open |
| v E. Hughes | 2-5 | 1st round | Benson & Hedges Irish Masters |
| v J. Campbell | 8-10 | 1st round | Embassy World Championship |
| v W. Jones | 5-4 | 3rd round | BCE International |
| v Gauvreau | 2-5 | 4th round | BCE International |
| v Chaperon | 3-5 | 3rd round | Rothmans Grand Prix |
| v M. Gibson | 9-6 | 3rd round | Tennents UK Open |
| v E. Hughes | 5-9 | 4th round | Tennents UK Open |
| 1987 v Hendry | 3-5 | 3rd round | Mercantile Credit Classic |
| v Johnson | 2-5 | 1st round | Benson & Hedges Masters |
| v Chappel | 4-6 | Quarter-final | Matchroom Welsh Championship |
| v O'Boye | 5-4 | 3rd round | Dulux British Open |
| v Murphy | 4-5 | 4th round | Dulux British Open |
| v West | 10-5 | 1st round | Embassy World Championship |
| v S. Davis | 4-13 | 2nd round | Embassy World Championship |
| v Rowswell | 5-4 | 2nd round | Fidelity International |
| v Charlton | 4-5 | 3rd round | Fidelity International |
| v Burke | 5-2 | 2nd round | Rothmans Grand Prix |
| v Dennis Taylor | 1-5 | 3rd round | Rothmans Grand Prix |
| v Van Rensberg | 9-7 | 2nd round | Tennents UK Open |
| v S. Francisco | 3-9 | 3rd round | Tennents UK Open |
| 1988 v Gary Wilkinson | 5-3 | 2nd round | Mercantile Credit Classic |

|  |  |  |  |  |
|---|---|---|---|---|
|  | v Thorburn | 3-5 | 3rd round | Mercantile Credit Classic |
|  | v W. Jones | 5-6 | Quarter-final | Welsh Championship |
|  | v Van Rensberg | 5-3 | 2nd round | MIM Britannia British Open |
|  | v S. Davis | 5-0 | 3rd round | MIM Britannia British Open |
|  | v Roe | 2-5 | 4th round | MIM Britannia British Open |
|  | v Oliver | 6-10 | Qualifying | Embassy World Championship |
|  | v Donnelly | 5-1 | 2nd round | Fidelity International |
|  | v Spencer | 4-5 | 3rd round | Fidelity International |
|  | v Morra | 4-5 | 2nd round | Rothmans Grand Prix |
|  | v J. Smith | 5-2 | 2nd round | BCE Canadian Masters |
|  | v Chaperon | 4-5 | 3rd round | BCE Canadian Masters |
|  | v D. Morgan | 9-5 | 2nd round | Tennents UK Open |
|  | v O'Kane | 8-9 | 3rd round | Tennents UK Open |
| 1989 | v Chambers | 5-4 | 2nd round | Mercantile Credit Classic |
|  | v Charlton | 5-1 | 3rd round | Mercantile Credit Classic |
|  | v Hendry | 4-5 | 4th round | Mercantile Credit Classic |
|  | v Williamson | 5-3 | 2nd round | European Open |
|  | v Virgo | 3-5 | 3rd round | European Open |
|  | v Mountjoy | 3-6 | Quarter-final | Senator Welsh Championship |
|  | v S. Campbell | 5-4 | 2nd round | Anglian British Open |
|  | v N. Foulds | 1-5 | 3rd round | Anglian British Open |
|  | v Fitzmaurice | 10-5 | Qualifying | Embassy World Championship |
|  | v Gary Wilkinson | 5-10 | Qualifying | Embassy World Championship |

## JIM REMPE (USA)

**Born** 4.11.47. **Turned professional** 1980. **World ranking** 129 (108).

|  |  |  |  |  |
|---|---|---|---|---|
| 1985 | v Burke | 5-3 | 1st round | Goya Matchroom Trophy |
|  | v Wych | 1-5 | 2nd round | Goya Matchroom Trophy |
|  | v Agrawal | 2-5 | 1st round | Rothmans Grand Prix |
| 1987 | v Smith | 10-9 | Qualifying | Embassy World Championship |
|  | v John Rea | 10-9 | Qualifying | Embassy World Championship |
|  | v Hendry | 4-10 | Qualifying | Embassy World Championship |
| 1988 | v Foldvari | 4-10 | Qualifying | Embassy World Championship |
|  | v Oliver | 3-5 | 1st round | BCE Canadian Masters |
| 1989 | v Bradley | 4-5 | 1st round | European Open |
|  | v Morra | 5-1 | 1st round | Anglian British Open |
|  | v Dodd | 0-5 | 2nd round | Anglian British Open |
|  | v Oliver | 5-10 | Qualifying | Embassy World Championship |

## DEAN REYNOLDS (England)

**Born** 11.1.63. **Turned professional** 1981. **World ranking** 15 (22). **Best professional performances** Runner-up 1989 Anglian British Open; winner 1988 English Championship.

|  |  |  |  |  |
|---|---|---|---|---|
| 1982 | v Sheehan | 9-5 | Qualifying | Embassy World Championship |
|  | v Edmonds | 9-6 | Qualifying | Embassy World Championship |
|  | v F. Davis | 10-7 | 1st round | Embassy World Championship |
|  | v S. Francisco | 8-13 | 2nd round | Embassy World Championship |
|  | v Morra | 5-1 | Qualifying | Jameson International |
|  | v Thorne | 5-3 | 1st round | Jameson International |
|  | v S. Davis | 0-5 | 2nd round | Jameson International |
|  | v Fitzmaurice | 5-0 | 2nd round | Professional Players Tournament |
|  | v Wilson | 5-1 | 3rd round | Professional Players Tournament |
|  | v Charlton | 2-5 | Quarter-final | Professional Players Tournament |
|  | v Fisher | 9-6 | 1st round | Coral UK Championship |
|  | v Higgins | 8-9 | 2nd round | Coral UK Championship |
| 1983 | v Reardon | 1-5 | 1st round | Benson & Hedges Masters |
|  | v Edmonds | 10-6 | Qualifying | Embassy World Championship |

*Dean Reynolds*

|      |                 |       |              |                                      |
|------|-----------------|-------|--------------|--------------------------------------|
|      | v Higgins       | 4-10  | 1st round    | Embassy World Championship           |
|      | v Williams      | 5-3   | Qualifying   | Jameson International                 |
|      | v Dennis Taylor | 3-5   | 1st round    | Jameson International                 |
|      | v Greaves       | 5-1   | 1st round    | Professional Players Tournament      |
|      | v Meo           | 0-5   | 2nd round    | Professional Players Tournament      |
|      | v Medati        | 3-9   | 1st round    | Coral UK Championship                |
| 1984 | v Griffiths     | 2-5   | Qualifying   | Lada Classic                         |
|      | v Morra         | 7-10  | Qualifying   | Embassy World Championship           |
|      | v Bales         | 5-4   | Qualifying   | Jameson International                 |
|      | v Knowles       | 1-5   | 1st round    | Jameson International                 |
|      | v Fowler        | 5-2   | 1st round    | Rothmans Grand Prix                  |
|      | v P. Francisco  | 5-4   | 2nd round    | Rothmans Grand Prix                  |
|      | v S. Francisco  | 5-1   | 3rd round    | Rothmans Grand Prix                  |
|      | v S. Davis      | 0-5   | Quarter-final| Rothmans Grand Prix                  |
|      | v Chappel       | 6-9   | Qualifying   | Coral UK Open                        |
| 1985 | v King          | 2-5   | Qualifying   | Mercantile Credit Classic            |
|      | v Fitzmaurice   | 9-2   | 1st round    | Tolly Cobbold English Championship   |
|      | v Thorne        | 9-6   | 2nd round    | Tolly Cobbold English Championship   |
|      | v Meo           | 4-9   | Quarter-final| Tolly Cobbold English Championship   |
|      | v Giannaros     | 6-3   | 1st round    | Dulux British Open                   |
|      | v Thorburn      | 3-5   | 2nd round    | Dulux British Open                   |
|      | v Gauvreau      | 10-1  | Qualifying   | Embassy World Championship           |
|      | v Higgins       | 4-10  | 1st round    | Embassy World Championship           |
|      | v Mikkelsen     | 5-0   | 3rd round    | Goya Matchroom Trophy                |
|      | v Gibson        | 5-0   | 4th round    | Goya Matchroom Trophy                |
|      | v White         | 1-5   | 5th round    | Goya Matchroom Trophy                |
|      | v Miles         | 3-5   | 3rd round    | Rothmans Grand Prix                  |
|      | v J. McLaughlin | 9-7   | 3rd round    | Coral UK Open                        |
|      | v Griffiths     | 7-9   | 4th round    | Coral UK Open                        |
| 1986 | v Houlihan      | 5-1   | 3rd round    | Mercantile Credit Classic            |
|      | v Dennis Taylor | 4-5   | 4th round    | Mercantile Credit Classic            |
|      | v Longworth     | 9-5   | 3rd round    | Tolly Cobbold English Championship   |
|      | v Thorne        | 9-8   | 4th round    | Tolly Cobbold English Championship   |
|      | v Meo           | 4-9   | Quarter-final| Tolly Cobbold English Championship   |
|      | v Wych          | 3-5   | 3rd round    | Dulux British Open                   |
|      | v Stevens       | 6-10  | 1st round    | Embassy World Championship           |
|      | v Dodd          | 5-2   | 3rd round    | BCE International                    |
|      | v Mountjoy      | 5-2   | 4th round    | BCE International                    |
|      | v David Taylor  | 5-1   | 5th round    | BCE International                    |
|      | v N. Foulds     | 2-5   | Quarter-final| BCE International                    |
|      | v Newbury       | 0-5   | 3rd round    | Rothmans Grand Prix                  |
|      | v Mikkelsen     | 9-6   | 3rd round    | Tennents UK Open                     |
|      | v S. Francisco  | 9-8   | 4th round    | Tennents UK Open                     |
|      | v S. Davis      | 5-9   | 5th round    | Tennents UK Open                     |
| 1987 | v King          | 5-4   | 3rd round    | Mercantile Credit Classic            |
|      | v Thorburn      | 5-4   | 4th round    | Mercantile Credit Classic            |
|      | v West          | 5-3   | 5th round    | Mercantile Credit Classic            |
|      | v Wilson        | 5-1   | Quarter-final| Mercantile Credit Classic            |
|      | v White         | 8-9   | Semi-final   | Mercantile Credit Classic            |
|      | v Edmonds       | 6-3   | 3rd round    | Tolly Ales English Championship      |
|      | v White         | 6-5   | 4th round    | Tolly Ales English Championship      |
|      | v Thorne        | 4-6   | Quarter-final| Tolly Ales English Championship      |
|      | v N. Gilbert    | 5-3   | 3rd round    | Dulux British Open                   |
|      | v Knowles       | 0-5   | 4th round    | Dulux British Open                   |
|      | v Oliver        | 10-7  | Qualifying   | Embassy World Championship           |
|      | v White         | 8-10  | 1st round    | Embassy World Championship           |
|      | v W. Jones      | 4-5   | 3rd round    | Fidelity International                |
|      | v Houlihan      | 4-5   | 3rd round    | Rothmans Grand Prix                  |
|      | v Chappel       | 5-9   | 3rd round    | Tennents UK Open                     |
| 1988 | v O'Boye        | 5-3   | 2nd round    | Mercantile Credit Classic            |
|      | v Murphy        | 4-5   | 4th round    | Mercantile Credit Classic            |
|      | v S. Davis      | 2-5   | 1st round    | Benson & Hedges Masters              |
|      | v D. Gilbert    | 6-3   | 3rd round    | English Championship                 |

| | v Parrott | 6-2 | 4th round | English Championship |
|---|---|---|---|---|
| | v Meo | 6-4 | Quarter-final | English Championship |
| | v Johnson | 9-8 | Semi-final | English Championship |
| | **v N. Foulds** | **9-5** | **Final** | **English Championship** |
| | v O'Boye | 2-5 | 3rd round | MIM Britannia British Open |
| | v Hendry | 6-10 | 1st round | Embassy World Championship |
| | v Johnson | 4-5 | 1st round | New Zealand Masters |
| | v T. Jones | 5-4 | 3rd round | Fidelity International |
| | v N. Foulds | 5-3 | 4th round | Fidelity International |
| | v Spencer | 5-2 | 5th round | Fidelity International |
| | v Johnson | 5-1 | Quarter-final | Fidelity International |
| | v White | 5-9 | Semi-final | Fidelity International |
| | v Dodd | 5-3 | 3rd round | Rothmans Grand Prix |
| | v Knowles | 3-5 | 4th round | Rothmans Grand Prix |
| | v Martin | 5-0 | 3rd round | BCE Canadian Masters |
| | v C. Wilson | 4-5 | 4th round | BCE Canadian Masters |
| | v Chappel | 9-4 | 3rd round | Tennents UK Open |
| | v C. Wilson | 9-3 | 4th round | Tennents UK Open |
| | v Griffiths | 6-9 | 5th round | Tennents UK Open |
| **1989** | v Duggan | 5-1 | 3rd round | Mercantile Credit Classic |
| | v Knowles | 4-5 | 4th round | Mercantile Credit Classic |
| | v A. Harris | 5-1 | 3rd round | English Championship |
| | v Rowswell | 4-5 | 4th round | English Championship |
| | v Dodd | 5-2 | 3rd round | Anglian British Open |
| | v White | *wo* | 4th round | Anglian British Open |
| | v C. Wilson | 5-0 | 5th round | Anglian British Open |
| | v Johnson | 5-4 | Quarter-final | Anglian British Open |
| | v Parrott | 9-8 | Semi-final | Anglian British Open |
| | v Meo | 6-13 | Final | Anglian British Open |
| | v Graham | 10-5 | Qualifying | Embassy World Championship |
| | v P. Francisco | 10-7 | 1st round | Embassy World Championship |
| | v W. Jones | 13-3 | 2nd round | Embassy World Championship |
| | v Meo | 9-13 | Quarter-final | Embassy World Championship |

## GINO RIGITANO (Canada)

**Born** 14.8.57. **Turned professional** 1983. **World ranking** 116 (91).

| | | | | |
|---|---|---|---|---|
| **1983** | v Gauvreau | 9-6 | 1st round | Canadian Championship |
| | v Mikkelsen | 4-9 | 2nd round | Canadian Championship |
| **1984** | v Gibson | 7-10 | Qualifying | Embassy World Championship |
| | v Foldvari | 2-5 | Qualifying | Jameson International |
| | v Edmonds | 5-3 | Qualifying | Rothmans Grand Prix |
| | v Thorburn | 4-5 | 1st round | Rothmans Grand Prix |
| | v Newbury | 6-9 | Qualifying | Coral UK Open |
| **1985** | v Fowler | 0-5 | Qualifying | Mercantile Credit Classic |
| | v Thorburn | 3-6 | 1st round | Dulux British Open |
| | v Sheehan | 10-9 | Qualifying | Embassy World Championship |
| | v B. Harris | 10-4 | Qualifying | Embassy World Championship |
| | v Kelly | 10-6 | Qualifying | Embassy World Championship |
| | v Fisher | 10-2 | Qualifying | Embassy World Championship |
| | v N. Foulds | 8-10 | Qualifying | Embassy World Championship |
| | v Black | 4-5 | 2nd round | Goya Matchroom Trophy |
| | v Miles | 4-5 | 2nd round | Rothmans Grand Prix |
| **1986** | v Dodd | 5-3 | 2nd round | Mercantile Credit Classic |
| | v Knowles | 4-5 | 3rd round | Mercantile Credit Classic |
| | v W. Jones | 1-5 | 2nd round | Dulux British Open |
| | v Foldvari | 6-10 | Qualifying | Embassy World Championship |
| | v Jonik | 1-6 | 1st round | Canadian Championship |
| | v Greaves | 5-3 | 1st round | BCE International |
| | v King | 0-5 | 2nd round | BCE International |
| | v Everton | 5-1 | 1st round | Rothmans Grand Prix |
| | v Medati | 1-5 | 2nd round | Rothmans Grand Prix |

|      |                  |          |              |                             |
|------|------------------|----------|--------------|-----------------------------|
|      | v James          | 5-9      | 1st round    | Tennents UK Open            |
| 1987 | v Grace          | 5-4      | 1st round    | Mercantile Credit Classic   |
|      | v Gauvreau       | 0-5      | 2nd round    | Mercantile Credit Classic   |
|      | v Demarco        | 5-1      | 1st round    | Dulux British Open          |
|      | v Browne         | 5-4      | 2nd round    | Dulux British Open          |
|      | v Hallett        | 0-5      | 3rd round    | Dulux British Open          |
|      | v Morgan         | 4-0 *retd* | Qualifying | Embassy World Championship  |
|      | v V. Harris      | 10-6     | Qualifying   | Embassy World Championship  |
|      | v Newbury        | 4-10     | Qualifying   | Embassy World Championship  |
|      | v Wych           | 4-6      | 1st round    | Canadian Championship       |
|      | v Gary Wilkinson | 1-5      | 1st round    | Fidelity International       |
|      | v Jack Rea       | 5-4      | 1st round    | Rothmans Grand Prix         |
|      | v Wright         | 0-5      | 2nd round    | Rothmans Grand Prix         |
|      | v P. Gibson      | 5-9      | 1st round    | Tennents UK Open            |
| 1988 | v Fowler         | 5-2      | 2nd round    | Mercantile Credit Classic   |
|      | v Virgo          | 2-5      | 3rd round    | Mercantile Credit Classic   |
|      | v Marshall       | 5-2      | 1st round    | MIM Britannia British Open  |
|      | v Chaperon       | 2-5      | 2nd round    | MIM Britannia British Open  |
|      | v Dunning        | 10-7     | Qualifying   | Embassy World Championship  |
|      | v M. Bennett     | 4-10     | Qualifying   | Embassy World Championship  |
|      | v D. Hughes      | 4-5      | 1st round    | Fidelity International       |
|      | v W. Jones       | 3-5      | 2nd round    | Rothmans Grand Prix         |
|      | v Watterson      | 3-5      | 1st round    | BCE Canadian Masters        |
|      | v Terry          | 5-9      | 1st round    | Tennents UK Open            |
| 1989 | v Watterson      | 4-5      | 1st round    | Mercantile Credit Classic   |
|      | v Burke          | 5-2      | 1st round    | European Open               |
|      | v W. Jones       | 4-5      | 2nd round    | European Open               |
|      | v Price          | 0-5      | 1st round    | Anglian British Open        |
|      | v Johnston-Allen | 3-10     | Qualifying   | Embassy World Championship  |

## ALAIN ROBIDOUX (Canada)

**Born** 25.7.60. **Turned professional** 1986 (earned full status 1988). **World ranking** 35 (102). **Best professional performances** Semi-finals 1988 Rothmans Grand Prix; winner 1988 Canadian Championship.

|      |                  |       |               |                             |
|------|------------------|-------|---------------|-----------------------------|
| 1988 | v Chaperon       | 6-3   | 1st round     | BCE Canadian Championship   |
|      | v Caggianello    | 6-5   | Quarter-final | BCE Canadian Championship   |
|      | v Mikkelsen      | 7-3   | Semi-final    | BCE Canadian Championship   |
|      | **v Wych**       | **8-4** | **Final**   | **BCE Canadian Championship** |
|      | v Black          | 5-1   | 1st round     | Fidelity International       |
|      | v Houlihan       | 5-2   | 2nd round     | Fidelity International       |
|      | v Charlton       | 5-2   | 3rd round     | Fidelity International       |
|      | v S. Davis       | 4-5   | 4th round     | Fidelity International       |
|      | v Van Rensberg   | 5-2   | 1st round     | Rothmans Grand Prix         |
|      | v Bales          | 5-1   | 2nd round     | Rothmans Grand Prix         |
|      | v Virgo          | 5-1   | 3rd round     | Rothmans Grand Prix         |
|      | v Meo            | 5-0   | 4th round     | Rothmans Grand Prix         |
|      | v Mountjoy       | 5-4   | 5th round     | Rothmans Grand Prix         |
|      | v N. Gilbert     | 5-4   | Quarter-final | Rothmans Grand Prix         |
|      | v Higgins        | 7-9   | Semi-final    | Rothmans Grand Prix         |
|      | v Glen Wilkinson | 5-3   | 1st round     | BCE Canadian Masters        |
|      | v Fisher         | 5-0   | 2nd round     | BCE Canadian Masters        |
|      | v Johnson        | 1-5   | 3rd round     | BCE Canadian Masters        |
|      | v Black          | 9-2   | 1st round     | Tennents UK Open            |
|      | v Bales          | 9-4   | 2nd round     | Tennents UK Open            |
|      | v Thorburn       | 4-9   | 3rd round     | Tennents UK Open            |
| 1989 | v B. Harris      | 5-1   | 1st round     | Mercantile Credit Classic   |
|      | v Werbeniuk      | 4-5   | 2nd round     | Mercantile Credit Classic   |
|      | v Meadowcroft    | 5-0   | 1st round     | European Open               |
|      | v Fisher         | 5-1   | 2nd round     | European Open               |

| | | | |
|---|---|---|---|
| v Newbury | 5-0 | 3rd round | European Open |
| v C. Wilson | 5-0 | 4th round | European Open |
| v Griffiths | 3-5 | 5th round | European Open |
| v B. Harris | 5-0 | 1st round | Anglian British Open |
| v King | 5-2 | 2nd round | Anglian British Open |
| v Spencer | 5-1 | 3rd round | Anglian British Open |
| v N. Foulds | 1-5 | 4th round | Anglian British Open |
| v Miles | 10-8 | Qualifying | Embassy World Championship |
| v Fisher | 10-2 | Qualifying | Embassy World Championship |
| v J. McLaughlin | 10-2 | Qualifying | Embassy World Championship |
| v O'Kane | 5-10 | Qualifying | Embassy World Championship |

## DAVID ROE (England)

**Born** 11.9.65. **Turned professional** 1986. **World ranking** 26 (39). **Best professional performances** Last 16 1989 Embassy World Championship, 1988 Tennents UK Open, 1988 MIM Britannia British Open, 1987 Tennents UK Open.

| | | | | |
|---|---|---|---|---|
| **1986** | v D. Hughes | 5-2 | 1st round | BCE International |
| | v Miles | 1-5 | 2nd round | BCE International |
| | v Hargreaves | 5-1 | 1st round | Rothmans Grand Prix |
| | v Van Rensberg | 5-3 | 2nd round | Rothmans Grand Prix |
| | v Knowles | 3-5 | 3rd round | Rothmans Grand Prix |
| | v G. Foulds | 7-1 | 1st round | Tennents UK Open |
| | v Van Rensberg | 9-6 | 2nd round | Tennents UK Open |
| | v Dennis Taylor | 6-9 | 3rd round | Tennents UK Open |
| **1987** | v Darrington | 5-0 | 1st round | Mercantile Credit Classic |
| | v Chaperon | 4-5 | 2nd round | Mercantile Credit Classic |
| | v Greaves | 6-1 | 1st round | Tolly Ales English Championship |
| | v Williamson | 4-6 | 2nd round | Tolly Ales English Championship |
| | v Watterson | 5-3 | 1st round | Dulux British Open |
| | v Black | 5-0 | 2nd round | Dulux British Open |
| | v N. Foulds | 1-5 | 3rd round | Dulux British Open |
| | v King | 4-10 | Qualifying | Embassy World Championship |
| | v Ellis | 5-4 | 1st round | Fidelity International |
| | v F. Davis | 5-3 | 2nd round | Fidelity International |
| | v Mountjoy | 5-4 | 3rd round | Fidelity International |
| | v James | 3-5 | 4th round | Fidelity International |
| | v Whitthread | 5-1 | 1st round | Rothmans Grand Prix |
| | v Wildman | 5-3 | 2nd round | Rothmans Grand Prix |
| | v Martin | 5-4 | 3rd round | Rothmans Grand Prix |
| | v Knowles | 2-5 | 4th round | Rothmans Grand Prix |
| | v Marshall | 9-3 | 1st round | Tennents UK Open |
| | v Owers | 9-7 | 2nd round | Tennents UK Open |
| | v Williams | 9-7 | 3rd round | Tennents UK Open |
| | v V. Harris | 9-5 | 4th round | Tennents UK Open |
| | v White | 5-9 | 5th round | Tennents UK Open |
| **1988** | v Kelly | 5-1 | 1st round | Mercantile Credit Classic |
| | v Dodd | 2-5 | 2nd round | Mercantile Credit Classic |
| | v Lawlor | 5-6 | 1st round | English Championship |
| | v Chambers | 5-3 | 1st round | MIM Britannia British Open |
| | v Edmonds | 5-1 | 2nd round | MIM Britannia British Open |
| | v Drago | 5-3 | 3rd round | MIM Britannia British Open |
| | v Reardon | 5-2 | 4th round | MIM Britannia British Open |
| | v O'Boye | 1-5 | 5th round | MIM Britannia British Open |
| | v Demarco | 10-2 | Qualifying | Embassy World Championship |
| | v Owers | 7-10 | Qualifying | Embassy World Championship |
| | v Sinclair | 5-1 | 2nd round | Fidelity International |
| | v Williams | 3-5 | 3rd round | Fidelity International |
| | v B. Harris | 5-2 | 2nd round | Rothmans Grand Prix |
| | v Higgins | 4-5 | 3rd round | Rothmans Grand Prix |
| | v Whitthread | 5-2 | 2nd round | BCE Canadian Masters |

|      | v White        | 3-5   | 3rd round      | BCE Canadian Masters        |
|------|----------------|-------|----------------|-----------------------------|
|      | v M. Gibson    | 9-3   | 2nd round      | Tennents UK Open            |
|      | v Meo          | 9-6   | 3rd round      | Tennents UK Open            |
|      | v P. Francisco | 9-7   | 4th round      | Tennents UK Open            |
|      | v Thorburn     | 8-9   | 5th round      | Tennents UK Open            |
| 1989 | v Ellis        | 5-0   | 2nd round      | Mercantile Credit Classic   |
|      | v Parrott      | 2-5   | 3rd round      | Mercantile Credit Classic   |
|      | v V. Harris    | 5-1   | 2nd round      | European Open               |
|      | v Meo          | 5-1   | 3rd round      | European Open               |
|      | v Johnson      | 2-5   | 4th round      | European Open               |
|      | v Lawlor       | 5-1   | 2nd round      | English Championship        |
|      | v West         | 5-4   | 3rd round      | English Championship        |
|      | v Thorne       | 1-5   | 4th round      | English Championship        |
|      | v Price        | 5-2   | 2nd round      | Anglian British Open        |
|      | v Williams     | 5-2   | 3rd round      | Anglian British Open        |
|      | v P. Francisco | 3-5   | 4th round      | Anglian British Open        |
|      | v Watchorn     | 10-5  | Qualifying     | Embassy World Championship  |
|      | v Murphy       | 10-7  | Qualifying     | Embassy World Championship  |
|      | v Williams     | 10-3  | Qualifying     | Embassy World Championship  |
|      | v Knowles      | 10-6  | 1st round      | Embassy World Championship  |
|      | v Hallett      | 12-13 | 2nd round      | Embassy World Championship  |

## COLIN ROSCOE (Wales)

**Born** 30.6.45. **Turned professional** 1981. **World ranking** 48 (67). **Amateur career** 1981 Welsh champion. **Best professional performances** Last 16 1989 Anglian British Open, 1988 Tennents UK Open, 1988 BCE Canadian Masters, 1988 Mercantile Credit Classic.

|      | v Macleod       | 9-7   | Qualifying     | Coral UK Championship            |
|------|-----------------|-------|----------------|----------------------------------|
| 1981 | v Macleod       | 9-7   | Qualifying     | Coral UK Championship            |
|      | v Williams      | 4-9   | Qualifying     | Coral UK Championship            |
|      | v Andrewartha   | 5-2   | Qualifying     | Jameson International            |
|      | v Sheehan       | 5-1   | Qualifying     | Jameson International            |
|      | v Meadowcroft   | 4-5   | Qualifying     | Jameson International            |
| 1982 | v Griffiths     | 2-6   | 1st round      | Welsh Championship               |
|      | v Mikkelsen     | 9-6   | Qualifying     | Embassy World Championship       |
|      | v Thorne        | 1-9   | Qualifying     | Embassy World Championship       |
|      | v Dunning       | 5-2   | Qualifying     | Jameson International            |
|      | v French        | 5-2   | Qualifying     | Jameson International            |
|      | v S. Davis      | 0-5   | 1st round      | Jameson International            |
|      | v Griffiths     | 1-5   | 1st round      | Professional Players Tournament  |
|      | v Jack Rea      | 9-6   | Qualifying     | Coral UK Championship            |
|      | v Wildman       | 4-9   | Qualifying     | Coral UK Championship            |
| 1983 | v C. Wilson     | 4-6   | Quarter-final  | Woodpecker Welsh Championship    |
|      | v Sinclair      | 2-10  | Qualifying     | Jameson International            |
|      | v Hallett       | 2-5   | Qualifying     | Jameson International            |
|      | v Meadowcroft   | 4-5   | 1st round      | Professional Players Tournament  |
|      | v N. Foulds     | 2-9   | Qualifying     | Coral UK Championship            |
| 1984 | v Ganim         | 5-3   | Qualifying     | Lada Classic                     |
|      | v Miles         | 5-2   | Qualifying     | Lada Classic                     |
|      | v Werbeniuk     | 5-4   | 1st round      | Lada Classic                     |
|      | v Griffiths     | 2-5   | 2nd round      | Lada Classic                     |
|      | v C. Wilson     | 2-6   | 1st round      | Strongbow Welsh Championship     |
|      | v Demarco       | 10-7  | Qualifying     | Embassy World Championship       |
|      | v Browne        | 4-10  | Qualifying     | Embassy World Championship       |
|      | v Mikkelsen     | 5-1   | Qualifying     | Jameson International            |
|      | v French        | 5-0   | Qualifying     | Rothmans Grand Prix              |
|      | v Reardon       | 1-5   | 1st round      | Rothmans Grand Prix              |
|      | v J. McLaughlin | 8-9   | Qualifying     | Coral UK Open                    |
| 1985 | v Medati        | 4-5   | Qualifying     | Mercantile Credit Classic        |

| | | | | |
|---|---|---|---|---|
| | v Giannaros | 1-6 | Qualifying | Dulux British Open |
| | v G. Foulds | 7-10 | Qualifying | Embassy World Championship |
| | v C. Wilson | 3-6 | Quarter-final | BCE Welsh Championship |
| | v G. Foulds | 5-3 | 2nd round | Goya Matchroom Trophy |
| | v C. Wilson | 1-5 | 3rd round | Goya Matchroom Trophy |
| | v Watson | 2-5 | 2nd round | Rothmans Grand Prix |
| | v West | 5-9 | 2nd round | Coral UK Open |
| 1986 | v V. Harris | 1-5 | 2nd round | Mercantile Credit Classic |
| | v Mountjoy | 4-6 | Quarter-final | Zetters Welsh Championship |
| | v Mikkelsen | 5-4 | 2nd round | Dulux British Open |
| | v Parrott | 2-5 | 3rd round | Dulux British Open |
| | v G. Foulds | 10-3 | Qualifying | Embassy World Championship |
| | v King | 5-10 | Qualifying | Embassy World Championship |
| | v Parkin | 5-1 | 1st round | BCE International |
| | v Chappel | 3-5 | 2nd round | BCE International |
| | v Burke | 3-5 | 1st round | Rothmans Grand Prix |
| | v Parkin | 9-1 | 1st round | Tennents UK Open |
| | v Wildman | 9-6 | 2nd round | Tennents UK Open |
| | v E. Hughes | 8-9 | 3rd round | Tennents UK Open |
| 1987 | v Whitthread | 5-1 | 1st round | Mercantile Credit Classic |
| | v Fagan | wo | 2nd round | Mercantile Credit Classic |
| | v Higgins | 2-5 | 3rd round | Mercantile Credit Classic |
| | v Everton | 6-2 | 1st round | Matchroom Welsh Championship |
| | v Mountjoy | 2-6 | Quarter-final | Matchroom Welsh Championship |
| | v Mienie | 5-2 | 1st round | Dulux British Open |
| | v Newbury | 5-3 | 2nd round | Dulux British Open |
| | v Dennis Taylor | 1-5 | 3rd round | Dulux British Open |
| | v Whitthread | 10-2 | Qualifying | Embassy World Championship |
| | v Duggan | 7-10 | Qualifying | Embassy World Championship |
| | v Lawlor | 5-4 | 1st round | Fidelity International |
| | v Browne | 5-2 | 2nd round | Fidelity International |
| | v Hallett | 3-5 | 3rd round | Fidelity International |
| | v T. Jones | 1-5 | 1st round | Rothmans Grand Prix |
| | v Chambers | 4-9 | 1st round | Tennents UK Open |
| 1988 | v Watchorn | 5-2 | 1st round | Mercantile Credit Classic |
| | v W. Jones | 5-4 | 2nd round | Mercantile Credit Classic |
| | v Charlton | 5-3 | 3rd round | Mercantile Credit Classic |
| | v Knowles | 0-5 | 4th round | Mercantile Credit Classic |
| | v Chappel | 4-6 | 1st round | Welsh Championship |
| | v P. Gibson | 5-4 | 1st round | MIM Britannia British Open |
| | v Wildman | 5-0 | 2nd round | MIM Britannia British Open |
| | v C. Wilson | 2-5 | 3rd round | MIM Britannia British Open |
| | v E. McLaughlin | 10-1 | Qualifying | Embassy World Championship |
| | v Murphy | 8-10 | Qualifying | Embassy World Championship |
| | v Terry | 5-2 | 1st round | Fidelity International |
| | v Dodd | 1-5 | 2nd round | Fidelity International |
| | v Johnston-Allen | 1-5 | 1st round | Rothmans Grand Prix |
| | v W. Jones | 5-4 | 2nd round | BCE Canadian Masters |
| | v Knowles | 5-2 | 3rd round | BCE Canadian Masters |
| | v David Taylor | 1-5 | 4th round | BCE Canadian Masters |
| | v Darrington | 9-7 | 1st round | Tennents UK Open |
| | v Houlihan | 9-8 | 2nd round | Tennents UK Open |
| | v Newbury | 9-7 | 3rd round | Tennents UK Open |
| | v Hendry | 3-9 | 4th round | Tennents UK Open |
| 1989 | v Whitthread | 5-3 | 1st round | Mercantile Credit Classic |
| | v Owers | 5-3 | 2nd round | Mercantile Credit Classic |
| | v Knowles | 4-5 | 3rd round | Mercantile Credit Classic |
| | v Watterson | 5-4 | 1st round | European Open |
| | v Cripsey | 4-5 | 2nd round | European Open |
| | v M. Bennett | 3-6 | 1st round | Senator Welsh Championship |
| | v Meakin | 5-1 | 1st round | Anglian British Open |
| | v Werbeniuk | wo | 2nd round | Anglian British Open |
| | v Dennis Taylor | 5-4 | 3rd round | Anglian British Open |

| | | | |
|---|---|---|---|
| v Meo | 3-5 | 4th round | Anglian British Open |
| v Fitzmaurice | 9-10 | Qualifying | Embassy World Championship |

## MARK ROWING (England)

**Born** 24.3.66. **Turned professional** 1988. **World ranking** 99. **Amateur career** 1987 English champion.

| | | | | |
|---|---|---|---|---|
| **1988** | v Sinclair | 0-5 | 1st round | Fidelity International |
| | v Bradley | 3-5 | 1st round | Rothmans Grand Prix |
| | v John Rea | 2-5 | 1st round | BCE Canadian Masters |
| | v G. Foulds | 9-4 | 1st round | Tennents UK Open |
| | v Wright | 9-7 | 2nd round | Tennents UK Open |
| | v N. Foulds | 4-9 | 3rd round | Tennents UK Open |
| **1989** | v M. Smith | 5-3 | 1st round | Mercantile Credit Classic |
| | v King | 4-5 | 2nd round | Mercantile Credit Classic |
| | v Foldvari | 5-4 | 1st round | European Open |
| | v Clark | 0-5 | 2nd round | European Open |
| | v Terry | 1-5 | Prelim | English Championship |
| | v M. Gibson | 0-5 | 1st round | Anglian British Open |
| | v Mizerak | 10-1 | Qualifying | Embassy World Championship |
| | v Dunning | 10-9 | Qualifying | Embassy World Championship |
| | v King | 10-7 | Qualifying | Embassy World Championship |
| | v Duggan | 6-10 | Qualifying | Embassy World Championship |

## BRIAN ROWSWELL (England)

**Born** 18.3.67. **Turned professional** 1986. **World ranking** 79 (70). **Best professional performance** Last 32 MIM Britannia British Open.

| | | | | |
|---|---|---|---|---|
| **1986** | v Sheehan | 5-4 | 1st round | BCE International |
| | v Wildman | 2-5 | 2nd round | BCE International |
| | v D. Gilbert | 1-5 | 1st round | Rothmans Grand Prix |
| | v F. Davis | 9-4 | 2nd round | Tennents UK Open |
| | v Longworth | 3-9 | 3rd round | Tennents UK Open |
| **1987** | v Watterson | 5-1 | 1st round | Mercantile Credit Classic |
| | v Bradley | 4-5 | 2nd round | Mercantile Credit Classic |
| | v Smith | 5-6 | 1st round | Tolly Ales English Championship |
| | v Jenkins | 5-1 | 1st round | Dulux British Open |
| | v O'Kane | 5-4 | 2nd round | Dulux British Open |
| | v S. Francisco | 0-5 | 3rd round | Dulux British Open |
| | v Bradley | 6-10 | Qualifying | Embassy World Championship |
| | v D. Hughes | 5-1 | 1st round | Fidelity International |
| | v Reardon | 4-5 | 2nd round | Fidelity International |
| | v J. Smith | 5-3 | 1st round | Rothmans Grand Prix |
| | v Chaperon | 4-5 | 2nd round | Rothmans Grand Prix |
| | v Everton | 4-9 | 1st round | Tennents UK Open |
| | v O'Kane | 2-9 | 2nd round | Tennents UK Open |
| **1988** | v Chambers | 5-2 | 1st round | Mercantile Credit Classic |
| | v O'Kane | 5-4 | 2nd round | Mercantile Credit Classic |
| | v S. Francisco | 3-5 | 3rd round | Mercantile Credit Classic |
| | v Gary Wilkinson | 1-6 | 1st round | English Championship |
| | v Jack Rea | 5-1 | 1st round | MIM Britannia British Open |
| | v J. McLaughlin | 5-2 | 2nd round | MIM Britannia British Open |
| | v Longworth | 5-4 | 3rd round | MIM Britannia British Open |
| | v Johnson | 2-5 | 4th round | MIM Britannia British Open |
| | v Thornley | 10-7 | Qualifying | Embassy World Championship |
| | v Werbeniuk | 6-10 | Qualifying | Embassy World Championship |
| | v Marshall | 4-5 | 1st round | Fidelity International |
| | v D. Morgan | 0-5 | 1st round | Rothmans Grand Prix |
| | v Ellis | 5-1 | 1st round | BCE Canadian Masters |

|        |                  |       |           |                              |
|--------|------------------|-------|-----------|------------------------------|
|        | v Fowler         | 4-5   | 2nd round | BCE Canadian Masters         |
|        | v Jenkins        | 9-4   | 1st round | Tennents UK Open             |
|        | v Gauvreau       | 9-2   | 2nd round | Tennents UK Open             |
|        | v Virgo          | 3-9   | 3rd round | Tennents UK Open             |
| 1989   | v Burke          | 5-2   | 1st round | Mercantile Credit Classic    |
|        | v W. Jones       | 3-5   | 2nd round | Mercantile Credit Classic    |
|        | v J. Smith       | 2-5   | 1st round | European Open                |
|        | v V. Harris      | 5-3   | 1st round | English Championship         |
|        | v Wright         | 5-2   | 2nd round | English Championship         |
|        | v Martin         | 5-2   | 3rd round | English Championship         |
|        | v Reynolds       | 5-4   | 4th round | English Championship         |
|        | v Gary Wilkinson | 1-5   | 5th round | English Championship         |
|        | v Ellis          | 5-1   | 1st round | Anglian British Open         |
|        | v W. Jones       | 0-5   | 2nd round | Anglian British Open         |
|        | v Burke          | 10-0  | Qualifying | Embassy World Championship  |
|        | v Gauvreau       | 10-7  | Qualifying | Embassy World Championship  |
|        | v Price          | 10-6  | Qualifying | Embassy World Championship  |
|        | v E. Hughes      | 9-10  | Qualifying | Embassy World Championship  |

## GEORGE SCOTT (England)

**Born** 16.9.29. **Turned professional** 1981. **World ranking** 73 (90). **Best professional performances** Last 32 1988 BCE Canadian Masters, 1985 Rothmans Grand Prix, 1985 Goya Matchroom Trophy.

|        |                  |       |            |                                      |
|--------|------------------|-------|------------|--------------------------------------|
| 1982   | v B. Harris      | 5-4   | Qualifying | Jameson International                |
|        | v Thorburn       | 1-5   | 1st round  | Jameson International                |
|        | v Meo            | 5-9   | Qualifying | Coral UK Championship                |
| 1983   | v Houlihan       | 5-0   | Qualifying | Jameson International                |
|        | v Gibson         | 5-3   | Qualifying | Jameson International                |
|        | v Werbeniuk      | 5-3   | 1st round  | Jameson International                |
|        | v Griffiths      | 0-5   | 2nd round  | Jameson International                |
|        | v Dennis Taylor  | 5-4   | 1st round  | Professional Players Tournament      |
|        | v S. Francisco   | 1-5   | 2nd round  | Professional Players Tournament      |
|        | v Parrott        | 7-9   | Qualifying | Coral UK Championship                |
| 1984   | v Heywood        | 10-7  | Qualifying | Embassy World Championship           |
|        | v Wych           | 6-10  | Qualifying | Embassy World Championship           |
|        | v W. Jones       | 0-5   | Qualifying | Jameson International                |
|        | v Chappel        | 1-5   | Qualifying | Rothmans Grand Prix                  |
|        | v O'Kane         | 9-7   | Qualifying | Coral UK Open                        |
|        | v Macleod        | 5-9   | Qualifying | Coral UK Open                        |
| 1985   | v J. McLaughlin  | 5-4   | Qualifying | Mercantile Credit Classic            |
|        | v J. Campbell    | 5-4   | Qualifying | Mercantile Credit Classic            |
|        | v Thorburn       | 1-5   | 1st round  | Mercantile Credit Classic            |
|        | v V. Harris      | 9-7   | Qualifying | Tolly Cobbold English Championship   |
|        | v Johnson        | 1-9   | 1st round  | Tolly Cobbold English Championship   |
|        | v Darrington     | 6-3   | Qualifying | Dulux British Open                   |
|        | v Dennis Taylor  | 2-6   | 1st round  | Dulux British Open                   |
|        | v Newbury        | 2-10  | Qualifying | Embassy World Championship           |
|        | v Van Rensberg   | 5-4   | 2nd round  | Goya Matchroom Trophy                |
|        | v Wildman        | 5-1   | 3rd round  | Goya Matchroom Trophy                |
|        | v Thorne         | 1-5   | 4th round  | Goya Matchroom Trophy                |
|        | v Chalmers       | 5-2   | 2nd round  | Rothmans Grand Prix                  |
|        | v Reardon        | 5-4   | 3rd round  | Rothmans Grand Prix                  |
|        | v C. Wilson      | 3-5   | 4th round  | Rothmans Grand Prix                  |
|        | v Sheehan        | 6-9   | 2nd round  | Coral UK Open                        |
| 1986   | v Mikkelsen      | 1-5   | 2nd round  | Mercantile Credit Classic            |
|        | v Bennett        | 9-1   | 2nd round  | Tolly Cobbold English Championship   |
|        | v Meo            | 1-9   | 3rd round  | Tolly Cobbold English Championship   |
|        | v Chalmers       | 5-1   | 2nd round  | Dulux British Open                   |
|        | v Griffiths      | 3-5   | 3rd round  | Dulux British Open                   |
|        | v Kearney        | 10-8  | Qualifying | Embassy World Championship           |

| | | | |
|---|---|---|---|
| v Fowler | 7-10 | Qualifying | Embassy World Championship |
| v Owers | 1-5 | 2nd round | BCE International |
| v Dodd | 2-5 | 2nd round | Rothmans Grand Prix |
| v Watchorn | 9-7 | 2nd round | Tennents UK Open |
| v Stevens | 2-9 | 3rd round | Tennents UK Open |
| **1987** v Jenkins | 4-5 | 2nd round | Mercantile Credit Classic |
| v Fitzmaurice | 2-6 | 2nd round | Tolly Ales English Championship |
| v Burke | 5-2 | 2nd round | Dulux British Open |
| v Martin | 3-5 | 3rd round | Dulux British Open |
| v Dunning | 10-7 | Qualifying | Embassy World Championship |
| v Oliver | 5-10 | Qualifying | Embassy World Championship |
| v Gary Wilkinson | 2-5 | 2nd round | Fidelity International |
| v Miles | 2-5 | 2nd round | Rothmans Grand Prix |
| v Oliver | 4-9 | 2nd round | Tennents UK Open |
| **1988** v Bear | 5-3 | 2nd round | Mercantile Credit Classic |
| v Drago | 3-5 | 3rd round | Mercantile Credit Classic |
| v Chambers | 3-6 | 2nd round | English Championship |
| v Dunning | 3-5 | 2nd round | MIM Britannia British Open |
| v Clark | 4-10 | Qualifying | Embassy World Championship |
| v Johnston-Allen | 2-5 | 1st round | Fidelity International |
| v T. Wilson | 3-5 | 1st round | Rothmans Grand Prix |
| v Everton | 5-0 | 1st round | BCE Canadian Masters |
| v Edmonds | 5-2 | 2nd round | BCE Canadian Masters |
| v Williams | 5-2 | 3rd round | BCE Canadian Masters |
| v S. Davis | 1-5 | 4th round | BCE Canadian Masters |
| v Fagan | 9-2 | 1st round | Tennents UK Open |
| v T. Jones | 5-9 | 2nd round | Tennents UK Open |
| **1989** v Johnston-Allen | 0-5 | 1st round | Mercantile Credit Classic |
| v Graham | 1-5 | 1st round | European Open |
| v Darrington | 4-5 | 2nd round | Anglian British Open |
| v T. Wilson | 4-10 | Qualifying | Embassy World Championship |

## DESSIE SHEEHAN (Republic of Ireland)

**Born** 3.9.49. **Turned professional** 1981. **World ranking** 109 (115). **Amateur career** 1970, 1971, 1980 Republic of Ireland champion.

| | | | |
|---|---|---|---|
| **1981** v V. Harris | 5-1 | Qualifying | Jameson International |
| v Roscoe | 1-5 | Qualifying | Jameson International |
| **1982** v E. Hughes | 1-6 | 1st round | Irish Championship |
| v V. Harris | 3-5 | Qualifying | Jameson International |
| v Dennis Taylor | 3-5 | 1st round | Benson & Hedges Irish Masters |
| v Reynolds | 5-9 | Qualifying | Embassy World Championship |
| v Fitzmaurice | 1-5 | 1st round | Professional Players Tournament |
| **1983** v Donnelly | 6-10 | Qualifying | Embassy World Championship |
| v Murphy | 2-5 | Qualifying | Jameson International |
| v Houlihan | 5-2 | Qualifying | Professional Players Tournament |
| v Williams | 1-5 | 1st round | Professional Players Tournament |
| **1984** v B. Harris | 3-10 | Qualifying | Embassy World Championship |
| v Bales | 2-5 | Qualifying | Jameson International |
| v Mikkelsen | 5-3 | Qualifying | Rothmans Grand Prix |
| v Hallett | 1-5 | 1st round | Rothmans Grand Prix |
| v P. Francisco | 5-9 | Qualifying | Coral UK Open |
| **1985** v John Rea | 5-2 | Qualifying | Mercantile Credit Classic |
| v E. McLaughlin | 2-5 | Qualifying | Mercantile Credit Classic |
| v Murphy | 3-6 | Qualifying | Dulux British Open |
| v J. McLaughlin | 3-6 | Qualifying | Irish Championship |
| v Rigitano | 9-10 | Qualifying | Embassy World Championship |
| v Smith | 2-5 | 1st round | Goya Matchroom Trophy |
| v Watson | 1-5 | 1st round | Rothmans Grand Prix |
| v Watchorn | 9-7 | 1st round | Coral UK Open |
| v Scott | 9-6 | 2nd round | Coral UK Open |

|      |                  |       |              |                                 |
|------|------------------|-------|--------------|---------------------------------|
|      | v S. Davis       | 1-9   | 3rd round    | Coral UK Open                   |
| 1986 | v Hendry         | 2-5   | 1st round    | Mercantile Credit Classic       |
|      | v Simngam        | 5-2   | 1st round    | Dulux British Open              |
|      | v Watterson      | wo    | 2nd round    | Dulux British Open              |
|      | v Thorburn       | 0-5   | 3rd round    | Dulux British Open              |
|      | v Houlihan       | 10-7  | Qualifying   | Embassy World Championship      |
|      | v King           | 4-10  | Qualifying   | Embassy World Championship      |
|      | v E. Hughes      | 0-5   | 1st round    | Strongbow Irish Championship    |
|      | v Rowswell       | 4-5   | 1st round    | BCE International               |
|      | v Demarco        | 5-1   | 1st round    | Rothmans Grand Prix             |
|      | v Browne         | 4-5   | 2nd round    | Rothmans Grand Prix             |
|      | v M. Bennett     | 9-8   | 1st round    | Tennents UK Open                |
|      | v Miles          | 8-9   | 2nd round    | Tennents UK Open                |
| 1987 | v M. Bennett     | 3-5   | 1st round    | Mercantile Credit Classic       |
|      | v Wright         | 5-2   | 1st round    | Dulux British Open              |
|      | v V. Harris      | 4-5   | 2nd round    | Dulux British Open              |
|      | v N. Gilbert     | 6-10  | Qualifying   | Embassy World Championship      |
|      | v J. McLaughlin  | 5-4   | 1st round    | Matchroom Irish Championship    |
|      | v Dennis Taylor  | 3-6   | Quarter-final| Matchroom Irish Championship    |
|      | v Dunning        | 1-5   | 1st round    | Fidelity International          |
|      | v Marshall       | 1-5   | 1st round    | Rothmans Grand Prix             |
|      | v Ellis          | 8-9   | 1st round    | Tennents UK Open                |
| 1988 | v Heaton         | 5-2   | 1st round    | Mercantile Credit Classic       |
|      | v O'Boye         | 3-5   | 2nd round    | Mercantile Credit Classic       |
|      | v O'Boye         | 0-5   | 1st round    | Irish Championship              |
|      | v N. Gilbert     | 3-5   | 1st round    | MIM Britannia British Open      |
|      | v P. Gibson      | 9-10  | Qualifying   | Embassy World Championship      |
|      | v Bradley        | 5-4   | 1st round    | Fidelity International          |
|      | v Macleod        | 0-5   | 2nd round    | Fidelity International          |
|      | v M. Smith       | 4-5   | 1st round    | Rothmans Grand Prix             |
|      | v Dunning        | 3-5   | 1st round    | BCE Canadian Masters            |
|      | v F. Davis       | 9-7   | 1st round    | Tennents UK Open                |
|      | v Gary Wilkinson | 5-9   | 2nd round    | Tennents UK Open                |
| 1989 | v Fisher         | 5-3   | 2nd round    | Mercantile Credit Classic       |
|      | v Johnson        | 2-5   | 3rd round    | Mercantile Credit Classic       |
|      | v Medati         | 1-5   | 1st round    | European Open                   |
|      | v Browne         | 2-5   | 1st round    | Irish Championship              |
|      | v Foldvari       | 1-5   | 1st round    | Anglian British Open            |
|      | v Black          | 8-10  | Qualifying   | Embassy World Championship      |

## EDDIE SINCLAIR (Scotland)

**Born** 5.5.37. **Turned professional** 1979. **World ranking** 94 (85). **Amateur career** 1960, 1963, 1967, 1968, 1973, 1975, 1976 Scottish champion. **Best professional performance** 1982 Scottish champion.

|      |                  |       |              |                                 |
|------|------------------|-------|--------------|---------------------------------|
| 1980 | v Meadowcroft    | 1-9   | Qualifying   | Embassy World Championship      |
|      | v Kennerley      | 9-1   | Qualifying   | Coral UK Championship           |
|      | v Miles          | 9-5   | 1st round    | Coral UK Championship           |
|      | v Dennis Taylor  | 6-9   | 2nd round    | Coral UK Championship           |
| 1981 | v Donnelly       | 0-5   | Quarter-final| Scottish Championship           |
|      | v Morgan         | 9-8   | Qualifying   | Embassy World Championship      |
|      | v Wilson         | 4-9   | Qualifying   | Embassy World Championship      |
|      | v E. Hughes      | 2-5   | Qualifying   | Jameson International           |
|      | v Wildman        | 9-8   | Qualifying   | Coral UK Championship           |
|      | v Hood           | 9-0   | Qualifying   | Coral UK Championship           |
|      | v Martin         | 7-9   | Qualifying   | Coral UK Championship           |
| 1982 | v Kelly          | 9-8   | Qualifying   | Embassy World Championship      |
|      | v Donnelly       | 8-9   | Qualifying   | Embassy World Championship      |
|      | v Phillips       | 6-3   | Quarter-final| Scottish Championship           |
|      | v Gibson         | 6-2   | Semi-final   | Scottish Championship           |
|      | **v Black**      | **11-7** | **Final**  | **Scottish Championship**       |

|      |         |  |         |                                     |
|------|-----------------|-------|--------------|------------------------------------------|
|      | v Higgins       | 1-5   | 1st round    | Langs Supreme Scottish Masters           |
|      | v Anderson      | 5-2   | Qualifying   | Jameson International                     |
|      | v Meo           | 5-3   | Qualifying   | Jameson International                     |
|      | v Knowles       | 2-5   | 1st round    | Jameson International                     |
|      | v F. Davis      | 5-2   | 1st round    | Professional Players Tournament          |
|      | v Meadowcroft   | 5-3   | 2nd round    | Professional Players Tournament          |
|      | v Griffiths     | 3-5   | 3rd round    | Professional Players Tournament          |
|      | v Murphy        | 9-5   | Qualifying   | Coral UK Championship                    |
|      | v Spencer       | 8-9   | 1st round    | Coral UK Championship                    |
| 1983 | v Roscoe        | 10-2  | Qualifying   | Embassy World Championship               |
|      | v E. Hughes     | 8-10  | Qualifying   | Embassy World Championship               |
|      | v Donnelly      | 6-5   | Semi-final   | Scottish Championship                    |
|      | v Macleod       | 9-11  | Final        | Scottish Championship                    |
|      | v Andrewartha   | 5-4   | Qualifying   | Jameson International                     |
|      | v Thorburn      | 0-5   | 1st round    | Jameson International                     |
|      | v E. Hughes     | 4-5   | 1st round    | Professional Players Tournament          |
|      | v T. Jones      | 3-9   | Qualifying   | Coral UK Championship                    |
| 1984 | v S. Davis      | 2-5   | Qualifying   | Lada Classic                             |
|      | v Browne        | 10-1  | Qualifying   | Embassy World Championship               |
|      | v Stevens       | 1-10  | 1st round    | Embassy World Championship               |
|      | v Duggan        | 5-0   | Qualifying   | Jameson International                     |
|      | v Mans          | 5-2   | Qualifying   | Jameson International                     |
|      | v Higgins       | 1-5   | 1st round    | Jameson International                     |
|      | v T. Jones      | 4-5   | Qualifying   | Rothmans Grand Prix                      |
|      | v P. Francisco  | 9-8   | Qualifying   | Coral UK Open                            |
|      | v S. Francisco  | 4-9   | Qualifying   | Coral UK Open                            |
|      | v Demarco       | 6-3   | 1st round    | Scottish Championship                    |
|      | v John Rea      | 6-2   | Semi-final   | Scottish Championship                    |
|      | v Macleod       | 2-10  | Final        | Scottish Championship                    |
| 1985 | v Newbury       | 3-6   | 1st round    | Dulux British Open                       |
|      | v T. Jones      | 2-10  | Qualifying   | Embassy World Championship               |
|      | v Darrington    | 5-0   | 2nd round    | Goya Matchroom Trophy                    |
|      | v Martin        | 1-5   | 3rd round    | Goya Matchroom Trophy                    |
|      | v Fitzmaurice   | 3-5   | 2nd round    | Rothmans Grand Prix                      |
|      | v G. Foulds     | 9-4   | 2nd round    | Coral UK Open                            |
|      | v Parrott       | 2-9   | 3rd round    | Coral UK Open                            |
| 1986 | v Greaves       | 5-1   | 2nd round    | Mercantile Credit Classic                |
|      | v Macleod       | 2-5   | 3rd round    | Mercantile Credit Classic                |
|      | v B. Harris     | 3-5   | 2nd round    | Dulux British Open                       |
|      | v Gibson        | 4-6   | Quarter-final| Canada Dry Scottish Championship         |
|      | v Morgan        | 10-8  | Qualifying   | Embassy World Championship               |
|      | v Van Rensberg  | 2-10  | Qualifying   | Embassy World Championship               |
|      | v Fagan         | 5-0   | 2nd round    | BCE International                        |
|      | v Higgins       | 3-5   | 3rd round    | BCE International                        |
|      | v John Rea      | 4-5   | 2nd round    | Rothmans Grand Prix                      |
|      | v Mikkelsen     | 8-9   | 2nd round    | Tennents UK Open                         |
| 1987 | v Miles         | 5-1   | 2nd round    | Mercantile Credit Classic                |
|      | v Johnson       | 0-5   | 3rd round    | Mercantile Credit Classic ·              |
|      | v M. Gibson     | 6-2   | 1st round    | Scottish Championship                    |
|      | v Donnelly      | 4-6   | Semi-final   | Scottish Championship                    |
|      | v Hendry        | 5-2   | 2nd round    | Dulux British Open                       |
|      | v P. Francisco  | 3-5   | 3rd round    | Dulux British Open                       |
|      | v Drago         | 10-9  | Qualifying   | Embassy World Championship               |
|      | v Edmonds       | 6-10  | Qualifying   | Embassy World Championship               |
|      | v Heaton        | 5-3   | 1st round    | Fidelity International                   |
|      | v Edmonds       | 5-4   | 2nd round    | Fidelity International                   |
|      | v Wilson        | 1-5   | 3rd round    | Fidelity International                   |
|      | v Ellis         | 5-4   | 1st round    | Rothmans Grand Prix                      |
|      | v Edmonds       | 2-5   | 2nd round    | Rothmans Grand Prix                      |
|      | v N. Gilbert    | 8-9   | 1st round    | Tennents UK Open                         |
| 1988 | v Lawlor        | 5-3   | 1st round    | Mercantile Credit Classic                |
|      | v Wright        | 3-5   | 2nd round    | Mercantile Credit Classic                |
|      | v John Rea      | 5-6   | Quarter-final| Scottish Championship                    |

| | | | | |
|---|---|---|---|---|
| | v Lawlor | 3-5 | 1st round | MIM Britannia British Open |
| | v Burke | 10-2 | Qualifying | Embassy World Championship |
| | v O'Kane | 10-9 | Qualifying | Embassy World Championship |
| | v B. Harris | 0-10 | Qualifying | Embassy World Championship |
| | v Rowing | 5-0 | 1st round | Fidelity International |
| | v Roe | 1-5 | 2nd round | Fidelity International |
| | v Terry | 3-5 | 1st round | Rothmans Grand Prix |
| | v Graham | 3-5 | 1st round | BCE Canadian Masters |
| | v Edwards | 8-9 | 1st round | Tennents UK Open |
| 1989 | v Meakin | 5-1 | 1st round | Mercantile Credit Classic |
| | v Dodd | 3-5 | 2nd round | Mercantile Credit Classic |
| | v Whitthread | 5-4 | 1st round | European Open |
| | v Houlihan | 5-1 | 2nd round | European Open |
| | v White | 3-5 | 3rd round | European Open |
| | v M. Gibson | 4-5 | 1st round | Scottish Championship |
| | v Mikkelsen | 5-3 | 1st round | Anglian British Open |
| | v Browne | 3-5 | 2nd round | Anglian British Open |
| | v Price | 9-10 | Qualifying | Embassy World Championship |

## JASON SMITH (England)

**Born** 6.1.64. **Turned professional** 1987. **World ranking** 104 (118).

| | | | | |
|---|---|---|---|---|
| 1987 | v Bradley | 1-5 | 2nd round | Fidelity International |
| | v Rowswell | 3-5 | 1st round | Rothmans Grand Prix |
| | v Black | 8-9 | 1st round | Tennents UK Open |
| 1988 | v Bear | 3-5 | 1st round | Mercantile Credit Classic |
| | v V. Harris | 6-3 | 1st round | English Championship |
| | v T. Jones | 6-5 | 2nd round | English Championship |
| | v Johnson | 5-6 | 3rd round | English Championship |
| | v Jenkins | 3-5 | 1st round | MIM Britannia British Open |
| | v Donnelly | 10-4 | Qualifying | Embassy World Championship |
| | v Wych | 3-10 | Qualifying | Embassy World Championship |
| | v Donnelly | 2-5 | 1st round | Fidelity International |
| | v G. Foulds | 5-3 | 1st round | Rothmans Grand Prix |
| | v Fisher | 3-5 | 2nd round | Rothmans Grand Prix |
| | v G. Foulds | 5-1 | 1st round | BCE Canadian Masters |
| | v Reardon | 2-5 | 2nd round | BCE Canadian Masters |
| | v Meadowcroft | 9-7 | 1st round | Tennents UK Open |
| | v Chappel | 6-9 | 2nd round | Tennents UK Open |
| 1989 | v Van Rensberg | 5-4 | 1st round | Mercantile Credit Classic |
| | v Bales | 5-1 | 2nd round | Mercantile Credit Classic |
| | v Thorne | 1-5 | 3rd round | Mercantile Credit Classic |
| | v Rowswell | 5-2 | 1st round | European Open |
| | v Browne | 4-5 | 2nd round | European Open |
| | v Gary Wilkinson | 3-5 | 2nd round | English Championship |
| | v G. Foulds | 5-3 | 1st round | Anglian British Open |
| | v M. Bennett | 4-5 | 2nd round | Anglian British Open |
| | v Foldvari | 10-4 | Qualifying | Embassy World Championship |
| | v T. Jones | 7-10 | Qualifying | Embassy World Championship |

## MARTIN SMITH (England)

**Born** 12.6.61. **Turned professional** 1985. **World ranking** 76 (72). **Best professional performance** Last 32 1987 Tennents UK Open.

| | | | | |
|---|---|---|---|---|
| 1985 | v Sheehan | 5-2 | 1st round | Goya Matchroom Trophy |
| | v W. Jones | 3-5 | 2nd round | Goya Matchroom Trophy |
| | v Bales | 1-5 | 1st round | Rothmans Grand Prix |
| | v Wilkinson | 4-9 | 1st round | Coral UK Open |
| 1986 | v Mienie | 5-1 | 1st round | Mercantile Credit Classic |
| | v Edmonds | 5-2 | 2nd round | Mercantile Credit Classic |

|      |               |       |           |                                      |
|------|---------------|-------|-----------|--------------------------------------|
|      | v Mans        | 4-5   | 3rd round | Mercantile Credit Classic            |
|      | v Edmonds     | 8-9   | 2nd round | Tolly Cobbold English Championship   |
|      | v Kearney     | 2-5   | 1st round | Dulux British Open                   |
|      | v Greaves     | 10-4  | Qualifying| Embassy World Championship           |
|      | v Donnelly    | 6-10  | Qualifying| Embassy World Championship           |
|      | v M. Bennett  | 4-5   | 1st round | BCE International                    |
|      | v Hines       | 5-2   | 1st round | Rothmans Grand Prix                  |
|      | v T. Jones    | 0-5   | 2nd round | Rothmans Grand Prix                  |
|      | v Wright      | 7-9   | 2nd round | Tennents UK Open                     |
| 1987 | v N. Gilbert  | 2-5   | 1st round | Mercantile Credit Classic            |
|      | v Rowswell    | 6-5   | 1st round | Tolly Ales English Championship      |
|      | v Dodd        | 3-6   | 2nd round | Tolly Ales English Championship      |
|      | v Ellis       | 2-5   | 1st round | Dulux British Open                   |
|      | v Rempe       | 9-10  | Qualifying| Embassy World Championship           |
|      | v Donnelly    | 5-3   | 1st round | Fidelity International               |
|      | v King        | 3-5   | 2nd round | Fidelity International               |
|      | v Black       | 5-0   | 1st round | Rothmans Grand Prix                  |
|      | v Gauvreau    | 3-5   | 2nd round | Rothmans Grand Prix                  |
|      | v Jonik       | 9-5   | 1st round | Tennents UK Open                     |
|      | v Browne      | 9-4   | 2nd round | Tennents UK Open                     |
|      | v Mountjoy    | 9-7   | 3rd round | Tennents UK Open                     |
|      | v J. Campbell | 8-9   | 4th round | Tennents UK Open                     |
| 1988 | v Fitzmaurice | 5-2   | 1st round | Mercantile Credit Classic            |
|      | v Browne      | 5-1   | 2nd round | Mercantile Credit Classic            |
|      | v David Taylor| 3-5   | 3rd round | Mercantile Credit Classic            |
|      | v Miles       | 6-1   | 1st round | English Championship                 |
|      | v B. Harris   | 6-4   | 2nd round | English Championship                 |
|      | v Martin      | 5-6   | 3rd round | English Championship                 |
|      | v Oliver      | 0-5   | 1st round | MIM Britannia British Open           |
|      | v V. Harris   | 10-6  | Qualifying| Embassy World Championship           |
|      | v J. McLaughlin| 10-3 | Qualifying| Embassy World Championship           |
|      | v Newbury     | 9-10  | Qualifying| Embassy World Championship           |
|      | v D. Morgan   | 5-3   | 1st round | Fidelity International               |
|      | v W. Jones    | 2-5   | 2nd round | Fidelity International               |
|      | v Sheehan     | 5-4   | 1st round | Rothmans Grand Prix                  |
|      | v Cripsey     | 5-0   | 2nd round | Rothmans Grand Prix                  |
|      | v James       | 3-5   | 3rd round | Rothmans Grand Prix                  |
|      | v Marshall    | 9-6   | 1st round | Tennents UK Open                     |
|      | v Werbeniuk   | 9-5   | 2nd round | Tennents UK Open                     |
|      | v Johnson     | 2-9   | 3rd round | Tennents UK Open                     |
| 1989 | v Rowing      | 3-5   | 1st round | Mercantile Credit Classic            |
|      | v Edwards     | 4-5   | 1st round | European Open                        |
|      | v Miles       | 4-5   | 1st round | English Championship                 |
|      | v D. Hughes   | 5-1   | 1st round | Anglian British Open                 |
|      | v Macleod     | 4-5   | 2nd round | Anglian British Open                 |
|      | v S. Campbell | 10-9  | Qualifying| Embassy World Championship           |
|      | v Wright      | 10-7  | Qualifying| Embassy World Championship           |
|      | v Graham      | 6-10  | Qualifying| Embassy World Championship           |

## JOHN SPENCER (England)

**Born** 18.9.35. **Turned professional** 1967. **World ranking** 38 (27). **Amateur career** 1966 English champion. **Best professional performances** Winner 1969, 1970, 1977 World Championship, 1975 Benson & Hedges Masters, 1978 Benson & Hedges Irish Masters.

|      |            |        |               |                              |
|------|------------|--------|---------------|------------------------------|
| 1969 | v Pulman   | 30-19  | Quarter-final | World Championship           |
|      | v Williams | 55-18  | Semi-final    | World Championship           |
|      | **v G. Owen** | **46-27** | **Final** | **World Championship**   |
| 1970 | v Jack Rea | 31-15  | Quarter-final | World Championship (Apr)     |
|      | v Reardon  | 33-37  | Semi-final    | World Championship (Apr)     |
|      | v Reardon  | 34-15  | Semi-final    | World Championship (Nov)     |

|      |                  |        |              |                                |
|------|------------------|--------|--------------|--------------------------------|
|      | **v Simpson**    | **42-31** | **Final**    | **World Championship (Nov)**   |
| 1972 | v F. Davis       | 31-21  | Quarter-final | World Championship            |
|      | v Charlton       | 37-32  | Semi-final   | World Championship            |
|      | v Higgins        | 32-37  | Final        | World Championship            |
| 1973 | v David Taylor   | 16-5   | 2nd round    | World Championship            |
|      | v Williams       | 16-7   | Quarter-final | World Championship            |
|      | v Reardon        | 22-23  | Semi-final   | World Championship            |
| 1974 | v Mans           | 13-15  | 2nd round    | World Championship            |
| 1975 | v Pulman         | 5-3    | Quarter-final | Benson & Hedges Masters       |
|      | v Charlton       | 5-2    | Semi-final   | Benson & Hedges Masters       |
|      | **v Reardon**    | **9-8** | **Final**    | **Benson & Hedges Masters**   |
|      | v Pulman         | 15-10  | 2nd round    | World Championship            |
|      | v Reardon        | 17-19  | Quarter-final | World Championship            |
| 1976 | v Miles          | 4-5    | Semi-final   | Benson & Hedges Masters       |
|      | v David Taylor   | 15-5   | 1st round    | Embassy World Championship    |
|      | v Higgins        | 14-15  | Quarter-final | Embassy World Championship    |
| 1977 | v Virgo          | 13-9   | 1st round    | Embassy World Championship    |
|      | v Reardon        | 13-6   | Quarter-final | Embassy World Championship    |
|      | v Pulman         | 18-16  | Semi-final   | Embassy World Championship    |
|      | **v Thorburn**   | **25-21** | **Final**  | **Embassy World Championship** |
|      | v Mountjoy       | 3-5    | 2nd round    | Super Crystalate UK Championship |
| 1978 | v Thorburn       | 3-5    | Semi-final   | Benson & Hedges Masters       |
|      | **v Mountjoy**   | **5-3** | **Final**    | **Benson & Hedges Irish Masters** |
|      | v Mans           | 8-13   | 1st round    | Embassy World Championship    |
|      | v Andrewartha    | 8-9    | 1st round    | Coral UK Championship         |
| 1979 | v Williams       | 6-2    | Semi-final   | Holsten Lager International    |
|      | **v Miles**      | **11-7** | **Final**   | **Holsten Lager International** |
|      | v Mountjoy       | 0-5    | Quarter-final | Benson & Hedges Masters       |
|      | v Werbeniuk      | 11-13  | 1st round    | Embassy World Championship    |
|      | v Werbeniuk      | 8-9    | 3rd round    | Coral UK Championship         |
| 1980 | v Charlton       | 5-2    | Quarter-final | Benson & Hedges Masters       |
|      | v Griffiths      | 0-5    | Semi-final   | Benson & Hedges Masters       |
|      | v Stevens        | 8-13   | 2nd round    | Embassy World Championship    |
|      | v Wildman        | 7-9    | 1st round    | Coral UK Championship         |
| 1981 | v Dennis Taylor  | 5-2    | 1st round    | Benson & Hedges Masters       |
|      | v Reardon        | 5-1    | Quarter-final | Benson & Hedges Masters       |
|      | v Griffiths      | 5-6    | Semi-final   | Benson & Hedges Masters       |
|      | v Houlihan       | 9-1    | 1st round    | John Courage English          |
|      | v S. Davis       | 7-9    | 2nd round    | John Courage English          |
|      | v Edmonds        | 10-9   | 1st round    | Embassy World Championship    |
|      | v Reardon        | 11-13  | 2nd round    | Embassy World Championship    |
|      | v Edmonds        | 5-3    | 2nd round    | Jameson International          |
|      | v Griffiths      | 2-5    | 3rd round    | Jameson International          |
|      | v Johnson        | 5-9    | 2nd round    | Coral UK Championship         |
| 1982 | v S. Davis       | 2-5    | 1st round    | Lada Classic                  |
|      | v Mountjoy       | 4-5    | 1st round    | Benson & Hedges Masters       |
|      | v Meo            | 3-5    | 1st round    | Benson & Hedges Irish Masters |
|      | v Dunning        | 10-4   | 1st round    | Embassy World Championship    |
|      | v Thorne         | 5-13   | 2nd round    | Embassy World Championship    |
|      | v Edmonds        | 5-2    | 1st round    | Jameson International          |
|      | v Virgo          | 4-5    | 2nd round    | Jameson International          |
|      | v G. Foulds      | 5-1    | 1st round    | Professional Players Tournament |
|      | v Martin         | 5-3    | 2nd round    | Professional Players Tournament |
|      | v Virgo          | 1-5    | 3rd round    | Professional Players Tournament |
|      | v Sinclair       | 9-8    | 1st round    | Coral UK Championship         |
|      | v Knowles        | 9-6    | 2nd round    | Coral UK Championship         |
|      | v Higgins        | 5-9    | Quarter-final | Coral UK Championship         |
| 1983 | v Reardon        | 5-3    | 1st round    | Lada Classic                  |
|      | v David Taylor   | 5-2    | Quarter-final | Lada Classic                  |
|      | v S. Davis       | 4-5    | Semi-final   | Lada Classic                  |
|      | v Hallett        | 10-7   | 1st round    | Embassy World Championship    |
|      | v Charlton       | 11-13  | 2nd round    | Embassy World Championship    |
|      | v Higgins        | 2-3    | 1st round    | **Winfield Masters**          |

|        |               |       |              |                                     |
|--------|---------------|-------|--------------|-------------------------------------|
|        | v Morgan      | 5-1   | 1st round    | Jameson International                |
|        | v Knowles     | 5-4   | 2nd round    | Jameson International                |
|        | v Griffiths   | 4-5   | Quarter-final| Jameson International                |
|        | v Black       | 5-2   | 1st round    | Professional Players Tournament      |
|        | v Thorne      | 1-5   | 2nd round    | Professional Players Tournament      |
|        | v Dunning     | 9-7   | 1st round    | Coral UK Championship                |
|        | v Meo         | 5-9   | 2nd round    | Coral UK Championship                |
| 1984   | v Johnson     | 5-4   | Qualifying   | Lada Classic                         |
|        | v S. Davis    | 1-5   | 1st round    | Lada Classic                         |
|        | v Thorburn    | 5-4   | 1st round    | Benson & Hedges Masters              |
|        | v Griffiths   | 4-5   | Quarter-final| Benson & Hedges Masters              |
|        | v Miles       | 10-3  | 1st round    | Embassy World Championship           |
|        | v S. Davis    | 5-13  | 2nd round    | Embassy World Championship           |
|        | v S. Francisco| 2-5   | 1st round    | Jameson International                |
|        | v P. Francisco| 2-5   | 1st round    | Rothmans Grand Prix                  |
|        | v Johnson     | 6-9   | 1st round    | Coral UK Open                        |
| 1985   | v King        | 2-5   | 1st round    | Mercantile Credit Classic            |
|        | v Charlton    | 5-3   | 1st round    | Benson & Hedges Masters              |
|        | v White       | 2-5   | Quarter-final| Benson & Hedges Masters              |
|        | v Medati      | 4-9   | 1st round    | Tolly Cobbold English Championship   |
|        | v Jonik       | 6-0   | 1st round    | Dulux British Open                   |
|        | v Miles       | 3-5   | 2nd round    | Dulux British Open                   |
|        | v Parrott     | 3-10  | 1st round    | Embassy World Championship           |
|        | v Foldvari    | 5-4   | 3rd round    | Goya Matchroom Trophy                |
|        | v Griffiths   | 1-5   | 4th round    | Goya Matchroom Trophy                |
|        | v B. Harris   | 2-5   | 3rd round    | Rothmans Grand Prix                  |
|        | v V. Harris   | 9-5   | 3rd round    | Coral UK Open                        |
|        | v Knowles     | 7-9   | 4th round    | Coral UK Open                        |
|        | v S. Davis    | 2-5   | 1st round    | Kit Kat                              |
| 1986   | v Cripsey     | 1-5   | 3rd round    | Mercantile Credit Classic            |
|        | v Houlihan    | 9-5   | 3rd round    | Tolly Cobbold English Championship   |
|        | v Johnson     | 7-9   | 4th round    | Tolly Cobbold English Championship   |
|        | v Browne      | 0-5   | 3rd round    | Dulux British Open                   |
|        | v Higgins     | 7-10  | 1st round    | Embassy World Championship           |
|        | v Williamson  | 5-2   | 2nd round    | BCE International                    |
|        | v Knowles     | 0-5   | 3rd round    | BCE International                    |
|        | v Burke       | 5-3   | 2nd round    | Rothmans Grand Prix                  |
|        | v S. Francisco| 4-5   | 3rd round    | Rothmans Grand Prix                  |
|        | v Foldvari    | 9-6   | 2nd round    | Tennents UK Open                     |
|        | v Wilson      | 9-5   | 3rd round    | Tennents UK Open                     |
|        | v Stevens     | 9-4   | 4th round    | Tennents UK Open                     |
|        | v Thorburn    | 2-9   | 5th round    | Tennents UK Open                     |
| 1987   | v D. Gilbert  | 5-4   | 2nd round    | Mercantile Credit Classic            |
|        | v Thorne      | 5-3   | 3rd round    | Mercantile Credit Classic            |
|        | v J. Campbell | 3-5   | 4th round    | Mercantile Credit Classic            |
|        | v Wright      | 6-1   | 2nd round    | Tolly Ales English Championship      |
|        | v Martin      | 5-6   | 3rd round    | Tolly Ales English Championship      |
|        | v Whitthread  | 5-2   | 2nd round    | Dulux British Open                   |
|        | v Meo         | 5-1   | 3rd round    | Dulux British Open                   |
|        | v Martin      | 5-2   | 4th round    | Dulux British Open                   |
|        | v Johnson     | 5-3   | 5th round    | Dulux British Open                   |
|        | v White       | 3-5   | Quarter-final| Dulux British Open                   |
|        | v Bales       | 10-3  | Qualifying   | Embassy World Championship           |
|        | v Chaperon    | 10-4  | Qualifying   | Embassy World Championship           |
|        | v West        | 5-10  | Qualifying   | Embassy World Championship           |
|        | v Jack Rea    | 5-0   | 3rd round    | Fidelity International               |
|        | v Hallett     | 2-5   | 4th round    | Fidelity International               |
|        | v Chappel     | 1-5   | 3rd round    | Rothmans Grand Prix                  |
|        | v Miles       | 5-9   | 3rd round    | Tennents UK Open                     |
| 1988   | v John Rea    | 5-3   | 3rd round    | Mercantile Credit Classic            |
|        | v White       | 1-5   | 4th round    | Mercantile Credit Classic            |
|        | v Fowler      | 3-6   | 3rd round    | English Championship                 |
|        | v F. Davis    | 5-0   | 3rd round    | MIM Britannia British Open           |

| | v Dennis Taylor | 5-0 | 4th round | MIM Britannia British Open |
|---|---|---|---|---|
| | v Williams | 4-5 | 5th round | MIM Britannia British Open |
| | v King | 7-10 | Qualifying | Embassy World Championship |
| | v Reardon | 5-4 | 3rd round | Fidelity International |
| | v Virgo | 5-1 | 4th round | Fidelity International |
| | v Reynolds | 2-5 | 5th round | Fidelity International |
| | v Johnston-Allen | 5-3 | 3rd round | Rothmans Grand Prix |
| | v J. McLaughlin | 3-5 | 4th round | Rothmans Grand Prix |
| | v Stevens | 5-3 | 3rd round | BCE Canadian Masters |
| | v Thorburn | 2-5 | 4th round | BCE Canadian Masters |
| | v N. Gilbert | 7-9 | 3rd round | Tennents UK Open |
| **1989** | v Clark | 2-5 | 3rd round | Mercantile Credit Classic |
| | v Edwards | 1-5 | 3rd round | English Championship |
| | v Robidoux | 1-5 | 3rd round | Anglian British Open |
| | v Duggan | 1-10 | Qualifying | Embassy World Championship |

## KIRK STEVENS (Canada)

**Born** 17.8.58. **Turned professional** 1978. **World ranking** 50 (37). **Best professional performances** Semi-finals 1980, 1984 Embassy World Championship; runner-up 1985 Dulux British Open.

| | v Amdor | 9-1 | Prelim | Embassy World Championship |
|---|---|---|---|---|
| **1979** | v Amdor | 9-1 | Prelim | Embassy World Championship |
| | v Pulman | 9-0 | Qualifying | Embassy World Championship |
| | v F. Davis | 8-13 | 1st round | Embassy World Championship |
| **1980** | v Hallett | 9-3 | Qualifying | Embassy World Championship |
| | v Miles | 10-3 | 1st round | Embassy World Championship |
| | v Spencer | 13-8 | 2nd round | Embassy World Championship |
| | v Charlton | 13-7 | Quarter-final | Embassy World Championship |
| | v Higgins | 13-16 | Semi-final | Embassy World Championship |
| **1981** | v F. Davis | 4-5 | 1st round | Benson & Hedges Masters |
| | v David Taylor | 3-5 | Semi-final | Yamaha International Masters |
| | v Dunning | 10-4 | 1st round | Embassy World Championship |
| | v Dennis Taylor | 11-13 | 2nd round | Embassy World Championship |
| | v Thorburn | 1-5 | Quarter-final | Langs Supreme Scottish Masters |
| | v Meadowcroft | 5-1 | 2nd round | Jameson International |
| | v David Taylor | 0-5 | 3rd round | Jameson International |
| | v Griffiths | 0-5 | 1st round | Northern Ireland Classic |
| | v Hallett | 9-4 | 2nd round | Coral UK Championship |
| | v Werbeniuk | 7-9 | 3rd round | Coral UK Championship |
| **1982** | v Fitzmaurice | 10-4 | 1st round | Embassy World Championship |
| | v Fagan | 13-7 | 2nd round | Embassy World Championship |
| | v White | 9-13 | Quarter-final | Embassy World Championship |
| | v Watterson | 5-3 | 1st round | Jameson International |
| | v Mans | 5-2 | 2nd round | Jameson International |
| | v Griffiths | 5-3 | Quarter-final | Jameson International |
| | v Knowles | 3-9 | Semi-final | Jameson International |
| | v E. Hughes | 5-2 | 1st round | Professional Players Tournament |
| | v Johnson | 1-5 | 2nd round | Professional Players Tournament |
| **1983** | v Knowles | 5-0 | 1st round | Lada Classic |
| | v Thorburn | 5-3 | Quarter-final | Lada Classic |
| | v Werbeniuk | 2-5 | Semi-final | Lada Classic |
| | v Griffiths | 3-5 | 1st round | Benson & Hedges Masters |
| | v Fisher | 10-2 | 1st round | Embassy World Championship |
| | v Mans | 13-3 | 2nd round | Embassy World Championship |
| | v Thorburn | 12-13 | Quarter-final | Embassy World Championship |
| | v Thorburn | 2-5 | Semi-final | Winfield Masters |
| | v Caggianello | 9-0 | Quarter-final | Canadian Championship |
| | v Jim Bear | 9-8 | Semi-final | Canadian Championship |
| | **v Jonik** | **9-8** | **Final** | **Canadian Championship** |
| | v Edmonds | 5-1 | 1st round | Professional Players Tournament |
| | v Murphy | 5-1 | 2nd round | Professional Players Tournament |

|      |   |                |       |              |                                   |
|------|---|----------------|-------|--------------|-----------------------------------|
|      | v | Wildman        | 5-0   | 3rd round    | Professional Players Tournament   |
|      | v | Meo            | 3-5   | Quarter-final| Professional Players Tournament   |
| 1984 | v | E. McLaughlin  | 5-4   | Qualifying   | Lada Classic                      |
|      | v | Macleod        | 5-1   | 1st round    | Lada Classic                      |
|      | v | Meo            | 2-5   | Quarter-final| Lada Classic                      |
|      | v | David Taylor   | 5-1   | 1st round    | Benson & Hedges Masters           |
|      | v | S. Davis       | 5-3   | Quarter-final| Benson & Hedges Masters           |
|      | v | White          | 4-6   | Semi-final   | Benson & Hedges Masters           |
|      | v | Charlton       | 5-3   | 1st round    | Tolly Cobbold Classic             |
|      | v | S. Davis       | 4-5   | Semi-final   | Tolly Cobbold Classic             |
|      | v | Sinclair       | 10-1  | 1st round    | Embassy World Championship        |
|      | v | David Taylor   | 13-10 | 2nd round    | Embassy World Championship        |
|      | v | Reardon        | 13-2  | Quarter-final| Embassy World Championship        |
|      | v | White          | 14-16 | Semi-final   | Embassy World Championship        |
|      | v | Meo            | 1-5   | Quarter-final| Winfield Australian Masters       |
|      | v | Higgins        | 2-5   | 1st round    | Langs Supreme Scottish Masters    |
|      | v | White          | 0-5   | 1st round    | Carlsberg Challenge               |
|      | v | Gauvreau       | 1-5   | 1st round    | Jameson International              |
|      | v | Chappel        | 5-3   | 1st round    | Rothmans Grand Prix               |
|      | v | Williams       | 5-3   | 2nd round    | Rothmans Grand Prix               |
|      | v | Hallett        | 5-3   | 3rd round    | Rothmans Grand Prix               |
|      | v | Dennis Taylor  | 2-5   | Quarter-final| Rothmans Grand Prix               |
|      | v | Chappel        | 9-7   | 1st round    | Coral UK Open                     |
|      | v | Johnson        | 9-2   | 2nd round    | Coral UK Open                     |
|      | v | Knowles        | 9-7   | Quarter-final| Coral UK Open                     |
|      | v | S. Davis       | 2-9   | Semi-final   | Coral UK Open                     |
| 1985 | v | Medati         | 5-4   | 1st round    | Mercantile Credit Classic         |
|      | v | Thorne         | 1-5   | 2nd round    | Mercantile Credit Classic         |
|      | v | Meo            | 2-5   | 1st round    | Benson & Hedges Masters           |
|      | v | Gauvreau       | 6-3   | 1st round    | Dulux British Open                |
|      | v | Wildman        | 5-2   | 2nd round    | Dulux British Open                |
|      | v | Miles          | 5-2   | 3rd round    | Dulux British Open                |
|      | v | Dennis Taylor  | 5-2   | Quarter-final| Dulux British Open                |
|      | v | S. Davis       | 9-7   | Semi-final   | Dulux British Open                |
|      | v | S. Francisco   | 9-12  | Final        | Dulux British Open                |
|      | v | Higgins        | 3-5   | Quarter-final| Benson & Hedges Irish Masters     |
|      | v | Edmonds        | 10-8  | 1st round    | Embassy World Championship        |
|      | v | Parrott        | 6-13  | 2nd round    | Embassy World Championship        |
|      | v | Chaperon       | 4-6   | Quarter-final| Canadian Championship             |
|      | v | Chappel        | 3-5   | 3rd round    | Goya Matchroom Trophy             |
|      | v | Watson         | 5-0   | 3rd round    | Rothmans Grand Prix               |
|      | v | Miles          | 5-2   | 4th round    | Rothmans Grand Prix               |
|      | v | Longworth      | 5-3   | 5th round    | Rothmans Grand Prix               |
|      | v | Knowles        | 4-5   | Quarter-final| Rothmans Grand Prix               |
|      | v | Newbury        | 9-7   | 3rd round    | Coral UK Open                     |
|      | v | Hallett        | 9-5   | 4th round    | Coral UK Open                     |
|      | v | Williams       | 9-7   | 5th round    | Coral UK Open                     |
|      | v | Dennis Taylor  | 1-9   | Quarter-final| Coral UK Open                     |
| 1986 | v | F. Davis       | 2-5   | 3rd round    | Mercantile Credit Classic         |
|      | v | Reardon        | 5-1   | 1st round    | BCE Belgian Classic               |
|      | v | Higgins        | 5-4   | Semi-final   | BCE Belgian Classic               |
|      | v | Griffiths      | 7-9   | Final        | BCE Belgian Classic               |
|      | v | Charlton       | 4-5   | 1st round    | Benson & Hedges Masters           |
|      | v | Miles          | 5-3   | 3rd round    | Dulux British Open                |
|      | v | Wilson         | 5-0   | 4th round    | Dulux British Open                |
|      | v | Thorne         | 4-5   | 5th round    | Dulux British Open                |
|      | v | Reynolds       | 10-6  | 1st round    | Embassy World Championship        |
|      | v | Charlton       | 13-12 | 2nd round    | Embassy World Championship        |
|      | v | Knowles        | 9-13  | Quarter-final| Embassy World Championship        |
|      | v | Thornley       | 6-2   | 2nd round    | Canadian Championship             |
|      | v | Wych           | 2-6   | Semi-final   | Canadian Championship             |
|      | v | Knowles        | 5-3   | 1st round    | Langs Scottish Masters            |

|       |                  |       |              |                            |
|-------|------------------|-------|--------------|----------------------------|
|       | v Higgins        | 2-6   | Semi-final   | Langs Scottish Masters     |
|       | v Bales          | 3-5   | 3rd round    | BCE International           |
|       | v Dodd           | 4-5   | 3rd round    | Rothmans Grand Prix        |
|       | v Scott          | 9-2   | 3rd round    | Tennents UK Open           |
|       | v Spencer        | 4-9   | 4th round    | Tennents UK Open           |
| 1987  | v Chaperon       | 5-3   | 3rd round    | Mercantile Credit Classic  |
|       | v West           | 3-5   | 4th round    | Mercantile Credit Classic  |
|       | v Thorne         | 3-5   | 1st round    | Benson & Hedges Masters    |
|       | v Chaperon       | 5-4   | 3rd round    | Dulux British Open         |
|       | v West           | 5-4   | 4th round    | Dulux British Open         |
|       | v David Taylor   | 2-5   | 5th round    | Dulux British Open         |
|       | v Thorne         | 1-5   | 1st round    | Benson & Hedges Irish Masters |
|       | v Longworth      | 4-10  | 1st round    | Embassy World Championship |
|       | v Caggianello    | 6-0   | Quarter-final| Canadian Championship      |
|       | v Bear           | 2-7   | Semi-final   | Canadian Championship      |
|       | v O'Boye         | 1-5   | 3rd round    | Fidelity International     |
|       | v W. Jones       | 5-1   | 3rd round    | Rothmans Grand Prix        |
|       | v Parrott        | 0-5   | 4th round    | Rothmans Grand Prix        |
|       | v O'Boye         | 9-8   | 3rd round    | Tennents UK Open           |
|       | v Knowles        | 8-9   | 4th round    | Tennents UK Open           |
| 1988  | v M. Bennett     | 2-5   | 3rd round    | Mercantile Credit Classic  |
|       | v M. Bennett     | 10-7  | Qualifying   | Embassy World Championship |
|       | v Thorburn       | 6-10  | 1st round    | Embassy World Championship |
|       | v Mikkelsen      | 5-6   | Quarter-final| BCE Canadian Masters       |
|       | v D. Hughes      | 5-2   | 2nd round    | Fidelity International*     |
|       | v S. Campbell    | 5-3   | 2nd round    | Rothmans Grand Prix        |
|       | v Meo            | 3-5   | 3rd round    | Rothmans Grand Prix        |
|       | v Kelly          | 5-1   | 2nd round    | BCE Canadian Masters       |
|       | v Spencer        | 3-5   | 3rd round    | BCE Canadian Masters       |
|       | v Edwards        | 9-4   | 2nd round    | Tennents UK Open           |
|       | v Charlton       | 9-7   | 3rd round    | Tennents UK Open           |
|       | v Thorne         | 3-9   | 4th round    | Tennents UK Open           |
| 1989  | v Edwards        | 5-4   | 2nd round    | Mercantile Credit Classic  |
|       | v Meo            | 3-5   | 3rd round    | Mercantile Credit Classic  |
|       | v Bear           | 5-2   | 2nd round    | European Open              |
|       | v Dennis Taylor  | 0-5   | 3rd round    | European Open              |
|       | v Marshall       | 4-5   | 2nd round    | Anglian British Open       |
|       | v Chambers       | 10-8  | Qualifying   | Embassy World Championship |
|       | v T. Jones       | 2-10  | Qualifying   | Embassy World Championship |

* Stevens scratched from the 3rd round.

## DAVID TAYLOR (England)

**Born** 29.7.43. **Turned professional** 1968. **World ranking** 33 (28). **Amateur career** 1968 World champion, 1968 English champion. **Best professional performances** Semi-finals 1980 Embassy World Championship; runner-up 1978 Coral UK Championship, 1982 Jameson International.

|       |             |       |              |                            |
|-------|-------------|-------|--------------|----------------------------|
| 1970  | v Bennett   | 11-8  | 1st round    | World Championship         |
|       | v Pulman    | 22-39 | Quarter-final| World Championship         |
| 1972  | v Charlton  | 25-31 | Quarter-final| World Championship         |
| 1973  | v Dunning   | 9-4   | 1st round    | World Championship         |
|       | v Spencer   | 5-16  | 2nd round    | World Championship         |
| 1974  | v Dunning   | 6-8   | 1st round    | World Championship         |
| 1975  | v King      | 15-8  | 1st round    | World Championship         |
|       | v Higgins   | 2-15  | 2nd round    | World Championship         |
| 1976  | v Greaves   | 8-1   | Qualifying   | Embassy World Championship |
|       | v Jack Rea  | 8-7   | Qualifying   | Embassy World Championship |
|       | v Spencer   | 5-15  | 1st round    | Embassy World Championship |
| 1977  | v Greaves   | 11-0  | Qualifying   | Embassy World Championship |
|       | v Charlton  | 5-13  | 1st round    | Embassy World Championship |

| | | | |
|---|---|---|---|
| | v Greaves | 5-4 | 1st round | Super Crystalate UK Championship |

| |  |  |  |  |
|---|---|---|---|---|
| | v Greaves | 5-4 | 1st round | Super Crystalate UK Championship |
| | v Higgins | 4-5 | 2nd round | Super Crystalate UK Championship |
| 1978 | v Morgan | 9-7 | Qualifying | Embassy World Championship |
| | v Miles | 10-13 | 1st round | Embassy World Championship |
| | v Parkin | 9-2 | Qualifying | Coral UK Championship |
| | v Fagan | 9-7 | 1st round | Coral UK Championship |
| | v Virgo | 9-2 | Quarter-final | Coral UK Championship |
| | v Higgins | 9-5 | Semi-final | Coral UK Championship |
| | v Mountjoy | 9-15 | Final | Coral UK Championship |
| 1979 | v Fagan | 5-4 | 1st round | Benson & Hedges Masters |
| | v Reardon | 2-5 | Quarter-final | Benson & Hedges Masters |
| | v Dunning | 9-8 | Qualifying | Embassy World Championship |
| | v Higgins | 5-13 | 1st round | Embassy World Championship |
| | v Meo | 7-9 | 2nd round | Coral UK Championship |
| 1980 | v Edmonds | 10-3 | 1st round | Embassy World Championship |
| | v F. Davis | 13-5 | 2nd round | Embassy World Championship |
| | v Reardon | 13-11 | Quarter-final | Embassy World Championship |
| | v Thorburn | 7-16 | Semi-final | Embassy World Championship |
| | v Williams | 7-9 | 2nd round | Coral UK Championship |
| 1981 | v Stevens | 5-3 | Semi-final | Yamaha International Masters |
| | v S. Davis | 6-9 | Final | Yamaha International Masters |
| | v Dunning | 8-9 | 1st round | John Courage English |
| | v Wilson | 10-6 | 1st round | Embassy World Championship |
| | v F. Davis | 13-3 | 2nd round | Embassy World Championship |
| | v Thorburn | 6-13 | Quarter-final | Embassy World Championship |
| | v Stevens | 5-0 | 3rd round | Jameson International |
| | v S. Davis | 1-5 | Quarter-final | Jameson International |
| | v Higgins | 5-9 | 3rd round | Coral UK Championship |
| 1982 | v Reardon | 1-5 | 1st round | Lada Classic |
| | v Meo | 2-5 | 1st round | Benson & Hedges Masters |
| | v Fagan | 9-10 | 1st round | Embassy World Championship |
| | v Fisher | 5-1 | 1st round | Jameson International |
| | v Werbeniuk | 5-2 | 2nd round | Jameson International |
| | v S. Davis | 5-3 | Quarter-final | Jameson International |
| | v Virgo | 9-5 | Semi-final | Jameson International |
| | v Knowles | 6-9 | Final | Jameson International |
| | v Anderson | 5-1 | 1st round | Professional Players Tournament |
| | v Dennis Taylor | 1-5 | 2nd round | Professional Players Tournament |
| | v Dodd | 9-7 | 1st round | Coral UK Championship |
| | v Meo | 6-9 | 2nd round | Coral UK Championship |
| 1983 | v White | 5-3 | 1st round | Lada Classic |
| | v Spencer | 2-5 | Quarter-final | Lada Classic |
| | v White | 2-5 | 1st round | Benson & Hedges Masters |
| | v Charlton | 4-5 | 1st round | Benson & Hedges Irish Masters |
| | v Meadowcroft | 10-2 | 1st round | Embassy World Championship |
| | v Werbeniuk | 10-13 | 2nd round | Embassy World Championship |
| | v Donnelly | 3-5 | 1st round | Jameson International |
| | v Morgan | 5-3 | 1st round | Professional Players Tournament |
| | v Wildman | 3-5 | 2nd round | Professional Players Tournament |
| | v N. Foulds | 9-4 | 1st round | Coral UK Championship |
| | v Johnson | 3-9 | 2nd round | Coral UK Championship |
| 1984 | v Macleod | 4-5 | Qualifying | Lada Classic |
| | v Stevens | 1-5 | 1st round | Benson & Hedges Masters |
| | v Gauvreau | 10-5 | 1st round | Embassy World Championship |
| | v Stevens | 10-13 | 2nd round | Embassy World Championship |
| | v Charlton | 4-5 | Quarter-final | Winfield Australian Masters |
| | v W. Jones | 5-4 | 1st round | Jameson International |
| | v S. Davis | 1-5 | 2nd round | Jameson International |
| | v O'Kane | 5-1 | 1st round | Rothmans Grand Prix |
| | v John Rea | 5-1 | 2nd round | Rothmans Grand Prix |
| | v S. Davis | 1-5 | 3rd round | Rothmans Grand Prix |
| | v Macleod | 9-6 | 1st round | Coral UK Open |

| | | | |
|---|---|---|---|
| | v Reardon | 4-9 | 2nd round | Coral UK Open |
| 1985 | v Longworth | 4-5 | 1st round | Mercantile Credit Classic |
| | v Reardon | 1-5 | 1st round | Benson & Hedges Masters |
| | v Cripsey | 9-5 | 1st round | Tolly Cobbold English Championship |
| | v Parrott | 9-6 | 2nd round | Tolly Cobbold English Championship |
| | v Knowles | 2-9 | Quarter-final | Tolly Cobbold English Championship |
| | v Bradley | 3-6 | 1st round | Dulux British Open |
| | v O'Kane | 10-4 | 1st round | Embassy World Championship |
| | v S. Davis | 4-13 | 2nd round | Embassy World Championship |
| | v White | 0-4 | 1st round | Winfield Australian Masters |
| | v T. Jones | 5-4 | 3rd round | Goya Matchroom Trophy |
| | v Werbeniuk | 5-4 | 4th round | Goya Matchroom Trophy |
| | v N. Foulds | 4-5 | 5th round | Goya Matchroom Trophy |
| | v Newbury | 5-2 | 3rd round | Rothmans Grand Prix |
| | v Longworth | 1-5 | 4th round | Rothmans Grand Prix |
| | v Mikkelsen | 9-6 | 3rd round | Coral UK Open |
| | v J. Campbell | 9-4 | 4th round | Coral UK Open |
| | v Knowles | 7-9 | 5th round | Coral UK Open |
| 1986 | v Gauvreau | 3-5 | 3rd round | Mercantile Credit Classic |
| | v S. Davis | 4-5 | 1st round | Benson & Hedges Masters |
| | v Edmonds | 6-9 | 3rd round | Tolly Cobbold English Championship |
| | v Medati | 1-5 | 3rd round | Dulux British Open |
| | v E. Hughes | 7-10 | 1st round | Embassy World Championship |
| | v Edmonds | 5-4 | 3rd round | BCE International |
| | v Johnson | 5-3 | 4th round | BCE International |
| | v Reynolds | 1-5 | 5th round | BCE International |
| | v W. Jones | 1-5 | 3rd round | Rothmans Grand Prix |
| | v Chaperon | 9-8 | 3rd round | Tennents UK Open |
| | v Thorburn | 4-9 | 4th round | Tennents UK Open |
| 1987 | v Bradley | 1-5 | 3rd round | Mercantile Credit Classic |
| | v Fitzmaurice | 6-1 | 3rd round | Tolly Ales English Championship |
| | v Williams | 2-6 | 4th round | Tolly Ales English Championship |
| | v Wilkinson | 5-4 | 3rd round | Dulux British Open |
| | v J. McLaughlin | 5-2 | 4th round | Dulux British Open |
| | v Stevens | 5-2 | 5th round | Dulux British Open |
| | v Thorburn | 3-5 | Quarter-final | Dulux British Open |
| | v Cripsey | 10-7 | Qualifying | Embassy World Championship |
| | v Mountjoy | 5-10 | 1st round | Embassy World Championship |
| | v Morra | 5-3 | 3rd round | Fidelity International |
| | v Knowles | 2-5 | 4th round | Fidelity International |
| | v Chaperon | 3-5 | 3rd round | Rothmans Grand Prix |
| | v Chaperon | 9-6 | 3rd round | Tennents UK Open |
| | v Higgins | 6-9 | 4th round | Tennents UK Open |
| 1988 | v M. Smith | 5-3 | 3rd round | Mercantile Credit Classic |
| | v Parrott | 0-5 | 4th round | Mercantile Credit Classic |
| | v Owers | 3-6 | 3rd round | English Championship |
| | v Medati | 4-5 | 3rd round | MIM Britannia British Open |
| | v Chaperon | 6-10 | Qualifying | Embassy World Championship |
| | v T. Wilson | 5-1 | 3rd round | Fidelity International |
| | v John Rea | 5-4 | 4th round | Fidelity International |
| | v S. Davis | 1-5 | 5th round | Fidelity International |
| | v Duggan | 1-5 | 3rd round | Rothmans Grand Prix |
| | v Dodd | 5-3 | 3rd round | BCE Canadian Masters |
| | v Roscoe | 5-1 | 4th round | BCE Canadian Masters |
| | v Dennis Taylor | 2-5 | 5th round | BCE Canadian Masters |
| | v M. Bennett | 4-9 | 3rd round | Tennents UK Open |
| 1989 | v Darrington | 5-2 | 3rd round | Mercantile Credit Classic |
| | v C. Wilson | 5-3 | 4th round | Mercantile Credit Classic |
| | v W. Jones | 3-5 | 5th round | Mercantile Credit Classic |
| | v Gary Wilkinson | 2-5 | 3rd round | European Open |
| | v Price | 1-5 | 3rd round | English Championship |
| | v Clark | 2-5 | 3rd round | Anglian British Open |
| | v W. Jones | 7-10 | Qualifying | Embassy World Championship |

## DENNIS TAYLOR (Northern Ireland)

**Born** 19.1.49. **Turned professional** 1971. **World ranking** 8 (10). **Best professional performances** Winner 1985 Embassy World Championship, 1984 Rothmans Grand Prix, 1987 Benson & Hedges Masters, 1985, 1987 Canadian Masters, 1982, 1985, 1986, 1987 Irish Championship.

| Year | Opponent | Score | Round | Tournament |
|---|---|---|---|---|
| 1973 | v Thorburn | 8-9 | 1st round | World Championship |
| 1974 | v M. Owen | 1-8 | Qualifying | World Championship |
| 1975 | v Mans | 15-12 | 1st round | World Championship |
| | v F. Davis | 15-14 | 2nd round | World Championship |
| | v G. Owen | 19-9 | Quarter-final | World Championship |
| | v Charlton | 12-19 | Semi-final | World Championship |
| 1976 | v G. Owen | 15-9 | 1st round | Embassy World Championship |
| | v Reardon | 2-15 | Quarter-final | Embassy World Championship |
| 1977 | v Karnehm | 11-0 | Qualifying | Embassy World Championship |
| | v Mans | 13-11 | 1st round | Embassy World Championship |
| | v Mountjoy | 13-11 | Quarter-final | Embassy World Championship |
| | v Thorburn | 16-18 | Semi-final | Embassy World Championship |
| 1978 | v F. Davis | 9-13 | 1st round | Embassy World Championship |
| | v Mountjoy | 4-9 | 1st round | Coral UK Championship |
| 1979 | v S. Davis | 13-11 | 1st round | Embassy World Championship |
| | v Reardon | 13-8 | Quarter-final | Embassy World Championship |
| | v Virgo | 19-12 | Semi-final | Embassy World Championship |
| | v Griffiths | 16-24 | Final | Embassy World Championship |
| | v Thorne | 9-8 | 3rd round | Coral UK Championship |
| | v Fagan | 9-6 | Quarter-final | Coral UK Championship |
| | v Virgo | 4-9 | Semi-final | Coral UK Championship |
| 1980 | v Reardon | 3-5 | Quarter-final | Benson & Hedges Masters |
| | v Wych | 10-13 | 2nd round | Embassy World Championship |
| | v Sinclair | 9-6 | 2nd round | Coral UK Championship |
| | v Griffiths | 2-9 | Quarter-final | Coral UK Championship |
| 1981 | v Spencer | 2-5 | 1st round | Benson & Hedges Masters |
| | v S. Davis | 2-5 | Semi-final | Yamaha International Masters |
| | v Stevens | 13-11 | 2nd round | Embassy World Championship |
| | v Mountjoy | 8-13 | Quarter-final | Embassy World Championship |
| | v Williams | 5-1 | 3rd round | Jameson International |
| | v Virgo | 5-2 | Quarter-final | Jameson International |
| | v Martin | 9-1 | Semi-final | Jameson International |
| | v S. Davis | 0-9 | Final | Jameson International |
| | v Mountjoy | 4-5 | 1st round | Northern Ireland Classic |
| | v White | 5-9 | 3rd round | Coral UK Championship |
| 1982 | v Higgins | 1-5 | 1st round | Lada Classic |
| | v Reardon | 3-5 | 1st round | Benson & Hedges Masters |
| | v Knowles | 5-2 | Semi-final | Tolly Cobbold Classic |
| | v S. Davis | 3-8 | Final | Tolly Cobbold Classic |
| | v Murphy | 6-0 | Semi-final | Irish Championship |
| | **v Higgins** | **16-13** | **Final** | **Irish Championship** |
| | v Sheehan | 5-3 | 1st round | Benson & Hedges Irish Masters |
| | v Reardon | 4-5 | Quarter-final | Benson & Hedges Irish Masters |
| | v S. Francisco | 7-10 | 1st round | Embassy World Championship |
| | v White | 5-4 | 1st round | Langs Supreme Scottish Masters |
| | v S. Davis | 1-6 | Semi-final | Langs Supreme Scottish Masters |
| | v Wildman | 5-2 | 1st round | Jameson International |
| | v Thorburn | 5-2 | 2nd round | Jameson International |
| | v Virgo | 3-5 | Quarter-final | Jameson International |
| | v Edmonds | 5-4 | 1st round | Professional Players Tournament |
| | v David Taylor | 5-1 | 2nd round | Professional Players Tournament |
| | v White | 3-5 | 3rd round | Professional Players Tournament |
| | v Meadowcroft | 9-7 | 1st round | Coral UK Championship |
| | v Griffiths | 7-9 | 2nd round | Coral UK Championship |
| 1983 | v S. Davis | 2-5 | 1st round | Lada Classic |

*Dennis Taylor*

|  |  |  |  |  |
|---|---|---|---|---|
|  | v S. Davis | 1-5 | Semi-final | Tolly Cobbold Classic |
|  | v Kelly | 6-0 | Quarter-final | Irish Championship |
|  | v Fagan | 6-1 | Semi-final | Irish Championship |
|  | v Higgins | 11-16 | Final | Irish Championship |
|  | v White | 4-5 | 1st round | Benson & Hedges Irish Masters |
|  | v S. Francisco | 10-9 | 1st round | Embassy World Championship |
|  | v S. Davis | 11-13 | 2nd round | Embassy World Championship |
|  | v Reynolds | 5-3 | 1st round | Jameson International |
|  | v Thorburn | 3-5 | 2nd round | Jameson International |
|  | v Scott | 4-5 | 1st round | Professional Players Tournament |
|  | v Murphy | 9-6 | 1st round | Coral UK Championship |
|  | v White | 4-9 | 2nd round | Coral UK Championship |
| 1984 | v Hallett | 4-5 | Qualifying | Lada Classic |
|  | v Knowles | 2-5 | 1st round | Benson & Hedges Masters |
|  | v E. Hughes | 5-1 | 1st round | Benson & Hedges Irish Masters |
|  | v Thorburn | 5-2 | Quarter-final | Benson & Hedges Irish Masters |
|  | v Griffiths | 4-5 | Semi-final | Benson & Hedges Irish Masters |
|  | v Johnson | 10-1 | 1st round | Embassy World Championship |
|  | v Parrott | 13-11 | 2nd round | Embassy World Championship |
|  | v Mountjoy | 13-8 | Quarter-final | Embassy World Championship |
|  | v S. Davis | 9-16 | Semi-final | Embassy World Championship |
|  | v Fowler | 5-0 | 1st round | Jameson International |
|  | v Watchorn | 5-1 | 1st round | Rothmans Grand Prix |
|  | v Virgo | 5-3 | 2nd round | Rothmans Grand Prix |
|  | v Reardon | 5-3 | 3rd round | Rothmans Grand Prix |
|  | v Stevens | 5-2 | Quarter-final | Rothmans Grand Prix |
|  | v N. Foulds | 9-3 | Semi-final | Rothmans Grand Prix |
|  | **v Thorburn** | **10-2** | **Final** | **Rothmans Grand Prix** |
|  | v King | 9-5 | 1st round | Coral UK Open |
|  | v Knowles | 2-9 | 2nd round | Coral UK Open |
| 1985 | v Williams | 3-5 | 1st round | Mercantile Credit Classic |
|  | v Thorburn | 3-5 | 1st round | Benson & Hedges Masters |
|  | v Scott | 6-2 | 1st round | Dulux British Open |
|  | v Parrott | 5-2 | 2nd round | Dulux British Open |
|  | v Newbury | 5-3 | 3rd round | Dulux British Open |
|  | v Stevens | 2-5 | Quarter-final | Dulux British Open |
|  | v Charlton | 4-5 | 1st round | Benson & Hedges Irish Masters |
|  | v Jack Rea | 6-0 | Quarter-final | Irish Championship |
|  | v E. Hughes | 6-5 | Semi-final | Irish Championship |
|  | **v Higgins** | **10-5** | **Final** | **Irish Championship** |
|  | v S. Francisco | 10-2 | 1st round | Embassy World Championship |
|  | v Charlton | 13-6 | 2nd round | Embassy World Championship |
|  | v Thorburn | 13-5 | Quarter-final | Embassy World Championship |
|  | v Knowles | 16-5 | Semi-final | Embassy World Championship |
|  | **v S. Davis** | **18-17** | **Final** | **Embassy World Championship** |
|  | v Thorne | 3-5 | 1st round | Langs Scottish Masters |
|  | v Cripsey | 5-1 | 3rd round | Goya Matchroom Trophy |
|  | v B. Harris | 5-3 | 4th round | Goya Matchroom Trophy |
|  | v Higgins | 5-1 | 5th round | Goya Matchroom Trophy |
|  | v Parrott | 5-1 | Quarter-final | Goya Matchroom Trophy |
|  | v Thorburn | 5-9 | Semi-final | Goya Matchroom Trophy |
|  | v West | 5-1 | 3rd round | Rothmans Grand Prix |
|  | v Williams | 5-2 | 4th round | Rothmans Grand Prix |
|  | v Meo | 5-3 | 5th round | Rothmans Grand Prix |
|  | v Wilson | 5-2 | Quarter-final | Rothmans Grand Prix |
|  | v Knowles | 9-6 | Semi-final | Rothmans Grand Prix |
|  | v S. Davis | 9-10 | Final | Rothmans Grand Prix |
|  | v Parrott | 5-1 | 1st round | BCE Canadian Masters |
|  | v Reardon | 8-3 | Semi-final | BCE Canadian Masters |
|  | **v S. Davis** | **9-5** | **Final** | **BCE Canadian Masters** |
|  | v Bear | 9-3 | 3rd round | Coral UK Open |
|  | v Cripsey | 9-2 | 4th round | Coral UK Open |
|  | v N. Foulds | 9-5 | 5th round | Coral UK Open |

|  |  |  |  |  |
|---|---|---|---|---|
|  | v Stevens | 9-1 | Quarter-final | Coral UK Open |
|  | v Thorne | 7-9 | Semi-final | Coral UK Open |
|  | v F. Davis | 5-0 | 1st round | Kit Kat |
|  | v Griffiths | 6-4 | Semi-final | Kit Kat |
|  | **v S. Davis** | **9-5** | **Final** | **Kit Kat** |
| 1986 | v Fitzmaurice | 5-1 | 3rd round | Mercantile Credit Classic |
|  | v Reynolds | 5-4 | 4th round | Mercantile Credit Classic |
|  | v Higgins | 4-5 | 5th round | Mercantile Credit Classic |
|  | v Higgins | 1-5 | 1st round | BCE Belgian Classic |
|  | v Mountjoy | 5-2 | 1st round | Benson & Hedges Masters |
|  | v White | 3-5 | Quarter-final | Benson & Hedges Masters |
|  | v Bales | 4-5 | 3rd round | Dulux British Open |
|  | v Thorne | 2-5 | Quarter-final | Benson & Hedges Irish Masters |
|  | v Hallett | 6-10 | 1st round | Embassy World Championship |
|  | v Kelly | 6-1 | Quarter-final | Strongbow Irish Championship |
|  | v Murphy | 6-3 | Semi-final | Strongbow Irish Championship |
|  | **v Higgins** | **10-7** | **Final** | **Strongbow Irish Championship** |
|  | v Griffiths | 5-4 | Semi-final | Camus Hong Kong Masters |
|  | v Thorne | 3-8 | Final | Camus Hong Kong Masters |
|  | v Johnson | 5-3 | 1st round | Carlsberg Challenge |
|  | **v White** | **8-3** | **Final** | **Carlsberg Challenge** |
|  | v Thorne | 5-6 | Semi-final | Matchroom Trophy |
|  | v Foldvari | 5-1 | 3rd round | BCE International |
|  | v Hendry | 5-3 | 4th round | BCE International |
|  | v S. Francisco | 0-5 | 5th round | BCE International |
|  | v Wright | 5-3 | 3rd round | Rothmans Grand Prix |
|  | v Virgo | 5-3 | 4th round | Rothmans Grand Prix |
|  | v Meo | 2-5 | 5th round | Rothmans Grand Prix |
|  | v Thorne | 4-5 | 1st round | BCE Canadian Masters |
|  | v Roe | 9-6 | 3rd round | Tennents UK Open |
|  | v W. Jones | 2-9 | 4th round | Tennents UK Open |
| 1987 | v W. Jones | 2-5 | 3rd round | Mercantile Credit Classic |
|  | v N. Foulds | 5-2 | 1st round | Benson & Hedges Masters |
|  | v S. Francisco | 5-3 | Quarter-final | Benson & Hedges Masters |
|  | v Thorburn | 6-5 | Semi-final | Benson & Hedges Masters |
|  | **v Higgins** | **9-8** | **Final** | **Benson & Hedges Masters** |
|  | v Roscoe | 5-1 | 3rd round | Dulux British Open |
|  | v Charlton | 5-1 | 4th round | Dulux British Open |
|  | v Griffiths | 5-4 | 5th round | Dulux British Open |
|  | v Knowles | 4-5 | Quarter-final | Dulux British Open |
|  | v E. Hughes | 5-4 | 1st round | Benson & Hedges Irish Masters |
|  | v Thorburn | 5-1 | Quarter-final | Benson & Hedges Irish Masters |
|  | v Thorne | 6-2 | Semi-final | Benson & Hedges Irish Masters |
|  | v M. Bennett | 10-4 | 1st round | Embassy World Championship |
|  | v N. Foulds | 10-13 | 2nd round | Embassy World Championship |
|  | v Sheehan | 6-3 | Quarter-final | Matchroom Irish Championship |
|  | v Browne | 6-1 | Semi-final | Matchroom Irish Championship |
|  | **v O'Boye** | **9-2** | **Final** | **Matchroom Irish Championship** |
|  | **v Griffiths** | **6-3** | **Final** | **British Caledonian Tokyo Masters (WS)** |
|  | v S. Davis | 4-5 | Semi-final | Riley Hong Kong Masters (WS) |
|  | v Hendry | 5-3 | 1st round | Carling Champions |
|  | **v Johnson** | **8-5** | **Final** | **Carling Champions** |
|  | v Thorburn | 2-5 | 1st round | Langs Scottish Masters |
|  | v Bradley | 5-0 | 3rd round | Fidelity International |
|  | v Clark | 0-5 | 4th round | Fidelity International |
|  | v Reardon | 5-1 | 3rd round | Rothmans Grand Prix |
|  | v Werbeniuk | 5-3 | 4th round | Rothmans Grand Prix |
|  | v Wilson | 5-2 | 5th round | Rothmans Grand Prix |
|  | v Newbury | 5-2 | Quarter-final | Rothmans Grand Prix |
|  | v P. Francisco | 9-4 | Semi-final | Rothmans Grand Prix |
|  | v Hendry | 7-10 | Final | Rothmans Grand Prix |
|  | v S. Davis | 5-1 | 1st round | Labatts Canadian Masters (WS) |
|  | v Thorburn | 8-5 | Semi-final | Labatts Canadian Masters (WS) |

|  | | | | |
|---|---|---|---|---|
| | v **White** | **9-7** | **Final** | **Labatts Canadian Masters (WS)** |
| | v White | 6-2 | 1st round | Matchroom Trophy |
| | v S. Davis | 6-3 | Semi-final | Matchroom Trophy |
| | v **Thorne** | **10-3** | **Final** | **Matchroom Trophy** |
| | v Dodd | 9-8 | 3rd round | Tennents UK Open |
| | v O'Kane | 7-9 | 4th round | Tennents UK Open |
| **1988** | v Whitthread | 5-2 | 3rd round | Mercantile Credit Classic |
| | v Drago | 5-0 | 4th round | Mercantile Credit Classic |
| | v P. Francisco | 5-3 | 5th round | Mercantile Credit Classic |
| | v Parrott | 1-5 | Quarter-final | Mercantile Credit Classic |
| | v Hallett | 3-5 | 1st round | Benson & Hedges Masters |
| | v Kearney | 6-3 | Quarter-final | Irish Championship |
| | v Browne | 6-5 | Semi-final | Irish Championship |
| | v J. McLaughlin | 4-9 | Final | Irish Championship |
| | v Miles | 5-1 | 3rd round | MIM Britannia British Open |
| | v Spencer | 0-5 | 4th round | MIM Britannia British Open |
| | v Higgins | 3-5 | 1st round | Benson & Hedges Irish Masters |
| | v Werbeniuk | 10-8 | 1st round | Embassy World Championship |
| | v Drago | 5-13 | 2nd round | Embassy World Championship |
| | v White | 2-5 | Semi-final | LEP Hong Kong Masters |
| | v Chappel | 5-1 | 3rd round | Fidelity International |
| | v J. Campbell | 5-4 | 4th round | Fidelity International |
| | v Wych | 5-2 | 5th round | Fidelity International |
| | v S. Davis | 2-5 | Quarter-final | Fidelity International |
| | v Meo | 6-4 | 1st round | LEP Matchroom Championship |
| | v N. Foulds | 6-3 | Semi-final | LEP Matchroom Championship |
| | v S. Davis | 7-10 | Final | LEP Matchroom Championship |
| | v Ellis | 5-1 | 3rd round | Rothmans Grand Prix |
| | v Chaperon | 5-4 | 4th round | Rothmans Grand Prix |
| | v Hallett | 5-2 | 5th round | Rothmans Grand Prix |
| | v White | 5-2 | Quarter-final | Rothmans Grand Prix |
| | v S. Davis | 1-9 | Semi-final | Rothmans Grand Prix |
| | v Owers | 5-1 | 3rd round | BCE Canadian Masters |
| | v Clark | 5-4 | 4th round | BCE Canadian Masters |
| | v David Taylor | 5-2 | 5th round | BCE Canadian Masters |
| | v White | 3-5 | Quarter-final | BCE Canadian Masters |
| | v J. McLaughlin | 9-5 | 3rd round | Tennents UK Open |
| | v O'Boye | 9-4 | 4th round | Tennents UK Open |
| | v Parrott | 4-9 | 5th round | Tennents UK Open |
| | v Knowles | 9-7 | 1st round | Everest World Matchplay |
| | v Hendry | 7-9 | Quarter-final | Everest World Matchplay |
| **1989** | v Fowler | 5-3 | 3rd round | Mercantile Credit Classic |
| | v Newbury | 4-5 | 4th round | Mercantile Credit Classic |
| | v Parrott | 1-5 | 1st round | Benson and Hedges Masters |
| | v Stevens | 5-0 | 3rd round | European Open |
| | v Mountjoy | 3-5 | 4th round | European Open |
| | v Roscoe | 4-5 | 3rd round | Anglian British Open |
| | v Parrott | 1-5 | 1st round | Benson and Hedges Irish Masters |
| | v E. Hughes | 10-3 | 1st round | Embassy World Championship |
| | v Parrott | 10-13 | 2nd round | Embassy World Championship |

## NICK TERRY (England)

**Born** 15.9.67. **Turned professional** 1988. **World ranking** 72. **Best professional performance** Last 32 1989 Mercantile Credit Classic.

|  | | | | |
|---|---|---|---|---|
| **1988** | v Roscoe | 2-5 | 1st round | Fidelity International |
| | v Sinclair | 5-3 | 1st round | Rothmans Grand Prix |
| | v Miles | 5-1 | 2nd round | Rothmans Grand Prix |
| | v N. Foulds | 4-5 | 3rd round | Rothmans Grand Prix |
| | v Donnelly | 5-1 | 1st round | BCE Canadian Masters |
| | v Gary Wilkinson | 3-5 | 2nd round | BCE Canadian Masters |

|         | v Rigitano       | 9-5    | 1st round    | Tennents UK Open              |
|---------|------------------|--------|--------------|-------------------------------|
|         | v King           | 7-9    | 2nd round    | Tennents UK Open              |
| 1989    | v John Rea       | 5-3    | 1st round    | Mercantile Credit Classic     |
|         | v M. Bennett     | 5-3    | 2nd round    | Mercantile Credit Classic     |
|         | v P. Francisco   | 5-4    | 3rd round    | Mercantile Credit Classic     |
|         | v Mountjoy       | 4-5    | 4th round    | Mercantile Credit Classic     |
|         | v V. Harris      | 2-5    | 1st round    | European Open                 |
|         | v Rowing         | 5-1    | Prelim       | English Championship          |
|         | v Marshall       | 3-5    | 1st round    | English Championship          |
|         | v Kearney        | 5-3    | 1st round    | Anglian British Open          |
|         | v Houlihan       | 2-5    | 2nd round    | Anglian British Open          |
|         | v Parkin         | 10-0   | Qualifying   | Embassy World Championship    |
|         | v Medati         | 10-8   | Qualifying   | Embassy World Championship    |
|         | v N. Gilbert     | 5-10   | Qualifying   | Embassy World Championship    |

## CLIFF THORBURN C.M. (Canada)

**Born** 16.1.48. **Turned professional** 1973. **World ranking** 7 (6). **Best professional performances** Winner 1980 Embassy World Championship, 1985 Goya Matchroom Trophy, 1983, 1985, 1986 Benson & Hedges Masters, 1985, 1986, 1987 Canadian Championship.

|         | v                | score   | round          | tournament                           |
|---------|------------------|---------|----------------|--------------------------------------|
| 1973    | v Dennis Taylor  | 9-8     | 1st round      | World Championship                   |
|         | v Williams       | 15-16   | 2nd round      | World Championship                   |
| 1974    | v Morgan         | 4-8     | 1st round      | World Championship                   |
| 1975    | v Pulman         | 3-5     | 1st round      | Benson & Hedges Masters              |
|         | v Morgan         | 15-6    | 1st round      | World Championship                   |
|         | v Miles          | 15-2    | 2nd round      | World Championship                   |
|         | v Charlton       | 12-19   | Quarter-final  | World Championship                   |
| 1976    | v Higgins        | 14-15   | 1st round      | Embassy World Championship           |
| 1977    | v Ross           | 11-0    | Qualifying     | Embassy World Championship           |
|         | v Williams       | 13-6    | 1st round      | Embassy World Championship           |
|         | v Charlton       | 13-12   | Quarter-final  | Embassy World Championship           |
|         | v Dennis Taylor  | 18-16   | Semi-final     | Embassy World Championship           |
|         | v Spencer        | 21-25   | Final          | Embassy World Championship           |
| 1978    | v Mountjoy       | 4-2     | Quarter-final  | Benson & Hedges Masters              |
|         | v Spencer        | 5-3     | Semi-final     | Benson & Hedges Masters              |
|         | v Higgins        | 5-7     | Final          | Benson & Hedges Masters              |
|         | v Houlihan       | 13-8    | 1st round      | Embassy World Championship           |
|         | v Charlton       | 12-13   | Quarter-final  | Embassy World Championship           |
| 1979    | v Mans           | 4-5     | Quarter-final  | Benson & Hedges Masters              |
|         | v Virgo          | 10-13   | 1st round      | Embassy World Championship           |
| 1980    | v Virgo          | 5-3     | 1st round      | Benson & Hedges Masters              |
|         | v Griffiths      | 3-5     | Quarter-final  | Benson & Hedges Masters              |
|         | v Mountjoy       | 13-10   | 2nd round      | Embassy World Championship           |
|         | v Wych           | 13-6    | Quarter-final  | Embassy World Championship           |
|         | v David Taylor   | 16-7    | Semi-final     | Embassy World Championship           |
|         | **v Higgins**    | **18-16** | **Final**    | **Embassy World Championship**       |
| 1981    | v Mans           | 5-4     | Quarter-final  | Benson & Hedges Masters              |
|         | v Higgins        | 5-6     | Semi-final     | Benson & Hedges Masters              |
|         | v Griffiths      | 5-6     | Semi-final     | Benson & Hedges Irish Masters        |
|         | v Miles          | 13-2    | 2nd round      | Embassy World Championship           |
|         | v David Taylor   | 13-6    | Quarter-final  | Embassy World Championship           |
|         | v S. Davis       | 10-16   | Semi-final     | Embassy World Championship           |
|         | v Stevens        | 5-1     | Quarter-final  | Langs Scottish Masters               |
|         | v Higgins        | 6-2     | Semi-final     | Langs Scottish Masters               |
|         | v White          | 4-9     | Final          | Langs Scottish Masters               |
|         | v Miles          | 0-5     | 3rd round      | Jameson International                 |
|         | v White          | 2-5     | 1st round      | Northern Ireland Classic             |
|         | v Meo            | 6-9     | 3rd round      | Coral UK Championship                |
| 1982    | v Griffiths      | 1-5     | 1st round      | Lada Classic                         |
|         | v Meo            | 0-5     | Quarter-final  | Benson & Hedges Masters              |

*Cliff Thorburn*

|  |  |  |  |  |
|---|---|---|---|---|
| | v Higgins | 4-5 | Quarter-final | Benson & Hedges Irish Masters |
| | v White | 4-10 | 1st round | Embassy World Championship |
| | v Scott | 5-1 | 1st round | Jameson International |
| | v Dennis Taylor | 2-5 | 2nd round | Jameson International |
| | v Medati | 5-1 | 1st round | Professional Players Tournament |
| | v Everton | 5-2 | 2nd round | Professional Players Tournament |
| | v Werbeniuk | 2-5 | 3rd round | Professional Players Tournament |
| **1983** | v Wilson | 5-3 | 1st round | Lada Classic |
| | v Stevens | 3-5 | Quarter-final | Lada Classic |
| | v Johnson | 5-2 | 1st round | Benson & Hedges Masters |
| | v Griffiths | 5-3 | Quarter-final | Benson & Hedges Masters |
| | v Charlton | 6-5 | Semi-final | Benson & Hedges Masters |
| | **v Reardon** | **9-7** | **Final** | **Benson & Hedges Masters** |
| | v J. Campbell | 10-5 | 1st round | Embassy World Championship |
| | v Griffiths | 13-12 | 2nd round | Embassy World Championship |
| | v Stevens | 13-12 | Quarter-final | Embassy World Championship |
| | v Knowles | 16-15 | Semi-final | Embassy World Championship |
| | v S. Davis | 6-18 | Final | Embassy World Championship |
| | v Stevens | 5-2 | Semi-final | Winfield Masters |
| | **v Werbeniuk** | **7-3** | **Final** | **Winfield Masters** |
| | v Mikkelsen | 9-2 | Quarter-final | Canadian Championship |
| | v Jonik | 6-9 | Semi-final | Canadian Championship |
| | v Griffiths | 5-1 | 1st round | Langs Scottish Masters |
| | v Knowles | 2-6 | Semi-final | Langs Scottish Masters |
| | v Sinclair | 5-0 | 1st round | Jameson International |
| | v Dennis Taylor | 5-3 | 2nd round | Jameson International |
| | v Mountjoy | 5-2 | Quarter-final | Jameson International |
| | v Griffiths | 9-8 | Semi-final | Jameson International |
| | v S. Davis | 4-9 | Final | Jameson International |
| | v V. Harris | 5-1 | 1st round | Professional Players Tournament |
| | v Meadowcroft | 5-1 | 2nd round | Professional Players Tournament |
| | v Wilson | 5-3 | 3rd round | Professional Players Tournament |
| | v Johnson | 1-5 | Quarter-final | Professional Players Tournament |
| **1984** | v S. Francisco | 1-5 | Qualifying | Lada Classic |
| | v Spencer | 4-5 | 1st round | Benson & Hedges Masters |
| | v Dennis Taylor | 2-5 | Quarter-final | Benson & Hedges Irish Masters |
| | v Meo | 5-4 | 1st round | Tolly Cobbold Classic |
| | v Knowles | 3-5 | Semi-final | Tolly Cobbold Classic |
| | v Morra | 10-3 | 1st round | Embassy World Championship |
| | v Thorne | 13-11 | 2nd round | Embassy World Championship |
| | v White | 8-13 | Quarter-final | Embassy World Championship |
| | v S. Davis | 2-5 | 1st round | Langs Scottish Masters |
| | v Virgo | 0-5 | 1st round | Jameson International |
| | v Rigitano | 5-4 | 1st round | Rothmans Grand Prix |
| | v J. Campbell | 5-1 | 2nd round | Rothmans Grand Prix |
| | v Meo | 5-4 | 3rd round | Rothmans Grand Prix |
| | v Mountjoy | 5-3 | Quarter-final | Rothmans Grand Prix |
| | v S. Davis | 9-7 | Semi-final | Rothmans Grand Prix |
| | v Dennis Taylor | 2-10 | Final | Rothmans Grand Prix |
| | v J. McLaughlin | 9-4 | 1st round | Coral UK Open |
| | v Wilson | 9-3 | 2nd round | Coral UK Open |
| | v Reardon | 9-8 | Quarter-final | Coral UK Open |
| | v Higgins | 7-9 | Semi-final | Coral UK Open |
| **1985** | v Scott | 5-1 | 1st round | Mercantile Credit Classic |
| | v Longworth | 5-3 | 2nd round | Mercantile Credit Classic |
| | v Griffiths | 5-4 | Quarter-final | Mercantile Credit Classic |
| | v Johnson | 9-2 | Semi-final | Mercantile Credit Classic |
| | v Thorne | 8-13 | Final | Mercantile Credit Classic |
| | v Dennis Taylor | 5-3 | 1st round | Benson & Hedges Masters |
| | v Reardon | 5-0 | Quarter-final | Benson & Hedges Masters |
| | v White | 6-4 | Semi-final | Benson & Hedges Masters |
| | **v Mountjoy** | **9-6** | **Final** | **Benson & Hedges Masters** |
| | v Rigitano | 6-3 | 1st round | Dulux British Open |

|        |                  |       |              |                                  |
|--------|------------------|-------|--------------|----------------------------------|
|        | v Reynolds       | 5-3   | 2nd round    | Dulux British Open               |
|        | v Higgins        | 2-5   | 3rd round    | Dulux British Open               |
|        | v White          | 3-5   | Quarter-final| Benson & Hedges Irish Masters    |
|        | v Hallett        | 10-8  | 1st round    | Embassy World Championship       |
|        | v Werbeniuk      | 13-3  | 2nd round    | Embassy World Championship       |
|        | v Dennis Taylor  | 5-13  | Quarter-final| Embassy World Championship       |
|        | v Caggianello    | 6-2   | Quarter-final| Canadian Championship            |
|        | v Wych           | 6-5   | Semi-final   | Canadian Championship            |
|        | **v Chaperon**   | **6-4** | **Final**  | **Canadian Championship**        |
|        | v Higgins        | 4-5   | Semi-final   | Carlsberg Trophy                 |
|        | v Macleod        | 5-1   | 1st round    | Langs Scottish Masters           |
|        | v S. Francisco   | 6-0   | Semi-final   | Langs Scottish Masters           |
|        | **v Thorne**     | **9-7** | **Final**  | **Langs Scottish Masters**       |
|        | v Longworth      | 5-3   | 3rd round    | Goya Matchroom Trophy            |
|        | v Martin         | 5-3   | 4th round    | Goya Matchroom Trophy            |
|        | v J. Campbell    | 5-0   | 5th round    | Goya Matchroom Trophy            |
|        | v Duggan         | 5-2   | Quarter-final| Goya Matchroom Trophy            |
|        | v Dennis Taylor  | 9-5   | Semi-final   | Goya Matchroom Trophy            |
|        | **v White**      | **12-10** | **Final**| **Goya Matchroom Trophy**        |
|        | v Oliver         | 5-0   | 3rd round    | Rothmans Grand Prix              |
|        | v Wildman        | 5-2   | 4th round    | Rothmans Grand Prix              |
|        | v Johnson        | 5-1   | 5th round    | Rothmans Grand Prix              |
|        | v Griffiths      | 5-1   | Quarter-final| Rothmans Grand Prix              |
|        | v S. Davis       | 5-9   | Semi-final   | Rothmans Grand Prix              |
|        | v White          | 5-3   | 1st round    | BCE Canadian Masters             |
|        | v S. Davis       | 1-8   | Semi-final   | BCE Canadian Masters             |
|        | v Dodd           | 9-4   | 3rd round    | Coral UK Open                    |
|        | v Parrott        | 9-6   | 4th round    | Coral UK Open                    |
|        | v Thorne         | 7-9   | 5th round    | Coral UK Open                    |
|        | v Higgins        | 4-5   | 1st round    | Kit Kat                          |
| **1986** | v J. McLaughlin | 5-1   | 3rd round    | Mercantile Credit Classic        |
|        | v Hallett        | 5-3   | 4th round    | Mercantile Credit Classic        |
|        | v Meo            | 5-1   | 5th round    | Mercantile Credit Classic        |
|        | v Johnson        | 5-4   | Quarter-final| Mercantile Credit Classic        |
|        | v Mountjoy       | 9-6   | Semi-final   | Mercantile Credit Classic        |
|        | v White          | 12-13 | Final        | Mercantile Credit Classic        |
|        | v Johnson        | 5-3   | 1st round    | Benson & Hedges Masters          |
|        | v Griffiths      | 5-2   | Quarter-final| Benson & Hedges Masters          |
|        | v Knowles        | 6-4   | Semi-final   | Benson & Hedges Masters          |
|        | **v White**      | **9-5** | **Final**  | **Benson & Hedges Masters**      |
|        | v Sheehan        | 5-0   | 3rd round    | Dulux British Open               |
|        | v Wildman        | 5-1   | 4th round    | Dulux British Open               |
|        | v Meo            | 3-5   | 5th round    | Dulux British Open               |
|        | v E. Hughes      | 5-1   | Quarter-final| Benson & Hedges Irish Masters    |
|        | v Thorne         | 4-6   | Semi-final   | Benson & Hedges Irish Masters    |
|        | v Werbeniuk      | 10-5  | 1st round    | Embassy World Championship       |
|        | v E. Hughes      | 13-6  | 2nd round    | Embassy World Championship       |
|        | v Thorne         | 13-6  | Quarter-final| Embassy World Championship       |
|        | v S. Davis       | 12-16 | Semi-final   | Embassy World Championship       |
|        | v Watson         | 6-1   | Quarter-final| Canadian Championship            |
|        | v Jonik          | 6-3   | Semi-final   | Canadian Championship            |
|        | **v Wych**       | **6-2** | **Final**  | **Canadian Championship**        |
|        | v Parrott        | 5-1   | 1st round    | Langs Scottish Masters           |
|        | v White          | 6-2   | Semi-final   | Langs Scottish Masters           |
|        | **v Higgins**    | **9-8** | **Final**  | **Langs Scottish Masters**       |
|        | v Burke          | 5-0   | 3rd round    | BCE International                 |
|        | v Wych           | 5-3   | 4th round    | BCE International                 |
|        | v Griffiths      | 5-4   | 5th round    | BCE International                 |
|        | v Wilson         | 5-1   | Quarter-final| BCE International                 |
|        | v P. Francisco   | 9-7   | Semi-final   | BCE International                 |
|        | v N. Foulds      | 9-12  | Final        | BCE International                 |
|        | v O'Boye         | 4-5   | 3rd round    | Rothmans Grand Prix              |
|        | v Knowles        | 1-5   | 1st round    | BCE Canadian Masters             |

|  | v Fowler | 9-7 | 3rd round | Tennents UK Open |
|---|---|---|---|---|
|  | v David Taylor | 9-4 | 4th round | Tennents UK Open |
|  | v Spencer | 9-2 | 5th round | Tennents UK Open |
|  | v N. Foulds | 2-9 | Quarter-final | Tennents UK Open |
| 1987 | v Cripsey | 5-0 | 3rd round | Mercantile Credit Classic |
|  | v Reynolds | 4-5 | 4th round | Mercantile Credit Classic |
|  | v Williams | 5-1 | 1st round | Benson & Hedges Masters |
|  | v Thorne | 5-3 | Quarter-final | Benson & Hedges Masters |
|  | v Dennis Taylor | 5-6 | Semi-final | Benson & Hedges Masters |
|  | v Wildman | 5-3 | 3rd round | Dulux British Open |
|  | v Cripsey | 5-2 | 4th round | Dulux British Open |
|  | v Mountjoy | 5-4 | 5th round | Dulux British Open |
|  | v David Taylor | 5-3 | Quarter-final | Dulux British Open |
|  | v White | 5-9 | Semi-final | Dulux British Open |
|  | v Dennis Taylor | 1-5 | Quarter-final | Benson & Hedges Irish Masters |
|  | v O'Kane | 5-10 | 1st round | Embassy World Championship |
|  | v Watson | 6-3 | Quarter-final | Canadian Championship |
|  | v Morra | 7-4 | Semi-final | Canadian Championship |
|  | **v Bear** | **8-4** | **Final** | **Canadian Championship** |
|  | v Dennis Taylor | 5-2 | 1st round | Langs Scottish Masters |
|  | v Johnson | 3-6 | Semi-final | Langs Scottish Masters |
|  | v Grace | 5-1 | 3rd round | Fidelity International |
|  | v Newbury | 5-3 | 4th round | Fidelity International |
|  | v James | 5-0 | 5th round | Fidelity International |
|  | v E. Hughes | 5-1 | Quarter-final | Fidelity International |
|  | v Hendry | 9-1 | Semi-final | Fidelity International |
|  | v S. Davis | 5-12 | Final | Fidelity International |
|  | v T. Jones | 5-2 | 3rd round | Rothmans Grand Prix |
|  | v Newbury | 0-5 | 4th round | Rothmans Grand Prix |
|  | v Johnson | 5-3 | 1st round | Labatts Canadian Masters (WS) |
|  | v Dennis Taylor | 5-8 | Semi-final | Labatts Canadian Masters (WS) |
|  | v Cripsey | 9-6 | 3rd round | Tennents UK Open |
|  | v Virgo | 9-6 | 4th round | Tennents UK Open |
|  | v J. Campbell | 9-4 | 5th round | Tennents UK Open |
|  | v Thorne | 8-9 | Quarter-final | Tennents UK Open |
| 1988 | v Reardon | 5-3 | 3rd round | Mercantile Credit Classic |
|  | v Newbury | 3-5 | 4th round | Mercantile Credit Classic |
|  | v Williams | 5-3 | 1st round | Benson and Hedges Masters |
|  | v Parrott | 4-5 | Quarter-final | Benson and Hedges Masters |
|  | v Newbury | 5-2 | 3rd round | MIM Britannia British Open |
|  | v Medati | 5-2 | 4th round | MIM Britannia British Open |
|  | v Thorne | 5-2 | 5th round | MIM Britannia British Open |
|  | v Williams | 5-2 | Quarter-final | MIM Britannia British Open |
|  | v Hendry | 5-9 | Semi-final | MIM Britannia British Open |
|  | v Higgins | 3-5 | Quarter-final | Benson & Hedges Irish Masters |
|  | v Stevens | 10-6 | 1st round | Embassy World Championship |
|  | v Parrott | 13-10 | 2nd round | Embassy World Championship |
|  | v James | 13-11 | Quarter-final | Embassy World Championship |
|  | v S. Davis | 8-16 | Semi-final | Embassy World Championship |
|  | v Jonik | 6-4 | Quarter-final | BCE Canadian Championship |
|  | v Wych | 5-7 | Semi-final | BCE Canadian Championship |
|  | v White | 4-6 | 1st round | LEP Matchroom Championship |
|  | v Chappel | 5-1 | 3rd round | BCE Canadian Masters |
|  | v Spencer | 5-2 | 4th round | BCE Canadian Masters |
|  | v Graham | 5-4 | 5th round | BCE Canadian Masters |
|  | v Hendry | 4-5 | Quarter-final | BCE Canadian Masters |
|  | v Robidoux | 9-4 | 3rd round | Tennents UK Open |
|  | v James | 9-6 | 4th round | Tennents UK Open |
|  | v Roe | 9-8 | 5th round | Tennents UK Open |
|  | v Hendry | 2-9 | Quarter-final | Tennents UK Open |
|  | v Johnson | 4-9 | 1st round | Everest World Matchplay |
| 1989 | v Glen Wilkinson | 5-2 | 3rd round | Mercantile Credit Classic |
|  | v Cripsey | 5-1 | 4th round | Mercantile Credit Classic |

|  |  |  |  |
|---|---|---|---|
| v Virgo | 5-3 | 5th round | Mercantile Credit Classic |
| v Hendry | 5-4 | Quarter-final | Mercantile Credit Classic |
| v Mountjoy | 5-9 | Semi-final | Mercantile Credit Classic |
| v Johnson | 5-2 | 1st round | Benson and Hedges Masters |
| v N. Foulds | 2-5 | Quarter-final | Benson and Hedges Masters |
| v Edmonds | 5-2 | 3rd round | European Open |
| v Macleod | 5-1 | 4th round | European Open |
| v Mountjoy | 5-0 | 5th round | European Open |
| v White | 3-5 | Quarter-final | European Open |
| v Browne | 5-0 | 3rd round | Anglian British Open |
| v D. Morgan | 5-4 | 4th round | Anglian British Open |
| v Hallett | 4-5 | 5th round | Anglian British Open |
| v Higgins | 4-5 | 1st round | Benson and Hedges Irish Masters |
| v Charlton | 9-10 | 1st round | Embassy World Championship |

## WILLIE THORNE (England)

**Born** 4.3.54. **Turned professional** 1975. **World ranking** 9 (13). **Best professional performances** Winner 1985 Mercantile Credit Classic; runner-up 1985 Coral UK Open, 1986 Dulux British Open, 1986 Canadian Masters.

|  |  |  |  |  |
|---|---|---|---|---|
| **1976** | v Condo | 8-3 | Qualifying | Embassy World Championship |
|  | v Meadowcroft | 5-8 | Qualifying | Embassy World Championship |
| **1977** | v Bennett | 11-4 | Qualifying | Embassy World Championship |
|  | v Miles | 4-13 | 1st round | Embassy World Championship |
|  | v Bennett | 5-1 | 1st round | Super Crystalate UK Championship |
|  | v Williams | 5-4 | 2nd round | Super Crystalate UK Championship |
|  | v Mountjoy | 4-5 | Quarter-final | Super Crystalate UK Championship |
| **1978** | v Williams | 9-3 | Qualifying | Embassy World Championship |
|  | v Charlton | 12-13 | 1st round | Embassy World Championship |
|  | v Bennett | 9-4 | Qualifying | Coral UK Championship |
|  | v Reardon | 9-6 | 1st round | Coral UK Championship |
|  | v Miles | 1-9 | Quarter-final | Coral UK Championship |
| **1979** | v Jim Charlton | 9-3 | Prelim | Embassy World Championship |
|  | v Virgo | 8-9 | Qualifying | Embassy World Championship |
|  | v Andrewartha | 9-4 | 2nd round | Coral UK Championship |
|  | v Dennis Taylor | 8-9 | 3rd round | Coral UK Championship |
| **1980** | v Jack Rea | 9-1 | Qualifying | Embassy World Championship |
|  | v Werbeniuk | 9-10 | 1st round | Embassy World Championship |
|  | v Meadowcroft | 9-1 | 1st round | Coral UK Championship |
|  | v Higgins | 7-9 | 2nd round | Coral UK Championship |
| **1981** | v Wildman | 9-2 | 1st round | John Courage English |
|  | v Dunning | 9-0 | 2nd round | John Courage English |
|  | v Meo | 8-9 | Semi-final | John Courage English |
|  | v Morra | 9-5 | Qualifying | Embassy World Championship |
|  | v Greaves | 9-3 | Qualifying | Embassy World Championship |
|  | v Mountjoy | 6-10 | 1st round | Embassy World Championship |
|  | v Medati | 9-6 | Qualifying | Coral UK Championship |
|  | v Edmonds | 9-4 | 2nd round | Coral UK Championship |
|  | v S. Davis | 2-9 | 3rd round | Coral UK Championship |
| **1982** | v Roscoe | 9-1 | Qualifying | Embassy World Championship |
|  | v Griffiths | 10-6 | 1st round | Embassy World Championship |
|  | v Spencer | 13-5 | 2nd round | Embassy World Championship |
|  | v Higgins | 10-13 | Quarter-final | Embassy World Championship |
|  | v Reynolds | 3-5 | 1st round | Jameson International |
|  | v Demarco | 5-3 | 1st round | Professional Players Tournament |
|  | v Macleod | 4-5 | 2nd round | Professional Players Tournament |
|  | v Wilson | 7-9 | 1st round | Coral UK Championship |
|  | v Virgo | 10-3 | 1st round | Embassy World Championship |
|  | v Higgins | 8-13 | 2nd round | Embassy World Championship |
| **1983** | v Murphy | 5-2 | Qualifying | Jameson International |
|  | v Virgo | 5-2 | 1st round | Jameson International |

*Willie Thorne*

| | | | | |
|---|---|---|---|---|
| | v Reardon | 5-0 | 2nd round | Jameson International |
| | v Charlton | 0-5 | Quarter-final | Jameson International |
| | v Everton | 5-1 | 1st round | Professional Players Tournament |
| | v Spencer | 5-1 | 2nd round | Professional Players Tournament |
| | v Reardon | 5-3 | 3rd round | Professional Players Tournament |
| | v E. Hughes | 5-1 | Quarter-final | Professional Players Tournament |
| | v Knowles | 7-9 | Semi-final | Professional Players Tournament |
| | v Wildman | 9-5 | 1st round | Coral UK Championship |
| | v S. Davis | 3-9 | 2nd round | Coral UK Championship |
| 1984 | v S. Davis | 2-5 | 1st round | Tolly Cobbold Classic |
| | v Mikkelsen | 10-3 | Qualifying | Embassy World Championship |
| | v Virgo | 10-9 | 1st round | Embassy World Championship |
| | v Thorburn | 11-13 | 2nd round | Embassy World Championship |
| | v Virgo | 3-5 | Quarter-final | Winfield Australian Masters |
| | v O'Kane | 5-3 | 1st round | Jameson International |
| | v Gauvreau | 5-3 | 2nd round | Jameson International |
| | v E. Hughes | 2-5 | Quarter-final | Jameson International |
| | v Newbury | 5-2 | 1st round | Rothmans Grand Prix |
| | v Macleod | 5-3 | 2nd round | Rothmans Grand Prix |
| | v N. Foulds | 1-5 | 3rd round | Rothmans Grand Prix |
| | v Parrot | 9-7 | 1st round | Coral UK Open |
| | v Charlton | 9-7 | 2nd round | Coral UK Open |
| | v Higgins | 5-9 | Quarter-final | Coral UK Open |
| 1985 | v Foldvari | 5-2 | 1st round | Mercantile Credit Classic |
| | v Stevens | 5-1 | 2nd round | Mercantile Credit Classic |
| | v Virgo | 5-1 | Quarter-final | Mercantile Credit Classic |
| | v S. Davis | 9-8 | Semi-final | Mercantile Credit Classic |
| | **v Thorburn** | **13-8** | **Final** | **Mercantile Credit Classic** |
| | v White | 2-5 | 1st round | Benson & Hedges Masters |
| | v Dodd | 9-1 | 1st round | Tolly Cobbold English Championship |
| | v Reynolds | 6-9 | 2nd round | Tolly Cobbold English Championship |
| | v Oliver | 6-3 | 1st round | Dulux British Open |
| | v Macleod | 0-5 | 2nd round | Dulux British Open |
| | v Fagan | 6-10 | 1st round | Embassy World Championship |
| | v Parrott | 0-5 | Quarter-final | Winfield Australian Masters |
| | v Dennis Taylor | 5-3 | 1st round | Langs Scottish Masters |
| | v White | 6-2 | Semi-final | Langs Scottish Masters |
| | v Thorburn | 7-9 | Final | Langs Scottish Masters |
| | v Fowler | 5-1 | 3rd round | Goya Matchroom Trophy |
| | v Scott | 5-1 | 4th round | Goya Matchroom Trophy |
| | v Duggan | 4-5 | 5th round | Goya Matchroom Trophy |
| | v W. Jones | 0-5 | 3rd round | Rothmans Grand Prix |
| | v Browne | 9-6 | 3rd round | Coral UK Open |
| | v Virgo | 9-8 | 4th round | Coral UK Open |
| | v Thorburn | 9-7 | 5th round | Coral UK Open |
| | v Griffiths | 9-7 | Quarter-final | Coral UK Open |
| | v Dennis Taylor | 9-7 | Semi-final | Coral UK Open |
| | v S. Davis | 14-16 | Final | Coral UK Open |
| 1986 | v T. Jones | 3-5 | 3rd round | Mercantile Credit Classic |
| | v Reardon | 5-4 | 1st round | Benson & Hedges Masters |
| | v S. Davis | 4-5 | Quarter-final | Benson & Hedges Masters |
| | v Medati | 9-2 | 3rd round | Tolly Cobbold English Championship |
| | v Reynolds | 8-9 | 4th round | Tolly Cobbold English Championship |
| | v Dodd | 5-2 | 3rd round | Dulux British Open |
| | v Mans | 5-1 | 4th round | Dulux British Open |
| | v Stevens | 5-4 | 5th round | Dulux British Open |
| | v Griffiths | 5-4 | Quarter-final | Dulux British Open |
| | v Virgo | 9-4 | Semi-final | Dulux British Open |
| | v S. Davis | 7-12 | Final | Dulux British Open |
| | v Griffiths | 5-2 | 1st round | Benson & Hedges Irish Masters |
| | v Dennis Taylor | 5-2 | Quarter-final | Benson & Hedges Irish Masters |
| | v Thorburn | 6-4 | Semi-final | Benson & Hedges Irish Masters |
| | v White | 5-9 | Final | Benson & Hedges Irish Masters |

| | | | |
|---|---|---|---|
| v Hendry | 10-8 | 1st round | Embassy World Championship |
| v J. Campbell | 13-9 | 2nd round | Embassy World Championship |
| v Thorburn | 6-13 | Quarter-final | Embassy World Championship |
| v S. Davis | 5-2 | Semi-final | Camus Hong Kong Masters |
| **v Dennis Taylor** | **8-3** | **Final** | **Camus Hong Kong Masters** |
| v N. Foulds | 6-3 | 1st round | Matchroom Trophy |
| v Dennis Taylor | 6-5 | Semi-final | Matchroom Trophy |
| **v S. Davis** | **10-9** | **Final** | **Matchroom Trophy** |
| v Drago | 2-5 | 3rd round | BCE International |
| v Duggan | 5-0 | 3rd round | Rothmans Grand Prix |
| v King | 5-2 | 4th round | Rothmans Grand Prix |
| v N. Foulds | 3-5 | 5th round | Rothmans Grand Prix |
| v Dennis Taylor | 5-4 | 1st round | BCE Canadian Masters |
| v Knowles | 8-7 | Semi-final | BCE Canadian Masters |
| v S. Davis | 3-9 | Final | BCE Canadian Masters |
| v Murphy | 9-4 | 3rd round | Tennents UK Open |
| v Grace | 9-1 | 4th round | Tennents UK Open |
| v Drago | 5-9 | 5th round | Tennents UK Open |
| **1987** v Spencer | 3-5 | 3rd round | Mercantile Credit Classic |
| v Stevens | 5-3 | 1st round | Benson & Hedges Masters |
| v Thorburn | 3-5 | Quarter-final | Benson & Hedges Masters |
| v B. Harris | 6-2 | 3rd round | Tolly Ales English Championship |
| v Martin | 6-3 | 4th round | Tolly Ales English Championship |
| v Reynolds | 6-4 | Quarter-final | Tolly Ales English Championship |
| v Meo | 3-9 | Semi-final | Tolly Ales English Championship |
| v R. Harris | 5-1 | 3rd round | Dulux British Open |
| v Duggan | 5-2 | 4th round | Dulux British Open |
| v N. Foulds | 2-5 | 5th round | Dulux British Open |
| v Stevens | 5-1 | 1st round | Benson & Hedges Irish Masters |
| v White | 5-4 | Quarter-final | Benson & Hedges Irish Masters |
| v Dennis Taylor | 6-2 | Semi-final | Benson & Hedges Irish Masters |
| v S. Davis | 1-9 | Final | Benson & Hedges Irish Masters |
| v Hendry | 7-10 | 1st round | Embassy World Championship |
| v John Rea | 5-3 | 3rd round | Fidelity International |
| v Virgo | 4-5 | 4th round | Fidelity International |
| v Bear | 5-1 | 3rd round | Rothmans Grand Prix |
| v Bales | 5-2 | 4th round | Rothmans Grand Prix |
| v Drago | 5-2 | 5th round | Rothmans Grand Prix |
| v P. Francisco | 3-5 | Quarter-final | Rothmans Grand Prix |
| v N. Foulds | 6-5 | Semi-final | Matchroom Trophy |
| v Dennis Taylor | 3-10 | Final | Matchroom Trophy |
| v Oliver | 9-3 | 3rd round | Tennents UK Open |
| v Murphy | 9-4 | 4th round | Tennents UK Open |
| v O'Kane | 9-7 | 5th round | Tennents UK Open |
| v Thorburn | 9-8 | Quarter-final | Tennents UK Open |
| v S. Davis | 2-9 | Semi-final | Tennents UK Open |
| **1988** v Bradley | 5-1 | 3rd round | Mercantile Credit Classic |
| v West | 2-5 | 4th round | Mercantile Credit Classic |
| v Johnson | 4-5 | 1st round | Benson & Hedges Masters |
| v Marshall | 6-3 | 3rd round | English Championship |
| v Virgo | 6-0 | 4th round | English Championship |
| v N. Foulds | 2-6 | Quarter-final | English Championship |
| v Wych | 5-1 | 3rd round | MIM Britannia British Open |
| v C. Wilson | 5-3 | 4th round | MIM Britannia British Open |
| v Thorburn | 2-5 | 5th round | MIM Britannia British Open |
| v Knowles | 3-5 | 1st round | Benson & Hedges Irish Masters |
| v P. Francisco | 10-6 | 1st round | Embassy World Championship |
| v Griffiths | 9-13 | 2nd round | Embassy World Championship |
| v N. Foulds | 4-5 | Semi-final | LEP Hong Kong Masters |
| v Chambers | 5-2 | 3rd round | Fidelity International |
| v Drago | 5-2 | 4th round | Fidelity International |
| v White | 4-5 | 5th round | Fidelity International |
| v S. Davis | 2-5 | Semi-final | Dubai Duty Free Masters |

|  |  | v S. Davis | 2-6 | 1st round | LEP Matchroom Championship |
|--|--|------------|-----|-----------|-----------------------------|
|  |  | v Gary Wilkinson | 3-5 | 3rd round | Rothmans Grand Prix |
|  |  | v Fitzmaurice | 5-0 | 3rd round | BCE Canadian Masters |
|  |  | v Mountjoy | 4-5 | 4th round | BCE Canadian Masters |
|  |  | v D. Gilbert | 9-3 | 3rd round | Tennents UK Open |
|  |  | v Stevens | 9-3 | 4th round | Tennents UK Open |
|  |  | v Hendry | 4-9 | 5th round | Tennents UK Open |
|  |  | v Hallett | 8-9 | 1st round | Everest World Matchplay |
| 1989 |  | v J. Smith | 5-1 | 3rd round | Mercantile Credit Classic |
|  |  | v O'Kane | 5-3 | 4th round | Mercantile Credit Classic |
|  |  | v Griffiths | 5-1 | 5th round | Mercantile Credit Classic |
|  |  | v Clark | 5-4 | Quarter-final | Mercantile Credit Classic |
|  |  | v W. Jones | 4-9 | Semi-final | Mercantile Credit Classic |
|  |  | v Hendry | 2-5 | 1st round | Benson and Hedges Masters |
|  |  | v Oliver | 5-0 | 3rd round | European Open |
|  |  | v Higgins | 5-1 | 4th round | European Open |
|  |  | v White | 3-5 | 5th round | European Open |
|  |  | v Clark | 5-1 | 3rd round | English Championship |
|  |  | v Roe | 5-1 | 4th round | English Championship |
|  |  | v N. Foulds | 3-5 | Quarter-final | English Championship |
|  |  | v Gary Wilkinson | 5-1 | 3rd round | Anglian British Open |
|  |  | v Marshall | 5-1 | 4th round | Anglian British Open |
|  |  | v S. Davis | 0-5 | 5th round | Anglian British Open |
|  |  | v Browne | 10-5 | 1st round | Embassy World Championship |
|  |  | v Hendry | 4-13 | 2nd round | Embassy World Championship |

## PAUL THORNLEY (Canada)

**Born** 15.4.44. **Turned professional** 1979. **World ranking** 111 (124).

| 1983 | v Caggianello | 7-9 | 2nd round | Canadian Championship |
|------|---------------|-----|-----------|-----------------------|
| 1984 | v Fisher | 8-10 | Qualifying | Embassy World Championship |
|  | v Cripsey | 3-5 | Qualifying | Jameson International |
|  | v Williamson | 2-5 | Qualifying | Rothmans Grand Prix |
| 1985 | v Chaperon | 1-5 | 1st round | Canadian Championship |
|  | v Mienie | 10-3 | Qualifying | Embassy World Championship |
|  | v Fagan | 10-7 | Qualifying | Embassy World Championship |
|  | v Murphy | 3-10 | Qualifying | Embassy World Championship |
| 1986 | v Morra | 6-4 | 1st round | Canadian Championship |
|  | v Stevens | 2-6 | 2nd round | Canadian Championship |
| 1987 | v Greaves | 6-10 | Qualifying | Embassy World Championship |
|  | v Watson | 4-6 | 1st round | Canadian Championship |
| 1988 | v V. Harris | 5-4 | 1st round | MIM Britannia British Open |
|  | v Wych | 1-5 | 2nd round | MIM Britannia British Open |
|  | v Rowswell | 7-10 | Qualifying | Embassy World Championship |
| 1989 | v Demarco | 10-3 | Qualifying | Embassy World Championship |
|  | v Bradley | 10-7 | Qualifying | Embassy World Championship |
|  | v Werbeniuk | *wo* | Qualifying | Embassy World Championship |
|  | v D. Gilbert | 4-10 | Qualifying | Embassy World Championship |

## JIMMY VAN RENSBERG (South Africa)

**Born** 24.10.31. **Turned professional** 1978. **World ranking** 103 (87). **Amateur career** 11 times South African champion between 1953 and 1973. **Best professional performance** Last 32 1986 Mercantile Credit Classic.

| 1979 | v Meadowcroft | 7-9 | Prelim | Embassy World Championship |
|------|---------------|-----|--------|-----------------------------|
| 1980 | v Meo | 1-9 | Qualifying | Embassy World Championship |
| 1984 | v V. Harris | 10-7 | Qualifying | Embassy World Championship |
|  | v Edmonds | 10-9 | Qualifying | Embassy World Championship |

|   | v S. Francisco | 3-10 | Qualifying | Embassy World Championship |
|---|---|---|---|---|
| 1985 | v Longworth | 10-7 | Qualifying | Embassy World Championship |
|   | v Gauvreau | 9-10 | Qualifying | Embassy World Championship |
|   | v Scott | 4-5 | 2nd round | Goya Matchroom Trophy |
|   | v E. McLaughlin | 5-4 | 2nd round | Rothmans Grand Prix |
|   | v J. Campbell | 4-5 | 3rd round | Rothmans Grand Prix |
|   | v Edmonds | 5-9 | 2nd round | Coral UK Open |
| 1986 | v W. Jones | 5-4 | 2nd round | Mercantile Credit Classic |
|   | v Parrott | 5-3 | 3rd round | Mercantile Credit Classic |
|   | v S. Davis | 1-5 | 4th round | Mercantile Credit Classic |
|   | v Wych | 0-5 | 2nd round | Dulux British Open |
|   | v Williamson | 10-9 | Qualifying | Embassy World Championship |
|   | v Sinclair | 10-2 | Qualifying | Embassy World Championship |
|   | v J. Campbell | 6-10 | Qualifying | Embassy World Championship |
|   | v Mienie | 7-1 | 2nd round | South African Championship |
|   | v Ellis | 2-8 | Semi-final | South African Championship |
|   | v Kearney | 5-3 | 2nd round | BCE International |
|   | v West | 3-5 | 3rd round | BCE International |
|   | v Roe | 3-5 | 2nd round | Rothmans Grand Prix |
|   | v Roe | 6-9 | 2nd round | Tennents UK Open |
| 1987 | v N. Gilbert | 5-3 | 2nd round | Mercantile Credit Classic |
|   | v S. Francisco | 4-5 | 3rd round | Mercantile Credit Classic |
|   | v Morra | 1-5 | 2nd round | Dulux British Open |
|   | v J. McLaughlin | 10-6 | Qualifying | Embassy World Championship |
|   | v T. Jones | 0-10 | Qualifying | Embassy World Championship |
|   | v O'Kane | 3-5 | 2nd round | Fidelity International |
|   | v Murphy | 5-4 | 2nd round | Rothmans Grand Prix |
|   | v Charlton | 1-5 | 3rd round | Rothmans Grand Prix |
|   | v Whitthread | 9-5 | 1st round | Tennents UK Open |
|   | v Reardon | 7-9 | 2nd round | Tennents UK Open |
| 1988 | v Grace | 5-3 | 2nd round | Mercantile Credit Classic |
|   | v Griffiths | 2-5 | 3rd round | Mercantile Credit Classic |
|   | v Reardon | 3-5 | 2nd round | MIM Britannia British Open |
|   | v Meakin | 4-5 | 1st round | Fidelity International |
|   | v Robidoux | 2-5 | 1st round | Rothmans Grand Prix |
|   | v Fitzmaurice | 3-5 | 1st round | BCE Canadian Masters |
|   | v Johnston-Allen | 4-9 | 1st round | Tennents UK Open |
| 1989 | v J. Smith | 4-5 | 1st round | Mercantile Credit Classic |
|   | v Marshall | 1-5 | 1st round | European Open |
|   | v Fowler | 1-5 | 2nd round | Anglian British Open |
|   | v A. Harris | 7-10 | Qualifying | Embassy World Championship |

## JOHN VIRGO (England)

**Born** 4.3.46. **Turned professional** 1976. **World ranking** 13 (15). **Best professional performance** Winner 1979 Coral UK Championship.

| 1977 | v Andrewartha | 11-1 | Prelim | Embassy World Championship |
|---|---|---|---|---|
|   | v Dunning | 11-6 | Qualifying | Embassy World Championship |
|   | v Spencer | 9-13 | 1st round | Embassy World Championship |
|   | v Dennis Taylor | 5-2 | 2nd round | Super Crystalate UK Championship |
|   | v Miles | 5-2 | Quarter-final | Super Crystalate UK Championship |
|   | v Fagan | 8-9 | Semi-final | Super Crystalate UK Championship |
| 1978 | v F. Davis | 8-9 | Qualifying | Embassy World Championship |
|   | v Edmonds | 9-4 | Qualifying | Coral UK Championship |
|   | v Pulman | 9-3 | 1st round | Coral UK Championship |
|   | v David Taylor | 2-9 | Quarter-final | Coral UK Championship |
| 1979 | v Parkin | 9-0 | Prelim | Embassy World Championship |
|   | v Thorne | 9-8 | Qualifying | Embassy World Championship |
|   | v Thorburn | 13-10 | 1st round | Embassy World Championship |
|   | v Werbeniuk | 13-9 | Quarter-final | Embassy World Championship |
|   | v Dennis Taylor | 12-19 | Semi-final | Embassy World Championship |

*John Virgo*

| | | | | |
|---|---|---|---|---|
| | v Meo | 9-6 | 3rd round | Coral UK Championship |
| | v S. Davis | 9-7 | Quarter-final | Coral UK Championship |
| | v Dennis Taylor | 9-4 | Semi-final | Coral UK Championship |
| | **v Griffiths** | **14-13** | **Final** | **Coral UK Championship** |
| 1980 | v Thorburn | 3-5 | 1st round | Benson & Hedges Masters |
| | v Meadowcroft | 10-2 | 1st round | Embassy World Championship |
| | v Charlton | 12-13 | 2nd round | Embassy World Championship |
| | v Meo | 1-9 | 2nd round | Coral UK Championship |
| 1981 | v Meo | 6-9 | 1st round | John Courage English |
| | v Meo | 6-10 | 1st round | Embassy World Championship |
| | v Knowles | 5-2 | 2nd round | Jameson International |
| | v Reardon | 5-3 | 3rd round | Jameson International |
| | v Dennis Taylor | 2-5 | Quarter-final | Jameson International |
| | v White | 6-9 | 2nd round | Coral UK Championship |
| 1982 | v Hallett | 10-4 | 1st round | Embassy World Championship |
| | v Reardon | 8-13 | 2nd round | Embassy World Championship |
| | v V. Harris | 5-2 | Qualifying | Jameson International |
| | v Charlton | 5-4 | 1st round | Jameson International |
| | v Spencer | 5-4 | 2nd round | Jameson International |
| | v Dennis Taylor | 5-3 | Quarter-final | Jameson International |
| | v David Taylor | 5-9 | Semi-final | Jameson International |
| | v Black | 5-2 | 1st round | Professional Players Tournament |
| | v Hallett | 5-2 | 2nd round | Professional Players Tournament |
| | v Spencer | 5-1 | 3rd round | Professional Players Tournament |
| | v Johnson | 5-1 | Quarter-final | Professional Players Tournament |
| | v White | 4-10 | Semi-final | Professional Players Tournament |
| | v Kelly | 9-2 | 1st round | Coral UK Championship |
| | v Mountjoy | 9-5 | 2nd round | Coral UK Championship |
| | v Meo | 6-9 | Quarter-final | Coral UK Championship |
| 1983 | v Charlton | 2-5 | 1st round | Lada Classic |
| | v Mountjoy | 1-5 | 1st round | Benson & Hedges Masters |
| | v Murphy | 10-8 | Qualifying | Embassy World Championship |
| | v Thorne | 3-10 | 1st round | Embassy World Championship |
| | v Thorne | 2-5 | 1st round | Jameson International |
| | v French | 5-4 | 1st round | Professional Players Tournament |
| | v Wilson | 2-5 | 2nd round | Professional Players Tournament |
| | v Johnson | 6-9 | 1st round | Coral UK Championship |
| 1984 | v Wildman | 2-5 | Qualifying | Lada Classic |
| | v Reardon | 3-5 | 1st round | Benson & Hedges Masters |
| | v Thorburn | 9-10 | 1st round | Embassy World Championship |
| | v Thorne | 5-3 | Quarter-final | Winfield Australian Masters |
| | v Meo | 6-2 | Semi-final | Winfield Australian Masters |
| | v Knowles | 3-7 | Final | Winfield Australian Masters |
| | v F. Davis | 5-3 | Qualifying | Jameson International |
| | v Thorburn | 5-0 | 1st round | Jameson International |
| | v S. Francisco | 2-5 | 2nd round | Jameson International |
| | v Bradley | 5-0 | 1st round | Rothmans Grand Prix |
| | v Dennis Taylor | 3-5 | 2nd round | Rothmans Grand Prix |
| | v King | 4-9 | Qualifying | Coral UK Open |
| 1985 | v Bales | 5-1 | Qualifying | Mercantile Credit Classic |
| | v Werbeniuk | 5-2 | 1st round | Mercantile Credit Classic |
| | v Macleod | 5-0 | 2nd round | Mercantile Credit Classic |
| | v Thorne | 1-5 | Quarter-final | Mercantile Credit Classic |
| | v Darrington | 9-0 | 1st round | Tolly Cobbold English Championship |
| | v Johnson | 9-4 | 2nd round | Tolly Cobbold English Championship |
| | v S. Davis | 2-9 | Quarter-final | Tolly Cobbold English Championship |
| | v P. Francisco | 6-2 | 1st round | Dulux British Open |
| | v S. Davis | 2-5 | 2nd round | Dulux British Open |
| | v Wych | 10-4 | Qualifying | Embassy World Championship |
| | v Meo | 6-10 | 1st round | Embassy World Championship |
| | v Meo | 3-5 | Quarter-final | Winfield Australian Masters |
| | v Miles | 5-2 | 3rd round | Goya Matchroom Trophy |
| | v S. Davis | 1-5 | 4th round | Goya Matchroom Trophy |

|  |  |  |  |
|---|---|---|---|
| v P. Francisco | 4-5 | 3rd round | Rothmans Grand Prix |
| v W. Jones | 9-7 | 3rd round | Coral UK Open |
| v Thorne | 8-9 | 4th round | Coral UK Open |
| 1986 v Gibson | 5-3 | 3rd round | Mercantile Credit Classic |
| v White | 2-5 | 4th round | Mercantile Credit Classic |
| v T. Jones | 9-7 | 3rd round | Tolly Cobbold English Championship |
| v Parrott | 9-6 | 4th round | Tolly Cobbold English Championship |
| v S. Davis | 2-9 | Quarter-final | Tolly Cobbold English Championship |
| v Fowler | 5-1 | 3rd round | Dulux British Open |
| v John Rea | 5-0 | 4th round | Dulux British Open |
| v Charlton | 5-4 | 5th round | Dulux British Open |
| v Meo | 5-3 | Quarter-final | Dulux British Open |
| v Thorne | 4-9 | Semi-final | Dulux British Open |
| v White | 7-10 | 1st round | Embassy World Championship |
| v Newbury | 5-4 | 3rd round | BCE International |
| v S. Francisco | 0-5 | 4th round | BCE International |
| v Fagan | 5-2 | 3rd round | Rothmans Grand Prix |
| v Dennis Taylor | 3-5 | 4th round | Rothmans Grand Prix |
| v Miles | 9-7 | 3rd round | Tennents UK Open |
| v Drago | 6-9 | 4th round | Tennents UK Open |
| 1987 v M. Bennett | 5-3 | 3rd round | Mercantile Credit Classic |
| v S. Davis | 2-5 | 4th round | Mercantile Credit Classic |
| v Medati | 6-1 | 3rd round | Tolly Ales English Championship |
| v Parrott | 2-6 | 4th round | Tolly Ales English Championship |
| v Morra | 5-3 | 3rd round | Dulux British Open |
| v S. Davis | 5-4 | 4th round | Dulux British Open |
| v Wilson | 5-2 | 5th round | Dulux British Open |
| v N. Foulds | 3-5 | Quarter-final | Dulux British Open |
| v T. Jones | 10-9 | Qualifying | Embassy World Championship |
| v N. Foulds | 4-10 | 1st round | Embassy World Championship |
| v Murphy | 5-1 | 3rd round | Fidelity International |
| v Thorne | 5-4 | 4th round | Fidelity International |
| v Knowles | 5-2 | 5th round | Fidelity International |
| v S. Davis | 2-5 | Quarter-final | Fidelity International |
| v Gauvreau | 5-1 | 3rd round | Rothmans Grand Prix |
| v Wilson | 3-5 | 4th round | Rothmans Grand Prix |
| v F. Davis | 9-4 | 3rd round | Tennents UK Open |
| v Thorburn | 6-9 | 4th round | Tennents UK Open |
| 1988 v Rigitano | 5-2 | 3rd round | Mercantile Credit Classic |
| v N. Foulds | 5-3 | 4th round | Mercantile Credit Classic |
| v Parrott | 0-5 | 5th round | Mercantile Credit Classic |
| v Dodd | 6-3 | 3rd round | English Championship |
| v Thorne | 0-6 | 4th round | English Championship |
| v Murphy | 5-1 | 3rd round | MIM Britannia British Open |
| v Parrott | 1-5 | 4th round | MIM Britannia British Open |
| v Duggan | 10-5 | Qualifying | Embassy World Championship |
| v S. Davis | 8-10 | 1st round | Embassy World Championship |
| v J. McLaughlin | 5-0 | 3rd round | Fidelity International |
| v Spencer | 1-5 | 4th round | Fidelity International |
| v Robidoux | 1-5 | 3rd round | Rothmans Grand Prix |
| v Medati | 5-1 | 3rd round | BCE Canadian Masters |
| v Newbury | 5-2 | 4th round | BCE Canadian Masters |
| v Parrott | 4-5 | 5th round | BCE Canadian Masters |
| v Rowswell | 9-3 | 3rd round | Tennents UK Open |
| v O'Kane | 9-8 | 4th round | Tennents UK Open |
| v Knowles | 9-3 | 5th round | Tennents UK Open |
| v Mountjoy | 8-9 | Quarter-final | Tennents UK Open |
| 1989 v Dodd | 5-2 | 3rd round | Mercantile Credit Classic |
| v Chaperon | 5-1 | 4th round | Mercantile Credit Classic |
| v Thorburn | 3-5 | 5th round | Mercantile Credit Classic |
| v White | 2-5 | 1st round | Benson and Hedges Masters |
| v Reardon | 5-3 | 3rd round | European Open |
| v Edwards | 5-3 | 4th round | European Open |

| v Charlton | 4-5 | 5th round | European Open |
|---|---|---|---|
| v Gary Wilkinson | 3-5 | 3rd round | English Championship |
| v Fowler | 5-2 | 3rd round | Anglian British Open |
| v Clark | 1-5 | 4th round | Anglian British Open |
| v D. Morgan | 10-4 | 1st round | Embassy World Championship |
| v White | 12-13 | 2nd round | Embassy World Championship |

## PAUL WATCHORN (Republic of Ireland)
### Born 19.7.58. Turned professional 1982. World ranking 114 (98).

| | | | | |
|---|---|---|---|---|
| **1983** | v Johnson | 0-10 | Qualifying | Embassy World Championship |
| | v Morra | 3-5 | Qualifying | Jameson International |
| | v Parrott | 0-5 | Qualifying | Professional Players Tournament |
| **1984** | v Donnelly | 7-10 | Qualifying | Embassy World Championship |
| | v W. Jones | 0-5 | Qualifying | Jameson International |
| | v Dennis Taylor | 1-5 | 1st round | Rothmans Grand Prix |
| | v B. Harris | 9-7 | Qualifying | Coral UK Open |
| | v Everton | 9-6 | Qualifying | Coral UK Open |
| | v Fisher | 5-9 | Qualifying | Coral UK Open |
| **1985** | v D. Hughes | 5-0 | Prelim | Mercantile Credit Classic |
| | v Mikkelsen | 5-1 | Qualifying | Mercantile Credit Classic |
| | v Donnelly | 1-5 | Qualifying | Mercantile Credit Classic |
| | v Fitzmaurice | 6-1 | Qualifying | Dulux British Open |
| | v E. Hughes | 4-6 | 1st round | Dulux British Open |
| | v Kelly | 2-6 | Qualifying | Irish Championship |
| | v Hines | 4-10 | Qualifying | Embassy World Championship |
| | v Agrawal | 2-5 | 1st round | Goya Matchroom Trophy |
| | v Drago | 2-5 | 1st round | Rothmans Grand Prix |
| | v Sheehan | 9-7 | 1st round | Coral UK Open |
| **1986** | v Greaves | 4-5 | 1st round | Mercantile Credit Classic |
| | v Wilkinson | 4-5 | 1st round | Dulux British Open |
| | v Longworth | 7-10 | Qualifying | Embassy World Championship |
| | v J. McLaughlin | 0-5 | 1st round | Strongbow Irish Championship |
| | v Bear | 1-5 | 1st round | BCE International |
| | v Darrington | 5-2 | 1st round | Rothmans Grand Prix |
| | v Drago | 3-5 | 2nd round | Rothmans Grand Prix |
| | v Kelly | 9-8 | 1st round | Tennents UK Open |
| | v Scott | 7-9 | 2nd round | Tennents UK Open |
| **1987** | v Donnelly | 5-0 | 1st round | Mercantile Credit Classic |
| | v Duggan | 1-5 | 2nd round | Mercantile Credit Classic |
| | v Dunning | 5-2 | 1st round | Dulux British Open |
| | v Cripsey | 4-5 | 2nd round | Dulux British Open |
| | v G. Foulds | 6-10 | Qualifying | Embassy World Championship |
| | v E. Hughes | 2-5 | 1st round | Matchroom Irish Championship |
| | v Oliver | 5-3 | 1st round | Fidelity International |
| | v Fowler | 1-5 | 2nd round | Fidelity International |
| | v Fisher | 4-5 | 1st round | Rothmans Grand Prix |
| | v Darrington | 9-2 | 1st round | Tennents UK Open |
| | v Bradley | 9-5 | 2nd round | Tennents UK Open |
| | v Meo | 1-9 | 3rd round | Tennents UK Open |
| **1988** | v Roscoe | 2-5 | 1st round | Mercantile Credit Classic |
| | v E. Hughes | 5-2 | 1st round | Irish Championship |
| | v J. McLaughlin | 5-6 | Quarter-final | Irish Championship |
| | v Morra | 1-5 | 1st round | MIM Britannia British Open |
| | v M. Gibson | 10-7 | Qualifying | Embassy World Championship |
| | v King | 4-10 | Qualifying | Embassy World Championship |
| | v B. Harris | 5-2 | 1st round | Fidelity International |
| | v Chappel | 4-5 | 2nd round | Fidelity International |
| | v Medati | 2-5 | 1st round | Rothmans Grand Prix |
| | v Miles | 5-2 | 1st round | BCE Canadian Masters |
| | v Macleod | 1-5 | 2nd round | BCE Canadian Masters |
| | v Miles | 6-9 | 1st round | Tennents UK Open |

| 1989 | v Glen Wilkinson | 3-5 | 1st round | Mercantile Credit Classic |
| | v B. Harris | 5-4 | 1st round | European Open |
| | v J. Campbell | 1-5 | 2nd round | European Open |
| | v Burke | 5-4 | 1st round | Irish Championship |
| | v Higgins | 2-5 | Quarter-final | Irish Championship |
| | v John Rea | 3-5 | 1st round | Anglian British Open |
| | v Grace | 10-6 | Qualifying | Embassy World Championship |
| | v Roe | 5-10 | Qualifying | Embassy World Championship |

## MIKE WATTERSON (England)

**Born** 26.8.42. **Turned professional** 1981. **World ranking** 110 (108). **Best professional performance:** Last 16 1983 Jameson International.

| 1981 | v Medati | 5-3 | Qualifying | Jameson International |
| | v Everton | 5-4 | Qualifying | Jameson International |
| | v Fagan | 2-5 | Qualifying | Jameson International |
| | v Bennett | 9-4 | Qualifying | Coral UK Championship |
| | v Johnson | 3-9 | Qualifying | Coral UK Championship |
| 1982 | v Demarco | 9-6 | Qualifying | Embassy World Championship |
| | v Meadowcroft | 7-9 | Qualifying | Embassy World Championship |
| | v Everton | 5-1 | Qualifying | Jameson International |
| | v Fagan | 5-1 | Qualifying | Jameson International |
| | v Stevens | 3-5 | 1st round | Jameson International |
| | v Donnelly | 5-4 | 1st round | Professional Players Tournament |
| | v Griffiths | 2-5 | 2nd round | Professional Players Tournament |
| | v B. Harris | 3-9 | Qualifying | Coral UK Championship |
| 1983 | v J. Campbell | 6-10 | Qualifying | Embassy World Championship |
| | v Demarco | 5-3 | Qualifying | Jameson International |
| | v Mans | 5-4 | Qualifying | Jameson International |
| | v Meo | 5-3 | 1st round | Jameson International |
| | v S. Davis | 0-5 | 2nd round | Jameson International |
| | v Higgins | 5-2 | 1st round | Professional Players Tournament |
| | v Martin | 4-5 | 2nd round | Professional Players Tournament |
| | v Everton | 9-6 | Qualifying | Coral UK Championship |
| | v F. Davis | 9-6 | Qualifying | Coral UK Championship |
| | v Mountjoy | 2-9 | 1st round | Coral UK Championship |
| 1984 | v Bennett | 10-5 | Qualifying | Embassy World Championship |
| | v King | 8-10 | Qualifying | Embassy World Championship |
| | v Black | 3-5 | Qualifying | Jameson International |
| | v W. Jones | 3-5 | Qualifying | Rothmans Grand Prix |
| | v Murphy | 4-9 | Qualifying | Coral UK Open |
| 1985 | v Edmonds | 2-5 | Qualifying | Mercantile Credit Classic |
| | v Kearney | 4-6 | Qualifying | Dulux British Open |
| | v W. Jones | 5-10 | Qualifying | Embassy World Championship |
| | v Fitzmaurice | 2-5 | 2nd round | Goya Matchroom Trophy |
| | v Caggianello | 5-1 | 2nd round | Rothmans Grand Prix |
| | v Williams | 2-5 | 3rd round | Rothmans Grand Prix |
| | v Jim Bear | 0-9 | 2nd round | Coral UK Open |
| 1986 | v Jenkins | 5-2 | 2nd round | Mercantile Credit Classic |
| | v Williams | 0-5 | 3rd round | Mercantile Credit Classic |
| | v G. Foulds | 1-9 | 2nd round | Tolly Cobbold English Championship |
| | v Mikkelsen | 10-2 | Qualifying | Embassy World Championship |
| | v Dodd | 1-10 | Qualifying | Embassy World Championship |
| | v Wright | 1-5 | 1st round | BCE International |
| | v M. Bennett | 1-5 | 1st round | Rothmans Grand Prix |
| | v Burke | 9-0 | 1st round | Tennents UK Open |
| | v Black | 9-3 | 2nd round | Tennents UK Open |
| | v P. Francisco | 4-9 | 3rd round | Tennents UK Open |
| 1987 | v Rowswell | 1-5 | 1st round | Mercantile Credit Classic |
| | v Roe | 3-5 | 1st round | Dulux British Open |
| | v James | 2-10 | Qualifying | Embassy World Championship |

| | v Anderson | 3-5 | 1st round | Fidelity International |
|---|---|---|---|---|
| | v Jack Rea | 6-9 | 1st round | Tennents UK Open |
| 1988 | v Chambers | 3-10 | Qualifying | Embassy World Championship |
| | v Kearney | 1-5 | 1st round | Fidelity International |
| | v Donnelly | 5-0 | 1st round | Rothmans Grand Prix |
| | v M. Bennett | 5-3 | 2nd round | Rothmans Grand Prix |
| | v Griffiths | 3-5 | 3rd round | Rothmans Grand Prix |
| | v Rigitano | 5-3 | 1st round | BCE Canadian Masters |
| | v Martin | 1-5 | 2nd round | BCE Canadian Masters |
| | v Kearney | 3-9 | 1st round | Tennents UK Open |
| 1989 | v Rigitano | 5-4 | 1st round | Mercantile Credit Classic |
| | v J. McLaughlin | 3-5 | 2nd round | Mercantile Credit Classic |
| | v Roscoe | 4-5 | 1st round | European Open |
| | v Edwards | 0-5 | 1st round | English Championship |
| | v Lawlor | 0-5 | 1st round | Anglian British Open |
| | v V. Harris | 5-10 | Qualifying | Embassy World Championship |

## BARRY WEST (England)

**Born** 24.10.58. **Turned professional** 1985. **World ranking** 21 (26). **Best professional performances** Quarter-finals 1988 Tennents UK Open, 1988 Fidelity International, 1985 Tennents UK Open.

| | v Hendry | 4-5 | 1st round | Goya Matchroom Trophy |
|---|---|---|---|---|
| 1985 | v Hendry | 4-5 | 1st round | Goya Matchroom Trophy |
| | v Meadowcroft | 5-2 | 2nd round | Rothmans Grand Prix |
| | v Dennis Taylor | 1-5 | 3rd round | Rothmans Grand Prix |
| | v Roscoe | 9-5 | 2nd round | Coral UK Open |
| | v E. Hughes | 9-3 | 3rd round | Coral UK Open |
| | v Mountjoy | 9-4 | 4th round | Coral UK Open |
| | v Macleod | 9-4 | 5th round | Coral UK Open |
| | v S. Davis | 1-9 | Quarter-final | Coral UK Open |
| 1986 | v Darrington | 5-0 | 1st round | Mercantile Credit Classic |
| | v Meadowcroft | 5-0 | 2nd round | Mercantile Credit Classic |
| | v Wildman | 5-2 | 3rd round | Mercantile Credit Classic |
| | v Meo | 1-5 | 4th round | Mercantile Credit Classic |
| | v Gilbert | 8-9 | 1st round | Tolly Cobbold English Championship |
| | v Bennett | 5-1 | 1st round | Dulux British Open |
| | v E. McLaughlin | 5-3 | 2nd round | Dulux British Open |
| | v J. Campbell | 4-5 | 3rd round | Dulux British Open |
| | v Dunning | 10-3 | Qualifying | Embassy World Championship |
| | v Donnelly | 10-5 | Qualifying | Embassy World Championship |
| | v Werbeniuk | 8-10 | Qualifying | Embassy World Championship |
| | v Van Rensberg | 5-3 | 3rd round | BCE International |
| | v Griffiths | 1-5 | 4th round | BCE International |
| | v J. McLaughlin | 1-5 | 3rd round | Rothmans Grand Prix |
| | v T. Jones | 4-9 | 3rd round | Tennents UK Open |
| 1987 | v Jonik | 5-4 | 3rd round | Mercantile Credit Classic |
| | v Stevens | 5-3 | 4th round | Mercantile Credit Classic |
| | v Reynolds | 3-5 | 5th round | Mercantile Credit Classic |
| | v V. Harris | 6-3 | 3rd round | Tolly Ales English Championship |
| | v Dodd | 3-6 | 4th round | Tolly Ales English Championship |
| | v Grace | 5-2 | 3rd round | Dulux British Open |
| | v Stevens | 4-5 | 4th round | Dulux British Open |
| | v Spencer | 10-5 | Qualifying | Embassy World Championship |
| | v Reardon | 5-10 | 1st round | Embassy World Championship |
| | v Chaperon | 4-5 | 3rd round | Fidelity International |
| | v Cripsey | 3-5 | 3rd round | Rothmans Grand Prix |
| | v Gauvreau | 9-6 | 3rd round | Tennents UK Open |
| | v Johnson | 6-9 | 4th round | Tennents UK Open |
| 1988 | v Oliver | 5-3 | 3rd round | Mercantile Credit Classic |
| | v Thorne | 5-2 | 4th round | Mercantile Credit Classic |
| | v Griffiths | 2-5 | 5th round | Mercantile Credit Classic |

|      | v Greaves      | 6-5   | 3rd round    | English Championship            |
|------|----------------|-------|--------------|---------------------------------|
|      | v White        | 6-2   | 4th round    | English Championship            |
|      | v Hallett      | 6-5   | Quarter-final| English Championship            |
|      | v N. Foulds    | 6-9   | Semi-final   | English Championship            |
|      | v Dunning      | 5-0   | 3rd round    | MIM Britannia British Open      |
|      | v Williams     | 0-5   | 4th round    | MIM Britannia British Open      |
|      | v Newbury      | 10-8  | Qualifying   | Embassy World Championship      |
|      | v Mountjoy     | 6-10  | 1st round    | Embassy World Championship      |
|      | v King         | 5-4   | 3rd round    | Fidelity International          |
|      | v Dodd         | 5-3   | 4th round    | Fidelity International          |
|      | v Williams     | 5-4   | 5th round    | Fidelity International          |
|      | v White        | 2-5   | Quarter-final| Fidelity International          |
|      | v Chambers     | 5-3   | 3rd round    | Rothmans Grand Prix             |
|      | v Griffiths    | 1-5   | 4th round    | Rothmans Grand Prix             |
|      | v Duggan       | 3-5   | 3rd round    | BCE Canadian Masters            |
|      | v T. Jones     | 9-5   | 3rd round    | Tennents UK Open                |
|      | v S. Francisco | 9-4   | 4th round    | Tennents UK Open                |
|      | v M. Bennett   | 9-4   | 5th round    | Tennents UK Open                |
|      | v Griffiths    | 5-9   | Quarter-final| Tennents UK Open                |
| 1989 | v A. Harris    | 4-5   | 3rd round    | Mercantile Credit Classic       |
|      | v Macleod      | 4-5   | 3rd round    | European Open                   |
|      | v Roe          | 4-5   | 3rd round    | English Championship            |
|      | v Graham       | 5-1   | 3rd round    | Anglian British Open            |
|      | v Knowles      | 5-0   | 4th round    | Anglian British Open            |
|      | v P. Francisco | 1-5   | 5th round    | Anglian British Open            |
|      | v O'Boye       | 7-10  | Qualifying   | Embassy World Championship      |

## JIMMY WHITE (England)

**Born** 2.5.62. **Turned professional** 1980. **World ranking** 4 (2). **Amateur career** 1980 World champion, 1979 English champion. **Best professional performances** Winner 1988 BCE Canadian Masters, 1987 Dulux British Open, 1986 Rothmans Grand Prix, 1986 Mercantile Credit Classic, 1984 Benson & Hedges Masters, 1985 and 1986 Benson & Hedges Irish Masters.

|      |                   |       |              |                                   |
|------|-------------------|-------|--------------|-----------------------------------|
| 1981 | v Mikkelsen       | 9-4   | Qualifying   | Embassy World Championship        |
|      | v Meadowcroft     | 9-8   | Qualifying   | Embassy World Championship        |
|      | v S. Davis        | 8-10  | 1st round    | Embassy World Championship        |
|      | v Reardon         | 5-4   | Quarter-final| Langs Supreme Scottish Masters    |
|      | v S. Davis        | 6-5   | Semi-final   | Langs Supreme Scottish Masters    |
|      | **v Thorburn**    | **9-4** | **Final**  | **Langs Supreme Scottish Masters**|
|      | v Williams        | 1-5   | 1st round    | Jameson International             |
|      | v Thorburn        | 5-2   | 1st round    | Northern Ireland Classic         |
|      | v Mountjoy        | 9-8   | Semi-final   | Northern Ireland Classic         |
|      | **v S. Davis**    | **11-9** | **Final** | **Northern Ireland Classic**     |
|      | v Everton         | 9-4   | Qualifying   | Coral UK Championship            |
|      | v Virgo           | 9-6   | 2nd round    | Coral UK Championship            |
|      | v Dennis Taylor   | 9-5   | 3rd round    | Coral UK Championship            |
|      | v Reardon         | 9-8   | Quarter-final| Coral UK Championship            |
|      | v S. Davis        | 0-9   | Semi-final   | Coral UK Championship            |
| 1982 | v Charlton        | 4-5   | 1st round    | Benson & Hedges Masters          |
|      | v Wildman         | 9-4   | Qualifying   | Embassy World Championship       |
|      | v Thorburn        | 10-4  | 1st round    | Embassy World Championship       |
|      | v Mans            | 13-6  | 2nd round    | Embassy World Championship       |
|      | v Stevens         | 13-9  | Quarter-final| Embassy World Championship       |
|      | v Higgins         | 15-16 | Semi-final   | Embassy World Championship       |
|      | v Dennis Taylor   | 4-5   | 1st round    | Langs Supreme Scottish Masters   |
|      | v Meadowcroft     | 5-1   | 1st round    | Jameson International             |
|      | v Wilson          | 2-5   | 2nd round    | Jameson International             |
|      | v Wych            | 5-0   | 2nd round    | Professional Players Tournament  |
|      | v Dennis Taylor   | 5-3   | 3rd round    | Professional Players Tournament  |
|      | v Griffiths       | 5-2   | Quarter-final| Professional Players Tournament  |

| | | | | |
|---|---|---|---|---|
| | v Virgo | 10-4 | Semi-final | Professional Players Tournament |
| | v Reardon | 5-10 | Final | Professional Players Tournament |
| | v Medati | 9-7 | 1st round | Coral UK Championship |
| | v Wilson | 9-5 | 2nd round | Coral UK Championship |
| | v Reardon | 8-9 | Quarter-final | Coral UK Championship |
| 1983 | v David Taylor | 3-5 | 1st round | Lada Classic |
| | v David Taylor | 5-2 | 1st round | Benson & Hedges Masters |
| | v Reardon | 2-5 | Quarter-final | Benson & Hedges Masters |
| | v Reardon | 6-9 | Final | Yamaha International Masters |
| | v Dennis Taylor | 5-4 | 1st round | Benson & Hedges Irish Masters |
| | v Higgins | 2-5 | Quarter-final | Benson & Hedges Irish Masters |
| | v Meo | 8-10 | 1st round | Embassy World Championship |
| | v Higgins | 3-5 | 1st round | Langs Supreme Scottish Masters |
| | v Morra | 3-5 | 1st round | Jameson International |
| | v Williamson | 5-2 | 1st round | Professional Players Tournament |
| | v Johnson | 3-5 | 2nd round | Professional Players Tournament |
| | v Black | 9-1 | 1st round | Coral UK Championship |
| | v Dennis Taylor | 9-4 | 2nd round | Coral UK Championship |
| | v Reardon | 9-4 | Quarter-final | Coral UK Championship |
| | v S. Davis | 4-9 | Semi-final | Coral UK Championship |
| 1984 | v J. Campbell | 5-1 | Qualifying | Lada Classic |
| | v Charlton | 3-5 | 1st round | Lada Classic |
| | v Charlton | 5-2 | 1st round | Benson & Hedges Masters |
| | v Reardon | 5-3 | Quarter-final | Benson & Hedges Masters |
| | v Stevens | 6-4 | Semi-final | Benson & Hedges Masters |
| | **v Griffiths** | **9-5** | **Final** | **Benson & Hedges Masters** |
| | v Meo | 4-5 | 1st round | Benson & Hedges Irish Masters |
| | v Knowles | 1-5 | 1st round | Tolly Cobbold Classic |
| | v Williams | 10-6 | 1st round | Embassy World Championship |
| | v Charlton | 13-7 | 2nd round | Embassy World Championship |
| | v Thorburn | 13-8 | Quarter-final | Embassy World Championship |
| | v Stevens | 16-14 | Semi-final | Embassy World Championship |
| | v S. Davis | 16-18 | Final | Embassy World Championship |
| | v Knowles | 3-5 | Quarter-final | Winfield Australian Masters |
| | v Macleod | 5-0 | 1st round | Langs Supreme Scottish Masters |
| | v Knowles | 6-5 | Semi-final | Langs Supreme Scottish Masters |
| | v S. Davis | 4-9 | Final | Langs Supreme Scottish Masters |
| | v Stevens | 5-0 | 1st round | Carlsberg Challenge |
| | **v Knowles** | **9-7** | **Final** | **Carlsberg Challenge** |
| | v Williams | 5-3 | 1st round | Jameson International |
| | v Meo | 5-1 | 2nd round | Jameson International |
| | v Knowles | 4-5 | Quarter-final | Jameson International |
| | v Oliver | 5-1 | 1st round | Rothmans Grand Prix |
| | v S. Francisco | 1-5 | 2nd round | Rothmans Grand Prix |
| | v J. Campbell | 9-7 | 1st round | Coral UK Open |
| | v Mountjoy | 9-2 | 2nd round | Coral UK Open |
| | v S. Davis | 4-9 | Quarter-final | Coral UK Open |
| 1985 | v Browne | 5-2 | 1st round | Mercantile Credit Classic |
| | v King | 2-5 | 2nd round | Mercantile Credit Classic |
| | v Thorne | 5-2 | 1st round | Benson & Hedges Masters |
| | v Spencer | 5-2 | Quarter-final | Benson & Hedges Masters |
| | v Thorburn | 4-6 | Semi-final | Benson & Hedges Masters |
| | v Chalmers | 9-5 | 1st round | Tolly Cobbold English Championship |
| | v N. Foulds | 9-7 | 2nd round | Tolly Cobbold English Championship |
| | v Longworth | 5-9 | Quarter-final | Tolly Cobbold English Championship |
| | v T. Jones | 6-5 | 1st round | Dulux British Open |
| | v S. Francisco | 4-5 | 2nd round | Dulux British Open |
| | v Meo | 5-1 | 1st round | Benson & Hedges Irish Masters |
| | v Thorburn | 5-3 | Quarter-final | Benson & Hedges Irish Masters |
| | v Knowles | 6-4 | Semi-final | Benson & Hedges Irish Masters |
| | **v Higgins** | **9-5** | **Final** | **Benson & Hedges Irish Masters** |
| | v W. Jones | 10-4 | 1st round | Embassy World Championship |
| | v Meo | 13-11 | 2nd round | Embassy World Championship |

|  |  |  |  |
|---|---|---|---|
| v Knowles | 10-13 | Quarter-final | Embassy World Championship |
| v Johnson | 5-4 | Quarter-final | Winfield Australian Masters |
| v Meo | 3-6 | Semi-final | Winfield Australian Masters |
| v Higgins | 5-0 | 1st round | Langs Scottish Masters |
| v Thorne | 2-6 | Semi-final | Langs Scottish Masters |
| v Parrott | 5-3 | Semi-final | Carlsberg Challenge |
| **v Higgins** | **8-3** | **Final** | **Carlsberg Challenge** |
| v Fagan | 5-2 | 3rd round | Goya Matchroom Trophy |
| v King | 5-2 | 4th round | Goya Matchroom Trophy |
| v Reynolds | 5-1 | 5th round | Goya Matchroom Trophy |
| v S. Davis | 5-3 | Quarter-final | Goya Matchroom Trophy |
| v N. Foulds | 9-5 | Semi-final | Goya Matchroom Trophy |
| v Thorburn | 10-12 | Final | Goya Matchroom Trophy |
| v Fitzmaurice | 5-0 | 3rd round | Rothmans Grand Prix |
| v O'Boye | 5-4 | 4th round | Rothmans Grand Prix |
| v S. Francisco | 4-5 | 5th round | Rothmans Grand Prix |
| v Thorburn | 3-5 | 1st round | BCE Canadian Masters |
| v Bradley | 9-4 | 3rd round | Coral UK Open |
| v Chappel | 9-5 | 4th round | Coral UK Open |
| v Higgins | 9-6 | 5th round | Coral UK Open |
| v Knowles | 9-4 | Quarter-final | Coral UK Open |
| v S. Davis | 5-9 | Semi-final | Coral UK Open |
| 1986 v Fowler | 5-1 | 3rd round | Mercantile Credit Classic |
| v Virgo | 5-2 | 4th round | Mercantile Credit Classic |
| v Gauvreau | 5-2 | 5th round | Mercantile Credit Classic |
| v S. Davis | 5-2 | Quarter-final | Mercantile Credit Classic |
| v Williams | 9-7 | Semi-final | Mercantile Credit Classic |
| **v Thorburn** | **13-12** | **Final** | **Mercantile Credit Classic** |
| v Knowles | 3-5 | 1st round | BCE Belgian Classic |
| v Meo | 5-4 | 1st round | Benson & Hedges Masters |
| v Dennis Taylor | 5-3 | Quarter-final | Benson & Hedges Masters |
| v S. Davis | 6-3 | Semi-final | Benson & Hedges Masters |
| v Thorburn | 5-9 | Final | Benson & Hedges Masters |
| v Williamson | 9-1 | 3rd round | Tolly Cobbold English Championship |
| v Williams | 9-5 | 4th round | Tolly Cobbold English Championship |
| v N. Foulds | 4-9 | Quarter-final | Tolly Cobbold English Championship |
| v P. Francisco | 4-5 | 3rd round | Dulux British Open |
| v Meo | 5-2 | Quarter-final | Benson & Hedges Irish Masters |
| v Fagan | 6-0 | Semi-final | Benson & Hedges Irish Masters |
| **v Thorne** | **9-5** | **Final** | **Benson & Hedges Irish Masters** |
| v Virgo | 10-7 | 1st round | Embassy World Championship |
| v Parrott | 13-8 | 2nd round | Embassy World Championship |
| v S. Davis | 5-13 | Quarter-final | Embassy World Championship |
| v Higgins | 5-1 | 1st round | Carlsberg Challenge |
| v Dennis Taylor | 3-8 | Final | Carlsberg Challenge |
| v Hendry | 5-1 | 1st round | Langs Scottish Masters |
| v Thorburn | 2-6 | Semi-final | Langs Scottish Masters |
| v Owers | 2-5 | 3rd round | BCE International |
| v T. Jones | 5-0 | 3rd round | Rothmans Grand Prix |
| v J. McLaughlin | 5-2 | 4th round | Rothmans Grand Prix |
| v Hallett | 5-3 | 5th round | Rothmans Grand Prix |
| v Hendry | 5-4 | Quarter-final | Rothmans Grand Prix |
| v S. Francisco | 9-6 | Semi-final | Rothmans Grand Prix |
| **v Williams** | **10-6** | **Final** | **Rothmans Grand Prix** |
| v S. Davis | 2-5 | 1st round | BCE Canadian Masters |
| v Edmonds | 9-4 | 3rd round | Tennents UK Open |
| v P. Francisco | 9-5 | 4th round | Tennents UK Open |
| v N. Foulds | 7-9 | 5th round | Tennents UK Open |
| 1987 v Newbury | 5-4 | 3rd round | Mercantile Credit Classic |
| v Bradley | 5-0 | 4th round | Mercantile Credit Classic |
| v Duggan | 5-2 | 5th round | Mercantile Credit Classic |
| v Griffiths | 5-3 | Quarter-final | Mercantile Credit Classic |
| v Reynolds | 9-8 | Semi-final | Mercantile Credit Classic |

*Jimmy White*

|  | | | | |
|---|---|---|---|---|
|  | v S. Davis | 12-13 | Final | Mercantile Credit Classic |
|  | v Meo | 4-5 | 1st round | Benson & Hedges Masters |
|  | v Cripsey | 6-4 | 3rd round | Tolly Ales English Championship |
|  | v Reynolds | 5-6 | 4th round | Tolly Ales English Championship |
|  | v Chappel | 5-1 | 3rd round | Dulux British Open |
|  | v Hallett | 5-2 | 4th round | Dulux British Open |
|  | v Williams | 5-0 | 5th round | Dulux British Open |
|  | v Spencer | 5-3 | Quarter-final | Dulux British Open |
|  | v Thorburn | 9-5 | Semi-final | Dulux British Open |
|  | **v N. Foulds** | **13-9** | **Final** | **Dulux British Open** |
|  | v Thorne | 4-5 | Quarter-final | Benson & Hedges Irish Masters |
|  | v Reynolds | 10-8 | 1st round | Embassy World Championship |
|  | v Parrott | 13-11 | 2nd round | Embassy World Championship |
|  | v O'Kane | 13-6 | Quarter-final | Embassy World Championship |
|  | v S. Davis | 11-16 | Semi-final | Embassy World Championship |
|  | v Hendry | 2-5 | Semi-final | Riley Hong Kong Masters (WS) |
|  | v Higgins | 5-3 | 1st round | Langs Scottish Masters |
|  | v Griffiths | 2-6 | Semi-final | Langs Scottish Masters |
|  | v M. Bennett | 5-3 | 3rd round | Fidelity International |
|  | v Longworth | 5-1 | 4th round | Fidelity International |
|  | v Hallett | 4-5 | 5th round | Fidelity International |
|  | v Wright | 5-4 | 3rd round | Rothmans Grand Prix |
|  | v Drago | 3-5 | 4th round | Rothmans Grand Prix |
|  | v Knowles | 5-1 | 1st round | Labatts Canadian Masters (WS) |
|  | v N. Foulds | 8-7 | Semi-final | Labatts Canadian Masters (WS) |
|  | v Dennis Taylor | 7-9 | Final | Labatts Canadian Masters (WS) |
|  | v Dennis Taylor | 2-6 | 1st round | Matchroom Trophy |
|  | v Dunning | 9-0 | 3rd round | Tennents UK Open |
|  | v E. Hughes | 9-4 | 4th round | Tennents UK Open |
|  | v Roe | 9-5 | 5th round | Tennents UK Open |
|  | v Griffiths | 9-7 | Quarter-final | Tennents UK Open |
|  | v Johnson | 9-4 | Semi-final | Tennents UK Open |
|  | v S. Davis | 14-16 | Final | Tennents UK Open |
| **1988** | v James | 5-1 | 3rd round | Mercantile Credit Classic |
|  | v Spencer | 5-1 | 4th round | Mercantile Credit Classic |
|  | v Martin | 2-5 | 5th round | Mercantile Credit Classic |
|  | v Mountjoy | 5-0 | 1st round | Benson & Hedges Masters |
|  | v Johnson | 3-5 | Quarter-final | Benson & Hedges Masters |
|  | v Clark | 6-5 | 3rd round | English Championship |
|  | v West | 2-6 | 4th round | English Championship |
|  | v Clark | 5-2 | 3rd round | MIM Britannia British Open |
|  | v James | 5-1 | 4th round | MIM Britannia British Open |
|  | v Gary Wilkinson | 5-1 | 5th round | MIM Britannia British Open |
|  | v Hendry | 4-5 | Quarter-final | MIM Britannia British Open |
|  | v Griffiths | 2-5 | Quarter-final | Benson & Hedges Irish Masters |
|  | v J. Campbell | 10-3 | 1st round | Embassy World Championship |
|  | v Hendry | 13-12 | 2nd round | Embassy World Championship |
|  | v Knowles | 13-6 | Quarter-final | Embassy World Championship |
|  | v Griffiths | 11-16 | Semi-final | Embassy World Championship |
|  | v Dennis Taylor | 5-2 | Semi-final | LEP Hong Kong Masters |
|  | **v N. Foulds** | **6-3** | **Final** | **LEP Hong Kong Masters** |
|  | v Clark | 5-2 | 3rd round | Fidelity International |
|  | v E. Hughes | 5-1 | 4th round | Fidelity International |
|  | v Thorne | 5-4 | 5th round | Fidelity International |
|  | v West | 5-2 | Quarter-final | Fidelity International |
|  | v Reynolds | 9-5 | Semi-final | Fidelity International |
|  | v S. Davis | 6-12 | Final | Fidelity International |
|  | v Thorburn | 6-4 | 1st round | LEP Matchroom Championship |
|  | v S. Davis | 4-6 | Semi-final | LEP Matchroom Championship |
|  | v Fowler | 5-0 | 3rd round | Rothmans Grand Prix |
|  | v W. Jones | 5-1 | 4th round | Rothmans Grand Prix |
|  | v J. McLaughlin | 5-2 | 5th round | Rothmans Grand Prix |
|  | v Dennis Taylor | 2-5 | Quarter-final | Rothmans Grand Prix |

| | | | | |
|---|---|---|---|---|
| | v Roe | 5-3 | 3rd round | BCE Canadian Masters |
| | v M. Bennett | 5-3 | 4th round | BCE Canadian Masters |
| | v Longworth | 5-3 | 5th round | BCE Canadian Masters |
| | v Dennis Taylor | 5-3 | Quarter-final | BCE Canadian Masters |
| | v Hallett | 9-2 | Semi-final | BCE Canadian Masters |
| | **v S. Davis** | **9-4** | **Final** | **BCE Canadian Masters** |
| | v J. Campbell | 9-5 | 3rd round | Tennents UK Open |
| | v M. Bennett | 6-9 | 4th round | Tennents UK Open |
| | v Griffiths | 9-5 | Quarter-final | Everest World Matchplay |
| | v S. Davis | 5-9 | Semi-final | Everest World Matchplay |
| | v S. Davis | 4-5 | Final | Norwich Union European Grand Prix |
| 1989 | v W. Jones | 3-5 | 3rd round | Mercantile Credit Classic |
| | v Virgo | 5-2 | 1st round | Benson and Hedges Masters |
| | v Parrott | 4-5 | Quarter-final | Benson and Hedges Masters |
| | v Sinclair | 5-3 | 3rd round | European Open |
| | v Williams | 5-2 | 4th round | European Open |
| | v Thorne | 5-3 | 5th round | European Open |
| | v Thorburn | 5-3 | Quarter-final | European Open |
| | v Griffiths | 4-5 | Semi-final | European Open |
| | v Houlihan | 5-3 | 3rd round | Anglian British Open |
| | v Reynolds | scr | 4th round | Anglian British Open |
| | v Parrott | 1-5 | Quarter-final | Benson and Hedges Irish Masters |
| | v O'Kane | 10-7 | 1st round | Embassy World Championship |
| | v Virgo | 13-12 | 2nd round | Embassy World Championship |
| | v Parrott | 7-13 | Quarter-final | Embassy World Championship |

## TERRY WHITTHREAD (England)

**Born** 7.7.64. **Turned professional** 1986. **World ranking** 100 (101). **Amateur career** 1985 English champion.

| | | | | |
|---|---|---|---|---|
| 1986 | v Kelly | 1-5 | 1st round | BCE International |
| | v Duggan | 1-5 | 1st round | Rothmans Grand Prix |
| | v Darrington | 8-9 | 1st round | Tennents UK Open |
| 1987 | v Roscoe | 1-5 | 1st round | Mercantile Credit Classic |
| | v Fisher | 3-6 | 1st round | Tolly Ales English Championship |
| | v D. Hughes | 5-1 | 1st round | Dulux British Open |
| | v Spencer | 2-5 | 2nd round | Dulux British Open |
| | v Roscoe | 2-10 | Qualifying | Embassy World Championship |
| | v Jenkins | 1-5 | 1st round | Fidelity International |
| | v Roe | 1-5 | 1st round | Rothmans Grand Prix |
| | v Van Rensberg | 5-9 | 1st round | Tennents UK Open |
| 1988 | v Fagan | 5-2 | 1st round | Mercantile Credit Classic |
| | v G. Foulds | 5-3 | 2nd round | Mercantile Credit Classic |
| | v Dennis Taylor | 2-5 | 3rd round | Mercantile Credit Classic |
| | v D. Gilbert | 1-6 | 1st round | English Championship |
| | v Glen Wilkinson | 5-4 | 1st round | MIM Britannia British Open |
| | v O'Kane | 2-5 | 2nd round | MIM Britannia British Open |
| | v Meadowcroft | 5-4 | 1st round | Fidelity International |
| | v O'Boye | 2-5 | 2nd round | Fidelity International |
| | v Grace | 5-4 | 1st round | Rothmans Grand Prix |
| | v Clark | 1-5 | 2nd round | Rothmans Grand Prix |
| | v Bear | 5-4 | 1st round | BCE Canadian Masters |
| | v Roe | 2-5 | 2nd round | BCE Canadian Masters |
| | v Donnelly | 9-8 | 1st round | Tennents UK Open |
| | v N. Gilbert | 5-9 | 2nd round | Tennents UK Open |
| 1989 | v Roscoe | 3-5 | 1st round | Mercantile Credit Classic |
| | v Sinclair | 4-5 | 1st round | European Open |
| | v D. Hughes | 5-1 | 1st round | English Championship |
| | v Cripsey | 2-5 | 2nd round | English Championship |
| | v Donnelly | 5-4 | 1st round | Anglian British Open |
| | v Murphy | 5-2 | 2nd round | Anglian British Open |

| | | | |
|---|---|---|---|
| v Johnson | 2-5 | 3rd round | Anglian British Open |
| v Donnelly | 10-7 | Qualifying | Embassy World Championship |
| v Fowler | 6-10 | Qualifying | Embassy World Championship |

## MARK WILDMAN (England)

**Born** 25.1.36. **Turned professional** 1979. **World ranking** 97 (76). **Best professional performance** Semi-final 1984 Lada Classic.

| | | | | |
|---|---|---|---|---|
| **1980** | v Jonik | 7-9 | Qualifying | Embassy World Championship |
| | v Wilson | 9-8 | Qualifying | Coral UK Championship |
| | v Spencer | 9-7 | 1st round | Coral UK Championship |
| | v F. Davis | 6-9 | 2nd round | Coral UK Championship |
| **1981** | v Bennett | 9-3 | Qualifying | John Courage English |
| | v Thorne | 2-9 | 1st round | John Courage English |
| | v Edmonds | 3-9 | Qualifying | Embassy World Championship |
| | v Morra | 5-3 | Qualifying | Jameson International |
| | v E. McLaughlin | 3-5 | Qualifying | Jameson International |
| | v Sinclair | 8-9 | Qualifying | Coral UK Championship |
| **1982** | v G. Foulds | 9-8 | Qualifying | Embassy World Championship |
| | v White | 4-9 | Qualifying | Embassy World Championship |
| | v Gibson | 5-1 | Qualifying | Jameson International |
| | v Hallett | 5-2 | Qualifying | Jameson International |
| | v Dennis Taylor | 2-5 | 1st round | Jameson International |
| | v Dunning | 5-4 | 1st round | Professional Players Tournament |
| | v Mans | 5-4 | 2nd round | Professional Players Tournament |
| | v Johnson | 4-5 | 3rd round | Professional Players Tournament |
| | v Roscoe | 9-4 | Qualifying | Coral UK Championship |
| | v Reardon | 5-9 | 1st round | Coral UK Championship |
| **1983** | v S. Davis | 2-5 | 1st round | Benson & Hedges Masters |
| | v B. Harris | 10-7 | Qualifying | Embassy World Championship |
| | v Griffiths | 8-10 | 1st round | Embassy World Championship |
| | v B. Harris | 5-2 | Qualifying | Jameson International |
| | v Mountjoy | 4-5 | 1st round | Jameson International |
| | v Jonik | 5-4 | 1st round | Professional Players Tournament |
| | v David Taylor | 5-3 | 2nd round | Professional Players Tournament |
| | v Stevens | 0-5 | 3rd round | Professional Players Tournament |
| | v Greaves | 9-5 | Qualifying | Coral UK Championship |
| | v Thorne | 5-9 | 1st round | Coral UK Championship |
| **1984** | v Virgo | 5-2 | Qualifying | Lada Classic |
| | v S. Francisco | 5-1 | 1st round | Lada Classic |
| | v Charlton | 5-4 | Quarter-final | Lada Classic |
| | v Meo | 3-5 | Semi-final | Lada Classic |
| | v Andrewartha | 9-10 | Qualifying | Embassy World Championship |
| | v W. Jones | 0-5 | Qualifying | Jameson International |
| | v J. McLaughlin | 5-3 | 1st round | Rothmans Grand Prix |
| | v Mountjoy | 0-5 | 2nd round | Rothmans Grand Prix |
| | v T. Jones | 2-9 | Qualifying | Coral UK Open |
| **1985** | v Fagan | 3-5 | Qualifying | Mercantile Credit Classic |
| | v Longworth | 3-9 | 1st round | Tolly Cobbold English Championship |
| | v Gibson | 6-1 | 1st round | Dulux British Open |
| | v Stevens | 2-5 | 2nd round | Dulux British Open |
| | v Edmonds | 7-10 | Qualifying | Embassy World Championship |
| | v Scott | 1-5 | 3rd round | Goya Matchroom Trophy |
| | v Duggan | 5-4 | 3rd round | Rothmans Grand Prix |
| | v Thorburn | 2-5 | 4th round | Rothmans Grand Prix |
| | v Drago | 5-9 | 3rd round | Coral UK Open |
| **1986** | v West | 2-5 | 3rd round | Mercantile Credit Classic |
| | v Cripsey | 9-5 | 3rd round | Tolly Cobbold English Championship |
| | v Meo | 3-9 | 4th round | Tolly Cobbold English Championship |
| | v Jenkins | 5-4 | 3rd round | Dulux British Open |
| | v Thorburn | 1-5 | 4th round | Dulux British Open |

|      | v Edmonds | 9-10 | Qualifying | Embassy World Championship |
|------|-----------|------|------------|----------------------------|
|      | v Rowswell | 5-2 | 2nd round | BCE International |
|      | v P. Francisco | 2-5 | 3rd round | BCE International |
|      | v Ellis | 5-1 | 2nd round | Rothmans Grand Prix |
|      | v Longworth | 5-2 | 3rd round | Rothmans Grand Prix |
|      | v Williams | 1-5 | 4th round | Rothmans Grand Prix |
|      | v Roscoe | 6-9 | 2nd round | Tennents UK Open |
| 1987 | v Kearney | 3-5 | 2nd round | Mercantile Credit Classic |
|      | v Parrott | 1-6 | 3rd round | Tolly Ales English Championship |
|      | v Chalmers | 5-0 | 2nd round | Dulux British Open |
|      | v Thorburn | 3-5 | 3rd round | Dulux British Open |
|      | v Foldvari | 10-5 | Qualifying | Embassy World Championship |
|      | v Wright | 0-10 | Qualifying | Embassy World Championship |
|      | v Miles | 5-3 | 2nd round | Fidelity International |
|      | v Griffiths | 1-5 | 3rd round | Fidelity International |
|      | v Roe | 3-5 | 2nd round | Rothmans Grand Prix |
|      | v Chambers | 5-9 | 2nd round | Tennents UK Open |
| 1988 | v Jonik | 5-4 | 2nd round | Mercantile Credit Classic |
|      | v Parrott | 2-5 | 3rd round | Mercantile Credit Classic |
|      | v D. Hughes | 0-6 | 2nd round | English Championship |
|      | v Roscoe | 0-5 | 2nd round | MIM Britannia British Open |
|      | v Mikkelsen | 10-5 | Qualifying | Embassy World Championship |
|      | v Foldvari | 1-10 | Qualifying | Embassy World Championship |
|      | v Jenkins | 1-5 | 1st round | Fidelity International |
|      | v Fagan | 5-1 | 1st round | Rothmans Grand Prix |
|      | v Martin | 1-5 | 2nd round | Rothmans Grand Prix |
|      | v Jenkins | 5-1 | 1st round | BCE Canadian Masters |
|      | v Duggan | 1-5 | 2nd round | BCE Canadian Masters |
|      | v Mienie | 9-4 | 1st round | Tennents UK Open |
|      | v Edmonds | 4-9 | 2nd round | Tennents UK Open |
| 1989 | v Morgan | 1-5 | 1st round | European Open |
|      | v Medati | 4-5 | 1st round | English Championship |
|      | v A. Harris | 4-5 | 1st round | Anglian British Open |
|      | v Ellis | 7-10 | Qualifying | Embassy World Championship |

## GARY WILKINSON (England)

**Born** 7.4.66. **Turned professional** 1987. **World ranking** 39 (45). **Best professional performances** Last 16 1988 MIM Britannia British Open, 1987 Rothmans Grand Prix.

|      | v Rigitano | 5-1 | 1st round | Fidelity International |
|------|-----------|------|------------|----------------------------|
| 1987 | v Rigitano | 5-1 | 1st round | Fidelity International |
|      | v Scott | 5-2 | 2nd round | Fidelity International |
|      | v Hendry | 4-5 | 3rd round | Fidelity International |
|      | v V. Harris | 5-0 | 1st round | Rothmans Grand Prix |
|      | v O'Kane | 5-2 | 2nd round | Rothmans Grand Prix |
|      | v Longworth | 5-4 | 3rd round | Rothmans Grand Prix |
|      | v S. Francisco | 5-3 | 4th round | Rothmans Grand Prix |
|      | v Newbury | 3-5 | 5th round | Rothmans Grand Prix |
|      | v Jenkins | 9-3 | 1st round | Tennents UK Open |
|      | v Grace | 9-5 | 2nd round | Tennents UK Open |
|      | v Griffiths | 5-9 | 3rd round | Tennents UK Open |
| 1988 | v Reardon | 3-5 | 2nd round | Mercantile Credit Classic |
|      | v Rowswell | 6-1 | 1st round | English Championship |
|      | v Edmonds | 6-3 | 2nd round | English Championship |
|      | v N. Foulds | 3-6 | 3rd round | English Championship |
|      | v Black | 5-2 | 1st round | MIM Britannia British Open |
|      | v Bales | 5-1 | 2nd round | MIM Britannia British Open |
|      | v Meo | 5-2 | 3rd round | MIM Britannia British Open |
|      | v S. Francisco | 5-3 | 4th round | MIM Britannia British Open |
|      | v White | 1-5 | 5th round | MIM Britannia British Open |
|      | v Medati | 9-10 | Qualifying | Embassy World Championship |

|      | v Chambers     | 4-5   | 2nd round    | Fidelity International        |
|------|----------------|-------|--------------|------------------------------|
|      | v D. Morgan    | 5-1   | 2nd round    | Rothmans Grand Prix          |
|      | v Thorne       | 5-3   | 3rd round    | Rothmans Grand Prix          |
|      | v Williams     | 2-5   | 4th round    | Rothmans Grand Prix          |
|      | v Terry        | 5-3   | 2nd round    | BCE Canadian Masters         |
|      | v C. Wilson    | 2-5   | 3rd round    | BCE Canadian Masters         |
|      | v Sheehan      | 9-5   | 2nd round    | Tennents UK Open             |
|      | v Chaperon     | 9-0   | 3rd round    | Tennents UK Open             |
|      | v S. Davis     | 3-9   | 4th round    | Tennents UK Open             |
| 1989 | v Medati       | 5-1   | 2nd round    | Mercantile Credit Classic    |
|      | v James        | 1-5   | 3rd round    | Mercantile Credit Classic    |
|      | v Graham       | 5-3   | 2nd round    | European Open                |
|      | v David Taylor | 5-2   | 3rd round    | European Open                |
|      | v Parrott      | 2-5   | 4th round    | European Open                |
|      | v J. Smith     | 5-3   | 2nd round    | English Championship         |
|      | v Virgo        | 5-3   | 3rd round    | English Championship         |
|      | v Graham       | 5-1   | 4th round    | English Championship         |
|      | v Rowswell     | 5-1   | Quarter-final| English Championship         |
|      | v Hallett      | 3-5   | Semi-final   | English Championship         |
|      | v Miles        | 5-2   | 2nd round    | Anglian British Open         |
|      | v Thorne       | 1-5   | 3rd round    | Anglian British Open         |
|      | v V. Harris    | 10-6  | Qualifying   | Embassy World Championship   |
|      | v Reardon      | 10-5  | Qualifying   | Embassy World Championship   |
|      | v Drago        | 10-9  | Qualifying   | Embassy World Championship   |
|      | v Hendry       | 9-10  | 1st round    | Embassy World Championship   |

## GLEN WILKINSON (Australia)

**Born** 4.7.59. **Turned professional** 1985. **World ranking** 91 (95). **Amateur career** 1985
Australian champion.

| 1985 | v Jenkins      | 6-2   | 1st round     | Australian Championship     |
|------|----------------|-------|---------------|-----------------------------|
|      | v Heywood      | 7-3   | 2nd round     | Australian Championship     |
|      | v Charlton     | 2-8   | Quarter-final | Australian Championship     |
|      | v Demarco      | 5-2   | 1st round     | Goya Matchroom Trophy       |
|      | v Longworth    | 0-5   | 2nd round     | Goya Matchroom Trophy       |
|      | v Gilbert      | 4-5   | 1st round     | Rothmans Grand Prix         |
|      | v Smith        | 9-4   | 1st round     | Coral UK Open               |
|      | v Fowler       | 6-9   | 2nd round     | Coral UK Open               |
| 1986 | v O'Boye       | 1-5   | 1st round     | Mercantile Credit Classic   |
|      | v Watchorn     | 5-4   | 1st round     | Dulux British Open          |
|      | v Donnelly     | 4-5   | 2nd round     | Dulux British Open          |
|      | v Kearney      | 5-10  | Qualifying    | Embassy World Championship  |
|      | v Heywood      | 6-0   | 2nd round     | Australian Championship     |
|      | v J. Campbell  | 1-6   | Quarter-final | Australian Championship     |
|      | v Bradley      | 4-5   | 2nd round     | BCE International            |
|      | v G. Foulds    | 3-5   | 1st round     | Rothmans Grand Prix         |
|      | v Jonik        | 9-8   | 1st round     | Tennents UK Open            |
|      | v Chappel      | 2-9   | 2nd round     | Tennents UK Open            |
| 1987 | v Fitzmaurice  | 5-2   | 1st round     | Mercantile Credit Classic   |
|      | v Fowler       | 1-5   | 2nd round     | Mercantile Credit Classic   |
|      | v Fitzmaurice  | 5-0   | 1st round     | Dulux British Open          |
|      | v Mans         | 5-2   | 2nd round     | Dulux British Open          |
|      | v David Taylor | 4-5   | 3rd round     | Dulux British Open          |
|      | v J. Campbell  | 4-6   | Quarter-final | Australian Championship     |
|      | v P. Gibson    | 3-5   | 1st round     | Fidelity International       |
|      | v Owers        | 5-4   | 2nd round     | Rothmans Grand Prix         |
|      | v Wilson       | 4-5   | 3rd round     | Rothmans Grand Prix         |
|      | v Meakin       | 0-9   | 1st round     | Tennents UK Open            |
| 1988 | v Chalmers     | 5-3   | 1st round     | Mercantile Credit Classic   |

|      | v Werbeniuk | 2-5 | 2nd round | Mercantile Credit Classic |
|------|-------------|-----|-----------|---------------------------|
|      | v Whitthread | 4-5 | 1st round | MIM Britannia British Open |
|      | v Everton | 10-2 | Qualifying | Embassy World Championship |
|      | v W. Jones | 4-10 | Qualifying | Embassy World Championship |
|      | v Potasznyk | 3-5 | 2nd round | Australian Championship |
|      | v Mienie | 5-2 | 1st round | Fidelity International |
|      | v Fisher | 4-5 | 2nd round | Fidelity International |
|      | v Graham | 5-4 | 1st round | Rothmans Grand Prix |
|      | v Macleod | 2-5 | 2nd round | Rothmans Grand Prix |
|      | v Robidoux | 3-5 | 1st round | BCE Canadian Masters |
|      | v Jack Rea | 9-0 | 1st round | Tennents UK Open |
|      | v Dodd | 6-9 | 2nd round | Tennents UK Open |
| 1989 | v Watchorn | 5-3 | 1st round | Mercantile Credit Classic |
|      | v Wych | 5-3 | 2nd round | Mercantile Credit Classic |
|      | v Thorburn | 2-5 | 3rd round | Mercantile Credit Classic |
|      | v A. Harris | 4-5 | 1st round | European Open |
|      | v D. Morgan | 0-5 | 1st round | Anglian British Open |
|      | v Kelly | 10-2 | Qualifying | Embassy World Championship |
|      | v Bales | 10-1 | Qualifying | Embassy World Championship |
|      | v Dodd | 4-10 | Qualifying | Embassy World Championship |

## REX WILLIAMS (England)

**Born** 20.7.33. **Turned professional** 1951. **World ranking** 32 (18). **Amateur career** 1951 English champion. **Best professional performance** Runner-up 1986 Rothmans Grand Prix.

|      | v Bennett | 38-11 | Quarter-final | World Championship |
|------|-----------|-------|---------------|--------------------|
| 1969 | v Bennett | 38-11 | Quarter-final | World Championship |
|      | v Spencer | 18-55 | Semi-final | World Championship |
| 1970 | v G. Owen | 11-31 | Quarter-final | World Championship (Apr) |
| 1972 | v Reardon | 25-23 | Quarter-final | World Championship |
|      | v Higgins | 30-31 | Semi-final | World Championship |
| 1973 | v Thorburn | 16-15 | 2nd round | World Championship |
|      | v Spencer | 7-16 | Quarter-final | World Championship |
| 1974 | v Pulman | 15-12 | 2nd round | World Championship |
|      | v Mans | 15-4 | Quarter-final | World Championship |
|      | v Miles | 7-15 | Semi-final | World Championship |
| 1975 | v Higgins | 5-3 | Quarter-final | Benson & Hedges Masters |
|      | v Reardon | 4-5 | Semi-final | Benson & Hedges Masters |
|      | v Anderson | 15-4 | 2nd round | World Championship |
|      | v Higgins | 12-19 | Quarter-final | World Championship |
| 1976 | v Meadowcroft | 7-15 | 1st round | Embassy World Championship |
| 1977 | v Thorburn | 6-13 | 1st round | Embassy World Championship |
| 1978 | v Thorne | 3-9 | Qualifying | Embassy World Championship |
|      | v Griffiths | 9-8 | Qualifying | Coral UK Championship |
|      | v Miles | 8-9 | 1st round | Coral UK Championship |
| 1979 | v Spencer | 2-6 | Semi-final | Holsten Lager International |
|      | v Greaves | 9-2 | Prelim | Embassy World Championship |
|      | v Miles | 5-9 | Qualifying | Embassy World Championship |
| 1980 | v Wych | 7-9 | Qualifying | Embassy World Championship |
|      | v Barrie | 9-1 | Qualifying | Coral UK Championship |
|      | v Mountjoy | 9-8 | 1st round | Coral UK Championship |
|      | v David Taylor | 9-7 | 2nd round | Coral UK Championship |
|      | v Reardon | 4-9 | Quarter-final | Coral UK Championship |
| 1981 | v Hood | 9-4 | Qualifying | Embassy World Championship |
|      | v Edmonds | 7-9 | Qualifying | Embassy World Championship |
|      | v French | 5-0 | Qualifying | Jameson International |
|      | v White | 5-1 | 1st round | Jameson International |
|      | v F. Davis | 5-0 | 2nd round | Jameson International |
|      | v Dennis Taylor | 1-5 | 3rd round | Jameson International |

|      |                 |       |              |                                     |
|------|-----------------|-------|--------------|-------------------------------------|
|      | v French        | 9-3   | Qualifying   | Coral UK Championship               |
|      | v Roscoe        | 9-4   | Qualifying   | Coral UK Championship               |
|      | v Dunning       | 9-4   | Qualifying   | Coral UK Championship               |
|      | v Meo           | 8-9   | 2nd round    | Coral UK Championship               |
| 1982 | v Black         | 9-2   | Qualifying   | Embassy World Championship          |
|      | v Mountjoy      | 3-10  | 1st round    | Embassy World Championship          |
|      | v Medati        | 5-3   | Qualifying   | Jameson International               |
|      | v E. McLaughlin | 5-1   | Qualifying   | Jameson International               |
|      | v Griffiths     | 2-5   | 1st round    | Jameson International               |
|      | v Ross          | 5-0   | 1st round    | Professional Players Tournament     |
|      | v Charlton      | 2-5   | 2nd round    | Professional Players Tournament     |
|      | v G. Foulds     | 9-7   | Qualifying   | Coral UK Championship               |
|      | v S. Davis      | 6-9   | 1st round    | Coral UK Championship               |
|      | v Darrington    | 10-0  | Qualifying   | Embassy World Championship          |
|      | v F. Davis      | 10-1  | Qualifying   | Embassy World Championship          |
|      | v S. Davis      | 4-10  | 1st round    | Embassy World Championship          |
| 1983 | v French        | 5-1   | Qualifying   | Jameson International               |
|      | v Reynolds      | 3-5   | Qualifying   | Jameson International               |
|      | v Sheehan       | 5-1   | 1st round    | Professional Players Tournament     |
|      | v Knowles       | 4-5   | 2nd round    | Professional Players Tournament     |
|      | v V. Harris     | 9-6   | Qualifying   | Coral UK Championship               |
|      | v Wilson        | 4-9   | 1st round    | Coral UK Championship               |
| 1984 | v Reardon       | 5-4   | Qualifying   | Lada Classic                        |
|      | v Meo           | 3-5   | 1st round    | Lada Classic                        |
|      | v Oliver        | 10-8  | Qualifying   | Embassy World Championship          |
|      | v White         | 6-10  | 1st round    | Embassy World Championship          |
|      | v Meadowcroft   | 5-4   | Qualifying   | Jameson International               |
|      | v White         | 3-5   | Qualifying   | Jameson International               |
|      | v Chalmers      | 5-0   | 1st round    | Rothmans Grand Prix                 |
|      | v Stevens       | 3-5   | 2nd round    | Rothmans Grand Prix                 |
|      | v Fisher        | 9-8   | Qualifying   | Coral UK Open                       |
|      | v Werbeniuk     | 9-1   | 1st round    | Coral UK Open                       |
|      | v Higgins       | 7-9   | 2nd round    | Coral UK Open                       |
| 1985 | v Donnelly      | 5-3   | Qualifying   | Mercantile Credit Classic           |
|      | v Dennis Taylor | 5-3   | 1st round    | Mercantile Credit Classic           |
|      | v Griffiths     | 3-5   | 2nd round    | Mercantile Credit Classic           |
|      | v T. Jones      | 9-6   | 1st round    | Tolly Cobbold English Championship  |
|      | v S. Davis      | 2-9   | 2nd round    | Tolly Cobbold English Championship  |
|      | v Fowler        | 4-6   | 1st round    | Dulux British Open                  |
|      | v F. Davis      | 10-6  | Qualifying   | Embassy World Championship          |
|      | v Griffiths     | 3-10  | 1st round    | Embassy World Championship          |
|      | v King          | 3-5   | 3rd round    | Goya Matchroom Trophy               |
|      | v Watterson     | 5-2   | 3rd round    | Rothmans Grand Prix                 |
|      | v Dennis Taylor | 2-5   | 4th round    | Rothmans Grand Prix                 |
|      | v King          | 9-5   | 3rd round    | Coral UK Open                       |
|      | v P. Francisco  | 9-7   | 4th round    | Coral UK Open                       |
|      | v Stevens       | 7-9   | 5th round    | Coral UK Open                       |
| 1986 | v Watterson     | 5-0   | 3rd round    | Mercantile Credit Classic           |
|      | v V. Harris     | 5-1   | 4th round    | Mercantile Credit Classic           |
|      | v Knowles       | 5-2   | 5th round    | Mercantile Credit Classic           |
|      | v Higgins       | 5-2   | Quarter-final| Mercantile Credit Classic           |
|      | v White         | 7-9   | Semi-final   | Mercantile Credit Classic           |
|      | v Miles         | 9-6   | 3rd round    | Tolly Cobbold English Championship  |
|      | v White         | 5-9   | 4th round    | Tolly Cobbold English Championship  |
|      | v Drago         | 5-1   | 3rd round    | Dulux British Open                  |
|      | v Bales         | 5-4   | 4th round    | Dulux British Open                  |
|      | v Werbeniuk     | 3-5   | 5th round    | Dulux British Open                  |
|      | v S. Francisco  | 4-10  | 1st round    | Embassy World Championship          |
|      | v O'Boye        | 5-0   | 3rd round    | BCE International                   |
|      | v Duggan        | 5-4   | 4th round    | BCE International                   |
|      | v S. Davis      | 4-5   | 5th round    | BCE International                   |
|      | v Bear          | 5-2   | 3rd round    | Rothmans Grand Prix                 |

| | | | |
|---|---|---|---|
| v Wildman | 5-1 | 4th round | Rothmans Grand Prix |
| v Higgins | 5-1 | 5th round | Rothmans Grand Prix |
| v S. Davis | 5-1 | Quarter-final | Rothmans Grand Prix |
| v N. Foulds | 9-8 | Semi-final | Rothmans Grand Prix |
| v White | 6-10 | Final | Rothmans Grand Prix |
| v Drago | 7-9 | 3rd round | Tennents UK Open |
| 1987 v Morra | 5-2 | 3rd round | Mercantile Credit Classic |
| v Charlton | 4-5 | 4th round | Mercantile Credit Classic |
| v Thorburn | 1-5 | 1st round | Benson & Hedges Masters |
| v T. Jones | 6-4 | 3rd round | Tolly Ales English Championship |
| v David Taylor | 6-2 | 4th round | Tolly Ales English Championship |
| v Johnson | 5-4 | Quarter-final | Tolly Ales English Championship |
| v Foldvari | 5-4 | 3rd round | Dulux British Open |
| v James | 5-2 | 4th round | Dulux British Open |
| v White | 0-5 | 5th round | Dulux British Open |
| v Macleod | 5-10 | 1st round | Embassy World Championship |
| v Foldvari | 0-5 | 3rd round | Fidelity International |
| v Edmonds | 3-5 | 3rd round | Rothmans Grand Prix |
| v Roe | 7-9 | 3rd round | Tennents UK Open |
| 1988 v Owers | 3-5 | 3rd round | Mercantile Credit Classic |
| v Thorburn | 3-5 | 1st round | Benson & Hedges Masters |
| v D. Hughes | 6-1 | 3rd round | English Championship |
| v Hallett | 3-6 | 4th round | English Championship |
| v N. Gilbert | 5-2 | 3rd round | MIM Britannia British Open |
| v West | 5-0 | 4th round | MIM Britannia British Open |
| v Spencer | 5-4 | 5th round | MIM Britannia British Open |
| v Thorburn | 2-5 | Quarter-final | MIM Britannia British Open |
| v Griffiths | 1-5 | 1st round | Benson & Hedges Irish Masters |
| v James | 6-10 | 1st round | Embassy World Championship |
| v Roe | 5-3 | 3rd round | Fidelity International |
| v Duggan | 5-4 | 4th round | Fidelity International |
| v West | 4-5 | 5th round | Fidelity International |
| v Medati | 5-2 | 3rd round | Rothmans Grand Prix |
| v Gary Wilkinson | 5-2 | 4th round | Rothmans Grand Prix |
| v Edmonds | 5-3 | 5th round | Rothmans Grand Prix |
| v Higgins | 4-5 | Quarter-final | Rothmans Grand Prix |
| v Scott | 2-5 | 3rd round | BCE Canadian Masters |
| v B. Harris | 9-4 | 3rd round | Tennents UK Open |
| v Johnson | 7-9 | 4th round | Tennents UK Open |
| 1989 v Wright | 0-5 | 3rd round | Mercantile Credit Classic |
| v King | 5-2 | 3rd round | European Open |
| v White | 2-5 | 4th round | European Open |
| v Graham | 3-5 | 3rd round | English Championship |
| v Roe | 2-5 | 3rd round | Anglian British Open |
| v Roe | 3-10 | Qualifying | Embassy World Championship |


## IAN WILLIAMSON (England)

**Born** 1.12.58. **Turned professional** 1982. **World ranking** 92 (89).

| | | | |
|---|---|---|---|
| 1982 v Donnelly | 5-3 | Qualifying | Jameson International |
| v Kelly | 1-5 | Qualifying | Jameson International |
| v Dodd | 1-9 | Qualifying | Coral UK Championship |
| 1983 v French | 10-8 | Qualifying | Embassy World Championship |
| v Dodd | 9-10 | Qualifying | Embassy World Championship |
| v Darrington | 3-5 | Qualifying | Jameson International |
| v White | 2-5 | 1st round | Professional Players Tournament |
| v Hargreaves | 9-4 | Qualifying | Coral UK Championship |
| v Black | 6-9 | Qualifying | Coral UK Championship |
| 1984 v Houlihan | 10-5 | Qualifying | Embassy World Championship |
| v Hines | 10-6 | Qualifying | Embassy World Championship |

|  | | | | |
|---|---|---|---|---|
| | v Miles | 6-10 | Qualifying | Embassy World Championship |
| | v V. Harris | 5-0 | Qualifying | Jameson International |
| | v G. Foulds | 4-5 | Qualifying | Jameson International |
| | v Thornley | 5-2 | Qualifying | Rothmans Grand Prix |
| | v Werbeniuk | 5-2 | 1st round | Rothmans Grand Prix |
| | v Johnson | 5-4 | 2nd round | Rothmans Grand Prix |
| | v Knowles | 2-5 | 3rd round | Rothmans Grand Prix |
| | v P. Francisco | 2-9 | Qualifying | Coral UK Open |
| 1985 | v Kearney | 5-3 | Qualifying | Mercantile Credit Classic |
| | v Fagan | 1-5 | Qualifying | Mercantile Credit Classic |
| | v Bradley | 8-9 | Qualifying | Tolly Cobbold English Championship |
| | v Chappel | 5-6 | Qualifying | Dulux British Open |
| | v Medati | 8-10 | Qualifying | Embassy World Championship |
| | v J. McLaughlin | 5-3 | 2nd round | Goya Matchroom Trophy |
| | v Werbeniuk | 2-5 | 3rd round | Goya Matchroom Trophy |
| | v Gilbert | 4-5 | 2nd round | Rothmans Grand Prix |
| | v Mikkelsen | 3-9 | 2nd round | Coral UK Championship |
| 1986 | v John Rea | 4-5 | 2nd round | Mercantile Credit Classic |
| | v Parkin | 9-4 | 2nd round | Tolly Cobbold English Championship |
| | v White | 1-9 | 3rd round | Tolly Cobbold English Championship |
| | v Cripsey | 5-4 | 2nd round | Dulux British Open |
| | v Knowles | 1-5 | 3rd round | Dulux British Open |
| | v Van Rensberg | 9-10 | Qualifying | Embassy World Championship |
| | v Spencer | 4-5 | 2nd round | BCE International |
| | v Hendry | 1-5 | 2nd round | Rothmans Grand Prix |
| | v Browne | 9-4 | 2nd round | Tennents UK Open |
| | v Martin | 5-9 | 3rd round | Tennents UK Open |
| 1987 | v Edmonds | 5-2 | 2nd round | Mercantile Credit Classic |
| | v Wilson | 4-5 | 3rd round | Mercantile Credit Classic |
| | v Roe | 6-4 | 2nd round | Tolly Ales English Championship |
| | v Hallett | 2-6 | 3rd round | Tolly Ales English Championship |
| | v King | 3-5 | 2nd round | Dulux British Open |
| | v Black | 8-10 | Qualifying | Embassy World Championship |
| | v Everton | 5-0 | 1st round | Fidelity International |
| | v Gauvreau | 5-1 | 2nd round | Fidelity International |
| | v Longworth | 4-5 | 3rd round | Fidelity International |
| | v Clark | 1-5 | 1st round | Rothmans Grand Prix |
| | v Kelly | 9-5 | 1st round | Tennents UK Open |
| | v Duggan | 7-9 | 2nd round | Tennents UK Open |
| 1988 | v D. Hughes | 3-5 | 1st round | Mercantile Credit Classic |
| | v Dunning | 6-5 | 1st round | English Championship |
| | v Duggan | 2-6 | 2nd round | English Championship |
| | v Meakin | 5-1 | 1st round | MIM Britannia British Open |
| | v Bradley | 5-3 | 2nd round | MIM Britannia British Open |
| | v Hallett | 0-5 | 3rd round | MIM Britannia British Open |
| | v Bradley | 9-10 | Qualifying | Embassy World Championship |
| | v Darrington | 5-1 | 1st round | Fidelity International |
| | v Wright | 1-5 | 2nd round | Fidelity International |
| | v Everton | 5-0 | 1st round | Rothmans Grand Prix |
| | v Wych | 5-4 | 2nd round | Rothmans Grand Prix |
| | v Hendry | 2-5 | 3rd round | Rothmans Grand Prix |
| | v Chalmers | 5-2 | 1st round | BCE Canadian Masters |
| | v Gauvreau | 1-5 | 2nd round | BCE Canadian Masters |
| | v Everton | 9-1 | 1st round | Tennents UK Open |
| | v O'Boye | 4-9 | 2nd round | Tennents UK Open |
| 1989 | v Jenkins | 5-2 | 1st round | Mercantile Credit Classic |
| | v Browne | 3-5 | 2nd round | Mercantile Credit Classic |
| | v D. Hughes | 5-1 | 1st round | European Open |
| | v Reardon | 3-5 | 2nd round | European Open |
| | v Owers | 5-4 | 2nd round | English Championship |
| | v Knowles | 2-5 | 3rd round | English Championship |
| | v Graham | 4-5 | 1st round | Anglian British Open |
| | v Grech | 7-10 | Qualifying | Embassy World Championship |

## CLIFF WILSON (Wales)

**Born** 10.5.34. **Turned professional** 1979. **World ranking** 18 (16). **Amateur career** 1978 World champion, 1956, 1977, 1979 Welsh champion. **Best professional performances** Quarter-finals 1987 Mercantile Credit Classic, 1986 BCE International, 1985 Rothmans Grand Prix, 1982 Jameson International.

| | | | | |
|---|---|---|---|---|
| 1979 | v Pulman | 9-7 | 2nd round | Coral UK Championship |
| | v Griffiths | 4-9 | 3rd round | Coral UK Championship |
| | v Reardon | 3-9 | 1st round | Woodpecker Welsh Championship |
| 1980 | v Jonik | 9-6 | Qualifying | Embassy World Championship |
| | v Mountjoy | 6-10 | 1st round | Embassy World Championship |
| | v Wildman | 8-9 | Qualifying | Coral UK Championship |
| 1981 | v Andrewartha | 6-5 | Prelim | Woodpecker Welsh Championship |
| | v Mountjoy | 9-6 | Semi-final | Woodpecker Welsh Championship |
| | v Reardon | 6-9 | Final | Woodpecker Welsh Championship |
| | v Andrewartha | 9-4 | Qualifying | Embassy World Championship |
| | v Sinclair | 9-4 | Qualifying | Embassy World Championship |
| | v David Taylor | 6-10 | 1st round | Embassy World Championship |
| | v Meadowcroft | 4-5 | 1st round | Jameson International |
| | v Johnson | 5-9 | Qualifying | Coral UK Championship |
| 1982 | v M. Owen | 6-0 | 1st round | Welsh Championship |
| | v Griffiths | 6-9 | Semi-final | Welsh Championship |
| | v Medati | 9-5 | Qualifying | Embassy World Championship |
| | v Charlton | 5-10 | 1st round | Embassy World Championship |
| | v Johnson | 5-4 | Qualifying | Jameson International |
| | v Mountjoy | 5-4 | 1st round | Jameson International |
| | v White | 5-2 | 2nd round | Jameson International |
| | v Knowles | 4-5 | Quarter-final | Jameson International |
| | v Morra | 5-2 | 1st round | Professional Players Tournament |
| | v Knowles | 5-4 | 2nd round | Professional Players Tournament |
| | v Reynolds | 1-5 | 3rd round | Professional Players Tournament |
| | v E. McLaughlin | 9-6 | Qualifying | Coral UK Championship |
| | v Thorne | 9-7 | 1st round | Coral UK Championship |
| | v White | 5-9 | 2nd round | Coral UK Championship |
| 1983 | v Thorburn | 3-5 | 1st round | Lada Classic |
| | v Roscoe | 6-4 | Quarter-final | Woodpecker Welsh Championship |
| | v Mountjoy | 3-9 | Semi-final | Woodpecker Welsh Championship |
| | v Everton | 10-1 | Qualifying | Embassy World Championship |
| | v Johnson | 10-8 | Qualifying | Embassy World Championship |
| | v Mountjoy | 2-10 | 1st round | Embassy World Championship |
| | v Donnelly | 1-5 | Qualifying | Jameson International |
| | v Bennett | 5-1 | 1st round | Professional Players Tournament |
| | v Virgo | 5-2 | 2nd round | Professional Players Tournament |
| | v Thorburn | 3-5 | 3rd round | Professional Players Tournament |
| | v Williams | 9-4 | 1st round | Coral UK Championship |
| | v Reardon | 4-9 | 2nd round | Coral UK Championship |
| 1984 | v Charlton | 0-5 | Qualifying | Lada Classic |
| | v Roscoe | 6-2 | 1st round | Strongbow Welsh Championship |
| | v Reardon | 9-4 | Semi-final | Strongbow Welsh Championship |
| | v Mountjoy | 3-9 | Final | Strongbow Welsh Championship |
| | v Mifsud | 8-10 | Qualifying | Embassy World Championship |
| | v Dodd | 1-5 | Qualifying | Jameson International |
| | v Donnelly | 5-2 | 1st round | Rothmans Grand Prix |
| | v Reardon | 4-5 | 2nd round | Rothmans Grand Prix |
| | v Dodd | 9-8 | Qualifying | Coral UK Open |
| | v Griffiths | 9-6 | 1st round | Coral UK Open |
| | v Thorburn | 3-9 | 2nd round | Coral UK Open |
| 1985 | v Fowler | 5-4 | Qualifying | Mercantile Credit Classic |
| | v Mountjoy | 5-4 | 1st round | Mercantile Credit Classic |
| | v Johnson | 0-5 | 2nd round | Mercantile Credit Classic |
| | v Longworth | 3-6 | 1st round | Dulux British Open |

*Cliff Wilson*

|  | | | | |
|---|---|---|---|---|
|  | v Fagan | 9-10 | Qualifying | Embassy World Championship |
|  | v Roscoe | 6-3 | Quarter-final | BCE Welsh Championship |
|  | v Mountjoy | 2-9 | Semi-final | BCE Welsh Championship |
|  | v Roscoe | 5-1 | 3rd round | Goya Matchroom Trophy |
|  | v Chappel | 5-0 | 4th round | Goya Matchroom Trophy |
|  | v Johnson | 1-5 | 5th round | Goya Matchroom Trophy |
|  | v Bales | 5-1 | 3rd round | Rothmans Grand Prix |
|  | v Scott | 5-3 | 4th round | Rothmans Grand Prix |
|  | v Drago | 5-2 | 5th round | Rothmans Grand Prix |
|  | v Dennis Taylor | 2-5 | Quarter-final | Rothmans Grand Prix |
|  | v Cripsey | 7-9 | 3rd round | Coral UK Open |
| 1986 | v Browne | 3-5 | 3rd round | Mercantile Credit Classic |
|  | v Newbury | 6-4 | Quarter-final | Zetters Welsh Championship |
|  | v Griffiths | 1-9 | Semi-final | Zetters Welsh Championship |
|  | v Chaperon | 5-3 | 3rd round | Dulux British Open |
|  | v Stevens | 0-5 | 4th round | Dulux British Open |
|  | v Charlton | 6-10 | 1st round | Embassy World Championship |
|  | v J. McLaughlin | 5-2 | 3rd round | BCE International |
|  | v Bales | 5-1 | 4th round | BCE International |
|  | v Knowles | 5-4 | 5th round | BCE International |
|  | v Thorburn | 1-5 | Quarter-final | BCE International |
|  | v Anderson | 5-4 | 3rd round | Rothmans Grand Prix |
|  | v N. Foulds | 0-5 | 4th round | Rothmans Grand Prix |
|  | v Spencer | 5-9 | 3rd round | Tennents UK Open |
| 1987 | v Williamson | 5-4 | 3rd round | Mercantile Credit Classic |
|  | v Dodd | 5-4 | 4th round | Mercantile Credit Classic |
|  | v W. Jones | 5-3 | 5th round | Mercantile Credit Classic |
|  | v Reynolds | 1-5 | Quarter-final | Mercantile Credit Classic |
|  | v Newbury | 2-6 | Quarter-final | Matchroom Welsh Championship |
|  | v G. Foulds | 5-3 | 3rd round | Dulux British Open |
|  | v S. Francisco | 5-4 | 4th round | Dulux British Open |
|  | v Virgo | 2-5 | 5th round | Dulux British Open |
|  | v Wright | 4-10 | Qualifying | Embassy World Championship |
|  | v Sinclair | 5-1 | 3rd round | Fidelity International |
|  | v D. Gilbert | 1-5 | 4th round | Fidelity International |
|  | v Glen Wilkinson | 5-4 | 3rd round | Rothmans Grand Prix |
|  | v Virgo | 5-3 | 4th round | Rothmans Grand Prix |
|  | v Dennis Taylor | 2-5 | 5th round | Rothmans Grand Prix |
|  | v W. Jones | 9-6 | 3rd round | Tennents UK Open |
|  | v S. Francisco | 1-9 | 4th round | Tennents UK Open |
| 1988 | v D. Gilbert | 5-3 | 3rd round | Mercantile Credit Classic |
|  | v Griffiths | 2-5 | 4th round | Mercantile Credit Classic |
|  | v Newbury | 6-3 | Quarter-final | Welsh Championship |
|  | v Griffiths | 7-9 | Semi-final | Welsh Championship |
|  | v Roscoe | 5-2 | 3rd round | MIM Britannia British Open |
|  | v Thorne | 3-5 | 4th round | MIM Britannia British Open |
|  | v Oliver | 10-6 | Qualifying | Embassy World Championship |
|  | v Johnson | 7-10 | 1st round | Embassy World Championship |
|  | v Duggan | 2-5 | 3rd round | Fidelity International |
|  | v Chappel | 5-2 | 3rd round | Rothmans Grand Prix |
|  | v Drago | 5-4 | 4th round | Rothmans Grand Prix |
|  | v S. Davis | 1-5 | 5th round | Rothmans Grand Prix |
|  | v Gary Wilkinson | 5-2 | 3rd round | BCE Canadian Masters |
|  | v Reynolds | 5-4 | 4th round | BCE Canadian Masters |
|  | v Hendry | 1-5 | 5th round | BCE Canadian Masters |
|  | v Edmonds | 9-1 | 3rd round | Tennents UK Open |
|  | v Reynolds | 3-9 | 4th round | Tennents UK Open |
| 1989 | v S. Campbell | 5-3 | 3rd round | Mercantile Credit Classic |
|  | v David Taylor | 3-5 | 4th round | Mercantile Credit Classic |
|  | v S. Davis | 2-5 | 1st round | Benson and Hedges Masters |
|  | v T. Jones | 5-3 | 3rd round | European Open |
|  | v Robidoux | 0-5 | 4th round | European Open |
|  | v M. Bennett | 1-6 | Quarter-final | Senator Welsh Championship |

| | | | |
|---|---|---|---|
| v John Rea | 5-2 | 3rd round | Anglian British Open |
| v Chappel | 5-3 | 4th round | Anglian British Open |
| v Reynolds | 0-5 | 5th round | Anglian British Open |
| v Duggan | 1-10 | 1st round | Embassy World Championship |

## TONY WILSON (Isle of Man)

**Born** 12.2.64. **Turned professional** 1988. **World ranking** 71. **Best professional performance** Last 32 1989 European Open.

| | | | | |
|---|---|---|---|---|
| **1988** | v M. Gibson | 5-1 | 1st round | Fidelity International |
| | v Browne | 5-3 | 2nd round | Fidelity International |
| | v David Taylor | 1-5 | 3rd round | Fidelity International |
| | v Scott | 5-3 | 1st round | Rothmans Grand Prix |
| | v Chappel | 1-5 | 2nd round | Rothmans Grand Prix |
| | v Grace | 5-2 | 1st round | BCE Canadian Masters |
| | v Clark | 3-5 | 2nd round | BCE Canadian Masters |
| | v Bradley | 7-9 | 1st round | Tennents UK Open |
| **1989** | v Foldvari | 4-5 | 1st round | Mercantile Credit Classic |
| | v M. Gibson | 5-3 | 1st round | European Open |
| | v Gauvreau | 5-3 | 2nd round | European Open |
| | v Spencer | *wo* | 3rd round | European Open |
| | v Fowler | 2-5 | 4th round | European Open |
| | v F. Davis | 5-1 | 1st round | Anglian British Open |
| | v N. Gilbert | 2-5 | 2nd round | Anglian British Open |
| | v M. Francisco | 10-5 | Qualifying | Embassy World Championship |
| | v Scott | 10-4 | Qualifying | Embassy World Championship |
| | v O'Boye | 8-10 | Qualifying | Embassy World Championship |

## JON WRIGHT (England)

**Born** 10.8.62. **Turned professional** 1986. **World ranking** 67 (61). **Best professional performances** Last 32 1987 Embassy World Championship, 1987, 1989 Mercantile Credit Classic.

| | | | | |
|---|---|---|---|---|
| **1986** | v Watterson | 5-1 | 1st round | BCE International |
| | v Black | 1-5 | 2nd round | BCE International |
| | v Fisher | 5-1 | 1st round | Rothmans Grand Prix |
| | v Bradley | 5-0 | 2nd round | Rothmans Grand Prix |
| | v Dennis Taylor | 3-5 | 3rd round | Rothmans Grand Prix |
| | v Smith | 9-7 | 1st round | Tennents UK Open |
| | v Fagan | 9-0 | 2nd round | Tennents UK Open |
| | v Johnson | 1-9 | 3rd round | Tennents UK Open |
| **1987** | v D. Hughes | 5-2 | 1st round | Mercantile Credit Classic |
| | v Chappel | 5-4 | 2nd round | Mercantile Credit Classic |
| | v E. Hughes | 5-4 | 3rd round | Mercantile Credit Classic |
| | v Hendry | 1-5 | 4th round | Mercantile Credit Classic |
| | v Chalmers | 6-5 | 1st round | Tolly Ales English Championship |
| | v Spencer | 1-6 | 2nd round | Tolly Ales English Championship |
| | v Sheehan | 2-5 | 1st round | Dulux British Open |
| | v Houlihan | 10-4 | Qualifying | Embassy World Championship |
| | v Browne | 10-6 | Qualifying | Embassy World Championship |
| | v Wildman | 10-0 | Qualifying | Embassy World Championship |
| | v Wilson | 10-4 | Qualifying | Embassy World Championship |
| | v Higgins | 6-10 | 1st round | Embassy World Championship |
| | v Kelly | 5-2 | 2nd round | Fidelity International |
| | v Meo | 2-5 | 3rd round | Fidelity International |
| | v Rigitano | 5-0 | 2nd round | Rothmans Grand Prix |
| | v White | 4-5 | 3rd round | Rothmans Grand Prix |
| | v Lawlor | 7-9 | 2nd round | Tennents UK Open |
| **1988** | v Sinclair | 5-3 | 2nd round | Mercantile Credit Classic |

| | v Knowles | 1-5 | 3rd round | Mercantile Credit Classic |
|---|---|---|---|---|
| | v Fisher | 6-2 | 2nd round | English Championship |
| | v Knowles | 2-6 | 3rd round | English Championship |
| | v D. Gilbert | 2-5 | 2nd round | MIM Britannia British Open |
| | v Chambers | 10-2 | Qualifying | Embassy World Championship |
| | v Owers | 10-8 | Qualifying | Embassy World Championship |
| | v Hendry | 4-10 | Qualifying | Embassy World Championship |
| | v Williamson | 5-1 | 2nd round | Fidelity International |
| | v James | 3-5 | 3rd round | Fidelity International |
| | v Foldvari | 4-5 | 2nd round | Rothmans Grand Prix |
| | v Graham | 2-5 | 2nd round | BCE Canadian Masters |
| | v Rowing | 7-9 | 2nd round | Tennents UK Open |
| **1989** | v G. Foulds | 5-4 | 2nd round | Mercantile Credit Classic |
| | v Williams | 5-0 | 3rd round | Mercantile Credit Classic |
| | v S. Francisco | 2-5 | 4th round | Mercantile Credit Classic |
| | v Johnston-Allen | 4-5 | 2nd round | European Open |
| | v Rowswell | 2-5 | 2nd round | English Championship |
| | v Grace | 5-1 | 2nd round | Anglian British Open |
| | v Parrott | 1-5 | 3rd round | Anglian British Open |
| | v M. Smith | 7-10 | Qualifying | Embassy World Championship |

## JIM WYCH (Canada)

**Born** 11.1.55. **Turned professional** 1979. **World ranking** 37 (38). **Amateur career** 1979 Canadian champion. **Best professional performances** Quarter-finals 1989 European Open, 1986 Dulux British Open, 1980 Embassy World Championship.

| | v John Bear | 9-5 | Qualifying | Embassy World Championship |
|---|---|---|---|---|
| **1980** | v John Bear | 9-5 | Qualifying | Embassy World Championship |
| | v Williams | 9-7 | Qualifying | Embassy World Championship |
| | v Pulman | 10-5 | 1st round | Embassy World Championship |
| | v Dennis Taylor | 13-10 | 2nd round | Embassy World Championship |
| | v Thorburn | 6-13 | Quarter-final | Embassy World Championship |
| **1981** | v Knowles | 3-9 | Qualifying | Embassy World Championship |
| | v Johnson | 2-5 | 1st round | Jameson International |
| **1982** | v Higgins | 3-5 | 1st round | Benson & Hedges Irish Masters |
| | v John Bear | 4-9 | Qualifying | Embassy World Championship |
| | v Bennett | 5-0 | Qualifying | Jameson International |
| | v Werbeniuk | 3-5 | 1st round | Jameson International |
| | v Kelly | 5-0 | 1st round | Professional Players Tournament |
| | v White | 0-5 | 2nd round | Professional Players Tournament |
| **1983** | v Jonik | 5-9 | Quarter-final | Canadian Championship |
| **1984** | v Ganim | 10-1 | Qualifying | Embassy World Championship |
| | v Scott | 10-6 | Qualifying | Embassy World Championship |
| | v Fagan | 10-3 | Qualifying | Embassy World Championship |
| | v Reardon | 7-10 | 1st round | Embassy World Championship |
| **1985** | v Bradley | 10-7 | Qualifying | Embassy World Championship |
| | v Virgo | 4-10 | Qualifying | Embassy World Championship |
| | v Sanderson | 5-2 | 1st round | Canadian Championship |
| | v John Bear | 6-3 | Quarter-final | Canadian Championship |
| | v Thorburn | 5-6 | Semi-final | Canadian Championship |
| | v Rempe | 5-1 | 2nd round | Goya Matchroom Trophy |
| | v Mountjoy | 1-5 | 3rd round | Goya Matchroom Trophy |
| | v V. Harris | 3-5 | 2nd round | Rothmans Grand Prix |
| | v Duggan | 9-5 | 2nd round | Coral UK Open |
| | v S. Francisco | 8-9 | 3rd round | Coral UK Open |
| **1986** | v Demarco | 5-0 | 2nd round | Mercantile Credit Classic |
| | v E. Hughes | 2-5 | 3rd round | Mercantile Credit Classic |
| | v Van Rensberg | 5-0 | 2nd round | Dulux British Open |
| | v Reynolds | 5-3 | 3rd round | Dulux British Open |
| | v Knowles | 5-4 | 4th round | Dulux British Open |
| | v Parrott | 5-4 | 5th round | Dulux British Open |
| | v S. Davis | 2-5 | Quarter-final | Dulux British Open |

|      |                    |       |               |                           |
|------|--------------------|-------|---------------|---------------------------|
|      | v Chappel          | 10-6  | Qualifying    | Embassy World Championship |
|      | v Duggan           | 10-5  | Qualifying    | Embassy World Championship |
|      | v Hallett          | 7-10  | Qualifying    | Embassy World Championship |
|      | v Mikkelsen        | 6-3   | 2nd round     | Canadian Championship     |
|      | v Stevens          | 6-2   | Semi-final    | Canadian Championship     |
|      | v Thorburn         | 2-6   | Final         | Canadian Championship     |
|      | v Bradley          | 5-2   | 3rd round     | BCE International         |
|      | v Thorburn         | 3-5   | 4th round     | BCE International         |
|      | v John Rea         | 5-2   | 3rd round     | Rothmans Grand Prix       |
|      | v Mountjoy         | 1-5   | 4th round     | Rothmans Grand Prix       |
|      | v B. Harris        | 9-6   | 3rd round     | Tennents UK Open          |
|      | v N. Foulds        | 3-9   | 4th round     | Tennents UK Open          |
| 1987 | v B. Harris        | 3-5   | 3rd round     | Mercantile Credit Classic |
|      | v Murphy           | 1-5   | 3rd round     | Dulux British Open        |
|      | v Bradley          | 10-7  | Qualifying    | Embassy World Championship |
|      | v Griffiths        | 4-10  | 1st round     | Embassy World Championship |
|      | v Bear             | 4-6   | Quarter-final | Canadian Championship     |
|      | v Jenkins          | 5-4   | 2nd round     | Fidelity International     |
|      | v Johnson          | 5-4   | 3rd round     | Fidelity International     |
|      | v E. Hughes        | 4-5   | 4th round     | Fidelity International     |
|      | v Marshall         | 5-2   | 2nd round     | Rothmans Grand Prix       |
|      | v Macleod          | 5-4   | 3rd round     | Rothmans Grand Prix       |
|      | v S. Davis         | 1-5   | 4th round     | Rothmans Grand Prix       |
|      | v Fisher           | 9-6   | 2nd round     | Tennents UK Open          |
|      | v Hendry           | 9-7   | 3rd round     | Tennents UK Open          |
|      | v Parrott          | 6-9   | 4th round     | Tennents UK Open          |
| 1988 | v Clark            | 2-5   | 2nd round     | Mercantile Credit Classic |
|      | v Thornley         | 5-1   | 2nd round     | MIM Britannia British Open |
|      | v Thorne           | 1-5   | 3rd round     | MIM Britannia British Open |
|      | v J. Smith         | 10-3  | Qualifying    | Embassy World Championship |
|      | v M. Bennett       | 5-10  | Qualifying    | Embassy World Championship |
|      | v Thornley         | 6-5   | 1st round     | BCE Canadian Championship |
|      | v Morra            | 6-5   | Quarter-final | BCE Canadian Championship |
|      | v Thorburn         | 7-5   | Semi-final    | BCE Canadian Championship |
|      | v Robidoux         | 4-8   | Final         | BCE Canadian Championship |
|      | v V. Harris        | 5-3   | 2nd round     | Fidelity International     |
|      | v Griffiths        | 5-0   | 3rd round     | Fidelity International     |
|      | v O'Kane           | 5-4   | 4th round     | Fidelity International     |
|      | v Dennis Taylor    | 2-5   | 5th round     | Fidelity International     |
|      | v Williamson       | 4-5   | 2nd round     | Rothmans Grand Prix       |
|      | v Foldvari         | 5-2   | 2nd round     | BCE Canadian Masters      |
|      | v Charlton         | 4-5   | 3rd round     | BCE Canadian Masters      |
|      | v Oliver           | 9-6   | 2nd round     | Tennents UK Open          |
|      | v Knowles          | 4-9   | 3rd round     | Tennents UK Open          |
| 1989 | v Glen Wilkinson   | 3-5   | 2nd round     | Mercantile Credit Classic |
|      | v G. Foulds        | 5-0   | 2nd round     | European Open             |
|      | v S. Francisco     | 5-1   | 3rd round     | European Open             |
|      | v Johnston-Allen   | 5-4   | 4th round     | European Open             |
|      | v Fowler           | 5-4   | 5th round     | European Open             |
|      | v Hallett          | 3-5   | Quarter-final | European Open             |
|      | v A. Harris        | 5-4   | 2nd round     | Anglian British Open      |
|      | v Knowles          | 2-5   | 3rd round     | Anglian British Open      |
|      | v Johnston-Allen   | 10-3  | Qualifying    | Embassy World Championship |
|      | v W. Jones         | 9-10  | Qualifying    | Embassy World Championship |

*At the end of the 1988–89 season, the following players became non-tournament playing members of the WPBSA:* **Billy Kelly (Republic of Ireland), Greg Jenkins (Australia), Ian Black (Scotland), Bernie Mikkelsen (Canada), Patsy Fagan (Republic of Ireland), Pascal Burke**

(Republic of Ireland), Dave Chalmers (England), Ian Anderson (Australia) and Jim Rempe (USA).

Other non-tournament playing members are: Derek Mienie (South Africa), Joe Grech* (Malta), Derek Heaton (England), Clive Everton (Wales), David Greaves (England), Bernard Bennett (England), Maurice Parkin (England), John Hargreaves (England), Bert Demarco (Scotland), Eddie McLaughlin (Scotland), Joe Caggianello (Canada), Mike Hines (South Africa), Lou Condo (Australia), Mannie Francisco (South Africa), James Giannaros (Australia), Steve Mizerak (USA), Paddy Morgan (Australia), Wayne Saunderson (Canada), Gerry Watson (Canada), Sam Frangie* (Australia) and Vladimir Potasnik* (Australia).
*denotes new member

George Ganim resigned during the 1987–88 season, and Perrie Mans at the end of the 1986–87 season. Bill Werbeniuk was expelled from membership for non payment of a disciplinary fine in March 1989.

The ten players who qualified for professional status for the 1989–90 season were: Nigel Bond (England), Ian Brumby (England), Andrew Cairns (England), Duncan Campbell (Scotland), Nick Dyson (England), Brady Gollan (Canada), Brian Morgan (England), Stephen Murphy (Republic of Ireland), Barry Pinches (England) and James Wattana (Thailand). Paul Thornley (Canada), by virtue of acquiring one merit point at the 1989 Embassy World Championship, qualified for tournament status.

## SNOOKER GREATS

### JOE DAVIS O.B.E. (1901–1978)

Although only one of the 'Big Four' at billiards, Joe Davis was undoubtedly the number one at snooker. With his friend Bill Camkin, a Birmingham billiard trader, he promoted and won the first World Professional Snooker Championship in 1927. He went on to win the title every year until 1940. The Championship was suspended until 1946, at which point Davis beat Horace Lindrum 78–67 to take the title for the 15th time,

Davis then retired from Championship play. He continued to play in other tournaments and in the public's mind he was still the champion, whoever had won the World Championship in his absence.

His expertise at the three-ball game carried him to four World Professional Billiards titles but his name will always be synonymous with snooker. It was he who developed the modern break-making methods, using the black as the key colour, and it was he who brought the sport to the public's attention.

### WALTER DONALDSON (1907–1973)

Consistent and steady, Walter Donaldson reached eight consecutive World Championship finals between 1948 and 1954. In 1947 and 1950 he beat Fred Davis to take the title.

As professional snooker's appeal dwindled in the mid-1950s, a disillusioned Donaldson turned his billiard room into a cowshed and broke up the slates of his table for crazy paving.

### JOHN PULMAN (born 1926)

After winning the English Amateur Championship in 1946, John Pulman turned professional but was at his peak when the professional game was going through a period in the doldrums. He was never able to capitalise fully on his natural talent.

He won the world title in 1957 and then successfully withstood a series of challengers. When the influx of new professionals led to the Championship being restored to a tournament format, he once reached the final, losing to Ray Reardon.

An accident led to his retirement from playing in 1982 but he is still involved on the circuit as a member of ITV's commentary team.

# THE CIRCUIT

## NEW ZEALAND MASTERS

**First staged** 1988. **Sponsors** Lion Brown. **Venue** Wellington. **Prize-money last season** £40,000. **TV** TVNZ.

**1988**
**First round:** J. Johnson beat D. Reynolds 5-4; S. Hendry beat D. Morgan 5-2; M. Hallett beat D. O'Kane 5-1; A. Knowles beat W. King 5-4
**Semi-finals:** Hendry beat Johnson 5-2; Hallett beat Knowles 5-3
**Final:** Hendry beat Hallett 6-1
*Play-off for third place: Johnson beat Knowles 5-4*


## LEP HONG KONG MASTERS

**First staged** 1984*. **Sponsors** Camus (1986–87), LEP (1988– ). **Venue** Queen Elizabeth Stadium. **Prize-money last season** £75,000. **TV** Hong Kong.
**The first two events, in 1984 and 1985, were small, pathfinding events which do not meet the conditions required for full inclusion in this book.*

**1986** (*Camus*)
**Semi-finals:** Dennis Taylor beat T. Griffiths 5-4; W. Thorne beat S. Davis 5-2
**Final:** Thorne beat Dennis Taylor 8-3

**1987** (*Rileys*)
**Quarter-finals:** S. Davis beat T. Griffiths 3-0; J. White beat W. Thorne 3-0; Dennis Taylor beat C. Thorburn 3-0; S. Hendry beat N. Foulds 3-2
**Semi-finals:** Davis beat Taylor 5-4; Hendry beat White 5-2
**Final:** Davis beat Hendry 9-3

**1988**
**Semi-finals:** N. Foulds beat W. Thorne 5-4; J. White beat Dennis Taylor 5-2
**Final:** White beat Foulds 6-3


## LANGS SCOTTISH MASTERS

**First staged** 1981. **Sponsors** Langs. **Venue** Kelvin Hall, Glasgow (1981), Holiday Inn, Glasgow (1982), Skean Dhu Hotel (re-named Hospitality Inn), Glasgow (1983– ). **Initial prize-money** £20,500. **Prize-money this season** £50,000. **TV** BBC Scotland.

**1981**
**Preliminary round:** V. Harris beat I. Black 4-0
**First round:** J. White beat R. Reardon 5-4; S. Davis beat D. Mountjoy 5-0; C. Thorburn beat K. Stevens 5-1; A. Higgins beat V. Harris 5-3
**Semi-finals:** White beat Davis 6-5; Thorburn beat Higgins 6-2
**Final:** White beat Thorburn 9-4

**1982**
**First round:** Dennis Taylor beat J. White 5-4; S. Davis beat A. Knowles 5-4; T. Griffiths beat R. Reardon 5-3; A. Higgins beat E. Sinclair 5-1
**Semi-finals:** S. Davis beat Dennis Taylor 6-1; Higgins beat Griffiths 6-5
**Final:** S. Davis beat Higgins 9-4

**1983**
**First round:** C. Thorburn beat T. Griffiths 5-1; S. Davis beat M. Macleod 5-1; A. Knowles beat T. Meo 5-4; A. Higgins beat J. White 5-3
**Semi-finals:** Knowles beat Thorburn 6-2; S. Davis beat Higgins 6-2
**Final:** S. Davis beat Knowles 9-6

**1984**
**First round:** A. Knowles beat T. Griffiths 5-3; J. White beat M. Macleod 5-0; S. Davis beat C. Thorburn 5-2; A. Higgins beat K. Stevens 5-2
**Semi-finals:** White beat Knowles 6-5; S. Davis beat Higgins 6-4
**Final:** S. Davis beat White 9-4

**1985**
**First round:** J. White beat A. Higgins 5-0; C. Thorburn beat M. Macleod 5-1; S. Francisco beat A. Knowles 5-4; W. Thorne beat Dennis Taylor 5-2
**Semi-finals:** Thorne beat White 6-2; Thorburn beat Francisco 6-0
**Final:** Thorburn beat Thorne 9-7

**1986**
**First round:** C. Thorburn beat J. Parrott 5-1; J. White beat S. Hendry 5-1; K. Stevens beat A. Knowles 5-3; A. Higgins beat J. Johnson 5-2
**Semi-finals:** Thorburn beat White 6-2; Higgins beat Stevens 6-2
**Final:** Thorburn beat Higgins 9-8

**1987**
**First round:** C. Thorburn beat Dennis Taylor 5-2; J. Johnson beat S. Hendry 5-2; T. Griffiths beat N. Foulds 5-4; J. White beat A. Higgins 5-3
**Semi-finals:** Johnson beat Thorburn 6-3; Griffiths beat White 6-2
**Final:** Johnson beat Griffiths 9-7

*The tournament was not held in 1988 but was due to be revived in 1989 under the sponsorship of Regal.*

# FIDELITY INTERNATIONAL

**First staged** 1981. **Sponsors** Jameson (1981-84), Goya (1985), BCE (1986), Fidelity (1987-88). **Venue** Assembly Rooms, Derby (1981-82), Eldon Square Recreation Centre, Newcastle upon Tyne (1983-84), Trentham Gardens, Stoke (1985- ). **Initial prize-money** £66,000. **Prize-money last season** £225,000. **TV** ITV.

**1981** (*Jameson*)
**Qualifying groups**
1  M. Gibson beat S. Hood 5-3; Gibson beat M. Parkin 5-3; J. Dunning beat Gibson 5-3
2  C. Roscoe beat R. Andrewartha 5-2; D. Sheehan beat V. Harris 5-1; Roscoe beat Sheehan 5-1; J. Meadowcroft beat Roscoe 5-4
3  C. Everton beat K. Kennerley 5-4; M. Watterson beat P. Medati 5-3; Watterson beat Everton 5-4; P. Fagan beat Watterson 5-2
4  P. Houlihan *wo* J. Barrie *scr*; D. French beat G. Foulds 5-2; French beat Houlihan 5-3; R. Williams beat French 5-0

5   B. Demarco *wo* B. Mikkelsen *scr*; D. Hughes beat Jack Rea 5-4; Demarco beat
    Hughes 5-1; M. Hallett beat Demarco 5-4
6   E. Hughes beat M. Owen 5-1; J. Fitzmaurice beat B. Bennett 5-1; E. Hughes beat
    Fitzmaurice 5-3; E. Hughes beat E. Sinclair 5-2
7   E. McLaughlin beat I. Black 5-3; M. Wildman beat M. Morra 5-3; E. McLaughlin
    beat Wildman 5-3; E. McLaughlin beat D. Greaves 5-1
8   M. Macleod beat B. Kelly 5-1; J. Johnson beat J. Donnelly 5-4; Johnson beat
    Macleod 5-1; Johnson *wo* J. Pulman *scr*
**First round:** J. Johnson beat J. Wych 5-2; D. Martin beat J. Dunning 5-2; R. Williams
beat J. White 5-1; A. Knowles beat M. Hallett 5-2; R. Edmonds beat E. Hughes 5-4;
J. Meadowcroft beat C. Wilson 5-4; T. Meo beat E. McLaughlin 5-2
**Second round:** G. Miles beat Johnson 5-3; Martin beat B. Werbeniuk 5-2; Williams beat
F. Davis 5-0; A. Higgins beat P. Fagan 5-3; J. Spencer beat Edmonds 5-3; J. Virgo beat
Knowles 5-2; K. Stevens beat Meadowcroft 5-1; P. Mans beat Meo 5-3
**Third round:** Miles beat C. Thorburn 5-0; Martin beat E. Charlton 5-2; Virgo beat
R. Reardon 5-3; David Taylor beat Stevens 5-0; Dennis Taylor beat Williams 5-1;
Higgins beat D. Mountjoy 5-1; T. Griffiths beat Spencer 5-2; S. Davis beat Mans 5-3
**Quarter-finals:** Martin beat Miles 5-1; Higgins beat Griffiths 5-2; Dennis Taylor beat
Virgo 5-2; S. Davis beat David Taylor 5-1
**Semi-finals:** Dennis Taylor beat Martin 9-1; S. Davis beat Higgins 9-8
**Final:** S. Davis beat Dennis Taylor 9-0

## 1982 (*Jameson*)
**Qualifying groups**
1   R. Edmonds beat D. Hughes 5-0; Edmonds beat G. Miles 5-1
2   V. Harris beat D. Sheehan 5-3; J. Virgo beat Harris 5-2
3   M. Fisher beat T. Murphy 5-1; Fisher beat F. Davis 5-3
4   B. Bennett beat M. Owen 5-2; J. Wych beat Bennett 5-0
5   M. Morra beat B. Demarco 5-2; D. Reynolds beat Morra 5-1
6   M. Watterson beat C. Everton 5-1; Watterson beat P. Fagan 5-1
7   E. Sinclair beat I. Anderson 5-2; Sinclair beat T. Meo 5-3
8   G. Scott beat B. Harris 5-4; Scott *wo* John Bear *scr*
9   J. Johnson *wo* J. Phillips *scr*; C. Wilson beat Johnson 5-4
10  E. Hughes beat M. Parkin 5-2; Hughes beat D. Martin 5-4
11  C. Ross *wo* D. Greaves *scr*; J. Meadowcroft beat Ross 5-0
12  I. Williamson beat J. Donnelly 5-3; B. Kelly beat G. Foulds 5-4; Kelly beat
    Williamson 5-1
13  C. Roscoe beat J. Dunning 5-2; D. French beat G. Cripsey 5-1; Roscoe beat French
    5-2
14  M. Hallett beat F. Jonik 5-2; M. Wildman beat M. Gibson 5-1; Wildman beat
    Hallett 5-2
15  J. Fitzmaurice beat I. Black 5-3; L. Dodd beat M. Macleod 5-1; Dodd beat
    Fitzmaurice 5-3
16  R. Williams beat P. Medati 5-3; E. McLaughlin beat P. Houlihan 5-2; Williams beat
    McLaughlin 5-1
**First round:** A. Knowles beat Sinclair 5-2; Reynolds beat W. Thorne 5-3; S. Davis beat
Roscoe 5-0; B. Werbeniuk beat Wych 5-3; David Taylor beat Fisher 5-1; K. Stevens beat
Watterson 5-3; T. Griffiths beat Williams 5-2; J. Spencer beat Edmonds 5-2; Dennis
Taylor beat Wildman 5-2; Virgo beat E. Charlton 5-4; P. Mans beat Dodd 5-3; J. White
beat Meadowcroft 5-1; R. Reardon beat E. Hughes 5-3; C. Thorburn beat Scott 5-1;
A. Higgins beat Kelly 5-3; Wilson beat D. Mountjoy 5-4
**Second round:** S. Davis beat Reynolds 5-0; David Taylor beat Werbeniuk 5-2; Stevens
beat Mans 5-2; Griffiths beat Higgins 5-2; Dennis Taylor beat Thorburn 5-2; Wilson
beat White 5-2; Virgo beat Spencer 5-4; Knowles beat Reardon 5-2
**Quarter-finals:** Virgo beat Dennis Taylor 5-3; David Taylor beat S. Davis 5-3; Knowles
beat Wilson 5-4; Stevens beat Griffiths 5-3

**Semi-finals:** Knowles beat Stevens 9-3; David Taylor beat Virgo 9-5
**Final:** Knowles beat David Taylor 9-6

## 1983 (*Jameson*)

**Qualifying groups**

1  M. Watterson beat B. Demarco 5-3; Watterson beat P. Mans 5-4
2  T. Murphy beat D. Sheehan 5-2; W. Thorne beat Murphy 5-2
3  R. Williams beat D. French 5-1; D. Reynolds beat Williams 5-3
4  J. Donnelly beat B. Bennett 5-1; Donnelly beat C. Wilson 5-1
5  M. Darrington beat I. Williamson 5-3; S. Francisco beat Darrington 5-2
6  W. King beat I. Black 5-3; G. Miles beat King 5-3
7  D. Hughes beat M. Parkin 5-0; J. Johnson beat Hughes 5-1
8  B. Harris beat J. Dunning 5-3; M. Wildman beat Harris 5-2
9  D. Martin beat D. Greaves 5-1; Martin beat P. Fagan 5-0
10  R. Andrewartha beat C. Everton 5-1; E. Sinclair beat Andrewartha 5-4
11  P. Medati beat V. Harris 5-0; M. Macleod beat Medati 5-3
12  F. Davis beat B. Kelly 5-1; P. Morgan beat J. Fitzmaurice 5-4; Morgan beat Davis 5-3
13  M. Hallett beat C. Roscoe 5-2; M. Morra beat P. Watchorn 5-3; Morra beat Hallett 5-3
14  G. Foulds beat P. Burke 5-2; E. Hughes beat M. Fisher 5-4; Hughes beat Foulds 5-1
15  M. Gibson beat L. Dodd 5-1; G. Scott beat P. Houlihan 5-0; Scott beat Gibson 5-3
16  E. McLaughlin beat J. Campbell 5-2; R. Edmonds beat Jack Rea 5-1; Edmonds beat McLaughlin 5-1

**First round:** Dennis Taylor beat Reynolds 5-3; R. Reardon beat Macleod 5-2; Thorne beat J. Virgo 5-2; Morra beat J. White 5-3; D. Mountjoy beat Wildman 5-4; Martin beat A. Higgins 5-2; Watterson beat T. Meo 5-3; Scott beat B. Werbeniuk 5-3; T. Griffiths beat Miles 5-2; S. Davis beat Hughes 5-1; Donnelly beat David Taylor 5-3; Francisco *wo* K. Stevens *scr*; E. Charlton beat Johnson 5-2; Thorburn beat Sinclair 5-0; J. Spencer beat Morgan 5-1; A. Knowles beat Edmonds 5-1

**Second round:** Griffiths beat Scott 5-0; Spencer beat Knowles 5-4; Thorburn beat Dennis Taylor 5-3; Mountjoy beat Martin 5-0; Charlton beat Morra 5-3; Thorne beat Reardon 5-0; S. Francisco beat Donnelly 5-1; S. Davis beat Watterson 5-0

**Quarter-finals:** Griffiths beat Spencer 5-4; Thorburn beat Mountjoy 5-2; Charlton beat Thorne 5-0; S. Davis beat S. Francisco 5-1

**Semi-finals:** Thorburn beat Griffiths 9-8; S. Davis beat Charlton 9-2
**Final:** S. Davis beat Thorburn 9-4

## 1984 (*Jameson*)

**Qualifying groups**

1  G. Foulds beat P. Francisco 5-4; I. Williamson beat V. Harris 5-0; Foulds beat Williamson 5-4; Foulds beat J. Donnelly 5-3; J. Campbell beat Foulds 5-3
2  W. Jones beat P. Watchorn 5-0; M. Gibson beat P. Medati 5-3; Jones beat Gibson 5-2; Jones beat G. Scott 5-0; Jones beat M. Wildman 5-0
3  T. Jones beat D. French 5-1; S. Duggan beat Jones 5-2; E. Sinclair beat Duggan 5-0; Sinclair beat P. Mans 5-2
4  B. Bennett beat B. Demarco 5-1; Bennett *wo* P. Morgan *scr*; Bennett *wo* J. Wych *scr*; N. Foulds beat Bennett 5-0
5  R. Foldvari beat G. Rigitano 5-2; Foldvari beat R. Edmonds 5-1; L. Dodd beat Foldvari 5-3; Dodd beat C. Wilson 5-1
6  B. Mikkelsen beat T. Chappel 5-4; Mikkelsen beat C. Everton 5-0; C. Roscoe beat Mikkelsen 5-1; E. Hughes beat Roscoe 5-1
7  D. O'Kane beat M. Parkin 5-2; O'Kane beat E. McLaughlin 5-1; O'Kane beat J. Fitzmaurice 5-4; O'Kane beat M. Hallett 5-4
8  J. McLaughlin beat D. Greaves 5-3; F. Jonik beat McLaughlin 5-2; M. Gauvreau beat Jonik 5-1; Gauvreau beat J. Parrott 5-4

9   G. Cripsey beat P. Thornley 5-3; J. Dunning beat Cripsey 5-3; F. Davis beat
Dunning 5-4; J. Virgo beat Davis 5-3
10   J. Hargreaves beat P. Houlihan 5-2; B. Kelly beat Hargreaves 5-2; Kelly beat
W. King 5-4; S. Francisco beat Kelly 5-3
11   D. Fowler beat R. Chaperon 5-0; Fowler *wo* P. Mifsud *scr*; Fowler beat
R. Andrewartha 5-0; Fowler beat D. Martin 5-0
12   M. Bradley beat M. Darrington 5-3; Bradley beat Jack Rea 5-2; M. Morra beat
Bradley 5-3; J. Johnson beat Morra 5-0
13   D. Chalmers *wo* Condo *scr*; W. Oliver beat D. Hughes 5-4; Chalmers beat Oliver
5-4; J. Meadowcroft beat Chalmers 5-1; R. Williams beat Meadowcroft 5-4
14   P. Browne beat John Rea 5-2; I. Black beat Browne 5-4; Black beat M. Watterson
5-3; M. Macleod beat Black 5-3
15   S. Newbury beat S. Longworth 5-4; P. Burke beat A. Kearney 5-4; Newbury beat
Burke 5-0; Newbury beat P. Fagan 5-0; Newbury beat G. Miles 5-1
16   R. Bales beat D. Sheehan 5-2; Bales beat T. Murphy 5-4; Bales beat M. Fisher 5-3;
D. Reynolds beat Bales 5-4
**First round:** S. Davis beat Campbell 5-1; A. Higgins beat Sinclair 5-1; T. Griffiths beat
N. Foulds 5-3; R. Reardon beat Dodd 5-4; E. Hughes beat D. Mountjoy 5-1; W. Thorne
beat O'Kane 5-3; Gauvreau beat K. Stevens 5-1; Virgo beat C. Thorburn 5-0;
S. Francisco beat J. Spencer 5-2; Dennis Taylor beat Fowler 5-0; Johnson beat
E. Charlton 5-1; J. White beat Williams 5-3; T. Meo beat Macleod 5-1; Newbury beat
B. Werbeniuk 5-2; A. Knowles beat Reynolds 5-1; David Taylor beat W. Jones 5-4
**Second round:** S. Davis beat David Taylor 5-1; Higgins beat Griffiths 5-4; E. Hughes
beat Reardon 5-1; Thorne beat Gauvreau 5-3; S. Francisco beat Virgo 5-2; Dennis
Taylor beat Johnson 5-2; White beat Meo 5-1; Knowles beat Newbury 5-4
**Quarter-finals:** S. Davis beat Higgins 5-1; E. Hughes beat Thorne 5-2; S. Francisco *wo*
Dennis Taylor *scr*; Knowles beat White 5-4
**Semi-finals:** S. Davis beat E. Hughes 9-3; Knowles beat S. Francisco 9-6
**Final:** S. Davis beat Knowles 9-2

## 1985 (*Goya Matchroom*)

**First round:** M. Darrington beat D. Gilbert 5-2; O. Agrawal beat P. Watchorn 5-2;
M. Smith beat D. Sheehan 5-2; S. Simngam beat D. Greaves 5-2; G. Wilkinson beat
B. Demarco 5-2; J. Rempe beat P. Burke 5-3; S. Hendry beat B. West 5-4; Jim Bear beat
P. Houlihan 5-2; J. Caggianello beat J. Hargreaves 5-2; D. Mienie *wo* G. Watson *scr*;
J. O'Boye beat M. Parkin 5-3; R. Bales beat T. Drago 5-2; D. Hughes beat A. Kearney
5-1; G. Cripsey beat B. Bennett 5-3
**Second round:** B. Mikkelsen beat M. Fisher 5-3; M. Gibson beat P. Francisco 5-4;
P. Fagan beat Mienie 5-4; W. King beat Caggianello 5-0; R. Chaperon beat D. Chalmers
5-2; Bales beat R. Edmonds 5-0; G. Miles beat O'Boye 5-2; J. Fitzmaurice beat
M. Watterson 5-2; T. Chappel beat J. Meadowcraft 5-2; C. Roscoe beat G. Foulds 5-3;
E. McLaughlin beat Hendry 5-3; Jim Bear beat J. Donnelly 5-2; T. Jones beat W. Kelly
5-3; M. Bradley beat John Rea 5-1; L. Dodd beat Simngam 5-4; Williamson beat
J. McLaughlin 5-3; J. Dunning beat C. Everton 5-2; M. Morra beat B. Oliver 5-1;
D. Fowler beat Agrawal 5-2; J. Wych beat Rempe 5-1; E. Sinclair beat Darrington 5-0;
S. Longworth beat Wilkinson 5-0; Cripsey beat P. Medati 5-2; S. Newbury beat F. Jonik
5-4; S. Duggan beat F. Davis 5-1; I. Black beat G. Rigitano 5-4; R. Foldvari beat
V. Harris 5-4; G. Scott beat J. Van Rensberg 5-4; T. Murphy beat Jack Rea 5-1;
B. Harris beat P. Browne 5-3; W. Jones beat Smith 5-3; D. Hughes beat M. Gauvreau 5-4
**Third round:** S. Davis beat Bales 5-2; J. Virgo beat Miles 5-2; Chaperon beat S. Francisco
5-3; M. Macleod beat Fitzmaurice 5-1; Gibson beat E. Charlton 5-4; D. Reynolds beat
Mikkelsen 5-0; J. White beat Fagan 5-2; King beat R. Williams 5-3; Chappel beat
K. Stevens 5-3; C. Wilson beat Roscoe 5-4; J. Johnson beat Jim Bear 5-1; Bradley beat
M. Hallett 5-4; David Taylor beat T. Jones 5-4; B. Werbeniuk beat Williamson 5-2;
A. Knowles beat E. McLaughlin 5-1; N. Foulds beat Dodd 5-3; C. Thorburn beat
Longworth 5-3; D. Martin beat Sinclair 5-1; D. Mountjoy beat Wych 5-1; J. Campbell

beat Morra 5-2; W. Thorne beat Fowler 5-1; Scott beat M. Wildman 5-1; Duggan beat R. Reardon 5-4; Black beat P. Mans 5-4; T. Griffiths beat Newbury 5-2; J. Spencer beat Foldvari 5-4; T. Meo beat Dunning 5-0; J. Parrott beat W. Jones 5-3; A. Higgins beat D. Hughes 5-1; Murphy beat E. Hughes 5-3; Dennis Taylor beat Cripsey 5-1; B. Harris beat D. O'Kane 5-3

**Fourth round:** S. Davis beat Virgo 5-1; Macleod beat Chaperon 5-4; Reynolds beat Gibson 5-0; White beat King 5-2; Wilson beat Chappel 5-0; Johnson beat Bradley 5-2; David Taylor beat Werbeniuk 5-4; N. Foulds beat Knowles 5-3; Thorburn beat Martin 5-3; Campbell beat Mountjoy 5-1; Thorne beat Scott 5-1; Duggan beat Black 5-1; Griffiths beat Spencer 5-1; Parrott beat Meo 5-4; Higgins beat Murphy 5-2; Dennis Taylor beat B. Harris 5-3

**Fifth round:** S. Davis beat Macleod 5-1; White beat Reynolds 5-1; Johnson beat Wilson 5-1; N. Foulds beat David Taylor 5-4; Thorburn beat Campbell 5-0; Duggan beat Thorne 5-4; Parrott beat Griffiths 5-1; Dennis Taylor beat Higgins 5-1

**Quarter-finals:** White beat S. Davis 5-3; N. Foulds beat Johnson 5-2; Thorburn beat Duggan 5-2; Dennis Taylor beat Parrott 5-1

**Semi-finals:** White beat N. Foulds 9-5; Thorburn beat Dennis Taylor 9-5

**Final:** Thorburn beat White 12-10

## 1986 *(BCE)*

**First round:** P. Burke beat J. Fitzmaurice 5-4; G. Wilkinson *wo* F. Jonik *scr*; A. Kearney *wo* S. Simngam *scr*; B. Kelly beat T. Whitthread 5-1; J. McLaughlin beat B. Bennett 5-0; J. Wright beat M. Watterson 5-1; B. Rowswell beat D. Sheehan 5-4; Jack Rea beat M. Darrington 5-4; G. Jenkins beat C. Everton 5-3; J. Dunning beat B. Demarco 5-4; M. Bennett beat M. Smith 5-4; P. Gibson beat J. Meadowcroft 5-2; I. Anderson *wo* E. McLaughlin *scr*; G. Rigitano beat D. Greaves 5-3; J. Bear beat P. Watchorn 5-1; P. Houlihan beat D. Chalmers 5-1; C. Roscoe beat M. Parkin 5-1; M. Morra beat F. Ellis 5-3; N. Gilbert beat O. Agrawal 5-0; K. Owers beat J. Hargreaves 5-3; B. Oliver beat D. Mienie 5-4; D. Roe beat D. Hughes 5-2; G. Foulds *wo* L. Heywood *scr*; M. Hines beat M. Fisher 5-2; J. Donnelly *wo* R. Grace *scr*; S. James beat D. Gilbert 5-2

**Second round:** Burke beat T. Jones 5-4; M. Bradley beat Wilkinson 5-4; P. Medati beat Kearney 5-3; J. Van Rensberg beat Kelly 5-1; R. Bales beat F. Davis 5-4; J. McLaughlin beat D. Fowler 5-2; J. Spencer beat I. Williamson 5-4; I. Black beat Wright 5-1; E. Sinclair beat P. Fagan 5-0; M. Wildman beat Rowswell 5-2; W. Jones beat Jack Rea 5-1; M. Gauvreau beat Jenkins 5-1; S. Newbury beat Dunning 5-4; M. Bennett beat P. Browne 5-1; R. Foldvari beat B. Harris 5-0; S. Hendry beat P. Gibson 5-2; John Rea beat Anderson 5-1; W. King beat Rigitano 5-0; J. O'Boye beat B. Mikkelsen 5-4; S. Duggan beat Bear 5-4; Houlihan beat G. Cripsey 5-1; T. Chappel beat Roscoe 5-3; J. Drago beat Morra 5-3; R. Chaperon beat N. Gilbert 5-3; Owers beat G. Scott 5-1; D. O'Kane beat Oliver 5-2; G. Miles beat Roe 5-1; G. Foulds beat V. Harris 5-4; M. Gibson beat Hines 5-1; L. Dodd *wo* P. Mans *scr*; T. Murphy beat Donnelly 5-2; R. Edmonds beat James 5-2

**Third round:** C. Thorburn beat Burke 5-0; J. Wych beat Bradley 5-2; T. Griffiths beat Medati 5-3; B. West beat Van Rensberg 5-3; Bales beat K. Stevens 5-3; C. Wilson beat J. McLaughlin 5-2; T. Knowles beat Spencer 5-0; E. Charlton beat Black 5-0; A. Higgins beat Sinclair 5-3; P. Francisco beat Wildman 5-2; R. Reardon beat W. Jones 5-4; Gauvreau beat M. Macleod 5-4; S. Francisco beat Newbury 5-4; J. Virgo beat M. Bennett 5-1; Dennis Taylor beat Foldvari 5-1; Hendry beat J. Parrott 5-3; S. Davis beat John Rea 5-1; King beat S. Longworth 5-0; R. Williams beat O'Boye 5-0; Duggan beat J. Campbell 5-3; Houlihan beat T. Meo 5-4; E. Hughes beat Chappel 5-4; Drago beat W. Thorne 5-2; Chaperon beat D. Martin 5-4; Owers beat J. White 5-2; O'Kane beat M. Hallet 5-1; N. Foulds beat Miles 5-2; G. Foulds beat B. Werbeniuk 5-2; D. Mountjoy beat M. Gibson 5-3; D. Reynolds beat Dodd 5-2; J. Johnson beat Murphy 5-4; David Taylor beat Edmonds 5-4

**Fourth round:** Thorburn beat Wych 5-3; Griffiths beat West 5-1; Wilson beat Bales 5-1; Knowles beat Charlton 5-1; P. Francisco beat Higgins 5-4; Gauvreau beat Reardon 5-2;

S. Francisco beat Virgo 5-0; Dennis Taylor beat Hendry 5-3; S. Davis beat King 5-4; Williams beat Duggan 5-4; E. Hughes beat Houlihan 5-1; Chaperon beat Drago 5-1; Owers beat O'Kane 5-0; N. Foulds beat G. Foulds 5-0; Reynolds beat Mountjoy 5-2; David Taylor beat Johnson 5-3
**Fifth round:** Thorburn beat Griffiths 5-4; Wilson beat Knowles 5-4; P. Francisco beat Gauvreau 5-2; S. Francisco beat Dennis Taylor 5-0; S. Davis beat Williams 5-4; E. Hughes beat Chaperon 5-0; N. Foulds beat Owers 5-1; Reynolds beat David Taylor 5-1
**Quarter-finals:** Thorburn beat Wilson 5-1; P. Francisco beat S. Francisco 5-3; E. Hughes beat S. Davis 5-4; N. Foulds beat Reynolds 5-2
**Semi-finals:** Thorburn beat P. Francisco 9-7; N. Foulds beat E. Hughes 9-8
**Final:** N. Foulds beat Thorburn 12-9

## 1987
**First round:** P. Gibson beat Glen Wilkinson 5-3; Gary Wilkinson beat G. Rigitano 5-1; E. Sinclair beat D. Heaton 5-3; D. Gilbert beat A. Harris 5-4; R. Foldvari beat S. Meakin 5-3; P. Fagan *wo* E. McLaughlin *scr*; J. Smith *wo* F. Jonik *scr*; M. Clark beat J. Bear 5-2; G. Jenkins beat T. Whitthread 5-1; J. Meadowcroft beat D. Greaves 5-1; M. Smith beat J. Donnelly 5-3; I. Anderson beat M. Watterson 5-3; D. Roe beat F. Ellis 5-4; J. Chambers *wo* B. Mikkelsen *scr*; M. Fisher *wo* J. Rempe *scr*; D. Chalmers beat J. Fitzmaurice 5-4; I. Williamson beat C. Everton 5-0; C. Roscoe beat E. Lawler 5-4; Jack Rea beat P. Burke 5-1; J. Dunning beat D. Sheehan 5-1; N. Gilbert beat I. Black 5-3; R. Rowswell beat D. Hughes 5-1; P. Watchorn beat B. Oliver 5-3; M. Morra beat J. Hargreaves 5-4; V. Harris beat R. Marshall 5-1; B. Kelly beat M. Darrington 5-4
**Second round:** P. Gibson beat T. Jones 5-4; Gary Wilkinson beat G. Scott 5-2; Sinclair beat R. Edmonds 5-4; D. Gilbert beat P. Houlihan 5-3; Foldvari beat A. Kearney 5-1; J. O'Boye beat Fagan 5-1; M. Bradley beat J. Smith 5-1; Clark beat S. Duggan 5-2; J. Wych beat Jenkins 5-4; K. Owers beat Meadowcroft 5-3; W. King beat M. Smith 5-3; G. Cripsey beat Anderson 5-4; Roe beat F. Davis 5-3; S. James beat B. Harris 5-0; R. Grace beat Chambers 5-4; S. Newbury beat Fisher 5-0; M. Bennett beat Chambers 5-4; Williamson beat M. Gauvreau 5-1; Roscoe beat P. Browne 5-2; Jack Rea beat G. Foulds 5-4; W. Jones beat Dunning 5-1; N. Gilbert beat J. McLaughlin 5-4; M. Wildman beat Miles 5-3; R. Reardon beat Rowswell 5-4; D. Fowler beat Watchorn 5-1; Morra beat L. Dodd 5-3; John Rea beat R. Bales 5-2; T. Murphy beat P. Medati 5-3; T. Chappel beat M. Gibson 5-2; R. Chaperon beat V. Harris 5-4; D. O'Kane beat J. Van Rensberg 5-3; J. Wright beat Kelly 5-2
**Third round:** N. Foulds beat P. Gibson 5-2; S. Hendry beat Gary Wilkinson 5-4; C. Wilson beat Sinclair 5-1; D. Gilbert beat D. Martin 5-2; Foldvari beat R. Williams 5-0; O'Boye beat K. Stevens 5-1; Dennis Taylor beat Bradley 5-0; Clark beat T. Drago 5-2; Wych beat J. Johnson 5-4; E. Hughes beat Owers 5-4; S. Francisco beat King 5-2; B. Werbeniuk beat Cripsey 5-1; Roe beat D. Mountjoy 5-4; James beat J. Campbell 5-4; C. Thorburn beat Grace 5-1; Newbury beat P. Francisco 5-2; J. White beat M. Bennett 5-3; S. Longworth beat Williamson 5-4; M. Hallett beat Roscoe 5-3; J. Spencer beat Jack Rea 5-0; W. Jones beat D. Reynolds 5-4; N. Gilbert beat M. Macleod 5-1; T. Griffiths beat Wildman 5-1; E. Charlton beat Reardon 5-4; A. Knowles beat Fowler 5-4; David Taylor beat Morra 5-3; W. Thorne beat John Rea 5-3; J. Virgo beat Murphy 5-1; J. Parrott beat Chappel 5-1; Chaperon beat B. West 5-4; S. Davis beat O'Kane 5-2; T. Meo beat Wright 5-2
**Fourth round:** Hendry beat N. Foulds 5-2; D. Gilbert beat Wilson 5-1; O'Boye beat Foldvari 5-4; Clark beat Dennis Taylor 5-0; E. Hughes beat Wych 5-4; S. Francisco beat Werbeniuk 5-3; James beat Roe 5-3; Thorburn beat Newbury 5-3; White beat Longworth 5-1; Hallett beat Spencer 5-2; N. Gilbert beat W. Jones 5-4; Charlton beat Griffiths 5-2; Knowles beat David Taylor 5-2; Virgo beat Thorne 5-4; Parrott beat Chaperon 5-1; S. Davis beat Meo 5-3
**Fifth round:** Hendry beat D. Gilbert 5-0; O'Boye beat Clark 5-2; E. Hughes beat S. Francisco 5-4; Thorburn beat James 5-0; Hallett beat White 5-4; Charlton beat N. Gilbert 5-0; Virgo beat Knowles 5-2; S. Davis beat Parrott 5-2

**Quarter-finals:** Hendry beat O'Boye 5-2; Thorburn beat E. Hughes 5-1; Hallett beat Charlton 5-4; S. Davis beat Virgo 5-2
**Semi-finals:** Thorburn beat Hendry 9-1; S. Davis beat Hallett 9-3
**Final:** S. Davis beat Thorburn 12-5

## 1988

**First round:** M. Smith beat D. Morgan 5-3; A. Robidoux beat I. Black 5-1; John Rea beat C. Edwards 5-2; T. Wilson beat M. Gibson 5-1; P. Watchorn beat B. Harris 5-2; D. Hughes beat G. Rigitano 5-4; V. Harris beat P. Burke 5-2; M. Johnston-Allen beat G. Scott 5-2; T. Whitthread beat J. Meadowcroft 5-4; J. Dunning beat B. Kelly 5-0; G. Jenkins beat M. Wildman 5-1; Glen Wilkinson beat D. Mienie 5-2; D. Sheehan beat M. Bradley 5-4; I. Williamson beat M. Darrington 5-1; Jim Bear beat D. Heaton 5-1; M. Price beat P. Medati 5-4; F. Davis beat S. Campbell 5-4; R. Foldvari beat A. Harris 5-1; E. Lawlor beat Jack Rea 5-2; J. Donnelly beat J. Smith 5-2; P. Gison *wo* F. Jonik *scr*; B. Mikkelsen beat J. Fitzmaurice 5-2; G. Foulds beat F. Ellis 5-2; R. Marshall beat B. Rowswell 5-4; C. Roscoe beat N. Terry 5-2; M. Morra beat C. Everton 5-2; B. Oliver beat P. Fagan 5-0; E. Sinclair beat M. Rowing 5-0; J. Chambers beat I. Graham 5-2; R. Grace *wo* D. Chalmers *scr*; T. Kearney beat M. Watterson 5-1; S. Meakin beat J. Van Rensberg 5-4
**Second round:** W. Jones beat M. Smith 5-2; Robidoux beat P. Houlihan 5-2; John Rea beat R. Bales 5-2; T. Wilson beat P. Browne 5-3; T. Chappel beat Watchorn 5-4; K. Stevens beat D. Hughes 5-2; J. Wych beat V. Harris 5-3; Johnston-Allen beat D. Gilbert 5-3; J. O'Boye beat Whitthread 5-2; N. Gilbert beat Dunning 5-0; K. Owers beat Jenkins 5-1; M. Fisher beat Glen Wilkinson 5-4; M. Macleod beat Sheehan 5-0; J. Wright beat Williamson 5-1; R. Edmonds beat Jim Bear 5-1; Price beat B. Werbeniuk 5-2; T. Murphy beat F. Davis 5-1; T. Jones beat Foldvari 5-4; J. McLaughlin beat Lawlor 5-3; R. Reardon beat Donnelly 5-1; G. Cripsey *wo* P. Gison *scr*; D. Martin beat Mikkelsen 5-4; G. Miles beat G. Foulds 5-3; M. Bennett beat Marshall 5-1; L. Dodd beat Roscoe 5-1; W. King beat Morra 5-4; S. Duggan beat Oliver 5-3; D. Roe beat Sinclair 5-1; Chambers beat Gary Wilkinson 5-4; D. Fowler beat Grace 5-3; M. Clark beat Kearney 5-3; Meakin beat M. Gauvreau 5-3
**Third round:** S. Davis beat W. Jones 5-1; Robidoux beat E. Charlton 5-2; John Rea beat P. Francisco 5-0; David Taylor beat T. Wilson 5-1; Dennis Taylor beat Chappel 5-1; J. Campbell *wo* K. Stevens *scr*; Wych beat T. Griffiths 5-0; D. O'Kane beat Johnston-Allen 5-3; M. Hallett beat O'Boye 5-3; T. Meo beat N. Gilbert 5-1; S. Francisco beat Owers 5-1; R. Chaperon beat Fisher 5-3; Macleod beat A. Higgins 5-2; S. James beat Wright 5-3; S. Hendry beat Edmonds 5-1; S. Longworth beat Price 5-4; N. Foulds beat Murphy 5-3; D. Reynolds beat T. Jones 5-4; J. Virgo beat J. McLaughlin 5-0; J. Spencer beat Reardon 5-4; J. Johnson beat Cripsey 5-3; D. Mountjoy beat Martin 5-1; A. Knowles beat Miles 5-4; S. Newbury beat M. Bennett 5-0; Dodd beat J. Parrott 5-4; B. West beat King 5-4; Duggan beat C. Wilson 5-2; R. Williams beat Roe 5-3; W. Thorne beat Chambers 5-2; T. Drago beat Fowler 5-3; J. White beat Clark 5-2; E. Hughes beat Meakin 5-0
**Fourth round:** S. Davis beat Robidoux 5-4; David Taylor beat John Rea 5-4; Dennis Taylor beat J. Campbell 5-4; Wych beat O'Kane 5-4; Meo beat Hallett 5-3; Chaperon beat S. Francisco 5-2; James beat Macleod 5-2; Hendry beat Longworth 5-3; Reynolds beat N. Foulds 5-3; Spencer beat Virgo 5-1; Johnson beat Mountjoy 5-4; Newbury beat Knowles 5-4; West beat Dodd 5-3; Williams beat Duggan 5-4; Thorne beat Drago 5-2; White beat E. Hughes 5-1
**Fifth round:** S. Davis beat David Taylor 5-1; Dennis Taylor beat Wych 5-2; Meo beat Chaperon 5-4; James beat Hendry 5-2; Reynolds beat Spencer 5-2; Johnson beat Newbury 5-2; West beat Williams 5-4; White beat Thorne 5-4
**Quarter-finals:** S. Davis beat Dennis Taylor 5-2; James beat Meo 5-1; Reynolds beat Johnson 5-1; White beat West 5-2
**Semi-finals:** S. Davis beat James 9-1; White beat Reynolds 9-5
**Final:** S. Davis beat White 12-6

# FOSTERS PROFESSIONAL

First staged 1984. Sponsors Carlsberg (1984–86), Carling (1987), Fosters (1988– ). Venue RTE Studios, Dublin. Initial prize-money £20,000. Prize-money last season £34,650. TV RTE.

1984 (*Carlsberg*)
First round: A. Knowles beat A. Higgins 5-3; J. White beat K. Stevens 5-0
Final: White beat Knowles 9-7

1985 (*Carlsberg*)
First round: J. White beat J. Parrott 5-3; A. Higgins beat C. Thorburn 5-4
Final: White beat Higgins 8-3

1986 (*Carlsberg*)
First round: J. White beat A. Higgins 5-1; Dennis Taylor beat J. Johnson 5-3
Final: Dennis Taylor beat White 8-3

1987 (*Carling*)
First round: J. Johnson beat N. Foulds 5-4; Dennis Taylor beat S. Hendry 5-3
Final: Taylor beat Johnson 8-5

1988
First round: M. Hallett beat J. Parrott 5-3; S. Hendry beat E. Hughes 5-1
Final: Hallett beat Hendry 8-5

# DUBAI DUTY FREE MASTERS

First staged 1988. Sponsors Dubai Duty Free. Venue Al Nasr Stadium, Dubai. Prize-money last season £130,000.

1988
Semi-finals: S. Davis beat W. Thorne 5-2; N. Foulds beat T. Meo 5-4
Final: N. Foulds beat S. Davis 5-4

# LEP MATCHROOM CHAMPIONSHIP

First staged 1986. Sponsors Matchroom (1986–87), LEP (1988– ). Venue Cliffs Pavilion, Southend. Initial prize-money £100,000. Prize-money last season £75,000. TV Super Channel.

1986 (*Matchroom*)
First round: T. Griffiths beat T. Meo 6-3; W. Thorne beat N. Foulds 6-3
Semi-finals: S. Davis beat Griffiths 6-2; Thorne beat Dennis Taylor 6-5
Final: Thorne beat S. Davis 10-9

1987 (*Matchroom*)
First round: S. Davis beat T. Meo 6-5; N. Foulds beat T. Griffiths 6-2; Dennis Taylor beat J. White 6-2
Semi-finals: W. Thorne beat Foulds 6-5; Dennis Taylor beat S. Davis 6-3
Final: Dennis Taylor beat Thorne 10-3

1988
First round: Dennis Taylor beat T. Meo 6-4; J. White beat C. Thorburn 6-4; N. Foulds beat T. Griffiths 6-4; S. Davis beat W. Thorne 6-2

**Semi-finals:** Dennis Taylor beat N. Foulds 6-3; S. Davis beat White 6-4
**Final:** S. Davis beat Dennis Taylor 10-7

# ROTHMANS GRAND PRIX

**First staged** 1982. **Sponsors** WPBSA (1982–83 when entitled Professional Players Tournament), Rothmans (1984– ). **Venue** La Reserve, Sutton Coldfield & International Snooker Club, Aston, Birmingham (1982), Redwood Lodge Country Club (1983), Hexagon, Reading (1984– ). **Initial prize-money** £32,000. **Prize-money last season** £325,000. **TV** BBC.

**1982** (*Professional Players Tournament*)
**First round:** E. Sinclair beat F. Davis 5-2; J. Meadowcroft beat B. Bennett 5-4; M. Watterson beat J. Donnelly 5-4; T. Griffiths beat C. Roscoe 5-1; A. Higgins beat D. French 5-3; R. Reardon beat T. Murphy 5-0; B. Werbeniuk beat P. Morgan 5-3; C. Everton beat P. Fagan 5-2; C. Thorburn beat P. Medati 5-1; David Taylor beat I. Anderson 5-1; Dennis Taylor beat R. Edmonds 5-4; J. Wych beat B. Kelly 5-0; R. Williams beat C. Ross 5-0; P. Mans beat E. McLaughlin 5-2; W. Thorne beat B. Demarco 5-3; M. Wildman beat J. Dunning 5-4; J. Johnson beat G. Miles 5-1; E. Charlton beat D. Hughes 5-2; F. Jonik beat D. Mountjoy 5-3; K. Stevens beat E. Hughes 5-2; T. Meo beat M. Owen 5-4; C. Wilson beat M. Morra 5-2; A. Knowles beat P Houlihan 5-4; J. Virgo beat I. Black 5-2; M. Hallett beat V. Harris 5-3; D. Martin beat M. Gibson 5-2; J. Fitzmaurice beat D. Sheehan 5-1; J. Spencer beat G. Foulds 5-1
**Second round:** Werbeniuk beat Jack Rea 5-2; Sinclair beat Meadowcroft 5-3; Thorburn beat Everton 5-2; Griffiths beat Watterson 5-2; Reardon beat Higgins 5-2; Dennis Taylor beat David Taylor 5-1; Wildman beat Mans 5-4; Charlton beat Williams 5-2; M. Macleod beat Thorne 5-4; White beat Wych 5-0; Johnson beat Stevens 5-1; Meo beat Jonik 5-0; Wilson beat Knowles 5-4; Virgo beat Hallett 5-2; Spencer beat Martin 5-3; Reynolds beat Fitzmaurice 5-0
**Third round:** Werbeniuk beat Thorburn 5-2; Johnson beat Wildman 5-4; Reynolds beat Wilson 5-1; Virgo beat Spencer 5-1; Charlton beat Meo 5-3; White beat Dennis Taylor 5-3; Griffiths beat Sinclair 5-3; Reardon beat Macleod 5-2
**Quarter-finals:** White beat Griffiths 5-2; Virgo beat Johnson 5-1; Reardon beat Werbeniuk 5-3; Charlton beat Reynolds 5-1
**Semi-finals:** White beat Virgo 10-4; Reardon beat Charlton 10-7
**Final:** Reardon beat White 10-5

**1983** (*Professional Players Tournament*)
**Qualifying:** G. Ganim Jr beat G. Cripsey 5-4; S. Duggan beat M. Darrington 5-4; T. Jones beat W. Oliver 5-2; D. French beat N. Foulds 5-2; B. Bennett beat B. Demarco 5-4; P. Burke beat G. Foulds 5-4; V. Harris wo P. Mifsud scr; P. Medati beat D. Hughes 5-1; T. Murphy beat P. Browne 5-2; J. Parrott beat P. Watchorn 5-0; D. Sheehan beat P. Houlihan 5-2; M. Morra beat J. Hargreaves 5-0; D. Greaves beat R. Andrewartha 5-2; W. King beat B. Harris 5-3; P. Morgan beat M. Gibson 5-4
**First round:** R. Reardon beat Ganim 5-4; C. Thorburn beat V. Harris 5-1; J. Meadowcroft beat C. Roscoe 5-4; Duggan beat J. Dunning 5-2; J. Virgo beat French 5-4; J. Spencer beat I. Black 5-2; W. Thorne beat C. Everton 5-1; C. Wilson beat Bennett 5-1; T. Griffiths beat L. Dodd 5-3; J. White beat I. Williamson 5-2; Parrott beat P. Fagan 5-2; J. Johnson beat Burke 5-3; E. Hughes beat E. Sinclair 5-4; M. Fisher beat F. Davis 5-4; B. Werbeniuk beat T. Jones 5-4; E. Charlton beat E. McLaughlin 5-0; M. Watterson beat A. Higgins 5-2; K. Stevens beat R. Edmonds 5-1; D. Martin beat J. Fitzmaurice 5-0; T. Murphy beat M. Macleod 5-0; J. Campbell beat D. Mountjoy 5-3; David Taylor beat P. Morgan 5-3; G. Miles beat M. Gauvreau 5-2; M. Wildman beat F. Jonik 5-4; G. Scott beat Dennis Taylor 5-4; T. Meo beat W. King 5-2; S. Francisco beat M. Morra 5-3; D. Reynolds beat D. Greaves 5-1; R. Williams beat D. Sheehan 5-1;

M. Hallett beat B. Kelly 5-0; A. Knowles beat P. Medati 5-1; S. Davis beat J. Donnelly 5-1
**Second round:** Reardon beat Duggan 5-2; Thorburn beat Meadowcroft 5-1; Thorne beat Spencer 5-1; Wilson beat Virgo 5-2; Griffiths beat Parrott 5-1; Johnson beat White 5-3; E. Hughes beat Werbeniuk 5-0; Charlton beat Fisher 5-4; Stevens beat Murphy 5-1; Martin beat Watterson 5-4; Wildman beat David Taylor 5-3; Campbell beat Miles 5-2; Meo beat Reynolds 5-0; S. Francisco beat Scott 5-1; Knowles beat Williams 5-4; Hallett beat S. Davis 5-2
**Third round:** Thorne beat Reardon 5-3; Thorburn beat Wilson 5-3; E. Hughes beat Griffiths 5-2; Johnson beat Charlton 5-0; Stevens beat Wildman 5-0; Campbell beat Martin 5-0; Knowles beat S. Francisco 5-0; Meo beat Hallett 5-3
**Quarter-finals:** Johnson beat Thorburn 5-1; Thorne beat E. Hughes 5-1; Meo beat Stevens 5-3; Knowles beat Campbell 5-3
**Semi-finals:** Knowles beat Thorne 9-7; Johnson beat Meo 9-6
**Final:** Knowles beat Johnson 9-8

**1984**
**Qualifying:** I. Williamson beat P. Thornley 5-2; Donnelly beat J. Hargreaves 5-4; B. Demarco *wo* P. Fagan *scr*; V. Harris beat F. Davis 5-1; J. Dunning beat D. Hughes 5-0; D. O'Kane beat B. Kelly 5-4; M. Gauvreau beat R. Foldvari 5-2; E. McLaughlin beat S. Longworth 5-2; M. Morra beat G. Cripsey 5-3; S. Duggan beat P. Browne 5-2; D. Sheehan *wo* L. Condo *scr*; Sheehan beat B. Mikkelsen 5-3; P. Burke beat M. Darrington 5-3; D. Chalmers beat R. Andrewartha 5-2; W. King beat D. Greaves 5-0; P. Medati beat L. Dodd 5-4; R. Chaperon beat A. Kearney 5-1; Chaperon beat M. Gibson 5-4; P. Francisco beat I. Black 5-4; G. Rigitano beat R. Edmonds 5-3; M. Bradley beat F. Jonik 5-1; W. Jones beat M. Watterson 5-3; John Rea beat J. Fitzmaurice 5-2; R. Bales *wo* J. Wych *scr*; S. Newbury beat M. Fisher 5-0; W. Oliver beat B. Bennett 5-3; C. Everton beat P. Houlihan 5-3; J. McLaughlin beat J. Meadowcroft 5-1; T. Chappel beat G. Scott 5-1; T. Murphy beat G. Foulds 5-1; T. Jones beat E. Sinclair 5-4; C. Roscoe beat D. French 5-0; P. Watchorn *wo* P. Morgan *scr*; D. Fowler *wo* P. Mifsud *scr*
**First round:** A. Knowles beat V. Harris 5-1; Dunning beat P. Mans 5-4; Williamson beat B. Werbeniuk 5-2; J. Johnson beat Medati 5-1; W. Thorne beat Newbury 5-2; M. Macleod beat King 5-4; N. Foulds beat Demarco 5-2; T. Jones beat T. Griffiths 5-3; R. Reardon beat Roscoe 5-1; C. Wilson beat Donnelly 5-2; Dennis Taylor beat Watchorn 5-1; J. Virgo beat Bradley 5-0; A. Higgins beat Bales 5-1; M. Hallett beat Sheehan 5-1; R. Williams beat Chalmers 5-0; K. Stevens beat Chappel 5-3; C. Thorburn beat Rigitano 5-4; J. Campbell beat W. Jones 5-4; T. Meo beat Burke 5-1; D. Martin beat Chaperon 5-4; D. Mountjoy beat E. McLaughlin 5-4; M. Wildman beat J. McLaughlin 5-3; J. Parrott beat Gauvreau 5-3; E. Charlton beat Everton 5-1; J. White beat Oliver 5-1; S. Francisco beat Duggan 5-3; P. Francisco beat J. Spencer 5-2; D. Reynolds beat Fowler 5-2; David Taylor beat O'Kane 5-1; John Rea beat E. Hughes 5-4; G. Miles beat Murphy 5-3; S. Davis beat Morra 5-2
**Second round:** Knowles beat Dunning 5-1; Williamson beat Johnson 5-4; Thorne beat Macleod 5-3; N. Foulds beat T. Jones 5-0; Reardon beat Wilson 5-4; Dennis Taylor beat Virgo 5-3; Hallett beat Higgins 5-3; Stevens beat Williams 5-3; Thorburn beat Campbell 5-1; Meo beat Martin 5-4; Mountjoy beat Wildman 5-0; Charlton beat Parrott 5-1; S. Francisco beat White 5-1; David Taylor beat John Rea 5-1; S. Davis beat Miles 5-0; Reynolds beat P. Francisco 5-4
**Third round:** Knowles beat Williamson 5-2; N. Foulds beat Thorne 5-1; Dennis Taylor beat Reardon 5-3; Stevens beat Hallett 5-3; Thorburn beat Meo 5-4; Mountjoy beat Charlton 5-4; Reynolds beat S. Francisco 5-1; S. Davis beat David Taylor 5-1
**Quarter-finals:** N. Foulds beat Knowles 5-2; Dennis Taylor beat Stevens 5-2; Thorburn beat Mountjoy 5-3; S. Davis beat Reynolds 5-0
**Semi-finals:** Dennis Taylor beat N. Foulds 9-3; Thorburn beat S. Davis 9-7
**Final:** Dennis Taylor beat Thorburn 10-2

**1985**
**First round:** B. West beat B. Demarco 5-2; P. Houlihan *wo* G. Robinson *scr*; S. Simngam
beat D. Mienie 5-3; T. Drago beat P. Watchorn 5-2; R. Bales beat M. Smith 5-1;
G. Watson beat D. Sheehan 5-1; J. Hargreaves beat G. Cripsey 5-1; A. Kearney beat Jim
Bear 5-3; D. Gilbert beat G. Wilkinson 5-4; J. O'Boye beat S. Hendry 5-4; D. Hughes
beat B. Bennett 5-4; M. Darrington beat D. Greaves 5-2; O. Agrawal beat J. Rempe 5-2
**Second round:** West beat J. Meadowcroft 5-2; M. Watterson beat J. Caggianello 5-1;
T. Jones beat Houlihan 5-4; Simngam beat F. Davis 5-3; G. Foulds beat Black 5-3;
Drago beat W. King 5-4; G. Scott beat D. Chalmers 5-2; Bales beat M. Fisher 5-3;
Watson beat C. Roscoe 5-2; G. Miles beat Rigitano 5-4; S. Newbury beat P. Burke 5-3;
S. Longworth beat Hargreaves 5-2; T. Chappel beat L. Dodd 5-2; J. Van Rensberg beat
E. McLaughlin 5-4; M. Gibson beat M. Bradley 5-4; R. Edmonds beat Kearney 5-2;
B. Oliver beat P. Fagan 5-4; S. Duggan beat M. Gauvreau 5-4; Gilbert beat I. Williams
5-4; B. Mikkelsen beat T. Murphy 5-4; W. Jones beat John Rea 5-0; P. Francisco beat
C. Everton 5-0; J. McLaughlin beat P. Medati 5-2; B. Harris beat P. Browne 5-3;
J. Fitzmaurice beat E. Sinclair 5-3; O'Boye beat R. Chaperon 5-3; B. Kelly beat
J. Donnelly 5-4; M. Morra beat D. Hughes 5-2; V. Harris beat J. Wych 5-3; Darrington
beat R. Foldvari 5-3; Agrawal *wo* J. Dunning *scr*; D. Fowler beat F. Jonik 5-4
**Third round:** Dennis Taylor beat West 5-1; R. Williams beat Watterson 5-2; T. Meo beat
T. Jones 5-2; E. Hughes beat Simngam 5-1; E. Charlton beat G. Foulds 5-1; Drago beat
M. Macleod 5-3; Scott beat R. Reardon 5-4; C. Wilson beat Bales 5-1; K. Stevens beat
Watson 5-0; Miles beat D. Reynolds 5-3; David Taylor beat Newbury 5-2; Longworth
beat J. Parrott 5-2; D. Mountjoy beat Chappel 5-1; J. Campbell beat Van Rensberg 5-4;
A. Knowles beat Gibson 5-1; Edmonds beat D. O'Kane 5-2; C. Thorburn beat Oliver
5-0; M. Wildman beat Duggan 5-4; J. Johnson beat Gilbert 5-2; M. Hallett beat
Mikkelsen 5-3; W. Jones beat W. Thorne 5-0; P. Francisco beat J. Virgo 5-4; T. Griffiths
beat J. McLaughlin 5-4; B. Harris beat J. Spencer 5-2; J. White beat Fitzmaurice 5-0;
O'Boye beat P. Mans 5-3; S. Francisco beat Kelly 5-2; D. Martin beat Morra 5-2;
A. Higgins beat V. Harris 5-1; N. Foulds beat Darrington 5-0; S. Davis beat Agrawal
5-0; Fowler beat B. Werbeniuk 5-1
**Fourth round:** Dennis Taylor beat Williams 5-2; Meo beat E. Hughes 5-3; Drago beat
Charlton 5-3; Wilson beat Scott 5-3; Stevens beat Miles 5-2; Longworth beat David
Taylor 5-1; Campbell beat Mountjoy 5-2; Knowles beat Edmonds 5-3; Thorburn beat
Wildman 5-2; Johnson beat Hallett 5-4; P. Francisco beat W. Jones 5-3; Griffiths beat
B. Harris 5-3; White beat O'Boye 5-4; S. Francisco beat Martin 5-3; Higgins beat
N. Foulds 5-3; S. Davis beat Fowler 5-1
**Fifth round:** Dennis Taylor beat Meo 5-3; Wilson beat Drago 5-2; Stevens beat
Longworth 5-3; Knowles beat Campbell 5-4; Thorburn beat Johnson 5-1; Griffiths beat
P. Francisco 5-2; S. Francisco beat White 5-4; S. Davis beat Higgins 5-0
**Quarter-finals:** Dennis Taylor beat Wilson 5-2; Knowles beat Stevens 5-4; Thorburn beat
Griffiths 5-1; S. Davis beat S. Francisco 5-2
**Semi-finals:** Dennis Taylor beat Knowles 9-6; S. Davis beat Thorburn 9-5
**Final:** S. Davis beat Dennis Taylor 10-9

**1986**
**First round:** D. Mienie beat J. Fitzmaurice 5-2; Watchorn beat M. Darrington 5-2;
M. Morra beat S. James 5-3; G. Foulds beat G. Wilkinson 5-3; J. Bear beat B. Bennett
5-2; F. Ellis *wo* E. McLaughlin *scr*; J. Meadowcroft beat D. Greaves 5-2; T. Whitthread
*wo* S. Simngam *scr*; J. Donnelly beat N. Gilbert 5-1; F. Jonik *wo* L. Heywood *scr*;
I. Anderson beat B. Oliver 5-4; A. Kearney beat G. Jenkins 5-3; P. Gibson beat
J. Dunning 5-1; J. Wright beat M. Fisher 5-1; R. Grace beat P. Houlihan 5-1; D. Gilbert
beat B. Rowswell 5-1; P. Burke beat C. Roscoe 5-3; Jack Rea beat D. Hughes 5-2;
D. Roe beat J. Hargreaves 5-1; G. Rigitano beat C. Everton 5-1; M. Smith beat M. Hines
5-2; J. McLaughlin beat K. Owers 5-2; B. Kelly beat M. Parkin 5-2; D. Chalmers beat
O. Agrawal 5-1; D. Sheehan beat B. Demarco 5-1; M. Bennett beat M. Watterson 5-1
**Second round:** M. Gibson beat Mienie 5-4; T. Drago beat Watchorn 5-3; Morra beat

I. Black 5-4; G. Foulds beat B. Mikkelsen 5-1; Bear beat D. Fowler 5-2; M. Wildman beat Ellis 5-1; F. Davis beat R. Bales 5-4; Meadowcroft *wo* P. Mans *scr*; S. Duggan beat Whitthread 5-1; W. King beat Donnelly 5-2; G. Miles beat Jonik 5-1; Anderson beat T. Murphy 5-4; T. Chappel beat Kearney 5-1; G. Cripsey beat P. Gibson 5-3; Wright beat M. Bradley 5-0; P. Fagan beat Grace 5-3; J. O'Boye beat R. Edmonds 5-2; S. Newbury beat D. Gilbert 5-1; J. Spencer beat Burke 5-3; W. Jones beat R. Foldvari 5-3; B. Harris beat Jack Rea 5-0; John Rea beat E. Sinclair 5-4; Roe beat J. Van Rensberg 5-3; P. Medati beat Rigitano 5-1; T. Jones beat Smith 5-0; J. McLaughlin beat M. Gauvreau 5-3; L. Dodd beat G. Scott 5-2; V. Harris beat Kelly 5-3; R. Chaperon beat Chalmers 5-2; S. Hendry beat I. Williamson 5-1; P. Browne beat Sheehan 5-4; M. Bennett beat D. O'Kane 5-1

**Third round:** S. Davis beat M. Gibson 5-1; Drago beat E. Charlton 5-4; T. Griffiths beat Morra 5-3; J. Campbell beat G. Foulds 5-0; R. Williams beat Bear 5-2; Wildman beat S. Longworth 5-2; A. Higgins beat F. Davis 5-0; D. Martin *wo* Meadowcroft *scr*; W. Thorne beat Duggan 5-0; King beat B. Werbeniuk 5-2; N. Foulds beat Miles 5-1; C. Wilson beat Anderson 5-4; T. Meo beat Chappel 5-1; J. Parrott beat Cripsey 5-4; Dennis Taylor beat Wright 5-3; J. Virgo beat Fagan 5-2; O'Boye beat C. Thorburn 5-4; Newbury beat D. Reynolds 5-0; S. Francisco beat Spencer 5-4; W. Jones beat David Taylor 5-1; D. Mountjoy beat B. Harris 5-2; J. Wych beat John Rea 5-2; A. Knowles beat Roe 5-3; P. Francisco beat Medati 5-1; J. White beat T. Jones 5-0; J. McLaughlin beat B. West 5-1; Dodd beat K. Stevens 5-4; M. Hallett beat V. Harris 5-2; Chaperon beat R. Reardon 5-3; Hendry beat E. Hughes 5-1; Browne beat J. Johnson 5-2; M. Bennett beat M. Macleod 5-1

**Fourth round:** S. Davis beat Drago 5-1; Griffiths beat Campbell 5-1; Williams beat Wildman 5-1; Higgins beat Martin 5-2; Thorne beat King 5-2; N. Foulds beat Wilson 5-0; Meo beat Parrott 5-3; Dennis Taylor beat Virgo 5-4; Newbury beat O'Boye 5-2; S. Francisco beat W. Jones 5-4; Mountjoy beat Wych 5-1; Knowles beat P. Francisco 5-3; White beat J. McLaughlin 5-2; Hallett beat Dodd 5-2; Hendry beat Chaperon 5-2; Browne beat M. Bennett 5-0

**Fifth round:** S. Davis beat Griffiths 5-2; Williams beat Higgins 5-1; N. Foulds beat Thorne 5-3; Meo beat Dennis Taylor 5-2; S. Francisco beat Newbury 5-2; Knowles beat Mountjoy 5-1; White beat Hallett 5-3; Hendry beat Browne 5-3

**Quarter-finals:** Williams beat S. Davis 5-1; N. Foulds beat Meo 5-3; S. Francisco beat Knowles 5-2; White beat Hendry 5-4

**Semi-finals:** Williams beat N. Foulds 9-8; White beat S. Francisco 9-6

**Final:** White beat Williams 10-6

## 1987
**First round:** G. Rigitano beat Jack Rea 5-4; J. Meadowcroft beat A. Harris 5-3; J. Bear beat D. Greaves 5-0; I. Anderson beat G. Jenkins 5-2; P. Gibson beat P. Fagan 5-0; P. Burke beat C. Everton 5-1; R. Foldvari beat J. Dunning 5-0; Glen Wilkinson *wo* J. Rempe *scr*; M. Smith beat I. Black 5-0; D. Gilbert beat E. Lawlor 5-2; Gary Wilkinson beat B. Harris 5-0; C. Roscoe *wo* J. Hargreaves *scr*; S. Meakin beat M. Morra 5-2; M. Clark beat I. Williamson 5-1; M. Fisher beat P. Watchorn 5-4; D. Heaton *wo* M. Watterson *scr*; B. Rowswell beat J. Smith 5-3; B. Kelly *wo* B. Mikkelsen *scr*; J. Donnelly beat D. Hughes 5-1; M. Darrington beat D. Chalmers 5-2; F. Jonik beat N. Gilbert 5-3; B. Oliver *wo* E. McLaughlin *scr*; D. Roe beat T. Whitthread 5-1; E. Sinclair beat F. Ellis 5-4; J. Chambers beat J. Fitzmaurice 5-2; R. Marshall beat D. Sheehan 5-1

**Second round:** J. Wright beat Rigitano 5-0; Meadowcroft beat P. Browne 5-3; Bear beat B. Harris 5-3; R. Bales beat Anderson 5-1; P. Gibson beat S. Duggan 5-4; G. Cripsey beat M. Gibson 5-2; S. James beat G. Foulds 5-0; John Rea beat M. Bradley 5-1; R. Reardon beat Burke 5-2; Foldvari beat W. King 5-4; Glen Wilkinson beat K. Owers 5-4; M. Gauvreau beat M. Smith 5-3; D. Fowler beat D. Gilbert 5-1; Gary Wilkinson beat D. O'Kane 5-2; T. Jones beat Roscoe 5-1; S. Newbury beat Meakin 5-1; Clark beat R. Grace 5-1; Fisher beat F. Davis 5-0; P. Houlihan beat Heaton 5-0; R. Chaperon beat

Rowswell 5-4; L. Dodd beat Kelly 5-2; W. Jones beat Donnelly 5-3; A. Kearney beat
Darrington 5-0; T. Chappel beat Jonik 5-4; J. McLaughlin beat Oliver 5-2; Roe beat
M. Wildman 5-3; R. Edmonds beat Sinclair 5-2; J. Van Rensberg beat T. Murphy 5-4;
Chambers beat J. O'Boye 5-3; M. Bennett beat R. Medati 5-4; G. Miles beat G. Scott
5-2; J. Wych beat Marshall 5-2
**Third round:** J. White beat Wright 5-4; T. Drago beat Meadowcroft 5-1; W. Thorne beat
Bear 5-1; Bales beat J. Campbell 5-3; P. Gibson beat M. Hallett 5-4; Cripsey beat
B. West 5-3; J. Johnson beat James 5-4; P. Francisco beat John Rea 5-3; Dennis Taylor
beat Reardon 5-1; B. Werbeniuk beat Foldvari 5-1; C. Wilson beat Glen Wilkinson 5-4;
J. Virgo beat Gauvreau 5-1; S. Francisco beat Fowler 5-1; Gary Wilkinson beat
S. Longworth 5-4; C. Thorburn beat T. Jones 5-2; Newbury beat T. Meo 5-0; Clark beat
N. Foulds 5-4; Fisher beat E. Hughes 5-4; Houlihan beat D. Reynolds 5-4; Chaperon
beat David Taylor 5-3; J. Parrott beat Dodd 5-1; K. Stevens beat W. Jones 5-1;
T. Griffiths beat Kearney 5-0; Chappel beat J. Spencer 5-1; T. Knowles beat
J. McLaughlin 5-0; Roe beat D. Martin 5-4; Edmonds beat R. Williams 5-3; E. Charlton
beat Van Rensberg 5-3; Chambers beat D. Mountjoy 5-2; S. Hendry beat M. Bennett
5-1; S. Davis beat Miles 5-1; Wych beat M. Macleod 5-4
**Fourth round:** Drago beat White 5-3; Thorne beat Bales 5-2; Cripsey beat P. Gibson 5-4;
P. Francisco beat Johnson 5-2; Dennis Taylor beat Werbeniuk 5-3; Wilson beat Virgo
5-3; Gary Wilkinson beat S. Francisco 5-3; Newbury beat Thorburn 5-0; Fisher beat
Clark 5-4; Chaperon beat Houlihan 5-0; Parrott beat Stevens 5-0; Griffiths beat Chappel
5-3; Knowles beat Roe 5-2; Charlton beat Edmonds 5-3; Hendry beat Chambers 5-1;
S. Davis beat Wych 5-1
**Fifth round:** Thorne beat Drago 5-2; P. Francisco beat Cripsey 5-1; Dennis Taylor beat
Wilson 5-2; Newbury beat Gary Wilkinson 5-3; Chaperon beat Fisher 5-2; Parrott beat
Griffiths 5-4; Knowles beat Charlton 5-0; Hendry beat S. Davis 5-2
**Quarter-finals:** P. Francisco beat Thorne 5-3; Dennis Taylor beat Newbury 5-2; Parrott
beat Chaperon 5-2; Hendry beat Knowles 5-2
**Semi-finals:** Dennis Taylor beat P. Francisco 9-4; Hendry beat Parrott 9-7
**Final:** Hendry beat Dennis Taylor 10-7

## 1988

**First round:** I. Williamson beat C. Everton 5-0; J. Smith beat G. Foulds 5-3; A. Robidoux
beat J. Van Rensberg 5-2; S. Campbell beat I. Black 5-1; B. Oliver beat J. Fitzmaurice
5-3; John Rea beat M. Darrington 5-4; G. Jenkins beat Jim Bear 5-4; M. Gibson beat
P. Burke 5-4; M. Morra *wo* D. Chalmers *scr*; J. Dunning beat D. Heaton 5-1; D. Morgan
beat B. Rowswell 5-0; P. Medati beat P. Watchorn 5-2; B. Harris beat Jack Rea 5-2;
D. Mienie *wo* J. Meadowcroft *scr*; N. Terry beat E. Sinclair 5-3; C. Edwards *wo*
P. Gibson *scr*; B. Kelly beat F. Davis 5-3; G. Rigitano *wo* F. Jonik 5-2; V. Harris beat
R. Marshall 5-3; M. Johnston-Allen beat C. Roscoe 5-1; F. Ellis beat E. Lawlor 5-4;
M. Wildman beat P. Fagan 5-1; B. Mikkelsen beat D. Hughes 5-4; M. Smith beat
D. Sheehan 5-4; M. Watterson beat J. Donnelly 5-0; J. Chambers beat S. Meakin 5-0;
M. Bradley beat M. Rowing 5-3; T. Whitthread beat R. Grace 5-4; T. Wilson beat
G. Scott 5-3; R. Foldvari beat M. Price 5-1; A. Harris beat T. Kearney 5-2; Glen
Wilkinson beat I. Graham 5-4
**Second round:** Williamson beat J. Wych 5-4; M. Fisher beat J. Smith 5-3; Robidoux beat
R. Bales 5-1; K. Stevens beat S. Campbell 5-3; N. Gilbert beat Oliver 5-4; P. Houlihan
beat John Rea 5-1; J. O'Boye beat Jenkins 5-1; L. Dodd beat M. Gibson 5-1; Morra beat
R. Reardon 5-4; R. Edmonds beat Dunning 5-3; Gary Wilkinson beat Morgan 5-1;
Medati beat W. King 5-1; D. Roe beat B. Harris 5-2; D. Gilbert beat Mienie 5-0; Terry
beat G. Miles 5-1; S. Duggan beat Edwards 5-4; D. Fowler beat Kelly 5-4; W. Jones beat
Rigitano 5-3; J. McLaughlin beat V. Harris 5-4; Johnston-Allen beat P. Browne 5-2; Ellis
beat M. Gauvreau 5-2; D. Martin beat Wildman 5-1; T. Jones beat Mikkelsen 5-3;
M. Smith beat G. Cripsey 5-0; Watterson beat M. Bennett 5-3; Chambers beat K. Owers
5-3; Bradley beat T. Murphy 5-3; M. Clark beat Whitthread 5-1; T. Chappel beat
T. Wilson 5-4; R. Foldvari beat Wright 5-4; B. Werbeniuk beat A. Harris 5-1;

M. Macleod beat Glen Wilkinson 5-3
**Third round:** S. Hendry beat Williamson 5-2; D. Mountjoy beat Fisher 5-1; Robidoux beat J. Virgo 5-1; T. Meo beat Stevens 5-3; N. Gilbert beat S. Francisco 5-4; E. Charlton beat Houlihan 5-3; A. Knowles beat O'Boye 5-4; D. Reynolds beat Dodd 5-3; J. Parrott beat Morra 5-3; Edmonds beat S. Longworth 5-3; Gary Wilkinson beat W. Thorne 5-3; R. Williams beat Medati 5-2; A. Higgins beat Roe 5-4; D. O'Kane beat D. Gilbert 5-4; N. Foulds beat Terry 5-4; S. Duggan beat David Taylor 5-1; White beat Fowler 5-0; W. Jones beat J. Campbell 5-2; J. McLaughlin beat P. Francisco 5-2; J. Spencer beat Johnston-Allen 5-3; Dennis Taylor beat Ellis 5-1; R. Chaperon beat Martin 5-0; M. Hallett beat T. Jones 5-2; S. James beat M. Smith 5-3; T. Griffiths beat Watterson 5-3; B. West beat Chambers 5-3; J. Johnson beat Bradley 5-2; E. Hughes beat Clark 5-3; C. Wilson beat Chappel 5-2; T. Drago beat Foldvari 5-3; S. Davis *wo* Werbeniuk *suspended*; S. Newbury beat Macleod 5-3
**Fourth round:** Mountjoy beat Hendry 5-1; Robidoux beat Meo 5-0; N. Gilbert beat Charlton 5-0; Knowles beat Reynolds 5-3; Edmonds beat Parrott 5-3; Williams beat Gary Wilkinson 5-2; Higgins beat O'Kane 5-0; N. Foulds beat Duggan 5-4; White beat W. Jones 5-1; J. McLaughlin beat Spencer 5-3; Dennis Taylor beat Chaperon 5-4; Hallett beat James 5-2; Griffiths beat West 5-1; E. Hughes beat Johnson 5-2; Wilson beat Drago 5-4; S. Davis beat Newbury 5-1
**Fifth round:** Robidoux beat Mountjoy 5-4; N. Gilbert beat Knowles 5-4; Williams beat Edmonds 5-3; Higgins beat N. Foulds 5-3; White beat J. McLaughlin 5-2; Dennis Taylor beat Hallett 5-2; Griffiths beat E. Hughes 5-2; S. Davis beat Wilson 5-1
**Quarter-finals:** Robidoux beat N. Gilbert 5-4; Higgins beat Williams 5-4; Dennis Taylor beat White 5-2; S. Davis beat Griffiths 5-3.
**Semi-finals:** Higgins beat Robidoux 9-7; S. Davis beat Dennis Taylor 9-1
**Final:** S. Davis beat Higgins 10-6

# BCE CANADIAN MASTERS

**First staged** 1985. **Sponsors** BCE. **Venue** CBC Studios, Toronto (1985–87), Minkler Auditorium, North York (1988– ). **Initial prize-money** £50,000. **Prize-money last season** £200,000. **TV** CBC.

## 1985
**First round:** Dennis Taylor beat J. Parrott 5-1; R. Reardon beat A. Knowles 5-2; C. Thorburn beat J. White 5-3; S. Davis beat T. Griffiths 5-4
**Semi-finals:** Taylor beat Reardon 8-3; S. Davis beat Thorburn 8-1
**Final:** Taylor beat S. Davis 9-5

## 1986
**First round:** W. Thorne beat Dennis Taylor 5-4; A. Knowles beat C. Thorburn 5-1; S. Davis beat J. White 5-2; A. Higgins beat J. Johnson 5-3
**Semi-finals:** Thorne beat Knowles 8-7; S. Davis beat Higgins 8-2
**Final:** S. Davis beat Thorne 9-3

## 1987
**First round:** N. Foulds beat T. Griffiths 5-4; J. White beat A. Knowles 5-1; C. Thorburn beat J. Johnson 5-3; Dennis Taylor beat S. Davis 5-1
**Semi-finals:** White beat N. Foulds 8-7; Dennis Taylor beat Thorburn 8-5
**Final:** Dennis Taylor beat White 9-7

## 1988
**First round:** M. Smith beat Jack Rea 5-1; G. Scott beat C. Everton 5-0; A. Robidoux beat Glen Wilkinson 5-3; J. Chambers beat P. Fagan 5-2; J. Fitzmaurice beat J. Van Rensberg 5-3; M. Prize beat J. Meadowcroft 5-0; B. Oliver beat J. Rempe 5-3; J. Smith beat G. Foulds 5-1; M. Darrington beat V. Harris 5-0; B. Kelly *wo* P. Gibson

*scr*; I. Graham beat E. Sinclair 5-3; R. Foldvari beat P. Burke 5-2; N. Terry beat
J. Donnelly 5-1; M. Watterson beat G. Rigitano 5-3; S. Campbell beat A. Kearney 5-2;
B. Rowswell beat F. Ellis 5-1; M Gibson beat D. Hughes 5-1; M. Wildman beat
G. Jenkins 5-1; A. Harris beat M. Morra 5-3; I. Williamson beat D. Chalmers 5-2;
P. Medati beat C. Edwards 5-3; M. Johnston-Allen beat B. Harris 5-4; J. Dunning beat
D. Sheehan 5-3; D. Morgan beat F. Davis 5-2; C. Roscoe *wo* F. Jonik *scr*; R. Marshall
beat I. Black 5-1; E. Lawlor beat B. Mikkelsen 5-2; T. Wilson beat R. Grace 5-2;
P. Watchorn beat G. Miles 5-2; M. Bradley beat S. Meakin 5-0; T. Whitthread beat Jim
Bear 5-4; John Rea beat M. Rowing 5-2

**Second round:** M. Smith beat P. Houlihan 5-2; Scott beat R. Edmonds 5-2; Robidoux
beat M. Fisher 5-0; T. Murphy beat J. Chambers 5-3; Fitzmaurice beat J. McLaughlin
5-2; Price beat D. Gilbert 5-4; Oliver beat J. Campbell 5-3; R. Reardon beat J. Smith
5-2; T. Chappel beat Darrington 5-1; K. Stevens beat Kelly 5-1; Graham beat J. Wright
5-2; J. Wych beat Foldvari 5-2; Gary Wilkinson beat Terry 5-3; D. Martin beat
Watterson 5-1; S. Campbell beat R. Bales 5-2; D. Fowler beat Rowswell 5-4; W. King
beat M. Gibson 5-3; S. Duggan beat Wildman 5-1; J. O'Boye beat A. Harris 5-3;
M. Gauvreau beat Williamson 5-1; Medati beat G. Cripsey 5-0; N. Gilbert beat
Johnston-Allen 5-4; B. Werbeniuk beat Dunning 5-3; D. Morgan beat T. Jones 5-0;
Roscoe beat W. Jones 5-4; L. Dodd beat Marshall 5-3; K. Owers beat Lawlor 5-2;
M. Clark beat T.Wilson 5-3; M. Macleod beat Watchorn 5-1; P. Browne beat Bradley
5-2; D. Roe beat Whitthread 5-2; M. Bennett beat John Rea 5-4

**Third round:** S. Davis beat M. Smith 5-0; Scott beat R. Williams 5-2; J. Johnson beat
Robidoux 5-1; S. James beat Murphy 5-3; W. Thorne beat Fitzmaurice 5-0; D. Mountjoy
beat Price 5-2; T. Griffiths beat Oliver 5-4; Reardon beat R. Chaperon 5-4; C. Thorburn
beat Chappel 5-1; J. Spencer beat Stevens 5-3; Graham beat P. Francisco 5-3;
E. Charlton beat Wych 5-4; C. Wilson beat Gary Wilkinson 5-2; D. Reynolds beat
Martin 5-0; S. Hendry beat S. Campbell 5-2; Fowler beat T. Drago 5-1; King beat
N. Foulds 5-3; Duggan beat B. West 5-3; M. Hallett beat O'Boye 5-0; Gauvreau beat
T. Meo 5-0; J. Virgo beat Medati 5-1; S. Newbury beat N. Gilbert 5-3; J. Parrott beat
Dunning 5-2; D. Morgan beat D. O'Kane 5-3; Roscoe beat A. Knowles 5-2; David
Taylor beat Dodd 5-3; Dennis Taylor beat Owers 5-1; Clark beat A. Higgins 5-3;
Macleod beat S. Francisco 5-4; S. Longworth beat Browne 5-4; J. White beat Roe 5-3;
M. Bennett beat E. Hughes 5-2

**Fourth round:** S. Davis beat Scott 5-1; James beat Johnson 5-4; Mountjoy beat Thorne
5-4; Griffiths beat Reardon 5-2; Thorburn beat Spencer 5-2; Graham beat Charlton 5-2;
C. Wilson beat Reynolds 5-4; Hendry beat Fowler 5-2; King beat Duggan 5-4; Hallett
beat Gauvreau 5-3; Virgo beat Newbury 5-2; Parrott beat D. Morgan 5-3; David Taylor
beat Roscoe 5-1; Dennis Taylor beat Clark 5-4; Longworth beat Macleod 5-3; White beat
M. Bennett 5-3

**Fifth round:** S. Davis beat James 5-0; Griffiths beat Mountjoy 5-4; Thorburn beat
Graham 5-4; Hendry beat Wilson 5-1; Hallett beat King 5-2; Parrott beat Virgo 5-4;
Dennis Taylor beat David Taylor 5-2; White beat Longworth 5-0

**Quarter-finals:** S. Davis beat Griffiths 5-3; Hendry beat Thorburn 5-4; Hallett beat
Parrott 5-3; White beat Dennis Taylor 5-3

**Semi-finals:** S. Davis beat Hendry 9-5; White beat Hallett 9-2

**Final:** White beat S. Davis 9-4

# TENNENTS UK OPEN

**First staged** 1977. **Sponsors** Super Crystalate (1977), Coral (1979-85), Tennents
(1986-  ). **Venue** Blackpool Tower Circus (1977), Guild Hall, Preston (1978-  ).
**Initial prize-money** £7,000. **Prize-money last season** £400,000. **TV** BBC.

**1977** (*Super Crystalate UK Championship*)
**First round:** J. Virgo *wo* J. Barrie *scr*; C. Ross beat J. Karnehm 5-4; P. Fagan
beat Jack Rea 5-1; J. Meadowcroft beat P. Houlihan 5-1; D. Mountjoy beat
R. Andrewartha 5-2; W. Thorne beat B. Bennett 5-1; J. Dunning beat M. Parkin 5-4;
David Taylor beat D. Greaves 5-4
**Second round:** Virgo beat Dennis Taylor 5-2; G. Miles beat Ross 5-1; Fagan beat
F. Davis 5-0; Meadowcroft beat R. Reardon 5-4; Mountjoy beat J. Spencer 5-3; Thorne
beat R. Williams 5-4; Dunning *wo* J. Pulman *scr*; A. Higgins beat David Taylor 5-4
**Quarter-finals:** Virgo beat Miles 5-2; Fagan beat Meadowcroft 5-4; Mountjoy beat
Thorne 5-4; Higgins beat Dunning 5-0
**Semi-finals:** Fagan beat Virgo 9-8; Mountjoy beat Higgins 9-2
**Final:** Fagan beat Mountjoy 12-9

**1978** (*Coral UK Championship*)
**Qualifying:** W. Thorne beat B. Bennett 9-4; R. Andrewartha beat P. Houlihan 9-3;
D. Mountjoy beat J. Barrie 9-5; R. Williams beat T. Griffiths 9-8; J. Dunning beat
D. Greaves 9-3; J. Virgo beat R. Edmonds 9-4; David Taylor beat M. Parkin 9-2;
J. Meadowcroft beat Jack Rea 9-5
**First round:** David Taylor beat Fagan 9-7; Virgo beat J. Pulman 9-3; F. Davis beat
Dunning 9-2; A. Higgins beat Meadowcroft 9-6; Thorne beat R. Reardon 9-6; G. Miles
beat Williams 9-8; Mountjoy beat Dennis Taylor 9-4; Andrewartha beat J. Spencer 9-8
**Quarter-finals:** David Taylor beat Virgo 9-2; Higgins beat F. Davis 9-4; Miles beat
Thorne 9-1; Mountjoy beat Andrewartha 9-4
**Semi-finals:** David Taylor beat Higgins 9-5; Mountjoy beat Miles 9-1
**Final:** Mountjoy beat David Taylor 15-9

**1979** (*Coral UK Championship*)
**Qualifying:** Jack Rea beat B. Bennett 9-8; M. Hallett beat M. Parkin 9-1; J. Dunning
beat D. Greaves 9-8
**First round:** W. Thorne beat R. Andrewartha 9-4; P. Houlihan beat Jack Rea 9-3;
S. Davis beat Dunning 9-3; P. Fagan beat Hallett 9-4; B. Werbeniuk beat J. Johnson 9-3;
R. Edmonds beat J. Meadowcroft 9-3; T. Meo beat David Taylor 9-7; C. Wilson beat
J. Pulman 9-7
**Second round:** S. Davis beat D. Mountjoy 9-5; T. Griffiths beat Wilson 9-4; A. Higgins
beat Houlihan 9-3; Fagan beat G. Miles 9-5; Werbeniuk beat J. Spencer 9-8; Dennis
Taylor beat Thorne 9-8; J. Virgo beat Meo 9-6; Edmonds beat F. Davis 9-6
**Quarter-finals:** Werbeniuk beat Edmonds 9-8; Dennis Taylor beat Fagan 9-6; Virgo beat
S. Davis 9-7; Griffiths beat Higgins 9-7
**Semi-finals:** Virgo beat Dennis Taylor 9-4; Griffiths beat Werbeniuk 9-3
**Final:** Virgo beat Griffiths 14-13

**1980** (*Coral UK Championship*)
**Preliminary round:** M. Hallett beat B. Bennett 9-4; S. Hood beat C. Ross 9-3
**Qualifying:** Hallett beat R. Edmonds 9-8; E. Sinclair beat K. Kennerley 9-1; M. Wildman
beat C. Wilson 9-8; J. Meadowcroft beat D. Greaves 9-1; R. Andrewartha beat
A. Knowles 9-8; R. Williams beat J. Barrie 9-1; J. Johnson beat J. Dunning 9-6; T. Meo
beat Hood 9-5
**First round:** Meo beat P. Houlihan 9-1; S. Davis beat Hallett 9-1; P. Fagan beat Johnson
9-4; Sinclair beat G. Miles 9-5; Thorne beat Meadowcroft 9-1; Wildman beat J. Spencer
9-7; Williams beat D. Mountjoy 9-8; Andrewartha beat J. Pulman 9-6
**Second round:** Meo beat J. Virgo 9-1; S. Davis beat B. Werbeniuk 9-3; Dennis Taylor
beat Sinclair 9-6; T. Griffiths beat Fagan 9-8; A. Higgins beat Thorne 9-7; F. Davis beat
Wildman 9-6; R. Reardon beat Andrewartha 9-3; Williams beat David Taylor 9-7
**Quarter-finals:** S. Davis beat Meo 9-5; Griffiths beat Dennis Taylor 9-2; Higgins beat
F. Davis 9-6; Reardon beat Williams 9-4
**Semi-finals:** S. Davis beat Griffiths 9-0; Higgins beat Reardon 9-7
**Final:** S. Davis beat Higgins 16-6

**1981** (*Coral UK Championship*)
**Qualifying groups**
1   P. Medati beat E. McLaughlin 9-5; Medati beat J. Donnelly 9-7; W. Thorne beat
    Medati 9-6
2   M. Hallett beat V. Harris 9-4; Hallett beat D. Hughes 9-6; Hallett beat P. Fagan 9-5
3   M. Gibson beat J. Fitzmaurice 9-6; C. Everton beat Gibson 9-7; J. White beat
    Everton 9-4
4   J. Johnson beat T. Murphy 9-1; M. Watterson beat B. Bennett 9-4; Johnson beat
    Watterson 9-3; Johnson beat C. Wilson 9-5
5   P. Houlihan beat K. Kennerley 9-1; Houlihan beat I. Black 9-4; Houlihan beat
    J. Meadowcroft 9-4
6   G. Foulds beat B. Kelly 9-7; A. Knowles beat Foulds 9-1
7   E. Sinclair beat M. Wildman 9-8; Sinclair beat S. Hood 9-0; D. Martin beat Sinclair
    9-7
8   R. Williams beat D. French 9-3; C. Roscoe beat M. Macleod 9-7; Williams beat
    Roscoe 9-4; Williams beat J. Dunning 9-4
**First round:** Thorne beat R. Edmonds 9-4; K. Stevens beat Hallet 9-4; White beat
J. Virgo 9-6; Johnson beat J. Spencer 9-5; G. Miles beat Houlihan 9-5; Knowles beat
F. Davis 9-6; A. Higgins beat Martin 9-7; T. Meo beat Williams 9-8
**Second round:** S. Davis beat Thorne 9-2; B. Werbeniuk beat Stevens 9-7; White beat
Dennis Taylor 9-5; R. Reardon beat Johnson 9-7; T. Griffiths beat Miles 9-4; Knowles
beat D. Mountjoy 9-6; Higgins beat David Taylor 9-5; Meo beat C. Thorburn 9-6
**Quarter-finals:** S. Davis beat Werbeniuk 9-5; White beat Reardon 9-8; Griffiths beat
Knowles 9-5; Meo beat Higgins 9-4
**Semi-finals:** S. Davis beat White 9-0; Griffiths beat Meo 9-3
**Final:** S. Davis beat Griffiths 16-3

**1982** (*Coral UK Championship*)
**Qualifying groups**
1   T. Meo beat G. Scott 9-5
2   C. Wilson beat E. McLaughlin 9-6
3   D. Martin beat M. Macleod 9-6
4   J. Meadowcroft beat D. Hughes 9-8
5   J. Donnelly beat C. Ross 9-5
6   P. Houlihan *wo* J. Dunning *scr*
7   M. Hallett beat B. Demarco 9-1
8   B. Kelly beat J. Fitzmaurice 9-0
9   G. Foulds beat M. Gibson 9-2; R. Williams beat Foulds 9-7
10  V. Harris beat M. Owen 9-4; J. Johnson beat Harris 9-8
11  T. Murphy beat C. Everton 9-4; E. Sinclair beat Murphy 9-5
12  B. Harris beat G. Cripsey 9-6; Harris beat M. Watterson 9-3
13  M. Fisher beat I. Black 9-3; Fisher beat R. Edmonds 9-8
14  L. Dodd beat I. Williamson 9-1; Dodd beat D. French 9-7
15  B. Bennett *wo* J. Phillips *scr*; P. Medati beat Bennett 9-1
16  C. Roscoe beat Jack Rea 9-6; M. Wildman beat Roscoe 9-4
**First round:** S. Davis beat Williams 9-6; P. Fagan beat B. Harris 9-6; T. Griffiths beat
Johnson 9-1; Dennis Taylor beat Meadowcroft 9-7; David Taylor beat Dodd 9-7; Meo
beat G. Miles 9-4; J. Virgo beat Kelly 9-2; D. Mountjoy beat Houlihan 9-3; R. Reardon
beat Wildman 9-5; Hallett beat F. Davis 9-7; Wilson beat W. Thorne 9-7; J. White beat
Medati 9-7; J. Spencer beat Sinclair 9-8; A. Knowles beat Donnelly 9-6; D. Reynolds
beat Fisher 9-6; A. Higgins beat Martin 9-7
**Second round:** S. Davis beat Fagan 9-3; Griffiths beat Dennis Taylor 9-7; Meo beat
David Taylor 9-6; Virgo beat Mountjoy 9-5; Reardon beat Hallett 9-8; White beat
Wilson 9-5; Spencer beat Knowles 9-6; Higgins beat Reynolds 9-8
**Quarter-finals:** Griffiths beat S. Davis 9-6; Meo beat Virgo 9-6; Reardon beat White 9-8;
Higgins beat Spencer 9-5

**Semi-finals:** Griffiths beat Meo 9-7; Higgins beat Reardon 9-6
**Final:** Griffiths beat Higgins 16-15

**1983** (*Coral UK Championship*)
**Qualifying groups**
1   J. Johnson beat M. Gibson 9-6
2   T. Jones beat E. Sinclair 9-3
3   M. Wildman beat D. Greaves 9-5
4   M. Macleod beat B. Bennett 9-0
5   M. Watterson beat C. Everton 9-6; Watterson beat F. Davis 9-6
6   M. Darrington beat G. Cripsey 9-3; M. Hallett beat Darrington 9-1
7   N. Foulds beat C. Roscoe 9-2; Foulds beat J. Meadowcroft 9-2
8   V. Harris beat P. Houlihan 9-6; R. Williams beat Harris 9-6
9   D. French beat Jack Rea 9-5; D. Martin beat French 9-3
10  G. Foulds beat S. Duggan 9-8; Foulds beat L. Dodd 9-7
11  J. Parrott beat G. Scott 9-7; Parrott beat M. Fisher 9-0
12  R. Andrewartha beat W. Oliver 9-1; J. Dunning beat Andrewartha 9-2
13  T. Murphy beat B. Demarco 9-4; Murphy beat Donnelly 9-4
14  P. Medati beat D. Hughes 9-3; Medati beat R. Edmonds 9-7
15  B. Harris beat E. McLaughlin 9-8; Harris beat J. Fitzmaurice 9-3
16  I. Williamson beat J. Hargreaves 9-4; I. Black beat Williamson 9-6
**First round:** T. Griffiths beat Martin 9-4; Hallett beat G. Miles 9-4; Johnson beat
J. Virgo 9-6; David Taylor beat N. Foulds 9-4; A. Knowles beat J. Jones 9-5;
D. Mountjoy beat Watterson 9-2; A. Higgins beat Macleod 9-6; Medati beat D. Reynolds
9-3; C. Wilson beat Williams 9-4; R. Reardon beat B. Harris 9-7; Dennis Taylor beat
Murphy 9-6; J. White beat Black 9-1; J. Spencer beat Dunning 9-7; T. Meo beat Parrott
9-7; W. Thorne beat Wildman 9-5; S. Davis beat G. Foulds 9-1
**Second round:** Griffiths beat Hallett 9-5; Johnson beat David Taylor 9-3; Knowles beat
Mountjoy 9-5; Higgins beat Medati 9-1; Reardon beat Wilson 9-4; White beat Dennis
Taylor 9-4; Meo beat Spencer 9-5; S. Davis beat Thorne 9-3
**Quarter-finals:** White beat Reardon 9-4; Griffiths beat Johnson 9-2; Higgins beat
Knowles 9-5; S. Davis beat Meo 9-4
**Semi-finals:** Higgins beat Griffiths 9-4; S. Davis beat White 9-4
**Final:** Higgins beat S. Davis 16-15

**1984** (*Coral UK Open*)
**Qualifying rounds**
1   T. Jones beat R. Chaperon 9-1; Jones beat P. Fagan 9-2; Jones beat M. Wildman 9-2
2   P. Watchorn beat B. Harris 9-7; Watchorn beat C. Everton 9-6; M. Fisher beat
    Watchorn 9-5; R. Williams beat Fisher 9-8
3   R. Foldvari beat D. Greaves 9-5; G. Cripsey beat Foldvari 9-7; J. Fitzmaurice beat
    Cripsey 9-8; J. Parrott beat Fitzmaurice 9-6
4   P. Francisco beat D. Sheehan 9-5; P. Francisco beat I. Williamson 9-2; E. Sinclair
    beat P. Francisco 9-8; S. Francisco beat Sinclair 9-4
5   D. Fowler beat B. Demarco 9-3; Fowler beat W. Oliver 9-3; Fowler beat F. Davis
    9-4; Fowler beat N. Foulds 9-6
6   D. O'Kane beat W. Jones 9-7; O'Kane beat S. Duggan 9-6; G. Scott beat O'Kane
    9-7; M. Macleod beat Scott 9-5
7   S. Newbury beat G. Rigitano 9-6; Newbury beat F. Jonik 9-3; L. Dodd beat
    Newbury 9-6; C. Wilson beat Dodd 9-8
8   J. McLaughlin beat D. French 9-3; McLaughlin *wo* P. Morgan *scr*; McLaughlin beat
    C. Roscoe 9-8; McLaughlin beat G. Miles 9-8
9   R. Bales beat D. Chalmers 9-2; Bales beat E. McLaughlin 9-4; M. Gauvreau beat
    Bales 9-8; Gauvreau beat P. Mans 9-6
10  G. Foulds beat D. Hughes 9-7; P. Browne beat Foulds 9-5; W. King beat Browne
    9-5; King beat J. Virgo 9-4

11   John Rea beat B. Bennett 9-5; Rea beat F. Dunning 9-3; Rea beat R. Edmonds 9-6;
J. Johnson beat Rea 9-6
12   T. Chappel beat P. Houlihan 9-3; Chappel beat I. Black 9-3; Chappel wo
R. Andrewartha scr; Chappel beat D. Reynolds 9-6
13   J. Hargreaves beat P. Medati 9-6; M. Gibson beat Hargreaves 9-8; J. Donnelly beat
Gibson 9-6; J. Campbell beat Donnelly 9-6
14   M. Bradley beat V. Harris 9-8; Bradley beat B. Kelly 9-6; Bradley beat
J. Meadowcroft 9-7; M. Hallett beat Bradley 9-8
15   S. Longworth beat M. Darrington 9-5; Longworth beat P. Burke 9-4; M. Morra beat
Longworth 9-1; E. Hughes beat Morra 9-8
16   T. Murphy beat A. Kearney 9-2; Murphy beat M. Watterson 9-4; Murphy beat
D. Martin 9-8
**First round:** A. Higgins beat T. Jones 9-7; S. Davis beat Murphy 9-1; J. White beat
Campbell 9-7; Williams beat B. Werbeniuk 9-1; W. Thorne beat Parrott 9-7; E. Charlton
beat S. Francisco 9-4; D. Mountjoy beat Hallett 9-2; T. Meo beat E. Hughes 9-4;
R. Reardon beat Fowler 9-2; K. Stevens beat Chappel 9-7; Dennis Taylor beat King 9-5;
Wilson beat T. Griffiths 9-6; Johnson beat J. Spencer 9-6; David Taylor beat Macleod
9-6; A. Knowles beat Gauvreau 9-5; C. Thorburn beat J. McLaughlin 9-4
**Second round:** Thorne beat Charlton 9-7; White beat Mountjoy 9-2; Higgins beat
Williams 9-7; Stevens beat Johnson 9-2; Reardon beat David Taylor 9-4; Thorburn beat
Wilson 9-3; Knowles beat Dennis Taylor 9-2; S. Davis beat Meo 9-7
**Quarter-finals:** Higgins beat Thorne 9-5; S. Davis beat White 9-4; Thorburn beat
Reardon 9-8; Stevens beat Knowles 9-7
**Semi-finals:** Higgins beat Thorburn 9-7; S. Davis beat Stevens 9-2
**Final:** S. Davis beat Higgins 16-8

## 1985 (*Coral UK Open*)

**First round:** D. Sheehan beat P. Watchorn 9-7; T. Drago beat D. Gilbert 9-5;
G. Wilkinson beat M. Smith 9-4; O. Agrawal beat S. Hendry 9-2; B. West wo
G. Robinson scr; G. Jenkins beat P. Burke 9-5; J. O'Boye beat B. Bennett 9-3;
M. Darrington wo M. Parkin scr; P. Houlihan beat G. Watson 9-4; J. Hargreaves beat
D. Mienie 9-7; D. Hughes beat A. Kearney 9-8; S. Simngam beat R. Bales 9-2; Jim Bear
beat B. Demarco 9-1; G. Cripsey beat D. Greaves 9-4
**Second round:** Sheehan beat G. Scott 9-6; Drago beat J. Donnelly 9-8; S. Longworth beat
M. Gibson 9-2; D. Fowler beat Wilkinson 9-6; M. Morra beat Agrawal 9-8; West beat
C. Roscoe 9-5; G. Miles beat B. Oliver 9-4; T. Murphy beat C. Everton 9-4; M. Bradley
beat Jenkins 9-3; T. Chappell wo J. McLaughlin scr; R. Edmonds beat J. Van Rensberg
9-5; F. Davis beat John Rea 9-8; B. Mikkelsen beat I. Williamson 9-3; P. Medati beat
W. Kelly 9-1; O'Boye beat M. Gauvreau 9-5; V. Harris beat I. Black 9-3; L. Dodd wo
Jack Rea scr; E. Sinclair beat G. Foulds 9-4; P. Browne beat D. Chalmers 9-4; W. Jones
beat J. Fitzmaurice 9-3; J. Wych beat S. Duggan 9-5; Darrington beat R. Foldvari 9-6;
T. Jones beat F. Jonik 9-4; J. McLaughlin beat R. Chaperon 9-5; S. Newbury beat
Houlihan 9-3; J. Meadowcroft beat Hargreaves 9-8; P. Francisco wo G. Rigitano scr;
W. King beat D. Hughes 9-0; Simngam beat M. Fisher 9-4; P. Fagan beat B. Harris 9-2;
Jim Bear beat M. Watterson 9-0; Cripsey wo J. Dunning scr
**Third round:** S. Davis beat Sheehan 9-1; Drago beat M. Wildman 9-5; T. Meo beat
Longworth 9-5; Fowler beat P. Mans 9-2; D. Mountjoy beat Morra 9-2; West beat
E. Hughes 9-3; R. Reardon beat Miles 9-4; M. Macleod beat Murphy 9-7; J. White beat
Bradley 9-4; Chappel beat D. O'Kane 9-5; A. Higgins beat Edmonds 9-8; F. Davis beat
B. Werbeniuk 9-7; David Taylor beat Mikkelsen 9-6; J. Campbell beat Medati 9-7;
A. Knowles beat O'Boye 9-5; J. Spencer beat V. Harris 9-5; C. Thorburn beat Dodd 9-4;
J. Parrott beat Sinclair 9-2; W. Thorne beat Browne 9-6; J. Virgo beat W. Jones 9-7;
S. Francisco beat Wych 9-8; D. Martin beat Darrington 9-3; T. Griffiths beat T. Jones
9-5; D. Reynolds beat J. McLaughlin 9-7; K. Stevens beat Newbury 9-7; M. Hallett beat
Meadowcroft 9-1; P. Francisco beat E. Charlton 9-5; R. Williams beat King 9-5;
J. Johnson beat Simngam 9-4; N. Foulds beat Fagan 9-5; Dennis Taylor beat Jim Bear

9-3; Cripsey beat C. Wilson 9-7
**Fourth round:** S. Davis beat Drago 9-2; Meo beat Fowler 9-2; West beat Mountjoy 9-4; Macleod beat Reardon 9-5; White beat Chappel 9-5; Higgins beat F. Davis 9-2; David Taylor beat Campbell 9-4; Knowles beat Spencer 9-7; Thorburn beat Parrott 9-6; Thorne beat Virgo 9-8; S. Francisco beat Martin 9-6; Griffiths beat Reynolds 9-7; Stevens beat Hallett 9-5; Williams beat P. Francisco 9-7; N. Foulds beat Johnson 9-8; Dennis Taylor beat Cripsey 9-2
**Fifth round:** S. Davis beat Meo 9-5; West beat Macleod 9-4; White beat Higgins 9-6; Knowles beat David Taylor 9-7; Thorne beat Thorburn 9-7; Griffiths beat S. Francisco 9-5; Stevens beat Williams 9-7; Dennis Taylor beat N. Foulds 9-5
**Quarter-finals:** S. Davis beat West 9-1; White beat Knowles 9-4; Thorne beat Griffiths 9-7; Dennis Taylor beat Stevens 9-7
**Semi-finals:** S. Davis beat White 9-5; Thorne beat Dennis Taylor 9-7
**Final:** S. Davis beat Thorne 16-14

## 1986
**First round:** G. Wilkinson beat F. Jonik 9-8; M. Fisher beat D. Greaves 9-4; K. Owers beat D. Gilbert 9-8; M. Morra beat B. Bennett 9-3; D. Sheehan beat M. Bennett 9-8; D. Hughes beat F. Ellis 9-6; R. Grace beat P. Houlihan 9-6; B. Oliver beat D. Chalmers 9-6; S. James beat G. Rigitano 9-5; J. Dunning beat A. Kearney 9-6; C. Roscoe beat M. Parkin 9-1; D. Roe beat G. Foulds 7-1 *(retd)*; J. Hargreaves *wo* L. Heywood *scr*; M. Darrington beat T. Whitthread 9-8; P. Watchorn beat B. Kelly 9-8; Jack Rea *wo* S. Simngam *scr*; J. Bear beat C. Everton 9-1; M. Watterson beat P. Burke 9-0; N. Gilbert beat J. Donnelly 9-8; J. Fitzmaurice beat M. Hines 9-4; P. Gibson beat O. Agrawal 9-6; G. Jenkins beat D. Mienie 9-6; B. Rowswell *wo* E. McLaughlin *scr*; J. Wright beat M. Smith 9-7; J. Meadowcroft beat B. Demarco 9-2
**Second round:** T. Chappel beat Wilkinson 9-2; V. Harris beat Fisher 9-4; Owers beat S. Newbury 9-8; B. Mikkelsen beat E. Sinclair 9-8; T. Drago beat Morra 9-6; G. Miles beat Sheehan 9-8; T. Murphy beat D. Hughes 9-0; Grace beat P. Medati 9-5; S. Hendry beat Oliver 9-1; I. Williamson beat P. Browne 9-4; J. O'Boye beat S. Duggan 9-4; W. King beat James 9-8; M. Gibson beat Dunning 9-2; Roscoe beat M. Wildman 9-6; Roe beat J. Van Rensberg 9-6; W. Jones beat Hargreaves 9-0; D. Fowler beat Darrington 9-6; R. Chaperon beat Dodd 9-4; G. Scott beat Watchorn 9-7; J. Spencer beat R. Foldvari 9-6; G. Cripsey beat R. Bales 9-6; B. Harris beat Jack Rea 9-5; R. Edmonds beat Bear 9-6; Watterson beat I. Black 9-3; John Rea beat N. Gilbert 9-8; T. Jones beat Fitzmaurice 9-0; P. Gibson *wo* P. Mans *scr*; D. O'Kane beat Jenkins 9-5; J. McLaughlin beat Gauvreau 9-8; Rowswell beat F. Davis 9-4; Wright beat P. Fagan 9-0; M. Bradley beat Meadowcroft 9-2
**Third round:** S. Davis beat Chappel 9-7; E. Charlton beat V. Harris 9-2; S. Francisco beat Owers 9-3; D. Reynolds beat Mikkelsen 9-6; Drago beat R. Williams 9-7; J. Virgo beat Miles 9-7; W. Thorne beat Murphy 9-4; Grace beat M. Macleod 9-6; A. Higgins beat Hendry 9-8; D. Martin beat Williamson 9-5; T. Meo beat O'Boye 9-3; M. Hallett beat King 9-5; R. Reardon beat M. Gibson 9-6; E. Hughes beat Roscoe 9-8; Dennis Taylor beat Roe 9-6; W. Jones beat J. Campbell 9-3; C. Thorburn beat Fowler 9-7; David Taylor beat Chaperon 9-8; K. Stevens beat Scott 9-2; Spencer beat C. Wilson 9-5; N. Foulds beat Cripsey 9-7; J. Wych beat B. Harris 9-6; J. White beat Edmonds 9-4; P. Francisco beat Watterson 9-4; A. Knowles beat John Rea 9-4; T. Jones beat B. West 9-4; T. Griffiths beat P. Gibson 9-3; O'Kane beat B. Werbeniuk 9-5; D. Mountjoy beat J. McLaughlin 9-6; S. Longworth beat Rowswell 9-3; J. Johnson beat Wright 9-1; J. Parrott beat Bradley 9-4
**Fourth round:** S. Davis beat Charlton 9-6; Reynolds beat S. Francisco 9-8; Drago beat Virgo 9-6; Thorne beat Grace 9-1; Higgins beat Martin 9-6; Hallett beat Meo 9-4; E. Hughes beat Reardon 9-5; W. Jones beat Dennis Taylor 9-2; Thorburn beat David Taylor 9-4; Spencer beat Stevens 9-4; N. Foulds beat Wych 9-3; White beat P. Francisco 9-5; Knowles beat T. Jones 9-2; Griffiths beat O'Kane 9-0; Longworth beat Mountjoy 9-1; Parrott beat Johnson 9-1

**Fifth round:** S. Davis beat Reynolds 9-5; Drago beat Thorne 9-5; Higgins beat Hallet 9-7; W. Jones beat E. Hughes 9-5; Thorburn beat Spencer 9-2; N. Foulds beat White 9-7; Knowles beat Griffiths 9-6; Parrott beat Longworth 9-6
**Quarter-finals:** S. Davis beat Drago 9-8; Higgins beat W. Jones 9-5; N. Foulds beat Thorburn 9-2; Parrott beat Knowles 9-4
**Semi-finals:** S. Davis beat Higgins 9-3; N. Foulds beat Parrott 9-3
**Final:** S. Davis beat N. Foulds 16-7

## 1987

**First round:** J. Meadowcroft *wo* E. McLaughlin *scr*; E. Lawlor beat J. Fitzmaurice 9-0; I. Williamson beat B. Kelly 9-5; Jack Rea beat M. Watterson 9-6; R. Foldvari beat M. Clark 9-8; M. Fisher *wo* J. Hargreaves *scr*; J. Donnelly beat I. Anderson 9-4; B. Rowswell beat C. Everton 9-4; B. Oliver beat P. Burke 9-1; M. Smith beat F. Jonik 9-5; J. Chambers beat C. Roscoe 9-4; P. Gibson beat G. Rigitano 9-5; F. Ellis beat D. Sheehan 9-8; P. Watchorn beat M. Darrington 9-2; D. Gilbert beat D. Heaton 9-5; I. Black beat J. Smith 9-8; J. Bear beat D. Chalmers 9-5; A. Harris beat M. Morra 9-8; Gary Wilkinson beat G. Jenkins 9-3; D. Hughes *wo* B. Mikkelsen *scr*; J. Van Rensberg beat T. Whitthread 9-5; S. Meakin beat Glen Wilkinson 9-0; D. Roe beat R. Marshall 9-3; V. Harris beat D. Greaves 9-1; J. Dunning beat P. Fagan 9-4; N. Gilbert beat E. Sinclair 9-8
**Second round:** W. King beat Meadowcroft 9-4; Lawlor beat J. Wright 9-7; S. Duggan beat Williamson 9-7; R. Chaperon beat Jack Rea 9-6; S. Newbury beat Foldvari 9-5; J. Wych beat Fisher 9-6; John Rea beat J. McLaughlin 9-5; J. O'Boye beat Donnelly 9-2; L. Dodd beat Medati 9-6; D. O'Kane beat Rowswell 9-2; Oliver beat G. Scott 9-4; T. Murphy beat M. Gibson 9-0; M. Smith beat P. Browne 9-4; Chambers beat M. Wildman 9-5; G. Cripsey beat P. Gibson 9-6; F. Davis beat Ellis 9-6; D. Fowler beat Kearney 9-7; Miles beat P. Houlihan 9-3; T. Jones beat S. James 9-6; Watchorn beat M. Bradley 9-5; T. Chappel beat D. Gilbert 9-2; B. Werbeniuk beat Black 9-5; Bear beat B. Harris 9-4; M. Gauvreau beat A. Harris 9-3; Gary Wilkinson beat R. Grace 9-5; R. Edmonds beat D. Hughes 9-4; R. Reardon beat Van Rensberg 9-7; W. Jones beat Meakin 9-1; Roe beat K. Owers 9-7; V. Harris beat M. Bennett 9-7; Dunning beat R. Bales 9-8; N. Gilbert beat G. Foulds 9-4
**Third round:** S. Davis beat King 9-2; P. Francisco beat Lawlor 9-4; A. Higgins beat Duggan 9-4; David Taylor beat Chaperon 9-6; J. Parrott beat Newbury 9-5; Wych beat S. Hendry 9-7; T. Knowles beat John Rea 9-6; K. Stevens beat O'Boye 9-8; Dennis Taylor beat Dodd 9-8; O'Kane beat E. Charlton 9-3; Thorne beat Oliver 9-3; Murphy beat T. Drago 9-7; M. Smith beat Mountjoy 9-7; J. Campbell beat Chambers 9-7; C. Thorburn beat Cripsey 9-6; J. Virgo beat F. Davis 9-4; Fowler beat N. Foulds 9-5; Miles beat J. Spencer 9-5; M. Hallett beat T. Jones 9-2; T. Meo beat Watchorn 9-1; Chappel beat D. Reynolds 9-5; S. Longworth beat Werbeniuk 9-5; J. Johnson beat Bear 9-5; B. West beat Gauvreau 9-6; T. Griffiths beat Gary Wilkinson 9-5; Edmonds beat M. Macleod 9-4; S. Francisco beat Reardon 9-3; C. Wilson beat W. Jones 9-6; Roe beat R. Williams 9-7; V. Harris beat D. Martin 9-7; J. White beat Dunning 9-0; E. Hughes beat N. Gilbert 9-7
**Fourth round:** S. Davis beat P. Francisco 9-6; Higgins beat David Taylor 9-6; Parrott beat Wych 9-6; Knowles beat Stevens 9-8; O'Kane beat Dennis Taylor 9-7; Thorne beat Murphy 9-4; Campbell beat M. Smith 9-8; Thorburn beat Virgo 9-6; Fowler beat Miles 9-4; Hallett beat Meo 9-5; Chappel beat Longworth 9-6; Johnson beat West 9-6; Griffiths beat Edmonds 9-5; S. Francisco beat Wilson 9-1; Roe beat V. Harris 9-5; White beat E. Hughes 9-4
**Fifth round:** S. Davis beat Higgins 9-2; Parrott beat Knowles 9-4; Thorne beat O'Kane 9-7; Thorburn beat Campbell 9-4; Hallett beat Fowler 9-4; Johnson beat Chappel 9-4; Griffiths beat S. Francisco 9-3; White beat Roe 9-5

**Quarter-finals:** S. Davis beat Parrott 9-5; Thorne beat Thorburn 9-8; Johnson beat Hallett 9-7; White beat Griffiths 9-7
**Semi-finals:** S. Davis beat Thorne 9-2; White beat Johnson 9-4
**Final:** S. Davis beat White 16-14

## 1988

**First round:** N. Terry beat G. Rigitano 9-5; D. Sheehan beat F. Davis 9-7; S. Campbell beat J. Dunning 9-5; F. Ellis beat Jim Bear 9-7; M. Bradley beat T. Wilson 9-7; I. Williamson beat C. Everton 9-1; G. Miles beat P. Watchorn 9-6; T. Whitthread beat J. Donnelly 9-8; A. Robidoux beat I. Black 9-2; T. Kearney beat M. Watterson 9-3; John Rea beat S. Meakin 9-6; M. Gibson beat A. Harris 9-8; E. Lawlor beat J. Fitzmaurice 9-1; C. Edwards beat E. Sinclair 9-8; M. Price beat R. Grace 9-3; C. Roscoe beat M. Darrington 9-7; M. Rowing beat G. Foulds 9-4; M. Johnston-Allen beat J. Van Rensberg 9-4; M. Smith beat R. Marshall 9-6; B. Harris beat I. Graham 9-4; B. Rowswell beat G. Jenkins 9-4; D. Morgan *wo* P. Gibson *scr*; B. Oliver beat B. Kelly 9-2; Glen Wilkinson beat Jack Rea 9-0; J. Chambers *wo* D. Chalmers *scr*; M. Morra beat D. Hughes 9-2; M. Wildman beat D. Mienie 9-4; J. Smith beat J. Meadowcroft 9-7; P. Medati *wo* F. Jonik *scr*; G. Scott beat P. Fagan 9-2; R. Foldvari beat P. Burke 9-0; V. Harris beat B. Mikkelsen 9-3
**Second round:** W. King beat Terry 9-7; Gary Wilkinson beat Sheehan 9-5; M. Clark beat S. Campbell 9-3; D. Fowler beat Ellis 9-3; J. McLaughlin beat Bradley 9-3; J. O'Boye beat Williamson 9-4; D. Martin beat Miles 9-7; N. Gilbert beat Whitthread 9-5; Robidoux beat R. Bales 9-4; Kearney beat P. Browne 9-6; John Rea beat G. Cripsey 9-2; D. Roe beat M. Gibson 9-3; D. Gilbert beat Lawlor 9-2; K. Stevens beat Edwards 9-4; T. Murphy beat Price 9-6; Roscoe beat P. Houlihan 9-8; Rowing beat J. Wright 9-7; W. Jones beat M. Johnston-Allen 9-8; M. Smith beat B. Werbeniuk 9-5; B. Harris beat M. Macleod 9-8; Rowswell beat M. Gauvreau 9-7; R. Reardon beat Morgan 9-5; J. Wych beat Oliver 9-6; L. Dodd beat Glen Wilkinson 9-6; K. Owers beat Chambers 9-4; S. Duggan beat Morra 9-8; R. Edmonds beat Wildman 9-4; T. Chappel beat J. Smith 9-6; Medati beat M. Fisher 9-3; T. Jones beat Scott 9-5; J. Campbell beat Foldvari 9-7; M. Bennett beat V. Harris 9-7
**Third round:** S. Davis beat King 9-7; Gary Wilkinson beat R. Chaperon 9-0; Clark beat M. Hallett 9-6; Fowler beat S. Longworth 9-8; Dennis Taylor beat J. McLaughlin 9-5; O'Boye beat E. Hughes 9-8; J. Parrott beat Martin 9-6; N. Gilbert beat J. Spencer 9-7; C. Thorburn beat Robidoux 9-4; S. James beat Kearney 9-1; P. Francisco beat John Rea 9-2; Roe beat T. Meo 9-6; W. Thorne beat D. Gilbert 9-3; Stevens beat E. Charlton 9-7; S. Hendry beat Murphy 9-4; Roscoe beat S. Newbury 9-7; N. Foulds beat Rowing 9-4; D. Mountjoy beat W. Jones 9-7; J. Johnson beat M. Smith 9-2; R. Williams beat B. Harris 9-4; J. Virgo beat Rowswell 9-3; D. O'Kane beat Reardon 9-8; A. Knowles beat Wych 9-4; T. Griffiths beat Owers 9-2; Duggan beat T. Drago 9-7; C. Wilson beat Edmonds 9-1; D. Reynolds beat Chappel 9-4; S. Francisco beat Medati 9-8; B. West beat T. Jones 9-5; J. White beat J. Campbell 9-5; M. Bennett beat David Taylor 9-4
**Fourth round:** S. Davis beat Gary Wilkinson 9-3; Fowler beat Clark 9-6; Dennis Taylor beat O'Boye 9-4; Parrott beat N. Gilbert 9-8; Thorburn beat James 9-6; Roe beat P. Francisco 9-7; Thorne beat Stevens 9-3; Hendry beat Roscoe 9-3; Mountjoy beat N. Foulds 9-4; Johnson beat Williams 9-7; Virgo beat O'Kane 9-8; Knowles beat Higgins 9-6; Griffiths beat Duggan 9-2; Reynolds beat C. Wilson 9-3; West beat S. Francisco 9-4; M. Bennett beat White 9-6
**Fifth round:** S. Davis beat Fowler 9-6; Parrott beat Dennis Taylor 9-4; Thorburn beat Roe 9-8; Hendry beat Thorne 9-4; Mountjoy beat Johnson 9-5; Virgo beat Knowles 9-3; Griffiths beat Reynolds 9-6; West beat Bennett 9-4
**Quarter-finals:** S. Davis beat Parrott 9-4; Hendry beat Thorburn 9-2; Mountjoy beat Virgo 9-8; Griffiths beat West 9-5
**Semi-finals:** Hendry beat S. Davis 9-3; Mountjoy beat Griffiths 9-4
**Final:** Mountjoy beat Hendry 16-12

# EVEREST WORLD MATCHPLAY

**First staged** 1988. **Sponsors** Everest. **Venue** International Hall, Brentwood. **Prize-money last season** £250,000. **TV** ITV.

**1988**
**First round:** M. Hallett beat W. Thorne 9-8; T. Griffiths beat P. Francisco 9-7; J. Johnson beat C. Thorburn 9-4; Dennis Taylor beat A. Knowles 9-7
**Quarter-finals:** S. Davis beat Hallett 9-2; J. White beat Griffiths 9-5; J. Parrott beat Johnson 9-7; S. Hendry beat Dennis Taylor 9-7
**Semi-finals:** S. Davis beat White 9-5; Parrott beat Hendry 9-6
**Final:** S. Davis beat Parrott 9-5

# NORWICH UNION EUROPEAN GRAND PRIX

**First staged** 1988. **Sponsors** Norwich Union. **Venues** Brussels, Paris, Madrid, Milan, Monte Carlo (Final)*. **Initial prize-money** £135,000. **TV** Canal Plus.
* *Four-man events in various venues produced four qualifiers for the final leg in Monte Carlo.*

**1988**
**Final:** S. Davis beat J. White 5-4

# MERCANTILE CREDIT CLASSIC

**First staged** 1980*. **Sponsors** Wilsons (1980–82), Lada (1983–84), Mercantile Credit (1985– ). **Venue** Civic Centre, Oldham (1982), Spectrum Arena, Warrington (1983–86), Norbreck Castle Hotel, Blackpool (1987– ). **Initial prize-money** £15,000 (1982). **Prize-money last season** £275,000. **TV** ITV.
* *The first two events, both in 1980, were small invitation events which do not meet the conditions required for full inclusion in this book.*

**1982** (*Wilsons*)
**First round:** T. Griffiths beat C. Thorburn 5-1; A. Higgins beat Dennis Taylor 5-1; R. Reardon beat David Taylor 5-1; S. Davis beat J. Spencer 5-2
**Semi-finals:** Griffiths beat Higgins 5-1; S. Davis beat Reardon 5-4
**Final:** Griffiths beat S. Davis 9-8

**1983** (*Lada Classic*)
**First round:** E. Charlton beat J. Virgo 5-2; J. Spencer beat R. Reardon 5-3; C. Thorburn beat C. Wilson 5-3; D. Mountjoy beat T. Griffiths 5-1; David Taylor beat J. White 5-3; B. Werbeniuk beat A. Higgins 5-4; K. Stevens beat A. Knowles 5-0; S. Davis beat Dennis Taylor 5-2
**Quarter-finals:** Spencer beat David Taylor 5-2; Werbeniuk beat Mountjoy 5-2; Stevens beat Thorburn 5-3; S. Davis beat Charlton 5-4
**Semi-finals:** S. Davis beat Spencer 5-4; Werbeniuk beat Stevens 5-2
**Final:** S. Davis beat Werbeniuk 9-5

**1984** (*Lada Classic*)
**First qualifying round:** G. Foulds beat M. Gauvreau 5-2; B. Demarco beat M. Gibson 5-2; N. Foulds beat P. Houlihan 5-3; M. Morra beat P. Burke 5-2; G. Ganim beat D. Hughes

5-2; I. Williamson beat D. French 5-1; J. Hargreaves beat W. King 5-3; W. Oliver beat
D. Sheehan 5-3; T. Jones beat P. Mifsud 5-3; P. Morgan beat M. Darrington 5-3;
G. Cripsey beat V. Harris 5-4; J. Parrott beat B. Bennett 5-0; P. Browne beat D. Greaves
5-2; P. Watchorn beat R. Andrewartha 5-2; S. Duggan beat B. Harris 5-2; P. Medati beat
T. Murphy 5-4
**Second qualifying round:** E. McLaughlin beat G. Foulds 5-1; G. Scott beat Demarco 5-2;
N. Foulds beat Jack Rea 5-1; Morra beat C. Everton 5-0; C. Roscoe beat Ganim 5-3;
F. Jonik beat Williamson 5-1; Hargreaves beat B. Kelly 5-4; Oliver beat J. Donnelly 5-4;
Morgan beat M. Watterson 5-3; T. Jones beat I. Black 5-0; J. Campbell beat Cripsey 5-3;
Parrott beat J. Fitzmaurice 5-2; R. Edmonds beat Browne 5-1; M. Fisher beat Watchorn
5-4; L. Dodd beat Duggan 5-2; E. Hughes beat Medati 5-1
**Third qualifying round:** E. McLaughlin beat W. Thorne 5-3; D. Reynolds beat Scott 5-3;
C. Wilson beat N. Foulds 5-4; S. Francisco beat Morra 5-1; Roscoe beat G. Miles 5-2;
J. Johnson beat Jonik 5-2; M. Wildman beat Hargreaves 5-1; P. Fagan beat Oliver 5-1;
E. Sinclair beat Morgan 5-2; M. Macleod beat T. Jones 5-2; Campbell beat F. Davis 5-0;
Parrott beat D. Martin 5-1; R. Williams beat Edmonds 5-1; J. Meadowcroft beat Fisher
5-0; M. Hallett beat Dodd 5-1; E. Hughes beat J. Dunning 5-4
**First round:** K. Stevens beat E. McLaughlin 5-4; T. Griffiths beat Reynolds 5-2;
E. Charlton beat Wilson 5-0; S. Francisco beat C. Thorburn 5-1; Roscoe beat
B. Werbeniuk 5-4; J. Spencer beat Johnson 5-4; Wildman beat J. Virgo 5-2; A. Higgins
beat Fagan 5-3; S. Davis beat Sinclair 5-2; Macleod beat David Taylor 5-4; J. White beat
Campbell 5-1; Parrott beat D. Mountjoy 5-4; Williams beat R. Reardon 5-4; T. Meo beat
Meadowcroft 5-1; Hallett beat Dennis Taylor 5-4; A. Knowles beat E. Hughes 5-1
**Second round:** S. Davis beat Spencer 5-1; Charlton beat White 5-2; Wildman beat
S. Francisco 5-1; Knowles beat Hallett 5-3; Stevens beat Macleod 5-1; Griffiths beat
Roscoe 5-2; Meo beat Williams 5-3; Parrott beat Higgins 5-2
**Quarter-finals:** Wildman beat Charlton 5-4; S. Davis beat Griffiths 5-4; Meo beat
Stevens 5-2; Parrott beat Knowles 5-1
**Semi-finals:** Meo beat Wildman 5-3; S. Davis beat Parrott 5-4
**Final:** S. Davis beat Meo 9-8

## 1985
**Preliminary round:** P. Watchorn beat D. Hughes 5-0; B. Mikkelsen beat D. Chalmers 5-1
**First qualifying round:** T. Jones beat D. Greaves 5-2; J. Giannaros beat T. Chappel 5-2;
S. Newbury beat V. Harris 5-3; G. Foulds beat R. Chaperon 5-3; D. Sheehan beat John
Rea 5-2; R. Bales beat B. Bennett 5-1; R. Foldvari beat P. Houlihan 5-1; P. Medati beat
G. Cripsey 5-4; J. McLaughlin beat B. Demarco 5-1; S. Longworth beat P. Francisco 5-4;
A. Kearney beat D. French 5-1; P. Browne beat M. Bradley 5-3; W. Jones beat
D. O'Kane 5-0; D. Fowler beat Rigitano 5-0; J. Hargreaves beat Darrington 5-2
**Second qualifying round:** T. Jones beat M. Gibson 5-0; Newbury beat P. Burke 5-1;
G. Foulds beat F. Jonik 5-2; E. McLaughlin beat Sheehan 5-2; Bales beat B. Kelly 5-3;
Foldvari beat Jack Rea 5-4; J. McLaughlin beat I. Black 5-0; Longworth beat B. Oliver
5-1; Watchorn beat Mikkelsen 5-1; I. Williamson beat Kearney 5-3; Browne beat
C. Everton 5-0; S. Duggan beat W. Jones 5-0; Fowler beat T. Murphy 5-0; R. Edmonds
beat Hargreaves 5-2
**Third qualifying round:** T. Jones beat L. Dodd 5-1; M. Gauvreau beat Giannaros 5-3;
Newbury beat M. Morra 5-2; G. Foulds beat J. Fitzmaurice 5-1; E. McLaughlin beat
F. Davis 5-1; Medati beat C. Roscoe 5-4; G. Scott beat J. McLaughlin 5-4; Longworth
beat M. Fisher 5-1; J. Donnelly beat Watchorn 5-1; P. Fagan beat Williamson 5-1;
W. King beat Duggan 5-4; Fowler beat J. Meadowcroft 5-2; Edmonds beat M. Watterson
5-2
**Fourth qualifying round:** S. Francisco beat T. Jones 5-1; Fagan beat M. Wildman 5-3;
M. Hallett beat G. Foulds 5-4; M. Macleod beat E. McLaughlin 5-4; Medati beat
J. Parrott 5-3; C. Wilson beat Fowler 5-4; Gauvreau beat E. Sinclair 5-1; J. Johnson beat
Edmonds 5-4; Scott beat J. Campbell 5-4; E. Hughes beat Newbury 5-3; King beat
D. Reynolds 5-2; R. Williams beat Donnelly 5-3; J. Virgo beat Bales 5-1; Longworth beat

N. Foulds 5-3; Foldvari beat D. Martin 5-2; Browne beat G. Miles 5-3
**First round:** Longworth beat David Taylor 5-4; Johnson beat A. Knowles 5-1;
C. Thorburn beat Scott 5-1; King beat J. Spencer 5-2; T. Griffiths beat Fagan 5-0;
J. White beat Browne 5-2; E. Hughes beat T. Meo 5-4; Macleod beat Charlton 5-1;
A. Higgins beat Gauvreau 5-3; Virgo beat B. Werbeniuk 5-2; Wilson beat D. Mountjoy
5-4; Williams beat Dennis Taylor 5-3; R. Reardon beat Hallett 5-3; S. Davis beat
S. Francisco 5-0; W. Thorne beat Foldvari 5-2; K. Stevens beat Medati 5-4
**Second round:** Reardon beat E. Hughes 5-1; S. Davis beat Higgins 5-2; Virgo beat
Macleod 5-0; Thorne beat Stevens 5-1; Thorburn beat Longworth 5-3; Griffiths beat
Williams 5-3; Johnson beat Wilson 5-0; King beat White 5-2
**Quarter-finals:** S. Davis beat Reardon 5-1; Thorburn beat Griffiths 5-4; Johnson beat
King 5-3; Thorne beat Virgo 5-1
**Semi-finals:** Thorne beat S. Davis 9-8; Thorburn beat Johnson 9-2
**Final:** Thorne beat Thorburn 13-8

## 1986
**First round:** D. Gilbert beat G. Watson 5-4; A. Kearney beat Jim Bear 5-0; S. Hendry
beat D. Sheehan 5-2; B. Demarco beat O. Agrawal 5-4; M. Smith beat D. Mienie 5-1;
J. O'Boye beat G. Wilkinson 5-1; B. West beat M. Darrington 5-0; P. Burke beat
D. Hughes 5-3; S. Simngam beat J. Hargreaves 5-1; R. Bales beat M. Parkin 5-0;
D. Greaves beat P. Watchorn 5-4; G. Jenkins *wo* G. Robinson *scr*; G. Cripsey beat
T. Drago 5-4; P. Houlihan beat B. Bennett 5-0
**Second round:** T. Jones beat Gilbert 5-3; G. Foulds beat I. Black 5-2; W. King beat
S. Duggan 5-2; P. Medati beat Kearney 5-2; Hendry beat G. Miles 5-1; M. Bradley beat
B. Oliver 5-3; B. Mikkelsen beat G. Scott 5-1; J. Donnelly beat D. Chalmers 5-0;
F. Davis beat B. Kelly 5-3; J. Wych beat Demarco 5-0; B. Harris beat M. Morra 5-3;
Smith beat R. Edmonds 5-2; O'Boye beat S. Longworth 5-1; West beat J. Meadowcroft
5-0; J. McLaughlin beat E. McLaughlin 5-2; John Rea beat I. Williamson 5-4;
R. Chaperon beat Burke 5-2; J. Van Rensberg beat W. Jones 5-4; P. Francisco beat
F. Jonik 5-2; T. Murphy beat T. Chappel 5-4; M. Gauvreau beat Simngam 5-1;
M. Gibson *wo* J. Dunning *scr*; P. Browne beat C. Everton 5-0; D. Fowler beat Bales 5-4;
G. Rigitano beat L. Dodd 5-3; E. Sinclair beat Greaves 5-1; V. Harris beat C. Roscoe
5-1; M. Watterson beat Jenkins 5-2; M. Fisher beat Jack Rea 5-3; Cripsey beat
S. Newbury 5-4; J. Fitzmaurice beat P. Fagan 5-3; Houlihan beat R. Foldvari 5-4
**Third round:** T. Jones beat W. Thorne 5-3; B. Werbeniuk beat G. Foulds 5-3;
D. Mountjoy beat King 5-4; D. O'Kane beat Medati 5-0; Hendry beat S. Francisco 5-4;
N. Foulds beat Bradley 5-3; Mikkelsen beat R. Reardon 5-3; J. Campbell beat Donnelly
5-2; F. Davis beat K. Stevens 5-2; E. Hughes beat Wych 5-2; J. Johnson beat B. Harris
5-4; P. Mans beat Smith 5-4; T. Meo beat O'Boye 5-3; West beat M. Wildman 5-2;
C. Thorburn beat J. McLaughlin 5-1; M. Hallett beat John Rea 5-2; S. Davis beat
Chaperon 5-1; Van Rensberg beat J. Parrott 5-3; P. Francisco beat E. Charlton 5-1;
D. Martin beat Murphy 5-3; Gauvreau beat David Taylor 5-3; Browne beat C. Wilson
5-3; J. White beat Fowler 5-1; J. Virgo beat Gibson 5-3; A. Knowles beat Rigitano 5-4;
M. Macleod beat Sinclair 5-2; V. Harris beat T. Griffiths 5-3; R. Williams beat
Watterson 5-0; A. Higgins beat Fisher 5-0; Cripsey beat J. Spencer 5-1; Dennis Taylor
beat Fitzmaurice 5-1; D. Reynolds beat Houlihan 5-1
**Fourth round:** Werbeniuk beat T. Jones 5-3; Mountjoy beat O'Kane 5-3; N. Foulds beat
Hendry 5-4; Campbell beat Mikkelsen 5-2; E. Hughes beat F. Davis 5-3; Johnson beat
Mans 5-2; Meo beat West 5-1; Thorburn beat Hallett 5-3; S. Davis beat Van Rensberg
5-1; P. Francisco beat Martin 5-2; Gauvreau beat Browne 5-3; White beat Virgo 5-2;
Knowles beat Macleod 5-3; Williams beat V. Harris 5-1; Higgins beat Cripsey 5-2;
Dennis Taylor beat Reynolds 5-4
**Fifth round:** Mountjoy beat Werbeniuk 5-3; N. Foulds beat Campbell 5-1; Johnson beat
E. Hughes 5-1; Thorburn beat Meo 5-1; S. Davis beat P. Francisco 5-0; White beat
Gauvreau 5-2; Williams beat Knowles 5-2; Higgins beat Dennis Taylor 5-4
**Quarter-finals:** Mountjoy beat N. Foulds 5-3; Thorburn beat Johnson 5-4; White beat

S. Davis 5-2; Williams beat Higgins 5-2
**Semi-finals:** Thorburn beat Mountjoy 9-6; White beat Williams 9-7
**Final:** White beat Thorburn 13-12

## 1987

**First round:** J. Meadowcroft *wo* L. Heywood *scr*; B. Rowswell beat M. Watterson 5-1;
P. Watchorn beat J. Donnelly 5-0; G. Foulds beat B. Bennett 5-2; C. Everton *wo*
E. McLaughlin *scr*; A. Kearney beat O. Agrawal 5-0; D. Roe beat M. Darrington 5-0;
F. Jonik beat S. James 5-4; D. Mienie *wo* J. Hargreaves *scr*; P. Burke *wo* J. Bear *scr*;
G. Jenkins beat M. Parkin 5-2; M. Bennett beat D. Sheehan 5-3; K. Owers beat
P. Houlihan 5-1; M. Morra beat F. Ellis 5-1; M. Fisher beat B. Demarco 5-0; C. Roscoe
beat T. Whitthread 5-1; B. Oliver beat D. Greaves 5-4; G. Wilkinson beat J. Fitzmaurice
5-2; Jack Rea beat B. Kelly 5-3; J. Wright beat D. Hughes 5-2; N. Gilbert beat M. Smith
5-0; P. Gibson *wo* S. Simngam *scr*; G. Rigitano beat R. Grace 5-4
**Second round:** S. Newbury beat Meadowcroft 5-1; M. Bradley beat Rowswell 5-4;
S. Duggan beat Watchorn 5-1; J. McLaughlin beat M. Gibson 5-3; J. O'Boye beat
V. Harris 5-1; G. Foulds beat D. O'Kane 5-4; J. Spencer beat D. Gilbert 5-4; P. Browne
beat Dunning 5-1; W. Jones beat Everton 5-0; Kearney beat M. Wildman 5-3; L. Dodd
beat Medati 5-4; I. Williamson beat R. Edmonds 5-2; R. Chaperon beat Roe 5-4; Jonik
beat T. Drago 5-2; G. Cripsey beat Mienie 5-0; W. King beat Burke 5-0; Jenkins beat
G. Scott 5-4; M. Bennett beat I. Black 5-3; John Rea beat Owers 5-2; T. Murphy beat
R. Bales 5-2; Morra *wo* P. Mans *scr*; Fisher beat F. Davis 5-2; Roscoe *wo* P. Fagan *scr*;
T. Jones beat Oliver 5-0; D. Fowler beat Wilkinson 5-1; B. Mikkelsen beat R. Foldvari
5-1; S. Hendry beat Jack Rea 5-1; Wright beat T. Chappel 5-4; J. Van Rensberg beat
N. Gilbert 5-3; R. Harris beat P. Gibson 5-3; E. Sinclair beat G. Miles 5-1; M. Gauvreau
beat Rigitano 5-0
**Third round:** J. White beat Newbury 5-4; Bradley beat David Taylor 5-1; Duggan beat
N. Foulds 5-3; B. Werbeniuk beat J. McLaughlin 5-1; T. Griffiths beat O'Boye 5-1;
D. Martin beat G. Foulds 5-4; Spencer beat W. Thorne 5-3; J. Campbell beat Browne
5-2; W. Jones beat Dennis Taylor 5-2; Kearney beat M. Macleod 5-0; Dodd beat
D. Mountjoy 5-4; C. Wilson beat Williamson 5-4; K. Stevens beat Chaperon 5-3; B. West
beat Jonik 5-4; C. Thorburn beat Cripsey 5-0; D. Reynolds beat King 5-4; S. Davis beat
Jenkins 5-0; J. Virgo beat M. Bennett 5-3; T. Meo beat John Rea 5-1; S. Longworth beat
Murphy 5-3; R. Williams beat Morra 5-2; E. Charlton beat Fisher 5-0; A. Higgins beat
Roscoe 5-2; J. Parrott beat T. Jones 5-2; Fowler beat A. Knowles 5-4; M. Hallett beat
Mikkelsen 5-3; Hendry beat R. Reardon 5-3; Wright beat E. Hughes 5-4; S. Francisco
beat Van Rensberg 5-4; B. Harris beat J. Wych 5-3; J. Johnson beat Sinclair 5-0;
P. Francisco beat Gauvreau 5-3
**Fourth round:** White beat Bradley 5-0; Duggan beat Werbeniuk 5-0; Griffiths beat
Martin 5-4; Campbell beat Spencer 5-3; W. Jones beat Kearney 5-1; Wilson beat Dodd
5-4; West beat Stevens 5-3; Reynolds beat Thorburn 5-4; S. Davis beat Virgo 5-2; Meo
beat Longworth 5-0; Charlton beat Williams 5-4; Parrott beat Higgins 5-2; Fowler beat
Hallett 5-4; Hendry beat Wright 5-1; S. Francisco beat N. Harris 5-3; P. Francisco beat
Johnson 5-3
**Fifth round:** White beat Duggan 5-2; Griffiths beat Campbell 5-3; Wilson beat W. Jones
5-3; Reynolds beat West 5-3; S. Davis beat Meo 5-2; Parrott beat Charlton 5-4; Hendry
beat Fowler 5-4; S. Francisco beat P. Francisco 5-1
**Quarter-finals:** White beat Griffiths 5-3; Reynolds beat Wilson 5-1; S. Davis beat Parrott
5-4; Hendry beat S. Francisco 5-0
**Semi-finals:** White beat Reynolds 9-8; S. Davis beat Hendry 9-3
**Final:** S. Davis beat White 13-12

## 1988

**First round:** D. Roe beat W. Kelly 5-1; J. Donnelly beat N. Gilbert 5-2; A. Harris beat
G. Jenkins 5-4; M. Morra beat R. Marshall 5-0; B. Rowswell beat J. Chambers 5-2;
R. Foldvari beat D. Greaves 5-3; D. Hughes beat I. Williamson 5-3; Glen Wilkinson beat

D. Chalmers 5-3; D. Gilbert beat Jack Rea 5-2; C. Everton beat J. Meadowcroft 5-3;
B. Oliver beat P. Burke 5-2; M. Clark *wo* B. Mikkelsen *scr*; Gary Wilkinson *wo*
M. Watterson *scr*; G. Rigitano *wo* J. Hargreaves *scr*; F. Jonik beat J. Dunning 5-2;
M. Smith beat J. Fitzmaurice 5-2; M. Fisher *wo* E. McLaughlin *scr*; T. Whitthread beat
P. Fagan 5-2; J. Bear beat J. Smith 5-3; E. Sinclair beat E. Lawlor 5-3; C. Roscoe beat
P. Watchorn 5-2; D. Sheehan beat D. Heaton 5-2; V. Harris beat F. Ellis 5-1; S. Meakin
beat M. Darrington 5-4; P. Gibson beat I. Black 5-2
**Second round:** L. Dodd beat Roe 5-2; Donnelly beat S. Duggan 5-4; T. Jones beat
A. Harris 5-2; Morra beat M. Gauvreau 5-4; Rowswell beat D. O'Kane 5-4; R. Edmonds
beat Foldvari 5-4; T. Chappel beat D. Hughes 5-3; B. Werbeniuk beat Glen Wilkinson
5-2; J. Van Rensberg beat R. Grace 5-3; D. Gilbert beat B. Harris 5-4; M. Bradley beat
Everton 5-2; Oliver beat W. King 5-3; Clark beat J. Wych 5-2; M. Bennett beat Miles
5-1; R. Reardon beat Gary Wilkinson 5-3; S. Newbury beat A. Kearney 5-1;
R. Chaperon beat P. Medati 5-3; Rigitano beat D. Fowler 5-2; M. Wildman beat Jonik
5-4; M. Smith beat P. Browne 5-1; K. Owers beat Fisher 5-0; G. Cripsey beat M. Gibson
5-4; Whitthread beat G. Foulds 5-3; G. Scott beat Bear 5-3; J. Wright beat Sinclair 5-3;
Roscoe beat W. Jones 5-4; J. O'Boye beat Sheehan 5-3; T. Murphy beat V. Harris 5-2;
F. Davis beat Meakin 5-4; J. McLaughlin beat P. Gibson 5-4; S. James beat P. Houlihan
5-2; John Rea beat R. Bales 5-0
**Third round:** S. Davis beat Dodd 5-0; Donnelly beat M. Macleod 5-4; A. Higgins beat
T. Jones 5-0; T. Meo beat Morra 5-1; S. Francisco beat Rowswell 5-3; S. Longworth beat
Edmonds 5-3; J. Johnson beat Chappel 5-2; S. Hendry beat Werbeniuk 5-2; T. Griffiths
beat Van Rensberg 5-2; C. Wilson beat D. Gilbert 5-3; W. Thorne beat Bradley 5-1;
B. West beat Oliver 5-3; Clark beat M. Hallett 5-4; M. Bennett beat K. Stevens 5-2;
C. Thorburn beat Reardon 5-3; Newbury beat E. Hughes 5-1; N. Foulds beat Chaperon
5-1; J. Virgo beat Rigitano 5-2; J. Parrott beat Wildman 5-2; David Taylor beat
M. Smith 5-3; Owers beat R. Williams 5-3; P. Francisco beat Cripsey 5-2; Dennis Taylor
beat Whitthread 5-2; T. Drago beat Scott 5-3; A. Knowles beat Wright 5-1; Roscoe beat
E. Charlton 5-3; D. Reynolds beat O'Boye 5-3; Murphy beat J. Campbell 5-3;
D. Mountjoy beat F. Davis 5-0; D. Martin beat J. McLaughlin 5-2; J. White beat James
5-1; J. Spencer beat John Rea 5-3
**Fourth round:** S. Davis beat Donnelly 5-0; Higgins beat Meo 5-3; S. Francisco beat
Longworth 5-2; Hendry beat Johnson 5-2; Griffiths beat Wilson 5-2; West beat Thorne
5-2; Clark beat M. Bennett 5-2; Newbury beat Thorburn 5-3; Virgo beat N. Foulds 5-3;
Parrott beat David Taylor 5-0; P. Francisco beat Owers 5-0; Dennis Taylor beat Drago
5-0; Knowles beat Roscoe 5-4; Murphy beat Reynolds 5-4; Martin beat Mountjoy 5-4;
White beat Spencer 5-1
**Fifth round:** S. Davis beat Higgins 5-0; Hendry beat S. Francisco 5-3; Griffiths beat West
5-2; Newbury beat Clark 5-2; Parrott beat Virgo 5-0; Dennis Taylor beat P. Francisco
5-3; Knowles beat Murphy 5-3; Martin beat White 5-2
**Quarter-finals:** S. Davis beat Hendry 5-3; Newbury beat Griffiths 5-4; Parrott beat
Dennis Taylor 5-1; Knowles beat Martin 5-1
**Semi-finals:** S. Davis beat Newbury 9-2; Parrott beat Knowles 9-4
**Final:** S. Davis beat Parrott 13-11

## 1989
**First round:** M. Johnston-Allen beat G. Scott 5-0; A. Harris beat Jim Bear 5-3;
I. Williamson beat G. Jenkins 5-2; P. Medati *wo* D. Chalmers *scr*; N. Terry beat John
Rea 5-3; D. Hughes *wo* P. Gibson *scr*; C. Roscoe beat T. Whitthread 5-3; J. Dunning
beat M. Price 5-3; Glen Wilkinson beat P. Watchorn 5-3; A. Kearney beat B. Kelly 5-3;
E. Sinclair beat S. Meakin 5-1; M. Watterson beat G. Rigitano 5-4; M. Wildman *wo*
F. Jonik *scr*; M. Bradley beat P. Fagan 5-3; Jack Rea beat M. Gibson 5-3; J. Chambers
beat D. Mienie 5-2; R. Foldvari beat T. Wilson 5-4; D. Morgan beat V. Harris 5-3;
D. Sheehan *wo* F. Davis *scr*; I. Graham beat R. Grace 5-4; J. Smith beat
J. Van Rensberg 5-4; J. Fitzmaurice beat J. Meadowcroft 5-2; M. Rowing beat M. Smith
5-3; R. Marshall beat I. Black 5-0; F. Ellis beat J. Donnelly 5-0; G. Foulds beat

C. Everton 5-0; A. Robidoux beat B. Harris 5-1; C. Edwards beat E. Lawlor 5-1;
S. Campbell beat B. Oliver 5-4; M. Darrington beat M. Morra 5-2; B. Rowswell beat
P. Burke 5-2; G. Miles beat B. Mikkelsen 5-3
**Second round:** T. Chappel beat Johnston-Allen 5-2; A. Harris beat D. Gilbert 5-4;
P. Browne beat Williamson 5-3; Gary Wilkinson beat Medati 5-1; Terry beat M. Bennett
5-3; D. Hughes beat J. O'Boye 5-1; Roscoe beat K. Owers 5-3; S. Duggan beat Dunning
5-2; Glen Wilkinson beat J. Wych 5-3; G. Cripsey beat Kearney 5-2; L. Dodd beat
Sinclair 5-3; J. McLaughlin beat Watterson 5-3; D. Fowler *wo* Wildman *scr*; Bradley beat
T. Jones 5-4; T. Murphy beat Jack Rea 5-0; R. Reardon beat Chambers 5-4; D. Martin
beat Foldvari 5-2; M. Clark beat Morgan 5-1; Sheehan beat M. Fisher 5-3; M. Macleod
beat Graham 5-4; J. Smith beat R. Bales 5-1; N. Gilbert beat Fitzmaurice 5-3; W. King
beat Rowing 5-4; Marshall beat R. Edmonds 5-2; D. Roe beat Ellis 5-0; J. Wright beat
G. Foulds 5-4; B. Werbeniuk beat Robidoux 5-4; K. Stevens beat Edwards 5-4;
S. Campbell beat J. Campbell 5-2; Darrington beat P. Houlihan 5-4; W. Jones beat
Rowswell 5-3; Miles beat M. Gauvreau 5-3
**Third round:** Chappel beat S. Davis 5-3; A. Harris beat B. West 5-4; Browne beat
M. Hallett 5-2; S. James beat Gary Wilkinson 5-1; Terry beat P. Francisco 5-4;
D. Mountjoy beat D. Hughes 5-0; A. Knowles beat Roscoe 5-4; D. Reynolds beat
Duggan 5-1; C. Thorburn beat Glen Wilkinson 5-2; Cripsey beat S. Longworth 5-3;
J. Virgo beat Dodd 5-2; R. Chaperon beat J. McLaughlin 5-3; Dennis Taylor beat Fowler
5-3; S. Newbury beat Bradley 5-3; S. Hendry beat Murphy 5-2; Reardon beat E. Charlton
5-1; N. Foulds beat Martin 5-1; Clark beat J. Spencer 5-2; J. Johnson beat Sheehan 5-2;
A. Higgins beat Macleod 5-2; W. Thorne beat J. Smith 5-1; D. O'Kane beat N. Gilbert
5-2; T. Griffiths beat King 5-2; T. Drago beat Marshall 5-1; J. Parrott beat Roe 5-2;
Wright beat R. Williams 5-0; S. Francisco *wo* Werbeniuk *scr*; T. Meo beat Stevens 5-3;
C. Wilson beat S. Campbell 5-3; David Taylor beat Darrington 5-2; W. Jones beat
J. White 5-3; E. Hughes beat Miles 5-2
**Fourth round:** Chappel beat A. Harris 5-1; Browne beat James 5-4; Mountjoy beat Terry
5-4; Knowles beat Reynolds 5-4; Thorburn beat Cripsey 5-1; Virgo beat Chaperon 5-1;
Newbury beat Dennis Taylor 5-4; Hendry beat Reardon 5-4; Clark beat N. Foulds 5-4;
Johnson beat Higgins 5-0; Thorne beat O'Kane 5-3; Griffiths beat Drago 5-0; Parrott
beat Wright 5-2; S. Francisco beat Meo 5-1; David Taylor beat C. Wilson 5-3; W. Jones
beat E. Hughes 5-1
**Fifth round:** Browne beat Chappel 5-1; Mountjoy beat Knowles 5-4; Thorburn beat Virgo
5-3; Hendry beat Newbury 5-1; Clark beat Johnson 5-3; Thorne beat Griffiths 5-1;
Parrott beat S. Francisco 5-1; W. Jones beat David Taylor 5-3
**Quarter-finals:** Mountjoy beat Browne 5-3; Thorburn beat Hendry 5-4; Thorne beat
Clark 5-4; W. Jones beat Parrott 5-4
**Semi-finals:** Mountjoy beat Thorburn 9-5; W. Jones beat Thorne 9-4
**Final:** Mountjoy beat W. Jones 13-11

# BENSON AND HEDGES MASTERS

**First staged** 1975. **Sponsors** Benson and Hedges. **Venue** West Centre Hotel
(1975), New London Theatre (1976–78), Wembley Conference Centre (1979– ).
**Initial prize-money** £5,000. **Prize-money last season** £250,000. **TV** BBC.

## 1975
**First round:** J. Pulman beat C. Thorburn 5-3; A. Higgins beat B. Werbeniuk 5-0
**Quarter-finals:** E. Charlton beat F. Davis 5-3; J. Spencer beat Pulman 5-3; R. Reardon
beat G. Miles 5-3; R. Williams beat Higgins 5-3
**Semi-finals:** Spencer beat Charlton 5-2; Reardon beat Williams 5-4
**Final:** Spencer beat Reardon 9-8

**1976**
First round: F. Davis beat C. Thorburn 4-2; J. Pulman beat Dennis Taylor 4-2
Quarter-finals: G. Miles beat A. Higgins 4-1; R. Reardon beat Pulman 4-1; J. Spencer beat F. Davis 4-0; E. Charlton beat R. Williams 4-1
Semi-finals: Miles beat Spencer 5-4; Reardon beat Charlton 5-4
Final: Reardon beat Miles 7-3

**1977**
First round: D. Mountjoy beat J. Pulman 4-2; J. Spencer beat Dennis Taylor 4-2
Quarter-finals: R. Reardon beat R. Williams 4-1; G. Miles beat Spencer 4-1; A. Higgins beat P. Mans 4-2; Mountjoy beat F. Davis 4-2
Semi-finals: Mountjoy beat Higgins 5-3; Reardon beat Miles 5-2
Final: Mountjoy beat Reardon 7-6

**1978**
First round: J. Pulman beat P. Fagan 4-2; G. Miles beat F. Davis 4-3
Quarter-finals: J. Spencer beat Pulman 4-2; A. Higgins beat Dennis Taylor 4-3; C. Thorburn beat D. Mountjoy 4-2; R. Reardon beat Miles 4-1
Semi-finals: Higgins beat Reardon 5-1; Thorburn beat Spencer 5-3
Final: Higgins beat Thorburn 7-5

**1979**
First round: D. Mountjoy beat F. Davis 5-2; David Taylor beat P. Fagan 5-4
Quarter-finals: A. Higgins beat E. Charlton 5-2; P. Mans beat C. Thorburn 5-4; Mountjoy beat Spencer 5-0; R. Reardon beat Taylor 5-2
Semi-finals: Higgins beat Mountjoy 5-1; Mans beat Reardon 5-3
Final: Mans beat Higgins 8-4

**1980**
First round: C. Thorburn beat J. Virgo 5-3; A. Higgins beat F. Davis 5-1
Quarter-finals: R. Reardon beat Dennis Taylor 5-3; T. Griffiths beat Thorburn 5-3; J. Spencer beat E. Charlton 5-2; Higgins beat P. Mans 5-1
Semi-finals: Griffiths beat Spencer 5-0; Higgins beat Reardon 5-2
Final: Griffiths beat Higgins 9-5

**1981**
First round: P. Mans beat S. Davis 5-3; D. Mountjoy beat E. Charlton 5-0; F. Davis beat K. Stevens 5-4; J. Spencer beat Dennis Taylor 5-2
Quarter-finals: A. Higgins beat Mountjoy 5-1; C. Thorburn beat Mans 5-4; Spencer beat R. Reardon 5-1; T. Griffiths beat F. Davis 5-2
Semi-finals: Higgins beat Thorburn 6-5; Griffiths beat Spencer 6-5
Final: Higgins beat Griffiths 9-6

**1982**
First round: R. Reardon beat Dennis Taylor 5-3; D. Mountjoy beat J. Spencer 5-4; T. Meo beat David Taylor 5-2; E. Charlton beat J. White 5-4
Quarter-finals: Meo beat C. Thorburn 5-0; S. Davis beat Mountjoy 5-2; A. Higgins beat Charlton 5-1; T. Griffiths beat Reardon 5-3
Semi-finals: S. Davis beat Meo 6-4; Griffiths beat Higgins 6-5
Final: S. Davis beat Griffiths 9-5

**1983**
First round: B. Werbeniuk beat A. Higgins 5-4; E. Charlton beat T. Meo 5-3; T. Griffiths beat K. Stevens 5-3; C. Thorburn beat J. Johnson 5-2; R. Reardon beat D. Reynolds 5-1; D. Mountjoy beat J. Virgo 5-1; S. Davis beat M. Wildman 5-2; J. White beat David Taylor 5-2
Quarter-finals: Charlton beat Werbeniuk 5-3; Thorburn beat Griffiths 5-3; Reardon beat White 5-2; Mountjoy beat S. Davis 5-4

**Semi-finals:** Thorburn beat Charlton 6-5; Reardon beat Mountjoy 6-3
**Final:** Thorburn beat Reardon 9-7

## 1984

**First round:** A. Knowles beat Dennis Taylor 5-2; R. Reardon beat J. Virgo 5-3;
J. Spencer beat C. Thorburn 5-4; T. Griffiths beat B. Werbeniuk 5-1; J. White beat
E. Charlton 5-2; A. Higgins beat D. Mountjoy 5-2; K. Stevens beat David Taylor 5-1;
S. Davis beat T. Meo 5-0
**Quarter-finals:** Griffiths beat Spencer 5-4; Knowles beat Higgins 5-1; White beat
Reardon 5-3; Stevens beat S. Davis 5-3
**Semi-finals:** Griffiths beat Knowles 6-4; White beat Stevens 6-4
**Final:** White beat Griffiths 9-5

## 1985

**First round:** J. White beat W. Thorne 5-2; J. Spencer beat E. Charlton 5-3; R. Reardon ·
beat David Taylor 5-1; C. Thorburn beat Dennis Taylor 5-3; D. Mountjoy beat
A. Knowles 5-3; T. Meo beat K. Stevens 5-2; T. Griffiths beat B. Werbeniuk 5-2;
A. Higgins beat S. Davis 5-4
**Quarter-finals:** White beat Spencer 5-2; Thorburn beat Reardon 5-0; Mountjoy beat Meo
5-4; Griffiths beat Higgins 5-1
**Semi-finals:** Thorburn beat White 6-4; Mountjoy beat Griffiths 6-2
**Final:** Thorburn beat Mountjoy 9-6

## 1986

**First round:** C. Thorburn beat J. Johnson 5-3; T. Griffiths beat A. Higgins 5-4;
E. Charlton beat K. Stevens 5-4; A. Knowles beat S. Francisco 5-1; S. Davis beat David
Taylor 5-4; W. Thorne beat R. Reardon 5-4; J. White beat T. Meo 5-4; Dennis Taylor
beat D. Mountjoy 5-2
**Quarter-finals:** Thorburn beat Griffiths 5-2; Knowles beat Charlton 5-4; S. Davis beat
Thorne 5-4; White beat Dennis Taylor 5-3
**Semi-finals:** Thorburn beat Knowles 6-4; White beat S. Davis 6-3
**Final:** Thorburn beat White 9-5

## 1987

**First round:** C. Thorburn beat R. Williams 5-1; W. Thorne beat K. Stevens 5-3;
S. Francisco beat A. Knowles 5-2; Dennis Taylor beat N. Foulds 5-2; D. Mountjoy beat
S. Davis 5-2; T. Meo beat J. White 5-4; A. Higgins beat T. Griffiths 5-4; J. Johnson beat
R. Reardon 5-2
**Quarter-finals:** Thorburn beat Thorne 5-3; Taylor beat S. Francisco 5-3; Meo beat
Mountjoy 5-4; Higgins beat Johnson 5-1
**Semi-finals:** Taylor beat Thorburn 6-5; Higgins beat Meo 6-2
**Final:** Taylor beat Higgins 9-8

## 1988

**First round:** M. Hallett beat Dennis Taylor 5-3; A. Higgins beat A. Knowles 5-4;
C. Thorburn beat R. Williams 5-3; J. Parrott beat N. Foulds 5-4; J. White beat
D. Mountjoy 5-0; J. Johnson beat W. Thorne 5-4; T. Griffiths beat S. Francisco 5-3;
S. Davis beat D. Reynolds 5-2
**Quarter-finals:** Hallett beat Higgins 5-2; Parrott beat Thorburn 5-4; Johnson beat White
5-3; S. Davis beat Griffiths 5-0
**Semi-finals:** Hallett beat Parrott 6-5; S. Davis beat Johnson 6-3
**Final:** S. Davis beat M. Hallett 9-0

## 1989

**First round:** S. Davis beat C. Wilson 5-2; A. Knowles beat M. Hallett 5-3; T. Griffiths
beat S. Francisco 5-1; S. Hendry beat W. Thorne 5-2; N. Foulds beat P. Francisco 5-2;
C. Thorburn beat J. Johnson 5-2; J. Parrott beat Dennis Taylor 5-1; J. White beat
J. Virgo 5-2

**Quarter-finals:** S. Davis beat Knowles 5-0; Hendry beat Griffiths 5-3; N. Foulds beat Thorburn 5-2; Parrott beat White 5-4
**Semi-finals:** Hendry beat S. Davis 6-3; Parrott beat N. Foulds 6-5
**Final:** Hendry beat Parrott 9-6

# EUROPEAN OPEN

**First staged** 1989. **Sponsors** ICI (quarter-finals onward). **Venue** Deauville Casino, France. **Initial prize-money** £200,000. **TV** packages on BBC, TF1, Eurosport.

**1989**
**First round:** J. Chambers beat B. Mikkelsen 5-3; D. Morgan beat W. Wildman 5-1; I. Williamson beat D. Hughes 5-1; C. Edwards beat M. Smith 5-4; P. Watchorn beat M. Harris 5-4; F. Davis beat C. Everton 5-0; E. Lawlor beat J. Fitzmaurice 5-0; I. Graham beat G. Scott 5-1; A. Harris beat Glen Wilkinson 5-4; T. Wilson beat M. Gibson 5-3; G. Foulds beat Jack Rea 5-4; M. Johnston-Allen beat J. Donnelly 5-3; F. Ellis beat A. Kearney 5-4; J. Smith beat B. Rowswell 5-2; M. Bradley beat J. Rempe 5-4; G. Rigitano beat P. Burke 5-2; M. Rowing beat R. Foldvari 5-4; M. Morra beat S. Campbell 5-3; C. Roscoe beat M. Watterson 5-4; V. Harris beat N. Terry 5-2; P. Medati beat D. Sheehan 5-1; A. Robidoux beat J. Meadowcroft 5-0; M. Price beat John Rea 5-4; M. Darrington beat J. Dunning 5-4; R. Grace beat S. Meakin 5-4; I. Black beat P. Fagan 5-1; Jim Bear beat B. Kelly 5-0; R. Marshall beat J. Van Rensberg 5-1; B. Oliver beat D. Chalmers 5-4; E. Sinclair beat T. Whitthread 5-4; G. Miles beat G. Jenkins 5-3
**Second round:** Chambers beat R. Bales 5-1; S. Duggan beat Morgan 5-4; R. Reardon beat Williamson 5-3; Edwards *wo* B. Werbeniuk *scr*; J. Campbell beat Watchorn 5-1; M. Bennett beat F. Davis 5-2; Lawlor beat K. Owers 5-4; Gary Wilkinson beat Graham 5-3; D. Fowler beat A. Harris 5-1; T. Wilson beat M. Gauvreau 5-3; J. Wych beat G. Foulds 5-0; Johnston-Allen beat J. Wright 5-4; D. Gilbert beat Ellis 5-2; P. Browne beat J. Smith 5-3; W. Jones beat Rigitano 5-4; M. Clark beat Rowing 5-0; Morra beat N. Gilbert 5-1; G. Cripsey beat Roscoe 5-4; D. Roe beat V. Harris 5-1; T. Jones beat Medati 5-2; Robidoux beat M. Fisher 5-1; J. McLaughlin beat Price 5-3; T. Chappel beat Darrington 5-0; R. Edmonds beat Grace 5-1; Macleod beat Black 5-1; K. Stevens beat Bear 5-2; T. Murphy beat Marshall 5-4; Oliver beat D. Martin 5-4; L. Dodd *wo* both P. Gibson & F. Jonik *scr*; Sinclair beat P. Houlihan 5-1; King beat Miles 5-2
**Third round:** Chambers *wo* S. Davis *scr*; E. Charlton beat Duggan 5-2; J. Virgo beat Reardon 5-3; Edwards beat R. Chaperon 5-3; J. Campbell beat P. Francisco 5-0; M. Bennett beat T. Drago 5-1; J. Parrott *wo* Lawlor *scr*; Gary Wilkinson beat David Taylor 5-2; Fowler beat A. Knowles 5-2; T. Wilson *wo* J. Spencer *scr*; Wych beat S. Francisco 5-1; Johnston-Allen beat S. James 5-1; M. Hallett beat D. Gilbert 5-3; Browne *wo* D. Reynolds *scr*; S. Hendry beat O'Boye 5-2; S. Longworth *wo* W. Jones *scr*; Clark beat N. Foulds 5-3; E. Hughes beat Morra 5-1; J. Johnson beat Cripsey 5-2; Roe beat T. Meo 5-1; C. Wilson beat T. Jones 5-3; Robidoux beat S. Newbury 5-0; T. Griffiths beat J. McLaughlin 5-3; Chappel beat D. O'Kane 5-0; C. Thorburn beat Edmonds 5-2; Macleod beat B. West 5-4; Dennis Taylor beat Stevens 5-0; D. Mountjoy beat Murphy 5-1; W. Thorne beat Oliver 5-0; A. Higgins beat Dodd 5-2; J. White beat Sinclair 5-3; R. Williams beat King 5-2
**Fourth round:** Charlton beat Chambers 5-2; Virgo beat Edwards 5-3; J. Campbell beat M. Bennett 5-3; Parrott beat Gary Wilkinson 5-2; Fowler beat T. Wilson 5-2; Wych beat Johnston-Allen 5-4; Hallett beat Browne 5-4; Hendry beat Longworth 5-0; Clark beat E. Hughes 5-1; Johnson beat Roe 5-2; Robidoux beat C. Wilson 5-0; Griffiths beat Chappel 5-2; Thorburn beat Macleod 5-1; Mountjoy beat Dennis Taylor 5-3; Thorne beat Higgins 5-1; White beat Williams 5-2

**Fifth round:** Charlton beat Virgo 5-4; Parrott beat J. Campbell 5-0; Wych beat Fowler 5-4; Hallett beat Hendry 5-3; Clark beat Johnson 5-4; Griffiths beat Robidoux 5-3; Thorburn beat Mountjoy 5-0; White beat Thorne 5-3
**Quarter-finals:** Parrott beat Charlton 5-1; Hallett beat Wych 5-3; Griffiths beat Clark 5-1; White beat Thorburn 5-3
**Semi-finals:** Parrott beat Hallett 5-4; Griffiths beat White 5-4
**Final:** Parrott beat Griffiths 9-8

# ANGLIAN BRITISH OPEN

**First staged** 1985. **Sponsors** Dulux (1985–87), MIM Britannia (1988), Anglian (1989). **Venue** Assembly Rooms, Derby. **Initial prize-money** £250,000. **Prize-money last season** £350,000. **TV** ITV.

**1985** (*Dulux*)
**Qualifying:** T. Chappel beat I. Williamson 6-5; D. Chalmers beat P. Burke 6-5; John Rea beat M. Fisher 6-0; W. King beat P. Medati 6-4; D. Fowler beat C. Everton 6-1; T. Murphy beat D. Sheehan 6-3; R. Foldvari beat S. Duggan 6-4; V. Harris beat L. Dodd 6-1; T. Jones beat G. Foulds 6-0; P. Francisco beat B. Kelly 6-3; D. O'Kane beat G. Cripsey 6-4; S. Newbury beat P. Browne 6-0; M. Bradley beat M. Morra 6-2; A. Kearney beat M. Watterson 6-4; D. French beat E. McLaughlin 6-0; R. Chaperon beat P. Fagan 6-5; B. Harris beat J. Meadowcroft 6-1; S. Longworth beat F. Davis 6-1; B. Mikkelsen beat D. Hughes 6-0; G. Scott beat M. Darrington 6-3; J. Giannaros beat C. Roscoe 6-1; F. Jonik beat J. McLaughlin 6-2; W. Jones beat J. Donnelly 6-1; P. Watchorn beat J. Fitzmaurice 6-1; R. Bales beat I. Black 6-4; M. Gauvreau beat D. Greaves 6-3; M. Gibson beat B. Demarco 6-1; R. Edmonds beat D. Mienie 6-1
**First round:** D. Reynolds beat Giannaros 6-3; M. Macleod beat Murphy 6-5; E. Hughes beat Watchorn 6-4; Longworth beat C. Wilson 6-3; W. Jones beat J. Johnson 6-5; M. Hallett *wo* Mikkelsen *scr*; C. Thorburn beat G. Rigitano 6-3; A. Higgins beat Bales 6-3; Chaperon beat B. Werbeniuk 6-1; S. Francisco beat Kearney 6-4; T. Meo beat Foldvari 6-0; W. Thorne beat W. Oliver 6-4; B. Harris beat E. Charlton 6-3; J. White beat T. Jones 6-5; A. Knowles beat French 6-2; N. Foulds beat J. Hargreaves 6-1; Newbury beat E. Sinclair 6-3; M. Wildman beat Gibson 6-1; J. Spencer beat Jonik 6-0; V. Harris beat D. Mountjoy 6-5; O'Kane beat J. Campbell 6-4; G. Miles beat Edmonds 6-1; T. Griffiths beat Chalmers 6-0; R. Reardon beat King 6-5; J. Parrott beat John Rea 6-4; Bradley beat David Taylor 6-3; K. Stevens beat Gauvreau 6-3; J. Virgo beat P. Francisco 6-2; Fowler beat R. Williams 6-4; D. Martin beat B. Bennett 6-0; S. Davis beat Chappel 6-5; Dennis Taylor beat Scott 6-2
**Second round:** Newbury beat Griffiths 5-3; Bradley beat Fowler 5-4; S. Davis beat Virgo 5-2; Knowles beat Longworth 5-2; O'Kane beat V. Harris 5-3; Thorburn beat Reynolds 5-3; Higgins beat N. Foulds 5-1; Dennis Taylor beat Parrott 5-2; Macleod beat Thorne 5-0; Martin beat Reardon 5-4; Miles beat Spencer 5-3; S. Francisco beat White 5-4; Meo beat Hallett 5-4; E. Hughes beat B. Harris 5-4; Stevens beat Wildman 5-2; Chaperon beat W. Jones 5-2
**Third round:** Meo beat Knowles 5-2; S. Davis beat Bradley 5-2; O'Kane beat Martin 5-4; S. Francisco beat Chaperon 5-2; Dennis Taylor beat Newbury 5-3; E. Hughes beat Macleod 5-2; Stevens beat Miles 5-2; Higgins beat Thorburn 5-2
**Quarter-finals:** Stevens beat Dennis Taylor 5-2; S. Davis beat O'Kane 5-1; S. Francisco beat Meo 5-4; Higgins beat E. Hughes 5-2
**Semi-finals:** Stevens beat S. Davis 9-7; S. Francisco beat Higgins 9-6
**Final:** S. Francisco beat Stevens 12-9

**1986** (*Dulux*)
**First round:** J. O'Boye beat Jim Bear 5-1; J. Hargreaves *wo* G. Watson *scr*; O. Agrawal beat D. Greaves 5-3; D. Gilbert beat P. Burke 5-1; S. Hendry beat D. Hughes 5-1;

G. Wilkinson beat P. Watchorn 5-4; D. Sheehan beat S. Simngam 5-2; G. Jenkins beat
B. Demarco 5-1; B. West beat B. Bennett 5-1; G. Cripsey beat M. Darrington 5-4;
P. Houlihan *wo* G. Robinson *scr*; A. Kearney beat M. Smith 5-2; R. Bales beat M. Parkin
5-1; T. Drago *wo* D. Mienie *scr*
**Second round:** T. Jones beat O'Boye 5-2; F. Davis beat W. Kelly 5-4; G. Scott beat
D. Chalmers 5-1; Hargreaves beat R. Edmonds 5-3; L. Dodd beat F. Jonik 5-4; W. Jones
beat G. Rigitano 5-1; G. Miles beat Agrawal 5-4; R. Chaperon beat V. Harris 5-0; John
Rea beat W. King 5-1; D. Fowler beat T. Chappel 5-4; Gilbert beat M. Morra 5-4;
P. Browne beat Hendry 5-0; J. Donnelly beat Wilkinson 5-4; S. Newbury beat W. Oliver
5-2; Sheehan *wo* M. Watterson *scr*; Jenkins beat J. Meadowcroft 5-2; I. Black beat
M. Gibson 5-0; B. Harris beat E. Sinclair 5-3; P. Medati beat C. Everton 5-1; West beat
E. McLaughlin 5-3; P. Fagan beat J. Fitzmaurice 5-4; C. Roscoe beat B. Mikkelsen 5-4;
I. Williamson beat Cripsey 5-4; J. Wych beat J. Van Rensberg 5-0; P. Francisco beat
G. Foulds 5-2; S. Longworth beat Houlihan 5-3; M. Bradley beat Jack Rea 5-1;
S. Duggan beat T. Murphy 5-1; J. McLaughlin beat M. Fisher 5-3; R. Foldvari beat
Kearney 5-2; Bales *wo* J. Dunning *scr*; Drago beat M. Gauvreau 5-3
**Third round:** S. Francisco beat T. Jones 5-2; M. Macleod beat F. Davis 5-4; T. Griffiths
beat Scott 5-3; N. Foulds beat Hargreaves 5-4; W. Thorne beat Dodd 5-2; P. Mans beat
W. Jones 5-2; K. Stevens beat Miles 5-3; C. Wilson beat Chaperon 5-3; John Rea beat
R. Reardon 5-3; J. Virgo beat Fowler 5-1; E. Charlton beat Gilbert 5-2; Browne beat
J. Spencer 5-0; T. Meo beat Donnelly 5-3; Newbury beat D. O'Kane 5-3; C. Thorburn
beat Sheehan 5-0; M. Wildman beat Jenkins 5-4; S. Davis beat Black 5-2; D. Martin
beat B. Harris 5-1; Medati beat David Taylor 5-1; J. Campbell beat West 5-4; Fagan
beat D. Mountjoy 5-1; J. Parrott beat Roscoe 5-2; A. Knowles beat Williamson 5-1;
Wych beat D. Reynolds 5-3; P. Francisco beat J. White 5-4; Longworth beat E. Hughes
5-4; A. Higgins beat Bradley 5-3; M. Hallett beat Duggan 5-3; J. Johnson beat
J. McLaughlin 5-2; B. Werbeniuk beat Foldvari 5-4; Bales beat Dennis Taylor 5-4;
R. Williams beat Drago 5-1
**Fourth round:** Macleod beat S. Francisco 5-1; Griffiths beat N. Foulds 5-3; Thorne beat
Mans 5-1; Stevens beat Wilson 5-0; Virgo beat John Rea 5-0; Charlton beat Browne 5-1;
Meo beat Newbury 5-0; Thorne beat Wildman 5-1; S. Davis beat Martin 5-1; Campbell
beat Medati 5-4; Parrott beat Fagan 5-0; Wych beat Knowles 5-4; P. Francisco beat
Longworth 5-2; Higgins beat Hallett 5-1; Werbeniuk beat Johnson 5-3; Williams beat
Bales 5-4
**Fifth round:** Griffiths beat Macleod 5-2; Thorne beat Stevens 5-4; Virgo beat Charlton
5-4; Meo beat Thorburn 5-3; S. Davis beat Campbell 5-0; Wych beat Parrott 5-4;
Higgins beat P. Francisco 5-2; Werbeniuk beat Williams 5-3
**Quarter-finals:** Thorne beat Griffiths 5-4; Virgo beat Meo 5-3; S. Davis beat Wych 5-2;
Higgins beat Werbeniuk 5-1
**Semi-finals:** Thorne beat Virgo 9-4; S. Davis beat Higgins 9-3
**Final:** S. Davis beat Thorne 12-7

## 1987 (*Dulux*)
**First round:** M. Morra beat M. Bennett 5-4; B. Rowswell beat G. Jenkins 5-1; G. Foulds
beat D. Greaves 5-3; D. Roe beat M. Watterson 5-3; B. Kelly beat B. Bennett 5-2;
P. Gibson beat O. Agrawal 5-0; N. Gilbert beat P. Houlihan 5-4; J. Hargreaves beat
M. Parkin 5-4; J. Donnelly *wo* L. Heywood *scr*; C. Roscoe beat D. Mienie 5-2; F. Ellis
beat M. Smith 5-2; D. Chalmers *wo* S. Simngam *scr*; P. Watchorn beat J. Dunning 5-2;
K. Owers beat F. Jonik 5-4; M. Fisher *wo* C. Everton *scr*; R. Grace beat J. Meadowcroft
5-4; G. Wilkinson beat J. Fitzmaurice 5-0; T. Kearney *wo* Jim Bear *scr*; G. Rigitano beat
B. Demarco 5-1; S. James beat M. Darrington 5-3; T. Whitthread beat D. Hughes 5-1;
P. Burke *wo* E. McLaughlin *scr*; B. Oliver beat Jack Rea 5-1; D. Sheehan beat J. Wright
5-2
**Second round:** M. Gauvreau beat R. Bales 5-0; Morra beat J. Van Rensberg 5-1;
Rowswell beat D. O'Kane 5-4; G. Foulds beat R. Edmonds 5-3; Roe beat I. Black 5-0;
W. King beat Williamson 5-3; B. Harris beat Kelly 5-2; S. Duggan beat Gibson 5-3;

D. Fowler beat Dodd 5-1; N. Gilbert beat W. Jones 5-3; J. O'Boye beat M. Bradley 5-1; T. Murphy beat D. Gilbert 5-4; Hargreaves beat John Rea 5-3; T. Jones beat Donnelly 5-2; Roscoe beat S. Newbury 5-3; P. Medati beat Ellis 5-0; M. Wildman beat Chalmers 5-0; G. Cripsey beat Watchorn 5-4; Owers beat F. Davis 5-3; E. Sinclair beat S. Hendry 5-2; R. Chaperon beat Fisher 5-2; Grace beat P. Fagan 5-3; J. McLaughlin beat M. Gibson 5-1; Wilkinson beat Mans 5-2; T. Chappel beat Kearney 5-3; Rigitano beat P. Browne 5-4; R. Foldvari beat B. Mikkelsen 5-3; James beat G. Miles 5-2; J. Spencer beat Whitthread 5-2; G. Scott beat Burke 5-2; T. Drago beat Oliver 5-1; V. Harris beat Sheehan 5-4

**Third round:** S. Davis beat Gauvreau 5-0; J. Virgo beat Morra 5-3; S. Francisco beat Rowswell 5-0; C. Wilson beat G. Foulds 5-3; N. Foulds beat Roe 5-1; King beat J. Parrott 5-1; W. Thorne beat B. Harris 5-1; Duggan beat S. Longworth 5-2; A. Knowles beat Fowler 5-4; D. Reynolds beat N. Gilbert 5-2; R. Reardon beat O'Boye 5-4; Murphy beat J. Wych 5-1; T. Griffiths beat John Rea 5-2; T. Jones beat M. Macleod 5-4; Dennis Taylor beat Roscoe 5-1; E. Charlton beat Medati 5-4; C. Thorburn beat Wildman 5-3; Cripsey beat B. Werbeniuk 5-2; D. Mountjoy beat Owers 5-1; P. Francisco beat Sinclair 5-3; K. Stevens beat Chaperon 5-4; B. West beat Grace 5-2; J. McLaughlin beat A. Higgins 5-4; David Taylor beat Wilkinson 5-4; J. White beat Chappel 5-1; M. Hallett beat Rigitano 5-1; R. Williams beat Foldvari 5-4; James beat J. Campbell 5-1; Spencer beat T. Meo 5-1; D. Martin beat Scott 5-3; J. Johnson beat Drago 5-0; E. Hughes beat V. Harris 5-1

**Fourth round:** Virgo beat S. Davis 5-4; Wilson beat S. Francisco 5-4; N. Foulds beat King 5-4; Thorne beat Duggan 5-2; Knowles beat Reynolds 5-0; Murphy beat Reardon 5-4; Griffiths beat T. Jones 5-3; Dennis Taylor beat Charlton 5-1; Thorburn beat Cripsey 5-2; Mountjoy beat P. Francisco 5-3; Stevens beat West 5-4; David Taylor beat J. McLaughlin 5-2; White beat Hallett 5-2; Williams beat James 5-2; Spencer beat Martin 5-2; Johnson beat E. Hughes 5-3

**Fifth round:** Virgo beat Wilson 5-2; N. Foulds beat Thorne 5-2; Knowles beat Murphy 5-3; Dennis Taylor beat Griffiths 5-4; Thorburn beat Mountjoy 5-4; David Taylor beat Stevens 5-2; White beat Williams 5-0; Spencer beat Johnson 5-3

**Quarter-finals:** N. Foulds beat Virgo 5-3; Knowles beat Dennis Taylor 5-4; Thorburn beat David Taylor 5-3; White beat Spencer 5-3

**Semi-finals:** N. Foulds beat Knowles 9-2; White beat Thorburn 9-5

**Final:** White beat N. Foulds 13-9

## 1988 (*MIM Britannia*)

**First round:** M. Clark beat M. Fisher 5-1; J. Bear beat A. Harris 5-2; Gary Wilkinson beat I. Black 5-2; J. Fitzmaurice *wo* C. Everton *scr*; G. Rigitano beat R. Marshall 5-2; M. Morra beat P. Watchorn 5-1; F. Ellis *wo* M. Watterson *scr*; D. Hughes beat P. Fagan 5-4; N. Gilbert beat D. Sheehan 5-3; J. Dunning beat F. Jonik 5-3; P. Thornley beat V. Harris 5-4; C. Roscoe beat P. Gibson 5-4; B. Oliver beat M. Smith 5-0; M. Darrington beat P. Burke 5-4; R. Foldvari beat D. Heaton 5-1; J. Meadowcroft beat B. Kelly 5-1; T. Whitthread beat Glen Wilkinson 5-4; D. Chalmers *wo* B. Mikkelsen *scr*; E. Lawlor beat E. Sinclair 5-3; B. Rowswell beat Jack Rea 5-1; D. Gilbert *wo* E. McLaughlin *scr*; I. Williamson beat S. Meakin 5-1; J. Donnelly beat D. Greaves 5-4; G. Jenkins beat J. Smith 5-3; J. Van Rensberg *wo* J. Hargreaves *scr*; D. Roe beat J. Chambers 5-3

**Second round:** Clark beat R. Grace 5-0; S. James beat W. King 5-2; Bear beat P. Houlihan 5-0; Gary Wilkinson beat R. Bales 5-1; T. Jones beat Fitzmaurice 5-3; R. Chaperon beat Rigitano 5-2; Morra beat M. Bennett 5-2; T. Chappel beat Ellis 5-0; G. Miles beat K. Owers 5-2; F. Davis beat D. Hughes 5-2; N. Gilbert beat Werbeniuk 5-1; Dunning beat G. Scott 5-3; J. Wych beat Thornley 5-1; Roscoe beat M. Wildman 5-0; S. Newbury beat Oliver 5-4; P. Medati beat M. Gauvreau 5-1; D. Fowler beat A. Kearney 5-1; Darrington beat L. Dodd 5-4; Foldvari beat G. Foulds 5-3; T. Murphy beat Meadowcroft 5-4; D. O'Kane beat Whitthread 5-2; P. Browne beat Chalmers 5-2; Lawlor beat B. Harris 5-2; Rowswell beat J. McLaughlin 5-2; M. Gibson beat S. Duggan 5-2; D. Gilbert beat J. Wright 5-2; Williamson beat M. Bradley 5-3; G. Cripsey beat

Donnelly 5-4; J. O'Boye beat Jenkins 5-1; W. Jones beat John Rea 5-3; R. Reardon beat Van Rensberg 5-3; Roe beat R. Edmonds 5-1
**Third round:** J. White beat Clark 5-2; James beat E. Charlton 5-2; S. Francisco beat Bear 5-0; Gary Wilkinson beat T. Meo 5-2; T. Jones beat A. Higgins 5-3; Chaperon *wo* K. Stevens *scr*; T. Griffiths beat Morra 5-1; S. Hendry beat Chappel 5-1; Dennis Taylor beat Miles 5-1; J. Spencer beat F. Davis 5-0; R. Williams beat N. Gilbert 5-2; B. West beat Dunning 5-0; W. Thorne beat Wych 5-1; C. Wilson beat Roscoe 5-2; C. Thorburn beat Newbury 5-2; Medati beat David Taylor 5-4; N. Foulds beat Fowler 5-3; P. Francisco beat Darrington 5-1; J. Parrott beat Foldvari 5-1; J. Virgo beat Murphy 5-1; O'Kane beat Mountjoy 5-3; Browne beat D. Martin 5-4; J. Johnson beat Lawlor 5-1; Rowswell beat S. Longworth 5-4; A. Knowles beat M. Gibson 5-4; M. Macleod beat D. Gilbert 5-4; M. Hallett beat Williamson 5-0; Cripsey beat E. Hughes 5-3; O'Boye beat Reynolds 5-2; J. Campbell beat W. Jones 5-3; Reardon beat S. Davis 5-0; Roe beat T. Drago 5-3
**Fourth round:** White beat James 5-1; Gary Wilkinson beat S. Francisco 5-3; T. Jones beat Chaperon 5-4; Hendry beat Griffiths 5-1; Spencer beat Dennis Taylor 5-0; Williams beat West 5-0; Thorne beat Wilson 5-3; Thorburn beat Medati 5-2; N. Foulds beat P. Francisco 5-3; Parrott beat Virgo 5-1; O'Kane beat Browne 5-2; Johnson beat Rowswell 5-2; Macleod beat Knowles 5-4; Hallett beat Cripsey 5-2; O'Boye beat Campbell 5-1; Roe beat Reardon 5-2
**Fifth round:** White beat Gary Wilkinson 5-1; Hendry beat T. Jones 5-3; Williams beat Spencer 5-4; Thorburn beat Thorne 5-2; Parrott beat N. Foulds 5-0; O'Kane beat Johnson 5-2; Hallett beat Macleod 5-2; O'Boye beat Roe 5-1
**Quarter-finals:** Hendry beat White 5-4; Thorburn beat Williams 5-2; Parrott beat O'Kane 5-2; Hallett beat O'Boye 5-4
**Semi-finals:** Hendry beat Thorburn 9-5; Hallett beat Parrott 9-8
**Final:** Hendry beat Hallett 13-2

## 1989
**First round:** C. Edwards beat I. Black 5-3; J. Meadowcroft beat G. Jenkins 5-4; C. Roscoe beat S. Meakin 5-1; J. Smith beat G. Foulds 5-3; M. Gibson beat M. Rowing 5-0; M. Price beat G. Rigitano 5-0; A. Harris beat M. Wildman 5-4; I. Graham beat I. Williamson 5-4; E. Sinclair beat M. Mikkelsen 5-3; D. Morgan beat Glen Wilkinson 5-0; T. Wilson beat F. Davis 5-1; J. Fitzmaurice beat J. Dunning 5-1; J. Van Rensberg *wo* F. Jonik *scr*; M. Darrington beat G. Scott 5-4; S. Campbell beat P. Medati 5-3; A. Robidoux beat B. Harris 5-0; N. Terry beat A. Kearney 5-3; J. Rempe beat M. Morra 5-1; John Rea beat P. Watchorn 5-3; E. Lawlor beat M. Watterson 5-0; T. Whitthread beat J. Donnelly 5-4; Jim Bear beat Jack Rea 5-4; M. Johnston-Allen beat V. Harris 5-1; B. Rowswell beat F. Ellis 5-1; R. Grace beat P. Fagan 5-2; P. Burke *wo* P. Gibson *scr*; M. Smith beat D. Hughes 5-1; B. Kelly beat B. Oliver 5-4; G. Miles beat D. Chalmers 5-4; R. Marshall beat J. Chambers 5-2; M. Bradley beat C. Everton 5-0; R. Foldvari beat D. Sheehan 5-1
**Second round:** Edwards beat J. O'Boye 5-4; T. Jones beat Meadowcroft 5-1; Roscoe *wo* B. Werbeniuk *scr*; M. Bennett beat J. Smith 5-4; J. Campbell beat M. Gibson 5-2; D. Roe beat Price 5-2; J. Wych beat A. Harris 5-4; Graham beat S. Duggan 5-2; P. Browne beat Sinclair 5-2; D. Morgan beat J. McLaughlin 5-0; N. Gilbert beat T. Wilson 5-2; R. Bales beat Fitzmaurice 5-1; D. Fowler beat Van Rensberg 5-1; M. Clark beat Darrington 5-2; R. Reardon beat S. Campbell 5-4; Robidoux beat W. King 5-2; P. Houlihan beat Terry 5-2; L. Dodd beat Rempe 5-0; John Rea beat D. Gilbert 5-3; T. Chappel beat Lawlor 5-2; Whitthread beat T. Murphy 5-2; Jim Bear beat D. Martin 5-2; Johnston-Allen beat R. Edmonds 5-4; W. Jones beat Rowswell 5-0; J. Wright beat Grace 5-1; K. Owers beat Burke 5-2; M. Macleod beat M. Smith 5-4; M. Gauvreau beat Kelly 5-0; Gary Wilkinson beat Miles 5-2; Marshall beat K. Stevens 5-4; G. Cripsey beat Bradley 5-4; Foldvari beat M. Fisher 5-0
**Third round:** S. Hendry beat Edwards 5-0; D. O'Kane beat T. Jones 5-4; Roscoe beat Dennis Taylor 5-4; T. Meo beat M. Bennett 5-1; P. Francisco beat J. Campbell 5-2; Roe

beat R. Williams 5-2; T. Knowles beat Wych 5-2; B. West beat Graham 5-1;
C. Thorburn beat Browne 5-0; D. Morgan beat E. Charlton 5-3; M. Hallett beat
N. Gilbert 5-3; R. Bales beat S. Newbury 5-3; J. Virgo beat Fowler 5-2; Clark beat
David Taylor 5-2; N. Foulds beat Reardon 5-1; Robidoux beat J. Spencer 5-1; J. White
beat Houlihan 5-3; D. Reynolds beat Dodd 5-2; C. Wilson beat John Rea 5-2; Chappel
beat S. James 5-3; J. Johnson beat Whitthread 5-2; T. Drago beat Jim Bear 5-2;
Johnston-Allen beat T. Griffiths 5-1; E. Hughes beat W. Jones 5-2; J. Parrott beat
Wright 5-1; S. Longworth beat Owers 5-1; Macleod beat S. Francisco 5-4; D. Mountjoy
beat Gauvreau 5-0; W. Thorne beat Gary Wilkinson 5-1; Marshall beat R. Chaperon
5-2; S. Davis beat Cripsey 5-1; A. Higgins beat Foldvari 5-1
**Fourth round:** Hendry beat O'Kane 5-2; Meo beat Roscoe 5-3; P. Francisco beat Roe 5-3;
West beat Knowles 5-0; Thorburn beat D. Morgan 5-4; Hallett beat Bales 5-0; Clark
beat Virgo 5-1; N. Foulds beat Robidoux 5-1; Reynolds *wo* White *scr*; C. Wilson beat
Chappel 5-3; Johnson beat Drago 5-3; Johnston-Allen beat E. Hughes 5-2; Parrott beat
Longworth 5-1; Mountjoy beat Macleod 5-0; Thorne beat Marshall 5-1; S. Davis beat
Higgins 5-0
**Fifth round:** Meo beat Hendry 5-3; P. Francisco beat West 5-1; Hallett beat Thorburn
5-4; Clark beat Foulds 5-4; Reynolds beat C. Wilson 5-0; Johnson beat Johnston-Allen
5-2; Parrott beat Mountjoy 5-2; S. Davis beat Thorne 5-0
**Quarter-finals:** Meo beat P. Francisco 5-3; Hallett beat Clark 5-3; Reynolds beat Johnson
5-4; Parrott beat S. Davis 5-1
**Semi-finals:** Meo beat Hallett 9-8; Reynolds beat Parrott 9-8
**Final:** Meo beat Reynolds 13-6

# FERSINA WORLD CUP

**First staged** 1979. **Sponsors** State Express (1979–83), Guinness (1985), Car Care
Plan (1986), Tuborg (1987), Fersina Windows (1988– ). **Venue** The Hexagon,
Reading (1979–83), Bournemouth International Centre (1985– ). **Initial
prize-money** £27,500. **Prize-money last season** £135,000. **TV** BBC.

**1979** (*State Express World Team Classic*)
**Group A**
England (F. Davis, G. Miles, J. Spencer) beat Rest of World (P. Mans, J. Van Rensberg,
P. Fagan) 8-7; England beat Northern Ireland (Jack Rea, A. Higgins, Dennis Taylor)
8-7; Northern Ireland beat Rest of World 8-7
**Group B**
Wales (R. Reardon, T. Griffiths, D. Mountjoy) beat Canada (C. Thorburn, K. Stevens,
B. Werbeniuk) 9-6; Australia (E. Charlton, G. Owen, P. Morgan) beat Canada 8-7;
Wales beat Australia 9-6
**Final:** Wales beat England 14-3

**1980** (*State Express World Team Classic*)
**Group A**
Wales (R. Reardon, T. Griffiths, D. Mountjoy) beat Canada (C. Thorburn, K. Stevens,
B. Werbeniuk) 10-5; Canada beat Rest of World (J. Rempe, E. Sinclair, P. Mans) 9-6;
Wales beat Rest of World 13-2
**Group B**
England (F. Davis, J. Virgo, David Taylor) beat Ireland (A. Higgins, Dennis Taylor,
P. Fagan) 11-4; Australia (E. Charlton, I. Anderson, P. Morgan) beat England 8-7;
Ireland beat Australia 10-5
**Semi-finals:** Wales beat Ireland 8-7; Canada beat England 8-5
**Final:** Wales beat Canada 8-5

**1981** (*State Express World Team Classic*)
**Preliminary match:** Republic of Ireland (E. Hughes, P. Fagan, D. Sheehan) beat Scotland
(I. Black, M. Macleod, E. Sinclair) 4-2
**Group A**
England (S. Davis, J. Spencer, David Taylor) beat Australia (I. Anderson, E. Charlton,
P. Morgan) 4-3; Northern Ireland (T. Murphy, Dennis Taylor, A. Higgins) beat Australia
4-1; England beat Northern Ireland 4-3
**Group B**
Wales (R. Reardon, D. Mountjoy, T. Griffiths) beat Canada (K. Stevens, C. Thorburn,
B. Werbeniuk) 4-2; Wales beat Republic of Ireland 4-0; Canada beat Republic of Ireland
4-2
**Semi-finals:** England beat Canada 4-2; Wales beat Northern Ireland 4-3
**Final:** England beat Wales 4-3

**1982** (*State Express World Team Classic*)
**Preliminary match:** Scotland (E. Sinclair, J. Donnelly, I. Black) beat Republic of Ireland
(E. Hughes, P. Fagan, D. Sheehan) 4-2
**Group A**
England (A. Knowles, S. Davis, J. White) beat Northern Ireland (A. Higgins,
T. Murphy, Dennis Taylor) 4-3; Scotland beat Northern Ireland 4-1; England beat
Scotland 4-1
**Group B**
Canada (C. Thorburn, B. Werbeniuk, K. Stevens) beat Wales (T. Griffiths, D. Mountjoy,
R. Reardon) 4-3; Canada beat Australia (E. Charlton, P. Morgan, I. Anderson) 4-0;
Wales beat Australia 4-1
**Semi-finals:** England beat Wales 4-2; Canada beat Scotland 4-0
**Final:** Canada beat England 4-2

**1983** (*State Express World Team Classic*)
**Preliminary match:** Scotland (E. Sinclair, M. Macleod, I. Black) beat Republic of Ireland
(B. Kelly, E. Hughes, P. Fagan) 4-2
**Group A**
Wales (D. Mountjoy, R. Reardon, T. Griffiths) beat Canada (C. Thorburn,
B. Werbeniuk, K. Stevens) 4-3; Canada beat Australia (E. Charlton, W. King,
J. Campbell) 4-2; Wales beat Australia 4-0
**Group B**
England (S. Davis, A. Knowles, T. Meo) beat Northern Ireland (A. Higgins, T. Murphy,
Dennis Taylor) 4-1; Northern Ireland beat Scotland 4-3; England beat Scotland 4-0
**Semi-finals:** Wales beat Northern Ireland 4-1; England beat Canada 4-2
**Final:** England beat Wales 4-2

**1985** (*Guinness World Cup*)
**First round:** Wales beat Australia 5-4 (T. Griffiths drew with E. Charlton 1-1;
D. Mountjoy beat J. Campbell 2-0; R. Reardon lost to W. King 0-2; Mountjoy drew with
Charlton 1-1; Griffiths beat King 1-0); England A beat Scotland 5-4 (S. Davis lost to
E. Sinclair 0-2; A. Knowles drew with M. Macleod 1-1; T. Meo beat J. Donnelly 2-0;
S. Davis drew with Sinclair 1-1; Knowles beat Macleod 1-0); England B beat Rest of
World 5-2 (J. White beat S. Francisco 2-0; W. Thorne drew with J. Rempe 1-1;
J. Spencer drew with D. O'Kane 1-1; White beat Francisco 1-0); Ireland beat Canada 5-2
(Dennis Taylor beat K. Stevens 2-0; E. Hughes drew with C. Thorburn 1-1; A. Higgins
drew with B. Werbeniuk 1-1; Higgins beat Thorburn 1-0)
**Semi-finals:** Ireland beat Wales 5-3 (Dennis Taylor drew with Mountjoy 1-1; E. Hughes
lost to Griffiths 0-2; Higgins beat Reardon 2-0; Higgins beat Mountjoy 2-0); England A
beat England B 5-2 (S. Davis beat Spencer 2-0; Knowles drew with Thorne 1-1; Meo
drew with White 1-1; S. Davis beat White 1-0)
**Final:** Ireland beat England A 9-7 (Dennis Taylor drew with Knowles 1-1; E. Hughes lost
to S. Davis 0-2; Higgins drew with Meo 1-1; Dennis Taylor drew with Knowles 1-1;

Dennis Taylor drew with S. Davis 1-1; E. Hughes drew with Knowles 1-1; Higgins beat Meo 2-0; Higgins beat S. Davis 2-0)

**1986** (*Car Care Plan World Cup*)
**First round:** Ireland A beat Ireland B 5-0 (A. Higgins beat P. Fagan 2-0; E. Hughes beat T. Murphy 2-0; Dennis Taylor beat P. Browne 1-0); Wales beat Scotland 5-1 (D. Mountjoy beat M. Macleod 2-0; R. Reardon drew with E. Sinclair 1-1; T. Griffiths beat J. Donnelly 2-0); Canada beat Rest of World 5-0 (C. Thorburn beat T. Drago 2-0; K. Stevens beat O. Agrawal 2-0; B. Werbeniuk beat S. Simngam 1-0); England beat Australia 5-2 (A. Knowles drew with J. Campbell 1-1; J. White drew with E. Charlton 1-1; S. Davis beat W. King 2-0; S. Davis beat Campbell 1-0)
**Semi-finals:** Ireland A beat Wales 5-2 (Higgins beat Mountjoy 2-0; Hughes lost to Reardon 0-2; Dennis Taylor beat Griffiths 2-0; Taylor beat Griffiths 1-0); Canada beat England 5-3 (Thorburn drew with Knowles 1-1; Stevens beat White 2-0; Werbeniuk drew with S. Davis 1-1; Thorburn drew with S. Davis 1-1)
**Final:** Ireland A beat Canada 9-7 (Dennis Taylor drew with Thorburn 1-1; Hughes lost to Stevens 0-2; Higgins beat Werbeniuk 2-0; Higgins drew with Stevens 1-1; Higgins drew with Thorburn 1-1; Hughes drew with Stevens 1-1; Taylor beat Werbeniuk 2-0; Taylor drew with Thorburn 1-1)

**1987** (*Tuborg World Cup*)
**First round:** Wales beat Australia 5-1 (R. Reardon drew with E. Charlton 1-1; D. Mountjoy beat W. King 2-0; T. Griffiths beat J. Campbell 2-0); Ireland A beat Ireland B 5-1 (E. Hughes beat P. Browne 2-0; A. Higgins beat P. Fagan 2-0; Dennis Taylor drew with T. Murphy 1-1); Canada beat Rest of World 5-4 (K. Stevens beat S. Francisco 2-0; C. Thorburn drew with T. Drago 1-1; B. Werbeniuk lost to D. O'Kane 0-2; Stevens drew with Drago 1-1; Thorburn beat Francisco 1-0); England beat Scotland 5-1 (J. Johnson drew with S. Hendry 1-1; S. Davis beat M. Gibson 2-0; T. Meo beat M. Macleod 2-0)
**Semi-finals:** Ireland A beat Wales 5-2 (Taylor lost to Griffiths 0-2; Hughes beat Reardon 2-0; Higgins beat Mountjoy 2-0; Higgins beat Griffiths 1-0); Canada beat England 5-4 (Stevens drew with Johnson 1-1; Thorburn beat Davis 2-0; Werbeniuk drew with Meo 1-1; Stevens lost to Davis 0-2; Thorburn beat Johnson 1-0)
**Final:** Ireland A beat Canada 9-2 (Hughes drew with Stevens 1-1; Higgins beat Thorburn 2-0; Taylor beat Werbeniuk 2-0; Taylor beat Stevens 2-0; Hughes drew with Stevens 1-1; Taylor beat Thorburn 1-0)

**1988**
**First round:** England beat Republic of Ireland 5-1 (S. Davis beat J. O'Boye 2-0; J. White beat E. Hughes 2-0; N. Foulds drew with P. Browne 1-1); Rest of World beat Northern Ireland 5-3 (D. O'Kane lost to D. Taylor 0-2; T. Drago beat A. Higgins 2-0; Drago drew with Taylor 1-1); Australia beat Canada 5-0 (J. Campbell beat J. Wych 2-0; W. King beat B. Werbeniuk 2-0; E. Charlton beat C. Thorburn 1-0); Scotland beat Wales 5-4 (M. Macleod beat D. Mountjoy 2-0; J. Rea drew with T. Griffiths 1-1; S. Hendry drew with C. Wilson 1-1; Hendry lost to Griffiths 0-2; Macleod beat Wilson 1-0)
**Semi-finals:** England beat Rest of World 5-3 (Davis drew with Drago 1-1; Foulds drew with O'Kane 1-1; White drew with Francisco 1-1; White beat Francisco 2-0); Australia beat Scotland 5-1 (Campbell beat Macleod 2-0; King beat Rea 2-0; Charlton drew with Hendry 1-1)
**Final:** England beat Australia 9-7 (Davis drew with Campbell 1-1; Foulds drew with King 1-1; White lost to Charlton 0-2; White drew with Charlton 1-1; White drew with King 1-1; Foulds drew with Campbell 1-1; Davis beat Charlton 2-0; Davis beat King 2-0)

**1989**
**First round:** England beat Republic of Ireland 5-1 (S. Davis beat E. Hughes 2-0; N. Foulds beat T. Kearney 2-0; J. White drew with P. Browne 1-1); Canada beat

Northern Ireland 5-1 (C. Thorburn beat A. Higgins 2-0; K. Stevens beat T. Murphy 2-0;
R. Chaperon drew with Dennis Taylor 1-1); Rest of World beat Australia 5-2 (T. Drago
beat J. Campbell 2-0; S. Francisco lost to E. Charlton 0-2; D. O'Kane beat W. King 2-0;
Drago beat Charlton 1-0); Wales beat Scotland 5-3 (T. Griffiths drew with S. Hendry 1-1;
C. Wilson beat M. Macleod 2-0; D. Mountjoy drew with J. Donnelly 1-1; Mountjoy drew
with Hendry 1-1)
**Semi-finals:** England beat Canada 5-2 (Davis beat Thorburn 2-0; White drew with
Stevens 1-1; Foulds drew with Chaperon 1-1; Foulds beat Thorburn 1-0); Rest of World
beat Wales 5-3 (O'Kane lost to Mountjoy 0-2; Drago beat Griffiths 2-0; Francisco drew
with Wilson 1-1; Drago beat Mountjoy 2-0)
**Final:** England beat Rest of World 9-8 (Davis drew with Drago 1-1; Foulds beat O'Kane
2-0; White lost to Francisco 1-3; White drew with Drago 1-1; Davis beat O'Kane 2-0;
Foulds drew with Francisco 1-1; Foulds lost to Drago 0-2; Davis beat O'Kane 1-0)

# BENSON AND HEDGES IRISH MASTERS

**First staged** 1978. **Sponsors** Benson and Hedges. **Venue** Goffs, Kill, Co Kildare.
**Initial prize-money** £3,000. **Prize-money last season** £113,445. **TV** RTE.

**1978**
**Final:** J. Spencer beat D. Mountjoy 5-3

**1979**
**Final:** D. Mountjoy beat R. Reardon 6-5

**1980**
**Final:** T. Griffiths beat D. Mountjoy 9-8

**1981**
**First round:** Dennis Taylor beat J. Spencer 4-2; S. Davis beat J. Virgo 4-3
**Quarter-finals:** T. Griffiths beat K. Stevens 4-0; Thorburn beat D. Mountjoy 4-0;
R. Reardon beat S. Davis 4-2; A. Higgins beat Dennis Taylor 4-2
**Semi-finals:** Griffiths beat Thorburn 6-5; Reardon beat Higgins 6-5
**Final:** Griffiths beat Reardon 9-7

**1982**
**First round:** Dennis Taylor beat D. Sheehan 5-3; T. Meo beat J. Spencer 5-3; A. Higgins
beat J. Wych 5-3; D. Mountjoy beat E. Hughes 5-4
**Quarter-finals:** T. Griffiths beat T. Meo 5-3; R. Reardon beat Dennis Taylor 5-4;
S. Davis beat Mountjoy 5-2; Higgins beat C. Thorburn 5-4
**Semi-finals:** Griffiths beat Reardon 6-3; S. Davis beat Higgins 6-2
**Final:** Griffiths beat S. Davis 9-5

**1983**
**First round:** J. White beat Dennis Taylor 5-4; T. Meo beat P. Burke 5-0; D. Mountjoy
beat A. Knowles 5-1; E. Charlton beat David Taylor 5-4
**Quarter-finals:** R. Reardon beat Meo 5-4; A. Higgins beat White 5-2; S. Davis beat
Charlton 5-1; T. Griffiths beat Mountjoy 5-4
**Semi-finals:** Reardon beat Higgins 6-3; S. Davis beat Griffiths 6-2
**Final:** S. Davis beat Reardon 9-2

**1984**
**First round:** T. Griffiths beat B. Werbeniuk 5-2; Dennis Taylor beat E. Hughes 5-1;
T. Meo beat J. White 5-4; A. Higgins beat E. Charlton 5-2
**Quarter-finals:** Dennis Taylor beat C. Thorburn 5-2; Griffiths beat A. Knowles 5-0;
Higgins beat R. Reardon 5-2; S. Davis beat Meo 5-4

**Semi-finals:** Griffiths beat Dennis Taylor 6-5; S. Davis beat Higgins 6-4
**Final:** S. Davis beat Griffiths 9-1

### 1985
**First round:** E. Charlton beat Dennis Taylor 5-4; J. White beat T. Meo 5-1; E. Hughes beat R. Reardon 5-0; A. Higgins beat T. Griffiths 5-2
**Quarter-finals:** A. Knowles beat Charlton 5-3; White beat C. Thorburn 5-3; S. Davis beat Hughes 5-4; Higgins beat K. Stevens 5-3
**Semi-finals:** White beat Knowles 6-4; Higgins beat S. Davis 6-2
**Final:** White beat Higgins 9-5

### 1986
**First round:** E. Hughes beat R. Reardon 5-2; W. Thorne beat T. Griffiths 5-2; T. Meo beat A. Higgins 5-4; P. Fagan *wo* K. Stevens *scr*
**Quarter-finals:** C. Thorburn beat Hughes 5-1; Thorne beat Dennis Taylor 5-2; J. White beat Meo 5-2; Fagan beat A. Knowles 5-4
**Semi-finals:** Thorne beat Thorburn 6-4; White beat Fagan 6-0
**Final:** White beat Thorne 9-5

### 1987
**First round:** W. Thorne beat K. Stevens 5-1; Dennis Taylor beat E. Hughes 5-4; T. Meo beat A. Knowles 5-2; T. Griffiths beat A. Higgins 5-1
**Quarter-finals:** Thorne beat J. White 5-4; Taylor beat C. Thorburn 5-1; S. Davis beat Meo 5-2; Griffiths beat J. Johnson 5-0
**Semi-finals:** Thorne beat Taylor 6-2; Davis beat Griffiths 6-2
**Final:** Davis beat Thorne 9-1

### 1988
**First round:** T. Griffiths beat R. Williams 5-1; T. Knowles beat W. Thorne 5-3; A. Higgins beat Dennis Taylor 5-3; J. Johnson beat E. Hughes 5-4
**Quarter-finals:** Griffiths beat J. White 5-2; N. Foulds beat Knowles 5-3; Higgins beat C. Thorburn 5-3; S. Davis beat Johnson 5-0
**Semi-finals:** Foulds beat Griffiths 6-4; Davis beat Higgins 6-2
**Final:** Davis beat Foulds 9-4

### 1989
**First round:** M. Hallett beat A. Knowles 5-0; T. Griffiths beat J. McLaughlin 5-4; A. Higgins beat C. Thorburn 5-4; J. Parrott beat Dennis Taylor 5-1
**Quarter-finals:** S. Hendry beat Griffiths 5-2; S. Davis beat Hallett 5-4; Parrott beat J. White 5-1; Higgins beat N. Foulds 5-2
**Semi-finals:** Higgins beat Parrott 6-4; Hendry beat Davis 6-4
**Final:** Higgins beat Hendry 9-8

# EMBASSY WORLD PROFESSIONAL CHAMPIONSHIP

**First staged** 1927. **Sponsors** Embassy (1976– ). **Venue** Crucible Theatre, Sheffield (1977– ). **Initial prize-money** £15,300. **Prize-money last season** £525,000. **TV** BBC.

### 1927
**First round:** M. Inman beat T. Newman 8-5; T. Carpenter beat N. Butler 8-3
**Second round:** T. A. Dennis beat F. Lawrence 8-7; A. Cope beat A. Mann 8-6; J. Davis beat J. Brady 10-5; Carpenter beat Inman 8-3
**Semi-finals:** J. Davis beat Cope 16-7; Dennis beat Carpenter 12-10
**Final:** J. Davis beat Dennis 20-11

**1928**
First round: T. Newman beat F. Smith 12-6; A. Mann beat A. Cope 14-9
Second round: Newman beat T. A. Dennis 12-5; F. Lawrence beat Mann 12-11
Third round: Lawrence beat Newman 12-7
Final: J. Davis beat Lawrence 16-13

**1929**
First round: F. Lawrence beat A. Mann 13-12
Semi-finals: J. Davis beat Lawrence 13-10; T. A. Dennis beat K. Prince 14-6
Final: J. Davis beat Dennis 19-14

**1930**
First round: F. Lawrence beat A. Mann 13-11; N. Butler beat T. Newman 13-11
Semi-finals: J. Davis beat Lawrence 13-2; T. A. Dennis beat Butler 13-11
Final: J. Davis beat Dennis 25-12

**1931**
Final: J. Davis beat T. A. Dennis 25-21

**1932**
First round: C. McConachy beat T. A. Dennis 13-11
Final: J. Davis beat McConachy 30-19

**1933**
First round: W. Donaldson beat W. Leigh 13-11
Semi-finals: J. Davis beat Donaldson 13-1; W. Smith beat T. A. Dennis 16-9
Final: J. Davis beat Smith 25-18

**1934**
Final: J. Davis beat T. Newman 25-23

**1935**
First round: W. Smith beat C. Stanbury 13-12
Semi-finals: Smith beat A. Mann 13-4; J. Davis beat T. Newman 15-10
Final: J. Davis beat Smith 25-20

**1936**
First round: C. O'Donnell beat S. Lee 16-15; H. Lindrum beat H. Terry 20-11; J. Davis beat T. Newman 29-2; W. Smith beat S. Smith 16-15; C. Stanbury beat A. Mann 22-9
Second round: Alec Brown beat Stanbury 16-15; Lindrum beat O'Donnell 19-6 (retd); J. Davis beat W. Smith 22-9; S. Newman wo
Semi-finals: J. Davis beat Alec Brown 21-10; Lindrum beat S. Newman 29-2
Final: J. Davis beat Lindrum 34-27

**1937**
First round: W. A. Withers beat F. Davis 17-14
Second round: J. Davis beat Withers 30-1; H. Lindrum beat S. Lee 20-11; W. Smith beat T. Newman 16-15; S. Smith beat Alec Brown 18-13
Semi-finals: Lindrum beat W. Smith 20-11; J. Davis beat S. Smith 18-13
Final: J. Davis beat Lindrum 32-29

**1938**
First qualifying round: H. Holt beat C. W. Read 21-10
Second qualifying round: F. Davis beat Holt 23-8
First round: F. Davis beat Alec Brown 14-6 (retd ill); S. Smith beat C. Stanbury 27-4; J. Davis beat S. Lee 24-7; W. Smith beat T. Newman 16-15
Semi-finals: J. Davis beat W. Smith (nrs); S. Smith beat F. Davis (nrs)
Final: J. Davis beat S. Smith 37-24

**1939**
**First qualifying round:** W. Donaldson beat H. Holt 18-13; H. W. Laws beat S. Newman 19-12
**Second qualifying round:** Donaldson beat Laws 18-13
**First round:** S. Smith beat S. Lee 21-10; W. Donaldson beat C. Falkiner 21-10; T. Newman beat A. Mann 19-12; F. Davis beat C. Stanbury 19-12
**Second round:** J. Davis beat W. Smith 19-12; F. Davis beat T. Newman 20-11; Alec Brown beat H. Lindrum 17-14; S. Smith beat Donaldson 16-15
**Semi-finals:** J. Davis beat F. Davis 17-14; S. Smith beat Alec Brown 20-11
**Final:** J. Davis beat S. Smith 43-30

**1940**
**Qualifying round:** H. Holt beat C. Stanbury 18-13
**First round:** W. Donaldson beat Holt 24-7; J. Davis beat Alec Brown 20-11; F. Davis beat S. Lee 20-11; S. Smith beat T. Newman 22-9
**Semi-finals:** J. Davis beat Donaldson 22-9; F. Davis beat S. Smith 17-14
**Final:** J. Davis beat F. Davis 37-36

**1946**
**First qualifying round:** K. Kennerley beat F. Lawrence 22-9; C. Stanbury beat J. Barrie 18-13; S. Newman beat W. Leigh 16-15
**Second qualifying round:** Kennerley beat T. Reece 8-2 (retd); S. Newman beat Stanbury 17-14
**Third qualifying round:** S. Newman beat Kennerley 21-10
**First round:** J. Davis beat W. Donaldson 21-10; S. Newman beat S. Lee 19-12; F. Davis beat Alec Brown 24-7; H. Lindrum beat H. Holt 17-14
**Semi-finals:** J. Davis beat S. Newman 21-10; Lindrum beat F. Davis 16-12
**Final:** J. Davis beat Lindrum 78-67

**1947**
**First qualifying round:** Albert Brown beat J. Pulman 21-14; W. Leigh beat H. F. Francis 19-16; S. Lee beat J. Lees 19-16; K. Kennerley beat C. Stanbury 23-12; E. Newman wo H. Holt scr
**Second qualifying round:** J. Barrie beat F. Lawrence 25-10; Albert Brown beat Newman 28-7; Kennerley beat A. Mann 23-12; Leigh beat Lee 25-10
**Third qualifying round:** Albert Brown beat Barrie 24-11; Kennerley beat Leigh 21-14
**Fourth qualifying round:** Albert Brown beat Kennerley 21-14
**First round:** H. Lindrum beat Albert Brown 39-34; S. Smith beat Alec Brown 43-28; W. Donaldson beat S. Newman 46-25; F. Davis beat C. McConachy 53-20
**Semi-finals:** Donaldson beat Lindrum 39-32; F. Davis beat Smith 39-32
**Final:** Donaldson beat F. Davis 82-63

**1948**
**First qualifying round:** C. Stanbury beat E. Newman 26-9; W. Leigh beat H. Holt 18-17; J. Barrie beat H. F. Francis 19-16; J. Pulman wo S. Lee scr
**Second qualifying round:** Leigh beat Barrie 21-14; Pulman beat Stanbury 19-16
**Third qualifying round:** Pulman beat Leigh 18-17
**First round:** F. Davis beat Alec Brown 43-28; C. McConachy beat J. Pulman 42-29; Albert Brown beat S. Smith 36-35; W. Donaldson beat K. Kennerley 46-25
**Semi-finals:** F. Davis beat McConachy 43-28; Donaldson beat Alec Brown 40-31
**Final:** F. Davis beat Donaldson 84-61

**1949**
**First qualifying round:** C. Stanbury beat H. F. Francis 18-17
**Second qualifying round:** Stanbury beat Jack Rea 18-17
**Third qualifying round:** Stanbury beat H. Holt 18-17
**First round:** W. Donaldson beat Stanbury 58-13; J. Pulman beat Albert Brown 42-29;

S. Smith beat Alec Brown 41-30; F. Davis beat K. Kennerley 50-21
**Semi-finals:** Donaldson beat Pulman 49-22; F. Davis beat Smith 42-29
**Final:** F. Davis beat Donaldson 80-65

### 1950

**First qualifying round:** W. Smith beat W. A. Withers 28-7; H. Holt beat H. W. Laws 26-9; S. Lee beat C. Stanbury 20-15; K. Kennerley beat J. Barrie 21-14
**Second qualifying round:** Kennerley beat Smith 22-13; Lee beat Holt 16-8 (*retd ill*)
**Third qualifying round:** Kennerley beat Lee 21-14
**First round:** Albert Brown beat J. Pulman 37-34; W. Donaldson beat K. Kennerley 42-29; G. Chenier beat P. Mans 37-34; F. Davis beat Alec Brown 44-27
**Semi-finals:** Donaldson beat Albert Brown 37-34; F. Davis beat Chenier 43-28
**Final:** Donaldson beat F. Davis 51-46

### 1951

**First qualifying round:** J. Barrie beat S. Lee 23-12
**Second qualifying round:** Barrie beat H. W. Laws 28-7
**First round:** F. Davis beat Barrie 42-29; H. Lindrum beat Albert Brown 43-28; W. Donaldson beat K. Kennerley 41-30; J. Pulman beat S. Smith 38-33
**Semi-finals:** Donaldson beat Lindrum 41-30; F. Davis beat Pulman 22-14 (*retd ill*)
**Final:** F. Davis beat Donaldson 58-39

### 1952

**First round:** Alec Brown beat R. Williams 39-22; Jack Rea beat J. Lees 38-32; Albert Brown beat J. Pulman 32-27 (*records incomplete*)
**Semi-finals:** W. Donaldson beat Albert Brown 31-30
**Final:** F. Davis beat Donaldson 38-35

### 1953

**First qualifying round:** W. Smith beat J. Lees 21-14; K. Kennerley beat R. Williams 25-12
**Second qualifying round:** Kennerley beat Smith 42-29
**First round:** Albert Brown beat Alec Brown 35-26; J. Pulman beat Jack Rea 36-25; W. Donaldson beat Kennerley 42-19; F. Davis beat J. Barrie 32-29
**Semi-finals:** Donaldson beat Brown (*nrs*); F. Davis beat Pulman 36-25
**Final:** F. Davis beat Donaldson 37-34

### 1954

**First round:** J. Pulman beat Jack Rea 31-30
**Semi-finals:** W. Donaldson beat Alec Brown 36-25; F. Davis beat Pulman 32-29
**Final:** F. Davis beat Donaldson 39-21

### 1955

**First round:** J. Pulman beat R. Williams 22-15; Jack Rea beat H. Stokes (*nrs*)
**Semi-finals:** F. Davis beat Rea 36-25; Pulman beat Alec Brown (*nrs*)
**Final:** F. Davis beat Pulman 37-34

### 1956

**Semi-finals:** J. Pulman beat Jack Rea 36-25; F. Davis beat R. Williams 35-26
**Final:** F. Davis beat Pulman 38-35

### 1957

**Semi-finals:** J. Pulman beat R. Williams 21-16; Jack Rea beat K. Kennerley 25-12
**Final:** Pulman beat Rea 39-34

Through lack of public support no Championship was organised between 1957 and 1964. After a truce with the BA and CC a new system was adopted whereby the champion defended his title against a series of single challengers. These matches resulted as follows:

**1964**
J. Pulman beat F. Davis 19-16; J. Pulman beat R. Williams 40-33

**1965**
J. Pulman beat F. Davis 37-36; J. Pulman beat R. Williams 25-22 (*matches*); J. Pulman beat F. Van Rensberg 39-12

**1966**
J. Pulman beat F. Davis 5-2 (*matches*)

**1968**
J. Pulman beat E. Charlton 39-34

**1969** (*Players No. 6*)
First round: J. Spencer beat J. Pulman 25-18; R. Williams beat B. Bennett 25-4; G. Owen beat Jack Rea 25-17; F. Davis beat R. Reardon 25-24
Semi-finals: Spencer beat Williams 37-12; G. Owen beat Davis 37-24
Final: Spencer beat Owen 37-24

**1970 (April)** (*Players No. 6*)
First round: David Taylor beat B. Bennett 11-8
Quarter-finals: J. Pulman beat David Taylor 31-20; G. Owen beat R. Williams 31-11; R. Reardon beat F. Davis 31-26; J. Spencer beat Jack Rea 31-15
Semi-finals: Pulman beat G. Owen 37-12; Reardon beat Spencer 37-33
Final: Reardon beat Pulman 37-33

**1970 (November)**
Round robin: J. Spencer beat P. Mans 20-17; beat N. Squire 27-10; beat J. Pulman 23-14
R. Reardon beat Mans 22-15; beat E. Charlton 21-16; beat Spencer 21-16
W. Simpson beat G. Owen 19-18; beat Pulman 21-16; beat Mans 19-18
Charlton beat Squire 27-10; beat Mans 26-11; beat Owen 23-14
Owen beat P. Morgan 26-11; beat Squire 26-11; Morgan beat Simpson 21-16
Semi-finals: Spencer beat Reardon 34-15; Simpson beat Charlton 27-22
Final: Spencer beat Simpson 37-29

**1972**
First qualifying round: A. Higgins beat R. Gross 15-6; M. Parkin beat G. Thompson 11-10; G. Miles beat B. Bennett 15-6; J. Dunning beat P. Houlihan 11-10
Second qualifying round: Higgins beat Parkin 11-3; Dunning beat Miles 11-5
First round: J. Pulman beat Dunning 19-7; Higgins beat Jack Rea 19-11
Quarter-finals: J. Spencer beat F. Davis 31-21; E. Charlton beat David Taylor 31-25; Higgins beat Pulman 31-23; R. Williams beat R. Reardon 25-23
Semi-finals: Higgins beat Williams 31-30; Spencer beat Charlton 37-32
Final: Higgins beat Spencer 37-32

**1973** (*Park Drive*)
First round: P. Houlihan beat Jack Rea 9-2; D. Greaves beat B. Bennett 9-8; G. Miles beat G. Thompson 9-5; P. Mans beat R. Gross 9-2; W. Simpson beat M. Parkin 9-3; C. Thorburn beat Dennis Taylor 9-8; David Taylor beat J. Dunning 9-4; J. Meadowcroft wo K. Kennerley scr
Second round: F. Davis beat Greaves 16-1; Miles beat J. Pulman 16-10; E. Charlton beat Mans 16-8; G. Owen beat Simpson 16-14; R. Reardon beat Meadowcroft 16-10; R. Williams beat Thorburn 16-15; J. Spencer beat David Taylor 16-5; A. Higgins beat

Houlihan 16-3
**Quarter-finals:** Higgins beat F. Davis 16-14; Spencer beat Williams 16-7; Charlton beat Miles 16-6; Reardon beat G. Owen 16-6
**Semi-finals:** Charlton beat Higgins 23-9; Reardon beat Spencer 23-22
**Final:** Reardon beat Charlton 38-32

## 1974 (*Park Drive*)

**Qualifying:** J. Dunning beat D. Greaves 8-2; W. Simpson beat Jack Rea 8-3; J. Meadowcroft beat P. Houlihan 8-5; C. Thorburn beat A. McDonald 8-3; J. Pulman beat J. Karnehm 8-0; David Taylor beat R. Gross 8-7; M. Owen beat Dennis Taylor 8-1
**First round:** B. Bennett beat Simpson 8-2; B. Werbeniuk beat G. Thompson 8-3; Meadowcroft beat K. Kennerley 8-5; M. Owen beat M. Parkin 8-5; P. Mans beat I. Anderson 8-1; Pulman beat S. Lee 8-0; Dunning beat David Taylor 8-6; P. Morgan beat Thorburn 8-4
**Second round:** Mans beat J. Spencer 15-13; Dunning beat E. Charlton 15-13; M. Owen beat G. Owen 15-8; A. Higgins beat Bennett 15-4; G. Miles beat Morgan 15-7; R. Williams beat Pulman 15-12; F. Davis beat Werbeniuk 15-5; R. Reardon beat Meadowcroft 15-3
**Quarter-finals:** Williams beat Mans 15-4; Reardon beat M. Owen 15-11; Miles beat Dunning 15-13; F. Davis beat Higgins 15-14
**Semi-finals:** Miles beat Williams 15-7; Reardon beat F. Davis 15-3
**Final:** Reardon beat Miles 22-12

## 1975

**Qualifying:** P. Tarrant beat B. Bennett 15-8; L. Condo beat M. Parkin 15-8; D. Greaves beat J. Charlton 15-14
**First round:** W. Simpson beat R. Mares 15-5; J. Pulman beat Tarrant 15-5; David Taylor beat R. King 15-8; I. Anderson beat Condo 15-8; Dennis Taylor beat P. Mans 15-12; G. Owen beat Greaves 15-3; B. Werbeniuk beat J. Meadowcroft 15-9; C. Thorburn beat P. Morgan 15-6
**Second round:** R. Reardon beat Simpson 15-11; J. Spencer beat Pulman 15-10; A. Higgins beat David Taylor 15-2; R. Williams beat Anderson 15-4; Dennis Taylor beat F. Davis 15-14; G. Owen beat J. Dunning 15-8; E. Charlton beat Werbeniuk 15-11; Thorburn beat G. Miles 15-2
**Quarter-finals:** Reardon beat Spencer 19-17; Higgins beat Williams 19-12; Dennis Taylor beat G. Owen 19-9; Charlton beat Thorburn 19-12
**Semi-finals:** Charlton beat Dennis Taylor 19-12; Reardon beat Higgins 19-14
**Final:** Reardon beat Charlton 31-30

## 1976

**First qualifying round:** Jack Rea beat I. Anderson 8-5; D. Greaves beat J. Charlton 8-5; J. Meadowcroft beat D. Wheelwright 8-1; R. Gross beat M. Parkin 8-5; L. Condo beat M. Owen 8-6
**Second qualifying round:** Jack Rea beat B. Bennett 8-5; David Taylor beat Greaves 8-1; Meadowcroft beat Gross 8-4; W. Thorne beat Condo 8-3
**First round:** R. Reardon beat J. Dunning 15-7; Dennis Taylor beat G. Owen 15-9; P. Mans beat G. Miles 15-10; Meadowcroft beat R. Williams 15-7; E. Charlton beat J. Pulman 15-9; F. Davis beat B. Werbeniuk 15-12; A. Higgins beat C. Thorburn 15-14; J. Spencer beat David Taylor 15-5
**Quarter-finals:** Reardon beat Dennis Taylor 15-2; Mans beat Meadowcroft 15-8; Charlton beat F. Davis 15-13; Higgins beat Spencer 15-14
**Semi-finals:** Reardon beat Mans 20-10; Higgins beat Charlton 20-18
**Final:** Reardon beat Higgins 27-16

## 1977

**First qualifying round:** J. Virgo beat R. Andrewartha 11-1
**Second qualifying round:** P. Fagan beat J. Meadowcroft 11-9; Virgo beat J. Dunning 11-6;

W. Thorne beat B. Bennett 11-4; J. Pulman wo; David Taylor beat D. Greaves 11-0;
C. Thorburn beat C. Ross 11-0; Dennis Taylor beat J. Karnehm 11-0; D. Mountjoy beat
Jack Rea 11-9
**First round:** R. Reardon beat Fagan 13-7; J. Spencer beat Virgo 13-9; G. Miles beat
Thorne 13-4; Pulman beat F. Davis 13-12; E. Charlton beat David Taylor 13-5;
Thorburn beat R. Williams 13-6; Dennis Taylor beat P. Mans 13-11; Mountjoy beat
A. Higgins 13-12
**Quarter-finals:** Spencer beat Reardon 13-6; Pulman beat Miles 13-10; Thorburn beat
Charlton 13-12; Dennis Taylor beat Mountjoy 13-11
**Semi-finals:** Spencer beat Pulman 18-16; Thorburn beat Dennis Taylor 18-16
**Final:** Spencer beat Thorburn 25-21

### 1978
**First qualifying round:** M. Parkin beat B. Bennett 9-4; R. Andrewartha beat J. Karnehm
9-0; J. Barrie beat D. Greaves 9-3; P. Houlihan beat C. Ross 9-1
**Second qualifying round:** D. Mountjoy beat Andrewartha 9-3; P. Fagan beat J. Dunning
9-5; W. Thorne beat R. Williams 9-3; B. Werbeniuk beat M. Parkin 9-2; P. Mans beat
Barrie 9-6; David Taylor beat P. Morgan 9-7; Houlihan beat J. Meadowcroft 9-6;
F. Davis beat J. Virgo 9-8
**First round:** Mans beat J. Spencer 13-8; G. Miles beat David Taylor 13-10; Fagan beat
A. Higgins 13-12; F. Davis beat Dennis Taylor 13-9; E. Charlton beat Thorne 13-12;
C. Thorburn beat Houlihan 13-8; Werbeniuk beat J. Pulman 13-4; R. Reardon beat
Mountjoy 13-9
**Quarter-finals:** Mans beat Miles 13-7; F. Davis beat Fagan 13-10; Charlton beat
Thorburn 13-12; Reardon beat Werbeniuk 13-6
**Semi-finals:** Mans beat F. Davis 18-16; Reardon beat Charlton 18-14
**Final:** Reardon beat Mans 25-18

### 1979
**First qualifying round:** D. Mountjoy beat D. Mienie 9-1; T. Griffiths beat B. Bennett 9-2;
P. Houlihan beat J. Barrie 9-5; W. Thorne beat J. Charlton 9-3; J. Virgo beat M. Parkin
9-0; J. Dunning beat Jack Rea 9-5; R. Williams beat D. Greaves 9-2; J. Meadowcroft
beat J. Van Rensberg 9-7; R. Andrewartha beat R. Edmonds 9-8; S. Davis beat
I. Anderson 9-1; K. Stevens beat R. Amdor 9-1
**Second qualifying round:** Virgo beat Thorne 9-8; B. Werbeniuk beat Andrewartha 9-2;
David Taylor beat Dunning 9-8; Mountjoy beat Houlihan 9-6; S. Davis beat P. Fagan
9-2; Griffiths beat Meadowcroft 9-6; Stevens beat J. Pulman 9-0; G. Miles beat Williams
9-5
**First round:** E. Charlton beat Mountjoy 13-6; Werbeniuk beat J. Spencer 13-11; Virgo
beat C. Thorburn 13-10; F. Davis beat Stevens 13-8; Dennis Taylor beat S. Davis 13-11;
A. Higgins beat David Taylor 13-5; Griffiths beat P. Mans 13-8; R. Reardon beat Miles
13-8
**Quarter-finals:** Charlton beat F. Davis 13-4; Dennis Taylor beat Reardon 13-8; Virgo
beat Werbeniuk 13-9; Griffiths beat Higgins 13-12
**Semi-finals:** Griffiths beat Charlton 19-17; Dennis Taylor beat Virgo 19-12
**Final:** Griffiths beat Dennis Taylor 24-16

### 1980
**Qualifying groups**
1  Jack Rea beat B. Bennett 9-1; W. Thorne beat K. Robitaille 9-4; Thorne beat Rea
   9-1
2  S. Davis beat C. Ross 9-3; P. Morgan beat P. Thornley 9-4; Davis beat Morgan 9-0
3  M. Hallett beat K. Kennerley 9-2; K. Stevens beat D. Greaves 9-3; Stevens beat
   Hallett 9-3
4  J. Johnson beat R. Andrewartha 9-5; P. Houlihan beat Johnson 9-6; T. Meo beat
   J. Van Rensberg 9-1; Meo beat Houlihan 9-1
5  R. Amdor beat B. Mikkelsen 9-7; R. Williams beat Amdor 9-4; J. Wych beat John

Bear 9-5; Wych beat Williams 9-7
6   F. Jonik beat M. Wildman 9-7; C. Wilson beat Jonik 9-6
7   R. Edmonds beat M. Parkin 9-2; S. Hood beat J. Dunning 16-7; Edmonds beat
    Hood 9-6
8   E. Sinclair beat M. Morra 9-5; Sinclair beat D. Mienie 9-7; J. Meadowcroft beat
    Sinclair 9-1
**First round:** S. Davis beat P. Fagan 10-6; A. Higgins beat Meo 10-9; D. Mountjoy beat
Wilson 10-6; Wych beat J. Pulman 10-5; J. Virgo beat Meadowcroft 10-2; Stevens beat
G. Miles 10-3; David Taylor beat Edmonds 10-3; B. Werbeniuk beat Thorne 10-9
**Second round:** S. Davis beat T. Griffiths 13-10; Higgins beat P. Mans 13-6; Stevens beat
J. Spencer 13-8; E. Charlton beat Virgo 13-12; C. Thorburn beat Mountjoy 13-10; Wych
beat Dennis Taylor 13-10; R. Reardon beat Werbeniuk 13-6; David Taylor beat F. Davis
13-5
**Quarter-finals:** David Taylor beat Reardon 13-11; Thorburn beat Wych 13-6; Stevens
beat Charlton 13-7; Higgins beat S. Davis 13-9
**Semi-finals:** Thorburn beat David Taylor 16-7; Higgins beat Stevens 16-13
**Final:** Thorburn beat Higgins 18-16

## 1981
**Qualifying groups**
1   W. Thorne beat M. Morra 9-5; D. Greaves beat M. Parkin 9-5; Thorne beat Greaves
    9-3
2   J. White beat B. Mikkelsen 9-4; White beat J. Meadowcroft 9-8
3   R. Edmonds beat M. Wildman 9-3; R. Williams beat S. Hood 9-4; Edmonds beat
    Williams 9-7
4   T. Meo beat J. Johnson 9-8; M. Hallett beat F. Jonik 9-1; Meo beat Hallett 9-4
5   J. Dunning beat B. Bennett 9-6; Dunning beat P. Fagan 9-7
6   D. Martin beat I. Anderson 9-3; Martin beat J. Pulman 9-2
7   C. Wilson beat R. Andrewartha 9-4; E. Sinclair beat P. Morgan 9-8; Wilson beat
    Sinclair 9-4
8   A. Knowles beat C. Ross 7-0 (*retd*); Knowles beat J. Wych 9-3
**First round:** G. Miles beat Knowles 10-8; David Taylor beat Wilson 10-6; D. Mountjoy
beat Thorne 10-6; K. Stevens beat Dunning 10-4; Meo beat J. Virgo 10-6; S. Davis beat
White 10-8; B. Werbeniuk beat Martin 10-4; J. Spencer beat Edmonds 10-9
**Second round:** C. Thorburn beat Miles 13-2; David Taylor beat F. Davis 13-3;
T. Griffiths beat
Meo 13-6; S. Davis beat Alex Higgins 13-8; Mountjoy beat E. Charlton 13-7; Dennis
Taylor beat Stevens 13-11; Werbeniuk beat P. Mans 13-5; R. Reardon beat Spencer
13-11
**Quarter-finals:** Thorburn beat David Taylor 13-6; S. Davis beat Griffiths 13-9; Mountjoy
beat Dennis Taylor 13-8; Reardon beat Werbeniuk 13-10
**Semi-finals:** S. Davis beat Thorburn 16-10; Mountjoy beat Reardon 16-10
**Final:** S. Davis beat Mountjoy 18-12

## 1982
**Qualifying groups**
1   John Bear beat F. Jonik 9-4; Bear beat J. Wych 9-4
2   D. Hughes beat C. Everton 9-4; T. Meo beat Hughes 9-4
3   D. Reynolds beat D. Sheehan 9-5; Reynolds beat R. Edmonds 9-6
4   E. Hughes *wo* D. Mienie *scr*; A. Knowles beat Hughes 9-7
5   M. Wildman beat G. Foulds 9-8; J. White beat Wildman 9-4
6   C. Roscoe beat B. Mikkelsen 9-6; W. Thorne beat Roscoe 9-1
7   P. Medati beat J. Phillips 9-3; C. Wilson beat Medati 9-5
8   P. Houlihan beat I. Anderson 9-5; D. Martin beat Houlihan 9-3
9   M. Macleod beat E. McLaughlin 9-8; J. Dunning beat Macleod 9-4
10  M. Watterson beat B. Demarco 9-6; J. Meadowcroft beat Watterson 9-7

11  D. French beat B. Bennett 9-3; P. Fagan beat French 9-6
12  I. Black beat M. Parkin 9-6; R. Williams beat Black 9-2
13  J. Johnson beat V. Harris 9-4; M. Hallett beat Johnson 9-8
14  J. Donnelly beat M. Gibson 9-8; E. Sinclair beat B. Kelly 9-8; Donnelly beat Sinclair 9-8
15  P. Morgan beat D. Greaves 9-2; S. Francisco beat C. Ross 9-0; Francisco beat Morgan 9-1
16  M. Morra beat T. Murphy 9-5; J. Fitzmaurice *wo* J. Pulman *scr*; Fitzmaurice beat Morra 9-7

**First round:** Knowles beat S. Davis 10-1; G. Miles beat Martin 10-5; B. Werbeniuk beat Bear 10-7; E. Charlton beat Wilson 10-5; S. Francisco beat Dennis Taylor 10-7; Reynolds beat F. Davis 10-7; J. Virgo beat Hallett 10-4; R. Reardon beat Donnelly 10-5; A. Higgins beat Meadowcroft 10-5; D. Mountjoy beat Williams 10-3; Fagan beat David Taylor 10-9; K. Stevens beat Fitzmaurice 10-4; P. Mans beat Meo 10-8; White beat C. Thorburn 10-4

**Second round:** Knowles beat Miles 13-7; Charlton beat Werbeniuk 13-5; S. Francisco beat Reynolds 13-8; Reardon beat Virgo 13-8; Thorne beat Spencer 13-5; Higgins beat Mountjoy 13-12; Stevens beat Fagan 13-7; White beat Mans 13-6

**Quarter-finals:** Charlton beat Knowles 13-11; Reardon beat S. Francisco 13-8; Higgins beat Thorne 13-10; White beat Stevens 13-9

**Semi-finals:** Reardon beat Charlton 16-11; Higgins beat White 16-15

**Final:** Higgins beat Reardon 18-15

## 1983
### Qualifying groups

1  B. Kelly beat B. Demarco 10-4; S. Francisco beat Kelly 10-5
2  P. Morgan beat P. Burke 10-9; G. Miles beat Morgan 10-6
3  T. Murphy beat P. Houlihan 10-9; J. Virgo beat Murphy 10-8
4  R. Williams beat M. Darrington 10-0; Williams beat F. Davis 10-1
5  M. Wildman beat B. Harris 10-7; Wildman *wo* J. Wych *scr*
6  R. Edmonds beat F. Jonik 10-4; D. Reynolds beat Edmonds 10-6
7  M. Fisher beat P. Fagan 10-8; E. McLaughlin beat D. Greaves 10-7; Fisher beat McLaughlin 10-9
8  T. Meo beat V. Harris 10-0; G. Foulds beat M. Gibson 10-6; Meo beat Foulds 10-4
9  I. Black beat M. Morra 10-9; P. Medati beat John Bear 10-7; Black beat Medati 10-4
10 C. Wilson beat C. Everton 10-1; J. Johnson beat P. Watchorn 10-0; Wilson beat Johnson 10-8
11 M. Macleod beat M. Owen 10-5; D. Martin beat M. Parkin 10-1; Martin beat Macleod 10-7
12 J. Meadowcroft beat B. Bennett 10-3; G. Cripsey beat D. Hughes 10-2; Meadowcroft beat Cripsey 10-6
13 J. Donnelly beat D. Sheehan 10-6; J. Campbell beat M. Watterson 10-6; Campbell beat Donnelly 10-2
14 L. Dodd *wo* J. Dunning *scr*; I. Williamson beat D. French 10-8; Dodd beat Williamson 10-9
15 M. Hallett beat R. Andrewartha 10-7; W. King beat I. Anderson 10-6; Hallett beat King 10-6
16 E. Hughes beat J. Fitzmaurice 10-7; E. Sinclair beat C. Roscoe 10-2; Hughes beat Sinclair 10-8

**First round:** A. Higgins beat Reynolds 10-4; W. Thorne beat Virgo 10-3; B. Werbeniuk beat Martin 10-4; David Taylor beat Meadowcroft 10-2; E. Charlton beat Dodd 10-7; J. Spencer beat Hallett 10-7; Dennis Taylor beat S. Francisco 10-9; S. Davis beat Williams 10-4; C. Thorburn beat Campbell 10-5; T. Griffiths beat Wildman 10-8; P. Mans beat Black 10-3; K. Stevens beat Fisher 10-2; D. Mountjoy beat Wilson 10-2; Meo beat J. White 10-8; A. Knowles beat Miles 10-3; R. Reardon beat E. Hughes 10-7

**Second round:** Higgins beat Thorne 13-8; Werbeniuk beat David Taylor 13-10; Charlton

beat Spencer 13-11; S. Davis beat Dennis Taylor 13-11; Thorburn beat Griffiths 13-12; Meo beat Mountjoy 13-11; Knowles beat Reardon 13-12; Stevens beat Mans 13-3
**Quarter-finals:** Higgins beat Werbeniuk 13-11; S. Davis beat Charlton 13-5; Thorburn beat Stevens 13-12; Knowles beat Meo 13-9
**Semi-finals:** Thorburn beat Knowles 16-15; S. Davis beat Higgins 16-5
**Final:** S. Davis beat Thorburn 18-6

## 1984

### Qualifying groups

1  J. Parrott beat D. Hughes 10-3; Parrott beat C. Everton 10-2; Parrott beat P. Mans 10-0
2  B. Mikkelsen beat P. Medati 10-8; Mikkelsen beat F. Jonik 10-9; W. Thorne beat Mikkelsen 10-3
3  M. Morra beat G. Foulds 10-2; T. Murphy beat J. Fitzmaurice 10-8; Morra beat Murphy 10-5; Morra beat D. Reynolds 10-7
4  W. Sanderson beat P. Morgan 10-8; P. Mifsud beat E. Hughes 10-5; Mifsud beat Sanderson 10-5; Mifsud beat C. Wilson 10-8
5  J. Van Rensberg beat V. Harris 10-7; R. Edmonds beat D. Greaves 10-0; Van Rensberg beat Edmonds 10-9; S. Francisco beat Van Rensberg 10-3
6  I. Williamson beat P. Houlihan 10-5; M. Hines beat I. Black 10-5; Williamson beat Hines 10-6; G. Miles beat Williamson 10-6
7  M. Gibson beat G. Rigitano 10-7; M. Fisher beat P. Thornley 10-8; Gibson beat Fisher 10-7; J. Johnson beat Gibson 10-3
8  E. McLaughlin beat J. Hargreaves 10-5; R. Andrewartha *wo* John Bear *scr*; Andrewartha beat McLaughlin 10-8; Andrewartha beat M. Wildman 10-9
9  J. Wych beat G. Ganim Jr 10-1; G. Scott beat L. Heywood 10-7; Wych beat Scott 10-6; Wych beat P. Fagan 10-3
10  P. Browne beat S. Duggan 10-9; C. Roscoe beat B. Demarco 10-7; Browne beat Roscoe 10-4; E. Sinclair beat Browne 10-1
11  M. Gauvreau beat J. Campbell 10-7; G. Cripsey beat M. Parkin 10-4; Gauvreau beat Cripsey 10-1; Gauvreau beat M. Macleod 10-6
12  I. Anderson beat G. Watson 10-4; J. Donnelly beat P. Watchorn 10-7; Donnelly beat Anderson 10-6; F. Davis beat Donnelly 10-5
13  W. King beat T. Jones 10-9; M. Watterson beat B. Bennett 10-5; King beat Watterson 10-8; King beat Dave Martin 10-8
14  J. Caggianello beat M. Darrington 10-7; W. Oliver beat J. Dunning 10-3; Oliver beat Caggianello 10-7; R. Williams beat Oliver 10-8
15  N. Foulds beat D. French 10-5; L. Dodd beat J. Giannaros 10-1; Foulds beat Dodd 10-4; Foulds beat J. Meadowcroft 10-2
16  B. Harris beat D. Sheehan 10-3; P. Burke beat B. Kelly 10-7; Burke beat Harris 10-4; M. Hallett beat Burke 10-5

**First round:** S. Davis beat King 10-3; J. Spencer beat Miles 10-3; T. Griffiths beat Mifsud 10-2; B. Werbeniuk beat F. Davis 10-4; N. Foulds beat A. Higgins 10-9; D. Mountjoy beat Hallett 10-4; Dennis Taylor beat Johnson 10-1; Parrott beat A. Knowles 10-7; C. Thorburn beat Morra 10-3; Thorne beat J. Virgo 10-9; J. White beat Williams 10-6; E. Charlton beat Andrewartha 10-4; K. Stevens beat Sinclair 10-1; David Taylor beat Gauvreau 10-5; S. Francisco beat T. Meo 10-5; R. Reardon beat Wych 10-7
**Second round:** S. Davis beat Spencer 13-5; Griffiths beat Werbeniuk 13-5; Mountjoy beat N. Foulds 13-6; Dennis Taylor beat Parrott 13-11; Thorburn beat Thorne 13-11; White beat Charlton 13-7; Stevens beat David Taylor 13-10; Reardon beat S. Francisco 13-8
**Quarter-finals:** S. Davis beat Griffiths 13-10; Dennis Taylor beat Mountjoy 13-8; White beat Thorburn 13-8; Stevens beat Reardon 13-2
**Semi-finals:** S. Davis beat Dennis Taylor 16-9; White beat Stevens 16-14
**Final:** S. Davis beat White 18-16

## 1985

**Qualifying groups**

1  G. Rigitano beat D. Sheehan 10-9; Rigitano beat B. Harris 10-4; Rigitano beat
   B. Kelly 10-6; Rigitano beat M. Fisher 10-2; N. Foulds beat Rigitano 10-8
2  D. O'Kane *wo* J. McLaughlin *scr*; O'Kane beat V. Harris 10-5; O'Kane beat
   F. Jonik 10-5; O'Kane beat L. Dodd 10-7; O'Kane beat D. Martin 10-8
3  S. Longworth beat J. Giannaros 10-1; Longworth beat G. Cripsey 10-8; J. Van
   Rensberg beat Longworth 10-7; M. Gauvreau beat Van Rensberg 10-9; D. Reynolds
   beat Gauvreau 10-1
4  R. Chaperon beat R. Bales 10-7; Chaperon beat L. Heywood 10-1; Chaperon beat
   P. Morgan 10-3; F. Davis beat Chaperon 10-9; R. Williams beat F. Davis 10-6
5  D. Hughes beat D. French 10-5; S. Newbury beat Hughes 10-9; Newbury beat
   P. Burke 10-3; Newbury beat G. Scott 10-2; E. Hughes beat Newbury 10-6
6  M. Hines beat T. Chappel 10-8; Hines beat P. Watchorn 10-4; M. Gibson beat
   Hines 10-7; P. Fagan beat Gibson 10-8; Fagan beat C. Wilson 10-9
7  D. Fowler beat J. Hargreaves 10-0; Fowler *wo* G. Watson *scr*; Fowler *wo*
   J. Caggianello *scr*; Fowler beat J. Donnelly 10-0; J. Parrott beat Fowler 10-2
8  R. Foldvari *wo* P. Thornley *scr*; Foldvari beat B. Oliver 10-3; R. Edmonds beat
   Foldvari 10-3; Edmonds beat M. Wildman 10-7
9  D. Chalmers beat D. Greaves 10-3; Chalmers beat E. McLaughlin 10-9; Chalmers
   beat I. Black 10-4; M. Hallett beat Chalmers 10-1
10 G. Foulds beat M. Parkin 10-6; Foulds beat C. Everton 10-2; Foulds beat C. Roscoe
   10-7; J. Johnson beat Foulds 10-6
11 P. Medati beat B. Bennett 10-4; Medati beat I. Williamson 10-8; Medati beat
   W. King 10-9; S. Francisco beat Medati 10-7
12 I. Anderson beat A. Kearney 10-8; P. Browne beat Anderson 10-5; M. Morra beat
   Browne 10-6; J. Campbell beat Morra 10-9
13 W. Jones beat John Rea 10-3; Jones beat J. Dunning 10-6; Jones beat M. Watterson
   10-5; Jones beat G. Miles 10-8
14 M. Bradley beat D. Mienie 10-4; Bradley beat B. Mikkelsen 10-9; J. Wych beat
   Bradley 10-7; J. Virgo beat Wych 10-4
15 P. Francisco beat B. Demarco 10-4; Francisco beat T. Murphy 10-4; Francisco beat
   J. Meadowcroft 10-5; M. Macleod beat Francisco 10-7
16 T. Jones beat M. Darrington 10-2; Jones beat S. Duggan 10-8; Jones beat
   J. Fitzmaurice 10-4; Jones beat E. Sinclair 10-2

**First round:** S. Davis beat N. Foulds 10-8; David Taylor beat O'Kane 10-4; A. Higgins
beat Reynolds 10-4; T. Griffiths beat Williams 10-3; R. Reardon beat E. Hughes 10-9;
Fagan beat W. Thorne 10-6; Parrott beat J. Spencer 10-3; K. Stevens beat Edmonds
10-8; C. Thorburn beat Hallett 10-8; B. Werbeniuk beat Johnson 10-8; Dennis Taylor
beat S. Francisco 10-2; E. Charlton beat Campbell 10-3; J. White beat W. Jones 10-4;
T. Meo beat Virgo 10-6; D. Mountjoy beat Macleod 10-5; A. Knowles beat T. Jones 10-8
**Second round:** S. Davis beat David Taylor 13-4; Griffiths beat Higgins 13-7; Reardon
beat Fagan 13-9; Parrott beat Stevens 13-6; Thorburn beat Werbeniuk 13-3; Dennis
Taylor beat Charlton 13-6; White beat Meo 13-11; Knowles beat Mountjoy 13-6
**Quarter-finals:** S. Davis beat Griffiths 13-6; Reardon beat Parrott 13-12; Dennis Taylor
beat Thorburn 13-5; Knowles beat White 13-10
**Semi-finals:** S. Davis beat Reardon 16-5; Dennis Taylor beat Knowles 16-5
**Final:** Dennis Taylor beat S. Davis 18-17

## 1986

**First qualifying round:** D. Gilbert beat R. Bales 10-7; O. Agrawal beat D. Hughes 10-6;
A. Kearney beat G. Wilkinson 10-5; B. Oliver beat J. O'Boye 10-8; D. Sheehan beat
P. Houlihan 10-7; M. Gibson beat G. Jenkins 10-4; S. Simngam beat B. Bennett 10-0;
Jim Bear beat P. Burke 10-8; T. Drago beat G. Cripsey 10-4; M. Smith beat D. Greaves
10-4; B. West *wo* J. Giannaros *scr*; P. Thornley beat D. Mienie 10-3; R. Grace beat
M. Parkin 10-8; S. Hendry beat B. Demarco 10-7; P. Watchorn *wo* J. Rempe *scr*;

B. Mikkelsen beat J. Hargreaves 10-7; M. Darrington *wo* W. Sanderson *scr*
**Second qualifying round:** J. Wych beat T. Chappel 10-6; S. Duggan beat M. Fisher 10-3;
T. Jones beat V. Harris 10-7; Gilbert beat M. Bradley 10-7; S. Newbury beat Agrawal
10-5; I. Black beat B. Harris 10-8; G. Scott beat Kearney 10-8; D. Fowler beat Oliver
10-8; C. Roscoe beat G. Foulds 10-3; W. King beat Sheehan 10-4; Gibson beat M. Morra
10-9; P. Medati beat Simngam 10-9; R. Chaperon beat F. Jonik 10-8; M. Gauvreau beat
Jim Bear 10-5; F. Davis beat D. Chalmers 10-6; P. Francisco beat Drago 10-4;
J. Donnelly beat Smith 10-6; West beat J. Dunning 10-3; T. Murphy beat J. McLaughlin
10-7; Thornley beat P. Fagan 10-7; W. Jones beat Grace 10-3; Hendry beat P. Browne
10-9; E. Sinclair beat P. Morgan 10-8; J. Van Rensberg beat I. Williamson 10-9; John
Rea beat E. McLaughlin 10-6; S. Longworth beat Watchorn 10-7; G. Miles beat
C. Everton 10-3; R. Foldvari beat G. Rigitano 10-6; M. Watterson beat Mikkelsen 10-2;
L. Dodd beat J. Fitzmaurice 10-6; Darrington beat J. Meadowcroft 10-6; R. Edmonds
beat B. Kelly 10-0
**Third qualifying round:** Wych beat Duggan 10-5; Gilbert beat T. Jones 10-7; Newbury
beat Black 10-2; Fowler beat Scott 10-7; King beat Roscoe 10-5; Medati beat Gibson
10-6; Gauvreau beat Chaperon 10-8; P. Francisco beat F. Davis 10-1; West beat
Donnelly 10-5; Murphy beat Thornley 10-3; Hendry beat W. Jones 10-8; Van Rensberg
beat Sinclair 10-2; Longworth beat John Rea 10-4; Foldvari beat Miles 10-7; Dodd beat
Watterson 10-1; Edmonds beat Darrington 10-5
**Fourth qualifying round:** M. Hallett beat Wych 10-7; D. Martin beat Gilbert 10-5;
J. Spencer beat Newbury 10-7; Fowler beat M. Macleod 10-6; D. Reynolds beat King
10-7; C. Wilson beat Medati 10-6; R. Williams beat Gauvreau 10-3; N. Foulds beat
P. Francisco 10-9; B. Werbeniuk beat West 10-8; E. Hughes beat Murphy 10-7; Hendry
beat O'Kane 10-9; J. Campbell beat Van Rensberg 10-6; J. Virgo beat Longworth 10-8;
J. Parrott beat Foldvari 10-6; P. Mans beat Dodd 10-7; Edmonds beat M. Wildman 10-9
**First round:** Hallett beat Dennis Taylor 10-6; J. Johnson beat Martin 10-3; A. Higgins
beat J. Spencer 10-7; T. Griffiths beat Fowler 10-2; K. Stevens beat Reynolds 10-6;
E. Charlton beat Wilson 10-6; S. Francisco beat Williams 10-4; A. Knowles beat
N. Foulds 10-9; C. Thorburn beat Werbeniuk 10-5; E. Hughes beat David Taylor 10-7;
W. Thorne beat Hendry 10-8; Campbell beat R. Reardon 10-8; J. White beat Virgo 10-7;
Parrott beat T. Meo 10-4; D. Mountjoy beat Mans 10-3; S. Davis beat Edmonds 10-4
**Second round:** Johnson beat Hallett 13-6; Griffiths beat Higgins 13-12; Stevens beat
Charlton 13-12; Knowles beat S. Francisco 13-10; Thorburn beat E. Hughes 13-6; Thorne
beat Campbell 13-9; White beat Parrott 13-8; S. Davis beat Mountjoy 13-5
**Quarter-finals:** Johnson beat Griffiths 13-12; Knowles beat Stevens 13-9; Thorburn beat
Thorne 13-6; S. Davis beat White 13-5
**Final:** Johnson beat S. Davis 18-12

## 1987
**First qualifying round:** J. Bear beat Jack Rea 10-5; A. Kearney *wo* F. Jonik *scr*; S. James
beat M. Watterson 10-2; G. Jenkins beat R. Grace 10-9; D. Greaves beat P. Thornley
10-6; M. Darrington beat B. Demarco 10-6; J. Rempe beat M. Smith 10-9; G. Rigitano
beat P. Morgan 4-0; C. Roscoe beat T. Whitthread 10-2; M. Morra beat P. Gibson 10-6;
D. Chalmers *wo* E. McLaughlin *scr*; M. Bennett beat J. Hargreaves 10-6; B. Kelly beat
B. Bennett 10-0; J. Meadowcroft beat D. Mienie 10-3; G. Foulds beat P. Watchorn 10-6;
D. Hughes beat M. Parkin 10-5; B. Oliver beat P. Burke 10-5; J. Dunning beat
J. Caggianello 10-7; J. Wright beat P. Houlihan 10-4; B. Rowswell *wo* S. Simngam *scr*;
J. Fitzmaurice beat C. Everton 10-2; D. Roe *wo* O. Agrawal *scr*; K. Owers beat M. Fisher
10-5
**Second qualifying round:** M. Gauvreau beat Bear 10-3; P. Medati beat Kearney 10-8;
E. Sinclair beat T. Drago 10-9; R. Edmonds beat James 10-1; T. Murphy beat Jenkins
10-4; G. Miles beat Greaves 10-7; S. Hendry beat Darrington 10-7; Rempe beat John
Rea 10-9; Rigitano beat V. Harris 10-6; S. Newbury beat L. Dodd 10-7; S. Duggan beat
Roscoe 10-7; T. Chappel beat Morra 10-8; T. Jones beat Chalmers 10-1; J. Van Rensberg
beat J. McLaughlin 10-6; M. Bennett beat B. Mikkelsen 10-4; W. Jones beat J. Donnelly

10-3; I. Black beat I. Williamson 10-8; D. O'Kane beat D. Gilbert 10-2; M. Gibson beat
Kelly 10-9; G. Cripsey beat Meadowcroft 10-9; D. Fowler beat G. Foulds 10-6; B. Harris
beat D. Hughes 10-2; Oliver beat P. Fagan 10-2; G. Scott beat Dunning 10-7;
M. Wildman beat Foldvari 10-5; Wright beat Browne 10-6; M. Bradley beat Rowswell
10-6; J. O'Boye beat N. Gilbert 10-5; J. Spencer beat R. Bales 10-2; R. Chaperon beat
Fitzmaurice 10-2; W. King beat Roe 10-4; Owers beat F. Davis 10-5
**Third qualifying round:** Medati beat Gauvreau 10-3; Edmonds beat Sinclair 10-6; Murphy
beat Miles 10-7; Hendry beat Rempe 10-4; Newbury beat Rigitano 10-4; Chappel beat
Duggan 10-3; T. Jones beat Van Rensberg 10-0; M. Bennett beat W. Jones 10-3; O'Kane
beat Black 10-2; Cripsey beat M. Gibson 10-4; Fowler beat B. Harris 10-5; Oliver beat
Scott 10-5; Wright beat Wildman 10-0; Bradley beat O'Boye 10-7; Spencer beat
Chaperon 10-4; King beat Owers 10-4
**Fourth qualifying round:** E. Hughes beat Medati 10-2; M. Macleod beat Edmonds 10-7;
S. Longworth beat Murphy 10-2; Hendry beat D. Martin 10-7; M. Hallett beat Newbury
10-4; J. Campbell beat Chappel 10-6; J. Virgo beat T. Jones 10-9; M. Bennett beat
W. Jones 10-3; O'Kane beat P. Francisco 10-5; David Taylor beat Cripsey 10-7;
J. Parrott beat Fowler 10-3; D. Reynolds beat Oliver 10-7; Wright beat C. Wilson 10-4;
J. Wych beat Bradley 10-7; B. West beat Spencer 10-5; King beat E. Charlton 10-4
**First round:** J. Johnson beat E. Hughes 10-9; Macleod beat R. Williams 10-5; Longworth
beat K. Stevens 10-4; Hendry beat W. Thorne 10-7; Hallett beat A. Knowles 10-6;
S. Francisco beat Campbell 10-3; N. Foulds beat Virgo 10-4; Dennis Taylor beat
M. Bennett 10-4; O'Kane beat Thorburn 10-5; D. Mountjoy beat David Taylor 10-5;
Parrott beat T. Meo 10-8; J. White beat Reynolds 10-8; A. Higgins beat Wright 10-6;
T. Griffiths beat Wych 10-4; R. Reardon beat West 10-5; S. Davis beat King 10-7
**Second round:** Johnson beat Macleod 13-7; Hendry beat Longworth 10-7; Hallett beat
S. Francisco 13-9; N. Foulds beat Dennis Taylor 13-10; O'Kane beat Mountjoy 13-5;
White beat Parrott 13-11; Griffiths beat Higgins 13-10; S. Davis beat Reardon 13-4
**Quarter-finals:** Johnson beat Hendry 13-12; N. Foulds beat Hallett 13-9; White beat
O'Kane 13-6; S. Davis beat Griffiths 13-5
**Semi-finals:** Johnson beat N. Foulds 16-9; S. Davis beat White 16-11
**Final:** S. Davis beat Johnson 18-14

## 1988
**Preliminary round:** A. Harris beat S. Mizerak 10-2
**First qualifying round:** P. Gibson beat D. Sheehan 10-9; A. Harris beat M. Fisher 10-4;
C. Roscoe beat E. McLaughlin 10-1; G. Miles beat D. Hughes 10-3; N. Gilbert beat
John Rea 10-5; I. Williamson *wo* J. Caggianello *scr*; B. Rowswell beat P. Thornley 10-7;
B. Oliver beat D. Chalmers 10-9; A. Robidoux *wo* F. Jonik *scr*; B. Kelly beat A. Kearney
10-4; S. James *wo* T. Whitthread *scr*; P. Watchorn beat M. Gibson 10-7; M. Clark beat
M. Darrington 10-5; G. Rigitano beat J. Dunning 10-7; J. Smith beat J. Donnelly 10-4;
Glen Wilkinson beat C. Everton 10-2; M. Morra beat S. Meakin 10-5; M. Smith beat
V. Harris 10-6; E. Lawlor *wo* J. Van Rensberg *scr*; B. Mikkelsen beat Jack Rea 10-3;
R. Foldvari beat J. Rempe 10-4; J. Meadowcroft beat B. Bennett 10-5; D. Gilbert beat
D. Heaton 10-2; P. Medati beat Gary Wilkinson 10-9; I. Black *wo* J. Hargreaves *scr*;
P. Fagan beat D. Greaves 10-3; E. Sinclair beat P. Burke 10-2; D. Roe beat B. Demarco
10-2; J. Chambers beat M. Watterson 10-3; J. Bear beat D. Mienie 10-4; J. Fitzmaurice
beat M. Parkin 10-6
**Second qualifying round:** P. Gibson beat M. Gauvreau 10-9; S. Duggan beat A. Harris
10-4; T. Murphy beat Roscoe 10-8; R. Chaperon beat Marshall 10-3; Miles beat R. Bales
10-7; T. Chappel beat N. Gilbert 10-8; M. Bradley beat Williamson 10-9; B. Werbeniuk
beat Rowswell 10-6; Oliver beat R. Reardon 10-6; Robidoux *wo* R. Grace *scr*; P. Browne
beat Kelly 10-8; James beat J. O'Boye 10-7; W. King beat Watchorn 10-4; Clark beat
G. Scott 10-4; M. Bennett beat Rigitano 10-4; J. Wych beat J. Smith 10-3; W. Jones beat
Glen Wilkinson 10-4; Morra beat R. Edmonds 10-8; M. Smith beat J. McLaughlin 10-3;
S. Newbury beat E. Lawlor 10-3; M. Wildman beat Mikkelsen 10-5; Foldvari beat
T. Jones 10-9; G. Cripsey beat Meadowcroft 10-3; P. Houlihan *wo* D. Gilbert *scr*;

L. Dodd beat Medati 10-6; D. Fowler beat Black 10-1; B. Harris beat Fagan 10-1;
Sinclair beat D. O'Kane 10-9; K. Owers beat Roe 10-7; J. Wright beat Chambers 10-2;
Bear beat G. Foulds 10-2; F. Davis beat Fitzmaurice 10-8
**Third qualifying round:** Duggan beat P. Gibson 10-9; Chaperon beat Murphy 10-5;
Chappel beat Miles 10-7; Werbeniuk beat Bradley 10-8; Oliver beat Robidoux 10-2;
James beat Browne 10-1; King beat Clark 10-9; M. Bennett beat Wych 10-5; W. Jones
beat Morra 10-8; Newbury beat M. Smith 10-9; Foldvari beat Wildman 10-1; Cripsey
beat Houlihan 10-4; Fowler beat Dodd 10-8; B. Harris beat Sinclair 10-0; Wright beat
Owers 10-8; F. Davis beat Bear 10-4
**Fourth qualifying round:** J. Virgo beat Duggan 10-5; Chaperon beat David Taylor 10-6;
T. Drago beat Chappel 10-7; Werbeniuk beat T. Meo 10-4; C. Wilson beat Oliver 10-6;
James beat E. Hughes 10-6; King beat J. Spencer 10-7; K. Stevens beat M. Bennett 10-7;
W. Jones beat D. Martin 10-5; B. West beat Newbury 10-8; P. Francisco beat Foldvari
10-5; S. Longworth beat Cripsey 10-2; Fowler beat M. Macleod 10-3; E. Charlton beat
B. Harris 10-4; S. Hendry beat Wright 10-4; J. Campbell beat F. Davis 10-3
**First round:** S. Davis beat Virgo 10-8; M. Hallett beat Chaperon 10-2; Drago beat
A. Higgins 10-2; Dennis Taylor beat Werbeniuk 10-8; J. Johnson beat Wilson 10-7;
James beat R. Williams 10-6; J. Parrott beat King 10-4; C. Thorburn beat Stevens 10-6;
N. Foulds beat W. Jones 10-7; D. Mountjoy beat West 10-6; W. Thorne beat
P. Francisco 10-6; T. Griffiths beat Longworth 10-1; T. Knowles beat Fowler 10-8;
Charlton beat S. Francisco 10-7; Hendry beat D. Reynolds 10-6; J. White beat Campbell
10-3
**Second round:** S. Davis beat Hallett 13-1; Drago beat Dennis Taylor 13-5; James beat
Johnson 13-9; Thorburn beat Parrott 13-10; N. Foulds beat Mountjoy 13-1; Griffiths
beat Thorne 13-9; Knowles beat Charlton 13-7; White beat Hendry 13-12
**Quarter-finals:** S. Davis beat Drago 13-4; Thorburn beat James 13-11; Griffiths beat
Foulds 13-9; White beat Knowles 13-6
**Semi-finals:** S. Davis beat Thorburn 16-8; Griffiths beat White 16-11
**Final:** S. Davis beat Griffiths 18-11

## 1989

**First qualifying round:** N. Terry beat M. Parkin 10-0; C. Edwards beat J. Giannaros
10-4; M. Rowing beat S. Mizerak 10-1; B. Bennett beat C. Everton 10-4; P. Thornley
beat B. Demarco 10-3; T. Wilson beat M. Francisco 10-5; D. Mienie beat V. Potasnik
10-6; M. Johnston-Allen beat E. McLaughlin 10-3; I. Graham beat D. Greaves 10-0;
S. Campbell *wo* G. Watson *scr*; J. Grech beat D. Heaton 10-6; M. Price *wo* P. Morgan
*scr*; R. Marshall beat M. Hines 10-1; D. Morgan beat S. Frangie 10-5
**Second qualifying round:** Terry beat P. Medati 10-8; Edwards beat Jim Bear 10-7;
Rowing beat J. Dunning 10-9; F. Davis beat B. Bennett 10-4; Thornley beat M. Bradley
10-7; P. Fagan beat G. Foulds 10-6; B. Oliver beat J. Rempe 10-5; P. Watchorn beat
R. Grace 10-6; M. Morra beat B. Mikkelsen 10-4; M. Gibson beat M. Darrington 10-0;
T. Whitthread beat J. Donnelly 10-7; T. Wilson beat G. Scott 10-4; J. Meadowcroft
beat Mienie 10-7; S. Meakin beat A. Kearney 10-3; J. Fitzmaurice beat C. Roscoe 10-9;
V. Harris beat M. Watterson 10-5; A. Harris beat J. Van Rensberg 10-7; Johnston-Allen
beat G. Rigitano 10-3; Graham *wo* B. Harris *scr*; M. Smith beat S. Campbell 10-9;
J. Smith beat R. Foldvari 10-4; J. Chambers beat I. Anderson 10-7; Grech beat
I. Williamson 10-7; Glen Wilkinson beat B. Kelly 10-2; John Rea beat D. Hughes 10-3;
I. Black beat D. Sheehan 10-8; Price beat E. Sinclair 10-9; B. Rowswell beat P. Burke
10-0; P. Gibson beat Marshall 10-3; D. Morgan beat E. Lawlor 10-2; F. Ellis beat
M. Wildman 10-7; A. Robidoux beat G. Miles 10-8
**Third qualifying round:** N. Gilbert beat Terry 10-5; Edwards beat T. Chappel 10-7;
Rowing beat W. King 10-7; S. Duggan beat F. Davis 10-3; Thornley *wo* B. Werbeniuk
*scr*; D. Gilbert beat Fagan 10-4; T. Murphy beat Oliver 10-8; D. Roe beat Watchorn
10-5; M. Clark beat Morra 10-6; D. Martin beat M. Gibson 10-7; D. Fowler beat
Whitthread 10-6; J. O'Boye beat T. Wilson 10-8; M. Macleod beat Meadowcroft 10-9;

P. Browne beat Meakin 10-9; R. Reardon beat Fitzmaurice 10-5; Gary Wilkinson beat
V. Harris 10-6; W. Jones beat A. Harris 10-4; J. Wych beat Johnston-Allen 10-3;
Graham beat G. Cripsey 10-2; M. Smith beat J. Wright 10-7; T. Jones beat J. Smith
10-7; K. Stevens beat Chambers 10-8; L. Dodd beat Grech 10-9; Glen Wilkinson beat
R. Bales 10-1; John Rea beat P. Houlihan 10-5; R. Edmonds beat Black 10-3; Price beat
M. Bennett 10-9; Rowswell beat M. Gauvreau 10-7; K. Owers beat P. Gibson 10-8;
D. Morgan beat J. Campbell 10-4; J. McLaughlin beat Ellis 10-9; Robidoux beat
M. Fisher 10-2
**Fourth qualifying round:** N. Gilbert beat Edwards 10-8; Duggan beat Rowing 10-6;
D. Gilbert beat Thornley 10-4; Roe beat Murphy 10-7; Clark beat Martin 10-2; O'Boye
beat Fowler 10-6; Browne beat Macleod 10-6; Gary Wilkinson beat Reardon 10-5;
W. Jones beat Wych 10-9; Graham beat M. Smith 10-6; T. Jones beat Stevens 10-2;
Dodd beat Glen Wilkinson 10-4; John Rea beat Edmonds 10-7; Rowswell beat Price
10-6; D. Morgan beat Owers 10-8; Robidoux beat J. McLaughlin 10-2
**Fifth qualifying round:** S. Newbury beat N. Gilbert 10-7; Duggan beat J. Spencer 10-1;
D. Mountjoy beat D. Gilbert 10-7; Roe beat R. Williams 10-3; R. Chaperon beat Clark
10-4; O'Boye beat B. West 10-7; Browne beat S. Longworth 10-0; Gary Wilkinson beat
T. Drago 10-9; W. Jones beat David Taylor 10-7; D. Reynolds beat Graham 10-5;
T. Meo beat T. Jones 10-7; E. Charlton beat Dodd 10-6; S. James beat John Rea 10-7;
E. Hughes beat Rowswell 10-9; D. Morgan beat A. Higgins 10-8; D. O'Kane beat
Robidoux 10-5
**First round:** S. Davis beat Newbury 10-5; Duggan beat C. Wilson 10-1; M. Hallett beat
Mountjoy 10-7; Roe beat A. Knowles 10-6; T. Griffiths beat Chaperon 10-6; S. Francisco
beat O'Boye 10-6; W. Thorne beat Browne 10-5; S. Hendry beat Gary Wilkinson 10-9;
W. Jones beat N. Foulds 10-9; Reynolds beat P. Francisco 10-7; Meo beat J. Johnson
10-5; Charlton beat C. Thorburn 10-9; J. Parrott beat James 10-9; Dennis Taylor beat
E. Hughes 10-3; J. Virgo beat D. Morgan 10-4; J. White beat O'Kane 19-7
**Second round:** S. Davis beat Duggan 13-3; Hallett beat Roe 13-12; Griffiths beat
S. Francisco 13-9; Hendry beat Thorne 13-4; Reynolds beat W. Jones 13-3; Meo beat
Charlton 13-8; Parrott beat Dennis Taylor 13-10; White beat Virgo 13-12
**Quarter-finals:** S. Davis beat Hallett 13-3; Hendry beat Griffiths 13-5; Meo beat
Reynolds 13-9; Parrott beat White 13-7
**Semi-finals:** S. Davis beat Hendry 16-9; Parrott beat Meo 16-7
**Final:** S. Davis beat Parrott 18-3

# WPBSA NON-RANKING EVENTS

In 1988–89 the WPBSA instituted three non-ranking events for players
knocked out in the early rounds of specific tournaments. Each carried prize-
money of £25,000 with the winner taking £5,000. The three finals resulted:

**Marcos Leisure, Glasgow**
Gary Wilkinson beat A. Higgins 5-4
**Pontins, Brixham**
P. Browne beat P. Francisco 5-1
**Excelsior Snooker Centre, Leeds**
David Taylor beat S. Meakin 9-1

# MATCHROOM LEAGUE

Steve Davis, with eight wins and only one loss, won the Matchroom League for the third consecutive year. Terry Griffiths and Alex Higgins, the bottom two finishers, were relegated to a new Matchroom European League for next season.

For the fourth year of the League, the top eight finishers will be joined by Dennis Taylor and Doug Mountjoy.

The squad for the six-man European League will be: Davis, Jimmy White, Griffiths, Tony Meo, Mike Hallett and Higgins.

## LEAGUE SCORECARD

*Match*

| | | | | |
|---|---|---|---|---|
| 1 | John Parrott | 5 | Terry Griffiths | 3 |
| 2 | Steve Davis | 5 | Neal Foulds | 3 |
| 3 | Cliff Thorburn | 5 | Stephen Hendry | 3 |
| 4 | Jimmy White | 4 | Willie Thorne | 4 |
| 5 | Cliff Thorburn | 4 | Tony Meo | 4 |
| 6 | Tony Meo | 5 | Terry Griffiths | 3 |
| 7 | John Parrott | 5 | Willie Thorne | 3 |
| 8 | Cliff Thorburn | 7 | Jimmy White | 1 |
| 9 | John Parrott | 5 | Neal Foulds | 3 |
| 10 | Jimmy White | 5 | Alex Higgins | 3 |
| 11 | Jimmy White | 5 | Terry Griffiths | 3 |
| 12 | Willie Thorne | 4 | Neal Foulds | 4 |
| 13 | Cliff Thorburn | 5 | Alex Higgins | 3 |
| 14 | John Parrott | 6 | Tony Meo | 2 |
| 15 | Steve Davis | 6 | Tony Meo | 2 |
| 16 | Willie Thorne | 5 | Terry Griffiths | 3 |
| 17 | Stephen Hendry | 4 | Neal Foulds | 4 |
| 18 | Steve Davis | 7 | Willie Thorne | 1 |
| 19 | Stephen Hendry | 5 | John Parrott | 3 |
| 20 | Neal Foulds | 7 | Jimmy White | 1 |
| 21 | Willie Thorne | 5 | Alex Higgins | 3 |
| 22 | Steve Davis | 5 | Stephen Hendry | 3 |
| 23 | Steve Davis | 6 | Cliff Thorburn | 2 |
| 24 | Stephen Hendry | 5 | Tony Meo | 3 |
| 25 | Neal Foulds | 4 | Tony Meo | 4 |
| 26 | Tony Meo | 5 | Jimmy White | 3 |
| 27 | Steve Davis | 5 | John Parrott | 3 |
| 28 | Neal Foulds | 5 | Alex Higgins | 3 |
| 29 | John Parrott | 7 | Alex Higgins | 1 |
| 30 | Terry Griffiths | 5 | Cliff Thorburn | 3 |
| 31 | Stephen Hendry | 5 | Willie Thorne | 3 |
| 32 | Stephen Hendry | 5 | Alex Higgins | 3 |
| 33 | Steve Davis | 7 | Terry Griffiths | 1 |
| 34 | Cliff Thorburn | 5 | Neal Foulds | 3 |
| 35 | Alex Higgins | 4 | Tony Meo | 4 |
| 36 | Jimmy White | 4 | John Parrott | 4 |
| 37 | Stephen Hendry | 6 | Jimmy White | 2 |

*Match*

| 38 | Stephen Hendry | 6 | Terry Griffiths | 2 |
| 39 | Terry Griffiths | 5 | Alex Higgins | 3 |
| 40 | Cliff Thorburn | 5 | Willie Thorne | 3 |
| 41 | Willie Thorne | 4 | Tony Meo | 4 |
| 42 | Steve Davis | 5 | Alex Higgins | 3 |
| 43 | Terry Griffiths | 6 | Neal Foulds | 2 |
| 44 | John Parrott | 7 | Cliff Thorburn | 1 |
| 45 | Jimmy White | 6 | Steve Davis | 2 |

## LEAGUE TABLE

| Player | Prize-money | P | W | D | L | F | A | Pts |
|---|---|---|---|---|---|---|---|---|
| Steve Davis | (£70,000) | 9 | 8 | 0 | 1 | 48 | 24 | 24 |
| John Parrott | (£30,000) | 9 | 6 | 1 | 2 | 45 | 27 | 19 |
| Stephen Hendry | (£25,000) | 9 | 6 | 1 | 2 | 42 | 30 | 19 |
| Cliff Thorburn | (£20,000) | 9 | 5 | 1 | 3 | 37 | 35 | 16 |
| Jimmy White | (£17,000) | 9 | 3 | 2 | 4 | 31 | 41 | 11 |
| Tony Meo | (£15,000) | 9 | 2 | 4 | 3 | 33 | 39 | 10 |
| Neal Foulds | (£13,000) | 9 | 2 | 3 | 4 | 35 | 37 | 9 |
| Willie Thorne | (£11,000) | 9 | 2 | 3 | 4 | 32 | 40 | 9 |
| Terry Griffiths | (£9,000) | 9 | 3 | 0 | 6 | 31 | 41 | 9 |
| Alex Higgins | (£5,000) | 9 | 0 | 1 | 8 | 26 | 46 | 1 |

**Highest break 147 points Cliff Thorburn** (£5,000 prize-money)

# NATIONAL PROFESSIONAL CHAMPIONSHIPS

The WPBSA's prize fund subsidy to national domestic championships of £1,000 per player from 1985 onwards enabled these events to be staged annually and scheduled properly.

There had previously been Australian and Canadian Championships but these had been played in a haphazard way. Eddie Charlton won the Australian title for the first time in 1964 and was beaten only in 1968 until he lost to John Campbell in 1985.

## ENGLISH CHAMPIONSHIP

**1981** (*John Courage*)
**Qualifying:** R. Edmonds beat M. Hallett 9-3; J. Johnson beat A. Knowles 9-2; M. Wildman beat B. Bennett 9-3; J. Dunning beat D. Greaves 9-4; J. Meadowcroft beat J. Barrie 9-3
**First round:** Edmonds beat F. Davis 9-6; T. Meo beat J. Virgo 9-6; G. Miles beat S. Hood 9-1; S. Davis beat Meadowcroft 9-2; J. Spencer beat P. Houlihan 9-1; W. Thorne beat Wildman 9-2; Johnson *wo*; Dunning beat David Taylor 9-8
**Quarter-finals:** S. Davis beat Spencer 9-7; Meo beat Miles 9-7; Thorne beat Dunning 9-0; Edmonds beat Johnson 9-5
**Semi-finals:** S. Davis beat Edmonds 9-0; Meo beat Thorne 9-8
**Final:** S. Davis beat Meo 9-3

**1985** (*Tolly Cobbold*)
**Qualifying:** D. Fowler beat W. Oliver 9-7; M. Bradley beat I. Williamson 9-8; T. Jones beat P. Houlihan 9-1; L. Dodd beat R. Bales 9-5; J. Fitzmaurice beat D. Greaves 9-3; M. Fisher beat D. French 9-8; S. Duggan beat B. Harris 9-8; D. Hughes beat M. Watterson 9-5; D. Chalmers beat J. Meadowcroft 9-3; S. Longworth beat R. Edmonds 9-4; P. Medati beat J. Hargreaves 9-8; G. Foulds beat F. Davis 9-2; G. Cripsey beat B. Bennett 9-0; G. Scott beat V. Harris 9-7
**First round:** S. Davis beat Fowler 9-3; M. Hallett beat Duggan 9-4; J. Johnson beat Scott 9-1; T. Meo beat Fisher 9-3; J. Virgo beat M. Darrington 9-0; D. Reynolds beat Fitzmaurice 9-2; R. Williams beat T. Jones 9-6; W. Thorne beat Dodd 9-1; Longworth beat M. Wildman 9-3; J. White beat Chalmers 9-5; Medati beat J. Spencer 9-4; N. Foulds beat D. Hughes 9-3; David Taylor beat Cripsey 9-5; J. Parrott beat G. Foulds 9-4; D. Martin beat G. Miles 9-7; A. Knowles beat Bradley 9-8
**Second round:** Virgo beat Johnson 9-4; Reynolds beat Thorne 9-6; S. Davis beat Williams 9-2; Meo beat Hallett 9-4; Knowles beat Martin 9-3; David Taylor beat Parrott 9-7; White beat N. Foulds 9-7; Longworth beat Medati 9-7
**Quarter-finals:** Meo beat Reynolds 9-4; Longworth beat White 9-5; Knowles beat David Taylor 9-2; S. Davis beat Virgo 9-2
**Semi-finals:** Knowles beat Longworth 9-6; S. Davis beat Meo 9-8
**Final:** S. Davis beat Knowles 9-2

**1986** (*Tolly Cobbold*)
**First round:** D. Gilbert beat B. West 9-8; P. Houlihan beat J. Hargreaves 9-5

**Second round:** M. Bradley beat Gilbert 9-5; F. Davis beat D. Hughes 9-6; T. Jones beat
B. Harris 9-5; W. Oliver beat L. Dodd 9-5; P. Medati beat D. Greaves 9-4; S. Longworth
beat S. Duggan 9-4; G. Cripsey beat J. Meadowcroft 9-1; G. Scott beat B. Bennett 9-1;
I. Williamson beat M. Watterson 9-1; R. Edmonds beat M. Smith 9-8; D. Fowler beat
M. Darrington 9-3; Houlihan *wo* J. Dunning *scr*; D. Chalmers beat Fisher 9-2; R. Bales
beat V. Harris 9-7
**Third round:** S. Davis beat Bradley 9-3; D. Martin beat F. Davis 9-8; J. Virgo beat
T. Jones 9-7; J. Parrott beat Oliver 9-0; W. Thorne beat Medati 9-2; D. Reynolds beat
Longworth 9-5; M. Wildman beat Cripsey 9-5; T. Meo beat Scott 9-1; J. White beat
Williamson 9-1; R. Williams beat Miles 9-6; N. Foulds beat G. Foulds 9-4; Edmonds
beat David Taylor 9-6; J. Johnson beat Fowler 9-7; J. Spencer beat Houlihan 9-5;
M. Hallett beat Chalmers 9-1; A. Knowles beat Bales 9-4
**Fourth round:** S. Davis beat Martin 9-4; Virgo beat Parrott 9-6; Reynolds beat Thorne
9-8; Meo beat Wildman 9-3; White beat Williams 9-5; N. Foulds beat Edmonds 9-4;
Johnson beat Spencer 9-7; Hallett beat Knowles 9-5
**Quarter-finals:** S. Davis beat Virgo 9-2; Meo beat Reynolds 9-4; N. Foulds beat White
9-4; Hallett beat Johnson 9-6
**Semi-finals:** Meo beat S. Davis 9-7; N. Foulds beat Hallett 9-8
**Final:** Meo beat Foulds 9-7

## 1987 (*Tolly Ales*)
**First round:** M. Fisher beat T. Whitthread 6-3; P. Gibson beat D. Hughes 6-3; J. Wright
beat D. Chalmers 6-5; B. Bennett beat N. Gilbert 6-5; D. Roe beat D. Greaves 6-1;
K. Owers *wo* P. Houlihan *scr*; S. James beat J. Hargeaves 6-5
**Second round:** S. Duggan beat Fisher 6-0; M. Bradley beat D. Gilbert 6-3; P. Medati beat
Gibson 6-2; M. Wildman *wo* M. Watterson *scr*; B. Harris beat G. Foulds 6-1; J. Spencer
beat Wright 6-1; R. Edmonds beat Bennett 6-1; G. Cripsey beat J. Dunning 6-1; L. Dodd
beat Smith 6-3; V. Harris beat M. Darrington 6-3; I. Williamson beat Roe 6-4; Owers
beat R. Bales 6-5; T. Jones beat B. Oliver 6-1; J. Fitzmaurice beat G. Scott 6-2; James
beat F. Davis 6-2; G. Miles *wo* J. Meadowcroft *scr*
**Third round:** T. Meo beat Duggan 6-3; D. Fowler beat Bradley 6-3; J. Virgo beat Medati
6-1; J. Parrott beat Wildman 6-1; W. Thorne beat B. Harris 6-2; D. Martin beat Spencer
6-5; D. Reynolds beat Edmonds 6-3; J. White beat Cripsey 6-4; Dodd beat A. Knowles
6-2; B. West beat V. Harris 6-3; M. Hallett beat Williamson 6-2; Owers beat N. Foulds
6-3; R. Williams beat Jones 6-4; David Taylor beat Fitzmaurice 6-1; James beat
S. Longworth 6-2; J. Johnson beat Miles 6-3
**Fourth round:** Meo beat Fowler 6-0; Parrott beat Virgo 6-2; Thorne beat Martin 6-3;
Reynolds beat White 6-5; Dodd beat West 6-3; Hallett beat Owers 6-2; Williams beat
David Taylor 6-2; Johnson beat James 6-3
**Quarter-finals:** Meo beat Parrott 6-3; Thorne beat Reynolds 6-4; Dodd beat Hallett 6-5;
Johnson beat Williams 6-5
**Semi-finals:** Meo beat Thorne 9-3; Dodd beat Johnson 9-5
**Final:** Meo beat Dodd 9-5

## 1988
**First round:** N. Gilbert beat A. Harris 6-3; J. Chambers beat P. Gibson 6-0; D. Gilbert
beat T. Whitthread 6-1; E. Lawlor beat D. Roe 6-5; D. Chalmers *wo* M. Fisher *scr*;
S. Meakin beat M. Darrington 6-3; M. Smith beat G. Miles 6-1; J. Smith beat V. Harris
6-3; Gary Wilkinson beat B. Rowswell 6-1; P. Medati beat N. Bennett 6-0; D. Heaton
beat J. Meadowcroft 6-0; R. Marshall beat B. Oliver 6-3; D. Hughes beat J. Fitzmaurice
6-3; I. Williamson beat J. Dunning 6-5; D. Greaves beat S. James 6-5; M. Clark *wo*
M. Watterson *scr*
**Second round:** F. Davis beat N. Gilbert 6-5; Chambers beat G. Scott 6-3; D. Gilbert beat
R. Bales 6-2; Lawlor beat M. Bradley 6-5; J. Wright beat Fisher 6-2; K. Owers beat
Meakin 6-2; M. Smith beat B. Harris 6-4; J. Smith beat T. Jones 6-5; Gary Wilkinson
beat R. Edmonds 6-3; L. Dodd beat Heaton 6-0; Marshall beat P. Houlihan 6-4;

D. Hughes beat M. Wildman 6-0; S. Duggan beat Williamson 6-2; Greaves beat
G. Cripsey 6-4; Clark beat G. Foulds 6-0
**Third round:** T. Meo beat F. Davis 6-3; S. Longworth beat Chambers 6-4; D. Reynolds
beat D. Gilbert 6-3; J. Parrott beat Lawlor 6-3; A. Knowles beat Wright 6-2; Owers beat
David Taylor 6-3; D. Martin beat M. Smith 6-5; J. Johnson beat J. Smith 6-5; N. Foulds
beat Gary Wilkinson 6-3; Fowler beat J. Spencer 6-3; J. Virgo beat Dodd 6-3; W. Thorne
beat Marshall 6-3; R. Williams beat D. Hughes 6-1; M. Hallett beat Duggan 6-3; B. West
beat Greaves 6-5; J. White beat Clark 6-5
**Fourth round:** Meo beat Longworth 6-4; Reynolds beat Parrott 6-2; Knowles beat Owers
6-4; Johnson beat Martin 6-4; N. Foulds beat Fowler 6-1; Thorne beat Virgo 6-0; Hallett
beat Williams 6-3; West beat White 6-2
**Quarter-finals:** Reynolds beat Meo 6-4; Johnson beat Knowles 6-3; N. Foulds beat
Thorne 6-2; West beat Hallett 6-5
**Semi-finals:** Reynolds beat Johnson 9-8; N. Foulds beat West 9-6
**Final:** Reynolds beat N. Foulds 9-5

**1989**
**Preliminary:** I. Graham beat D. Heaton 5-1; M. Johnston-Allen beat B. Bennett 5-2;
N. Terry beat M. Rowing 5-1; C. Edwards *wo* D. Greaves *scr*
**First round:** A. Harris *wo* G. Scott *scr*; B. Rowswell beat V. Harris 5-3; Graham beat
M. Darrington 5-3; J. Smith *wo* P. Gibson *scr*; J. Fitzmaurice beat B. Harris 5-4;
M. Price beat Johnston-Allen 5-4; R. Marshall beat Terry 5-3; I. Williamson *wo*
S. Meakin *scr*; G. Miles beat M. Smith 5-4; S. Campbell beat J. Dunning 5-3; Edwards
beat M. Watterson 5-0; M. Bradley beat J. Chambers 5-2; B. Oliver beat G. Foulds 5-1;
E. Lawlor beat F. Davis 5-2; T. Whitthread beat D. Hughes 5-1; P. Medati beat
M. Wildman 5-4
**Second round:** A. Harris beat T. Jones 5-3; Rowswell beat J. Wright 5-2; Graham beat
S. Duggan 5-2; Gary Wilkinson beat J. Smith 5-3; P. Houlihan beat Fitzmaurice 5-4;
Price beat R. Edmonds 5-4; Marshall beat N. Gilbert 5-4; Williamson beat Owers 5-4;
Miles beat M. Fisher 5-4; D. Fowler beat Campbell 5-1; Edwards beat Dodd 5-1;
D. Gilbert beat Bradley 5-4; M. Clark beat Oliver 5-2; D. Roe beat Lawlor 5-1;
G. Cripsey beat Whitthread 5-0; Medati beat R. Bales 5-3
**Third round:** D. Reynolds beat A. Harris 5-1; Rowswell beat D. Martin 5-2; Graham beat
R. Williams 5-3; Wilkinson beat J. Virgo 5-3; M. Hallett beat Houlihan 5-2; Price beat
David Taylor 5-1; S. Longworth beat Marshall 5-3; T. Knowles beat Williamson 5-2;
J. Parrott beat Miles 5-3; Fowler beat T. Meo 5-3; Edwards beat J. Spencer 5-1;
J. Johnson beat D. Gilbert 5-2; W. Thorne beat Clark 5-1; Roe beat B. West 5-4; Cripsey
beat S. James 5-3; N. Foulds beat Medati 5-3
**Fourth round:** Rowswell beat Reynolds 5-4; Wilkinson beat Graham 5-1; Hallett beat
Price 5-4; Longworth beat Knowles 5-4; Parrott beat Fowler 5-4; Johnson beat Edwards
5-0; Thorne beat Roe 5-1; N. Foulds beat Cripsey 5-1
**Quarter-finals:** Wilkinson beat Rowswell 5-1; Hallett beat Longworth 5-1; Parrott beat
Johnson 5-4; N. Foulds beat Thorne 5-3
**Semi-finals:** Hallett beat Wilkinson 5-3; Parrott beat N. Foulds 5-4
**Final:** Hallett beat Parrott 9-7

# IRISH CHAMPIONSHIP

**1972**
**Challenge:** A. Higgins beat Jack Rea 28-12
**1978**
**Challenge:** A. Higgins beat Dennis Taylor 21-7
**1979**
**Challenge:** A. Higgins beat P. Fagan 21-13

**1980**
Challenge: Dennis Taylor beat A. Higgins 21-15

**1981**
Challenge: Dennis Taylor beat P. Fagan 22-21

**1982**
First round: E. Hughes beat D. Sheehan 6-1
Quarter-finals: E. Hughes beat Jack Rea 6-0; T. Murphy beat P. Fagan 6-2
Semi-finals: Dennis Taylor beat Murphy 6-0; A. Higgins beat E. Hughes 6-2
Final: Taylor beat Higgins 16-13

**1983**
First round: Dennis Taylor beat B. Kelly 6-0; P. Fagan beat T. Murphy 6-4; A. Higgins beat Jack Rea 6-3; E. Hughes beat P. Burke 6-2
Semi-finals: Higgins beat E. Hughes 6-2; Taylor beat Fagan 6-1
Final: Higgins beat Taylor 16-11

**1985** (*Strongbow*)
Preliminary: J. McLaughlin beat D. Sheehan 6-3
Qualifying: P. Burke beat A. Kearney 6-4; T. Murphy beat P. Browne 6-3; B. Kelly beat P. Watchorn 6-2; Jack Rea beat McLaughlin 6-5
Quarter-finals: P. Fagan beat Murphy 6-2; Dennis Taylor beat Jack Rea 6-0; A. Higgins beat Burke 6-0; E. Hughes beat Kelly 6-2
Semi-finals: Taylor beat Hughes 6-5; Higgins beat Fagan 6-3
Final: Taylor beat Higgins 10-5

**1986** (*Strongbow*)
First round: B. Kelly beat Jack Rea 5-0; T. Murphy beat J. O'Boye 5-0; E. Hughes beat D. Sheehan 5-0; A. Kearney beat P. Fagan 5-0; J. McLaughlin beat P. Watchorn 5-0; P. Burke beat P. Browne 5-4
Quarter-finals: Dennis Taylor beat Kelly 6-1; Murphy beat Kearney 6-2; A. Higgins beat McLaughlin 6-2; Hughes beat Burke 6-3
Semi-finals: Taylor beat Murphy 6-3; Higgins beat Hughes 6-2
Final: Taylor beat Higgins 10-7

**1987** (*Matchroom*)
First round: D. Sheehan beat J. McLaughlin 5-4; P. Browne beat Jack Rea 5-3; T. Kearney beat T. Murphy 5-1; J. O'Boye beat B. Kelly 5-0; P. Burke beat P. Fagan 5-3; E. Hughes beat P. Watchorn 5-2
Quarter-finals: Dennis Taylor beat Sheehan 6-3; Hughes beat Kearney 6-1; Browne beat Burke 6-2; O'Boye *wo* Higgins *scr*
Semi-finals: Taylor beat Browne 6-1; O'Boye beat Hughes 6-3
Final: Taylor beat O'Boye 9-2

**1988**
First round: A. Kearney beat P. Fagan 5-3; T. Murphy beat B. Kelly 5-1; P. Browne beat Jack Rea 5-0; P. Watchorn beat E. Hughes 5-2; J. McLaughlin beat P. Burke 5-3; J. O'Boye beat D. Sheehan 5-0
Quarter-finals: Dennis Taylor beat Kearney 6-3; Browne beat Murphy 6-5; McLaughlin beat Watchorn 6-5; O'Boye beat A. Higgins 6-4
Semi-finals: Taylor beat Browne 6-5; McLaughlin beat O'Boye 6-4
Final: McLaughlin beat Taylor 9-4

**1989**
First round: Jack Rea *wo* P. Fagan *scr*; P. Browne beat D. Sheehan 5-2; A. Kearney beat B. Kelly 5-2; P. Watchorn beat B. Burke 5-4
Quarter-finals: J. McLaughlin beat Rea 5-0; Browne beat T. Murphy 5-3; E. Hughes beat Kearney 5-1; A. Higgins beat Watchorn 5-2

**Semi-finals:** McLaughlin beat Browne 6-3; Higgins beat Hughes 6-2
**Final:** Higgins beat McLaughlin 9-7

# SCOTTISH CHAMPIONSHIP

## 1980
**Challenge:** E. Sinclair beat C. Ross 11-6

## 1981
**First round:** M. Gibson beat B. Demarco 5-3; J. Donnelly beat E. Sinclair 5-0;
E. McLaughlin beat C. Ross 5-3; I. Black beat M. Macleod 5-4
**Semi-finals:** Gibson beat Donnelly 6-4; Black beat E. McLaughlin 6-3
**Final:** Black beat Gibson 11-7

## 1982
**First round:** M. Macleod beat J. Donnelly 6-5
**Quarter-finals:** C. Ross beat B. Demarco 6-5; M. Gibson beat E. McLaughlin 6-3;
I. Black beat Macleod 6-0; E. Sinclair beat J. Phillips 6-3
**Semi-finals:** Black beat Ross 6-4; Sinclair beat Gibson 6-2
**Final:** Sinclair beat Black 11-7

## 1983
**First round:** J. Donnelly beat B. Demarco 6-4; I. Black beat E. McLaughlin 6-4;
M. Macleod beat M. Gibson 6-5
**Semi-finals:** E. Sinclair beat Donnelly 6-5; Macleod beat Black 6-2
**Final:** Macleod beat Sinclair 11-9

## 1985
**First round:** M. Macleod beat E. McLaughlin 6-4; M. Gibson beat I. Black 6-2; John Rea
beat J. Donnelly 6-2; E. Sinclair beat B. Demarco 6-3
**Semi-final:** Macleod beat Gibson 6-4; Sinclair beat John Rea 6-2
**Final:** Macleod beat Sinclair 10-2

## 1986 (*Canada Dry*)
**First round:** S. Hendry beat B. Demarco 6-1
**Quarter-finals:** Hendry beat M. Macleod 6-5; I. Black beat E. McLaughlin 6-4; John Rea
beat J. Donnelly 6-1; M.Gibson beat E. Sinclair 6-4
**Semi-finals:** Hendry beat Black 6-2; Gibson beat John Rea 6-0
**Final:** Hendry beat Gibson 10-5

## 1987
**First round:** S. Hendry beat B. Demarco 6-2; John Rea beat I. Black 6-1; E. Sinclair beat
M. Gibson 6-2; J. Donnelly beat M. Macleod 6-2
**Semi-finals:** Hendry beat Rea 6-0; Donnelly beat Sinclair 6-4
**Final:** Hendry beat Donnelly 10-7

## 1988 (*Swish*)
**First round:** B. Demarco beat E. McLaughlin 6-0
**Quarter-finals:** S. Hendry beat Demarco 6-0; M. Gibson beat I. Black 6-2; John Rea beat
E. Sinclair 6-5; M. Macleod beat J. Donnelly 6-5
**Semi-finals:** Hendry beat Gibson 6-1; Macleod beat Rea 6-5
**Final:** Hendry beat Macleod 10-4

## 1989
**First round:** M. Macleod beat E. McLaughlin 5-0; M. Gibson beat E. Sinclair 5-4; John
Rea beat I. Black 5-3; J. Donnelly beat B. Demarco 5-1
**Semi-finals:** Macleod beat Gibson 5-1; Rea beat Donnelly 5-1
**Final:** Rea beat Macleod 9-7

# WELSH CHAMPIONSHIP

**1977** (*William Hill*)
**Challenge:** R. Reardon beat D. Mountjoy 12-8

**1980** (*Woodpecker*)
**First round:** D. Mountjoy beat T. Griffiths 9-6; R. Reardon beat C. Wilson 9-3
**Final:** Mountjoy beat Reardon 9-6

**1981** (*Woodpecker*)
**Qualifying:** C. Wilson beat R. Andrewartha 6-5
**First round:** Wilson beat D. Mountjoy 9-6; R. Reardon beat T. Griffiths 9-6
**Final:** Reardon beat Wilson 9-6

**1982** (*Woodpecker*)
**First round:** C. Wilson beat M. Owen 6-0; T. Griffiths beat C. Roscoe 6-2; R. Reardon beat C. Everton 6-1; D. Mountjoy beat R. Andrewartha 6-3
**Semi-finals:** Griffiths beat Wilson 9-6; Mountjoy beat Reardon 9-7
**Final:** Mountjoy beat Griffiths 9-8

**1983** (*Woodpecker*)
**First round:** T. Griffiths beat C. Everton 6-1; R. Reardon beat R. Andrewartha 6-2; C. Wilson beat C. Roscoe 6-4; D. Mountjoy beat M. Owen 6-0
**Semi-finals:** Reardon beat Griffiths 9-4; Mountjoy beat Wilson 9-3
**Final:** Reardon beat Mountjoy 9-1

**1984** (*Strongbow*)
**First round:** D. Mountjoy beat C. Everton 6-1; T. Griffiths beat R. Andrewartha 6-1; R. Reardon beat M. Owen 6-1; C. Wilson beat C. Roscoe 6-2
**Semi-finals:** Mountjoy beat Griffiths 9-5; Wilson beat Reardon 9-4
**Final:** Mountjoy beat Wilson 9-3

**1985** (*BCE*)
**First round:** S. Newbury beat W. Jones 6-2; T. Chappel beat M. Owen 6-0
**Quarter finals:** R. Reardon beat C. Everton 6-2; D. Mountjoy beat Newbury 6-5; C. Wilson beat C. Roscoe 6-3; T. Griffiths beat Chappel 6-0
**Semi-finals:** Griffiths beat Reardon 9-3; Mountjoy beat Wilson 9-2
**Final:** Griffiths beat Mountjoy 9-4

**1986** (*Zetters*)
**First round:** T. Chappel *wo* M. Owen *scr*; W. Jones beat C. Everton 6-2
**Quarter-finals:** T. Griffiths beat Chappel 6-4; C. Wilson beat S. Newbury 6-4; D. Mountjoy beat C. Roscoe 6-4; W. Jones beat Reardon 6-4
**Semi-finals:** Griffiths beat Wilson 9-1; Mountjoy beat W. Jones 9-7
**Final:** Griffiths beat Mountjoy 9-3

**1987** (*Matchroom*)
**First round:** W. Jones beat M. Bennett 6-3; C. Roscoe beat C. Everton 6-2
**Quarter-finals:** T. Griffiths beat Jones 6-2; S. Newbury beat C. Wilson 6-2; T. Chappel beat R. Reardon 6-4; D. Mountjoy beat Roscoe 6-2
**Semi-finals:** Newbury beat Griffiths 9-6; Mountjoy beat Chappel 9-2
**Final:** Mountjoy beat Newbury 9-7

**1988** (*Senator*)
**First round:** M. Bennett beat C. Everton 6-0; T. Chappel beat C. Roscoe 6-4
**Quarter-finals:** D. Mountjoy beat Bennett 6-3; W. Jones beat R. Reardon 6-5; C. Wilson beat S. Newbury 6-3; T. Griffiths beat Chappel 6-4

**Semi-finals:** Jones beat Mountjoy 9-5; Griffiths beat Wilson 9-7
**Final:** Griffiths beat Jones 9-3

**1989** (*Senator*)
**First round:** D. Morgan beat T. Chappel 6-5; M. Bennett beat C. Roscoe 6-3
**Quarter-finals:** T. Griffiths beat Morgan 6-5; S. Newbury beat W. Jones 6-5;
D. Mountjoy beat R. Reardon 6-3; Bennett beat C. Wilson 6-1
**Semi-finals:** Griffiths beat Newbury 9-7; Mountjoy beat Bennett 9-5
**Final:** Mountjoy beat Griffiths 9-6

# AUSTRALIAN CHAMPIONSHIP

## 1985
**First round:** G. Wilkinson beat G. Jenkins 6-2; G. Robinson beat J. Charlton* 6-0;
L. Condo beat E. Charlton* 6-2
**Second round:** Wilkinson beat L. Heywood 7-3; R. Foldvari beat Robinson 7-2;
J. Giannaros beat Condo 7-2; I. Anderson *wo* G. Ganim *scr*
**Quarter-finals:** E. Charlton beat Wilkinson 8-2; P. Morgan beat Giannaros 8-4; W. King
beat Anderson 8-2; J. Campbell beat Foldvari 8-5
**Semi-finals:** Charlton beat Morgan 9-3; Campbell beat King 9-6
**Final:** Campbell beat Charlton 10-7

## 1986
**First-round:** G. Jenkins beat G. Ganim** 6-2; L. Condo** beat E. Charlton Jr* 6-0;
J. Charlton* beat G. Robinson* 6-4
**Second round:** Condo beat J. Giannaros 6-4; I. Anderson beat J. Charlton 6-2;
G. Wilkinson beat L. Heywood 6-0; R. Foldvari beat Jenkins 6-3
**Quarter-finals:** J. Campbell beat Wilkinson 6-1; Foldvari beat P. Morgan 6-2; W. King
beat Condo 6-3; E. Charlton beat Anderson 6-2
**Semi-finals:** Campbell beat Foldvari 8-3; King beat Charlton 8-6
**Final:** King beat Campbell 10-3

## 1987
**Qualifying round:** S. Frangie* beat W. Potasnyk* 6-4
**First round:** G. Jenkins beat L. Condo** 6-1; I. Anderson beat L. Heywood* 6-4;
G. Wilkinson beat J. Charlton* 6-0; Frangie beat P. Morgan** 6-5
**Quarter-finals:** W. King beat Jenkins 6-4; R. Foldvari beat Frangie 6-2; E. Charlton beat
Anderson 6-2; J. Campbell beat Wilkinson 6-4
**Semi-finals:** King beat Foldvari 8-1; Charlton beat Campbell 8-6
**Final:** King beat Charlton 10-7

## 1988
**Qualifying round:** W. Potasznyk* beat Edward Charlton* 5-1
**Second round:** S. Frangie* beat L. Condo** 5-2; G. Jenkins beat P. Morgan** 5-3;
I. Anderson beat J. Giannaros** 5-2; Potasznyk beat Glen Wilkinson 5-3
**Quarter-finals:** Eddie Charlton beat Jenkins 5-0; W. King beat Frangie 5-4; R. Foldvari
beat Potasznyk 5-3; J. Campbell beat Anderson 5-0
**Semi-finals:** Foldvari beat King 8-4; Campbell beat Charlton 8-6
**Final:** Campbell beat Foldvari 9-7

\* Member of Australian Professional Association only
\*\* Non-tournament playing member of WPBSA

# CANADIAN CHAMPIONSHIP

## 1983
**First round:** G. Rigitano beat M. Gauvreau 9-6; R. Chaperon beat G. Watson 9-5;
J. Caggianello beat W. Sanderson 9-5

**Second round:** B. Mikkelsen beat Rigitano 9-4; F. Jonik beat Chaperon 9-4; Jim Bear beat M. Morra 9-8; Caggianello beat P. Thornley 9-7
**Quarter-finals:** C. Thorburn beat Mikkelsen 9-2; Jonik beat J. Wych 9-5; Jim Bear beat John Bear 9-5; K. Stevens beat Caggianello 9-0
**Semi-finals:** Jonik beat Thorburn 9-6; Stevens beat Jim Bear 9-8
**Final:** Stevens beat Jonik 9-8

### 1985
**First round:** J. Caggianello beat Jim Bear 5-4; R. Chaperon beat P. Thornley 5-1; B. Mikkelsen beat G. Watson 5-3; John Bear beat M. Morra 5-4; J. Wych beat W. Sanderson 5-2
**Quarter-finals:** Chaperon beat K. Stevens 6-4; F. Jonik beat Mikkelsen 6-4; C. Thorburn beat Caggianello 6-2; Wych beat John Bear 6-3
**Semi-finals:** Chaperon beat Jonik 6-3; Thorburn beat Wych 6-5
**Final:** Thorburn beat Chaperon 6-4

### 1986
**First round:** G. Watson beat J. Caggianello 6-1; F. Jonik beat G. Rigitano 6-1; R. Chaperon beat J. Bear 6-3; B. Mikkelsen beat W. Sanderson 6-1; P. Thornley beat M. Morra 6-4
**Second round:** C. Thorburn beat Watson 6-1; Jonik beat Chaperon 6-3; J. Wych beat Mikkelsen 6-3; K. Stevens beat Thornley 6-2
**Semi-finals:** Thorburn beat Jonik 6-3; Wych beat Stevens 6-2
**Final:** Thorburn beat Wych 6-2

### 1987 (*BCE*)
**First round:** G. Watson beat P. Thornley 6-4; F. Jonik beat W. Sanderson 6-0; M. Morra beat R. Chaperon 6-5; J. Wych beat G. Rigitano 6-4; Jim Bear beat B. Mikkelsen 6-0; J. Caggianello beat M. Gauvreau 6-3
**Quarter-finals:** Morra beat Jonik 6-2; C. Thorburn beat Watson 6-3; Bear beat Wych 6-4; K. Stevens beat Caggianello 6-0
**Semi-finals:** Bear beat Stevens 7-2; Thorburn beat Morra 7-4
**Final:** Thorburn beat Bear 8-4

### 1988 (*BCE*)
**First round:** F. Jonik *wo* G. Rigitano *scr*; M. Morra beat G. Watson 6-2; J. Wych beat P. Thornley 6-5; A. Robidoux beat R. Chaperon 6-3; J. Caggianello beat Jim Bear 6-3; B. Mikkelsen beat M. Gauvreau 6-2
**Quarter-finals:** C. Thorburn beat Jonik 6-4; Wych beat Morra 6-4; Robidoux beat Caggianello 6-4; Mikkelsen beat K. Stevens 6-5
**Semi-finals:** Wych beat Thorburn 7-5; Robidoux beat Mikkelsen 7-3
**Final:** Robidoux beat Wych 8-4

# SOUTH AFRICAN CHAMPIONSHIP

### 1986
**First round:** P. Francisco beat V. Blignaut* 6-3; D. Mienie beat M. Hines 6-5; F. Ellis beat R. Amdor* 6-2
**Second round:** S. Francisco beat G. Johnston* 7-0; P. Francisco beat R. Grace 7-1; J. Van Rensberg beat Mienie 7-1; Ellis beat P. Mans 7-6
**Semi-finals:** S. Francisco beat P. Francisco 8-3; Ellis beat Van Rensberg 8-2
**Final:** S. Francisco beat Ellis 9-1

### 1987
**Semi-finals:** F. Ellis beat R. Grace 9-8; J. Van Rensberg beat P. Mans* 9-4
**Final:** Ellis beat Van Rensberg 9-4

* Member of the South African Professional Association but not the WPBSA

# PROFESSIONAL BILLIARDS

## THE WORLD PROFESSIONAL BILLIARDS CHAMPIONSHIP

Founded in 1870, the World Professional Billiards Championship is the oldest of all the game's events but since snooker has become by far the most popular of the billiard table games it has declined steadily in public appeal.

The problems started in the 1930s when the four best players in the world, Walter Lindrum, Joe Davis, Tom Newman and Clark McConachy, mastered all aspects of the game so completely that they effectively killed it as a public entertainment. They did such a thorough job that there was only one Championship between 1934 and 1968 that they did not claim – when Rex Williams travelled to New Zealand and beat McConachy, then 73 and suffering from Parkinson's disease.

Williams successfully defended the title three times against various challengers but lost it in June 1980 to Joe's younger brother Fred, who thus became only the second player to have held world titles at both billiards and snooker – the first, of course, was Joe.

In November 1980, the event reverted to a tournament format and a variety of playing systems was tried: time-limit games, points-up games and, for the first time last season, the best of five games of 400-up. This formula gave frequent climaxes, as in frames of snooker, and also eliminated the possibility of very large breaks.

1985 also saw Channel 4 attempt a 'Pot Black'-style billiards event, the Blue Arrow Masters. Viewing figures for this were encouraging and the BBC agreed to televise the final of the 1986 World Professional Championship which was again played over the best of five games of 400-up.

In 1987, from the Albert Hall, Bolton, both the semi-finals and final were televised. Norman Dagley, who had earlier in the season won the UK Championship, added the professional title to his two world amateur victories by beating Robby Foldvari 3-1 in the final.

For the 1987–88 season, the format of the World and UK Championships was altered to the best of seven games (except for finals) of 150-up.

This format was also adopted for two new events, the European Championship and Yorkshire Bank Open. Dagley retained the 1988 world title at Bolton and the 1989 Championship was due to be promoted in Australia in July 1989.

## World Professional Billiards Championship (1870–1920)

| | | | |
|---|---|---|---|
| 1870 (Feb) | W. Cook | J. Roberts Sr | 1,200-1,083 |
| (Apr) | J. Roberts Jr | W. Cook | 1,000- 522 |
| (June) | J. Roberts Jr | A. Bowles | 1,000- 759 |
| (Nov) | J. Bennett | J. Roberts Jr | 1,000- 905 |
| 1871 (Jan) | J. Roberts Jr | J. Bennett | 1,000- 637 |
| (May) | W. Cook | J. Roberts Jr | 1,000- 985 |
| (Nov) | W. Cook | J. Bennett | 1,000- 942 |
| 1872 (Mar) | W. Cook | J. Roberts Jr | 1,000- 799 |
| 1874 (Feb) | W. Cook | J. Roberts Jr | 1,000- 784 |
| 1875 (May) | J. Roberts Jr | W. Cook | 1,000- 837 |
| (Dec) | J. Roberts Jr | W. Cook | 1,000- 865 |
| 1877 (May) | J. Roberts Jr | W. Cook | 1,000- 779 |
| 1880 (Nov) | J. Bennett | W. Cook | 1,000- 949 |
| 1881 (Jan) | J. Bennett | T. Taylor | 1,000- 910 |
| 1885 (Apr) | J. Roberts Jr | W. Cook | 3,000-2,908 |
| (June) | J. Roberts Jr | J. Bennett | 3,000-1,360 |
| 1899 | C. Dawson | J. North | 9,000-4,715 |
| 1900 | C. Dawson | H. W. Stevenson | 9,000-6,775 |
| 1901 | H. W. Stevenson | C. Dawson | 9,000-6,406 |
| | C. Dawson | H. W. Stevenson | 9,000-5,796 |
| | H. W. Stevenson (declared champion – no contest) | | |
| 1903 | C. Dawson | H. W. Stevenson | 9,000-8,700 |
| 1908 | M. Inman (declared champion – no contest) | | |
| 1909 | M. Inman | A. Williams | 9,000-7,662 |
| Under Billiards Control Club Rules | | | |
| 1909 | H. W. Stevenson (declared champion – no contest) | | |
| 1910 | H. W. Stevenson | M. Inman | 13,370-13,212 |
| | | (match abandoned) | |
| | H. W. Stevenson | M. Inman | 18,000-16,907 |
| 1911 | H. W. Stevenson | M. Inman | 18,000-16,914 |
| 1912 | M. Inman | T. Reece | 18,000- 9,675 |
| 1913 | M. Inman | T. Reece | 18,000-16,627 |
| 1914 | M. Inman | T. Reece | 18,000-12,826 |
| 1919 | M. Inman | H. W. Stevenson | 16,000- 9,468 |
| 1920 | W. Smith | C. Falkiner | 16,000-14,500 |

## World Professional Billiards Championship (1921–88)

### 1921

**First round:** C. Falkiner beat H. W. Stevenson 7,334-5,084; T. Newman beat T. Tothill 8,000-3,267

**Semi-finals:** Newman beat Falkiner 8,000-6,627; T. Reece beat F. Lawrence *nr*

**Final:** Newman beat Reece 16,000-10,744

## 1922
First round: T. Reece beat M. McConachy 8,000-6,767
Semi-finals: T. Newman beat J. Davis 8,000-5,181; C. Falkiner beat Reece 8,000-7,289
Final: Newman beat Falkiner 16,000-15,167

## 1923
First round: M. Inman beat A. Peall 16,000-11,758; C. Falkiner beat T. Reece 16,000-14,952
Semi-finals: T. Newman beat Inman 16,000-14,506; W. Smith beat Falkiner 16,000-8,695
Final: Smith beat Newman 16,000-15,180

## 1924
First round: T. Newman beat C. McConachy 16,000-8,703
Final: Newman beat T. Reece 16,000-14,845

## 1925
T. Newman beat T. Reece 16,000-10,092

## 1926
T. Newman beat J. Davis 16,000-9,505

## 1927
First round: M. Inman beat T. Reece 8,000-5,527
Second round: J. Davis beat Inman 8,000-6,895
Challenge round: T. Newman beat Davis 16,000-14,763

## 1928
First round: T. Carpenter beat T. Reece 8,000-7,283
Second round: J. Davis beat Carpenter 8,000-5,602
Challenge round: Davis beat T. Newman 16,000-14,874

## 1929
First round: T. Newman beat T. Carpenter 8,000-5,984
Final: J. Davis beat Newman 18,000-17,219

## 1930
First round: T. Newman beat M. Inman 24,001-10,104; J. Davis beat C. Falkiner 21,975-19,815
Final: Davis beat Newman 20,918-20,117

## 1932
First round: J. Davis beat C. McConachy 25,161-19,259

## 1933
First round: W. Lindrum beat T. Newman 21,470-20,252
Final: Lindrum beat Davis 21,815-21,121

## 1934
First round: W. Lindrum beat C. McConachy 21,903-20,795
Final: Lindrum beat J. Davis 23,533-22,678

## 1951
C. McConachy beat J. Barrie 6,681-5,057

## 1968
R. Williams beat C. McConachy 5,499-5,234

**1971**
R. Williams beat B. Bennett 9,250-4,058

**1973**
R. Williams beat J. Karnehm 8,360-4,336

**1974**
R. Williams beat E. Charlton 7,017-4,916

**1976**
R. Williams beat E. Charlton 9,105-5,149

**1980** (*May*)
F. Davis beat R. Williams 5,978-4,452

**1980** (*Nov*)
Qualifying: P. Morgan beat J. Dunning 1,655-1,107; M. Wildman beat B. Bennett 1,968-678;
S. Davis beat K. Kennerley 1,809-965
Quarter-finals: J. Barrie beat S. Davis 2,186-870; F. Davis beat Morgan 1,907-978;
R. Edmonds beat J. Karnehm 1,513-1,306; Wildman beat R. Williams 1,476-1,415
Semi-finals: F. Davis beat Barrie 1,253-1,153; Wildman beat Edmonds 1,629-955
Final: F. Davis beat Wildman 3,037-2,064

**1982**
First round: C. Everton beat B. Bennett 1,500-556
Quarter-finals: F. Davis beat Everton 1,500-652; R. Williams beat J. Karnehm 1,500-569;
R. Edmonds beat K. Kennerley 1,500-753; M. Wildman beat J. Fitzmaurice 1,500-721
Semi-finals: Williams beat Davis 1,500-1,494; Wildman beat Edmonds 1,500-765
Final: Williams beat Wildman 3,000-1,785

**1983**
Qualifying: I. Williamson beat D. Martin 1,000-710; B. Bennett beat G. Cripsey 1,000-683
First round: J. Karnehm beat M. Darrington 1,500-1,199; Bennett beat J. Fitzmaurice
1,500-1,396; C. Everton beat Williamson 1,500-1,085; E. Charlton beat T. Murphy
1,500-1,105
Quarter-finals: R. Williams beat Bennett 1,500-443; F. Davis beat Everton 1,500-477;
R. Edmonds beat Karnehm 1,500-1,075; Charlton beat M. Wildman 1,500-778
Semi-finals: Davis beat Charlton 1,500-956; Williams beat Edmonds 1,500-671
Final: Williams beat Davis 1,500-605

**1984**
Qualifying: T. Murphy beat M. Darrington 1,021-861
First round: P. Morgan beat B. Bennett 1,021-639; I. Williamson beat C. Everton 746-496;
J. Karnehm beat G. Ganim jnr 1,270-733; Murphy beat J. Fitzmaurice 1,050-868
Quarter-finals: F. Davis beat Murphy 1,242-852; E. Charlton beat Karnehm 944-931;
Williamson beat R. Edmonds 918-805; M. Wildman beat Morgan 1,347-759
Semi-finals: Charlton beat Davis 1,436-829; Wildman beat Williamson 1,501-849
Final: Wildman beat Charlton 1,045-1,012

**1985**
First round: P. Francisco beat M. Darrington 3-0; I. Williamson beat B. Bennett 3-0;
J. Karnehm beat E. Charlton 3-0; R. Edmonds beat A. Higgins 3-0; M. Wildman beat
T. Jones 3-0; N. Dagley beat J. Fitzmaurice 3-0; R. Foldvari *wo* B. Oliver *scr*; F. Davis
beat C. Everton 3-1

**Quarter-finals:** Dagley beat Karnehm 3-0; Foldvari beat Davis 3-0; Wildman beat Francisco 3-0; Edmonds beat Williamson 3-1
**Semi-finals:** Edmonds beat Wildman 3-0; Dagley beat Foldvari 3-0
**Final:** Edmonds beat Dagley 3-1

## 1986

**Qualifying:** R. Close beat E. Hughes 3-1; G. Scott beat B. Oliver 3-0
**First round:** E. Charlton beat T. Jones 3-0; I. Williamson beat Scott 3-0; R. Foldvari beat J. Fitzmaurice 3-0; N. Dagley beat B. Bennett 3-0; Close beat F. Davis 3-0; P. Francisco beat C. Everton 3-0; M. Wildman beat G. Thompson 3-0
**Quarter-finals:** Edmonds beat Francisco 3-0; Dagley beat Charlton 3-0; Foldvari beat Close 3-0; Wildman beat Williamson 3-2
**Semi-finals:** Dagley beat Edmonds 3-1; Foldvari beat Wildman 3-1
**Final:** Foldvari beat Dagley 3-1

## 1987

**First round:** G. Thompson beat J. Fitzmaurice 2-0; G. Miles *wo* L. Dielis *scr*; T. Jones *wo* R. Ceulemans *scr*; C. Everton beat H. Griffiths 2-1
**Second round:** R. Foldvari beat E. Hughes 3-0; F. Davis beat Thompson 3-0; P. Francisco beat Miles 3-0; R. Edmonds beat B. Bennett 3-0; N. Dagley beat R. Close 3-0; I. Williamson *wo* Jones *scr*; E. Charlton beat J. Karnehm 3-1; M. Wildman beat Everton 3-0
**Quarter-finals:** Foldvari beat Davis 3-1; Edmonds beat Francisco 3-0; Dagley beat Williamson 3-1; Wildman beat Charlton 3-1
**Semi-finals:** Foldvari beat Edmonds 3-1; Dagley beat Wildman 3-0
**Final:** Dagley beat Foldvari 3-1

## 1988

**Preliminary round:** H. Griffiths beat G. Cripsey 4-2; M. Ferreira beat J. Fitzmaurice 4-1; T. Murphy beat C. Everton 4-2; H. Nimmo beat G. Thompson 4-3; D. Heaton beat B. Bennett 4-2; E. Hughes *wo* G. Scott *scr*
**First round:** N. Dagley beat M. Russell 4-0; Griffiths beat J. Karnehm 4-2; I. Williamson beat R. Close 4-2; Ferreira beat M. Wildman 4-2; R. Edmonds beat Hughes 4-0; E. Charlton beat Murphy 4-1; Nimmo beat F. Davis 4-2; R. Foldvari beat Heaton 4-0
**Quarter-finals:** Dagley beat Griffiths 4-1; Williamson beat Ferreira 4-2; Charlton beat Edmonds 4-3; Foldvari beat Nimmo 4-2
**Semi-finals:** Dagley beat Williamson 4-1; Charlton beat Foldvari 4-1
**Final:** Dagley beat Charlton 7-4

# United Kingdom Professional Billiards Championship (1934-88)

## 1934

J. Davis beat T. Newman 18,745-18,301

## 1935

J. Davis beat T. Newman 21,733-19,919

## 1936

**First round:** W. Smith beat S. Lee 10,373-7,212
**Semi-finals:** T. Newman beat S. Smith 9,561-7,792; J. Davis beat W. Smith 10,965-9,566
**Final:** Davis beat Newman 21,710-19,790

## 1937
**First round:** S. Smith beat S. Lee 8,135-4,209
**Semi-finals:** T. Newman *wo* W. Smith *scr*; J. Davis beat S. Smith 12,046-8,516
**Final:** Davis beat Newman 22,601-18,321

## 1938
**Semi-finals:** T. Newman beat S. Smith 8,959-7,227; J. Davis beat S. Lee 15,238-6,048
**Final:** Davis beat Newman 20,933-19,542

## 1946
J. Barrie beat W. Leigh 8,972-6,782

## 1950
**First round:** J. Barrie beat S. Lee 7,645-5,593
**Semi-finals:** Barrie beat W. Smith 7,009-5,941; K. Kennerley *wo*
**Final:** Barrie beat Kennerley 9,046-5,069

## 1951
F. Davis beat K. Kennerley 8,120-6,011

## 1979 *(Super Crystalate)*
**Quarter-finals:** J. Karnehm beat J. Dunning 2,041-760; R. Williams beat R. Edmonds
1,537-1,350; J. Barrie beat S. Davis 2,292-629; F. Davis beat B. Bennett 1,953-679
**Semi-finals:** Williams beat Karnehm 1,539-1,182; Barrie beat F. Davis 1,548-1,031
**Final:** Williams beat Barrie 2,952-2,116

## 1980
**First round:** S. Davis beat S. Hood 1,670-1,029; B. Bennett beat C. Ross 1,093-933
**Quarter-finals:** J. Barrie beat M. Wildman 2,001-815; J. Karnehm beat Kennerley
1,990-842; R. Edmonds beat Bennett 1,380-914; R. Williams beat S. Davis 1,871-862
**Semi-finals:** Karnehm beat Barrie 1,755-1,085; Williams beat Edmonds 2,159-789
**Final:** Karnehm beat Williams 2,518-2,423

## 1981
**Qualifying:** S. Davis beat N. Bennett 980-770; R. Edmonds beat G. Miles 1,881-473;
J. Pulman beat K. Kennerley 1,078-879
**Quarter-finals:** J. Karnehm beat Edmonds 1,307-935; J. Barrie beat Pulman 1,743-509;
R. Williams beat S. Davis 1,575-579; F. Davis beat M. Wildman 1,304-805
**Semi-finals:** Karnehm beat Barrie 1,338-1,074; Williams beat F. Davis 2,003-999
**Final:** Williams beat Karnehm 1,592-1,112

## 1983
**First round:** B. Bennett beat D. Greaves 750-280; C. Everton beat M. Darrington 750-177;
I. Williamson beat T. Murphy 750-625; R. Edmonds beat J. Fitzmaurice 750-505
**Quarter-finals:** Edmonds beat J. Karnehm 1,500-1,194; M. Wildman beat Everton
1,500-1,170; F. Davis beat Williamson 1,500-604; R. Williams beat Bennett 1,500-230
**Semi-finals:** Wildman beat Williams 1,500-1,272; F. Davis beat Edmonds 1,500-936
**Final:** Wildman beat Davis 1,500-1,032

## 1987
**First round:** C. Everton beat J. Fitzmaurice 2-1; H. Griffiths beat G. Thompson 2-1;
B. Bennett beat D. Greaves 2-0

**Second round:** M. Wildman *wo* G. Miles *scr*; R. Close *wo* T. Jones *scr*; E. Hughes *wo*
P. Francisco *scr*; R. Edmonds beat M. Darrington 3-0; N. Dagley *wo* J. Karnehm *scr*;
I. Williamson beat Everton 3-1; F. Davis beat Griffiths 3-0; R. Foldvari beat Bennett 3-0
**Quarter-finals:** Wildman beat Close 3-1; Edmonds beat Hughes 3-2; Dagley beat
Williamson 3-1; Foldvari beat Davis 3-2
**Semi-finals:** Edmonds beat Wildman 3-0; Dagley beat Foldvari 3-2
**Final:** Dagley beat Edmonds 3-1

**1988** (*Strachan*) (*January*)
**Preliminary round:** C. Everton beat T. Murphy 4-2; M. Russell beat G. Scott 4-0;
G. Cripsey beat H. Griffiths 4-2; H. Nimmo beat B. Bennett 4-0
**First round:** N. Dagley beat Everton 4-1; I. Williamson beat E. Hughes 4-0; E. Charlton
beat G. Thompson 4-2; Russell beat M. Wildman 4-3; R. Close beat R. Edmonds 4-3;
F. Davis beat Cripsey 4-0; Nimmo beat J. Karnehm 4-2; R. Foldvari beat M. Ferreira
4-1
**Quarter-finals:** Williamson beat Dagley 4-2; Russell beat Charlton 4-2; Close beat Davis
4-0; Foldvari beat Nimmo 4-0
**Semi-finals:** Williamson beat Russell 4-2; Foldvari beat Close 4-1
**Final:** Williamson beat Foldvari 7-3

**1988** (*Strachan*) (*Nov*)
**Qualifying:** C. Everton beat J. Dunning 4-0; P. Gilchrist beat B. Bennett 4-0
**First round:** I. Williamson beat F. Davis 4-1; R. Close beat H. Griffiths 4-0; M. Ferreira
beat M. Wildman 4-2; Everton *wo* R. Edmonds *scr*; R. Foldvari beat G. Thompson 4-0;
M. Russell beat H. Nimmo 4-0; Gilchrist beat E. Charlton 4-1; N. Dagley beat
J. Karnehm 4-0
**Quarter-finals:** Close beat Williamson 4-0; Ferreira beat Everton 4-1; Russell beat
Foldvari 4-1; Dagley beat Gilchrist 4-3
**Semi-finals:** Close beat Ferreira 4-1; Russell beat Dagley 4-0
**Final:** Russell beat Close 7-0

# EUROPEAN BILLIARDS CHAMPIONSHIP

**1987**
**First round:** Robbie Foldvari (Australia) beat Clive Everton (Wales) 4-0; Mike Russell
(England) beat Bob Close (England) 4-2; Jack Karnehm (England) beat Howard
Griffiths (Wales) 4-1; Michael Ferreira (India) beat Ray Edmonds
(England) 4-3; Norman Dagley (England) beat Graham Cripsey (England) 4-0; Ian
Williamson (England) beat Eugene Hughes (Republic of Ireland) 4-3;
Eddie Charlton (Australia) beat Bernard Bennett (England) 4-0; Mark Wildman
(England) beat Geoff Thompson (England) 4-1
**Quarter-finals:** Foldvari beat Russell 4-1; Karnehm beat Ferreira 4-3; Dagley beat
Williamson 4-2; Wildman beat Charlton 4-1
**Semi-finals:** Foldvari beat Karnehm 4-2; Dagley beat Wildman 4-2
**Final:** Dagley beat Foldvari 7-5

**1988**
**Group A:** M. Ferreira beat H. Nimmo 4-0; N. Dagley beat B. Close 4-1; Close beat
Nimmo 4-1; Dagley beat Ferreira 4-1; Close beat Ferreira 4-1; Dagley beat Nimmo 4-1

**Group B:** I. Williamson beat C. Everton 4-0
**Group C:** G. Cripsey beat H. Griffiths 4-1; R. Edmonds beat Griffiths 4-0; Edmonds beat Cripsey 4-0
**Group D:** M. Russell beat G. Thompson 4-0; R. Foldvari beat J. Karnehm 4-2; Thompson beat Karnehm 4-2; Foldvari beat Russell 4-0; Russell beat Karnehm 4-0; Foldvari beat Thompson 4-1
**Semi-final Group A:** Close beat Williamson 4-3; Dagley beat Everton 4-3; Close beat Everton 4-1; Dagley beat Williamson 4-0; Dagley beat Close 4-2; Williamson beat Everton 4-0
**Semi-final Group B:** Foldvari beat Cripsey 4-0; Russell beat Edmonds 4-0; Edmonds beat Foldvari 4-3; Russell beat Cripsey 4-0; Edmonds beat Cripsey 4-0; Russell beat Foldvari 4-3
**Semi-finals:** Dagley beat Edmonds 4-1; Russell beat Close 4-3
**Final:** Russell beat Dagley 7-4

# YORKSHIRE BANK OPEN

**1988**
**Preliminary round:** H. Nimmo beat B. Bennett 4-0; H. Griffiths beat D. Heaton 4-0; C. Everton beat G. Cripsey 4-2; M. Russell *wo* G. Scott *scr*
**First round:** N. Dagley beat E. Hughes 4-1; R. Close beat F. Davis 4-3; Nimmo beat I. Williamson 4-3; M. Ferreira beat M. Wildman 4-3; R. Edmonds beat Griffiths 4-0; G. Thompson beat J. Karnehm 4-0; E. Charlton beat Everton 4-0; Russell beat R. Foldvari 4-2
**Quarter finals:** Dagley beat Close 4-1; Ferreira beat Nimmo 4-0; Edmonds beat Thompson 4-2; Russell beat Charlton 4-3
**Semi-finals:** Ferreira beat Dagley 4-2; Edmonds beat Russell 4-0
**Final:** Edmonds beat Ferreira 7-3

**1989**
**Qualifying:** T. Jones beat B. Bennett 4-1
**First round:** M. Russell beat H. Nimmo 4-0; I. Williamson beat H. Griffiths 4-0; N. Dagley beat M. Ferreira 4-1; P. Gilchrist beat R. Close 4-3; R. Foldvari beat J. Dunning 4-0; M. Wildman beat G. Thompson 4-0; R. Edmonds beat Jones 4-0; E. Charlton beat C. Everton 4-0
**Quarter-finals:** Gilchrist beat Edmonds 4-2; Williamson beat Wildman 4-1; Russell beat Foldvari 4-1; Dagley beat Charlton 4-1
**Semi-finals:** Williamson beat Gilchrist 4-2; Russell beat Dagley 4-1
**Final:** Russell beat Williamson 7-2

# BRITISH OPEN

*Two-and-a-half-hour matches except for final, five hours.*

**1989**
**Qualifying:** E. Hughes beat P. Burke 641-521; P. Gilchrist beat G. Thompson 784-495; J. Karnehm beat V. Potasnik 832-423; C. Everton beat J. Dunning 481-451; H. Griffiths *wo* T. Jones *scr*

**First round:** Gilchrist beat R. Edmonds 702-583; N. Dagley beat Hughes 756-541; Everton beat R. Foldvari 466-314; I. Williamson beat Griffiths 765-239; H. Nimmo beat M. Wildman 647-473; R. Close beat F. Davis 576-467; M. Russell beat Karnehm 888-726; M. Ferreira beat E. Charlton 716-461
**Quarter-finals:** Russell beat Williamson 709-549; Nimmo beat Everton 449-416; Gilchrist beat Ferreira 782-632; Close beat Dagley 622-561
**Semi-finals:** Gilchrist beat Nimmo 946-518; Russell beat Close 1,054-576
**Final:** Gilchrist beat Russell 1,489-974

# ROTHMANS WORLD MATCHPLAY CHAMPIONSHIP

**1989**
**Qualifying:** J. McLaughlin *wo* T. Jones *scr*
**First round:** N. Dagley beat H. Griffiths 4-0; J. Karnehm beat H. Nimmo 4-1; M. Wildman beat McLaughlin 4-1; M. Russell beat B. Bennett 4-0; I. Williamson beat C. Everton 4-1; R. Close beat J. Dunning 4-0; M. Ferreira beat P. Burke 4-0; R. Foldvari beat P. Gilchrist 4-0
**Quarter-finals:** Dagley beat Karnehm 4-0; Russell beat Wildman 4-1; Williamson beat Close 4-1; Ferreira beat Foldvari 4-1
**Semi-finals:** Russell beat Dagley 4-3; Williamson beat Ferreira 4-2
**Final:** Russell beat Williamson 6-1

*Mike Russell*

# BILLIARDS PROFESSIONALS

It was not until 1984 that Norman Dagley could envisage a financial return from professional billiards appropriate for him to relinquish an amateur career which brought him two world and fifteen English amateur titles. After twice losing in the final of the World Professional Billiards Championship, he won the event in 1987 to complete a unique set of titles: English Amateur, World Amateur, UK Professional (1987) and World Professional. In the 1986–87 season, in fact, he won all three professional billiards titles on offer – the World, UK and European Championships. In 1987–88 he retained the world title and did well enough in the UK, European and a new ranking event, the Yorkshire Bank Open, to retain top place in the world rankings. The season saw, though, initial professional titles for Ian Williamson (UK) and Mike Russell (European), the latter making the 18-year-old Tees-sider the youngest-ever winner of a professional billiards title. Ray Edmonds, the 1985 world champion, won the Yorkshire Bank Open.

In 1988-89, Russell emerged as the leading professional, winning the UK, Yorkshire Bank and Rothmans World Matchplay titles. His fellow Teessider Peter Gilchrist, in his first professional season, won the new British Open. The European Championship fell into abeyance. The World Professional Championship was rescheduled for Australia in July 1989.

## RANKING LIST

All snooker members of the WPBSA are entitled to play in the WPBSA's billiards events. The WPBSA also has a number of billiards-only members who are entitled to play only in billiards events. These are: Bob Close (England), Norman Dagley (England), Michael Ferreira (India), Peter Gilchrist (England), Howard Griffiths (Wales), Jack Karnehm (England), Hugh Nimmo (Scotland), Mike Russell (England) and Geoff Thompson (England).

*Ranking List for the 1988–89 season with the World Championship still to be added:*
1. Norman Dagley (29 pts); 2. Mike Russell (24); 3. Ian Williamson (18); 4. Robby Foldvari (17); 5. Ray Edmonds (13); 6. Bob Close (12); 7. Michael Ferreira (10); 8. Mark Wildman (8); 9. Peter Gilchrist (7); 10. Hugh Nimmo (5); 11. Eddie Charlton (5); 12. Clive Everton (3); 13. Jack Karnehm (3); 14. Fred Davis (3); 15. Howard Griffiths (1); 16. Geoff Thompson (1); 16. Graham Cripsey (1); 18. Peter Francisco (1); 19 Eugene Hughes (1).

# THE WOMEN'S GAME

Allison Fisher, 21, is by popular consent the finest female player snooker has seen, but in the last twelve months her dominance has become slightly less pronounced as her nearest rivals, stepping up their efforts to match her, have made substantial improvements, so much so that the women's No 1 has sustained a few defeats in minor events.

In the 1988 Women's World Championship at Pontins, Brixham, however, Fisher carried off the £3,500 first prize by beating Ann-Marie Farren, the 1987 champion, 6-1 in the final. This was the only frame she dropped in the entire event. Her 82 break was the highest of the championship and only two short of her own championship record.

Fisher, beaten by Stacey Hillyard in the 1987 semi-final, thus regained the title she had won for the first time in 1986. She and Hillyard each won one Women's World Amateur title before all distinctions between professionals and amateurs were abolished in the women's game.

With Fisher not defending the Women's UK title she had won for the two previous seasons, there was a new UK champion in Tessa Davidson, 19, a newcomer from Banbury, who also made the highest break of the tournament, 84.

Hillyard became the first woman to make a century in competition when, in January 1985, she made a break of 114 in the Bournemouth League. Fisher made a break of 103 in the final of the Billiards and Snooker Control Council's women's tournament in May 1987, the first century in an event confined to women. Kim Shaw made a 104 break in a women's tournament at Breaks, Coventry in 1988.

## WOMEN'S WORLD CHAMPIONSHIP

### 1986

**Last 16:** A. Fisher (England) beat L. Horsbrough (England) 3-0; G. Aplin (England) beat C. Walch (England) 3-1; M. Fisher (England) beat S. Newbury (Wales) 3-0; A. Jones (England) beat S. Martin (Australia) 3-0; S. Hillyard (England) beat J. Dowen (England) 3-1; S. LeMaich (Canada) beat A. Davies (Wales) 3-1; K. Shaw (England) beat S. Sinanan (England) 3-1; M. Tart (England) beat H. Isitt (Wales) 3-0
**Quarter-finals:** A. Fisher beat Aplin 4-0; Jones beat M. Fisher 4-1; LeMaich beat Hillyard 4-3; Shaw beat Tart 4-0
**Semi-finals:** A. Fisher beat Jones 4-1; LeMaich beat Shaw 4-3
**Final:** A. Fisher beat LeMaich 5-0

### 1987

**Last 16:** A-M. Farren (England) beat A. Davies (Wales) 3-1; A. Jones (England) beat L. Horsbrugh (England) 3-1; J. Banks (England) beat

M. O'Driscoll (Republic of Ireland) 3-2; M. Fisher (England) beat R. Clements (England) 3-1; S. Hillyard (England) beat J. Heyhurst (England) 3-1; G. Aplin (England) beat J. Dowen (England) 3-0; K. Leech (England) beat M. Tart (England) 3-0; A. Fisher (England) beat L. Gordon (England) 3-0
**Quarter-finals:** Farren beat Jones 4-1; M. Fisher beat Banks 4-1; Hillyard beat Aplin 4-1; A. Fisher beat Leech 4-0
**Semi-finals:** Farren beat M. Fisher 4-0; Hillyard beat A. Fisher 4-3
**Final:** Farren beat Hillyard 5-1

**1988**
**Last 16:** A-M. Farren (England) beat T. Davidson (England) 4-3; K. Corr (England) beat M. O'Driscoll (Rep. of Ireland) 4-3; L. Gordon (England) beat J. Bedford (England) 4-0; M. Fisher (England) beat M. Brown (England) 4-0; S. Hillyard (England) beat A. Ratcliffe (England) 4-1; L. Horsburgh (England) beat K. Shaw (England) 4-3; L. Jones (Denmark) beat C. Walch (England) 4-1; A. Fisher (England) beat R. Abbot (England) 4-0
**Quarter-finals:** Farren beat Corr 4-0; M. Fisher beat Gordon 4-2; Hillyard beat Horsburgh 4-3; A. Fisher beat Jones 4-0
**Semi-finals:** Farren beat M. Fisher 5-4; A. Fisher beat Hillyard 5-0
**Final:** A. Fisher beat Farren 6-1

# TUBORG WOMEN'S UK CHAMPIONSHIP

**1987**
**Quarter-finals:** A. Fisher (England) beat M. Tart (England) 4-0; A-M. Farren (England) beat S. Hillyard (England) 4-3; G. Aplin (England) beat K. Shaw (England) 4-1; M. Fisher (England) beat R. Clements (England) 4-1
**Semi-finals:** A. Fisher beat Farren 4-0; M. Fisher beat Aplin 4-0
**Finals:** A. Fisher beat M. Fisher 5-1

**1988**
**Quarter-finals:** A-M. Farren (England) beat C. Walch (England) 4-3; S. Hillyard (England) beat L. Gordon (England) 4-0; J. Dowen (England) beat M. Fisher (England) 4-3; A. Fisher (England) beat K. Corr (England) 4-0
**Semi-finals:** Hillyard beat Farren 4-1; A. Fisher beat Dowen 4-0
**Final:** A. Fisher beat Hillyard 5-2

**1989**
**Last 16:** S. Hillyard (England) beat S. Dick (Wales) 3-0; L. Horsburgh (England) beat L. Gordon (England) 3-0; K. Corr (England) beat J. Banks (England) 3-0; G. Aplin (England) beat M. O'Driscoll (Rep. of Ireland) 3-0; M. Fisher (England) beat G. Jones (England) 3-0; K. Shaw (England) beat J. Dowen (England) 3-0; T. Davidson (England) beat C. Walch (England) 3-0; A-M. Farren (England) beat R. Abbott (England) 3-2
**Quarter-finals:** Hillyard beat Horsburgh 4-0; Corr beat Aplin 4-2; Shaw beat Fisher 4-1; Davidson beat Farren 4-1
**Semi-finals:** Hillyard beat Corr 4-2; Davidson beat Shaw 4-1
**Final:** Davidson beat Hillyard 4-1

# THE AMATEUR
# GAME

## THE WORLD AMATEUR SNOOKER CHAMPIONSHIP

The English Amateur Billiards Championship is the oldest domestic amateur title. It was started in 1888 and was followed in 1916 by the English Amateur Snooker Championship. It was not until 1926 that the first World Amateur Billiards Championship, then called the British Empire Championship, was staged, and in 1963, the inaugural World Amateur Snooker Championship was held in Calcutta.

The two events then took place in alternate years until it was decided that from 1985 the snooker would become an annual event. For that first Championship in 1963 there were only five entries from four countries – England, Australia, India and Ceylon (now Sri Lanka). The 1987 Championship in Bangalore, India, attracted 47 players representing 26 countries – an indication of just how fast the game is developing all over the world.

Before India's Omprakesh Agrawal captured the title in Dublin, the event had been dominated by British players. Gary Owen (England) won it in 1963 and 1966 and another Englishman, David Taylor, in 1968. Jonathan Barron gave England their fourth title in 1970 and Ray Edmonds made it six in a row when he won both in 1972 and 1974.

Welshman Doug Mountjoy broke the stranglehold by taking the 1976 title and his fellow countryman Cliff Wilson won it in 1978 before England gave the Championship its youngest ever titleholder when Jimmy White won in 1980 at the age of 18. The title went back to Wales with Terry Parsons in 1982 and Parsons again reached the final in 1984 only to lose to Agrawal.

Each country affiliated to the International Billiards and Snooker Federation is entitled to send two competitors who are initially split into round robin groups with the quarter-finals onwards being knockout.

The biggest innovation in amateur snooker came in 1972 when the then world governing body, the Billiards and Snooker Control Council (now effectively the English body), lifted all restrictions on amateurs accepting prize-money or fees for exhibitions. This brought about a new breed of full-time amateur players who capitalise fully on a variety of privately organised tournaments which carry thousands of pounds in prize-money.

However, the money available in the 'amateur' game pales into insignificance when compared to the prosperity at the top of the professional game. Consequently, there is a high turnover of top amateurs who, as soon as they become eligible, join the professional ranks.

## World Amateur Snooker Championships

|  | Wins | For | Agst |
|---|---|---|---|
| **1963** (*Calcutta*) | | | |
| G. Owen (England) | 4 | 23 | 7 |
| F. Harris (Australia) | 3 | 21 | 17 |
| M. J. M. Lafir (Ceylon) | 2 | 19 | 18 |
| T. Monteiro (India) | 1 | 14 | 19 |
| W. Jones (India) | 0 | 7 | 24 |
| **1966** (*Karachi*) | | | |
| G. Owen (England) | 5 | 30 | 7 |
| J. Spencer (England) | 4 | 26 | 14 |
| W. Barrie (Australia) | 3 | 23 | 22 |
| M. J. M. Lafir (Ceylon) | 2 | 22 | 20 |
| L. U. Demarco (Scotland) | 1 | 14 | 28 |
| H. Karim (Pakistan) | 0 | 6 | 30 |
| **1968** (*Sydney*) | | | |
| *Group A* | | | |
| David Taylor (England) | 4 | 24 | 13 |
| J. Van Rensberg (S. Africa) | 3 | 22 | 14 |
| H. Andrews (Australia) | 2 | 17 | 16 |
| T. Monteiro (India) | 1 | 17 | 22 |
| L. Napper (N. Zealand) | 0 | 9 | 24 |
| *Group B* | | | |
| M. Williams (Australia) | 3 | 22 | 14 |
| P. Morgan (Ireland) | 3 | 19 | 14 |
| M. J. M. Lafir (Ceylon) | 2 | 19 | 16 |
| S. Shroff (India) | 2 | 20 | 19 |
| R. Flutey (N. Zealand) | 0 | 7 | 24 |

*Play-offs*
*Semi-finals*: Williams beat Van Rensberg 8-7; David Taylor beat Morgan 8-3
*Final*: David Taylor beat Williams 8-7

| **1970** (*Edinburgh*) | | | |
|---|---|---|---|
| *Group A* | | | |
| S. Hood (England) | 5 | 20 | 9 |
| P. Mifsud (Malta) | 4 | 22 | 11 |
| M. J. M. Lafir (Sri Lanka) | 4 | 20 | 16 |
| J. Phillips (Scotland) | 4 | 19 | 18 |
| D. Sneddon (Scotland) | 2 | 17 | 17 |
| L. Glozier (N. Zealand) | 2 | 10 | 21 |
| J. Clint (N. Ireland) | 0 | 8 | 24 |
| *Group B* | | | |
| J. Barron (England) | 5 | 21 | 13 |
| D. May (Wales) | 4 | 22 | 18 |
| S. Shroff (India) | 3 | 18 | 14 |
| E. Sinclair (Scotland) | 3 | 16 | 16 |
| J. Rogers (Ireland) | 3 | 16 | 19 |
| L. U. Demarco (Scotland) | 2 | 15 | 19 |

|  | Wins | For | Agst |
|---|---|---|---|
| H. Andrews (Australia) | 1 | 13 | 22 |

*Final*: Barron beat Hood 11-7

**1972** (*Cardiff*)

*Group A*

|  | Wins | For | Agst |
|---|---|---|---|
| J. Van Rensberg (S. Africa) | 3 | 12 | 6 |
| K. Tristram (N. Zealand) | 1 | 8 | 8 |
| G. Thomas (Wales) | 1 | 6 | 8 |
| L. U. Demarco (Scotland) | 1 | 6 | 10 |

*Group B*

|  | Wins | For | Agst |
|---|---|---|---|
| M. Francisco (S. Africa) | 3 | 15 | 5 |
| J. Barron (England) | 3 | 15 | 10 |
| A. Borg (Malta) | 2 | 12 | 11 |
| A. Lloyd (Wales) | 2 | 11 | 14 |
| T. Monteiro (India) | 0 | 3 | 16 |

*Group C*

|  | Wins | For | Agst |
|---|---|---|---|
| P. Mifsud (Malta) | 4 | 16 | 5 |
| R. Edmonds (England) | 3 | 14 | 7 |
| J. Rogers (Ireland) | 2 | 8 | 8 |
| M. Berni (Wales) | 1 | 7 | 12 |
| B. Bennett (N. Zealand) | 0 | 3 | 16 |

*Group D*

|  | Wins | For | Agst |
|---|---|---|---|
| A. Savur (India) | 2 | 10 | 6 |
| M. Williams (Australia) | 2 | 9 | 7 |
| D. Sneddon (Scotland) | 2 | 9 | 9 |
| D. May (Wales) | 0 | 6 | 12 |

*Semi-final groups*

*Group A*

|  | Wins | For | Agst |
|---|---|---|---|
| Barron | 3 | 12 | 4 |
| Savur | 2 | 10 | 8 |
| Tristram | 1 | 6 | 8 |
| Mifsud | 0 | 6 | 12 |

*Group B*

|  | Wins | For | Agst |
|---|---|---|---|
| M. Francisco | 2 | 11 | 9 |
| Edmonds | 2 | 11 | 9 |
| Van Rensberg | 1 | 8 | 10 |
| Williams | 1 | 9 | 11 |

*Semi-finals*: Edmonds beat Barron 8-6; M. Francisco beat Savur 8-7(51, 72)

*Final*: Edmonds beat M. Francisco 11-10

**1974** (*Dublin*)

*Group A*

|  | Wins | For | Agst |
|---|---|---|---|
| R. Edmonds (England) | 7 | 31 | 11 |
| M. J. M. Lafir (Sri Lanka) | 6 | 30 | 19 |
| E. Sinclair (Scotland) | 6 | 28 | 21 |
| G. Thomas (Wales) | 4 | 24 | 22 |
| D. Sheehan (Ireland) | 4 | 25 | 24 |
| P. Donnelly (N. Ireland) | 3 | 21 | 28 |
| S. Shroff (India) | 3 | 16 | 26 |
| N. Stockman (N. Zealand) | 2 | 18 | 29 |
| J. Sklazeski (Canada) | 1 | 18 | 31 |

|  | Wins | For | Agst |
|---|---|---|---|
| *Group B* | | | |
| A. Lloyd (Wales) | 8 | 32 | 14 |
| W. Hill (N. Zealand) | 5 | 26 | 21 |
| P. Burke (Ireland) | 4 | 26 | 20 |
| L. Condo (Australia) | 4 | 26 | 21 |
| A. Borg (Malta) | 4 | 27 | 23 |
| D. Sneddon (Scotland) | 4 | 23 | 21 |
| A. Savur (India) | 4 | 24 | 23 |
| R. Cowley (Isle of Man) | 3 | 16 | 27 |
| N. J. Rahim (Sri Lanka) | 0 | 2 | 32 |

*Quarter-finals*: Edmonds beat Condo 4(60)-3; Sinclair beat Hill 4-2; Burke beat Lafir 4-3; Thomas beat Lloyd 4-2
*Semi-finals*: Edmonds beat Sinclair 8(54)-4(79); Thomas beat Burke 8-2
*Final*: Edmonds beat Thomas 11-9

**1976** (*Johannesburg*)

|  | Wins | For | Agst |
|---|---|---|---|
| *Group A* | | | |
| D. Mountjoy (Wales) | 7 | 28 | 9 |
| J. Van Rensberg (S. Africa) | 5 | 24 | 16 |
| R. Edmonds (England) | 4 | 20 | 18 |
| N. Stockman (N. Zealand) | 4 | 21 | 19 |
| E. Sinclair (Scotland) | 4 | 21 | 21 |
| P. Burke (Ireland) | 2 | 17 | 25 |
| J. Van Niekerk (S. Africa) | 1 | 17 | 27 |
| P. Reynolds (Isle of Man) | 1 | 14 | 27 |
| *Group B* | | | |
| P. Mifsud (Malta) | 6 | 25 | 9 |
| S. Francisco (S. Africa) | 6 | 27 | 12 |
| T. Griffiths (Wales) | 5 | 23 | 14 |
| C. Ross (England) | 4 | 19 | 17 |
| R. Paquette (Canada) | 4 | 22 | 22 |
| E. Swaffield (N. Ireland) | 1 | 16 | 26 |
| L. Heywood (Australia) | 1 | 13 | 27 |
| L. Watson (Ireland) | 1 | 9 | 27 |
| *Group C* | | | |
| M. Francisco (S. Africa) | 6 | 27 | 12 |
| R. Atkins (Australia) | 6 | 25 | 12 |
| R. Andrewartha (England) | 5 | 25 | 14 |
| J. Clint (N. Ireland) | 4 | 17 | 18 |
| L. U. Demarco (Scotland) | 3 | 21 | 21 |
| B. Mikkelsen (Canada) | 3 | 19 | 22 |
| K. Tristram (N. Zealand) | 1 | 9 | 27 |
| R. Cowley (Isle of Man) | 0 | 11 | 28 |

*Elimination match*: Griffiths beat Andrewartha 4(51)-0
*Quarter-finals*: Mountjoy beat Atkins 5(80)-1; Van Rensberg beat Griffiths 5-3(52); S. Francisco beat M. Francisco 5-1; Mifsud beat Edmonds 5-1
*Semi-finals*: Mountjoy beat S. Francisco 8(51)-2; Mifsud beat Van Rensberg 8(50)-4
*Final*: Mountjoy beat Mifsud 11(62, 79)-1

|  | Wins | For | Agst |
|---|---|---|---|
| **1978** (*Malta*) | | | |
| *Group A* | | | |
| K. Burles (Australia) | 6 | 26 | 10 |
| P. Mifsud (Malta) | 6 | 26 | 10 |
| J. Johnson (England) | 5 | 23 | 9 |
| J. Donnelly (Scotland) | 5 | 20 | 13 |
| D. McVeigh (N. Ireland) | 2 | 15 | 20 |
| P. Reynolds (Isle of Man) | 2 | 10 | 22 |
| V. Cremona (Malta) | 2 | 9 | 25 |
| M. Mohideen (Sri Lanka) | 0 | 8 | 28 |
| *Group B* | | | |
| A. Lloyd (Wales) | 6 | 26 | 12 |
| K. Stevens (Canada) | 5 | 23 | 16 |
| J. Grech (Malta) | 4 | 23 | 16 |
| E. Hughes (Ireland) | 4 | 23 | 21 |
| M. J. M. Lafir (Sri Lanka) | 3 | 19 | 20 |
| D. Meredith (N. Zealand) | 3 | 18 | 20 |
| S. Shroff (India) | 2 | 14 | 23 |
| L. McCann (N. Ireland) | 1 | 10 | 27 |
| *Group C* | | | |
| C. Wilson (Wales) | 8 | 32 | 10 |
| R. Paquette (Canada) | 5 | 24 | 14 |
| D. Kwok (N. Zealand) | 5 | 23 | 20 |
| A. Savur (India) | 5 | 26 | 22 |
| I. Williamson (England) | 3 | 22 | 24 |
| R. Atkins (Australia) | 3 | 21 | 24 |
| R. Miller (Scotland) | 3 | 18 | 24 |
| A. Borg (Malta) | 2 | 15 | 27 |
| C. Cooper (Isle of Man) | 2 | 13 | 29 |

*Elimination match*: Grech beat Kwok 4-0
*Quarter-finals*: Burles beat Paquette 5-4; Stevens beat Mifsud 5-0; Johnson beat Lloyd 5(72)-0; Wilson beat Grech 5-4
*Semi-finals*: Johnson beat Burles 8(85)-4; Wilson beat Stevens 8(64)-2(81)
*Final*: Wilson beat Johnson 11(87)-5(66)

|  | Wins | For | Agst |
|---|---|---|---|
| **1980** (*Launceston*) | | | |
| *Group A* | | | |
| J. White (England) | 6 | 24 | 9 |
| A. Savur (India) | 4 | 20 | 11 |
| E. Hughes (Ireland) | 4 | 21 | 13 |
| J. Grech (Malta) | 3 | 19 | 18 |
| L. Adams (N. Zealand) | 3 | 15 | 18 |
| Loo Yap Long (Singapore) | 1 | 6 | 23 |
| R. Burke (N. Ireland) | 0 | 11 | 24 |
| *Group B* | | | |
| J. Giannaros (Australia) | 6 | 24 | 11 |
| S. Newbury (Wales) | 4 | 20 | 14 |
| R. Paquette (Canada) | 4 | 20 | 15 |
| D. Meredith (N. Zealand) | 4 | 20 | 16 |
| G. Parikh (India) | 2 | 17 | 18 |

|  | Wins | For | Agst |
|---|---|---|---|
| S. Clarke (N. Ireland) | 1 | 10 | 22 |
| Lau Weng Yew (Singapore) | 0 | 8 | 24 |
| J. Bonner (Australia) | 4 | 17 | 17 |
| W. King (Australia) | 3 | 19 | 15 |
| E. McLaughlin (Scotland) | 3 | 16 | 16 |
| J. O'Boye (England) | 1 | 14 | 21 |
| S. Padayachi (Fiji) | 0 | 2 | 24 |
| *Group D* | | | |
| A. Lloyd (Wales) | 6 | 24 | 4 |
| J. Campbell (Australia) | 5 | 22 | 8 |
| D. Sheehan (Ireland) | 4 | 17 | 14 |
| M. Gibson (Scotland) | 3 | 16 | 20 |
| H. Boteju (Sri Lanka) | 2 | 16 | 20 |
| P. Reynolds (Isle of Man) | 1 | 11 | 23 |
| W. Barrie (Australia) | 0 | 7 | 24 |

*Quarter-finals*: Savur beat Lloyd 5(54)-3; Atkins beat Giannaros 5(53)-3(82); Mifsud beat Campbell 5(63)-3; White beat Newbury 5(70)-4
*Semi-finals*: Atkins beat Savur 8-6; White beat Mifsud 8(100)-6(83)
*Final*: White beat Atkins 11(80, 101)-2(60)

**1982** (*Calgary*)
*Group A*

|  | Wins | For | Agst |
|---|---|---|---|
| J. Grech (Malta) | 6 | 28 | 13 |
| A. Kearney (Ireland) | 6 | 26 | 15 |
| D. O'Kane (N. Zealand) | 6 | 28 | 18 |
| B. McConnell (Canada) | 5 | 26 | 19 |
| P. Kippie (Scotland) | 5 | 23 | 16 |
| S. Habib (India) | 4 | 22 | 21 |
| V. Saengthong (Thailand) | 3 | 20 | 28 |
| Lui Yew Keong (Singapore) | 1 | 13 | 30 |
| J. A. Wahid (Sri Lanka) | 0 | 6 | 32 |
| *Group B* | | | |
| T. Parsons (Wales) | 7 | 31 | 7 |
| P. Browne (Ireland) | 7 | 31 | 12 |
| G. Kwok Kwan Shing (Hong Kong) | 7 | 28 | 12 |
| G. Parikh (India) | 5 | 27 | 21 |
| A. Thomson (Zimbabwe) | 4 | 17 | 23 |
| G. Kwok (N. Zealand) | 3 | 17 | 26 |
| H. Boteju (Sri Lanka) | 2 | 15 | 28 |
| W. Craig (Isle of Man) | 1 | 14 | 29 |
| T. Dada (Pakistan) | 0 | 10 | 32 |
| *Group C* | | | |
| J. Bear (Canada) | 7 | 30 | 12 |
| M. Bradley (England) | 7 | 30 | 12 |
| J. Jorgensen (Canada) | 6 | 25 | 17 |
| W. Mills (N. Ireland) | 5 | 26 | 17 |
| J. Giannaros (Australia) | 5 | 25 | 21 |
| P. Reynolds (Isle of Man) | 3 | 23 | 23 |
| Cheung Che-Ming (Hong Kong) | 2 | 17 | 25 |

|  | Wins | For | Agst |
|---|---|---|---|
| E. Amro (Egypt) | 1 | 11 | 31 |
| V. Yassa (Sudan) | 0 | 3 | 32 |

*Group D*

|  | Wins | For | Agst |
|---|---|---|---|
| W. Jones (Wales) | 6 | 27 | 13 |
| P. Mifsud (Malta) | 6 | 29 | 15 |
| W. King (Australia) | 6 | 29 | 17 |
| R. Chaperon (Canada) | 5 | 24 | 18 |
| D. Chalmers (England) | 5 | 25 | 24 |
| R. Lane (Scotland) | 3 | 23 | 23 |
| S. Pavis (N. Ireland) | 3 | 19 | 27 |
| Lau Weng Yew (Singapore) | 2 | 15 | 29 |
| S. Sherif (Egypt) | 0 | 7 | 32 |

*Quarter-finals*: W. Jones beat Kearney 5-1; Parsons beat Bradley 5(69, 54)-0; Grech beat Browne 5(55)-3; Bear beat Mifsud 5-2
*Semi-finals*: Parsons beat Jones 8(103, 87)-5(54); Bear beat Grech 8-7
*Final*: Parsons beat Bear 11(61, 58, 58)-8(57, 69)

**1984** (*Dublin*)

*Group A*

|  | Wins | For | Agst |
|---|---|---|---|
| A. Micallef (Malta) | 9 | 38 | 16 |
| T. Parsons (Wales) | 8 | 37 | 11 |
| P. Ennis (Ireland) | 8 | 34 | 28 |
| V. Saengthong (Thailand) | 7 | 34 | 19 |
| J. Sigurossonn (Iceland) | 6 | 29 | 29 |
| T. Finstad (Canada) | 4 | 28 | 28 |
| B. Bjorkman (Sweden) | 4 | 26 | 27 |
| A. Thomson (Zimbabwe) | 3 | 24 | 34 |
| D. Feeney (U.S.A.) | 3 | 21 | 35 |
| K. Sirisoma (Sri Lanka) | 3 | 16 | 33 |
| L. Talman (Belgium) | 0 | 11 | 40 |

*Group B*

|  | Wins | For | Agst |
|---|---|---|---|
| D. John (Wales) | 9 | 37 | 10 |
| T. Drago (Malta) | 8 | 35 | 15 |
| A. Robidou (Canada) | 8 | 36 | 20 |
| S. Simngam (Thailand) | 7 | 33 | 20 |
| J. Long (Ireland) | 6 | 30 | 24 |
| M. G. Jayaram (India) | 5 | 30 | 23 |
| A. Campbell (Australia) | 4 | 25 | 29 |
| J. McIntyre (N. Ireland) | 4 | 21 | 30 |
| R. Cowley (Isle of Man) | 3 | 20 | 30 |
| M. Sedupathi (Sri Lanka) | 1 | 6 | 36 |
| C. D'Avoine (Mauritius) | 0 | 3 | 40 |

*Group C*

|  | Wins | For | Agst |
|---|---|---|---|
| G. Wilkinson (Australia) | 8 | 30 | 13 |
| J. Wright (England) | 7 | 27 | 14 |
| H. Haenga (N. Zealand) | 7 | 26 | 14 |
| H. Bakahati (Egypt) | 6 | 26 | 21 |
| M. Colquitt (Isle of Man) | 5 | 24 | 20 |
| S. Hendry (Scotland) | 5 | 23 | 22 |
| T. Kollins (U.S.A.) | 3 | 16 | 27 |

| | Wins | For | Agst |
|---|---|---|---|
| K. Friopjofssonn (Iceland) | 3 | 15 | 28 |
| H. Thwaites (Belgium) | 1 | 3 | 32 |
| Lui Yew Keong (Singapore) | scr | | |
| *Group D* | | | |
| C. Archer (England) | 9 | 32 | 15 |
| O. Agrawal (India) | 7 | 33 | 16 |
| D. Kwok (N. Zealand) | 5 | 27 | 21 |
| G. Kwok Kwan Shing (Hong Kong) | 5 | 26 | 23 |
| H. Morgan (N. Ireland) | 5 | 27 | 27 |
| J. Selby (Wales) | 4 | 24 | 23 |
| L. Yew (Singapore) | 3 | 25 | 28 |
| G. Carnegie (Scotland) | 3 | 22 | 32 |
| M. Hallgren (Sweden) | 2 | 17 | 32 |
| M. Sadek (Egypt) | 2 | 15 | 31 |

*Quarter-finals*: Agrawal beat John 5-4; Wright beat A. Micallef 5(69, 70)-1; Archer beat Drago 5-4; Parsons beat Wilkinson 5(66)-2
*Semi-finals*: Agrawal beat Wright 8(75)-5; Parsons beat Archer 8(58, 78, 52)-3
*Final*: Agrawal beat Parsons 11(69, 74, 62, 54)-7

**1985** (*Blackpool*)
*Group A*

| | | | |
|---|---|---|---|
| P. Mifsud (Malta) | 8 | 37 | 16 |
| R. Marshall (England) | 7 | 33 | 21 |
| G. Lackenby (Australia) | 7 | 35 | 23 |
| S. Robertson (N. Zealand) | 7 | 33 | 24 |
| J. Long (Ireland) | 6 | 31 | 28 |
| A. Essam (Egypt) | 5 | 28 | 25 |
| K. Erwin (Ireland) | 5 | 28 | 27 |
| J. Allan (Scotland) | 5 | 27 | 29 |
| M. Lemoy (Belgium) | 3 | 22 | 35 |
| M. Hallgren (Sweden) | 2 | 23 | 32 |
| I. Adam (Mauritius) | 0 | 3 | 40 |

*Group B*

| | | | |
|---|---|---|---|
| J. McNellan (Scotland) | 10 | 40 | 11 |
| T. Whitthread (England) | 8 | 34 | 11 |
| T. Saelim (Thailand) | 8 | 37 | 18 |
| D. Kwok (N. Zealand) | 6 | 28 | 22 |
| S. Sawant (India) | 6 | 28 | 22 |
| L. K. Guan (Singapore) | 5 | 25 | 27 |
| T. Dada (Pakistan) | 4 | 27 | 27 |
| A. Thomson (Zimbabwe) | 3 | 20 | 31 |
| H. Boteju (Sri Lanka) | 3 | 17 | 32 |
| P. Reynolds (Isle of Man) | 2 | 18 | 35 |
| P. Rivet (Mauritius) | 0 | 2 | 40 |

*Group C*

| | | | |
|---|---|---|---|
| J. Grech (Malta) | 9 | 39 | 12 |
| D. John (Wales) | 8 | 37 | 14 |
| J. Bonner (Australia) | 8 | 35 | 20 |
| G. Kwok Kwan Shing (Hong Kong) | 7 | 35 | 22 |
| W. Pu-Ob-Orm (Thailand) | 6 | 29 | 23 |

|  | Wins | For | Agst |
|---|---|---|---|
| M. Sobala (Canada) | 5 | 29 | 27 |
| L. A. Bux (Pakistan) | 5 | 24 | 28 |
| H. Bakhaty (Egypt) | 3 | 23 | 31 |
| K. Sirisoma (Sri Lanka) | 2 | 14 | 33 |
| H. Ramj (Kenya) | 1 | 13 | 37 |
| A. Agustsson (Iceland) | 1 | 10 | 38 |
| *Group D* | | | |
| M. Bennett (Wales) | 11 | 40 | 16 |
| G. Sethi (India) | 9 | 34 | 15 |
| A. Robidoux (Canada) | 8 | 34 | 22 |
| G. Burns (Ireland) | 8 | 30 | 23 |
| J. Wright (England) | 6 | 25 | 19 |
| S. Pavis (N. Ireland) | 5 | 28 | 27 |
| B. Bjorkman (Sweden) | 5 | 26 | 30 |
| M. Colquitt (Isle of Man) | 5 | 25 | 30 |
| K. Fridthjofsson (Iceland) | 3 | 14 | 32 |
| L. Nazarali (Kenya) | 3 | 15 | 34 |
| D. Barron (Zimbabwe) | 3 | 22 | 35 |

*Quarter-finals*: Marshall beat McNellan 5(50)-1; John beat Bennett 5(44, 37)-2(30); Mifsud beat Whitthread 5(32, 39, 39)-2; Grech beat Sethi 5(42, 59, 50)-2(41, 30)
*Semi-finals*: John beat Marshall 8(37, 30, 40, 30, 46, 40, 32, 31)-4; Mifsud beat Grech 8(41, 58, 35)-4(56, 82, 40)
*Final*: Mifsud beat John 11(68, 32, 34, 59, 31, 39)-6(31, 47, 31, 48)

**1986** (*New Zealand*)
*Group A*

| G. Burns (Ireland) | 9 | 36 | 15 |
|---|---|---|---|
| J. Griffiths (Wales) | 7 | 29 | 20 |
| B. Lui (Singapore) | 6 | 26 | 21 |
| A. Harris (England) | 6 | 31 | 22 |
| N. Nopachorn (Thailand) | 6 | 30 | 22 |
| P. Hawkes (Australia) | 4 | 27 | 23 |
| M. Lannoye (Belgium) | 3 | 23 | 26 |
| B. Bjorkman (Sweden) | 2 | 15 | 30 |
| P. De Groot (N. Zealand) | 1 | 19 | 33 |
| A. Thomson (Zimbabwe) | 1 | 11 | 35 |

*Group B*

| K. Jones (Wales) | 7 | 29 | 9 |
|---|---|---|---|
| M. Colquitt (Isle of Man) | 6 | 24 | 12 |
| M. Haenga (N. Zealand) | 4 | 25 | 20 |
| L. Amir Bux (Pakistan) | 4 | 20 | 20 |
| G. Sethi (India) | 3 | 23 | 19 |
| C. Sewell (N. Ireland) | 3 | 20 | 19 |
| M. Raibin (Sri Lanka) | 1 | 10 | 24 |
| A. Verny (Mauritius) | 0 | 1 | 28 |

*Group C*

| G. Grennan (England) | 9 | 36 | 17 |
|---|---|---|---|
| S. Sawant (India) | 6 | 31 | 15 |
| J. Allan (Scotland) | 5 | 28 | 22 |
| W. Pu-Ob-Orm (Thailand) | 5 | 26 | 22 |

|  | Wins | For | Agst |
|---|---|---|---|
| K. Doherty (Rep. of Ireland) | 5 | 26 | 27 |
| R. Johansson (Sweden) | 4 | 23 | 27 |
| G. Natale (Canada) | 4 | 22 | 31 |
| G. Campbell (N. Ireland) | 3 | 23 | 31 |
| F. Chan (Hong Kong) | 2 | 23 | 33 |
| H. Bakhaty (Egypt) | 2 | 20 | 33 |
| *Group D* | | | |
| P. Mifsud (Malta) | 9 | 36 | 10 |
| B. Gollan (Canada) | 8 | 34 | 8 |
| G. Miller (Australia) | 6 | 29 | 17 |
| S. Leung (Hong Kong) | 5 | 25 | 19 |
| L. Weng Yew (Singapore) | 5 | 26 | 24 |
| T. Dada (Pakistan) | 3 | 20 | 28 |
| R. Young (N. Zealand) | 3 | 16 | 29 |
| L. Cameron (Scotland) | 2 | 15 | 29 |
| H. Boteju (Sri Lanka) | 2 | 14 | 34 |
| Y. Van Velthoven (Belgium) | 1 | 15 | 32 |

*Quarter-finals*: Grennan beat Griffiths 5(38, 91)-2(39, 88, 39, 48); Jones beat Gollan 5(64)-1; Burns beat Colquitt 5(60)-0; Mifsud beat Sawant 5(66, 81)-2

*Semi-finals*: Mifsud beat Burns 8(52, 56)-5(57, 60); Jones beat Grennan 8(37, 41, 51, 83, 40)-7(45, 38, 48, 36)

*Final*: Mifsud beat Jones 11(41, 55, 60, 34, 43, 42)-9(99, 57, 63, 45, 43, 44, 52, 45, 66)

**1987** (*Bangalore*)

*Group A*

| | | | |
|---|---|---|---|
| J. Allan (Scotland) | 5 | 20 | 7 |
| P. Mifsud (Malta) | 4 | 19 | 6 |
| B. Bjorkman (Sweden) | 3 | 15 | 14 |
| B. Lui (Singapore) | 2 | 14 | 16 |
| R. Karaitiana (N.Z.) | 1 | 8 | 16 |
| S. Mahboob (Bangladesh) | 0 | 3 | 20 |

*Group B*

| | | | |
|---|---|---|---|
| J. Wattana (Thailand) | 5 | 20 | 9 |
| J. White (Canada) | 3 | 17 | 14 |
| S. Tong (Hong Kong) | 3 | 14 | 13 |
| Y. Mirza (India) | 3 | 13 | 12 |
| M. Rowing (England) | 1 | 14 | 17 |
| M. Loon Hong (Malaysia) | 0 | 7 | 20 |

*Group C*

| | | | |
|---|---|---|---|
| D. Morgan (Wales) | 5 | 20 | 3 |
| S. McClarey (N. Ireland) | 3 | 15 | 10 |
| S. Lannigan (England) | 3 | 15 | 10 |
| P. Su Liang (Malaysia) | 3 | 13 | 11 |
| M. Yousef (Pakistan) | 1 | 3 | 16 |

*Group D*

| | | | |
|---|---|---|---|
| A. Robidoux (Canada) | 5 | 20 | 2 |
| J. Long (Rep. of Ireland) | 3 | 14 | 9 |
| F. Chan (Hong Kong) | 3 | 14 | 11 |
| H. Boteju (Sri Lanka) | 3 | 13 | 12 |
| P. Houke (Netherlands) | 1 | 10 | 16 |

|  | Wins | For | Agst |
|---|---|---|---|
| *Group E* | | | |
| G. Sethi (India) | 4 | 19 | 11 |
| M. Henson (W. Germany) | 4 | 17 | 12 |
| K. Doherty (Rep. of Ireland) | 3 | 18 | 8 |
| R. Farebrother (Australia) | 3 | 13 | 12 |
| T. Dada (Pakistan) | 1 | 10 | 18 |
| A. Borg (Malta) | 0 | 4 | 20 |
| *Group F* | | | |
| J. Swail (N. Ireland) | 5 | 20 | 4 |
| P. Hawkes (Australia) | 4 | 17 | 8 |
| D. Barron (Zimbabwe) | 2 | 13 | 15 |
| S. Agrawal (India) | 2 | 13 | 16 |
| S. Lemmens (Belgium) | 1 | 8 | 14 |
| R. Ameen (Bangladesh) | 0 | 6 | 20 |
| *Group G* | | | |
| J. Grech (Malta) | 6 | 24 | 9 |
| B. L'Orange (Norway) | 4 | 22 | 13 |
| S. Nivison (Scotland) | 4 | 19 | 14 |
| J. Herbert (Wales) | 3 | 19 | 15 |
| Lim Koon Guan (Singapore) | 2 | 16 | 19 |
| A. A. Aziz (Egypt) | 2 | 10 | 17 |
| K. Hossen (Mauritius) | 0 | 1 | 24 |
| *Group H* | | | |
| U. Kaimuk (Thailand) | 5 | 20 | 5 |
| M. Lanoye (Belgium) | 3 | 14 | 14 |
| D. Meredith (N.Z.) | 2 | 15 | 14 |
| R. Dikstra (Netherlands) | 2 | 12 | 13 |
| P. Reynolds (Isle of Man) | 2 | 12 | 17 |
| K. Sirisoma (Sri Lanka) | 1 | 9 | 18 |

*Pre-quarter finals:* Darren Morgan beat B. L'Orange 5-0: 69(40)-45(34), 64(44)-30, 67(50)-28, 70(61)-2, 108(89)-0; J. Wattana beat M. Lanoye 5-3: 96(44, 39)-8, 13-71, 18-56, 72(52)-50, 72-15, 16-64(40), 86(45)-5, 68(50)-41; A. Robidoux beat M. Henson 5-1: 27-76(38), 49-34, 67(54)-61(36), 84(55)-10, 66(39)-41, 86(32)-36; J. Allan beat P. Hawkes 5-3: 45-72(32), 67-55, 31-88(38, 35), 40-62, 80(41)-38, 88(42)-29, 61-28, 88-31; P. Mifsud beat J. Swail 5-3: 0-102(102), 23-79(59), 73(36)-16, 55-18, 62-8, 63-64(42), 57-50, 60-19; G. Sethi beat J. White: 65(36)-17, 97(55)-5, 33-74(30, 31), 75(31, 36)-58(43), 77(36)-5, 24-67(32), 54-52; J. Grech beat S. McClarey 5-0: 66-28, 60(38)-22, 69(30, 33)-21, 56-24, 76(35, 32); U. Kaimuk beat J. Long 5-3: 13-73, 72(36)-30, 92(34)-17, 92(32)-28, 41-64, 8-82(65), 64-20, 65(37)-10

*Quarter-finals:* D. Morgan beat J. Wattana 5-3: 95(36, 35)-2, 67(37)-23, 20-114(71), 78(77)-0, 5-66(60), 29-76(60), 73-35, 84(80)-47(45); A. Robidoux beat J. Allan 5-4: 84(67)-34, 78(36)-14, 64(32)-42, 45-78(37), 1-74(67), 38-61, 13-93(68), 51-31, 63-34; G. Sethi beat P. Mifsud 5-4: 104(40)-48, 22-70(38), 89(48)-31, 61(33)-39, 8-71, 6-71(69), 75(58)-1, 7-61, 80(49)-42; J. Grech beat U. Kaimuk 5-4: 26-81(30), 71(31)-63, 63(40)-67(67), 84(32)-35, 69(40)-56, 9-90(71), 55-62, 84(31)-28, 59-56(44)

*Semi-finals:* D. Morgan beat A. Robidoux 8-5: 72(38)-14, 83(82)-43, 94(64)-8, 87(53)-24, 72(40)-9, 64(37)-49, 21-79(44, 35); 39-71(48), 47-86(56), 39(34)-75, 19-73(59), 102(69, 33)-23, 63-52(30); J. Grech beat G. Sethi 8-3: 72-29, 72-45(40), 46-71, 69-44(35), 71(63)-17, 26-86(60), 101(45, 56)-45(3); 116(86)-13, 6-58(36), 55-35, 70(31)-13

*Match for 3rd and 4th place*: A. Robidoux beat G. Sethi 4-1: 55-67, 136(81, 42)-0, 81(52)-46(38), 84(84)-5, 64(31, 33)-62

*Final:* D. Morgan beat J. Grech 11-4: 86(30)-11, 92(60)-28, 62(37)-51, 18-94(52), 89(68)-31, 73(42)-30, 98(90)-0; 22-71(50), 31-73(49), 69-29, 84(66)-15, 78(50)-20, 33-73(38), 84(39)-7, 73(40)-59

| | Wins | For | Agst |
|---|---|---|---|
| **1988** (*Sydney*) | | | |
| *Group A* | | | |
| J. Wattana (Thailand) | 5 | 20 | 2 |
| B. Gollan (Canada) | 4 | 19 | 9 |
| H. Bakhaty (Egypt) | 3 | 12 | 11 |
| Y. Merchant (India) | 2 | 13 | 12 |
| W. Braam (Netherlands) | 1 | 7 | 16 |
| M. Gutowski (W. Germany) | 0 | 0 | 20 |
| *Group B* | | | |
| B. Pinches (England) | 6 | 24 | 6 |
| M. Colquitt (Isle of Man) | 5 | 22 | 10 |
| N. O'Neill (N. Ireland) | 3 | 19 | 14 |
| F. Chan (Hong Kong) | 3 | 16 | 14 |
| B. Choo (Malaysia) | 3 | 15 | 14 |
| A. Helmy (Egypt) | 1 | 5 | 21 |
| Mahboob Syed (Bangladesh) | 0 | 2 | 24 |
| *Group C* | | | |
| P. Mifsud (Malta) | 4 | 19 | 6 |
| K. G. Lim (Singapore) | 4 | 18 | 7 |
| G. Burns (Rep. of Ireland) | 3 | 15 | 14 |
| D. Collins (Australia) | 2 | 10 | 13 |
| H. Boteju (Sri Lanka) | 2 | 11 | 15 |
| S. Hamdan (Brunei) | 0 | 2 | 20 |
| *Group D* | | | |
| J. Allan (Scotland) | 6 | 24 | 8 |
| J. Buckley (Rep. of Ireland) | 6 | 24 | 8 |
| B. Anderson (New Zealand) | 5 | 21 | 12 |
| M. Y. Mirad (Pakistan) | 4 | 20 | 14 |
| E. Van Der Linden (Belgium) | 3 | 19 | 26 |
| M. Mansoor (Sri Lanka) | 2 | 15 | 21 |
| S. Lal (Fiji) | 2 | 13 | 23 |
| H. H. J. Tengah (Brunei) | 0 | 1 | 28 |
| *Group E* | | | |
| J. Peplow (Malta) | 5 | 20 | 9 |
| N. Nopachorn (Thailand) | 3 | 16 | 10 |
| S. Robertson (New Zealand) | 3 | 17 | 11 |
| L. Weng Yew (Singapore) | 2 | 13 | 12 |
| A. Thomson (Zimbabwe) | 2 | 11 | 15 |
| A. Verny (Mauritius) | 0 | 0 | 20 |
| *Group F* | | | |
| P. Doran (N. Ireland) | 4 | 17 | 8 |
| B. L'Orange (Norway) | 4 | 19 | 11 |
| S. Gorski (Australia) | 3 | 16 | 11 |
| G. Sethi (India) | 3 | 16 | 12 |

|  | Wins | For | Agst |
|---|---|---|---|
| D. Barron (Zimbabwe) | 1 | 8 | 18 |
| R. Ameen (Bangladesh) | 0 | 4 | 20 |
| *Group G* | | | |
| R. Jones (Wales) | 4 | 19 | 6 |
| S. Ventham (England) | 4 | 17 | 10 |
| J. Bonner (Australia) | 3 | 16 | 10 |
| R. Dikstra (Netherlands) | 3 | 13 | 10 |
| N. Bohling (Sweden) | 1 | 5 | 16 |
| D. Nanji (Fiji) | 0 | 2 | 20 |
| *Group H* | | | |
| P. Dawkins (Wales) | 5 | 23 | 10 |
| D. Henry (Scotland) | 4 | 21 | 10 |
| K. Kwok (Hong Kong) | 4 | 17 | 12 |
| J. Bear (Canada) | 4 | 18 | 16 |
| R. Johansson (Sweden) | 2 | 14 | 16 |
| M. Lannoye (Belgium) | 2 | 13 | 21 |
| H. Yoshida (Japan) | 0 | 3 | 24 |

*Pre-quarter-finals:* R. Hones beat B. L'Orange 5-0: 64-39, 57(31)-45, 69-37, 65-40, 56-37; D. Henry beat P. Mifsud 5-3: 54-23, 17-60(39), 91(33)-20, 20-85, 73(49)-26, 74(34)-28, 3-66(40), 69(44)-40(40); B. Gollan beat P. Doran 5-0: 54-46(40), 93(68)-16, 105(105)-0, 88(87)-31(31), 69(39)-11; J. Allan beat N. Nopachorn 5-2: 53-34, 34-49, 82(31, 52)-1, 80(39, 30)-5, 58-41, 22-62, 75(53)-5; J. Wattana beat M. Colquitt 5-0: 99(47)-17, 102(31, 40)-7, 100(46, 46)-29, 78(78)-17, 76(45, 30)-0; J. Peplow beat K. G. Lim 5-0: 67(42)-34, 82(65)-13, 60-30, 61-60, 56-35; P. Dawkins beat J. Buckley 5-1: 15-84, 52(31)-42, 62-51, 74(40)-18, 68(54)-36, 64(32)-5; B. Pinches beat S. Ventham 5-0: 64-54, 60-48, 68(55)-13, 71(35)-49(39), 69(60)-39

*Quarter-finals:* Pinches beat Gollan 5-0: 125(91, 33)-11, 80(54)-51(33), 74(32)-10, 66(42)-15, 123(107)-1; Peplow beat Dawkins 5-4: 82-28, 83(67)-48(32), 49-41, 36-77, 77(32)-20, 7-78, 30-75(52), 36-57, 91(67)-29; Henry beat Allan 5-1: 22-73, 70(34)-51, 79(50)-1, 74-14, 76(48)-1, 91(32)-47(34); Wattana beat Jones 5-0: 68-33, 62-24, 84(39)-18, 67(67)-19, 63(31)-52(30)

*Semi-finals:* Wattana beat Peplow 8-2: 107(77)-17, 70(49)-53(38), 34-68(35), 56-44, 49-60, 87-17, 81(49)-17, 64-38, 87(60)-21, 77(44)-0; Pinches beat Henry 8-5: 75-33, 61(60)-54(37), 0-99(50, 31), 66(37)-41, 10-76(52), 29-101(53, 40), 7-83(56), 64-46, 100(53, 47)-20, 75(34, 41)-53(53), 89(89)-19, 8-80, 85-19

*Final:* Wattana beat Pinches 11-8: 55-43, 47-65(31), 76-30, 67-54(31), 17-78(34, 32), 49-84(38), 71-48, 60(33)-74(61), 59-34, 22-77(56), 0-140(35, 105), 79-23, 143(78, 65)-0, 73(32)-40, 119(99)-1, 62-69(30), 99(69)-9, 15-95(41), 96(96)-0

## World Amateur Billiards Championships

|  | Won | Score (average) | Highest break | No of centuries |
|---|---|---|---|---|
| **1926** (*London*) | | | | |
| J. Earlham (England) | 4 | 8,000 (25.6) | 282 | 18 |
| G. Shailer (Australia) | 3 | 7,394 (16.8) | 203 | 13 |
| M. Smith (Scotland) | 2 | 6,569 (12.7) | 130 | 4 |
| P. Rutledge (S. Africa) | 1 | 5,902 (12.5) | 142 | 2 |
| T. McCluney (N. Ireland) | 0 | 5,617 (11.9) | 144 | 4 |
| **1927** (*London*) | | | | |
| A. Prior (S. Africa) | 3 | 6,000 (16.6) | 184 | 9 |
| H. F. Coles (Wales) | 2 | 5,533 (12.2) | 164 | 2 |

| | Won | Score (average) | Highest break | No of centuries |
|---|---|---|---|---|
| L. Steeples (England) | 1 | 5,506 (14.8) | 236 | 9 |
| M. Smith (Scotland) | 0 | 4,499 (12.6) | 158 | 1 |
| **1929** (*Johannesburg*) | | | | |
| L. Hayes (Australia) | 3 | 6,000 (15.5) | 136 | 6 |
| A. Prior (S. Africa) | 2 | 5,512 (16.0) | 226 | 7 |
| H. F. Coles (England) | 1 | 5,592 (14.7) | 170 | 7 |
| P. Rutledge (S. Africa) | 0 | 2,882 (10.9) | 164 | 1 |
| **1931** (*Sydney*) | | | | |
| L. Steeples (England) | 4 | 8,000 (37.3) | 461 | 24 |
| S. Lee (England) | 3 | 7,126 (22.1) | 433 | 18 |
| L. Hayes (Australia) | 2 | 6,113 (15.3) | 167 | 6 |
| H. Goldsmith (Australia) | 1 | 4,995 (13.0) | 179 | 4 |
| W. Hackett (N. Zealand) | 0 | 3,549 (7.7) | 97 | 0 |
| **1933** (*London*) | | | | |
| S. Lee (England) | 4 | 12,402 (28.0) | 394 | 31 |
| T. Jones (Wales) | 3 | 9,883 (18.7) | 144 | 8 |
| A. Prior (S. Africa) | 2 | 9,113 (18.3) | 235 | 13 |
| M. Smith (Scotland) | 1 | 8,292 (17.5) | 166 | 5 |
| J. Blackburn (N. Ireland) | 0 | 6,362 (12.5) | 94 | 0 |
| **1935** (*London*) | | | | |
| H. F. Coles (England) | 4 | 13,665 (28.4) | 267 | 33 |
| J. McGhie (Scotland) | 3 | 9,359 (19.4) | 207 | 11 |
| I. Edwards (Wales) | 2 | 9,814 (18.1) | 196 | 11 |
| S. Fenning (Ireland) | 1 | 9,068 (17.4) | 161 | 6 |
| P. Deb (India) | 0 | 7,461 (13.1) | 123 | 5 |
| **1936** (*Johannesburg*) | | | | |
| R. Marshall (Australia) | 3 | 8,526 (22.0) | 248 | 24 |
| A. Prior (S. Africa) | 2 | 7,014 (17.7) | 197 | 11 |
| J. Thompson (England) | 1 | 7,705 (21.2) | 245 | 15 |
| A. Bowlly (S. Africa) | 0 | 4,548 (9.0) | 93 | 0 |
| *Three 2 hour sessions* | | | | |
| **1938** (*Melbourne*) | | | | |
| R. Marshall (Australia) | 6 | 17,626 (39.0) | 427 | 59 |
| K. Kennerley (England) | 5 | 14,528 (30.1) | 472 | 45 |
| T. Cleary (Australia) | 4 | 8,535 (19.7) | 322 | 17 |
| S. Moses (N. Zealand) | 2 | 6,727 (13.1) | 129 | 4 |
| M. M. Begg (India) | 2 | 6,685 (13.4) | 111 | 2 |
| A. Burke (S. Africa) | 1 | 5,993 (12.0) | 119 | 1 |
| A. Albertson (N. Zealand) | 1 | 5,805 (12.4) | 107 | 1 |
| **1951** (*London*) | | | | |
| R. Marshall (Australia) | 6 | 14,735 (38.1) | 423 | 42 |
| F. Edwards (England) | 5 | 13,459 (26.7) | 345 | 36 |
| T. Cleary (Australia) | 4 | 12,373 (25.5) | 330 | 31 |
| W. Ramage (Scotland) | 3 | 7,638 (19.1) | 151 | 8 |
| W. Pierce (Wales) | 2 | 6,029 (13.6) | 225 | 3 |
| W. Jones (India) | 1 | 7,202 (16.6) | 138 | 10 |
| E. Haslem (N. Ireland) | 0 | 5,896 (14.1) | 125 | 3 |

|  | Won | Score (average) | Highest break | No of centuries |
|---|---|---|---|---|
| **1952** (*Calcutta*) | | | | |
| L. Driffield (England) | 5 | 8,529 (34.5) | 278 | 31 |
| R. Marshall (Australia) | 3 | 9,237 (37.3) | 351 | 27 |
| C. Hirjee (India) | 3 | 7,701 (22.7) | 230 | 14 |
| W. Ramage (Scotland) | 3 | 6,525 (20.8) | 211 | 10 |
| W. Jones (India) | 1 | 6,731 (23.3) | 253 | 6 |
| A. Yunoos (Burma) | 0 | 3,768 (11.0) | 79 | 0 |
| **1954** (*Sydney*) | | | | |
| T. Cleary (Australia) | 4 | 11,496 (33.5) | 682 | 35 |
| R. Marshall (Australia) | 3 | 11,488 (36.0) | 407 | 35 |
| F. Edwards (England) | 2 | 9,053 (24.7) | 328 | 26 |
| W. Jones (India) | 1 | 8,523 (20.5) | 209 | 17 |
| T. G. Rees (S. Africa) | 0 | 6,271 (16.9) | 207 | 6 |
| **1958** (*Calcutta*) | | | | |
| W. Jones (India) | 5 | 16,493 | 501 | 56 |
| L. Driffield (England) | 4 | 14,370 | 499 | 48 |
| T. Cleary (Australia) | 3 | 13,626 | 431 | 52 |
| C. Hirjee (India) | 2 | 12,853 | 226 | 38 |
| W. Asciak (Malta) | 1 | 6,329 | 154 | 7 |
| M. Hman (Burma) | 0 | 5,633 | 215 | 8 |
| **1960** (*Edinburgh*) | | | | |
| J. H. Beetham (England) | 7 | 9,351 | 277 | 29 |
| J. Long (Australia) | 6 | 10,634 | 353 | 26 |
| W. Jones (India) | 5 | 12,397 | 589 | 30 |
| M. Francisco (S. Africa) | 4 | 7,773 | 148 | 11 |
| W. Ramage (Scotland) | 3 | 7,938 | 283 | 12 |
| W. Asciak (Malta) | 2 | 8,408 | 194 | 11 |
| W. Dennison (N. Ireland) | 1 | 6,231 | 155 | 4 |
| A. Ramage (Scotland) | 0 | 5,706 | 101 | 2 |
| **1962** (*Perth*) | | | | |
| R. Marshall (Australia) | 5 | 12,367 (35.6) | 348 | 57 |
| W. Jones (India) | 5 | 10,805 (26.9) | 489 | 34 |
| T. Cleary (Australia) | 4 | 9,808 (27.0) | 315 | 27 |
| J. H. Beetham (England) | 3 | 7,626 (22.9) | 283 | 18 |
| S. Benajee (India) | 3 | 8,332 (17.2) | 219 | 9 |
| R. A. Karim (Pakistan) | 1 | 5,657 (11.9) | 130 | 3 |
| W. Harcourt (N. Zealand) | 0 | 5,623 (14.3) | 123 | 5 |
| *Play off:* Marshall beat Jones 3,623-2,891 | | | | |
| **1964** (*Pukekohe*) | | | | |
| W. Jones (India) | 9 | 16,628 (24.5) | 294 | 49 |
| J. Karnehm (England) | 8 | 12,953 (21.8) | 390 | 28 |
| M. Ferreira (India) | 7 | 13,345 (19.0) | 182 | 29 |
| M. Francisco (S. Africa) | 6 | 12,957 (22.0) | 518 | 38 |
| A. Nolan (England) | 5 | 12,126 (19.9) | 259 | 26 |
| T. Cleary (Australia) | 4 | 10,781 (13.9) | 241 | 19 |
| H. Robinson (N. Zealand) | 3 | 7,643 (10.5) | 85 | 0 |
| T. Yesberg (N. Zealand) | 2 | 7,528 (10.4) | 80 | 0 |
| M. Mavalwala (Pakistan) | 1 | 8,404 (11.3) | 174 | 1 |

|  | Won | Score (average) | Highest break | No of centuries |
|---|---|---|---|---|
| A. E. Redmond (S. Africa) | 0 | 6,914 (9.0) | 107 | 1 |
| **1967** (*Colombo*) | | | | |
| L. Driffield (England) | 8 | 13,556 (30.5) | 421 | 53 |
| M. J. M. Lafir (Ceylon) | 7 | 12,562 (18.4) | 218 | 31 |
| M. Francisco (S. Africa) | 6 | 12,477 (20.4) | 301 | 32 |
| M. Ferreira (India) | 5 | 11,140 (19.5) | 507 | 22 |
| J. Long (Australia) | 4 | 11,068 (17.5) | 261 | 27 |
| T. Cleary (Australia) | 3 | 9,252 (11.6) | 322 | 15 |
| N. J. Rahim (Ceylon) | 2 | 6,895 (8.8) | 116 | 3 |
| M. S. M. Marzuq (Ceylon) | 1 | 7,153 (7.9) | 88 | 0 |
| F. Holz (N. Zealand) | 0 | 5,350 (7.1) | 68 | 0 |
| **1969** (*London*) | | | | |
| J. Karnehm (England) | 9 | 12,902 | 232 | 27 |
| M. Ferreira (India) | 7 | 14,115 | 629 | 34 |
| M. Francisco (S. Africa) | 7 | 13,760 | 335 | 35 |
| M. J. M. Lafir (Ceylon) | 7 | 12,934 | 296 | 28 |
| R. Marshall (Australia) | 6 | 13,033 | 216 | 33 |
| M. Wildman (England) | 6 | 11,739 | 274 | 22 |
| R. Oriel (Wales) | 5 | 13,306 | 297 | 30 |
| S. Mohan (India) | 5 | 13,407 | 219 | 24 |
| P. Mifsud (Malta) | 2 | 10,410 | 173 | 8 |
| A. Twohill (N. Zealand) | 1 | 10,016 | 146 | 12 |
| F. Holz (N. Zealand) | 0 | 6,061 | 65 | 0 |
| **1971** (*Malta*) | | | | |
| *Group A* | | | | |
| M. Francisco (S. Africa) | 4 | 6,450 | 321 | 15 |
| M. J. M. Lafir (Ceylon) | 3 | 4,757 | 233 | 4 |
| P. Mifsud (Malta) | 2 | 4,142 | 134 | 2 |
| D. Sneddon (Scotland) | 1 | 3,160 | 121 | 2 |
| L. Napper (N. Zealand) | 0 | 3,798 | 87 | 0 |
| *Group B* | | | | |
| S. Mohan (India) | 4 | 5,839 | 188 | 11 |
| N. Dagley (England) | 3 | 5,454 | 330 | 11 |
| M. Ferreira (India) | 2 | 4,423 | 227 | 4 |
| C. Everton (Wales) | 1 | 3,893 | 205 | 5 |
| W. Asciak (Malta) | 0 | 4,511 | 188 | 7 |
| *Play-offs:* | | | | |
| Dagley | 3 | 6,041 | 348 | 17 |
| M. Francisco | 2 | 3,981 | 353 | 11 |
| Mohan | 1 | 3,822 | 327 | 11 |
| Lafir | 0 | 2,514 | 211 | 5 |
| **1973** (*Bombay*) | | | | |
| M. J. M. Lafir (Sri Lanka) | 9 | 16,956 (34.1) | 859 | 43 |
| S. Mohan (India) | 7 | 17,016 (30.8) | 468 | 53 |
| M. Ferreira (India) | 7 | 15,639 (25.4) | 421 | 41 |
| P. Tarrant (Australia) | 6 | 13,200 (24.4) | 373 | 36 |
| C. Everton (Wales) | 5 | 9,921 (18.2) | 240 | 17 |
| A. Nolan (England) | 4 | 12,709 (20.8) | 265 | 31 |

| | Won | Score (average) | Highest break | No of centuries |
|---|---|---|---|---|
| P. Mifsud (Malta) | 4 | 12,253 (18.8) | 203 | 23 |
| E. Simons (N. Zealand) | 2 | 8,521 (12.4) | 94 | 0 |
| B. Kirkness (N. Zealand) | 1 | 8,464 (13.5) | 195 | 7 |
| L. U. Demarco (Scotland) | 0 | 7,488 (10.4) | 87 | 0 |

**1975** (*Auckland*)

*Group A*

| | | | | |
|---|---|---|---|---|
| N. Dagley (England) | 5 | 9,257 | 477 | 24 |
| D. Sneddon (Scotland) | 4 | 6,272 | 124 | 4 |
| G. Parikh (India) | 3 | 6,471 | 197 | 16 |
| J. Reece (Australia) | 2 | 4,058 | 125 | 4 |
| H. Robinson (N. Zealand) | 1 | 4,529 | 123 | 2 |
| M. Shaharwardi (Sri Lanka) | 0 | 4,032 | 121 | 1 |

*Group B*

| | | | | |
|---|---|---|---|---|
| M. Ferreira (India) | 5 | 9,022 | 411 | 26 |
| C. Everton (Wales) | 4 | 6,043 | 272 | 13 |
| R. Close (England) | 3 | 5,449 | 164 | 10 |
| T. Yesberg (N. Zealand) | 2 | 4,373 | 131 | 3 |
| J. Long (Australia) | 1 | 4,598 | 157 | 5 |
| B. Bennett (N. Zealand) | 0 | 3,684 | 95 | 0 |

*Play-offs*

*Semi-finals*: Dagley beat Everton 1,293(222)-775; Ferreira beat Sneddon 2,470(211)-681
*Final*: Dagley beat Ferreira 3,385(200, 228, 202, 314)-2,268(281)

**1977** (*Melbourne*)

*Group A*

| | | | | |
|---|---|---|---|---|
| N. Dagley (England) | 5 | 7,546 | 272 | 16 |
| C. Everton (Wales) | 4 | 4,962 | 170 | 7 |
| S. Aleem (India) | 3 | 7,028 | 263 | 11 |
| G. Ganim Sr (Australia) | 2 | 6,322 | 231 | 6 |
| H. Robinson (N. Zealand) | 1 | 4,133 | 93 | 0 |
| J. Nugent (Scotland) | 0 | 4,131 | 68 | 0 |

*Group B*

| | | | | |
|---|---|---|---|---|
| M. Ferreira (India) | 5 | 12,554 | 519 | 33 |
| R. Close (England) | 4 | 7,252 | 207 | 15 |
| G. Ganim Jr (Australia) | 3 | 6,424 | 192 | 9 |
| T. Yesberg (N. Zealand) | 2 | 4,349 | 109 | 1 |
| W. Weerasinghe (Sri Lanka) | 1 | 4,364 | 97 | 0 |
| D. Pratt (Scotland) | 0 | 4,316 | 108 | 1 |

*Play-offs*

*Semi-finals*: Ferreira beat Everton 2,155-1,310; Close beat Dagley 1,912(234)-1,781(236)
*Final*: Ferreira beat Close 2,683-2,564(231)

**1979** (*Colombo*)

*Group A*

| | | | | |
|---|---|---|---|---|
| M. Ferreira (India) | 7 | 14,695 | 467 | 40 |
| M. J. M. Lafir (Sri Lanka) | 5 | 12,456 | 370 | 30 |
| K. Shirley (England) | 5 | 10,656 | 195 | 13 |
| W. Barrie (Australia) | 4 | 8,255 | 128 | 2 |
| B. Kirkness (N. Zealand) | 4 | 7,283 | 214 | 8 |
| H. Nimmo (Scotland) | 2 | 7,022 | 105 | 2 |

| | Won | Score (average) | Highest break | No of centuries |
|---|---|---|---|---|
| M. S. U. Mohideen (Sri Lanka) | 1 | 6,408 | 76 | 0 |
| R. Lim Sin Foo (Singapore) | 0 | 6,433 | 97 | 0 |
| *Group B* | | | | |
| N. Dagley (England) | 6 | 12,539 | 466 | 39 |
| P. Mifsud (Malta) | 6 | 12,193 | 325 | 31 |
| S. Agrawal (India) | 6 | 11,924 | 355 | 30 |
| G. Ganim Jr (Australia) | 3 | 8,486 | 267 | 15 |
| C. Everton (Wales) | 3 | 6,905 | 211 | 11 |
| W. A. J. Weerasinghe (Sri Lanka) | 3 | 7,883 | 202 | 7 |
| B. Bennett (N. Zealand) | 1 | 6,083 | 101 | 1 |
| E. Fisher (Canada) | 0 | 4,198 | 88 | 0 |

*Play-offs*
*Semi-finals*: Mifsud beat Ferreira 2,489(338, 285)-1,856; Dagley beat Lafir 2,694(266, 444, 289)-1,692(240)
*Final*: Mifsud beat Dagley 2,943(361)-2,152

**1981** (*New Delhi*)
*Group A*

| | | | | |
|---|---|---|---|---|
| N. Dagley (England) | 6 | 11,982 | 416 | 42 |
| S. Agrawal (India) | 5 | 12,967 | 384 | 39 |
| G. Ganim Jr (Australia) | 4 | 7,934 | 178 | 13 |
| A. K. B. Giles (N. Zealand) | 3 | 6,895 | 162 | 5 |
| D. Sneddon (Scotland) | 2 | 7,071 | 123 | 6 |
| J. W. H. Boteju (Sri Lanka) | 1 | 6,312 | 107 | 1 |
| A. A. Essam (Egypt) | 0 | 3,948 | 59 | – |
| *Group B* | | | | |
| M. Ferreira (India) | 6 | 13,862 | 630 | 58 |
| L. A. Bux (Pakistan) | 5 | 8,712 | 257 | 21 |
| R. Close (England) | 3 | 7,161 | 217 | 15 |
| J. Grech (Malta) | 3 | 7,388 | 402 | 9 |
| D. Meredith (N. Zealand) | 3 | 6,507 | 154 | 7 |
| H. Roberts-Thomson (Australia) | 2 | 6,535 | 151 | 5 |
| S. M. Shahawardi (Sri Lanka) | 0 | 5,111 | 77 | – |

*Semi-finals*: Dagley beat Bux 2,890(229, 277, 218)-1,505(257); Ferreira beat Agrawal 3,272(213, 532, 327, 527, 630)-1,964(233, 253)
*Final*: Ferreira beat Dagley 2,725(208, 349, 245, 244)-2,631(223, 296, 281)

**1983** (*Malta*)
*Group A*

| | | | | |
|---|---|---|---|---|
| M. Ferreira (India) | 6 | | 463 | 31 |
| R. Foldvari (Australia) | 5 | | 302 | 30 |
| L. A. Bux (Pakistan) | 4 | | 177 | 9 |
| H. Nimmo (Scotland) | 3 | | 224 | 6 |
| D. Meredith (N. Zealand) | 2 | | 157 | 7 |
| H. Griffiths (Wales) | 1 | | 112 | 1 |
| A. Micallef (Malta) | 0 | | 122 | 6 |
| *Group B* | | | | |
| S. Agrawal (India) | 5 | | 635 | 42 |
| N. Dagley (England) | 5 | | 368 | 30 |
| J. Grech (Malta) | 5 | | 286 | 31 |

|  | Won | Score (average) | Highest break | No of centuries |
|---|---|---|---|---|
| V. Ellul (Malta) | 2 | | 145 | 2 |
| R. Lim (Singapore) | 2 | | 96 | – |
| W. Loughan (N. Ireland) | 2 | | 198 | 5 |
| H. Boteju (Sri Lanka) | 0 | | 120 | 2 |

Semi-finals: Agrawal beat Foldvari 2,047(240, 503)-1,900(302, 225, 231); Ferreira beat Dagley 1,983(463)-1,919(258)

Final: Ferreira beat Agrawal 3,933(353, 398, 201, 254)-2,744(242, 212)

**1985** (Malta)

Group A

| | | |
|---|---|---|
| R. Marshall (Australia) | 7 | 396* |
| M. Ferreira (India) | 6 | 341 |
| L. A. Bux (Pakistan) | 5 | 229 |
| R. Robinson (N. Zealand) | 4 | 100 |
| D. Sneddon (Scotland) | 3 | 190 |
| T. Ward (England) | 2 | 106 |
| Lau Weng Yew (Singapore) | 1 | 92 |
| S. Clarke (N. Ireland) | 0 | 101 |

Group B

| | | |
|---|---|---|
| G. Sethi (India) | 7 | 604 |
| S. Agrawal (India) | 6 | 599 |
| R. Close (England) | 5 | 182 |
| H. Nimmo (Scotland) | 3 | 146 |
| D. Meredith (N. Zealand) | 3 | 263 |
| K. Sirisoma (Sri Lanka) | 2 | 118 |
| F. Humphries | 1 | 131 |
| A. Micallef (Malta) | 1 | 138 |

*unfinished

Semi-finals: Sethi beat Ferreira 2,513(201, 303)-2,379; Marshall beat Agrawal 2,782(300, 204)-1,872

Final: Sethi beat Marshall 3,809(546, 235, 348, 232, 257)-2,453(201)

**1987** (Belfast)

Group A

| | | | |
|---|---|---|---|
| G. Sethi (India) | 8 | 364 | 51 |
| D. Edwards (Wales) | 7 | 215 | 19 |
| D. Elliott (Northern Ireland) | 6 | 192 | 9 |
| T. Ward (England) | 5 | 130 | 5 |
| B. Kirkness (New Zealand) | 4 | 196 | 8 |
| D. Collins (Australia) | 3 | 183 | 18 |
| J. McIntyre (Northern Ireland) | 2 | 132 | 1 |
| M. Spoormans (Belgium) | 1 | 77 | – |
| R. Brennan (Republic of Ireland) | 0 | 88 | – |

Group B

| | | | |
|---|---|---|---|
| J. Grech (Malta) | 7 | 447 | 43 |
| S. Agrawal (India) | 7 | 491 | 50 |
| P. Gilchrist (England) | 7 | 242 | 23 |
| D. Meredith (New Zealand) | 5 | 243 | 21 |
| B. Kelly (Scotland) | 4 | 218 | 1 |
| S. McClarey (Northern Ireland) | 3 | 136 | 4 |

|                              | Won | Score (average) | *Highest break* | *No of centuries* |
|------------------------------|-----|-----------------|-----------------|-------------------|
| J. Millen (Australia)        | 2   |                 | 112             | 2                 |
| T. Martin (Republic of Ireland) | 1 |               | 95              | –                 |
| M. De Sutter (Belgium)       | 0   |                 | 174             | 1                 |

*Semi-finals:* Grech beat Edwards 2971(271, 236, 480)-1748(212); Sethi beat Agrawal 2959(242, 288, 366, 221)-2456

*Final:* Sethi beat Grech 4846(760, 206, 202, 224, 248, 460)-3256(200, 244, 360, 253, 358, 238)

## World Amateur Championship Records

**Snooker**

B. Gollan (Canada)   135   1988

**Billiards**

| | | |
|---|---|---|
| T. Cleary (Australia) | 682 (2 pots) | 1954 |
| M. J. M. Lafir (Sri Lanka) | 859 (5 pots) | 1973 |
| M. Ferreira (India) | 467 (3 pots) | 1979 |

# NATIONAL AMATEUR CHAMPIONSHIPS

## ENGLAND
### Snooker

| | | | | | |
|---|---|---|---|---|---|
| 1916 | C. N. Jacques | 1940 | K. Kennerley | 1967 | M. Owen |
| 1917 | C. N. Jacques | 1941–45 | No contests | 1968 | David Taylor |
| 1918 | T. N. Palmer | 1946 | H. J. Pulman | 1969 | R. Edmonds |
| 1919 | S. H. Fry | 1947 | H. Morris | 1970 | J. Barron |
| 1920 | A. R. Wisdom | 1948 | S. Battye | 1971 | J. Barron |
| 1921 | M. J. Vaughan | 1949 | T. C. Gordon | 1972 | J. Barron |
| 1922 | J. McGlynn | 1950 | A. Nolan | 1973 | M. Owen |
| 1923 | W. Coupe | 1951 | R. Williams | 1974 | R. Edmonds |
| 1924 | W. Coupe | 1952 | C. Downey | 1975 | S. Hood |
| 1925 | J. McGlynn | 1953 | T. C. Gordon | 1976 | C. Ross |
| 1926 | W. Nash | 1954 | G. Thompson | 1977 | T. Griffiths |
| 1927 | O. T. Jackson | 1955 | M. Parkin | 1978 | T. Griffiths |
| 1928 | P. H. Matthews | 1956 | T. C. Gordon | 1979 | J. White |
| 1929 | L. Steeples | 1957 | R. Gross | 1980 | J. O'Boye |
| 1930 | L. Steeples | 1958 | M. Owen | 1981 | V. Harris |
| 1931 | P. H. Matthews | 1959 | M. Owen | 1982 | D. Chalmers |
| 1932 | W. E. Bach | 1960 | R. Gross | 1983 | T. Jones |
| 1933 | E. Bedford | 1961 | A. Barnett | 1984 | S. Longworth |
| 1934 | C. H. Beavis | 1962 | R. Gross | 1985 | T. Whitthread |
| 1935 | C. H. Beavis | 1963 | G. Owen | 1986 | A. Harris |
| 1936 | P. H. Matthews | 1964 | R. Reardon | 1987 | M. Rowing |
| 1937 | K. Kennerley | 1965 | P. Houlihan | 1988 | B. Pincher |
| 1938 | P. H. Matthews | 1966 | J. Spencer | 1989 | N. Bond |
| 1939 | P. Bendon | | | | |

### Billiards

| | | | | | |
|---|---|---|---|---|---|
| 1888 | { H. A. O. Lonsdale / A. P. Gaskell | 1893 | { A. R. Wisdom / S. H. Fry | 1902 | { A. W. T. Good / A. W. T. Good |
| 1889 | { A. P. Gaskell / A. P. Gaskell | 1894 | { A. H. Vahid / H. Mitchell / W. T. Maughan | 1903 | { A. R. Wisdom / S. S. Christey |
| 1890 | { A. P. Gaskell / A. P. Gaskell / W. D. Courtney | 1895 | *No contest* | 1904 | W. A. Lovejoy |
| | | 1896 | S. H. Fry | 1905 | A. W. T. Good |
| 1891 | { W. D. Courtney / A. P. Gaskell | 1897–98 | *No contests* | 1906 | E. C. Breed |
| | | 1899 | A. R. Wisdom | 1907 | H. C. Virr |
| 1892 | { A. R. Wisdom / S. S. Christey | 1900 | S. H. Fry | 1908 | H. C. Virr |
| | | 1901 | S. S. Christey | 1909 | Major Fleming |
| | | | | 1910 | H. A. O Lonsdale |

| Year | Winner | Year | Winner | Year | Winner |
|---|---|---|---|---|---|
| 1911 | H. C. Virr | 1936 | J. Thompson | 1965 | N. Dagley |
| 1912 | H. C. Virr | 1937 | K. Kennerley | 1966 | N. Dagley |
| 1913 | H. C. Virr | 1938 | K. Kennerley | 1967 | A. L. Driffield |
| 1914 | H. C. Virr | 1939 | K. Kennerley | 1968 | M. Wildman |
| 1915 | A. W. T. Good | 1940 | K. Kennerley | 1969 | J. Karnehm |
| 1916 | S. H. Fry | 1941-45 | No contests | 1970 | N. Dagley |
| 1917 | J. Graham-Symes | 1946 | M. Showman | 1971 | N. Dagley |
| 1918 | J. Graham-Symes | 1947 | J. Thompson | 1972 | N. Dagley |
| 1919 | S. H. Fry | 1948 | J. Thompson | 1973 | N. Dagley |
| 1920 | S. H. Fry | 1949 | F. Edwards | 1974 | N. Dagley |
| 1921 | S. H. Fry | 1950 | F. Edwards | 1975 | N. Dagley |
| 1922 | J. Graham-Symes | 1951 | F. Edwards | 1976 | R. Close |
| 1923 | W. P. McLeod | 1952 | A. L. Driffield | 1977 | R. Close |
| 1924 | W. P. McLeod | 1953 | A. L. Driffield | 1978 | N. Dagley |
| 1925 | S. H. Fry | 1954 | A. L. Driffield | 1979 | N. Dagley |
| 1926 | J. Earlam | 1955 | F. Edwards | 1980 | N. Dagley |
| 1927 | L. Steeples | 1956 | F. Edwards | 1981 | N. Dagley |
| 1928 | A. Wardle | 1957 | A. L. Driffield | 1982 | N. Dagley |
| 1929 | H. F. E Coles | 1958 | A. L. Driffield | 1983 | N. Dagley |
| 1930 | L. Steeples | 1959 | A. L. Driffield | 1984 | N. Dagley |
| 1931 | S. Lee | 1960 | J. H. Beetham | 1985 | R. Close |
| 1932 | S. Lee | 1961 | J. H. Beetham | 1986 | K. Shirley |
| 1933 | S. Lee | 1962 | A. L. Driffield | 1987 | D. Edwards |
| 1934 | S. Lee | 1963 | J. H. Beetham | 1988 | P. Gilchrist |
| 1935 | H. F. E. Coles | 1964 | A. Nolan | 1989 | D. Edwards |

## NORTHERN IRELAND
### Snooker

| Year | Winner | Year | Winner | Year | Winner |
|---|---|---|---|---|---|
| 1927 | G. Barron | 1950 | J. Bates | 1970 | J. Clint |
| 1928 | J. Perry | 1951 | J. Stevenson | 1971 | S. Crothers |
| 1929 | W. Lyttle | 1952 | J. Stevenson | 1972 | P. Donnelly |
| 1930 | J. Luney | 1953 | J. Stevenson | 1973 | J. Clint |
| 1931 | J. McNally | 1954 | W. Seeds | 1974 | P. Donnelly |
| 1932 | Capt. J. Ross | 1955 | J. Stevenson | 1975 | J. Clint |
| 1933 | J. French | 1956 | S. Brooks | 1976 | E. Swaffield |
| 1934 | Capt. J. Ross | 1957 | M. Gill | 1977 | D. McVeigh |
| 1935 | W. Agnew | 1958 | W. Agnew | 1978 | D. McVeigh |
| 1936 | W. Lowe | 1959 | W. Hanna | 1979 | R. Burke |
| 1937 | J. Chambers | 1960 | M. Gill | 1980 | S. Clarke |
| 1938 | J. McNally | 1961 | D. Anderson | 1981 | T. Murphy |
| 1939 | J. McNally | 1962 | S. McMahon | 1982 | S. Pavis |
| 1940 | No contest | 1963 | D. Anderson | 1983 | J. McLaughlin Jr |
| 1941 | J. McNally | 1964 | P. Morgan | 1984 | J. McLaughlin Jr |
| 1942-44 | No contests | 1965 | M. Gill | 1985 | S. Pavis |
| 1945 | J. McNally | 1966 | S. Crothers | 1986 | C. Sewell |
| 1946 | J. McNally | 1967 | D. Anderson | 1987 | S. McClarey |
| 1947 | J. Rea | 1968 | A. Higgins | 1988 | P. Doran |
| 1948 | J. Bates | 1969 | D. Anderson | 1989 | H. Morgan |
| 1949 | J. Bates | | | | |

### Billiards

| Year | Winner | Year | Winner | Year | Winner |
|---|---|---|---|---|---|
| 1925 | T. McCluney | 1940 | No contest | 1957 | W. Scanlon |
| 1926 | T. McCluney | 1941 | E. Haslem | 1958 | W. Hanna |
| 1927 | J. Sloan | 1942-44 | No contests | 1959 | W. Hanna |
| 1928 | A. Davison | 1945 | E. Haslem | 1960 | W. Dennison |
| 1929 | J. Blackburn | 1946 | J. Holness | 1961 | R. Hanna |
| 1930 | J. Blackburn | 1947 | J. Bates | 1962 | N. McQuay |
| 1931 | J. Blackburn | 1948 | J. Bates | 1963 | W. Hanna |
| 1932 | W. Lowe | 1949 | J. Bates | 1964 | { D. Anderson / D. Turley |
| 1933 | W. Mills | 1950 | J. Bates | | |
| 1934 | W. Lowe | 1951 | E. Haslem | 1965 | W. Ashe |
| 1935 | W. Morrison | 1952 | R. Taylor | 1966 | D. Anderson |
| 1936 | J. Blackburn | 1953 | W. Scanlon | 1967 | W. Loughan |
| 1937 | J. Blackburn | 1954 | W. Scanlon | 1968 | D. Anderson |
| 1938 | W. Lowe | 1955 | D. Turley | 1969 | W. Loughan |
| 1939 | W. Lowe | 1956 | J. Stevenson | 1970 | S. Crothers |

| Year | Name | Year | Name | Year | Name |
|---|---|---|---|---|---|
| 1971 | J. Bates | 1978 | W. Loughan | 1984 | D. Elliott |
| 1972–73 | No contests | 1979 | J. Bates | 1985 | S. Clarke |
| 1974 | P. Donnelly | 1980 | S. Clarke | 1986 | D. Elliott |
| 1975 | P. Donnelly | 1981 | W. Loughan | 1987 | D. Elliott |
| 1976 | P. Donnelly | 1982 | P. Donnelly | 1988 | J. McIntyre |
| 1977 | T. Taylor | 1983 | F. Clarke | | |

## REPUBLIC OF IRELAND
### Snooker

| Year | Name | Year | Name | Year | Name |
|---|---|---|---|---|---|
| 1931 | J. Ayres | 1953 | S. Brooks | 1972 | J. Rogers |
| 1932 | No contest | 1954 | S. Fenning | 1973 | F. Murphy |
| 1933 | S. Fenning | 1955 | S. Fenning | 1974 | P. Burke |
| 1934 | No contest | 1956 | W. Brown | 1975 | F. Nathan |
| 1935 | S. Fenning | 1957 | J. Connolly | 1976 | P. Burke |
| 1936 | No contest | 1958 | G. Gibson | 1977 | J. Clusker |
| 1937 | P. J. O'Connor | 1959–60 | No contests | 1978 | E. Hughes |
| 1938–39 | No contests | 1961 | W. Brown | 1979 | E. Hughes |
| 1940 | P. Merrigan | 1962 | J. Weber | 1980 | D. Sheehan |
| 1941 | No contest | 1963 | J. Rogers | 1981 | A. Kearney |
| 1942 | P. J. O'Connor | 1964 | J. Rogers | 1982 | P. Browne |
| 1943 | No contest | 1965 | W. Fields | 1983 | J. Long |
| 1944 | S. Fenning | 1966 | G. Hanway | 1984 | P. Ennis |
| 1945–46 | No contests | 1967 | P. Morgan | 1985 | G. Burns |
| 1947 | C. Downey | 1968 | G. Hanway | 1986 | G. Burns |
| 1948 | P. Merrigan | 1969 | D. Dally | 1987 | K. Doherty |
| 1949 | S. Fenning | 1970 | D. Sheehan | 1988 | J. Buckley |
| 1950–51 | No contests | 1971 | D. Sheehan | 1989 | K. Doherty |
| 1952 | W. Brown | | | | |

### Billiards

| Year | Name | Year | Name | Year | Name |
|---|---|---|---|---|---|
| 1931 | J. Ayres | 1953 | D. Turley | 1970 | L. Drennan |
| 1932 | No contest | 1954 | M. Nolan | 1971 | L. Codd |
| 1933 | J. Ayres | 1955 | M. Nolan | 1972 | L. Codd |
| 1934 | S. Fenning | 1956 | M. Nolan | 1973 | T. Martin |
| 1935 | S. Fenning | 1957 | M. Nolan | 1974 | T. Doyle |
| 1936 | S. Fenning | 1958 | W. Dennison | 1975 | P. Fenelon |
| 1937 | T. O'Brien | 1959–60 | No contests | 1976 | J. Rogers |
| 1938–41 | No contests | 1961 | K. Smyth | 1977 | E. Hughes |
| 1942 | S. Fenning | 1962 | K. Smyth | 1978 | E. Hughes |
| 1943 | No contest | 1963 | J. Bates | 1979 | L. Drennan |
| 1944 | S. Fenning | 1964 | J. Bates | 1980 | P. Burke |
| 1945–47 | No contests | 1965 | L. Codd | 1981 | P. Burke |
| 1948 | W. Brown | 1966 | L. Codd | 1982 | D. Elliott |
| 1949 | S. Fenning | 1967 | P. Morgan | 1984 | A. Murphy |
| 1950–51 | No contests | 1968 | P. Morgan | 1985 | A. Roche |
| 1952 | M. Nolan | 1969 | J. Rogers | 1987 | L. Drennan |

## SCOTLAND
### Snooker

| Year | Name | Year | Name | Year | Name |
|---|---|---|---|---|---|
| 1931 | G. Brown | 1960 | E. Sinclair | 1975 | E. Sinclair |
| 1932–45 | No contests | 1961 | J. Phillips | 1976 | E. Sinclair |
| 1946 | J. Levey | 1962 | A. Kennedy | 1977 | R. Miller |
| 1947 | J. Levey | 1963 | E. Sinclair | 1978 | J. Donnelly |
| 1948 | I. Wexelstein | 1964 | J. Phillips | 1979 | S. Nivison |
| 1949 | W. Ramage | 1965 | L. U. Demarco | 1980 | M. Gibson |
| 1950 | W. Ramage | 1966 | L. U. Demarco | 1981 | R. Lane |
| 1951 | A. Wilson | 1967 | E. Sinclair | 1982 | P. Kippie |
| 1952 | D. Emerson | 1968 | E. Sinclair | 1983 | G. Carnegie |
| 1953 | P. Spence | 1969 | A. Kennedy | 1984 | S. Hendry |
| 1954 | D. Edmond | 1970 | D. Sneddon | 1985 | S. Hendry |
| 1955 | L. U. Demarco | 1971 | J. Phillips | 1986 | S. Muir |
| 1956 | W. Barrie | 1972 | D. Sneddon | 1987 | S. Nivison |
| 1957 | T. Paul | 1973 | E. Sinclair | 1988 | D. Henry |
| 1958 | J. Phillips | 1974 | D. Sneddon | 1989 | M. Campbell |
| 1959 | J. Phillips | | | | |

## Billiards

| Year | Name | Year | Name | Year | Name |
|---|---|---|---|---|---|
| 1913 | Capt. Croneen | 1946 | J. Levey | 1966 | W. Ramage |
| *1914–21* | *No contests* | 1947 | A. Ramage | 1967 | W. Ramage |
| 1922 | H. L. Fleming | 1948 | W. Ramage | 1968 | A. Kennedy |
| 1923 | M. Smith | 1949 | W. Ramage | 1969 | A. Kennedy |
| *1924* | *No contest* | 1950 | A. Ramage | 1970 | D. Sneddon |
| 1925 | W. D. Greenlees | 1951 | W. Ramage | 1971 | D. Sneddon |
| 1926 | M. Smith | 1952 | J. Murray | 1972 | L. U. Demarco |
| 1927 | M. Smith | 1953 | J. Bates | 1973 | D. Sneddon |
| 1928 | M. Smith | 1954 | J. Bates | 1974 | D. Sneddon |
| 1929 | J. McGhee | 1955 | W. Ramage | 1975 | D. Sneddon |
| 1930 | M. Smith | 1956 | W. Ramage | 1976 | D. Sneddon |
| 1933 | A. Ramage | 1957 | W. Ramage | 1977 | J. Nugent |
| 1934 | N. Canney | 1958 | W. Ramage | 1978 | D. Sneddon |
| 1935 | H. King | 1959 | W. Ramage | 1979 | H. Nimmo |
| 1936 | N. Canney | 1960 | A. Ramage | 1980 | D. Sneddon |
| 1937 | J. McGhee | 1961 | P. Spence | 1981 | D. Sneddon |
| 1938 | J. McGhee | 1962 | W. Ramage | 1982 | W. Kelly |
| *1939* | *No contest* | 1963 | W. Ramage | 1983 | H. Nimmo |
| 1940 | W. McCann | 1964 | W. Ramage | 1984 | D. Sneddon |
| *1941–45* | *No contests* | 1965 | W. Ramage | 1987 | W. Kelly |

## WALES

### Snooker

| Year | Name | Year | Name | Year | Name |
|---|---|---|---|---|---|
| 1930 | T. Jones | 1954 | R. Reardon | 1972 | G. Thomas |
| 1931 | T. Jones | 1955 | R. Reardon | 1973 | A. Lloyd |
| 1932 | T. Jones | 1956 | C. Wilson | 1974 | A. Lloyd |
| 1933 | T. Jones | 1957 | R. D. Meredith | 1975 | T. Griffiths |
| 1934 | T. Jones | 1958 | A. Kemp | 1976 | D. Mountjoy |
| 1935 | T. Jones | 1959 | J. R. Price | 1977 | C. Wilson |
| 1936 | T. Jones | 1960 | L. Luker | 1978 | A. Lloyd |
| 1937 | G. Howells | 1961 | T. Parsons | 1979 | C. Wilson |
| 1938 | B. Gravenor | 1962 | A. J. Ford | 1980 | S. Newbury |
| 1939 | W. E. James | 1963 | R. D. Meredith | 1981 | C. Roscoe |
| *1940–46* | *No contests* | 1964 | M. L. Berni | 1982 | T. Parsons |
| 1947 | T. Jones | 1965 | T. Parsons | 1983 | W. Jones |
| 1948 | R. Smith | 1966 | L. L. O'Neill | 1984 | T. Parsons |
| 1949 | A. J. Ford | 1967 | L. L. O'Neill | 1985 | M. Bennett |
| 1950 | R. Reardon | 1968 | D. Mountjoy | 1986 | K. Jones |
| 1951 | R. Reardon | 1969 | T. Parsons | 1987 | D. Morgan |
| 1952 | R. Reardon | 1970 | D. T. May | 1988 | P. Dawkins |
| 1953 | R. Reardon | 1971 | D. T. May | 1989 | P. Dawkins |

### Billiards

| Year | Name | Year | Name | Year | Name |
|---|---|---|---|---|---|
| 1920 | H. F. E. Coles | 1939 | B. Gravenor | 1963 | R. W. Oriel |
| 1921 | H. F. E. Coles | *1940–45* | *No contests* | 1964 | R. W. Oriel |
| 1922 | H. F. E. Coles | 1946 | T. G. Rees | 1965 | R. W. Oriel |
| 1923 | H. F. E. Coles | 1947 | T. C. Morse | 1966 | R. W. Oriel |
| 1924 | H. F. E. Coles | 1948 | J. Tregoning | 1967 | R. W. Oriel |
| 1925 | Unknown | 1949 | I. Edwards | 1968 | D. E. Edwards |
| 1926 | Unknown | 1950 | W. Pierce | 1969 | R. W. Oriel |
| 1927 | Unknown | 1951 | W. Pierce | 1970 | R. W. Oriel |
| 1928 | G. Moore | 1952 | J. Tregoning | 1971 | R. W. Oriel |
| 1929 | J. Tregoning | 1953 | B. Sainsbury | 1972 | C. Everton |
| 1930 | Unknown | 1954 | R. Smith | 1973 | C. Everton |
| 1931 | L. Prosser | 1955 | J. Tregoning | 1974 | R. W. Oriel |
| 1932 | T. Jones | 1956 | A. J. Ford | 1975 | R. W. Oriel |
| 1933 | T. Jones | 1957 | R. Smith | 1976 | C. Everton |
| 1934 | Unknown | 1958 | R. W. Oriel | 1977 | C. Everton |
| 1935 | I. Edwards | 1959 | A. J. Ford | 1978 | R. W. Oriel |
| 1936 | J. Tregoning | 1960 | C. Everton | 1979 | R. W. Oriel |
| 1937 | B. Gravenor | 1961 | R. W. Oriel | | *No further contests* |
| 1938 | J. Tregoning | 1962 | R. W. Oriel | | |

## AUSTRALIA
### Snooker

| | | | | | |
|---|---|---|---|---|---|
| 1953 | W. Simpson | 1965 | W. Barrie | 1977 | R. Atkins |
| 1954 | W. Simpson | 1966 | M. Williams | 1978 | K. Burles |
| 1955 | E. Pickett | 1967 | M. Williams | 1979 | J. Campbell |
| 1956 | R. Marshall | 1968 | M. Williams | 1980 | W. King |
| 1957 | W. Simpson | 1969 | W. Barrie | 1981 | W. King |
| 1958 | F. Harris | 1970 | M. Williams | 1982 | J. Giannaros |
| 1959 | K. Burles | 1971 | M. Williams | 1983 | G. Lackenby |
| 1960 | K. Burles | 1972 | M. Williams | 1984 | G. Wilkinson |
| 1961 | M. Williams | 1973 | M. Williams | 1985 | J. Bonner |
| 1962 | W. Barrie | 1974 | L. Condo | 1986 | G. Miller |
| 1963 | F. Harris | 1975 | R. Atkins | 1987 | P. Hawkes |
| 1964 | W. Barrie | 1976 | R. Atkins | 1988 | J. Bonner |

### Billiards

| | | | | | |
|---|---|---|---|---|---|
| 1913 | G. B. Shailer | 1940–45 | No contests | 1967 | J. Long |
| 1914–19 | No contests | 1946 | R. Marshall | 1968 | J. Long |
| 1920 | J. R. Hooper | 1947 | T. Cleary | 1969 | R. Marshall |
| 1921 | G. B. Shailer | 1948 | R. Marshall | 1970 | R. Marshall |
| 1922 | G. B. Shailer | 1949 | R. Marshall | 1971 | M. Williams |
| 1923 | G. B. Shailer | 1950 | T. Cleary | 1972 | P. Tarrant |
| 1924 | E. Eccles | 1951 | R. Marshall | 1973 | P. Tarrant |
| 1925 | G. B. Shailer | 1952 | R. Marshall | 1974 | J. Reece |
| 1926 | L. W. Hayes | 1953 | R. Marshall | 1975 | J. Long |
| 1927 | L. W. Hayes | 1954 | R. Marshall | 1976 | G. Ganim Jr |
| 1928 | L. W. Hayes | 1955 | R. Marshall | 1977 | G. Ganim Jr |
| 1929 | A. H. Hearndon | 1956 | J. Long | 1978 | G. Ganim Jr |
| 1930 | S. Ryan | 1957 | R. Marshall | 1979 | G. Ganim Jr |
| 1931 | H. L. Goldsmith | 1958 | T. Cleary | 1980 | G. Ganim Jr |
| 1932 | A. Sakzewski | 1959 | R. Marshall | 1981 | G. Ganim Jr |
| 1933 | L. W. Hayes | 1960 | J. Long | 1982 | R. Foldvari |
| 1934 | L. W. Hayes | 1961 | R. Marshall | 1983 | R. Foldvari |
| 1935 | L. W. Hayes | 1962 | R. Marshall | 1984 | F. Humphreys |
| 1936 | R. Marshall | 1963 | R. Marshall | 1985 | R. Marshall |
| 1937 | R. Marshall | 1964 | J. Long | 1986 | R. Marshall |
| 1938 | R. Marshall | 1965 | T. Cleary | 1987 | P. Tarrant |
| 1939 | R. Marshall | 1966 | T. Cleary | 1988 | P. Tarrant |

## CANADA
### Snooker

| | | | | | |
|---|---|---|---|---|---|
| 1979 | J. Wych | 1981 | R. Chaperon | 1984 | T. Finstad |
| 1980 | Jim Bear | 1983 | A. Robidoux | 1985 | A. Robidoux |

### Billiards

| | | | | | |
|---|---|---|---|---|---|
| 1979 | E. Fisher | 1981 | R. Chaperon | 1982 | R. Chaperon |
| 1980 | S. Holden | | | | |

## INDIA
### Snooker

| | | | | | |
|---|---|---|---|---|---|
| 1939 | P. K. Deb | 1956 | M. J. M. Lafir | 1971 | T. Monteiro |
| 1940 | P. K. Deb | 1957 | M. J. M. Lafir | 1972 | S. Shroff |
| 1941 | V. R. Freer | 1958 | W. Jones | 1973 | S. Shroff |
| 1942 | P. K. Deb | 1959 | M. J. M. Lafir | 1974 | M. J. M. Lafir |
| 1943–45 | No contests | 1960 | W. Jones | 1975 | M. J. M. Lafir |
| 1946 | T. A. Selvaraj | 1961 | M. J. M. Lafir | 1976 | A. Savur |
| 1947 | T. Sadler | 1962 | R. Marshall | 1977 | M. J. M. Lafir |
| 1948 | W. Jones | | (Aust) | 1978 | A. Savur |
| 1949 | T. A. Selvaraj | 1963 | M. J. M. Lafir | 1979 | A. Savur |
| 1950 | F. Edwards (Eng) | 1964 | S. Shroff | 1980 | J. White (Eng) |
| 1951 | T. A. Selvaraj | 1965 | S. Shroff | 1981 | G. Parikh |
| 1952 | W. Jones | 1966 | T. Monteiro | 1984 | G. Sethi |
| 1953 | A. L. Driffield | 1967 | S. Shroff | 1985 | G. Sethi |
| | (Eng) | 1968 | S. Mohan | 1986 | G. Sethi |
| 1954 | W. Jones | 1969 | S. Shroff | 1987 | G. Sethi |
| 1955 | T. A. Selvaraj | 1970 | S. Shroff | 1988 | G. Sethi |

## Billiards

| | | | | | |
|---|---|---|---|---|---|
| 1935 | P. K. Deb | 1955 | W. Jones | 1973 | S. Mohan |
| 1936 | P. K. Deb | 1956 | C. Hirjee | 1974 | M. Ferreira |
| 1937 | M. M. Begg | 1957 | W. Jones | 1975 | G. C. Parikh |
| 1938 | P. K. Deb | 1958 | C. Hirjee | 1976 | M. Ferreira |
| 1939 | P. K. Deb | 1959 | T. Cleary (Aust) | 1977 | M. J. M. Lafir |
| 1940 | S. H. Lyth | 1960 | W. Jones | 1978 | M. Ferreira |
| 1941 | V. R. Freer | 1961 | W. Jones | 1979 | M. Ferreira |
| 1942 | V. R. Freer | 1962 | R. Marshall (Aust) | 1980 | M. Ferreira |
| *1943-45* | *No contests* | 1963 | W. Jones | 1981 | G. Sethi |
| 1946 | C. Hirjee | 1964 | W. Jones | 1982 | M. Ferreira |
| 1947 | C. Hirjee | 1965 | W. Jones | 1983 | S. Agrawal |
| 1948 | V. R. Freer | 1966 | W. Jones | 1984 | G. Sethi |
| 1949 | T. A. Selvaraj | 1967 | A. Savur | 1985 | M. Ferreira |
| 1950 | W. Jones | 1968 | S. Mohan | 1986 | G. Sethi |
| 1951 | W. Jones | 1969 | M. Ferreira | 1987 | G. Sethi |
| 1952 | W. Jones | 1970 | S. Mohan | 1988 | G. Sethi |
| 1953 | L. Driffield (Eng) | 1971 | S. Mohan | | |
| 1954 | W. Jones | 1972 | S. Mohan | | |

## MALTA
## Snooker

| | | | | | |
|---|---|---|---|---|---|
| 1947 | L. Galea | 1961 | A. Borg | 1975 | P. Mifsud |
| 1948 | T. B. Oliver | 1962 | A. Borg | 1976 | P. Mifsud |
| 1949 | L. Galea | 1963 | M. Tonna | 1977 | A. Borg |
| 1950 | W. Asciak | 1964 | A. Borg | 1978 | P. Mifsud |
| 1951 | W. Asciak | 1965 | A. Borg | 1979 | P. Mifsud |
| 1952 | A. Borg | 1966 | A. Borg | 1980 | J. Grech |
| 1953 | A. Borg | 1967 | A. Borg | 1981 | J. Grech |
| 1954 | W. Asciak | 1968 | P. Mifsud | 1982 | P. Mifsud |
| 1955 | A. Borg | 1969 | P. Mifsud | 1983 | P. Mifsud |
| 1956 | W. Asciak | 1970 | P. Mifsud | 1984 | T. Drago |
| 1957 | W. Asciak | 1971 | P. Mifsud | 1985 | P. Mifsud |
| 1958 | W. Asciak | 1972 | P. Mifsud | 1988 | P. Mifsud |
| 1959 | A. Borg | 1973 | A. Borg | | |
| 1960 | A. Borg | 1974 | A. Borg | | |

## Billiards

| | | | | | |
|---|---|---|---|---|---|
| 1947 | V. Micallef | 1959 | A. Asciak | 1972 | W. Asciak |
| *1948* | *No contests* | 1960 | A. Asciak | 1973 | P. Mifsud |
| 1949 | E. Bartolo | 1961 | A. Borg | 1974 | P. Mifsud |
| 1950 | W. Asciak | 1962 | J. Bartolo | 1975 | P. Mifsud |
| 1951 | W. Asciak | 1963 | J. Bartolo | 1976 | P. Mifsud |
| 1952 | W. Asciak | 1964 | W. Asciak | 1977 | P. Mifsud |
| 1953 | W. Asciak | 1965 | A. Asciak | 1978 | J. Grech |
| 1954 | W. Asciak | 1966 | A. Asciak | 1979 | P. Mifsud |
| 1955 | W. Asciak | 1967 | A. Asciak | 1980 | J. Grech |
| 1956 | W. Asciak | 1969 | P. Mifsud | *1981* | *No contest* |
| 1957 | W. Asciak | 1970 | W. Asciak | 1982 | V. Ellul |
| 1958 | A. Asciak | 1971 | P. Mifsud | 1983 | J. Grech |

## NEW ZEALAND
## Snooker

| | | | | | |
|---|---|---|---|---|---|
| 1945 | S. Moses | 1959 | W. Thomas | 1973 | W. Hill |
| 1946 | J. Munro | 1960 | T. Yesberg | 1974 | K. Tristram |
| 1947 | W. Thompson | 1961 | F. Franks | 1975 | K. Tristram |
| 1948 | L. Stout | 1962 | K. Murphy | 1976 | D. Kwok |
| 1949 | L. Stout | 1963 | W. Harcourt | 1977 | D. Meredith |
| 1950 | L. Stout | 1964 | T. Yesberg | 1978 | D. Meredith |
| 1951 | N. Lewis | 1965 | L. Napper | 1979 | D. Meredith |
| 1952 | L. Stout | 1966 | L. Napper | 1980 | D. O'Kane |
| 1953 | L. Stout | 1967 | R. Flutey | 1981 | D. Kwok |
| 1954 | R. Franks | 1968 | L. Napper | 1982 | D. Kwok |
| 1955 | L. Stout | 1969 | L. Glozier | 1983 | D. Kwok |
| 1956 | L. Stout | 1970 | K. Tristram | 1984 | D. Kwok |
| 1957 | W. Harcourt | 1971 | B. J Bennett | 1985 | P. de Groot |
| 1958 | W. Harcourt | 1972 | N. Stockman | 1986 | R. Karaitiana |

## Billiards

| Year | Winner | Year | Winner | Year | Winner |
|---|---|---|---|---|---|
| 1908 | J. Ryan | 1935 | L. Holdsworth | 1962 | W. Harcourt |
| *1909* | *No contests* | 1936 | S. Moses | 1963 | H. C. Robinson |
| 1910 | F. Lovelock | 1937 | S. Moses | 1964 | T. Yesberg |
| 1911 | F. Lovelock | 1938 | L. Holdsworth | 1965 | L. Napper |
| 1912 | H. Valentine | 1939 | R. Carrick | 1966 | A. Twohill |
| 1913 | H. Valentine | 1940 | S. Moses | 1967 | A. Twohill |
| 1914 | N. Lynch | 1941 | R. Carrick | 1968 | A. Twohill |
| 1915 | W. E. Warren | 1942 | R. Carrick | 1969 | E. Simmons |
| 1916 | H. Siedeberg | 1943 | A. Albertson | 1970 | L. Napper |
| 1917 | H. Siedeberg | 1944 | S. Moses | 1971 | W. Harcourt |
| 1918 | W. E. Warren | 1945 | J. Shepherd | 1972 | B. Kirkness |
| 1919 | H. Siedeberg | 1946 | R. Carrick | 1973 | H. C. Robinson |
| 1920 | W. E. Warren | 1947 | C. Peek | 1974 | H. C. Robinson |
| 1921 | H. Siedeberg | 1948 | R. Carrick | 1975 | T. Yesberg |
| 1922 | E. V. Roberts | 1949 | R. Carrick | 1976 | H. C. Robinson |
| 1923 | E. V. Roberts | 1950 | R. Carrick | 1977 | B. Kirkness |
| 1924 | R. Fredotovich | 1951 | R. Carrick | 1978 | B. Kirkness |
| 1925 | C. Mason | 1952 | L. Stout | 1979 | R. Adams |
| 1926 | E. V. Roberts | 1953 | A. Twohill | 1980 | D. Meredith |
| 1927 | E. V. Roberts | 1954 | A. Twohill | 1981 | D. Meredith |
| 1928 | A. Bowie | 1955 | A. Twohill | 1982 | D. Meredith |
| 1929 | L. Stout | 1956 | A. Twohill | 1983 | D. Meredith |
| 1930 | W. E. Hackett | 1957 | A. Twohill | 1984 | D. Meredith |
| 1931 | A. Duncan | 1958 | A. Albertson | 1985 | D. Meredith |
| 1932 | C. Mason | 1959 | A. Twohill | 1986 | B. Kirkness |
| 1933 | A. Albertson | 1960 | W. Harcourt | | |
| 1934 | H. McLean | 1961 | A. Albertson | | |

## SOUTH AFRICA

### Snooker

| Year | Winner | Year | Winner | Year | Winner |
|---|---|---|---|---|---|
| 1937 | A. Prior | 1957 | J. Van Rensberg | 1972 | J. Van Rensberg |
| 1938 | A. H. Ashby | 1958 | R. Walker | 1973 | J. Van Rensberg |
| 1939 | A. Prior | 1959 | M. Fancisco | 1974 | S. Francisco |
| *1940–45* | *No contests* | 1960 | P. Mans Jr | 1975 | M. Francisco |
| 1946 | F. Walker | 1961 | J. Van Rensberg | *1976* | *No contest* |
| *1947* | *No contest* | 1962 | J. Van Rensberg | 1977 | S. Francisco |
| 1948 | F. Walker | 1963 | J. Van Rensberg | 1978 | J. van Niekerk |
| 1949 | E. Kerr | 1964 | M. Francisco | 1979 | F. Ellis |
| 1950 | T. G. Rees | 1965 | M. Francisco | 1980 | F. Ellis |
| 1951 | T. G. Rees | 1966 | M. Francisco | 1981 | P. Francisco |
| 1952 | T. G. Rees | 1967 | J. Van Rensberg | 1982 | P. Francisco |
| 1953 | J. Van Rensberg | 1968 | S. Francisco | 1983 | P. Francisco |
| 1954 | J. Van Rensberg | 1969 | S. Francisco | 1984 | N. van Niekerk |
| 1955 | J. Van Rensberg | 1970 | J. Van Rensberg | 1985 | P. Smallshaw |
| 1956 | F. Walker | 1971 | M. Francisco | 1986 | S. Mouton |

### Billiards

| Year | Winner | Year | Winner | Year | Winner |
|---|---|---|---|---|---|
| 1920 | Sgt Bruyns | 1949 | T. G. Rees | 1968 | M. Francisco |
| 1921 | A. Prior | 1950 | T. G. Rees | 1969 | M. Francisco |
| 1922 | A. Prior | 1951 | I. Drapin | 1970 | M. Francisco |
| *1923* | *No contest* | 1952 | T. G. Rees | 1971 | M. Francisco |
| 1924 | A. Prior | 1953 | T. G. Rees | 1972 | S. Francisco |
| 1925 | P. Rutledge | 1954 | F. Walker | 1973 | S. Francisco |
| 1926 | A. Prior | 1955 | F. Walker | 1974 | M. Francisco |
| 1927 | A. Percival | 1956 | G. Povall | 1975 | S. Francisco |
| 1928 | P. Rutledge | 1957 | F. Walker | *1976* | *No contests* |
| *1929–30* | *No contests* | 1958 | F. Walker | 1977 | M. Francisco |
| 1931 | A. Prior | 1959 | M. Francisco | 1978 | C. van Dijk |
| *1932–36* | *No contests* | 1960 | R. Walker | 1979 | C. van Dijk |
| 1937 | A. M. Burke | 1961 | M. Francisco | 1980 | C. van Dijk |
| 1938 | A. Prior | 1962 | M. Francisco | 1981 | P. Spence |
| 1939 | A. Prior | 1963 | M. Francisco | 1982 | P. Francisco |
| *1940–45* | *No contests* | 1964 | M. Francisco | 1983 | C. van Dijk |
| 1946 | P. G. Kempen | 1965 | M. Francisco | 1984 | C. van Dijk |
| *1947* | *No contest* | 1966 | M. Francisco | 1985 | C. van Dijk |
| 1948 | P. G. Kempen | 1967 | J. Van Rensberg | 1986 | C. van Dijk |

## SRI LANKA

### Snooker

| | | | | | |
|---|---|---|---|---|---|
| 1951 | M. S. A. Hassan | 1963 | M. J. M. Izzath | 1975 | N. A. Rahim |
| 1952 | M. J. M Lafir | 1964 | M. J. M. Lafir | 1976 | M. S. U. Mohideen |
| 1953 | M. J. M. Lafir | 1965 | M. J. M. Lafir | 1977 | M. S. U. Mohideen |
| 1954 | M. J. M Lafir | 1966 | M. J. M. Lafir | 1978 | N. A. Rahim |
| 1955 | M. J. M. Lafir | 1967 | N. J. Rahim | 1981 | J. W. H. Boteju |
| 1956 | M. J. M. Lafir | *1968* | *No contest* | 1982 | J. A. Wahid |
| 1957 | M. J. M. Lafir | 1969 | M. J. M. Lafir | 1983 | J. W. H. Boteju |
| 1958 | M. J. M. Lafir | 1970 | N. J. Rahim | 1984 | K. Scrisoma |
| 1959 | M. J. M. Lafir | *1971* | *No contest* | 1985 | J. W. H. Boteju |
| 1960 | M. J. M. Lafir | 1972 | N. J. Rahim | 1986 | J. W. H. Boteju |
| 1961 | M. J. M. Lafir | 1973 | M. J. M. Lafir | 1987 | J. W. H. Boteju |
| 1962 | M. J. M. Lafir | 1974 | *Abandoned* | | |

### Billiards

| | | | | | |
|---|---|---|---|---|---|
| 1951 | M. J. M. Lafir | 1962 | M. J. M. Lafir | 1976 | W. Weerasinghe |
| 1952 | M. J. M. Lafir | 1963 | M. H. M. Mujahid | 1977 | W. Weerasinghe |
| 1953 | M. J. M. Lafir | 1964 | M. J. M. Lafir | 1978 | J. W. H Boteju |
| 1954 | A. C. Cambal | 1966 | M. J. M. Lafir | 1979 | W. Weerasinghe |
| 1955 | T. A. Selvaraj | 1967 | J. K. Bakshani | 1981 | J. W. H Boteju |
| 1956 | T. A. Selvaraj | 1969 | M. J. M. Lafir | 1982 | J. W. H Boteju |
| 1957 | M. J. M. Lafir | 1970 | M. J. M. Lafir | 1983 | W. Weerasinghe |
| 1958 | M. J. M. Lafir | 1972 | M. J. M. Lafir | 1984 | J. W. H Boteju |
| 1959 | M. J. M. Lafir | 1973 | M. J. M. Lafir | 1985 | K. Scrisoma |
| 1960 | M. J. M. Lafir | 1974 | S. Shaharwardi | 1986 | J. W. H. Boteju |
| 1961 | M. J. M. Lafir | 1975 | M. S. U. Mohideen | | |

# FIXTURES 1989–90

| | |
|---|---|
| **August 7–13** | 555 HONG KONG OPEN |
| | at Hong Kong Convention and Exhibition Centre |
| **August 17–27** | 555 ASIAN OPEN |
| | at Channel 12 Studios, Bangkok |
| **September 13–17** | REGAL SCOTTISH MASTERS |
| | at Scottish Exhibition Centre, Glasgow |
| **September 18–30** | INTERNATIONAL |
| | at Trentham Gardens, Stoke |
| | Box office: (0782) 657341 |
| **October 9–22** | ROTHMANS GRAND PRIX |
| | at Hexagon, Reading |
| | Box office: (0734) 591591 |
| **October 27–** | DUBAI CLASSIC |
| **November 3** | at Al Nasr Stadium, Dubai |
| **November 17–** | STORMSEAL UK OPEN |
| **December 3** | at Guild Hall, Preston |
| | Box office: (0772) 21721 |
| **December 8–17** | EVEREST WORLD MATCHPLAY |
| | at International Hall, Brentwood |
| | Box office: (0277) 229621 |
| **January 2–14** | MERCANTILE CREDIT CLASSIC |
| | at Norbreck Castle Hotel, Blackpool |
| | Box office: (0253) 52341 |
| **February 4–11** | BENSON AND HEDGES MASTERS |
| | at Wembley Conference Centre |
| | Box office: (01) 901 1234 |
| **February 18–** | BRITISH OPEN |
| **March 4** | at Assembly Rooms, Derby |
| | Box office: (0332) 369311 |
| **March 6–17** | OVERSEAS RANKING EVENT |
| | country and venue to be announced |
| **March 20–23** | FERSINA WORLD CUP |
| | at International Centre, Bournemouth |
| | Box office: (0202) 297297 |
| **March 27–April 1** | BENSON AND HEDGES IRISH MASTERS |
| | at Goffs, Kill, Co Kildare |
| **April 13–29** | EMBASSY WORLD CHAMPIONSHIP |
| | at Crucible Theatre, Sheffield |
| | Box office (by post): |
| | Crucible Theatre, Norfolk Street, |
| | Sheffield SA 1DA |

*Note:* These dates are subject to amendment.